Interact with your textbook

* **each book in the *DIRECTIONS* series offers free teaching and learning solutions online**

www.oxfordtextbooks.co.uk/orc/directions/

 online resource centre

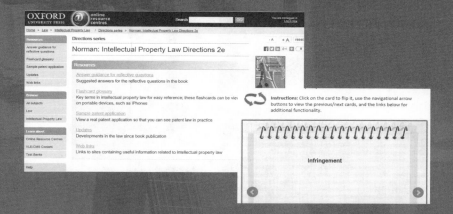

www.oxfordtextbooks.co.uk/orc/norman_directions2e/

Visit the website for access to additional resources.

For Students

* Pointers on answering end-of-chapter questions

* A flashcard glossary providing a useful reference point for key words and terms

* Sample patent applications to allow you to see patent law in practice

* Annotated web links

* Updates providing easy access to changes and developments in the law

See the **Guide to the Online Resource Centre** on p. viii for full details.

intellectual property law

DIRECTIONS

2nd edition

HELEN E NORMAN

LLM (Birmingham)
Unregistered Barrister
Senior Associate Teacher
University of Bristol Law School

OXFORD
UNIVERSITY PRESS

OXFORD
UNIVERSITY PRESS

Great Clarendon Street, Oxford, OX2 6DP,
United Kingdom

Oxford University Press is a department of the University of Oxford.
It furthers the University's objective of excellence in research, scholarship,
and education by publishing worldwide. Oxford is a registered trade mark of
Oxford University Press in the UK and in certain other countries

© Helen Norman 2014

The moral rights of the author have been asserted

First edition 2011

Impression: 1

Public sector information reproduced under Open Government Licence v1.0
(http://www.nationalarchives.gov.uk/doc/open-government-licence/open-government-licence.htm)

Crown Copyright material reproduced with the permission of the
Controller, HMSO (under the terms of the Click Use licence)

Published in the United States of America by Oxford University Press
198 Madison Avenue, New York, NY 10016, United States of America

British Library Cataloguing in Publication Data
Data available

Library of Congress Control Number: 2013955897

ISBN 978–0–19–968810–4

Printed in Great Britain by
Ashford Colour Press Ltd, Gosport, Hampshire

For Richard

Guide to using the book

Intellectual Property Law Directions is enriched with a range of special features designed to support and reinforce your learning. This brief guide to those features will help you use the book to the full and get the most out of your study.

Learning objectives

Upon completion of this chapter, you should have acquir

- an overview of the family of rights called 'intellectual proper
- an appreciation of the debate whether further protection th

Learning objectives

Each chapter begins with a list of learning objectives to enable you to draw out the main themes of the chapter. They should also be helpful when you are revising as a quick check that you have a grasp of the key knowledge requirements.

example

Imagine that Household Appliances plc is about to launch
to be marketed under the name BROWNIE. Its shape is unu
pictures of country landscapes. A special safety feature is th
made from a new metal alloy which is very light but which
outside remains cool to the touch. The metal alloy is obtain
pliers, the identity of whom is known only to the company.
From this information, the intellectual property rights re
are as follows:

Examples

We encounter real examples of intellectual property law every day, whether we recognise them or not. In each chapter you will find scenarios of intellectual property law in practice

cross reference
The unregistered design right is explained in section 11.4.

been created and recorded. The criteria for protectic
design must be **original** (in the copyright sense), not
document. The duration of protection is, however, m
mum period of protection of 15 years from creatio
marketing if articles bearing the design are sold anyw
design having been created. The design right owne
else from reproducing the design (ie, copying it) by
and the right to stop anyone else dealing in infringi
a design right infringement action, the owner has t

Highlighted key terms

Key terms are highlighted and clearly explained when they first appear. These terms are then collated into a glossary which appears at the end of the book for your ease of reference.

Summary

This chapter has explained:

- the range of rights available under United Kingdom law to p lect, together with their characteristics;

Chapter summaries

The brief summaries at the end of each chapter outline the key points covered in the chapter and help to reinforce your understanding of each topic.

case close-up

Rocknroll v News Group Newspapers [2013] EWHC 2

The claimant had sought an injunction to restrain the publi
taken at a private party. At [5] Briggs J summarised what h
ciples' of privacy:

'(1) The first stage is to ascertain whether the applicant ha
    so as to engage Article 8; if not, the claim fails.

Case close-up boxes

Summaries of key and landmark cases are highlighted so you can easily pick out the significant facts and details.

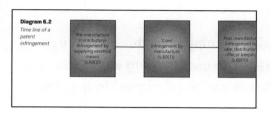

Statute boxes

Relevant provisions are set out in boxes and explained in the text.

The Statute of Venice

The Statute of Venice is considered to be one of the earliest to It reads:

Be it enacted that, by the authority of this Council, every pers and ingenious device in this City, not previously made in our

Tables and figures

Tables and figures appear throughout the book. Use these in conjunction with the text to gain a clear understanding of even the most complex concepts.

Diagram 6.2
Time line of a patent infringement

| Pre-manufacture (contributory) infringement by supplying essential means (s.60(2)) | → | 'Core' infringement by manufacture (s.60(1)) | → | Post manufacture infringement by sale, distribution, offer, or keeping (s.60(1)) |

Cross references

Connections between topics are carefully cross-referenced so you can see how they interlink. Links are highlighted to aid quick and accurate navigation through the book.

cross reference
The unregistered design right is explained in section 11.4.

been created and recorded. The criteria for protectic design must be **original** (in the copyright sense), no document. The duration of protection is, however, m mum period of protection of 15 years from creatio marketing if articles bearing the design are sold anyv design having been created. The design right owne else from reproducing the design (ie, copying it) by and the right to stop anyone else dealing in infringi

Thinking points

Thinking points allow you to pause and reflect on what you are reading. They give you the opportunity to form your own views on issues discussed in the book, and provide valuable practice in critical thinking.

thinking point
Is it correct to state that intellectual property rights are monopolistic in nature? If they are, is that such a

the intellectual property right. Failure to exploit a pa failure to use a trade mark for more than five years me for non-use at the instance of any third party. In the c tition authorities may intervene in the case of the ov of the unregistered design right, **licences of right** ca of the term of protection. With the exception of tra are of finite duration. Finally, in the case of all regist provides for the right to be declared invalid in certa

Reflective questions

Reflective questions at the end of each chapter encourage you to consider the key areas of debate discussed and provide useful exam practice in responding critically to discussion points.

? Reflective questio

1 Would United Kingdom law benefit from the introductic competition or would the doctrine of misappropriation be the interests of other traders?

2 Which is likely to be more effective as a means of changing

Annotated further reading

Selected further reading is included at the end of each chapter to provide a springboard for further study. The author has annotated the list to explain why a certain book or article might be useful to you in your studies.

📖 Annotated further reading

Arup, C. 'TRIPs: Across the Global Field of Intellectual Proper

Guide to the Online Resource Centre

The Online Resource Centre that accompanies this book provides students and lecturers with ready to use teaching and learning resources. They are free of charge and are designed to maximise the learning experience.

www.oxfordtextbooks.co.uk/orc/norman_directions2e

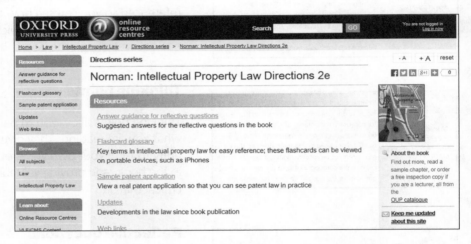

Accessible to all, with no registration or password required, enabling you to get the most from your textbook.

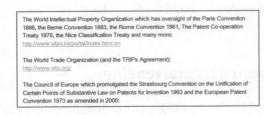

Web links

A selection of annotated web links chosen by the author to allow you to easily research those topics that are of particular interest to you. These links are checked regularly to ensure they remain up to date.

Updates to the law

An indispensable resource providing access to recent cases and developments in the law that have occurred since publication of the book.

INTELLECTUAL PROPERTY DIRECTIONS: ORC

END OF CHAPTER REFLECTIVE QUESTIONS: SUGGESTED ANSWERS

Chapter 1

Would United Kingdom law benefit from the introduction of protection against unfair competition or would the doctrine of misappropriation be a better means of protecting the interests of other traders?

Suggested answer:

The good answer would:

- Begin with a definition of 'unfair competition', that is, conduct which, whilst not

Pointers on answering end of chapter questions

All the questions posed at the end of each chapter have some suggestions on how you might tackle answering them.

Norman: Intellectual Property Flashcards

Instructions: Click on the card to flip it, use the navigational arrow buttons to view the previous/next cards, and the links below for additional functionality.

Flashcard glossary

A series of interactive flaschards containing key terms and concepts to test your understanding of intellectual property law terminology.

Sample patent application documents

Access the links below to view the sample patents (available via the Intellectual Property Office website):

Trevor Baylis - clockwork radio

Mandy Haberman - 'anyway up cup'

Sample patent application

Walking you through a real patent application so that you can see patent law in practice.

New to this edition

Key new materials and cases covered in the second edition include:

- ECtHR and United Kingdom case law developments on breach of confidence and privacy;

- EPO decisions on the patenting of biological processes and EPO/ECJ cases on patenting human embryonic stem cells;

- the introduction of the EU Unitary Patent;

- United Kingdom Supreme Court decisions on patent infringement, and on remedies for patent infringement;

- ECJ and United Kingdom Supreme Court decisions on originality in copyright and the temporary copies exception;

- changes to the Copyright, Designs and Patents Act 1988 (CDPA) concerning the duration of protection for industrially exploited artistic works, the duration of protection for sound recordings and performances, and the amendment of defences to copyright infringement as a result of the Hargreaves Report;

- changes to the Registered Designs Act 1949 and to the CDPA concerning the registered and unregistered design right brought about by the Intellectual Property Act 2014;

- the EU's proposed 'recasting' of the Trade Marks Directive and the EU Trade Mark Regulation;

- case law developments from United Kingdom and EU courts on the protection for and infringement of copyright, design right and trade marks, including the use of trade marks as 'ad words'.

Preface

When preparing the second edition of this book, I felt as if I had been a victim of the ancient curse 'may you live in interesting times'. The torrent of domestic and EU case law and legislation has continued unabated since the first edition appeared. Case law developments have ranged from breach of confidence and privacy, to trade marks as 'ad words', to the patenting of human embryonic stem cells and patent infringement, to originality in copyright and the copyright defence of making temporary copies. Legislation (or what is even worse for an author writing a legal textbook, draft legislation), has dealt (or will deal with) the introduction of the EU's Unitary Patent, the increase in the duration of protection for copyright in sound recordings and for performers' rights, changes to registered and unregistered design right, defences to copyright infringement, and the recasting of the EU Trade Marks Directive and Regulation. All this has presented the challenge of trying to accommodate additional material without increasing the length of the book, a battle which I fear I have lost.

I have, however, attempted to remain true to the original vision of the book. It aims to provide the student with an introduction to the United Kingdom law of intellectual property from a practical perspective as enterprises endeavour to protect their investment in the 'knowledge economy'. Patents, brand names and copyright works are seen as the key to success for many businesses. The *real* driving force for the subject is litigation as IP practitioners seek to enforce their clients' interests. The book will continue to provide historical references (in order to aid understanding of why the current law takes the form it does), theoretical references (to enable a critical appreciation of the legal rules), and minor comparative references (in order to highlight the deficiencies of domestic law). Nevertheless, the text seeks to set out the key domestic statutory provisions and the case law which has interpreted them in a manner which helps to understand how the subject *works*. Space does not permit a discussion of any of the pan-European rights nor of the way in which the international IP system operates.

The caveat remains that the student should not expect the principal categories of IP rights which provide protection for human creativity, namely patents, copyright, designs, trade marks and breach of confidence, to be a homogeneous entity. The rights have little in common with each other. Some are statute-based, others are of case law origin. Some are the product of domestic law alone, whilst others are the result of external influences in the shape of international conventions and EU legislation. Even though it is possible to impose a structure on these categories by describing the rules which exist for the creation, infringement and ownership of each type of right, the differences between them mean that no clear pattern emerges. In addition, each area of intellectual property presents its own challenge. In the case of copyright, the statutory provisions are detailed to the point of absurdity; in the case of patents, students who do not have a science background may baulk at reading details of a dispute about recombinant DNA (even though patent *law* itself is straightforward); whilst in the case of trade marks, an appreciation of how human beings send and receive messages through words and other signs is essential to understanding the case law.

It is customary in a preface to list those to whom thanks are due. I am very grateful to Carol Barber at OUP for her patience in reminding me of deadlines and for putting up with my not-so-inventive excuses as to why the revised chapters had *still* not been despatched. The biggest vote of thanks, however, is reserved for all those students whom I have tried to inspire over the years with my own love of Intellectual Property. Their countless questions have prompted me to find better ways of explaining the complexities of what at times can seem an impenetrable thicket.

I have endeavoured to state the law as it stood on 1 November 2013. I have assumed (hopefully correctly) that the Intellectual Property Bill 2013 will complete its Parliamentary stages in the Spring of 2014 and have referred to it throughout as the Intellectual Property Act 2014. Likewise, I have incorporated the Hargreaves Report's changes to copyright defences in Chapter 9 even though at proof stage there was no sign of their implementation. Sadly, it was not possible to deal with the ECJ's ruling in Case C-466/12 *Svensson* in the discussion of the communication right in Chapter 9. All errors are mine alone.

HEN

17 February 2014

Outline contents

Detailed contents

Part 3 Patents   83

Chapter 4 Introduction to patents   85

Chapter 5 Patentability   111

Chapter 6 Infringement of patents   149

Table of cases

Table of cases

xxiii

Table of legislation

Table of statutory instruments

Part 1
General matters

General introduction

Learning objectives

Upon completion of this chapter, you should have acquired:

- an overview of the family of rights called 'intellectual property';

- an appreciation of the debate whether further protection through the action for unfair competition would be desirable;

- an understanding of the common characteristics of intellectual property rights;

- knowledge of some of the theoretical justifications advanced in support of intellectual property rights; and

- an ability to identify the sources which have influenced the current law of intellectual property in the United Kingdom.

Introduction

The purpose of this chapter is to provide a general introduction to the material which follows. We begin with an overview of the various types of right recognised under United Kingdom law, with a brief account of the principal criteria for the protection and infringement of each one. The overview should be seen as a prelude to the more detailed discussion in subsequent chapters. The opportunity is also taken to debate whether there is a gap in the scheme of protection, as United Kingdom law does not give redress against unfair competition. We then proceed to identify the common characteristics of intellectual property rights and to consider the theoretical justifications which are advanced for them (we shall look further at the theories underpinning each type of right in the chapters dealing with the individual rights). Last, there is an account of the sources of United Kingdom intellectual property law, with particular emphasis on the external forces which have played a major part in shaping domestic law over the last four decades.

1.1 Overview of the different types of right

In *Phillips v Mulcaire* [2012] UKSC 28 at [21] Lord Walker declared that there was no particular potency to the term 'intellectual property'. There was general consensus as to its core content but not as to its limits. The core can be said to consist of the following:

1.1.1 Patents

A **patent** is concerned with *applied technology*, with how things work, not with abstract ideas. The subject matter of a patent, called an *invention*, can be either a product (a tangible item or thing) or a process (a method of making something or using something or doing something). Whether a patent relates to a product or a process is determined by reference to the wording of its **claims**. Thus, a claim to a product might relate to a new chemical compound, whilst a claim to a process would relate to how to make that compound, or how to use it. A patent might have only a few claims (if it is a relatively simple mechanical invention) or tens of claims. In turn, these claims might be product claims only, or process claims. More complex inventions will have separate product and process claims.

cross reference

Novelty is explained in section 5.5, inventive step in section 5.6.

cross reference

Industrial applicability is explained in section 5.7, the exclusions from and exceptions to patentability in sections 5.3 to 5.4.

The four criteria for patentability are that the invention must be new, contain an inventive step, be capable of industrial application and not fall within the statutory list of **excluded subject matter**. In relation to the first two (sometimes called 'external' criteria), the invention as set out in the patent document (the specification) is compared with all information made available to the public at the date the patent was filed (the **priority date).** Such information is called 'the **prior art**'. The other two so-called 'internal' characteristics of patentability, namely whether the invention is susceptible of industrial application (ie, is useful) or falls outside the statutory list of exclusions and exceptions, do not involve a comparison with what has been known or used before. Instead they involve an examination of the way in which the claims have been drafted by the **patentee**, and whether these meet the relevant statutory conditions.

A patent can be granted either by the **United Kingdom Intellectual Property Office ('UKIPO')** under the Patents Act 1977, as amended, or by the European Patent Office ('**EPO**') under the European Patent Convention 1973 ('**EPC**') as amended in 2000. If the EPO route is chosen, a **European patent**, once granted, is treated as a bundle of national patents. Whether the national or European route is taken, the patent's maximum duration will be 20 years, calculated from the application date, subject to the payment of annual renewal fees from the fifth year onwards. A patent confers on its owner (the **patentee**) the exclusive right to make, offer, dispose of, keep or use the product, or to use or offer the process which is the subject matter of the patent. If another person infringes a patent, the fact that they created the same invention independently is not a defence. A patent is an absolute monopoly.

1.1.2 **Copyright**

Copyright is the right to stop the copying and distribution of different categories of work. Under the Copyright, Designs and Patents Act 1988 ('CDPA'), works include books, plays, music, paintings, films, sound recordings and broadcasts.

It should not be assumed, however, that United Kingdom copyright law protects only those works resulting from great creativity. Traditionally, the threshold for protection has been very low, so that everyday items (such as lists of TV programmes) are protected. To qualify for protection, the work must be original (meaning 'not copied'), be recorded in a permanent form, and the **author** must be a '**qualifying person**'. Unlike other statute-based forms of intellectual property, copyright protection does not depend on registration, but arises automatically once the work is created and recorded. Copyright protection lasts for a long time, generally speaking the lifetime of the author plus 70 years. The copyright owner has the exclusive right to stop anyone else from reproducing the work (that is, copying it); issuing (that is, distributing) *tangible* copies of the work (including renting out copies); performing the work in public; communicating the work to the public by *intangible* means (either by broadcast or the internet); or adapting the work. They also have the right to stop secondary infringers, such as retailers, dealing in infringing copies of the work by way of trade. However, to succeed in a copyright infringement action, the owner has to prove their work has been copied. Independent creation is therefore always a defence to copyright infringement.

cross reference

Originality and qualification for protection are explained in sections 8.2 and 8.3. Section 8.2 also considers whether the traditionally low threshold for United Kingdom copyright protection can continue in the light of EU developments.

1.1.3 **Designs**

The law of designs is concerned with the appearance of **products**, that is, with *how things look*. In design law, what is protected is not the underlying **article**, which could be an everyday item such as a teapot (*Ocular Sciences Ltd v Aspect Vision Care Ltd* [1997] RPC 289 at p. 422) but the design features applied to it. Under United Kingdom law, a designer has three potential means of protecting their design, namely registered design protection, unregistered design right or copyright. Under EU law, a designer has two further options, namely an EU registered or unregistered design right. We shall, however, be concerned only with the United Kingdom system of protection.

cross reference

Registered designs are explained in section 11.2.

In the case of registered designs, the criteria for protection under both the Registered Designs Act 1949 ('RDA'), as amended, and EU law, are that the design must be new and have 'individual character'. The latter phrase means that the design must produce on the **informed user** (a potential customer but not necessarily a consumer of the product) an overall impression which is different from that of previous designs. A United Kingdom registered design is granted by the Designs Registry (part of UKIPO) whilst an **EU design** is granted by the **Office for Harmonisation in the Internal Market (Trade Marks and Designs) ('OHIM')**. Each lasts for a maximum of 25 years, calculated from the application date, subject to the payment of renewal fees every five years. A registered design confers on its owner the exclusive right to prevent anyone else from using the design on *any* product, ie, from making, offering, putting on the market, importing, exporting, using or stocking *a product* in which the design is incorporated or to which it is applied. Like patents, independent creation is not a defence to an action for registered design infringement, so a registered design is also an absolute monopoly.

For some industries, especially those in which the design of products changes rapidly, the formality and delays inherent in a registration system are felt to be inappropriate. The alternative means of protection is the **unregistered design right**. Under United Kingdom law, this is a copyright-type right to protect *the shape or configuration of the whole or part of an article*. The right arises automatically, without the need for registration, once the design has been created and recorded. The criteria for protection under Part III of the CDPA are that the design must be **original** (in the copyright sense), not **commonplace**, and recorded in a design document. The duration of protection is, however, much shorter than copyright, with a maximum period of protection of 15 years from creation, reduced further to 10 years from first marketing if articles bearing the design are sold anywhere in the world within five years of the design having been created. The design right owner has the exclusive right to stop anyone else from reproducing the design (ie, copying it) by making articles for commercial purposes, and the right to stop anyone else dealing in infringing copies by way of trade. To succeed in a design right infringement action, the owner has to prove that their design was copied, so that independent creation is a defence to design right infringement, just as it is to copyright infringement.

cross reference
The unregistered design right is explained in section 11.4.

Lastly, under United Kingdom law, a designer may able to claim copyright protection (just as they could before the CDPA) for the appearance of an article. The CDPA curtails the availability of copyright as a matter of public policy, echoing the decision in *British Leyland v Armstrong Patents* [1986] AC 577. Copyright may be claimed where the article is an artistic work in its own right, for example, a sculpture or a work of artistic craftsmanship, such as hand-carved furniture. The criteria for and scope of protection are the same as for copyright.

cross reference
Copyright protection for designs is explained at section 11.3.

1.1.4 Trade marks

A **trade mark** is a **sign** or symbol used in the course of trade to indicate the origin of goods or services. It is an integral part of consumer society, enabling customers to distinguish one product from another and to choose between competing brands, returning to those which have given satisfaction and avoiding those which have not. Under United Kingdom law, a trader can choose between two means of protection, either registration, or bringing an action in tort for **passing off**. In relation to registration, there are further choices, either obtaining a United Kingdom registration from the Trade Marks Registry under the provisions of the Trade Marks Act 1994 ('TMA'), or by obtaining an **EU trade mark** from OHIM (valid for all the Member

States of the EU) under the terms of the Community Trade Mark Regulation. Again, this book will concern itself with the United Kingdom system.

In the case of registered trade marks, the criterion for protection (identical under both domestic and EU law) is that there must be a sign which is capable of graphic representation and capable of distinguishing the goods or services of one undertaking from those of another. It must not fall within the list of **Absolute Grounds** for refusal (that is, objections which relate to the inherent nature of the mark itself), nor must it fall within any of the **Relative Grounds** for refusal (that is, it must not conflict with any prior rights).

cross reference

The definition of 'trade mark', and the absolute and relative grounds for refusal are explained in sections 14.3, 14.4 and 14.5 respectively.

Once registered (by whichever route is taken to obtain protection), a trade mark is capable of lasting indefinitely, subject only to the payment of renewal fees every 10 years. Registration does not mean that the mark is safe from counter-attack. Where the proprietor has failed to look after the mark, the mark is vulnerable to an action for **revocation** by any third party, and like any other registered intellectual property right, a third party can always seek to have the registration declared **invalid** because it does not comply with the statutory requirements. Registration gives the proprietor the exclusive right to prevent others from using the same or similar sign in the course of trade in relation to the same or similar goods or services (or, in some instances, dissimilar goods or services) for which the mark is registered.

cross reference

Revocation and invalidity of trade marks are dealt with in section 15.5, infringement in section 15.3.

However, it is not compulsory for a trader to register the brand name they wish to use in the course of trade. Protection for unregistered trade marks (sometimes called 'common law' trade marks) is available through the tort of passing off. Passing off is entirely judge-made law. At times the cases appear to be contradictory. The inconsistencies may in part be explained by the fact that passing off is highly dependent on the circumstances of each case and on the quality of evidence put forward by the claimant.

cross reference

Passing off is considered in chapter 13.

---

case close-up

Reckitt & Colman v Borden (JIF LEMON) [1990] 1 WLR 491

It is generally accepted that the basic ingredients of passing off are as stated by Lord Oliver in *Reckitt & Colman v Borden (JIF LEMON)* [1990] 1 WLR 491. To be successful, the claimant must prove that:

- his name, trade mark, logo or other visual symbol has, through use, acquired a reputation which has generated business **goodwill**;

- that the defendant, by using this symbol, has made a misrepresentation in the course of trade to customers that his goods or services are in some way 'connected with' the claimant; and

- that the claimant has suffered or will suffer damage to his business goodwill as a result.

The onus is on the claimant to prove each element of the *JIF LEMON* definition. If any one of these ingredients is missing, the passing off action will fail. This may help to explain why registering a trade mark is preferable to relying on the vagaries of the passing off action.

cross reference

Breach of confidence is dealt with in chapter 3.

1.1.5 **Confidential information**

The action for **breach of confidence** is the means of protecting trade secrets. It can also be used to protect personal and state information, but not information already known to the public ('in the public domain'). It is the one area of intellectual property providing protection for ideas themselves, as opposed to their tangible embodiment in **inventions**, **works**, brand names or the appearance of products. The action for breach of confidence is another area of intellectual property law which does not depend on statute, but on case law.

case close-up

Coco v AN Clark (Engineers) Ltd [1969] RPC 41

The accepted ingredients of the action for breach of confidence were set out by Megarry J in *Coco v AN Clark (Engineers) Ltd* [1969] RPC 41 at p. 47. They require the successful claimant to prove that:

- there existed confidential information;
- the defendant owed the claimant a duty of confidence (which may be inferred from the circumstances, such as the parties being in a joint venture); and
- there has been breach of that duty by the misuse or wrongful disclosure of that information by the defendant.

example

Imagine that Household Appliances plc is about to launch a new type of toaster. The toaster is to be marketed under the name BROWNIE. Its shape is unusual, and its sides are decorated with pictures of country landscapes. A special safety feature is that the outside walls of the toaster are made from a new metal alloy which is very light but which does not conduct heat, so that the outside remains cool to the touch. The metal alloy is obtainable only from certain specialist suppliers, the identity of whom is known only to the company.

From this information, the intellectual property rights relevant to the features of the toaster are as follows:

- the name, BROWNIE, could be protected as a trade mark. Dependent on the size of its business, the company could register the name just in the United Kingdom or throughout the EU; alternatively, once the name has been used so that goodwill has been established, it could seek protection under the tort of passing off;

- the shape of the toaster could be protected as a design. Again, the company has a choice whether to seek registration either nationally or under the EU system, or rely on national or EU unregistered design protection. The toaster is unlikely to be treated as an artistic work in its own right, so copyright protection would not be available;

- the picture on the side of the toaster, however, could be protected as an artistic work under copyright law;

- the metal alloy used in the outer wall could be protected by a patent, provided the invention satisfies the requirements of patentability in the Patents Act 1977; and

- the list of suppliers of the alloy could amount to confidential information.

1.2 The absence of any protection against unfair competition in United Kingdom law

1.2.1 The Paris Convention obligation

Despite the wide range of items protected by intellectual property law, there appears to be a gap in the United Kingdom régime. There is no protection for a business against **unfair competition**. By 'unfair competition' we mean conduct which, whilst not amounting to infringement of a specific intellectual property right, involves taking advantage of or benefiting from the effort, skill and investment of another enterprise in such a way as to affect that enterprise's ability to compete. It may conveniently, if emotively, be described as 'free-riding' or 'reaping without sowing'. Unfair competition should be distinguished from competition law, which seeks to regulate the conduct of businesses who seek to restrict competition from others by means of cartels or monopoly power.

Many other EU Member States, for example France and Germany, have specific laws against unfair competition. As Gerhard Schricker explains (in 'Twenty-five Years of Protection against Unfair Competition' (1995) 26 *IIC* 782), these derive from provisions in the **Paris Convention** for the Protection of Industrial Property 1883. The Paris Convention principles on unfair competition came at a relatively late stage of the development of industrial property and can be regarded as no more than a basic outline. Besides giving redress to businesses affected by unfair conduct (the main thrust of unfair competition is to protect competitors), action may be brought to protect consumers and even the public interest in general. Examples include misleading advertising, price discounting and loss-leading. Schricker & Henning-Bodewig (in 'New Initiatives for the Harmonisation of Unfair Competition Law in Europe' [2002] *EIPR* 271) point out that within those countries which do have protection against unfair competition considerable divergences exist and that the United Kingdom and Ireland stand out as EU Member States who do not have such protection.

cross reference
The Paris Convention is explained at section 1.5.1.1.

Article 10*bis* of the Paris Convention contains the basic obligation for its Contracting States to provide effective redress against unfair competition. 'Unfair competition' is defined as being 'any act of competition contrary to honest practices in industrial or commercial matters'. The Article gives a non-exhaustive list of examples, including creating confusion with the activities of a competitor, making false allegations in the course of trade such as to discredit a competitor, and misleading the public as to the nature of goods.

It has been argued that there *ought* to be effective redress against unfair competition under United Kingdom law. At least three unsuccessful attempts have been made since 1994 to introduce this by statute, but the official Government response in blocking such proposals has always been that the existing law of passing off is adequate. In 2006, the *Gowers Review of Intellectual Property* received a number of submissions calling for the introduction of a general unfair competition law. It noted that the EU had legislated to regulate unfair business-to-consumer transactions by means of Directive 2005/29/EC of the European Parliament and of the Council of 11 May 2005 [2005] OJ L 149/22 (the 'Unfair Commercial Practices Directive') but added that the Directive might not provide sufficient redress for unfair 'business-to-business' anti-competitive practices (although Wadlow in 'The Emergent European Law of Unfair Competition and its Consumer Law Origins' [2012] *IPQ* 1 argues to the contrary). The Gowers Review identified (in para 5.82) one area of activity where legislation might be desirable, namely copycat packaging of famous brands by supermarkets, recommending that the Government should monitor whether current measures to combat unfair competition were effective and if need be consult on appropriate changes. No action has so far been taken.

1.2.2 The judicial view: free competition is to be preferred

United Kingdom courts have traditionally adopted a robust attitude: any form of business conduct is regarded as fair, provided that it does not breach the criminal law (*Crofter Hand Woven Harris Tweed v Veitch* [1942] AC 435; *Mogul v McGregor Gow* (1889) LR 23 QBD 598) and provided there is no conspiracy to injure the claimant by unlawful means (*Lonrho Ltd v Shell Petroleum Co Ltd* [1982] AC 173). Therefore there should *not* be a law of unfair competition in the United Kingdom. Intellectual property is divided into discrete rights and where a claimant seeks protection for something falling outside such categories, the action should fail. The judiciary (as befits the common law tradition) are reluctant to expand the boundaries of the existing rights, particularly those which are statute based. Indeed, there are powerful *dicta* against the introduction of a general tort of unfair competition, for example the views expressed in *Victoria Park Racing v Taylor* (1937) 58 CLR 479 at p. 509 (*per* Dixon J) (Australian HC) and *Moorgate Tobacco v Philip Morris* [1985] RPC 291 at pp. 236–240 (*per* Deane J) (also Australian HC). In the former case it was said that generalised protection should not be given to intangible elements falling outside the traditional areas of intellectual property which resulted from the exercise by an individual in the organisation of a business, or the use of ingenuity, knowledge, skill or labour.

thinking point
Should the claimant in the INS *case have been given protection in respect of the time and trouble taken to organise its news gathering service?*

These *dicta* should be compared with the thinking of the US Supreme Court in the case of *International News Service v Associated Press* (1918) 248 US 215 (the *INS* case), where the majority of the court held that taking news stories of World War I collected by the **claimant** and telegraphing them from the East Coast to the West Coast of the USA in order to publish the news there first before the claimant's own newspapers could do so amounted to an act of unfair competition. There are, however, two powerful dissenting judgments in the case (by Justices Holmes and Brandeis), and the case has since been criticised and confined. Libling, however, (in 'The Concept of Property: Property in Intangibles' (1978) 94 *LQR* 103) argues that Justice Brandeis misunderstood earlier United Kingdom case law. Further, he says, Justice Brandeis was used as authority by Dixon J in the *Victoria Park Racing* case, so the latter decision is unsound. Libling argues that the remedy in the *INS* case was correctly granted to protect the claimant's property right, not in the copyright in the newspaper stories, but to the commercial exploitation of its investment in gathering news.

1.2.3 Passing off as a possible mechanism

In the United Kingdom, breach of confidence, copyright and passing off are the categories of intellectual property most likely to be utilised in litigation in an attempt to provide protection against unfair competition. In particular, it is possible to identify passing off cases where the judges seem more willing to expand the boundaries of protection. An early example is *Vine Products v MacKenzie* [1969] RPC 1 where Cross J (as he then was), when allowing Spanish sherry producers to enjoin the use of the term 'British Sherry', referred to the 'new-fangled tort of unfair competition'. The high-water mark of such expansionism is the opinion of Lord Diplock in *Erven Warnink BV v Townend & Sons* [1979] AC 731 at pp. 741–743, where he argued that the common law should follow Parliament's lead and impose a higher standard of commercial conduct than envisaged in the early days of passing off, founded as it was on the narrow basis of the action of deceit.

Equally, there are cases where the judges declare that existing forms of redress should not be expanded to encompass unfair competition. An instance is the decision of the Privy Council in *Cadbury-Schweppes v Pub Squash Co* [1981] RPC 429, where Lord Scarman (who ironically had concurred with Lord Diplock in *Erven* two years earlier) was adamant that competition must remain free, and that free competition is best safeguarded by requiring the claimant to establish all the ingredients of the passing off action in its orthodox form.

At first glance the views of Lord Diplock and Lord Scarman cannot be reconciled. Lord Diplock argued that the common law, through the tort of passing off, must develop and remain flexible to deal with changing business practices. He commented that passing off is a 'protean' tort, that is, one that can change its shape to suit the needs of the case. Lord Scarman, on the other hand, contended that passing off must stay within its traditional boundaries, adding that if the key elements of the action were not present, there should be no redress simply because it was felt intuitively that the defendant's conduct was 'unfair'. In the instant case, the defendants had not committed passing off by taking the underlying theme of the claimant's advertising campaign nor by copying the rather common colour scheme of the claimant's product (green and yellow for cans of lemonade was not unusual), even though they had set out quite deliberately to 'free-ride' on the claimant's success.

Despite these differences of attitude about the response of the common law to unfair trading, the two cases can be reconciled at a factual level. In the *Pub Squash* case, the Privy Council were constrained by Powell J's finding that the defendant's conduct had not caused any customer confusion. The facts as found did not even meet the list of ingredients for passing off suggested by Lord Diplock in *Erven Warnink* (and Lord Diplock himself pointed out that just because all the elements of the tort were established did not guarantee redress for the claimant—though why that should be so he did not explain). By contrast, in *Erven Warnink*, Goulding J had held that the claimants had sustained damage to goodwill as a result of the defendant having called its 'egg flip' drink 'Advocaat'. The contrasting outcomes emphasise how small differences in evidence can have a disproportionate effect in passing off cases.

1.2.4 **An alternative solution**

Hazel Carty (in 'The Common Law and the Quest for the IP Effect' [2007] *IPQ* 237) identifies a number of areas in current law where protection is said to be weak against the theft (or misappropriation) of investment. The creation of a general action for unfair competition is one solution; another would be to adopt the notion of unjust enrichment; another would be to use misappropriation. Arguably, this last is what happened in *Irvine v Talksport* [2002] 2 All ER 414 at [38–45], where Laddie J hinted that passing off has moved on (perhaps influenced by the Human Rights Act 1998) and can indeed protect against the value of the claimant's investment in their name or image. Davis (in 'Why the United Kingdom Should Have a Law against Misappropriation' [2012] *CLJ* 561) considers whether such an extension to passing off is appropriate, as does Carty in 'Passing Off: Frameworks of Liability Debated' [2012] *IPQ* 106.

Others, too, have debated whether misappropriation *should* be used as the basis of a new tort of unfair competition. Libling argues that there are property rights in intangibles, particularly where there has been investment resulting from the expenditure of effort: such investment should be protected against taking by others. Equally, Ricketson (in ' "Reaping without Sowing": Unfair Competition and Intellectual Property Rights in Anglo Australian Law' (1984) 7 *UNSWLJ* 1) argues that although the traditional categories of intellectual property rights have been expanded over the years to deal with many instances of unfair competition, there is scope for a general doctrine of misappropriation. This is particularly so, he says, where there is an actual or potential competitive advantage to the defendant or an actual or potential competitive disadvantage to the claimant. By contrast, Spence (in 'Passing Off and the Misappropriation of Valuable Intangibles' (1996) 112 *LQR* 472), having outlined four possible justifications for the recognition of misappropriation (causing harm to the creator, the fact that the creator deserves to own their creation, unjust enrichment of the defendant, and the autonomy of the creator) concludes that passing off is best confined within its traditional boundaries.

Relying on misappropriation as the basis for protection against unacceptable business practices is not without difficulty. The courts or Parliament would have to define what is capable of protection (a matter not addressed by Libling), and whether protection should have a proprietary or tortious basis. If the basis of protection is the investment which a company has made, would that not simply lead to monopoly power, so that the law would be protecting the large enterprise rather than the individual innovator? Further, how to draw the boundary between acceptable and unacceptable behaviour in business? Lastly, why should competition, indeed imitation, not be encouraged?

1.2.5 **Recent judicial views**

It has been suggested that passing off *ought* to be regarded as unfair competition by Aldous LJ in two cases, *BT plc v One in a Million* [1999] FSR 1 at p. 18 and *Arsenal Football Club v Matthew Reed* [2003] RPC 696 at [70]. This view is diametrically opposite that of Jacob J (as he then was) in *Hodgkinson & Corby v Wards Mobility Service* [1995] FSR 169: ' there is no tort of copying. There is no tort of taking another man's market or customers. Neither the market nor the customers are the plaintiff's to own.' Subsequently, Jacob LJ (as he had become) observed in *L'Oréal SA v Bellure NV* [2008] RPC 196 at [141] that,

> the basic economic rule is that competition is not only lawful but a mainspring of the economy. The legislator has recognised that there should be exceptions. It has laid down the rules for these: the laws of patents, trade marks, copyrights, and designs have all been fashioned for the purpose. Each of them have rules for their existence and (save for trade marks) set time periods for existence. Each has their own justification. It is not for the judges to step in and legislate into existence new categories of intellectual property rights. And if they were to do so they would be entering wholly uncertain territory.

Interestingly, when the case reached the European Court of Justice (ECJ) in Case C-487/07 *L'Oréal SA v Bellure NV* [2009] ECR I-5185 civil law notions of unfair competition are evident. The Court stated that there can be liability in the law of trade marks for taking unfair advantage of another's mark, even though the senior mark's distinctive character is not harmed and even though there is no damage to the reputation of the senior mark. In appropriate circumstances, 'free-riding' on another's investment can be prevented. The same Court had previously stated (again in the context of trade mark law) that unfair competition involves 'the duty to act fairly in relation to the legitimate interests of the trade mark proprietor' (Case C-100/02 *Gerolsteiner Brunnen GmbH v Putsch GmbH* [2004] ECR I-691). When *L'Oréal SA v Bellure NV* returned to the Court of Appeal ([2010] RPC 687), the ECJ's ruling was accepted with marked reluctance. Not only are there diverging judicial views within United Kingdom courts, there is a cultural divide between those EU Member States which recognise unfair competition as a form of actionable harm, and the common law tradition.

thinking point
Should 'free-riding' on the efforts and investment of others be permitted? If not, in what circumstances should the right to object to unfair competition arise?

1.3 The principal characteristics of intellectual property rights

1.3.1 Property rights

Intellectual property rights are, self-evidently, proprietary in nature. They can be bought and sold, mortgaged and **licensed**, just like any other type of property. A valuation can be put on them for contractual or accounting purposes. Nevertheless, it is important to distinguish between property rights in a tangible item and the intangible intellectual property rights which may be embodied in that item. For example, if A writes a letter to B, the piece of paper received by B will belong to B as it was intended as a gift by the sender. However, the copyright in the words contained in the letter will belong to the creator, A. Further, A may use a pen to write the letter. The pen will be A's personal property, but there may be a patent for the pen belonging to C Ltd, or perhaps, if the pen is of an unusual shape, C Ltd might own a design right in respect of the pen. The fact that there are intellectual property rights over the pen does not prevent the use or ownership of the tangible item by A, just as A's ownership of copyright in the letter does not affect B's ownership of the piece of paper on which the letter is written. However, were B to attempt to do something falling within the scope of A's copyright (such as to include it in his autobiography which is about to be published in a newspaper) then A's copyright may (depending on the circumstances) be infringed.

1.3.2 Territorial nature

Intellectual property rights are territorial in nature, that is, they arise as a result of national legislation which authorises an official 'grant' of the right by a national intellectual property office. In the case of copyright, which does not depend on registration, the 'grant' of the right by United Kingdom law is automatic, providing the conditions in the CDPA are fulfilled. For actions in passing off or breach of confidence, the 'grant' of the right is as a result of a judicial decision in favour of the claimant.

'Territorial nature' means that an intellectual property right is only effective in the territory of the state granting that right. A patent granted by UKIPO only has effect for the territory of the United Kingdom. It does not give the patentee any rights outside the United Kingdom and can only be infringed by conduct which occurs within the territory of the United Kingdom.

cross reference
These conventions are explained in section 1.5.1.2.

There are various consequences. First, where protection is required for a patent or trade mark or registered design in more than one country, it is necessary to obtain separate registration for that right in each country. Various international conventions exist which assist an **applicant** to make multiple simultaneous applications in several countries. Also, one of the developments of EU law has been the creation of pan-European rights, so that it possible to obtain a single registration for a plant variety, trade mark or design effective in all 28 Member States of the EU.

Next, the content of a particular intellectual property right may vary from country to country. Despite the existence of international conventions attempting to standardise intellectual property laws, differences do exist between the laws of those conventions' Contracting States. These differences may relate to the detailed rules concerning the creation or infringement of a particular intellectual property right, or to the legal systems within which the right is enforced, or to the social and cultural values which that legal system seeks to uphold.

One final consequence of the territorial nature of intellectual property rights must be mentioned at this stage. The various statutory provisions setting out what conduct infringes intellectual property rights (for example, the TMA s.10(4)(c)) entitle the proprietor to prohibit the importation of goods (there are similar provisions for patents, designs and copyright). Staying with trade marks as our example (because almost all the case law involves trade marks), what if trade marked goods have been sold by the trade mark owner in another country? Does the United Kingdom registration entitle the trade mark owner to sue the importer for infringement, so as to keep legitimate (as opposed to pirated) goods out of the country? Such a right would enable the trade mark owner to protect their United Kingdom distributors from price competition, as the importer may have acquired the branded goods more cheaply elsewhere. The answer is, 'it depends'. If the trade mark owner first sold the goods in a Contracting State of the **European Economic Area ('EEA')** (the 28 EU Member States plus Iceland, Norway and Liechtenstein) then EU law provides that the trade mark owner's rights are exhausted (or spent). No objection can be made to further dealing in these parallel imports within the EEA unless the importer does something to undermine the value of the trade mark. However, if the goods were first sold by the United Kingdom trade mark owner outside the EEA (for example, in Japan), then under EU law the principle of **exhaustion of rights** does not apply, and national trade mark rights enable the owner to sue for trade mark infringement (Case C-414/99 *Zino Davidoff SA v A & G Imports Ltd* [2001] ECR I-8691). National trade mark rights can therefore be used to prevent parallel imports of non-EEA goods, insulating the trade mark owner against price competition.

cross reference
Exhaustion of rights is dealt with in chapter 16.

1.3.3 **Monopolistic nature**

The descriptions of the various categories of intellectual property rights discussed in preceding paragraphs used the phrase 'exclusive right'. This embodies two important concepts. First, that intellectual property rights are negative in nature, because the owner is given the right to *exclude* others. To go back to the example given earlier, A's copyright in the letter written to B does not give A any positive rights of ownership over the physical medium of the piece of paper. Rather, it gives A the right to prevent B (or anyone else) from infringing any one of the particular rights conferred on the copyright owner by statute, for example, the right to stop the letter being copied or communicated to the public. Second, the phrase 'exclusive right' means that the owner of the intellectual property right is the *only* person who can exploit the right. In the case of a patent, the patentee is the only person who can make the patented product, offer it for sale, dispose of it, keep it, or use it by way of trade. In the case of a registered trade mark, the owner is the only person who can apply the mark to goods, sell goods bearing the mark, import or export the goods, or advertise goods bearing the mark. In other words, an intellectual property right gives rise to a legal monopoly. Whether such a right gives rise to a monopoly in the sense understood by economists is a different matter, and unfortunately one rarely discussed by the courts.

Whether monopolies (in the economic sense) are good or bad is the subject of much debate. At common law, since the case of *Darcy v Allin (Case of Monopolies)* (1602) 11 Co Rep 84b, all monopolies are viewed as contrary to public policy. Such policy was confirmed by Parliament in the Statute of Monopolies 1623, to which patents are declared to be an exception in s.6. Arguably, therefore, United Kingdom intellectual property law can be viewed as an exception to a general principle prohibiting monopolies. Indeed, case law contains numerous instances where the judges have been reluctant to find in favour of the claimant on the ground that this would create an 'unfair monopoly' (see, for example, the decision of the House of Lords in *Re COCA COLA Trade Marks* [1986] RPC 421). Add to this the assumption that free competition is a good thing, and it is easy to see why at times the Patents Court gives the impression of being against intellectual property owners.

Present-day intellectual property legislation contains many built-in safeguards to ensure that a balance is struck between the rights of the intellectual property owner and free competition. Some of these safeguards require the owner to pay renewal fees regularly (in the case of patents, registered designs and trade marks). Others require the owner to make effective use of the intellectual property right. Failure to exploit a patent may result in **compulsory licensing**; failure to use a trade mark for more than five years means that the registration may be revoked for non-use at the instance of any third party. In the case of copyright and designs, the competition authorities may intervene in the case of the owner's abuse of the right, and in the case of the unregistered design right, **licences of right** can be demanded during the last five years of the term of protection. With the exception of trade marks, all intellectual property rights are of finite duration. Finally, in the case of all registered intellectual property rights, statute provides for the right to be declared invalid in certain instances, so unlike real property and tangible personal property, intellectual property rights are always vulnerable to destruction.

thinking point
Is it correct to state that intellectual property rights are monopolistic in nature? If they are, is that such a bad thing?

1.4 The theoretical justifications for intellectual property rights

Intellectual property rights ultimately protect information. Assuming that property rights over real and personal property can themselves be justified (and certain philosophies deny this), is it correct to treat information in the same way? Should information be the subject of private rights or should it be regarded as public property? Further, if private property rights are allowed to exist over information, what safeguards should be created to ensure the protection of the public interest in such information, so that it is left free for others to enjoy?

1.4.1 Possible justifications

William Fisher has argued (see 'Theories of Intellectual Property', in Munzer *New Essays in the Legal and Political Theory of Property* (ed) (2001), Cambridge University Press) that there are potentially four different theoretical justifications found in current academic literature. The arguments which follow are rarely articulated in United Kingdom case law (although for an exception, see *Dranez Anstalt v Hayek* [2003] FSR 561 at [25]). As Fisher says, the theories are not as helpful as might be supposed in assisting legislators and the judiciary to determine the precise limits of intellectual property law in the information age. Each is hampered by internal inconsistency, and by the lack of empirical evidence to support it. No one theory is sustainable across the entire range of intellectual property rights. Moreover, the extensive literature supporting the various theories can be viewed as a product of a particular era or a particular society.

First, influenced by the writings of Jeremy Bentham, is the utilitarian theory of intellectual property. Bentham's ideal was to achieve 'the greatest good of the greatest number' by the maximisation of net social welfare. In the context of intellectual property, utilitarianism propounds that authors and inventors be given a limited monopoly, either as an incentive to create or as a reward for their efforts, because society will be improved and enriched by their resultant endeavours. The theory requires a balance to be struck between the exclusive rights of the owner and the rights of public enjoyment over what has been created.

Next, there is the natural law theory attributed to the writings of John Locke. Locke's arguments (often referred to as the 'labour theory' or the 'desert theory' and advanced in an era when society was largely agrarian) state that a person may legitimately acquire property rights by mixing his labour with resources held 'in common' provided that there is enough left in common for others. So if a worker ploughs a field and grows a crop of wheat, the wheat belongs to him.

Third, derived from the writings of Kant and Hegel, there is the argument that private property rights are essential to the satisfaction of human need. Intellectual creations are seen as an extension of the individual's personality. Last, and encountered less often, there is the theory that property rights in general should be shaped so as to achieve a desirable society. Fisher calls this the 'social planning' theory, arguing that it is different from utilitarianism.

An alternative structure is put forward by Merges (in *Justifying Intellectual Property* (2011), Harvard University Press). He argues that there are three first order principles which justify the existence of intellectual property, Lockean appropriation, Kantian individualism and Rawlsian distributive effects of property, with utilitarianism ('efficiency') being a second-tier rather than foundation principle.

1.4.2 Criticisms of the theories

Utilitarianism (which permeates US law because of the constitutional foundations for patent and copyright protection) holds that the law should provide incentives for those creative efforts which benefit society as a whole. What evidence is there that the availability of legal protection actually provides an incentive? Consider how the computer software industry developed in the 1970s despite the absence of any form of legal protection. Henry Ford refined the system of mass-producing motor cars long before the US Patent Office granted patents for 'methods of doing business'. Even if it is concluded that society is better off if authors and inventors are rewarded, is an intellectual property régime necessarily the best means of providing that reward? The founders of the US Constitution contemplated, but eventually abandoned, the idea of state-funded rewards for creativity. If intellectual property law is deemed the best solution, how far should the rights of authors and inventors extend? Should the owner of a copyright work be entitled to control all subsequent works based on it? Should a patentee be able to prevent others from conducting experiments on his invention? If protection is taken too far, then monopoly power is created. Monopoly power in turn creates inefficiency as the patentee's competitors waste time and money trying to 'invent around' the earlier patent without being liable for infringement.

Similar problems occur with the labour theory. It is by no means clear that Locke's writings do support any sort of protection for intellectual property rights: they were certainly not within his contemplation at the time of writing. Even if this obstacle is overcome, what should count as 'labour' in the context of intellectual property rights, when it is very easy to think up a brand name or when the threshold for copyright protection is so low? In the information society, what are the 'commons': is it facts, or culture, or ideas? To quote Fisher's example, granting a patent on a better mousetrap prevents others from making *that* mousetrap, but not from reading the patent document and using the information which it contains to make an even better one. Finally, how should intellectual property legislation ensure that enough is left from 'the commons' for others to enjoy?

Reliance on property rights as an aspect of personality to justify intellectual property equally causes problems. Which rights should be treated as capable of individual ownership and which should be left to the public? Even if it is possible to identify which rights can be privately owned, should they be capable of alienation? How much autonomy should an individual have? How much public property should they be able to monopolise? And what conduct should amount to infringement? Last, the social policy theory begs the question what sort of society we want, and who should make that decision? Should society's values be based on consumer welfare, the artistic tradition or distributive justice? Here, an individual's political vision will affect the answer to the question, on which there is accordingly little consensus.

Further, it is impossible to apply a particular theory to every single type of intellectual property right. Can copyright be supported by the same arguments as patents? Does the same reasoning apply to the protection of designs or trade secrets? The odd one out here is clearly the trade mark right. The reasons for having trade mark law are much more to do with the workings of consumer society rather than rewarding creativity or protecting an individual against theft. However, the pro-competitive benefits of brand names still have to be balanced by the need to avoid anti-competitive behaviour by large, multi-national brand owners.

Next, there is no empirical evidence that a society with intellectual property protection is any better or worse than a society without it. If intellectual property rights are accepted as a good thing, one would expect that the protection conferred on their owners would reflect the justifications for such rights. Regrettably, the law does not distinguish between 'good' and 'bad' intellectual property rights. There is no difference in the scope or duration of protection accorded to a patent for a new life-saving drug and one for a very minor modification to the

internal combustion engine. The composer of a great choral work receives no better protection than the person who writes a jingle for a television advertisement. Ironically (depending on one's point of view) the latter may receive far more royalties for the performance of their work than the former.

Finally, if intellectual property rights are accepted as beneficial to society, there remains the question of how to strike the balance between the interests of the owner and the interests of society. Should the task of striking this balance fall to the discretion of the judges, or should it be built into the legislation creating the intellectual property rights, or should it be left to those with authority to administer competition law? Whichever is preferable (and again there is no consensus), as Sir Robin Jacob has argued (in 'The Stephen Stewart Memorial Lecture: Industrial Property—Industry's Enemy' [1997] *IPQ* 3), intellectual property rights continue to expand and strengthen, with little attention being paid to protecting the interests of others.

thinking point

Which theoretical justification for granting intellectual property rights do you find the most convincing? Which is the least?

1.5 Sources of intellectual property law

We now consider the origins of United Kingdom intellectual property law. It should not be assumed that intellectual property law is purely domestic. External influences in the shape of international conventions have played a major role in deciding the contents of United Kingdom law since the late nineteenth century. In the last three decades, the EU's harmonisation programme in the form of Regulations and Directives has led to a stream of further revisions. Whatever reforms the *Gowers* and *Hargreaves Reviews of Intellectual Property* eventually produce will be at the margins, as any room for manoeuvre is constrained by the United Kingdom's international and European obligations.

In terms of hierarchy, the sources of United Kingdom intellectual property law can be classified as international conventions, EU legislation, domestic legislation and case law, both European and domestic. In principle, no international convention is part of United Kingdom domestic law unless and until it is enacted by Parliament. It used to be said that once enacted, United Kingdom courts would refer to the implementing legislation rather than the convention itself in determining the rights of the individual, as international agreements are not capable of direct effect: see *Lenzing AG's European Patent* [1997] RPC 245, dealing specifically with the effect of the **EPC**. Less than a decade later, however, United Kingdom courts hearing intellectual property disputes refer directly to the original source in the interests of clarity: see *Aerotel Ltd v Telco Holdings Ltd/Macrossan's Application* [2007] RPC 117 where the Court of Appeal looked to the wording of the EPC rather than s.1(2) of the Patents Act 1977.

In contrast, many of the **Articles of the Treaty on the Functioning of the European Union (TFEU)** (formerly the Treaty of Rome 1957) together with those Regulations creating pan-European intellectual property rights will have direct effect in United Kingdom law; harmonisation Directives have prompted much domestic legislation. United Kingdom courts must therefore apply the guidance of the ECJ as to the meaning of the TFEU, the Regulations and Directives.

cross reference

Section 1(2) of the Patents Act 1977 is explained in section 5.3.

cross reference

The significance of complying with ECJ guidance is explained at section 1.5.4.

1.5.1 **International conventions administered by WIPO**

Most, but not all, international intellectual property conventions are administered by the **World Intellectual Property Organisation ('WIPO')**, an agency of the United Nations. WIPO's chief objectives are to encourage and assist countries to establish effective protection for intellectual property rights, and to work towards an international consensus on the standardisation of national laws. According to WIPO's own description, its conventions are subdivided into three main types, namely protection treaties, global protection systems and classification treaties.

1.5.1.1 WIPO protection treaties

Protection treaties specify the types of right which are to be recognised, the criteria for their protection, and the minimum standards to be applied to each type of right. Contracting States are obliged to adhere to these criteria and standards in their domestic legislation.

The Paris Convention

The prime example of a protection treaty is the Paris Convention for the Protection of Industrial Property 1883 (as revised at Stockholm 1967). The Paris Convention deals with those intellectual property rights obtainable by registration (patents, trade marks and designs). It also requires Contracting States to provide protection against unfair competition. Membership of the Convention obliges a Contracting State to establish its own patent office, and, once established, for that Office to issue certain publications (for example, a *Patents Journal* and a *Trade Marks Journal*). There are, however, two particular substantive rights created by the Convention, **priority** claiming and **national treatment**, which deserve particular mention.

cross reference
Patent application procedure is dealt with at section 4.4.

Priority claiming (Article 4) enables an applicant for a patent, trade mark or design, once they have filed an application in one of the Contracting States, to backdate all subsequent national filings made within a specified period to the date of that first national filing, provided the later filings relate to the same subject matter. The specified periods are 12 months for patents, and six months for trade marks and designs. The ability to backdate a patent application by up to 12 months is of great practical importance in 'the race to the patent office door'.

National treatment (Article 2) is the cornerstone of the Paris Convention and of many other international intellectual property conventions. Any state which becomes a signatory to the Convention is required to provide the same protection under domestic law to foreign nationals as it does to its own nationals. So, for example, the fact that the United Kingdom is a Contracting State to the Paris Convention means that it must offer nationals from other Contracting States (for example Japan) the same treatment under United Kingdom law as it gives to United Kingdom nationals. However, because intellectual property laws differ from state to state, national treatment does *not* mean that in our example, United Kingdom law must offer Japanese nationals the same protection as they receive under Japanese law. Japanese law might provide better (or worse) protection than United Kingdom law, but that can have no bearing on the duty of the United Kingdom under Article 2 not to discriminate against those from other Contracting States.

WIPO copyright conventions

Besides the Paris Convention, WIPO oversees conventions concerned with rights which are not registrable, namely copyright and related rights (these latter are sometimes referred to as 'neighbouring rights'). The chief of these conventions is the **Berne Convention** for the Protection of Literary and Artistic Works 1886 (as revised at Paris in 1971). The Berne Convention deals with literary, dramatic, musical and artistic works, and films. It sets out the criteria for the existence of each one of these rights and the extent of protection conferred on the owner. Two key features deserve a brief mention. First, the Convention, just like the Paris Convention, contains the principle of national treatment in Article 5, and, second, in the same Article, declares that copyright protection is not dependent on registration. The consequence is that copyright protection arises automatically once a work comes into existence.

The remaining categories of copyright and related rights are dealt with by another WIPO Convention, namely the **Rome Convention** for the Protection of Performers, Record Makers and Broadcasting Organisations 1961 (sometimes called the 'Neighbouring Rights Convention'). The Rome Convention sets out the obligations of Contracting States with regard to the protection of sound recordings (called 'phonograms' in the Convention), broadcasts and performances. Like the Berne Convention, it specifies the criteria for the existence of each right and the scope of protection accorded to the owner. Similarly, it contains the principle of national treatment and declares that protection is not dependent on registration. It does, however, provide for the formality of a copyright notice to be affixed to each copy of the work, but only in the case of sound recordings (the ℗ symbol).

cross reference

How the Berne and Rome Conventions are implemented in United Kingdom law is explained in chapter 8.

Lastly, in relation to copyright and neighbouring rights, in 1996 WIPO concluded two further treaties, namely the WIPO Copyright Treaty ('WCT') and the WIPO Performers and Phonograms Treaty ('WPPT'). The objective of these two Conventions is to spell out more clearly the rights of the copyright owner in the digital era, especially with regard to the exploitation of copyright works on the internet. They build, respectively, on the Berne Convention and the Rome Convention. Their main impact in United Kingdom law is in relation to copyright infringement. The WPPT has also prompted recent revisions to the law on **moral rights**.

1.5.1.2 WIPO global protection systems

Global protection systems exist because of the territorial nature of intellectual property rights and the consequent need to assist businesses who want to obtain registration for their rights in more than one country. Essentially these systems provide procedural shortcuts to enable an applicant to make multiple national filings in respect of patents, trade marks and designs. The two principal global protection systems operated by WIPO are the Patent Co-operation Treaty 1970 ('**PCT**') (which provides for the multiple filing of patent applications) and the Madrid Agreement for the International Registration of Marks 1891 (revised Stockholm 1967) as amended by the Protocol to the Madrid Agreement 1989 (the '**Madrid System**' which provides a mechanism for filing multiple applications for trade marks). These will not be discussed further in this text.

1.5.1.3 WIPO classification treaties

cross reference

See further chapter 14.

Last, classification treaties exist primarily to standardise the internal workings of national patent offices, and trade marks and designs registries, by providing (for example) a standard classification for the subject matter of patents or designs. The one most commonly encountered is the **Nice Agreement** for the International Classification of Goods and Services 1957, incorporated into United Kingdom law by means of Sch. 4 of the Trade Marks (Amendment) Rules 2001.

1.5.2 Conventions administered by other international organisations

1.5.2.1 The World Trade Organization: TRIPs

The World Trade Organization ('**WTO**') was established in 1995, replacing another international organisation known as the General Agreement on Tariffs and Trade ('GATT'). The WTO has a much broader scope than GATT, in that it is not concerned simply with trade in goods. The principal objective of the WTO is to promote free trade between states by overseeing and enforcing the rules of international trade. One of its underlying assumptions is that free trade helps to raise living standards. Nevertheless, it has come to be associated with the perceived evils of globalisation.

One of the conventions concluded under the auspices of the WTO is the Agreement on the Trade Related Aspects of Intellectual Property ('**TRIPs**'). Membership of the WTO obliges a Contracting State to sign up to TRIPs. TRIPs contains provisions setting out a minimum 'floor of rights' for all major categories of intellectual property. It builds on what has gone before by incorporating the fundamental principles of the Paris and Berne Conventions, and requires its Contracting States to accede to the latest versions of these (and other) treaties. Like them it adopts the principle of national treatment.

The most significant feature of TRIPs is that where a state is in breach of its obligations, another dissatisfied state may initiate the WTO dispute settlement procedure. If a complaint is upheld, then the complainant may (once all the lengthy procedures have been exhausted) impose trade sanctions on the defaulting state (including import quotas and duties). These sanctions can be imposed on products other than those which were the subject matter of the complaint. Arguably, the enforcement mechanism makes the WTO a more powerful force for change than WIPO. However, WIPO can hardly be considered a spent force, because since the advent of the WTO it has secured the two 1996 Conventions detailed earlier, as well as the ICANN dispute resolution system for domain names.

WIPO or WTO?

Some have asserted (see Arup, 'TRIPs: Across the Global Field of Intellectual Property' [2004] *EIPR* 7) that WIPO is the better organisation to advance global standards in intellectual property because of its extensive experience (over five decades) and because it strives to be more balanced in its approach, preferring education and persuasion to coercion. The drawback is that its consultation procedures are more formalised and protracted. As Samuelson points out (in 'Challenges for WIPO and TRIPs in Regulating Intellectual Property Rights in the Information Age' [1999] *EIPR* 578), TRIPs was in part adopted because of dissatisfaction with WIPO, in particular its inability to enforce change on its Contracting States and the fact that its conventions allow states to enter reservations, thereby 'opting out' of certain obligations. Ultimately, it was felt, WIPO deferred too much to its members and left too much to their discretion. The absolute nature of the obligations in TRIPs together with the WTO enforcement mechanism was perceived by some as the more effective régime.

Criticisms of TRIPs

TRIPs is not without its critics. As Samuelson contends, there is a cultural difference between the language of free trade and that of authors' rights. Further, as May argues (in 'Why IPRs Are a Global Political Issue' [2003] *EIPR* 1), the 'one size fits all' approach of TRIPs does not accord with reality for less-developed nations. Ironically, 500 years ago developed countries were in the same position as less-developed countries are today and have spent the intervening years establishing a workable balance between the rights of the author or inventor and 'the commons'. Conversely, as Arup comments, TRIPs itself is 'backwards looking' as it builds on existing WIPO treaties, themselves a product of nineteenth-century industrialisation.

The most trenchant criticisms of TRIPs are to be found in *Integrating Intellectual Property Rights and Development Policy* (the Report of the Commission on Intellectual Property Rights, London, 2002). Amongst other things, the Report considers the impact of granting patents for animals and plants, the relationship between patents and health care, bio-prospecting, the protection of traditional knowledge, and how the standards of patentability ought to be applied. Many of the Report's underlying assumptions are challenged by Crespi (in 'IPRs under Siege: First Impressions of the Report of the Commission on Intellectual Property Rights' [2003] *EIPR* 242). He argues that the Commission failed to keep in mind the difference between an intellectual property right *per se* and the use made of it. Crespi questions whether intellectual property rights should be an instrument of public policy, as such rights on their own do not have an economic impact unless and until they are exploited.

thinking point
Are the criticisms of TRIPs justified?

1.5.2.2 The Council of Europe

Next, there are intellectual property conventions promulgated by the Council of Europe. Although often considered as dealing only with the European Convention on Human Rights, the Council has since its foundation in 1949 concerned itself with a wide range of scientific and cultural issues, and has created two conventions dealing with patents, the most important of which is the **EPC**. Membership of this is open to any state which belongs to the Council of Europe. Consequently, the membership of the EPC is far broader than that of the EU. It should be remembered that the EPC is *not* a legal instrument of the EU, and so is not subject to the jurisdiction of the ECJ.

The EPC established the EPO in Munich. In contrast to the PCT mentioned earlier (which enables an applicant to make multiple national patent filings worldwide), the EPC is a regional intellectual property system providing centralised grant. One application to the EPO will, if successful, result in the grant of national patents in all the Contracting States of the EPC (at present there are over 30) unless the applicant indicates otherwise. A European patent bypasses national patent offices. A European patent has the same effect in a Contracting State as a national patent granted by that state's own patent office. So, in the United Kingdom, there are in force national patents granted by UKIPO, and European Patents (UK) granted by the EPO in Munich. Each type of patent has exactly the same effect and confers exactly the same type of rights once granted.

1.5.2.3 UNESCO and the Universal Copyright Convention

An alternative route designed to assist citizens of developing countries obtain copyright protection in developed countries is the **Universal Copyright Convention ('UCC')**. The UCC was initially agreed in Geneva in 1952 and revised in Paris in 1971. It is unusual in that it is administered not by WIPO but by the United Nations Educational, Scientific and Cultural Organisation ('UNESCO'). The scope of the UCC is the same as the Berne Convention, in that it deals with literary, dramatic, musical and artistic works, and films. Just like the Berne Convention, it contains the principle of national treatment, but in contrast it does require the use of a copyright notice on a work as a precondition to protection (the © symbol). The intention of its creators was that when former colonies obtained their independence, membership of the UCC would ensure national treatment for their citizens in the countries which had previously governed those territories. Since the advent of the TRIPs Agreement, the number of new accessions to the UCC has declined noticeably. This is because membership of the WTO obliges Contracting States to adhere to the Berne Convention. The UCC could therefore be regarded as something of an anachronism.

1.5.3 European Union legislation

At a fairly early point in the development of the European Economic Community (as it was then called), it was realised that intellectual property rights were one of the main non-tariff barriers to trade and an obstacle to the creation of what is now known as the internal market. The internal market means the 28 Member States are regarded as a single territory without internal boundaries. National intellectual property rights are an obstacle to attaining the internal market because of their territorial nature. Another obstacle was that Member States had enacted different criteria for the protection, duration and scope of the various intellectual property rights. The EU Commission therefore adopted a two-pronged strategy designed to overcome these problems, namely a series of harmonisation Directives, addressed to Member States, requiring them to standardise their national laws, and the creation of pan-European rights by means of directly applicable Regulations.

1.5.3.1 Harmonisation Directives

Harmonisation Directives in the field of intellectual property have had a significant effect on United Kingdom law (and indeed the law of other Member States) in relation to trade marks, designs and copyright, but so far have had only a limited effect in relation to patents.

Trade marks

The *First Trade Marks Directive* (Council Directive 89/104/EEC of 21 December 1988 on the approximation of the laws of Member States relating to trade marks [1989] OJ L 40/1) (now codified as Directive 2008/95/EC of the European Parliament and of the Council of 22 October 2008 [2008] OJ L 299/25) is declared to be a partial harmonisation measure, dealing only with those aspects of trade mark law which directly affect the functioning of the internal market. It deals with what signs can be trade marks, the absolute and relative grounds on which a trade mark application may be refused, the scope of protection afforded by registration to the proprietor of the mark to prevent infringing conduct by others, the defences to infringement, and provisions dealing with the licensing of marks and the loss of registration. All of these key provisions are reflected in the wording of the TMA, though in some instances, it must be said, the enactment of the Directive in the United Kingdom has been less than perfect. Other aspects of trade mark law, such as registration procedure, ownership and enforcement, are left to the domestic laws of Member States.

cross reference
The implementation of the Directive in the TMA is discussed further in chapters 14 and 15.

One way in which a registered trade mark can be used by a competitor is in comparative advertising. The Trade Marks Directive did not deal with whether comparative advertising was a form of trade mark infringement. Subsequently, the EU adopted the Comparative Advertising Directive (Directive 97/55/EC of the European Parliament and of the Council of 6 October 1997 amending Directive 84/450/EEC concerning misleading advertising so as to include

cross reference

Comparative advertising as a defence to trade mark infringement is considered in section 15.4.7. The impact of the proposed changes to the Trade Marks Directive is considered throughout chapters 14, 15 and 16.

comparative advertising [1997] OJ L 290/18, now consolidated as Directive 2006/114/EC of the European Parliament and of the Council of 12 December 2006 [2006] OJ L 376/21) (the 'CAD'). The CAD has been implemented into United Kingdom law by means of administrative regulation (the Business Protection from Misleading Marketing Regulations 2008), with enforcement being by way of complaint to the Advertising Standards Authority. No change was made to the provisions of the 1994 Act. Subsequently, however, the ECJ in Case C-533/06 *O2 Holdings Ltd v Hutchinson 3G Ltd* [2008] ECR I-4231 has read the two Directives together.

In March 2013, the EU Commission published a proposal to modernise and improve the Trade Marks Directive. Its wording codifies the ruling in *O2*.

Designs

cross reference

The impact of the Directive is considered in chapter 11.

In relation to registered designs, the Designs Directive (Council Directive 98/71/EC of 13 October 1998 on the legal protection of designs [1998] OJ L 289/28) has had a major impact on the content of United Kingdom law on registered designs. Again, it is declared to be a partial harmonisation measure only, leaving Member States to decide on ownership, registration procedure and remedies. The Directive therefore deals with those aspects of the law of registered designs which most affected the functioning of the internal market, namely the conditions for acquiring protection (including the definition of a design and the key criteria of novelty and individual character), the exclusions from protection, and the scope of the infringement action. The Directive allows Member States to provide other legal methods of protecting designs (such as copyright and unregistered design right).

Copyright

It is in relation to copyright that the EU has adopted the most number of Directives. However, their impact has been in relation to specific aspects of copyright, and in contrast to trade marks and designs, there has been no attempt to standardise the core criteria for protection. Whether a 'work' meets the minimum standards for protection is therefore left still to the domestic laws of the Member States.

General copyright Directives

cross reference

Duration of copyright is dealt with in chapter 8; duration of performers' rights in chapter 10.

Two Directives have had an impact on general copyright principles. First, the Rental Rights Directive (Council Directive 92/100/EEC of 19 November 1992 on rental right and lending rights and on certain rights related to copyright in the field of intellectual property [1992] OJ L 346/61, now codified as Directive 2006/115/EC of the European Parliament and of the Council of 12 December 2006 [2006] OJ L 376/28) clarified that the copyright owner has the right to control the hire and rental of copies of the work. Second, the Copyright Term Directive (Council Directive 93/98/EC of 29 October 1993 harmonising the term of copyright protection [1993] OJ L 290/9, now codified as Directive 2006/116/EC of the European Parliament and of the Council of 12 December 2006 [2006] OJ L 372/12) standardised the duration of protection for the various categories of copyright work throughout the EU. So, for example, in respect of those works covered by the Berne Convention, the term is to be the duration of the author's life plus 70 years, provided the author is a national of one of the EEA Contracting States or the work's 'country of origin' is an EEA Contracting State. The 2006 Directive has been amended by Directive 2011/77/EU of the European Parliament and of the Council of 27 September 2011 [2011] OJ L 265/1 with regard to the duration of copyright in sound recordings and of performers' rights.

The impact of technology

Another group of Directives has, over the years, endeavoured to deal with the impact of new technology on copyright and related rights. The first, and most specific, of these was the Semiconductor Directive (Council Directive 87/54/EEC of 16 December 1986 on the legal protection of topographies of semiconductor products [1987] OJ L 24/36), which, in response to legislation in the USA, provided protection for the three-dimensional layout of computer chips. The Computer Programs Directive (Council Directive 91/250/EEC of 14 May 1991 on the legal protection of computer programs [1991] OJ L 122/42 now codified as Directive 2009/24/EC of the European Parliament and of the Council of 23 April 2009 [2009] OJ L 111/16) provided that computer programs were to be accorded copyright protection 'as literary works'. Lastly, the Database Directive (Directive 96/9/EC of 11 March 1996 on the legal protection of databases [1996] OJ L 77/20) created a two-tier system of protection for collections of works, data and other materials.

cross reference
Computer programs and databases are treated as literary works, explained at section 8.2.1.

New media

Two further Directives attempted to ensure that the owner of a copyright work is protected against exploitation of the work in new forms of communication. First, the Copyright Broadcasting Directive (Council Directive 93/83/EEC of 27 September 1993 on the co-ordination of certain rules concerning copyright and neighbouring rights applicable to satellite broadcasting and cable retransmission [1993] OJ L 246/15) established the principle that the rights of owners of existing copyright works were to be protected when the works became the subject of satellite or cable broadcasts. Next, the Information Society Directive (Directive 2001/29/EC of the European Parliament and of the Council of 22 May 2001 on the harmonisation of certain aspects of copyright and related rights in the information society [2001] OJ L 167/10) implemented the WCT and the WPPT by declaring the rights of authors to control the reproduction, issuing and communication of their works in the digital era.

cross reference
The Directive is explained in chapter 10.

Miscellaneous

Lastly, two recent Directives have dealt with specific problems. The Droit de Suite Directive (Directive 2001/84/EC of the European Parliament and of the Council of 27 September 2001 on the resale right for the benefit of the author of an original work of art [2001] OJ L 272/32) implemented a particular provision of the Berne Convention, namely the right of an artist to be remunerated when the original version of his/her work is sold. By contrast, the worldwide problem with counterfeiting (which of course is not confined to copyright, but applies equally to trade marks) is dealt with by the Enforcement Directive (Directive 2004/48/EC of the European Parliament and of the Council of 29 April 2004 on the enforcement of intellectual property rights [2004] OJ L 157/45) which requires Member States to harmonise the civil remedies available to the intellectual property owner.

cross reference
Remedies are considered in chapter 2.

Patents

The tortured history of the **EU Patent** (its title since the Lisbon Treaty) shows that creating pan-European rights is not easy. The original twin-track approach was to leave the EPC to deal with the issuing of patents, whilst the EU Patent ensured that the post-grant rights of patentees throughout the EU with regard to infringement, licensing, renewal and invalidity were harmonised. The intention was to have a **unitary patent** for the whole of the EU, as a special type of European patent granted by the EPO. So little progress was made in the ratification of the draft Community Patent Convention 1975 that the EU Commission decided in 2000 to restart the process by using a different legal instrument, namely a Council Regulation under what was then Article 308 EC (now Article 352 TFEU) (the implied powers provision). Again, little progress was made.

The ratification of the Lisbon Treaty in December 2009 reactivated the process yet again. Article 118 TFEU provided for the creation of European intellectual property rights in the context of the internal market. The 2009 proposal for the EU patent envisaged the enactment of a Regulation so that the EU itself would accede to the EPC thereby becoming a 'Contracting State' for which a European patent having unitary effect throughout the Union would be granted. There was to be a European and EU Patents court system with exclusive jurisdiction in respect of validity and infringement issues concerning European and EU patents, consisting of a Court of First Instance and a Court of Appeal. The establishment of such a system required an agreement between EU Member States and non-EU Member States of the EPC but in March 2011 the ECJ ruled that this was not compatible with the EU Treaties. Meanwhile, in the same month, 25 of the then 27 Member States (the exceptions being Spain and Italy) decided to go ahead with 'enhanced co-operation' in the matter of the EU Patent under Title III of the TFEU. Subsequently, the EU Parliament and the Council of Ministers agreed two Regulations: No 1257/2012 (OJ [2012] L 361/1) implementing enhanced co-operation in the area of the creation of unitary patent protection; and No 1260/2012 (OJ [2012] L 361/89) implementing enhanced co-operation in the area of the creation of unitary patent protection with regard to the applicable translation arrangements. The Regulations entered into force on 20 January 2013. However, they will only apply from 1 January 2014 or the date of entry into force of the Agreement on a Unified Patent Court, whichever is the later. The Agreement on the Unified Patent Court was published on 11 January 2013 and was formally signed on 19 February 2013. It has to be ratified by 1 November 2013 with a minimum of 13 states required, including France, Germany and the United Kingdom (at the time of writing 25 Member States have signed the agreement; Poland, Croatia and Spain have not signed, but only Austria has ratified). It was intended that the new system would be ready for business early in 2014, although the Unified Patent Court Preparatory Committee believes that early 2015 would be a more 'realistic target date for the entry into operation of the Court'. The net result is the creation of a patent for the EU which despite its name, is not unitary, in that it will not have effect in those Member States who did not participate in the enhanced co-operation procedure. It does seem, however, that the thorny issue of translation has been resolved, because the unitary patent will have the same working languages as the EPC, namely English, French and German.

There has only been one EU Directive in the field of patent law, namely the Biotechnological Patents Directive (Directive 98/44/EC of the European Parliament and of the Council of 6 July 1998 on the legal protection of biotechnological inventions [1998] OJ L 213/13) ('the Biotech Directive'). It was passed in response to the practice of the United States Patent and Trademark Office of granting patents in relation to genetically engineered plants and animals, and because Member States' national patent offices had adopted varying attitudes to such patents. It declared that, provided the normal criteria for patentability are met, inventions consisting of biological material shall *in principle* be patentable. There are a number of exceptions, concerned primarily with ethical objections to such inventions, and the Directive also spells out the rights of the owner of such an invention against infringers.

cross reference
The Directive is considered further in chapter 5.

1.5.3.2 Pan-European rights

In three areas, the EU has seen fit to create an EU-wide system whereby the intellectual property owner can, in a single registration procedure, obtain protection throughout all Member States. Such rights are unitary in nature, that is, the rights are valid for the whole of the EU, but equally, if they are invalid in one part of the EU (for example, because the right in question does not meet all the criteria for protection or because of an earlier conflicting right) then they are invalid for the whole (an 'all or nothing' system). The three systems are: the Council Regulation on Plant Variety Rights (Council Regulation (EC) 2100/94 of 27 July 1994 on Community Plant Variety Rights [1994] OJ L 227/1); the Community Trademark Regulation (Council Regulation (EC) 40/94 of 20 December 1993 [1994] OJ L 11/1, now consolidated as Council Regulation (EC) No 207/2009 of 26 February 2009 on the Community trade mark [2009] OJ L 78/1); and the Council Regulation on the Community Design (Council Regulation EC 6/2002 of 12 December 2001 on Community Designs [2002] OJ L 3/1). It is beyond the scope of this book to deal with these three Regulations, but as indicated earlier, there are parallel Directives which seek to harmonise national laws. One result of these parallel systems (applicants can still elect to seek only national registration for their trade mark or design) is that the case law on the Directives can be interchanged with the case law under the Regulations. The role of the ECJ in this aspect of harmonisation should not be underestimated.

1.5.4 **United Kingdom legislation**

There are four principal statutes governing intellectual property law in the United Kingdom. All were enacted or have been modified to take account of international or regional conventions, or EU secondary legislation.

1.5.4.1 Summary of domestic legislation

- The RDA, as amended by the Design Regulations 2001, incorporates the Designs Directive.

- The Patents Act 1977, as amended by the Patents Act 2004, was enacted to fulfil the United Kingdom's obligations under the EPC 1973, whilst the 2004 Act takes account of the revisions in the EPC 2000.

- The CDPA was initially a domestic measure (although it did enable the United Kingdom to ratify the 1971 version of the Berne Convention). It has since been amended on a number of occasions in order to implement EU Directives dealing with copyright and related rights. The latest changes (intended to come into force in October 2013) will give effect to some of the proposals in the *Hargreaves Review of IP and Growth* (2011).

- The TMA was passed so that the United Kingdom could implement the EU Trade Marks Directive and the Community Trade Mark Regulation.

Because of these outside influences, United Kingdom tribunals are constrained in their interpretation of domestic legislation. The Patents Act 1977 s.130 declares that key provisions in the Act (specifically those dealing with **patentability**, infringement and revocation) are intended to have the same effect as the corresponding provisions in the EPC, the EU patent and the PCT have in other states which are members of these conventions. In particular, the section imposes an obligation on United Kingdom tribunals to take note of the case law of the Boards of Appeal and the Enlarged Board of Appeal of the EPO (that is, the EPO's internal judicial organs) with regard to the interpretation of the criteria for patentability: see *Merrell Dow v Norton* [1996] RPC 76 at p. 82 (HL) and *Kirin Amgen Inc and others v Hoechst Marion Roussel Ltd and others* [2005] 1 All ER 667 at [101] (HL), in each case *per* Lord Hoffmann.

Where domestic law has been enacted or amended to give effect to EU harmonisation Directives, then the position of United Kingdom tribunals is even more constrained. It is a principle of EU law that the tribunals of a Member State are obliged to interpret national legislation adopted in implementation of a Directive in such a way that the objectives of a Directive are achieved (Case 14/83 *Von Colson and Kamann v Land Nordrhein-Westfalen* [1984] ECR 1891). Even where there has been non-implementation or mis-implementation of a Directive, national law must, after the deadline for implementation has passed, be interpreted in such a way as to comply with the wording and purpose of the Directive (Case C-106/89 *Marleasing* [1990] ECR I-4135 at [8] and Case C-91/92 *Faccini Dori v Recreb* [1994] ECR I-3325 at [26]). These principles of EU law should be remembered when considering those provisions in the RDA, the TMA and the CDPA based on the wording of EU Directives. Further, the only court which can give an authoritative ruling on the meaning of a provision in such a Directive is the ECJ.

1.5.5 **Case law**

When reading intellectual property cases it is important to understand two key points: which tribunal dealt with the matter and in which context. Dealing with the latter point first, intellectual property case law can arise in the context of an application to register a patent, trade mark or design. Here, the tribunal (ie a national or regional patent office, design registry or trade mark registry) will be concerned only with whether the application complies with the relevant statutory criteria. Second, case law can arise in the context of an action to restrain the infringement of any intellectual property right. It is important to remember that in the United Kingdom (in contrast to some other countries), the tribunal hearing the infringement action can also deal with any counterclaim that the registered right is invalid. Such a case may therefore discuss the criteria to be met by the successful claimant when suing for infringement, as well as the criteria for the validity of the claimant's right.

In the United Kingdom, decisions concerned with applications in respect of registrable intellectual property rights will be handed down by UKIPO, or, when dealing with applications to register trade marks or designs, the Trade Marks Registry or the Designs Registry or their respective appellate tribunals. Infringement actions are dealt with either by the Patents Court (a specialist court within the Chancery Division) or the Patents County Court.

As will have become apparent from the material already discussed, intellectual property rights effective in the United Kingdom can be granted by bodies other than UKIPO. In respect of patents, therefore, the decisions of the EPO are relevant, as are the decisions of OHIM in respect of trade marks and registered designs.

Lastly, there is an increasingly large body of case law being handed down in intellectual property cases by the ECJ, particularly in relation to trade marks. The ECJ's case law has two bases. First, where a national court in any Member State of the EU is required to apply a provision originating in one of the EU harmonisation Directives, a definitive interpretation of

thinking point
Is it correct to say that the United Kingdom does not really have a domestic law of intellectual property?

that Directive may only be given by the ECJ under the preliminary ruling mechanism set out in Article 267 TFEU (formerly Article 234 EC). Second, where OHIM has made a decision relating to the registrability or otherwise of an EU trade mark or design application, appeal from OHIM lies initially to the General Court (formerly the Court of First Instance of the European Community), with a further appeal (on a point of law only) to the ECJ. The ECJ thus acts in two capacities: as the final appellate body for the registration of pan-European rights and as the only judicial body which can interpret harmonisation Directives.

Summary

This chapter has explained:

- the range of rights available under United Kingdom law to protect the product of the intellect, together with their characteristics;

- the theoretical reasons why such rights might be protected; and

- the sources, both internal and external, from which United Kingdom law is derived.

Reflective questions

1 Would United Kingdom law benefit from the introduction of protection against unfair competition or would the doctrine of misappropriation be a better means of protecting the interests of other traders?

2 Which is likely to be more effective as a means of changing domestic intellectual property law, WIPO or WTO?

Annotated further reading

Arup, C. 'TRIPs: Across the Global Field of Intellectual Property' [2004] *EIPR* 7
Compares the WTO with WIPO.

Carty, H. 'The Common Law and the Quest for the IP Effect' [2007] *IPQ* 237
Considers those areas of intellectual property law where there are gaps in protection and discusses whether unfair competition or misappropriation could provide a solution.

Carty, H. 'Passing Off: Frameworks of Liability Debated' [2012] *IPQ* 106
Argues that passing off should remain firmly based in Lord Oliver's 'classic trinity'.

Crespi, S. 'IPRs under Siege: First Impressions of the Report of the Commission on Intellectual Property Rights' [2003] *EIPR* 242
Argues that the Report fails to understand the nature of IP rights, particularly as they affect developing countries, and relies heavily on emotive language when so doing.

Davis, J. 'Why the United Kingdom Should Have a Law against Misappropriation' [2012] *CLJ* 561
Argues that trends in passing off show that remedies for misappropriation are necessary to protect investment in the attractiveness of brands.

Fisher, W. 'Theories of Intellectual Property' in Munzer (ed) *New Essays in the Legal and Political Theory of Property* (2001), Cambridge University Press
Sets out in detail the various theories put forward to justify the protection of intellectual property.

Jacob, R. 'The Stephen Stewart Memorial Lecture: Industrial Property—Industry's Enemy' [1997] *IPQ* 3
Argues that the continued expansion of intellectual property rights is unjustified.

Libling, D.F. 'The Concept of Property: Property in Intangibles' (1978) 94 *LQR* 103
Argues on the basis of the *INS* case that there should be a property right in intangible property arising from effort and investment.

May, C. 'Why IPRs Are a Global Political Issue' [2003] *EIPR* 1
Argues that there needs to be a global mechanism to deal with the balance between IP owners' interests and social need.

Merges, R. *Justifying Intellectual Property* (2011), Harvard University Press
A wide-ranging synthesis of three philosophies which he argues are the true, workable foundations for intellectual property protection.

Ricketson, S. ' "Reaping without Sowing": Unfair Competition and Intellectual Property Rights in Anglo Australian Law' (1984) 7 *UNSWLJ* 1
Argues that there should be protection against misappropriation on the ground either that the defendant has gained a competitive advantage or the claimant has suffered a competitive disadvantage.

Samuelson, P. 'Challenges for WIPO and TRIPs in Regulating Intellectual Property Rights in the Information Age' [1999] *EIPR* 578
Considers the background to the TRIPs Agreement.

Schricker, G. 'Twenty-five Years of Protection against Unfair Competition' (1995) 26 *IIC* 782
Explains how unfair competition actions can be classified and gives a summary of key cases (mainly from Germany).

Schricker, G. and Henning-Bodewig, F. 'New Initiatives for the Harmonisation of Unfair Competition Law in Europe' [2002] *EIPR* 271

Discusses what areas might be the subject matter of EU harmonisation of unfair competition law.

Spence, M. 'Passing Off and the Misappropriation of Valuable Intangibles' (1996) 112 *LQR* 472

Considers four arguments in favour of adopting misappropriation as a basis for protection but concludes that none is viable.

Wadlow, C. 'The Emergent European Law of Unfair Competition and its Consumer Law Origins' [2012] *IPQ* 1

Argues that the Unfair Commercial Practices Directive could form the basis of an EU law against unfair competition.

Enforcement of intellectual property rights

Learning objectives

Upon completion of this chapter, you should have acquired:

- an understanding of the context in which intellectual property rights are enforced;
- knowledge of remedies available to a claimant before the action is heard;
- knowledge of remedies available to a successful claimant;
- an appreciation of the subtle differences which exist between the remedies for different forms of intellectual property; and
- an understanding of the role of the court, when granting relief, in trying to strike a balance between the protection of the intellectual property owner and the needs of free competition.

Introduction

In this chapter, we consider the means available to the owner of an intellectual property right (whether a patent, trade mark, design or copyright) to obtain redress for infringement. It may seem a little odd to deal with the issue of remedies so early in a study of intellectual property. However, understanding what relief an intellectual property owner may obtain will assist with the process of obtaining an overall view of the subject. It will also emphasise the practical *raison d'être* for a business to obtain intellectual property protection, namely the ability to maintain a competitive edge by keeping rival undertakings out of the marketplace by means of an injunction, or to receive some sort of monetary compensation for another's wrongful use of a patent, design, copyright or trade mark.

The importance of litigation in the development of intellectual property law should not be underestimated. It is, after all, a case-based subject and those cases come about because clients approach their legal advisors for assistance in stopping competitors and counterfeiters from misappropriating the effort and investment in creating an intellectual property portfolio. In turn, this produces judicial decisions which interpret and apply the statutory rules.

cross reference

The need to balance intellectual property with free competition was discussed at section 1.2.

It might be assumed that such litigation (which in the United Kingdom is very expensive) would be the prerogative of powerful, multi-national corporations who are able to drive smaller enterprises out of business. We shall therefore return to one of our recurring themes, namely how to balance the interests of the intellectual property owner with the needs of free competition.

As this chapter will show, most remedies are common to all intellectual property rights. Whether the action concerns the infringement of a patent, design, copyright or trade mark, the relief a successful claimant can obtain is basically the same. Nevertheless, there are a host of minor differences between the available remedies. The reason for these discrepancies is not immediately apparent. In many cases the idiosyncrasies can be attributed to history or to the fact that United Kingdom intellectual property legislation has developed on a piecemeal basis. Unlike other jurisdictions, there is no overarching civil code to ensure a consistency of approach. However, Directive 2004/48/EC of the European Parliament and of the Council of 29 April 2004 on the enforcement of intellectual property rights [2004] OJ L 157/45 ('the Enforcement Directive') has produced a degree of standardisation previously lacking, but equally has raised questions about some well-established principles of United Kingdom law.

2.1 General matters

2.1.1 Forum

Under the Supreme Court Act 1981 (now renamed the Senior Courts Act by the Constitutional Reform Act 2005) all actions for the **infringement** of intellectual property rights are allocated to the Patents Court, part of the Chancery Division (see s.6(1)(a), ss.61, 62 and Sch. 1). Despite its name, the Patents Court deals with all types of intellectual property rights. It has a number of specialist judges.

In addition, there is the Intellectual Property Enterprise Court (IPEC) (formerly, the Patents County Court) (Copyright, Designs and Patents Act 1988 ('CDPA') s.287), intended to provide a less costly and more speedy means of litigation for small businesses (for the reasons why the court was established, see the *Report of the Oulton Committee on Patent Litigation*, Lord Chancellor's Department, November 1987). The IPEC is part of the county court system and therefore it has the ordinary jurisdiction of such a court. Its intellectual property jurisdiction is 'special jurisdiction', which is subdivided into 'multi-track' and 'small claims track'. There is one specialist judge appointed to the court and there is a ceiling on the amount of **damages** or an **account of profits** (£500,000) and costs (£50,000) which can be awarded. The creation of the small claims track was a response to the concerns of the *Hargreaves Report* and came into effect in October 2012. It covers cases involving **copyright**, **trade marks**, **passing off** and unregistered designs where the sum claimed is less than £10,000. Guidelines concerned with the transfer of cases between the Patents Court and the IPEC are set out in the Patents County Court Guide: factors include the size of the parties, the complexity of the claim, the nature of the evidence (hearings are strictly limited to two days), and the value of the claim. Appeals on questions of either law or fact lie from either the Patents Court or the IPEC to the Court of Appeal. Further appeal to the Supreme Court (formerly the House of Lords) is only possible with leave.

2.1.2 Choice of defendant

The statutory rules on infringement impose liability not only on primary infringers of the right in question, such as those who affix trade marks to goods or who make copies of sound recordings and films, but on **contributory infringers** (those who assist the primary infringer to commit an infringing act, by the pre-manufacture supply of essential materials, equipment or packaging) and on secondary infringers (those who post-manufacture sell, distribute or otherwise deal in infringing products by way of trade). An important question for any **claimant** will therefore be 'whom should I sue'? Tempting though it may be to sue anyone and everyone, a claimant will need to consider likely expense and complexity if there is a large number of defendants. There is also the possible loss of **goodwill** if retailers are sued, bearing in mind that the claimant may want those retailers to sell its own goods.

2.1.2.1 Conduct outside the jurisdiction

Suing importers, wholesalers or retailers may, however, be necessary where the primary infringer is an overseas undertaking which has manufactured infringing copies abroad, as all the statutory infringement provisions require acts of infringement to be committed within the United Kingdom: see the Patents Act 1977 s.60; the Trade Marks Act 1994 ('TMA') s.9; and CDPA s.16. No such restriction appears in s.7 Registered Designs Act 1949 ('RDA') but common sense would indicate that a United Kingdom **registered design** can be infringed only by conduct committed within the jurisdiction.

The Brussels Regulation (Council Regulation (EU) No 1215/2012 of 12 December 2012 on Jurisdiction and the Recognition and Enforcement of Judgments in Civil and Commercial Matters, [2012] OJ L 351/1) (the 'recast Regulation' which will be effective in January 2015), like its predecessor, (Council Regulation (EC) No 44/2001 of 22 December 2000 on Jurisdiction and the Recognition and Enforcement of Judgments in Civil and Commercial Matters, [2001] OJ L 12/1) enables United Kingdom courts to accept jurisdiction either on the basis of the domicile of the defendant (Article 4) (currently Article 2) or the place where the harm was committed (Article 7) (currently Article 5). However, in the case of registered intellectual property rights, the wording of Article 24(4) (currently Article 22(4)) confers exclusive jurisdiction on the state granting the right (*Coin Controls Ltd v Suzo International (UK) Ltd* [1997] 3 All ER 45). The ability to sue an enterprise before United Kingdom courts for infringing conduct committed abroad is therefore limited to copyright infringement and passing off. Thus in *Pearce v Ove Arup Partnership Ltd* [1999] 1 All ER 769, jurisdiction for copyright infringement allegedly committed in the Netherlands was accepted on the basis of the defendant's domicile as a United Kingdom company, although ultimately the defendant was found not to have infringed. In *Mecklermedia Corp v DC Congress GmbH* [1997] 3 WLR 479, jurisdiction was accepted for passing off, where although the misrepresentation had been made in Germany, the harm to goodwill occurred in the United Kingdom. The recast Regulation will require further amendment to accommodate the **Unitary Patent**.

cross reference
The Unitary Patent was explained at section 1.5.3.

It may, however, be possible for an intellectual property owner to sue for infringement where a primary infringer is located outside the United Kingdom, but an undertaking within the jurisdiction arranges for them to make the infringing product. In such a case, the claimant would be able to argue that the overseas defendant is a joint tortfeasor, either by virtue of having induced the infringing act, or because it was party to a common design. So, for example, in *Puschner v Tom Parker (Scotland)* [1989] RPC 430 there was held to be a common design where as part of a joint marketing agreement, the foreign supplier had provided promotional literature to and trained the sales staff of the United Kingdom customer. However, the mere supply of infringing goods to a United Kingdom purchaser is not enough for this type of liability: 'Each person must make the infringing acts his own' (*Sabaf SpA v Meneghetti* [2003] RPC 264 at [58] (CA)).

2.1.3 **Who can sue**

It may seem self-evident that an action in respect of the infringement of an intellectual property right can only be brought by its proprietor. Nevertheless, case law is full of examples of claimants failing because they are not the owners of the right. Examples include an employee suing for copyright infringement when the **work** was owned by the employer by virtue of a contract of employment (*Beloff v Pressdram Ltd* [1973] RPC 765) or a widow suing for infringement of copyright in photographs taken by her late husband where it could not be established that she had letters of administration to his estate (*Gabrin v Universal Music Operations Ltd*

[2004] ECDR 18). In the case of registrable rights, the relevant register (of **patents**, **designs** or trade marks) should be checked to see that the claimant is actually entered as the owner of the right alleged to have been infringed before the claim form is issued. Any transactions (such as **assignments**) affecting entitlement to sue must have been recorded (see Patents Act s.68, TMA s.25). It is also useful to check that all **renewal fees** have been paid!

All intellectual property legislation (the Patents Act s.67, TMA s.31, CDPA s.101, RDA s.24) confers the right to commence proceedings on an **exclusive licensee** of the right. Such right is procedural only and does not confer any proprietary interest (*Northern & Shell plc v Condé Nast & National Magazine Distributors Ltd* [1995] RPC 117). In the case of registrable rights, the existence of the exclusive **licence** must be entered on the register. As a result of the Enforcement Directive, the penalty for failing to record a licence is that the successful claimant may not be awarded costs, whereas previously the penalty for failing to record a licence promptly was loss of compensatory relief. In the case of copyright, the exclusive licence must be in writing in order for the procedural rights in s.101 CDPA to be exercised. Subject to certain conditions, similar rights may also be conferred on a **non-exclusive licensee** under s.101A.

2.1.4 Statutory basis of relief

For those intellectual property rights which are statute based (that is, copyright, designs, patents and trade marks), the remedies are prescribed by the relevant statute. These statutes are largely declaratory of prior case law (*Coflexip SA v Stolt Comex Seaway MS Ltd* [2001] 1 All ER 952). Remedies for passing off and **breach of confidence** are the result of case law alone and reflect the historical influence of the Court of Chancery over the development of these causes of action.

2.1.5 The effect of the Civil Procedure Rules

As a result of the Woolf Reforms, the Civil Procedure Rules ('CPR') were introduced in 1999. So far as practicable, in giving effect to the overall objective of dealing with cases justly, courts must seek to:

* ensure that the parties are on an equal footing;
* save expense;
* deal with the case in ways which are proportionate; and
* ensure that the case is dealt with expeditiously and fairly.

The key word in the CPR's objectives is 'expeditiously'. It seeks to address the concerns previously raised about unnecessary delays in litigation. The reforms have also led to changes in terminology, so that 'plaintiff' becomes 'claimant', 'writs' become 'claim forms', 'interlocutory injunctions' become 'interim injunctions', *Anton Piller* orders become '**search orders**' and *Mareva* orders become '**freezing injunctions**'. Latin words and phrases are to be avoided. CPR Part 63, together with supplementary Practice Direction 63 and the Patents Court Guide, govern intellectual property litigation. CPR Part 63 and its Practice Direction are stated to apply to both the Patents Court and the IPEC.

2.1.6 Summary

Before commencing proceedings for the infringement of an intellectual property right, the potential claimant ought to consider the following:

- which court should I use?
- do I have title to sue?
- in the case of registrable rights, is the register entry correct and have all renewal fees been paid?
- has an act of primary infringement (eg manufacture) been committed in the United Kingdom or have the infringing products been made abroad?
- if the latter is the case, is there a suitable defendant within the jurisdiction (a subsidiary of the manufacturer, or an importer, wholesaler or retailer) who can be sued?
- if the most obvious defendant is a retailer, is it worth the loss of goodwill if litigation is started?
- if the manufacturer is based abroad, might it be possible to allege a common design with another enterprise within the United Kingdom?

2.2 Pre-trial orders

If an intellectual property owner wishes to sue someone for infringement, a successful action may be of little value to the claimant if, in the meantime, the defendant is allowed to continue trading, thereby increasing their share of the market or doing other harm to the claimant's business. Equally, issuing a claim form may have the effect of encouraging a defendant to destroy evidence of their infringing conduct, or to remove assets out of the United Kingdom so that no funds exist out of which to pay damages. Finally, an intellectual property owner may decide to sue a retailer who is selling infringing copies, but ideally would like to know who has been making these copies. All these difficulties can be overcome by the award of various pre-trial orders.

2.2.1 Interim injunctions

Interim injunctions (formerly called interlocutory injunctions) are governed by the Senior Courts Act 1981, s.37 together with CPR Part 25. An interim injunction is a court order directing that certain acts do or do not take place or should continue, pending the final determination of the parties' rights by the court. An **injunction** may be ordered in all cases in which it appears to the court to be just and convenient to do so. The objective of an interim injunction is to preserve the **status quo** in order to prevent irremediable harm. As with other interim remedies, an interim injunction may be sought before or after the claim form is issued, although seeking interim relief before proceedings have been started can only be done in cases of urgency. Speed is of the essence in seeking interim relief: whilst not commencing proceedings for several weeks after the claimant becomes aware of the infringement may not be fatal, a delay of several months usually will be. The claimant must offer a cross-undertaking in damages, that is, pay money into court as security in case they lose at the main hearing. If they do not have the means to do so, then interim relief will not be available.

2.2.1.1 Relevant principles

The principles governing the grant of interim injunctions were stated by Lord Diplock in *American Cyanamid v Ethicon* [1975] AC 396, itself a patent infringement case. At the time, Lord Diplock was attempting to restate the basic rule that the award of an interim injunction is essentially a discretionary matter. This was because, he said, the Court of Appeal in *Cyanamid* had treated the matter as if it were a 'rule of law' by demanding that the claimant establish a *prima facie* case. The principal issue, according to Lord Diplock, is whether there is a serious issue to be tried, arguably a more relaxed test than that of showing a *prima facie* case.

The matter was revisited by Laddie J in *Series 5 Software v Clarke* [1996] FSR 273. Laddie J declared that the most important factor to be taken into account by the court in the exercise of its discretion was the strength of each party's case. The effect of *Series 5*, when combined with the emphasis in the CPR on the expeditious conduct of litigation, means that where a successful claimant's damages would be based on a reasonable licence fee (the normal remedy in many infringement cases) an interim injunction is unlikely to be awarded. Where, however, the right to be protected is incapable of compensation (for example, the right of privacy in photographs) then interim relief ought to be granted (*Douglas v Hello! Ltd (No 2)* [2005] 4 All ER 128 (CA) at [253–255], relying on *Von Hannover v Germany* (2005) 40 EHRR 1).

At first glance, the views of Laddie J in *Series 5* appear to contradict those of Lord Diplock in *American Cyanamid*. The question is often asked 'how can that be?' because under the doctrine of precedent, a decision of the House of Lords (now the Supreme Court) is binding on all lower courts. It is, however, instructive to compare in more detail what was said in the two cases.

case close-up

American Cyanamid v Ethicon [1975] AC 396

Lord Diplock listed the factors to be considered when granting interim relief:

- whether there is a serious issue to be tried;
- whether damages are an adequate remedy. Adequacy has to be considered from the viewpoint of both parties. If the claimant succeeds at trial and obtains a permanent injunction, could they be compensated adequately if the defendant is allowed to continue the harmful conduct between the date of the application for interim relief and the date of the trial? That being so, if the defendant were to succeed at trial, could they be compensated adequately if an injunction were granted between the date of the application and the date of the trial?
- where the balance of convenience lies;
- if factors are evenly balanced, the court should endeavour to preserve the **status quo**; and
- which party has the stronger case?

Series 5 Software v Clarke [1996] FSR 273

Laddie J stated that the issues for the court were:

- interim relief is always a matter of discretion, depending on the facts of the case;
- the rule is that there are no rules—the relief must be kept flexible;
- the court should avoid dealing with complex issues of disputed fact or law at an interim hearing; and
- the major factors to be considered are the adequacy of damages, the balance of convenience, the maintenance of the **status quo**; and whether there is any clear view of the relative strengths of each of the parties' case.

One obvious difference between the views of Lord Diplock and Laddie J is that the latter places greater stress on the relative strengths of the parties' case. However, looked at more closely, both judgments are saying the same thing. Interim injunctions are always a matter of discretion and flexibility must be maintained. Each case will depend on a number of factors. The conclusion to be drawn from both cases is that periodically the courts need to remind themselves of the discretionary nature of the award. Laddie J was doing no more than Lord Diplock had done 20 years before.

2.2.1.2 Effect of the Human Rights Act 1998

Where the action involves a claim for copyright infringement or breach of confidence, and the defendant is a newspaper, magazine or broadcasting organisation, s.12(3) Human Rights Act 1998 provides that no relief (for example, an interim injunction) which might affect the exercise of the right to freedom of expression is to be granted so as to restrain publication before trial, unless the court is satisfied that the applicant is likely to establish that publication should not be allowed. The relationship between this provision and the *American Cyanamid* test was explored by the House of Lords in *Cream Holdings Ltd v Banerjee* [2004] 3 WLR 918. Lord Nicholls, having declared that the purpose of s.12(3) was to buttress the protection afforded to freedom of speech at the interlocutory stage (sic), thought that likelihood of success at trial was an essential element in the court's consideration of whether to make an interim order. Flexibility meant that there could be no single, rigid standard. The court should not grant an interim order restraining publication unless satisfied that the applicant's prospects of success were 'sufficiently favourable' in the circumstances. 'Sufficiently favourable' meant that relief should not be granted where the applicant had not satisfied the court that he would probably succeed at trial.

2.2.1.3 The balance of convenience

One of the issues mentioned in Lord Diplock's opinion in *American Cyanamid*, the balance of convenience, needs further elaboration. Much will depend on the circumstances of each individual case, but the court may consider one or more of the following factors, most of which are of a commercial nature:

- the relative size of the parties. They may be equal in size, for example, both being large, multi-nationals. If that is so, both will be able to pay damages if the other succeeds at trial, and both will be able to survive competition in the marketplace in the meantime, as in *Polaroid v Kodak* [1977] FSR 25. In such a case, an interim injunction will *not* be granted. On the other hand, the claimant may be small and the defendant a large enterprise with 'muscle', as in *Corruplast v Harrison* [1978] RPC 761, in which case relief will be granted. Alternatively, relief may be denied where the defendant is relatively new to the market but the claimant is well established and thus able financially to withstand competition until trial, as in *Catnic v Stressline* [1976] FSR 157;

- whether there are **public interest** grounds for refusing relief. Examples of the public interest prevailing include where an interim injunction would prevent a new life-saving drug from reaching the market (*Roussel-Uclaf v G.D. Searle* [1977] FSR 125) or the need for a 'whistle-blower' to disclose the wrongdoing of their former employer even though this involved breach of the employee's duty of confidentiality (*Cream Holdings Ltd v Banerjee*);

- whether there was any delay by the claimant. Interim relief should be sought promptly, ie within days or weeks of the infringing conduct, not months;

- whether the parties are in direct competition, and how close their products are in terms of characteristics and quality. Direct competition from a product which is a cheap imitation of the claimant's is more likely to lead to relief being granted, because of the risk of loss of reputation, and hence loss of long-term sales, to the claimant's product;

- whether granting or not granting an injunction might put one of the parties out of business; and

- the risk to either party's investment (as in *Catnic v Stressline* [1976] FSR 157), including the risk of redundancies amongst their employees.

It can therefore be seen that the balance of convenience is far from straightforward. Ultimately, however, the CPR ensure that in many cases, interim relief will be refused and a speedy trial ordered instead.

thinking point

Is it fair to deny a claimant interim relief where there is clear evidence that there has been infringement? Do the principles set out by Lord Diplock in American Cyanamid *and Laddie J in* Series 5 *ensure that a fair balance is maintained between the interests of the intellectual property owner and those of any competitors?*

2.2.2 **Search orders**

These are now governed by the Civil Procedure Act 1997 s.7, together with CPR Part 25. Often mis-described as a 'civil search warrant', the order is addressed to the defendant who, it is thought, might destroy vital evidence of infringing conduct. It requires the defendant to admit the claimant's solicitor to the defendant's premises with a view to copying or removing such evidence. The defendant is not given notice of the request for the order and hence is not in court when it is granted. Surprise is of the essence.

case close-up

Anton Piller KG v Manufacturing Processes Ltd [1976] Ch 55

. . . .

The search order originated in Lord Denning's judgment in *Anton Piller KG v Manufacturing Processes Ltd* [1976] Ch 55, where he laid down the primary criteria:

- the claimant must have an extremely strong *prima facie* case;
- there must be a serious risk of damage to the claimant's interests;
- there must be compelling evidence that the defendant will dispose of or destroy documents if given warning (for example, on receipt of the claim form); but
- the risk to the defendant's business must not be excessive.

The purpose of the order must be to fulfil a legitimate purpose, such as protecting the claimant's copyright or other intellectual property right (*Columbia Pictures v Robinson* [1986] FSR 367) but the court is required to bear in mind the right to private life enshrined in Article 8 of the ECHR (*Chappell v UK* [1989] FSR 617).

Search orders have always been of a draconian nature. Indeed, a former Master of the Rolls once described the *Anton Piller* order as 'one of the law's two nuclear weapons', the other 'nuclear weapon' being the *Mareva* order (*per* Donaldson LJ, as he then was, in *Bank Mellat v Nikpour* [1985] FSR 87 at p. 92). At one time, *Anton Piller* orders were granted relatively readily. By the late 1980s, the perception was that they were being misused. Such misuse was that either claimants were using them as a 'fishing expedition' to gain information about a rival's business rather than evidence of infringing conduct, or they were being administered in a very aggressive manner. These concerns led Nicholls VC to state clear guidelines for the grant of an *Anton Piller* order in *Universal Thermosensors v Hibben* [1992] 3 All ER 257. These guidelines have now been incorporated into and updated by the Practice Direction supplementing CPR Part 25.

case close-up

Universal Thermosensors v Hibben [1992] 3 All ER 257

. . . .

Nicholls VC gave the following guidelines for search orders:

- the order is to be executed during office hours so that the defendant can contact his/her solicitor;
- a female solicitor must be present if unaccompanied female family members or office staff will be on the defendant's premises;
- the defendant must be given a list of items which are being removed;
- the injunction restraining the defendant from giving a 'tip off' to third parties is to be limited in time;
- the order must be executed only at company premises before a responsible officer of the defendant's business;
- the claimant is not allowed to make a thorough search of the defendant's premises (that is, the order should not be a 'fishing expedition'); and
- there must be an experienced supervising solicitor who should report back to the court.

As with interim injunctions, the claimant must give a cross-undertaking in damages. The search order must not have the effect of putting the defendant out of business. If documents are copied, these must be returned to the defendant within two days. The CPR contain further detailed guidance where the evidence to be obtained is stored on the defendant's computers.

thinking point
Do the current rules on the award of a search order meet the concerns expressed by Nicholls VC in Universal Thermosensors v Hibben?

The guidelines are indicative of the sorts of misuse which occurred before the *Hibben* decision, which may well have justified the description of the order as a 'nuclear weapon'. Because the application for the order is heard in the defendant's absence, the onus is on the claimant to put all material facts before the court. Failure to do so may lead to the order being discharged or the evidence obtained not being admissible (*Naf Naf v Dickens* [1993] FSR 424). The current Practice Direction, when coupled with the requirement to give a cross-undertaking in damages and the risk that evidence incorrectly obtained may be rendered inadmissible, suggests that the opportunity for abuse is much reduced.

2.2.3 Freezing injunctions

These are governed by the Senior Courts Act 1981, s.37 and CPR Part 25. A freezing injunction (again, obtained without notice, that is, without the defendant being notified or being present in court) is designed to prevent the defendant from moving assets out of the jurisdiction or otherwise dissipating them or concealing them so as to deprive the claimant of any monetary compensation in the event of success at trial. It may relate to assets within the jurisdiction or worldwide. The order originated in *Mareva Compania Naviera SA v International Bulk Carriers SA* [1980] 1 All ER 213. The case established the following requirements:

- a cause of action justiciable within England and Wales;
- a good arguable case on the merits;
- the defendant has assets within the jurisdiction; and
- there is a real risk of removal or disposal.

The safeguards for such a draconian order are that the defendant must be left with enough money to live on and to carry on his day-to-day business. Nevertheless, the order can affect third parties, such as banks.

2.2.4 Discovery

The last interim order to consider is that of **discovery**. In *Norwich Pharmacal v Commissioners of Customs & Excise* [1974] AC 133 the House of Lords confirmed that an order could be made against the Commissioners of Customs and Excise to reveal the names of a company importing pharmaceutical products which infringed the claimant's patent. In *Ashworth Security Hospital v MGN* [2003] FSR 311, a similar order was granted against a newspaper journalist, requiring him to disclose the name of the person who had supplied the journalist with the medical records of a convicted criminal being held in a secure hospital. The information had been disclosed to the journalist in breach of confidence. The House of Lords stressed, however, that the order in the instant case was issued because of a pressing social need, and that a court issuing such an order should bear in mind the Human Rights Act 1998, in particular s.10(2) (the freedom of the press). Last, in *The Rugby Football Union v Consolidated Information*

Services Ltd [2012] 1 WLR 3333, the Supreme Court rejected the defendant's argument that an order requiring it to reveal the names of those who had supplied it with tickets in breach of the claimant's conditions of sale was unnecessary and disproportionate: it did not breach Article 8 of the EU's Charter of Fundamental Rights.

As with other interim relief, the onus is on the claimant to establish that there has been infringement of an intellectual property right. The court will limit the use of the information obtained under the order, so that it can only be used to support further intellectual property litigation.

The order for discovery of names (as a prelude to further litigation) should not be confused with an order for discovery of documents. The latter is one of a range of directions which may be made by the court as part of the case management process under the CPR.

thinking point

Do the various forms of interim relief (injunctions, search orders, freezing injunctions and discovery of names) provide effective protection for the intellectual property owner against a serial counterfeiter?

2.3 Post-trial remedies

The successful claimant in an intellectual property infringement action has a range of well-established remedies available to them. These comprise injunctive relief, compensation for financial loss and a range of court orders intended to ensure that infringing copies do not remain in circulation. Some of these remedies will, however, have to be re-evaluated as the impact of the Enforcement Directive becomes clearer.

2.3.1 Final injunctions

Each of the principal statutes (RDA s.24A, TMA s.14, CDPA s.96 and the Patents Act 1977, s.61) provides for the award of a final injunction. Once it has been established that there has been infringement of an intellectual property right and the infringement has not completely ceased at the date of trial, an injunction is the normal form of remedy: *Cantor Gaming Ltd v Gameaccount Global Ltd* [2007] EWHC 1914. The injunction protects the claimant from a continuation of the infringements of his rights. The court assumes that the infringement is not a one-off activity and so grants relief to avoid repetition: *Coflexip SA v Stolt Comex Seaway MS Ltd* at [6–7].

Nevertheless, even a final injunction is discretionary in nature. It must be fair to the defendant and will not be awarded where it is unlikely that the defendant will repeat any acts of infringement, because, for example, undertakings have been given: *Landor & Hawa International Ltd v Azure Designs Ltd* [2007] FSR 181 at [46] *per* Neuberger LJ. Equally, a final injunction will not be granted if the interference with the claimant's right is trivial. The injunction will be discharged if the intellectual property right in question is declared **invalid** in other, parallel proceedings against a different defendant: *Coflexip SA v Stolt Offshore MS Ltd* [2004] FSR 34 at [32]. The same principle also applies to the award of damages: *Virgin Atlantic Airways Ltd v Zodiac Seats UK Ltd* [2013] UKSC 46.

The form of the injunction is governed by the wording of the relevant statutory provision rather than the actual conduct of the defendant: *Coflexip SA v Stolt Comex Seaway MS Ltd per* Aldous LJ at [60]. Thus, even though the defendant may only have infringed the claimant's patent by manufacture, the formula of the injunction will reflect the list of infringing acts set out in the legislation. Normally, the injunction is limited in time to the balance of the term of protection for the intellectual property right in question. However, where the defendant has obtained an unfair competitive advantage from its infringing conduct, so that on the expiry of the claimant's right the defendant could immediately recommence manufacture of a rival product, the duration of the injunction may be extended beyond the expiry date of the right. The defendant will be restrained from competing with the claimant for the length of time it would normally take the defendant, starting afresh and without the knowledge which it has already gained by its infringing conduct, to analyse the claimant's product and set up a manu-facturing facility (see *Dyson Appliances Ltd v Hoover Ltd (No 2)* [2001] RPC 544 for an example of this so-called 'springboard' relief).

The principles concerning the grant of final injunctions were developed in an era when infring-ers were primarily manufacturers or those who supplied manufacturers with key ingredients or those who supplied the infringing goods to the public. In the age of the internet, however, what should the position be regarding those enterprises whose services are used by a third party infringer, but who have not themselves committed an infringing act? Specifically, are internet companies, such as Google, eBay and Yahoo, to be subjected to injunctive relief where their websites are used by others to sell infringing products? The Enforcement Directive provides, in Article 11, that Member States are required to ensure that owners of intellec-tual property rights are in a position to apply for an injunction against intermediaries whose services are used by third party infringers. The United Kingdom has not taken any steps to implement Article 11, it being assumed by the Government that existing law is in compliance with the Directive. However, in *L'Oréal SA v eBay International AG* [2009] EWHC 1094 (Ch) Arnold J pointed out that such an intermediary could not be liable under existing law as a joint infringer under the principle of *CBS Songs Ltd v Amstrad Consumer Electronics plc* [1988] AC 1013 as it had not procured the infringing conduct by inducement, incitement or persuasion, nor had it participated in a common design. Facilitation was not enough, and eBay was under no legal duty to prevent infringement. Arnold J added that it was unclear whether Article 11 of the Enforcement Directive had changed these principles so that a domestic court would be obliged to apply s.37 of the Senior Courts Act to intermediaries. He therefore referred this point to the ECJ for guidance. The reply from the Court (in Case C-324/09 *L'Oréal SA v eBay International AG* [2011] RPC 777) was to the effect that Member States are required to empower their courts to order the operators of online marketplaces to terminate existing infringements and to prevent further ones.

2.3.2 **Monetary remedies**

A successful claimant in an intellectual property infringement action will normally want to be compensated for the trespass to its right. Two forms of monetary remedy are available, com-mon law damages and the equitable action for an account of profits.

2.3.2.1 Damages: general principles

Damages for the infringement of intellectual property rights are tortious in nature, their object-ive being to restore the claimant to the position they would have been in had the defendant not infringed. The principles governing the award of damages for intellectual property rights are set out in detail in *General Tire v Firestone* [1976] RPC 197 by Lord Wilberforce. In the case of patent infringement, where the claimant is in the business of manufacturing goods, and so in competition with the defendant, the measure of damages will be lost profits. In all other cases of patent infringement the measure of damages will be a reasonable licence fee. Lost profits is also the measure of damages adopted in trade mark infringement actions, and where there has been wrongful use of a competitor's **trade secret** (*Cadbury Schweppes Inc v FBI Foods Ltd* [2000] FSR 491). In the case of copyright infringement, the normal measure will be a reasonable licence fee.

2.3.2.2 'Parasitic' damages

If damages are meant to compensate the claimant for the trespass to the intangible property right, can a **patentee** recover damages in respect of non-patented items which are normally sold as part of a patented product or process? The original view expressed in *Polaroid v Eastman Kodak* [1977] RPC 379 was that such 'parasitic' damages were not available because the mon-etary compensation must reflect the precise scope of the patentee's monopoly. Consequently, the patentee could only claim for patented items and not any ancillary equipment. However, a more liberal attitude was shown in *Gerber v Lectra* [1997] RPC 443 where Jacob J held that the loss of sales of ancillary items which were invariably sold with the patented equipment were recoverable as being a direct result of the infringing conduct.

2.3.2.3 Additional damages for copyright infringement

In the case of copyright infringement and **unregistered design right** infringement (CDPA ss.97(2) and 229(3)) but not any other form of intellectual property right, the court may award **additional damages**. A similar provision existed in the Copyright Act 1956 (in relation to copyright only), its purpose being explained in *Williams v Settle* [1960] 1 WLR 1072 to deal with cases of flagrant infringement, where the defendant had exhibited total disregard of the claimant's copyright.

Section 97(2) was considered in *Nottinghamshire Healthcare NHS Trust v News Group Newspapers* [2002] RPC 962 by Pumfrey J. Having reiterated the general principles appli-cable to damages for the infringement of all intellectual property rights, the judgment reviewed the difference of wording between s.97(2) and its predecessor. Pumfrey J pointed out that the exact nature of additional damages for copyright infringement under the CDPA had been left undecided by the House of Lords in *Redrow Homes Ltd v Bett Brothers plc* [1998] 2 WLR 198. It had been suggested that the award under s.97(2) was *sui generis*, but, Pumfrey J explained, a consensus was emerging that such damages were similar to aggravated damages. The reasons for this were, first, the policy restrictions laid down by the House of Lords in *Rookes v Barnard* [1964] AC 1129 on the award of exemplary dam-ages, the latter phrase meaning, according to Pumfrey J at [33], 'an award of damages intended both to compensate the claimant for his loss and to teach the defendant that tort does not pay', this definition reflecting the punitive nature of the award. Second, the possibility of bringing criminal proceedings against the infringer under the CDPA s.107

pointed to additional damages for copyright infringement being aggravated damages, that is, the award had an element of restitution which took into account the benefit gained by the defendant, and where the normal compensation to the claimant 'left the defendant still enjoying the fruits of his infringement'. These conclusions suggest that there has been a change in the nature of additional damages under the CDPA, as the Court of Appeal in *Williams v Settle* clearly regarded the predecessor to s.97(2) as giving power to award exemplary damages.

An example of additional damages can be found in *Phonographic Performance Ltd v Reader* [2005] FSR 891, where a disc jockey had failed to obtain a licence for the public performance of sound recordings for at least two years despite previous undertakings. Pumfrey J held, applying his own ruling in *Nottinghamshire Health Care NHS Trust v Newsgroup Newspapers*, that it is permissible for an award of statutory additional damages to include a punitive element provided that the purpose was not simply to punish the defendant. Here, the defendant was well aware of the need for a licence, had previously obtained one only under the threat of legal proceedings, and had no excuse for his failure to seek the appropriate licence. It was therefore a case of deliberate and flagrant infringement.

2.3.2.4 Damages: the effect of the defendant's innocence

The various statutes dealing with the award of damages for intellectual property infringement contain provisions dealing with the effect of the defendant's innocence on the claimant's ability to obtain such relief. The defendant's innocence must be as to the *existence* of the right, an objective standard being applied. Innocence prevents the award of damages for copyright, design right, registered design and patent infringement, by virtue of the CDPA ss.97(1) and 233(1), RDA as amended, s.24B and Patents Act 1977, s.62(1). There is no such provision in the TMA 1994.

As to why innocence does not affect the award of damages for trade mark infringement (and likewise passing off), the matter was considered in *Gillette UK Ltd v Edenwest Ltd* [1994] RPC 279. Blackburne J pointed out that the trade mark infringement action was derived, historically, from the tort of deceit. What mattered was *the effect* of the defendant's misrepresentation on the claimant's customer, not the defendant's state of mind. If the consumer was misled, it mattered not whether the misrepresentation was innocent.

2.3.2.5 Damages: the effect of the defendant's knowledge

The Enforcement Directive may yet have a further impact on the calculation of damages. Article 13 of the Directive is incorporated in Regulation 3 of the Intellectual Property (Enforcement etc) Regulations 2006 (SI 2006/1028). It provides that where a defendant knew or had reasonable grounds to know that he was engaged in infringing activity, the damages awarded should be 'appropriate to the actual prejudice suffered as a result of the infringement'. The court is required to take into account all appropriate aspects, in particular the negative economic consequences, including any lost profits which the claimant has suffered and any unfair profits made by the defendant and any elements other than economic factors, including moral prejudice caused to the claimant by the infringement. As yet there have been no cases where Regulation 3 has been raised, so it remains a matter of speculation whether the principles elaborated by Lord Wilberforce in *General Tire* will need revising or whether the notion of additional damages, currently confined to copyright and unregistered design right, will have to be extended to other forms of intellectual property.

2.3.2.6 Account of profits

Equity provides an alternative form of monetary remedy through the order for an account of profits. The aim here is to transfer to the claimant the profits which the defendant has made from his/her infringing conduct, rather than to compensate the claimant for lost revenue from the intellectual property right. An account of profits can also be the appropriate remedy where there has been either breach of a fiduciary duty or breach of a civil servant's duty to the Crown, as illustrated by *AG v Blake* [2001] AC 268, although the House of Lords was at pains to point out that this was an extreme case.

The remedy of an account of profits can be complex to apply, and has the effect of condoning past acts of infringement. Nevertheless, there are instances when it is more advantageous than damages. The decision of *Potton v Yorkclose* [1990] FSR 11 is a good example of when an account is preferable. *Potton* was a case of copyright infringement where the copyright work consisted of an architect's plans for houses. Had the defendant sought a licence before building the houses, the fee would have been governed by the rules of the Royal Institute of British Architects and would have been relatively low. However, by copying without permission and by building houses at a time of a rising housing market, the defendant gained much more from its infringing activities. Despite the complexity of the calculation, an account was a more effective remedy.

Like the award of damages, a plea of innocent infringement by a defendant may have the effect of denying a claimant an account, though the statutory provisions are more inconsistent here. The Patents Act 1977, s.62(1), and the RDA s.24B both provide that innocence (again, to be determined objectively) will prevent the award of an account of profits. Innocence does not, however, affect the award of an account for copyright and unregistered design right infringement (see the CDPA ss.97(1) and 233(1)). Innocence cannot prevent the award of an account of profits for trade mark infringement or passing off for the same reason as innocence does not prevent the award of damages (*Gillette v Edenwest*). Proposed amendments to the RDA s.24B in the Intellectual Property Act 2014 will result in the award of an account of profits (but not damages) being available against the innocent infringer of a registered design.

2.3.2.7 Account or damages?

A claimant cannot have both damages and an account, but must elect between them. However, they do not have to do so until after the conclusion of the trial: *Island Records v Tring* [1995] FSR 560. Where, however, a claimant elects for an account, they may not also claim additional damages under s.97(2) CDPA: *Redrow Homes Ltd v Bett Brothers plc*.

2.3.2.8 Remedies: discrepancies

As will have become apparent, there are a number of minor discrepancies between the statutory provisions on damages, the most obvious examples being the effect of innocence and the availability of additional damages. Dealing with the latter first, the availability of additional damages for copyright and unregistered design right infringement, but not for the infringement of other forms of intellectual property right, seems at first glance intuitively wrong.

Copyright and unregistered design right are not registrable intellectual property rights, so there is no means whereby the defendant can ascertain the existence of the right. By contrast, anyone can check the registers of trade marks, designs and patents, so why should they not be penalised if they infringe in a flagrant manner? However, additional damages for copyright and unjustified design right infringement can be justified because *copying* the work is the kernel of liability for both types of right. Further, the normal measure of damages will be a reasonable licence fee, which a persistent defendant may regard as an incidental cost. If, therefore, a defendant has deliberately and flagrantly copied a work, or persisted in committing another of the restricted acts, then it seems entirely appropriate that such additional compensation be available to 'top up' the reasonable licence fee normally awarded under the CDPA.

With regard to the effect of innocence on the availability of monetary relief, *Gillette v Edenwest* contains a convincing explanation as to why trade marks and passing off are different from other forms of intellectual property right. What mattered, historically, was the effect of the defendant's conduct on the claimant's customers, not the defendant's state of mind. However, there remain differences between patents, copyright, unregistered design right and registered design right as regards the effect of innocence on the award of damages and an account of profits. For both patents and registered designs, at present, innocence is a complete bar to any monetary award, whilst with copyright and unregistered design right, innocence prevents the award of damages but not an account. The origin of this may lie in the difference between registered and unregistered rights, or because of the normal measure of damages for copyright and unregistered design right infringement. Equally, one is tempted to put the matter down to Parliamentary oversight which in one regard the Intellectual Property Act 2014 appears to redress. It remains to be seen whether in the longer term the Enforcement Directive will have any impact here.

thinking point

Would it be better to do away with the remedy of account of profits and repeal all the statutory provisions on the award of damages, replacing the latter with a simple rule which leaves the award of damages at the discretion of the court, guided only by the principles set out in Article 13 of the Enforcement Directive?

2.3.3 Moral rights and rights in performances

Mention has not been made so far of the remedies available for the two rights specifically created by the CDPA 1988, namely **moral rights** and **rights in performances**. The CDPA declares (in ss.103 and 194, respectively) that infringement of such rights is to be actionable as a breach of statutory duty. The correctness of treating these rights as analogous with the protection of employees under the Factories Acts is questionable.

2.3.4 Additional statutory remedies

Various ancillary remedies are prescribed by legislation to assist the intellectual property owner in the fight against counterfeiting. These include an order for the erasure of an infringing sign under the TMA s.15, and an order for the delivery up and destruction of infringing copies of copyright works, performances, designs, patents and trade marks (see, respectively ss.99 and 114 of the CDPA in relation to copyright works; ss.195 and 204 CDPA in relation to illicit copies of performances; ss.230 and 231 CDPA in relation to designs; s.61 of the Patents Act 1977; and ss.16 and 19 of the TMA). The wording of these various provisions means that a court order can be made against an innocent retailer who just happens to have infringing copies in its possession, and not merely the counterfeiter who has made the products in question: *Lagenes Ltd v It's At (UK) Ltd* [1991] FSR 492. Lastly, a copyright owner and a performer have, as a result of the CDPA 1988, ss.100 and 196 respectively, the 'self-help' remedy whereby infringing copies can be seized. However, there are stringent conditions imposed on this remedy, including the requirement that due notice must be given to the local police. Because the remedy cannot be executed against anyone operating from permanent business premises (which phrase includes market stalls), in effect it is only available against pavement vendors. It is therefore most likely to be used against those selling counterfeit merchandise outside sports venues and rock concerts.

thinking point
Why should the self-help remedy in CDPA ss.100 and 196 not be available for other forms of intellectual property?

2.4 State assistance for the intellectual property owner

Because of the widespread problem of counterfeiting (it has been estimated to cause a loss of between 10–15 per cent to world trade), United Kingdom law provides for the intellectual property owner to invoke the assistance of the state in protecting what is essentially a right of private property. One might question the value judgement inherent in such state support. Why should the infringement of a private property right attract the opprobrium of the criminal law, when the owner of the right in question might be a multi-national corporation, such undertakings being perceived, rightly or wrongly, as being key players in globalisation? Why should a company, which has perhaps outsourced the manufacture of branded goods to less-developed countries so as to take advantage of low wage-rates, be able to invoke state assistance if imitations of those goods are being supplied to brand-conscious United Kingdom consumers? Whatever one's views, the implicit assumption in United Kingdom law is that the taking of intangible property should be treated as criminal conduct, a point reinforced by those who contend that counterfeiting forms part of organised crime.

Counterfeiting is facilitated by modern technology. Items which have required the investment of labour and capital to create are easily copied, depriving the creator of their expected return. In particular, films and sound recordings, computer software, fashion garments, shoes and perfumes are frequently the subject of counterfeiting. More recently (and more worryingly) counterfeiting has extended to pharmaceuticals. The assistance provided by the state is twofold.

2.4.1 Criminal liability

First, to commit copyright and trade mark infringement by way of trade gives rise to criminal liability: see the CDPA 1988, s.107 (copyright) and s.198 (performances); and the TMA ss.92 and 93. There is no such liability in relation to patents, registered designs, the unregistered design right, nor the theft of **trade secrets**, although the Intellectual Property Act 2014 proposes the imposition of criminal liability for the deliberate copying of a registered design. Prosecution, however, is not confined to those who are counterfeiters, but may be brought against the intellectual property owner's competitors: *Thames & Hudson v Design & Copyright Artists Society* [1995] FSR 153. The inconsistencies which formerly existed between copyright law and trade mark law as regards criminal penalties have been removed by the Copyright, etc and Trade Marks (Offences and Enforcement) Act 2002. The enforcement of these criminal provisions is delegated to Local Authority Trading Standards Departments. Besides raiding premises where counterfeit goods, often worth thousands of pounds, are being made, a fertile hunting ground for such products is the ubiquitous car boot sale. Under the Criminal Justice Act 1988 (Confiscation Orders) Order 1995, a magistrates' court can impose a confiscation order in respect of the criminal offences found in the CDPA and the Trade Marks Act 1994. The maximum penalties were increased by the Digital Economy Act 2010.

thinking point

Is it right that infringement of a private property right should give rise to criminal liability?

2.4.2 **HM Revenue and Customs**

Regulation (EU) No 608/2013 of the European Parliament and of the Council of 12 June 2013 concerning customs enforcement of intellectual property rights, [2013] OJ L 181/15 (effective 1 January 2014) applies to counterfeit goods and pirated goods. It allows the intellectual property owner to notify the customs authorities, who have power to prevent the importation of suspect goods at the point of entry. The goods in question are liable to forfeiture and destruction. One gap in the predecessor to the Regulation was revealed by the ECJ's ruling in Joined Cases C-446/09 and C-495/09 *Philips/Nokia* [2012] ETMR 248 which held that goods entering the EU in transit to a non-Member State did not infringe any intellectual property rights as conferred by the EU and its Member States: they could only be treated as counterfeit once there was proof that they were the subject matter of a commercial act directed at EU consumers. This gap will be closed by draft Article 10(5) of the proposed revised Trade Marks Directive.

cross reference

The proposed revised Trade Marks Directive is considered throughout chapters 14, 15 and 16.

2.5 **Policy restrictions on the intellectual property owner's rights**

cross reference

For the monopolistic nature of intellectual property rights see section 1.3.3.

Civil litigation is the normal means for an intellectual property owner to protect their rights. However, because of the monopolistic nature of intellectual property rights, it would be very easy for a large, multi-national corporation to use the power of litigation to put competitors out of business. United Kingdom intellectual property litigation is estimated to be one of the most expensive in the world, and these costs may act as a deterrent to small businesses. There are therefore various statutory provisions which curtail the litigious intellectual property owner.

2.5.1 **Threats actions**

United Kingdom statutes contain provisions restricting the right of the intellectual property owner to threaten another with litigation. The presence of the **threats action** in United Kingdom legislation can be seen as a safeguard to ensure that the intellectual property owner does not attempt to stifle competition by excessive use of their monopoly power. The underlying assumption is that small competitors may otherwise be intimidated by a 'letter before action', particularly in view of the high costs of litigation. Nevertheless, the threats action sits uneasily with the CPR, the aim of which is to encourage litigants to set out the case in full in pre-action correspondence. There are a number of 'pre-action protocols' which set out how such correspondence should be conducted. Unfortunately, in relation to intellectual property litigation, no such protocol exists, only a code of conduct.

2.5.1.1 The nature of the threats action

cross reference

The requirement of trade mark use is discussed at section 15.3.2.

Where an intellectual property owner makes an unjustified threat to bring infringement proceedings, any person *affected* by the threat (who need not be the suspected infringer nor the recipient of the threat) can commence an action, so that the author of the threat (who need not be the intellectual property owner) becomes the defendant to that action, rather than the claimant in an infringement action. The claimant in a threats action can be awarded a declaration that an unjustified threat has been made, an injunction restraining further threats, and damages. They can also take the opportunity to challenge the **validity** of the intellectual property right itself. If they are successful, then the intellectual property owner may end up with nothing. Besides enabling the alleged infringer to make a pre-emptive strike (important tactically in the business of intellectual property litigation), the threats action has the effect of shifting the onus to the intellectual property owner to show that there had been infringing conduct and that the right in question is valid. As an example of this shift of onus, we may note *Trebor Bassett Ltd v The Football Association* [1997] FSR 211 where a sweet manufacturer successfully argued that the FA had wrongly threatened litigation for trade mark infringement. No infringing conduct had occurred because the appearance of the three lions logo in collectible pictures of football players found in sweet packets was not trade mark use under ss.9 and 10 TMA.

2.5.1.2 Which rights are protected by the threats action?

Provisions curtailing the intellectual property owner's ability to threaten a third party with litigation are to be found in respect of those rights regarded, traditionally, as '**industrial property**', namely patents, trade marks, unregistered design rights and registered designs (see Patents Act 1977, s.70 as amended; TMA s.21; CDPA 1988 s.253; and RDA s.26). It may be noted that the unregistered design right receives the same treatment as registrable rights, even though it is a copyright-type right and not dependent on registration. Not just nationally registered rights are protected, but also **EU trade marks** and **EU designs**.

There are no such restrictions in relation to copyright infringement, infringement of moral rights, rights in performances, plant breeders' rights, **database rights**, nor in relation to passing off or breach of confidence (the last two are not statute based anyway). It may be questioned why, if excessive zeal in litigation is regarded as undesirable, the threats action does not apply to all categories of rights.

A further difficulty is that the Patents Act 2004 amended the wording of s.70 Patents Act 1977. The opportunity was not taken to amend the parallel provisions in the RDA, the CDPA 1988 and the TMA, so there are unfortunate differences between the statutory régimes.

2.5.1.3 The breadth of protection

The wording of the statutory provisions is very wide. It is not just the proprietor of a patent, trade mark, unregistered design right and registered design who can be made liable for issuing threats, but anyone acting on their behalf, such as their solicitor. It is consequently the *author* of the threat who can be made liable. The threats action can be brought by any 'person aggrieved', who need not be the direct recipient of the threat, merely someone affected by it. For example, where a patentee (or their solicitor) writes to a third party threatening to sue them for supplying an allegedly infringing product to another, and the recipient of the letter then ceases the supply of that product, the other party to the contract of supply as well as the addressee of those threats can sue the patentee (or their solicitor) for making unjustified threats. Another example can be found in *Quads 4 Kids v Campbell* [2006] EWHC 2482 (Ch) where the defendant claimed to be the owner of various EU designs and wrote to eBay informing them that goods advertised by the claimant infringed his right. The response of eBay was to remove the advert, which Pumfrey J construed as an actionable threat, especially in view of the fact that the defendant was unwilling (due to lack of money) to start infringement proceedings. In *Best Buy Co Inc v Worldwide Sales Corp Espana SL* [2011] FSR 742, the Court of Appeal agreed with Floyd J that a letter sent by the defendant's lawyers amounted to a threat under TMA s.21: it indicated the range of options which the defendant could take should the claimant commence opening a chain of retail premises in the United Kingdom and elsewhere in the EU; any reasonable businessman would have understood that the defendant contemplated action in the United Kingdom if the negotiations between the two parties failed. However, the Court of Appeal disagreed with the trial judge that the defendant's letter was privileged from use in court because it was written in the context of negotiations. Viewed overall, the substance of the letter could not be viewed as 'without prejudice'.

2.5.1.4 What amounts to a threat?

The court will consider the wording of the communication from the intellectual property owner (it may be written or oral) to see whether viewed through the eyes of a reasonable third party it constitutes a threat to sue. A 'working definition' of an actionable threat was given by Pumfrey J in *Quads 4 Kids v Campbell* at [23] as 'a statement from which a reasonable man in the position of a person to whom the statement is made understands is a statement that might well be the subject of infringement proceedings at some point in the future'. Lightman J in *L'Oréal (UK) Ltd v Johnson & Johnson* [2000] FSR 686 stated that 'the term "threat" covers any intimation that would convey to a reasonable man that some person has...rights and intends to enforce them against another. It matters not that the threat may be veiled or covert, conditional or future. Nor does it matter that the threat is made in response to an enquiry from the party threatened.' The words in question do not have to be intimidatory so that even vague language counts, indeed in the *L'Oréal* case the letter in question was described by the judge as 'Delphic' but sufficient to unsettle the alleged infringer. Further, where an intellectual property owner with rights in another country (for example, the owner of a USA trade mark) writes to a United Kingdom business intimating that they will take action for trade mark infringement because the United Kingdom business operates a website with a domain name identical to the foreign trade mark, then such correspondence is actionable if the threat is received in the United Kingdom: *Prince plc v Prince Sports Group Inc* [1998] FSR 21.

2.5.1.5 The exceptions

There are several exceptions to the threats action. First, the intellectual property owner can threaten to sue someone for acts of manufacture or importation (see TMA s.21(3), CDPA 1988, s.253(3) and RDA s.26(2A)). The threats action can therefore be seen to protect those further along the supply chain, such as wholesalers and retailers rather than those who commit the 'core' acts of infringement. The intellectual property owner can still threaten to sue primary infringers, namely importers and manufacturers, but they cannot threaten to sue someone merely for keeping, selling or disposing of infringing goods. However, in relation to patents, following the 2004 amendments, the exception is somewhat broader. A patentee can threaten to sue someone for manufacture, importation *and subsequent disposal* of the infringing product (Patents Act 1977 s.70(4) as amended). Further, but in relation only to patents, the defendant to a threats action (ie the patentee) can argue by way of exoneration that at the time of making the threats they did not know and had no reason to suspect that the patent was invalid (Patents Act 1977 s.70(2A)). The amendment to the 1977 Act was intended to deal with the situation whereby a patent can be declared invalid because of some obscure piece of **prior art**, unknown to the patentee at the date the patent application was made.

cross reference
Revocation of patents for invalidity is dealt with at section 6.4.1.

Next, all of the previously mentioned provisions contain another exception, whereby it does not constitute an actionable threat merely to notify a third party that a particular intellectual property right exists. By way of case law addition to this, 'without prejudice' correspondence is inadmissible as evidence of a threat to sue: *Unilever v Procter & Gamble* [2000] FSR 344, although as suggested earlier, the *Best Buy* case indicates the court will examine the substance of the correspondence to see if it really does merit treatment as a privileged communication.

Finally, the amended s.70 of the Patents Act contains two further exceptions which apply only to patents. In s.70(5) the patentee can make enquiries of a retailer (without incurring liability) for the sole purpose of discovering by whom the infringing product has been imported or made, and under s.70(6), the patentee can argue that in making the threat, he had used his best endeavours without success to find the identity of the primary infringer.

2.5.1.6 Criticisms of the provisions

There are several criticisms which can be made of the threats action. Schwartz and Gardner (in 'Groundless Threats of Proceedings for IP Infringement: An Introduction to and Critique of the Statutory Provisions' [2006] *Comms L* 85) argue first that the threats action conflicts with the ethos of the CPR, which is that parties should settle their disputes without recourse to litigation. Because of this, rights-holders may be tempted to sue first rather than resolve matters through correspondence. Second, as a matter of policy it is wrong to make a professional advisor liable, especially if the latter is simply following his or her client's instructions.

Davies and Scourfield (in 'Threats: Is the Current Régime Still Justified' [2007] *EIPR* 259) point out that the United Kingdom is the only EU Member State to have a specific statutory provision dealing with unjustified threats. Other countries deal with such oppressive behaviour through the action for unfair competition. This discrepancy is even more marked when it is remembered that the threats action is available not just in respect of United Kingdom registered rights, but also EU registered rights. The consensus in the legal profession is that the threats action is a 'shambles'.

The Law Commission is currently considering reform of the threats action: its report is due in the Spring of 2014.

2.5.1.7 Threats: conclusion

The message is, therefore, that before warning potential defendants of litigation, the claimant needs to be sure that (a) there has been an act of infringement; and (b) the right which has been infringed is valid. The wording of the sections does not restrict the intellectual property owner's rights with regard to *whom* they threaten to sue, but with regard to *what* they threaten to sue for. In other words, you can write to someone alleging that they have infringed your trade mark by manufacture or importation, but not that they have infringed by manufacture and *sale*. The case of *Cavity Trays Ltd v RMC Panel Products* [1996] RPC 361 is a good illustration of this, although it should be noted that the case itself, which concerned a patent, would be decided differently today because of the 2004 amendments to the Patents Act.

thinking point
Does the threats action strike a workable balance between the interests of the intellectual property owner in protecting its right and the interests of third parties in free competition?

Summary

This chapter has explained:

- the context in which intellectual property disputes are heard;

- the remedies which can be obtained before the full hearing of the case;

- the remedies which the successful claimant may be awarded;

- the various inconsistencies which are to be found in United Kingdom legislation regarding remedies; and

- the role of the threats action as a restriction on the intellectual property owner's freedom to litigate.

Reflective question

Do the United Kingdom statutory provisions on remedies give too much power to the intellectual property owner, enabling them to stifle competition?

Annotated further reading

Bently, L. 'Account of Profits for infringement of Copyright: Potton Ltd v Yorkclose Ltd and Others' [1990] *EIPR* 106

Davies, I. and Scourfield, T. 'Threats: Is the Current Régime Still Justified' [2007] *EIPR* 259
Argues that the United Kingdom is out of step with the rest of Europe over liability for threats and that a better solution would be to develop the law on unfair competition or rely on the tort of abuse of process.

Edenborough, M. and Tritton, G. 'American Cyanamid Revisited' [1996] *EIPR* 234
Considers the relationship between *American Cyanamid* and *Series 5* with regard to the grant of interim injunctions.

Hall, S. '*Anton Piller* Orders: A Doorstep Too Far' [1995] *EIPR* 50
Explains the background to the guidelines set out by Nicholls LJ in the *Hibben* case.

Philips, J. 'Interlocutory Injunctions and Intellectual Property: A Review of *American Cyanamid v Ethicon* in the Light of *Series 5 Software*' [1997] *JBL* 486
Considers the relationship between *American Cyanamid* and *Series 5* with regard to the grant of interim injunctions.

Russell, F. '*Anton Pillers* after *Universal Thermosensors*: Has the Pendulum Swung Too Far' [1992] *EIPR* 243
Explains the background to the guidelines set out by Nicholls VC in the *Hibben* case.

Schwartz, G. and Gardner, M. 'Groundless Threats of Proceedings for IP Infringement: An Introduction to and Critique of the Statutory Provisions' [2006] *Comms L* 85
Points out the inherent conflict between the CPR and the statutory provisions on threats and argues that the liability imposed on professional advisors is unjustified.

Part 2

Breach of confidence

Breach of confidence

Learning objectives

Upon completion of this chapter, you should have acquired:

- an understanding of how breach of confidence can protect ideas and information;
- knowledge of the criteria governing the action for breach of confidence, and the defences thereto;
- an appreciation of how breach of confidence, when used in conjunction with the Human Rights Act, can be used to protect celebrities against media intrusion; and
- an understanding of some specific issues concerning remedies for breach of confidence.

Introduction

The purpose of this chapter is to explain how the action for breach of confidence fits within intellectual property law. It will set out the circumstances in which the action for breach of confidence will arise, the defences which may be available, and consider some particular problems which have arisen with regard to remedies.

Breach of confidence is judge-made law. In consequence, it has developed in a piece-meal and sometimes contradictory fashion, so that the rationale for the action has not always been clear. Key points remain unresolved. It is an area of recent judicial activity, owing to the interaction of the Human Rights Act 1998 with the 'cult of the celebrity'.

3.1 Types of information: commercial, state and personal

3.1.1 Protection for information as such

The action for **breach of confidence** provides the only legal mechanism in United Kingdom law to protect ideas and information as such. Other categories of intellectual property require ideas and information to be embodied in a tangible form, such as brand names (**trade marks**), **inventions** (**patents**), **works** (**copyright**) or the appearance of products (**designs**). Although there can be no property rights in information (*Boardman v Phipps* [1967] 2 AC 46 at pp.127–8 *per* Lord Upjohn; *Douglas v Hello! Ltd (No 2)* [2005] 4 All ER 128 (CA) at [119]), where information, which is not in the public domain, has been disclosed in circumstances which impose an obligation on the recipient, then its use or further disclosure may be restrained by **injunction**. A monetary remedy may also be available where the defendant has exploited the information for their own ends.

thinking point
Should breach of confidence be treated as an aspect of unfair competition and so 'fill the gaps' in the intellectual property régime?

We may note that the **TRIPs** Agreement, in Article 39, regards the protection of 'undisclosed information' as an aspect of **unfair competition** under Article 10*bis* of the **Paris Convention** for the Protection of Industrial Property 1883. Chapter 1 explained how there is a lack of protection for unfair competition in the United Kingdom intellectual property régime. Whether the action for breach of confidence is one way of filling the gap remains to be seen in view of two comments by Lord Walker in *Douglas and Zeta-Jones v Hello! Ltd* [2008] 1 AC 1 (HL). At [300] he states that relying on the law of confidence to protect 'the exclusivity in a spectacle' would go against the well-established view in *Victoria Park Racing v Taylor* (1937) 58 CLR 479 and at [292] he remarks that 'uncontrolled growth of the law of confidence would...tend to bring incoherence into the law of intellectual property'.

3.1.2 **Types of information**

Information protected by the action for breach of confidence may be commercial, governmental or personal. Commercial information might relate to an idea for a new television series or a 'themed' nightclub, a new product (which might or might not be capable of patent protection), steps to be taken in a manufacturing process or in creating software, test data or a list of valued customers or suppliers. Government information concerns official secrets and other material about the internal workings of the state and its agencies, which the Government would prefer not to be made public. Such information may have been obtained by Crown servants in the course of their duties, or by politicians whilst in Government.

By contrast, personal information will involve facts about an individual which they regard as sensitive, and therefore private. Within this category of personal information we include photographs. Special considerations attach to photographs, because they are not merely an alternative to words, but can be a particularly intrusive way of conveying information. 'A picture is worth a thousand words' (*per* Baroness Hale in *Naomi Campbell v Mirror Group Newspapers* [2004] 2 AC 457 at [155]; *per* Lord Walker in *Douglas and Zeta-Jones v Hello! Ltd* (HL) at [288]).

cross reference
See further chapter 18.

The leading cases in breach of confidence are drawn from each of these three areas and are often used interchangeably. However, what is clear is that there are two distinct groups of cases, those dealing with 'traditional' breach of confidence (ie commercial and governmental information) and those dealing with what is now termed 'misuse of personal information'. These two should be kept separate: *Naomi Campbell v MGN* at [14] *per* Lord Nicholls; *Douglas and Zeta-Jones v Hello! Ltd* (HL) at [255] again, *per* Lord Nicholls. The test for what is 'confidential' differs depending on whether the disputed information is commercial or personal. However, many cases involving misuse of personal information arise in situations where there is already a contractual obligation in place (for example, an exclusive deal with a magazine to publish photographs of a celebrity wedding) and so could be regarded as commercial rather than personal in nature: see Lord Hoffmann at [124] in *Douglas and Zeta-Jones v Hello! Ltd* (HL).

Our principal focus is on the way in which the action for breach of confidence operates in the commercial world to protect **trade secrets**, but we will later consider the interaction of the principles of breach of confidence with the Human Rights Act 1998 to create a remedy for the invasion of privacy. Many of the cases in this particular area (usually, but not always, about high-profile celebrities) involve unique facts. The courts were initially reluctant to establish any general right of privacy in the absence of legislation (*Wainwright v Home Office* [2004] AC 406 at [15–35] *per* Lord Hoffmann), and have to balance Article 8 of the European Convention on Human Rights ('ECHR') (respect for private and family life) with Article 10 (freedom of expression). It has been declared by the Court of Appeal in *Douglas v Hello! Ltd (No 2)* at [49] that the decision of the European Court of Human Rights ('ECtHR') in *Von Hannover v Germany (No 1)* (2004) 40 EHHR 1 imposed a positive obligation on Member States to protect an individual against the unjustified invasion of their private life by another individual, and a further obligation on the courts of a Member State to interpret domestic legislation in a way which will achieve that result. The significance of the privacy cases from the intellectual property perspective is twofold: they provide a first step towards the creation of a right of personality; and they enable the individual to exercise a degree of control over the commercial exploitation of their image.

thinking point
Is it correct to expand breach of confidence to cover misuse of personal information?

The role of breach of confidence in intellectual property law

In relation to commercial information (often termed 'trade secrets'), breach of confidence has several practical applications, as follows.

3.2.1 **An alternative to patents**

thinking point

In view of advances in technology, is a company wise to rely on breach of confidence to protect an invention?

Confidentiality has always been an alternative to patent protection. An inventor may decide not to bother with obtaining patent protection for their invention, but instead to rely on secrecy (which after all is instant and free). So, for instance, the Coca Cola Company never obtained a patent on the recipe for its drink, and to this day relies on secrecy to protect the details of the recipe. A case law example is *Seager v Copydex (No 1)* [1967] RPC 349 where an inventor had not obtained patent protection for a new type of carpet grip but nevertheless was able to argue successfully that the defendants had misappropriated his ideas. However, relying on secrecy to protect an invention will only be worthwhile if it is not possible for a third party to 'reverse engineer' the invention, that is, having acquired a legitimate copy of the product, to analyse it to find out how it works before making their own version of the product.

3.2.2 **An alternative to copyright**

Confidentiality can be used to protect ideas which are not yet sufficiently permanent to fall within the scope of copyright. As an example, in *Fraser v Thames Television* [1983] 2 All ER 101 an experienced television script writer approached the defendants with an idea for a new drama series. His idea was rejected, but some time later the company broadcast a series, 'Rock Follies' based on the **claimant**'s proposal. He was awarded extensive **damages**.

3.2.3 **A supplement to copyright**

cross reference
See section 8.1.2.

Confidentiality can offer parallel protection to copyright, so that there can be liability for publication even though there has not been copying. An example of this is *Creation Records v News Group Newspapers* [1997] EMLR 444. Here, there had been a 'photo-shoot' to create the cover for the CD *Be Here Now* by the group Oasis, which entailed assembling a number of objects in a swimming pool which were then photographed. Lloyd J declined to hold that the collection of objects in the pool amounted to a collage for the purposes of artistic copyright. Equally, the claimant's photograph had not been copied by the defendant's photographer (a prerequisite for copyright **infringement**). However, the conduct of the newspaper in taking its own photograph amounted to breach of confidence as it was clear that their employee knew that the session was secret (Lord Walker in *Douglas and Zeta-Jones v Hello! Ltd* (HL) (at [290–291]) regarded the decision as 'scraping the barrel', not least because it involved trivial information). Breach of confidence and copyright were also combined in *Shelley Films v Rex Features* [1994] EMLR 134 (an application for interim relief) where a photographer obtained unauthorised photographs of the film set of Kenneth Branagh's *Frankenstein*. Michael Mann QC held that there was both breach of confidence (the photographer knew that the taking of photographs of the film set was forbidden) and breach of copyright (the costumes, masks and sets were arguably works of artistic craftsmanship so that taking photographs of them infringed).

3.2.4 **Ensuring the novelty of a patent or registered design**

The use of a confidentiality undertaking is vital to protect the disclosure of potential patents or designs where it is necessary to have the item evaluated prior to filing the application. The reason for this is that s.2(4) Patents Act 1977 and s.1(6) Registered Designs Act 1949, as amended, provide that the **novelty** of a patent or design is not destroyed by a prior disclosure in breach of confidence. Keeping an intended patent or **registered design** secret is a key aspect to the successful management of intellectual property rights.

3.2.5 **Know-how**

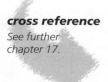

cross reference
See further
chapter 17.

Imposing confidentiality undertakings is the means (in the context of **licensing** agreements) to protect non-patentable but commercially valuable information ('**know-how**') relating to the procedures etc to be used in the manufacture of goods. Such information could relate to a particular sequence to be adopted in a manufacturing process, instruction manuals, systems analysis, software or other similar technical knowledge. It should be noted that there are competition law implications in the licensing of technology.

thinking point
Do you think that businesses fully appreciate the importance of breach of confidence as a means of protecting information?

3.3

The historical development of breach of confidence and the basis for its protection

3.3.1 **Early cases**

It is generally accepted that the first breach of confidence case was *Prince Albert v Strange* (1849) 1 H & Tw 1, where private drawings by Prince Albert had been sent to a printer to be copied professionally. The defendant had made unauthorised copies which he had intended to put on public display. An injunction was granted to restrain him. As Lord Cottenham, LC, remarked, 'privacy is the right invaded'. A more typical trade secret case was *Morison v Moat* (1851) 9 Hare 241, where the son of one of two business partners was restrained by the other partner, after the partnership had been dissolved, from making use of a secret recipe for a medicine.

3.3.2 **Basis of protection**

The theoretical basis for many of the early decisions on breach of confidence was not entirely clear. Arguments deployed included contract, property rights and conscience. Because many breach of confidence claims arise when the parties are in a contractual relationship, there were a number of other cases where the courts strove to find some sort of implied contract to justify the outcome, even if the parties were not contractually linked. Such artificiality masked the true nature of the action.

Equally, the proximity of breach of confidence to other intellectual property rights, especially patents and copyright, led to arguments that the basis of the action should be some notion of property. In the leading case on breach of confidence, *Coco v AN Clark (Engineers) Ltd* [1969] RPC 41 (discussed in detail later), Megarry J remarked that 'whether it is described as originality or novelty or ingenuity or otherwise . . . there must be some *product* of the human brain' (emphasis supplied), language which has property implications. Tempting though it is to utilise property concepts, the overwhelming weight of authority is against using property law as the basis of the action. Apart from the statement of Lord Upjohn in *Boardman v Phipps*, mentioned earlier, the Court of Appeal in *Douglas v Hello! Ltd (No 2)* at [126] has made clear that property law should *not* be used. The court saw fit to distinguish earlier cases which had apparently treated secret information as having the attributes of property, namely *Gilbert v Star Newspaper Co Ltd* (1894) 51 TLR 4 and *Mustad & Sons Ltd v Allcock & Dosen* (1928) [1964] 1 WLR 109, HL. Nevertheless, the Court of Appeal's conclusion that the rights of the claimant's exclusive publishers rested entirely in contract, so that they had no remedy under the law of confidence to restrain a rival magazine from publishing surreptitiously obtained pictures of the claimant's wedding, was overturned by a majority of the House of Lords who held that, as the recipient of commercial **confidential information**, the defendant's conscience was affected. In order for the recipient's conscience to be affected, they must have agreed, or must know, that the information is confidential: *Vestergaard Frandsen A/S v Bestnet Europe Ltd* [2013] UKSC 31 at [23].

Even before the pronouncements in *Douglas v Hello! Ltd (No 2)* (CA), case law had moved away from any theories of implied contract or property law, and had instead declared that the action was based on the equitable concept of 'good faith'. The first statement that breach of confidence is underpinned by a general notion of conscience was in *Saltman Engineering Co Ltd v Campbell Engineering Co Ltd* (1948) 65 RPC 203. Subsequent reiterations include those by Lord Denning in *Fraser v Evans* [1969] 1 QB 349 at 361 ('It is based not so much on property or on contract as on a duty to be of good faith') and Lord Keith in *AG v Guardian Newspapers (No 2)* [1990] 1 AC 109 (hereafter '*Spycatcher*') ('The obligation may be imposed by an express or implied term in a contract but it may also exist independently of any contract on the basis of an independent equitable principle of confidence').

thinking point

Does the statement that breach of confidence rests on a general notion of 'good faith' provide for legal certainty? Wouldn't contract or property provide a better solution?

3.4 Conditions for protection

case close-up

Coco v AN Clark (Engineers) Ltd [1969] RPC 41

· ·

The leading case on breach of confidence is *Coco v AN Clark (Engineers) Ltd*. At p. 47 Megarry J set out the ingredients of the action. First, the information must be of a confidential nature; second, it must have been communicated in circumstances 'importing an obligation of confidence'; and third, there must be subsequent unauthorised use or disclosure of that information.

3.4.1 Confidential information

The types of information protected by the action for breach of confidence are very wide. The form which the information takes is irrelevant: it may be in writing, in drawings, in photographs or oral. It need not be permanent, and does not have to be recorded in a document (*Douglas v Hello! Ltd (No 2)* (CA) at [61]). But according to Lord Goff in *Spycatcher*, it must not be useless, trivial, vague or immoral. Further, the information must be capable of being identified and certain.

An illustration of this last point is *De Maudsley v Palumbo* [1996] FSR 447 where it was held that vague, preliminary ideas for the 'Ministry of Sound' nightclub were not protectable. The case should be contrasted with *Fraser v Thames Television* (discussed earlier) where the claimant's ideas for a television drama series were much more fully developed. The argument that information cannot be protected if it discloses illegality was at the heart of the case of *Mosley v News Group Newspapers* [2008] EWHC 1777. Eady J dismissed the defendant's contention that the claimant's sado-masochistic behaviour was not protectable: it was not for the media to expose sexual conduct which did not involve any significant breach of the criminal law:

> It is not for journalists to undermine human rights, or for judges to refuse to enforce them, merely on grounds of taste or moral disapproval. Everyone is naturally entitled to espouse moral or religious beliefs to the effect that certain types of sexual behaviour are wrong or demeaning...[but] that does not mean that they are entitled to hound those who practise them.

However, whatever the information may be, the one key requirement is that it must not already be in the public domain. Megarry J in *Coco v Clark* referred to the statement of Lord Greene MR in *Saltman Engineering Co Ltd v Campbell Engineering Co Ltd* to the effect that the information must not be 'something which is public property and public knowledge'. In the words of Lord Goff in *Spycatcher*, it must be secret information. Once factual information is in the public domain, then it will no longer be entitled to protection in the law of confidence (*Spycatcher per* Lord Goff at p. 282; *Douglas and Zeta-Jones v Hello! Ltd* (HL) at [122] *per* Lord Hoffmann; *BBC v HarperCollins Publishers Ltd* [2010] EWHC 2424 (Ch)). Thus, in *Woodward v Hutchins* [1977] 1 WLR 760, an injunction preventing disclosure was refused, as gossip about the behaviour of certain pop stars on a transatlantic flight was already known. However, the same is not true of photographs: 'in so far as a photograph does more than convey information and intrudes on privacy by enabling the viewer to focus on intimate personal detail, there will be a fresh intrusion of privacy when each additional viewer sees the photograph' (*Douglas v Hello! Ltd (No 2)* (CA) at [105]). Republication of a photograph is therefore misuse of personal information.

cross reference
See further section 5.5.

Unlike the law of patents, the action for breach of confidence is based on the concept of relative not absolute secrecy (*Vestergaard Frandsen A/S v BestNet Europe Ltd* [2010] FSR 29 at [77]). Consequently, disclosure to a select few may not destroy confidentiality. But what if the information is a mixture of public and private information? It has been held that protection is still available if the defendant uses the information as a 'springboard' to gain a commercial advantage over competitors. The 'springboard' doctrine is the product of the judgment of Roxburgh J in *Terrapin v Builders' Supply Co* [1960] RPC 128 where 'mixed' information was protected. Where the 'springboard' test applies, any remedy will be limited to the time it would take a competitor to reverse engineer the claimant's information: *Cadbury Schweppes Inc v FBI Foods Ltd* [2000] FSR 491 (a decision of the Supreme Court of Canada), the information in question here being a secret recipe for a drink, 'Clamato'. It was held that it would take a competitor 12 months to analyse the composition of the product using laboratory equipment, to test their findings, and bring their own version of the product to market. The injunction against the defendant was accordingly limited to that period of time. The effects of the 'springboard' cannot be indefinite (*Potters Ballotini v Weston Baker* [1977] RPC 202) and will not apply if the information is already in the public domain (*Vestergaard Frandsen A/S v BestNet Europe Ltd* [2010] FSR 29).

thinking point
How easy is it to apply Lord Goff's test of what is protectable information?

3.4.2 **An obligation of confidence**

The second requirement from *Coco v Clark* is that the information must have been disclosed by the confider to the confidant in circumstances of confidence. The duty of secrecy can arise in a number of ways. Commonly, it may arise from a contract between the parties. There may be an express term imposing the duty of secrecy, or the court may impose an implied term in the interests of business efficacy, in accordance with the principles established by the House of Lords in *Liverpool City Council v Irwin* [1977] AC 239 and the speech of Lord Simon in *BP Refinery (Westernport) Pty Ltd v The President, Councillors and Ratepayers of the Shire of Hastings* (1978) 52 ALJR 20. However, it is not necessary to show that there was a contractual relationship, even though evidentially this will help the claimant's case considerably. Instead, the court can infer that there is a duty of confidence either from the parties' relationship or simply from the circumstances of the disclosure, objectively assessed.

Examples of relationships which would give rise to an implied duty of confidentiality include those of employment, banker/customer, professional adviser/client or a commercial joint venture (*Re Gallay* [1959] RPC 141). The relationship, however, must be of the type which imposes an equitable duty of good faith. An example of where the *circumstances* of the disclosure, as opposed to the parties' relationship, were sufficient to give rise to a duty to keep the information secret is *Stephens v Avery* [1988] Ch 449, discussed further later.

3.4.2.1 **An objective test**

At one time, there were suggestions in *Thomas Marshall (Exports) Ltd v Guinle* [1978] 3 All ER 193 and in *Schering Chemicals v Falkman* [1982] 1 QB 1 that the test was *subjective*, that is, whether the confider believed that the circumstances imposed secrecy. However, the weight of authority is now overwhelmingly in favour of an objective test. The courts have consistently preferred the approach of Megarry J in *Coco v Clark*:

> It seems to me that if the circumstances are such that any reasonable man standing in the shoes of the recipient of the information would have realised that upon reasonable grounds the information was being given to him in confidence, then this should suffice to impose upon him the equitable obligation of confidence ([1969] RPC 41 at p. 48).

The objective test was by implication approved in *Spycatcher* by Lords Goff and Keith, and was expressly approved by Lindsay J at first instance in *Douglas and Zeta-Jones v Hello! Ltd* [2003] 3 All ER 996 and by the House of Lords in *Naomi Campbell v MGN*. An example of an application of the objective test for the existence of the duty of secrecy arising from the circumstances of the disclosure itself is *Stephens v Avery*. Here, one friend disclosed to another that she was in a lesbian relationship. It was held that the confidant should have realised from the circumstances of the disclosure that the information was confidential and not to be disclosed, least of all to a tabloid newspaper.

When dealing with the obligation of confidence, there are three distinct groups of recipients where greater discussion is required.

3.4.2.2 Employees

An employee owes their employer a duty of fidelity, that is, to further the interests of the employer's business (*Robb v Green* [1895] 2 QB 315). The duty varies depending on the seniority and skill of the employee and not all employees will necessarily receive the same treatment. Very senior employees will be treated as fiduciaries. The duty of good faith can encompass the duty not to compete with or injure the employer's business (*Hivac Ltd v Park Royal Scientific Instruments Ltd* [1964] 1 All ER 350) as well as the obligation to maintain secrecy (*Printers and Finishers Ltd v Holloway* [1965] 1 WLR 1).

3.4.2.3 Ex-employees

Whether a former employee owes an obligation of secrecy to the employer depends again on the status, knowledge and skills of the employee. Further, there are three principal categories of information which must be kept distinct, namely trade secrets as such, commercially sensitive or valuable information, and the employee's general skill and knowledge (*Faccenda v Fowler* [1986] 1 All ER 617). The first category is automatically protected during and after the contract of employment. The second is automatically protected during the contract of employment because of the employee's general duty of fidelity, but will require an express clause to protect it after termination of employment. Such a clause must be limited appropriately in time, geographical area, and as to the relevant activities of the ex-employee, otherwise it may be held void as being in restraint of trade (*Fellowes v Fisher* [1976] QB 122, *Commercial Plastics v Vincent* [1964] 3 All ER 546). The only exception to the requirement to tailor the restriction to the ex-employee's activities would appear to be senior members of the Intelligence Service: *AG v Blake* [2001] AC 268. The final category of information, the employee's general skill and knowledge, is not protectable on grounds of public policy, so that the employee is free to make use of his/her skills in subsequent employment (*Herbert*

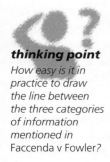

thinking point

How easy is it in practice to draw the line between the three categories of information mentioned in Faccenda v Fowler?

Morris v Saxelby [1916] AC 688). 'The law should not discourage former employees from benefiting society and advancing themselves by imposing unfair potential difficulties on their honest attempts to compete with their former employers' (*Vestergaard Frandsen A/S v Bestnet Europe Ltd* [2013] UKSC 31 at [44]). Nevertheless, as the decision in *Faccenda v Fowler* itself shows, the first and second categories are not easy to separate in practice: is a list of customers a trade secret as such or simply valuable commercial information?

3.4.2.4 Involuntary third party recipients

The starting point here is fairly obvious: unless protection is available against a third party recipient, the action for breach of confidence would be worthless (*per* Lord Griffiths in *Spycatcher*; and *per* Lords Hoffmann and Brown in *Douglas and Zeta-Jones v Hello! Ltd* at [120–122] and [325] respectively). However, it is in this area that the cases are most contradictory. This stems in part from the difficulty the courts have experienced in deciding the true rationale for breach of confidence. In the absence of a contractual relationship, the justification for the action for breach of confidence is either that information should be treated as a form of property, or that liability rests on whether the defendant's conscience was affected.

There is a certain attractiveness in adopting the property solution to decide whether an involuntary third party recipient of secret information is bound by a duty of confidence. Treating information as property would enable the court to adopt concepts such as the *bona fide* purchaser to determine the third party's liability. Nevertheless, there are intrinsic difficulties in applying rules developed in relation to transactions in land in a commercial context (*Bank of Credit & Commerce International (Overseas) Ltd v Akindele* [2001] Ch 437). Alternatively, the third party's conduct could be equated to theft of the information. Here, too, English law has always experienced difficulty in applying the law of theft to intangible property (*Oxford v Moss* (1979) 68 Cr App R 183). There is now extensive authority that the property law approach is not to be adopted: *Boardman v Phipps* at pp. 127–8 *per* Lord Upjohn; *Douglas v Hello! Ltd (No 2)* (CA) at [119]; *Douglas and Zeta-Jones v Hello! Ltd* (HL) *per* Lord Walker at [282]. Such authority avoids the need to consider whether a third party recipient can be treated as a *bona fide* purchaser of the information (see *Valeo Vision SA v Flexible Lamps* [1995] RPC 203 for the difficulties which Aldous J encountered in attempting to apply the *bona fide* purchaser rule to trade secrets).

Even if the conscience of the recipient is the key to liability, there is the further difficulty as to what level of knowledge is required. The classic example given by Lord Goff in *Spycatcher*, is of a confidential document left lying on a desk in an office. The document may come into the hands of a third party in a variety of ways, for example by being stolen, acquired by sale or gift from the thief, or blown through an open window onto the street below where it is accidentally found by a passer-by. Consider the implications of these different situations for the recipient's conscience. The third party may acquire the information from the original confidant, either with actual knowledge at the time of the receipt, actual knowledge subsequently acquired, or with some form of constructive knowledge. The recipient may acquire the information from someone who is not themselves bound by secrecy, or the recipient may be a complete stranger. An example of the latter would be the burglar or passer-by.

The variety of circumstances in which a third party may acquire secret information may help to explain the inconsistency in the cases. In some instances, where information has been obtained by unlawful means, the courts have focused on the *conduct* of the third party acquiring the information. There are two decisions which on their facts appear impossible to reconcile. In *Malone v Commissioner of Police* [1979] Ch 344 Megarry J held that there was no duty of secrecy in respect of information obtained when the police intercepted the claimant's telephone calls. By contrast, in *Francome v Mirror Group Newspapers* [1984] 2 All ER 408, the court held that there *was* an obligation of confidence where information was obtained when the claimant's telephone calls were overheard by a private investigator. The Court of Appeal distinguished *Malone* on the basis that the `phone tap there was authorised. Because of legislative changes relating to human rights, data protection and telecommunications laws, these cases today would have different outcomes as regards the legality of the defendants' conduct. One possible way of reconciling them as regards the law of breach of confidence might be to adopt the approach of Lord Woolf in *A v B (a Company)* [2002] 3 WLR 542, at [11(x)], that is, that the obtaining of information by unlawful means is an issue which goes to the exercise of the court's discretion as to the award of an injunction.

In most other instances, it is the knowledge of the recipient which determines whether they are bound by confidentiality. Hence, it is necessary to identify whether the subsequent recipient of information steals it, receives it with actual notice, receives it with constructive notice ('turning a blind eye'), or receives it innocently. Ultimately it is a question of conscience. An objective test is applied to determine whether the third party should in conscience be bound. In *Shelley Films v Rex Features* (at p. 146), Michael Mann QC stressed that what mattered was

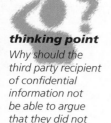

thinking point
Why should the third party recipient of confidential information not be able to argue that they did not appreciate that the information was secret?

not whether the photographer was a trespasser, but whether the photographer knew that taking photographs was prohibited and therefore confidential. In *Douglas v Hello! Ltd (No 2)* the Court of Appeal confirmed that Lindsay J had been correct to apply the objective test in deciding whether the defendant magazine was bound by a duty of secrecy in respect of the unauthorised wedding photographs taken by the uninvited paparazzo. In the same case in the House of Lords, Lord Hoffmann (at [121]–[125]) thought that the defendant should be liable to *OK Magazine*, as well as to Michael Douglas and Catherine Zeta Jones, because it was well aware of the confidential nature of the photographs.

3.4.3 **Wrongful use or disclosure**

The final element from the *Coco v Clark* formula which must be proved is that the defendant has gone beyond the purpose of the original disclosure. This may entail using the information for another purpose, or, more usually, passing the information on to somebody else. Even here, there are some unresolved issues in the cases. For example, does there have to be some sort of detriment or harm suffered by the claimant (a useful comparison can be made with the tort of defamation) or is wrongful use *per se* enough? The matter was left open by the House of Lords in *Spycatcher*. Normally in the case of commercial information, the loss of potential sales as a result of the defendant's use of the information to make its own competing product will mean that detriment is not an issue. In the case of personal information, there are cases which hold that the mere fact that there has been disclosure suffices (see *Argyll v Argyll* [1967] Ch 302 and *Michael Barrymore v News Group Newspapers* [1997] FSR 600). By contrast, in the substantive action in *Douglas and Zeta-Jones v Hello! Ltd* (at [199]), Lindsay J suggested that there must be some more tangible detriment to the claimants. The point was not discussed by the Court of Appeal or the House of Lords. The question remains, therefore, whether, for example, in the case of a photograph it is mere publication which suffices, or does the photograph have to show the celebrity in an unfavourable light? If the latter is the case, is it enough

that the photograph is of poor quality or shows the 'wrong side' of the celebrity's face, or must there be something more?

These apparent difficulties can be resolved by arguing that the question of detriment is something which goes to the issue of the remedy to be awarded rather than the existence of liability, so that minimal harm will result in the award of nominal rather than substantial damages. However, in *Douglas v Hello Ltd (No 2)*, the Court of Appeal did not disturb Lindsay J's 'modest award' for the mental distress caused by the invasion of the claimants' privacy. The low quantum of damages can be contrasted with the force of the court's statement as regards the duty imposed by the ECHR to ensure respect for private life, and its comments about the incorrect discharge of the interim injunction by a differently constituted Court of Appeal.

thinking point

Should the victim of a wrongful breach of confidence have to show detriment or should the mere fact of disclosure suffice? If detriment is required, how is this to be determined? If disclosure alone suffices, is that not tantamount to treating the information as property?

3.5 Privacy

3.5.1 The pre-1998 Act cases

Prior to the implementation of the Human Rights Act 1998, United Kingdom courts had declared on more than one occasion that there was no right of privacy in United Kingdom law. Whilst this state of affairs was regrettable, it was not for the courts to depart from well-established principle. The clearest statement of regret is to be found in *Kaye v Robertson* [1991] FSR 62 where the court was unable to give redress under the law of privacy to the claimant, a well-known actor. He had been the victim of a fictitious report published in the defendant's newspaper whilst he was lying unconscious in hospital recovering from a serious car accident. The court did, however, find that the defendant had committed **malicious falsehood** and awarded damages to the claimant on that basis. Similar regrets were expressed by the court in *Creation Records v News Group Newspapers* concerning the pre-emptive publication by *The Sun* newspaper of the CD cover for the Oasis album *Be Here Now*, although a remedy was granted because the claimants had established all the elements of the 'classical' action for breach of confidence: the photographer was aware of the confidential nature of the session during which the album cover was created.

3.5.2 The impact of the Human Rights Act 1998

Since *Kaye v Robertson*, there has been a change of judicial attitude. The turning point was the interim (interlocutory) decision of the Court of Appeal in *Douglas and Zeta-Jones v Hello! Ltd* [2001] 2 WLR 992. The Court of Appeal discharged the interim injunction granted by Hunt J to restrain the defendant magazine from publishing unauthorised photographs of the claimants' wedding, on the basis that damages would be an adequate remedy. The subsequent Court of Appeal decision in the substantive action, *Douglas v Hello! Ltd (No 2)* at [251], thought that the discharge was wrong. To return to the interim ruling of the Court of Appeal, a majority of the judges were of the view that the extensive imposition of confidentiality undertakings upon guests and staff at the wedding was enough, when coupled with the Human Rights Act, to create a right of privacy. Whilst Brooke and Keene LJJ were somewhat cautious in their approach, the comments of Sedley LJ were much more forthright as to the significance of the 1998 Act and its relationship with the action for breach of confidence. Nevertheless, despite Sedley LJ's assertion that the law recognised and would protect a right of privacy, the most significant factual aspect of the case was that the claimants had entered into detailed arrangements to ensure that their wedding was as private as possible, thereby enabling the court to utilise the action for breach of confidence as a means of redress.

Even more 'dramatic' in its use of the law of confidence to protect privacy (*per* the Court of Appeal in *Douglas v Hello! Ltd (No 2)* at [68]) was the decision of Dame Elizabeth Butler-Sloss P in *Venables & Thompson v News Group Newspapers Ltd* [2001] 1 All ER 908. The President granted a permanent injunction against all news media in the United Kingdom preventing them from disclosing the whereabouts and new identities of the claimants, two boys, who had been convicted of murder, and who, having served their prison sentences, wished to preserve their anonymity in case of revenge attacks. The key factor in this case, however, was the very real risk to the boys' safety should their location become public knowledge. The nature of the information alone gave rise to a duty of confidence.

Until the decision in *Douglas v Hello! Ltd (No 2)* (CA), there were repeated assertions that despite the Human Rights Act, in the absence of confidentiality undertakings there could be no free-standing right of privacy in United Kingdom law. Further, it was said, it was for Parliament, not the courts, to create such a right. Such assertions are to be found in particular in the substantive action in *Douglas and Zeta-Jones v Hello! Ltd* at [229] *per* Lindsay J, and in *Wainwright v Home Office* at [15–35] *per* Lord Hoffmann, and were no doubt influenced by the decision in *Peck v United Kingdom* (2003) 36 EHRR 719. Here the applicant had complained that there was a lack of domestic remedy under pre-Human Rights Act law for the infringement of his right to respect for private life. He had been photographed in a public place by closed circuit television with a knife in his hands after attempting to commit suicide. The film had been released to the media and widely publicised. The ECtHR had found it unlikely that the applicant would have been granted a remedy if he had sued for breach of confidence.

3.5.3 **Privacy: a general right?**

The assumption that there is no free-standing right to privacy must now be discounted. Two cases paved the way for the Court of Appeal's declaration in *Douglas v Hello! Ltd (No 2)* at [53] that United Kingdom courts are required (in fulfilment of their duties under the ECHR) to adopt the cause of action formerly described as breach of confidence as the appropriate vehicle for ensuring the protection of private information. The court was obliged to develop the action in such a manner as to give effect to the rights found in Articles 8 and 10 ECHR, taking account of the Strasbourg jurisprudence, although it must be said the court did not find it satisfactory to use breach of confidence in this way. The statements in *Douglas v Hello! Ltd (No 2)* (CA) are the clearest indication yet that the Human Rights Act 1998 has had an indirect horizontal effect in creating an action for the invasion of privacy.

Chronologically, the first of these pivotal cases was *Naomi Campbell v MGN*.

case close-up

Naomi Campbell v Mirror Group Newspapers [2004] 2 AC 457

A majority of the House of Lords held that the claimant's privacy had been invaded by detailed accounts appearing in the defendant's newspaper of her attendance at a drug rehabilitation clinic in London. The newspaper was entitled to 'set the record straight' after the claimant had denied her drug addiction, but had gone too far in disclosing the details of her attendance at the clinic and in publishing pictures, taken surreptitiously, of her leaving a counselling session. According to Lord Hope at [88], at issue were five pieces of information:

- the fact that Naomi Campbell was a drug addict;
- the fact that she was receiving treatment for her addiction;
- the fact that such treatment was provided by Narcotics Anonymous;
- the details of the treatment; and
- photographs of her leaving a treatment session.

The division of opinion in the House of Lords was as to whether the last three items were wrongfully disclosed, not whether there *should* in principle be protection of privacy. On this latter point there was unanimity. Hence, despite being in the minority in his conclusion on the facts, Lord Nicholls accepted that protecting privacy through the action for breach of confidence was a fast developing area of the law. He suggested that the essence of the action was not so much wrongful disclosure of private information but the *misuse* of private information. The other minority Law Lord, Lord Hoffmann, commented that instead of relying on the duty of good faith, it was better to focus on the protection of human autonomy and dignity, and the right to control the dissemination of information about one's private life. Baroness Hale thought that the cause of action of breach of confidence had within its scope what might be termed 'protection of the individual's informational autonomy'.

The other key case is that of the ECtHR in *Von Hannover v Germany (No 1)*, occurring some six weeks after *Naomi Campbell v MGN*.

case close-up

Von Hannover v Germany (No 1) (2004) 40 EHRR 1

The applicant, Princess Caroline of Monaco, had applied unsuccessfully on several occasions to the German courts to prevent a number of German magazines from publishing photographs of her and her children. The German Federal Constitutional Court held that as a 'figure of contemporary society' she had to tolerate the publication of the photographs of her in a public place even though she was not engaged in official duties but daily routine, such as shopping and collecting her children from school. The Strasbourg court disagreed, drawing a distinction between facts contributing to a debate about politicians in the exercise of their duties and the reporting of details about the private life of an individual who does not exercise official functions. In the former case, the press had a vital role to play as the 'watchdog' of democracy, but this did not apply where photographs and articles had the sole purpose of satisfying the public's curiosity. In this context, freedom of expression had to be interpreted more narrowly.

The forthright nature of the ECtHR's judgment really left the Court of Appeal in *Douglas v Hello! Ltd (No 2)* little choice but to develop a right of privacy.

3.5.4 **The correct test for liability**

One remaining issue was whether the *Coco v Clark* formula for breach of confidence should be applied in cases of misuse of personal information, or whether an alternative test should be developed. What has emerged is that rather than ask whether information is confidential, one should ask whether it is private: *per* Lord Woolf in *A v B (a Company)*. There is a line to be drawn between public and private information, a distinction which is easy to state but less simple to apply. How does one decide whether information is public or private? One test suggested in the context of media intrusion is that of Gleeson CJ in *Australian Broadcasting Corporation v Lenah Game Meats Pty Ltd* (2001) 185 ALR 1:

> There is no bright line which can be drawn between that which is private and what is not. Use of the term 'public' is often a convenient method of contrast, but there is a large area in between what is necessarily public and what is necessarily private…The requirement that disclosure or observation of information or conduct would be highly offensive to a reasonable person of ordinary sensibilities is in many circumstances a useful practical test of what is private.

The 'highly offensive' test was cited with approval in *A v B (a Company)*. However, in *Naomi Campbell v MGN*, Lord Nicholls thought the test was more appropriate to the issue of whether it was proportionate to disclose the information, rather than whether that information was protected in the first place. He thought (at [21]) that the correct test was whether there was a reasonable expectation of privacy. Lord Hope (at [99]) put this a slightly different way, namely what would a reasonable person of ordinary sensibilities feel if she were placed in the same position as the claimant and faced with the same publicity?

case close-up

Murray v Express Newspapers [2009] Ch 481
. . . .

The Court of Appeal at [35] blends the statements by Lords Nicholls and Hope in *Naomi Campbell v MGN*. The preferred test is whether there is a reasonable expectation of privacy, assessed objectively through the eyes of the reasonable third party. The court provided a list of factors to be considered in deciding whether such an expectation existed. These were:

- the attributes of the claimant;
- the nature of the activity in which the claimant was engaged;
- the place at which it was happening;
- the nature and purpose of the intrusion;
- the absence of consent and whether it was known or could be inferred;
- the effect on the claimant; and
- the circumstances in which and the purposes for which the information came into the hands of the publisher.

Once it is established that there is a reasonable expectation of privacy, the court then has to balance the competing claims of Articles 8 and 10 ECHR.

The same approach was adopted by Eady J in *Mosley v News Group Newspapers* and has also been used in cases where the confider and confidant were in an existing contractual relationship. In *McKennitt v Ash* [2007] 3 WLR 194 the claimant was a successful composer and performer of folk music, whilst the defendant was a former friend who had worked closely with her in connection with merchandising activities, accompanying her on tour as a personal assistant. The defendant wrote a book called *Travels with Loreena McKennitt: My Life as a Friend*. Eady J, confirmed by the Court of Appeal, held that there had been a reasonable expectation of privacy. **Public interest** had to yield to effective protection of private life. The defendant would have been aware that much of the book would cause distress because of its intrusive nature. A number of passages should not have been published. A similar outcome can be found in *HRH Prince of Wales v Associated Newspapers Ltd* [2007] 3 WLR 222. The claimant had for some 30 years kept personal journals recording his thoughts on various visits he had made to different parts of the world. On his return to the United Kingdom, his journals would be photocopied by his staff and selectively distributed to close friends. The copies and any covering letter were marked 'private and confidential'. The originals were kept in a locked safe and it was not anticipated that they would be published during the claimant's lifetime. The defendant had acquired a copy of the claimant's journal (recording his thoughts on the return of Hong Kong to the People's Republic of China) from an undisclosed intermediary who in turn had obtained it from a former secretary. The secretary had tried to retrieve the copy of the journal without success. Blackburne J, having established that there was a reasonable expectation of privacy, carried out the balancing exercise required under the ECHR, holding that as there had been no hypocrisy or wrongdoing on the part of the claimant, the public interest did not favour disclosure. The influence of *Naomi Campbell v MGN* and *Von Hannover v Germany (No 1)* on both these cases is very evident.

case close-up

Rocknroll v News Group Newspapers [2013] EWHC 24 (Ch)

The claimant had sought an injunction to restrain the publication on Facebook of a photograph taken at a private party. At [5] Briggs J summarised what he described as the 'well-settled principles' of privacy:

(1) The first stage is to ascertain whether the applicant has a reasonable expectation of privacy so as to engage Article 8; if not, the claim fails.

(2) The question of whether or not there is a reasonable expectation of privacy in relation to the information: '...is a broad one, which takes account of all the circumstances of the case. They include the attributes of the claimant, the nature of the activity in which the claimant was engaged, the place at which it was happening, the nature and purpose of the intrusion, the absence of consent and whether it was known or could be inferred, the effect on the claimant and the circumstances in which and the purposes for which the information came into the hands of the publisher': see *Murray v Express Newspapers* [2009] Ch 481 at [36].

The test established in *Campbell v MGN Ltd* [2004] 2 AC 457 is to ask whether a reasonable person of ordinary sensibilities, if placed in the same situation as the subject of the disclosure, rather than the recipient, would find the disclosure offensive.

(3) The protection may be lost if the information is in the public domain. In this regard there is, *per Browne v Associated Newspapers Ltd* [2008] QB 103 at [61],'... potentially

an important distinction between information which is made available to a person's circle of friends or work colleagues and information which is widely published in a newspaper.'

(4) If Article 8 is engaged then the second stage of the inquiry is to conduct 'the ultimate balancing test' which has the four features identified by Lord Steyn in *In Re S (A Child) (Identification: Restrictions on Publication* [2005] 1 AC 593 at [17]:

'First, neither article [8 or 10] has *as such* precedence over the other. Secondly, where the values under the two articles are in conflict, an intense focus on the comparative importance of the specific rights being claimed in the individual case is necessary. Thirdly, the justifications for interfering with or restricting each right must be taken into account. Finally, the proportionality test must be applied to each.'

(5) As *Von Hannover v Germany* (2004) 40 EHRR 1 makes clear at [76]: 'the decisive factor in balancing the protection of private life against freedom of expression should lie in the contribution that the published photos and articles make to a debate of general interest.'

(6) Pursuant to section 12(3) of the Human Rights Act 1998 an interim injunction should not be granted unless a court is satisfied that the applicant is likely—in the sense of more likely than not—to obtain an injunction following a trial.

3.5.5 **Loss of privacy**

One counter-argument which is often raised in cases involving media intrusion is that those who court publicity have by their own conduct diminished their right of privacy. This was certainly the view of Lord Woolf in *A v B (a Company)* at [11(xii)] where the court refused to restrain the disclosure in the newspapers of the extramarital affairs of a well-known footballer. In *Theakston v MGN* [2002] EWHC 137, Ouseley J likewise refused to restrain the publication of a story concerning the visit to a brothel by a television personality, although he did restrain publication of photographs of the event (again, we may note the more stringent treatment accorded to photographic information).

These two decisions appear to treat the defence of 'in the public interest' as if it meant 'of public interest', thereby lending an aura of respectability to the activities of the media in their attempt to satisfy public curiosity about the rich and famous. This should be contrasted with what was said in *Von Hannover v Germany (No 1)* about the status of someone who was in the public eye but not holding any office of state, and with the treatment of the public interest argument in *McKennitt v Ash*, the *Prince of Wales* case and *Mosley v News Group Newspapers*. As the Court of Appeal remarked in *Douglas v Hello! Ltd (No 2)*, English courts for a time appeared to take a less generous view of the protection which a celebrity could expect than the Strasbourg court. There may be a general public interest in maintaining a free press, but in striking a balance between Articles 8 and 10 ECHR, 'one does not start with the balance tilted in favour of Article 10' (*Douglas v Hello! Ltd (No 2)* at [254], [82]). The comments of the Court of Appeal in *Douglas v Hello! Ltd (No 2)* (which the court itself stated were *obiter*) must be considered as critical of the treatment of the public interest defence in *A v B (a Company)* and *Theakston*. Nevertheless, the ECtHR itself has recognised that there are circumstances in which the right to privacy may be lost. In *Von Hannover v Germany (No 2)* [2012] ECHR 228, Princess Caroline sought to restrain the publication of photographs taken of herself and her family on a skiing holiday at a time when her father, Prince Rainier, was gravely ill. The court was of the view that 'not only does the press have the task of imparting information and ideas on all matters of public interest, the public also has a right to receive them'. Here the Prince's illness was an event in contemporary society; in the particular factual context it would be wrong to treat the claimant as an ordinary private individual.

Equally, where the claimant has been untruthful or hypocritical, then the press are entitled to set the record straight (*Woodward v Hutchins per* Bridge LJ). Thus in *Browne v Associated Newspapers* [2007] 3 WLR 289, the Court of Appeal applied the public interest defence by permitting the defendant to publish details of the claimant's homosexual relationship because the claimant had previously committed perjury about it. However, even 'setting the record straight' has its limits. In *Naomi Campbell v MGN* the majority of the House of Lords held that only two out of the five pieces of information (the fact that the claimant was a drug addict and the fact that she was receiving treatment for her addiction) should have been disclosed by the defendant in its attempt to counter the lies which she had told: 'It should [not] necessarily be in the public interest that an individual who has been adopted as a role model . . . should be demonstrated to have feet of clay' (*Naomi Campbell v Mirror Group Newspapers Ltd* [2003] 1 All ER 224 at [41] (CA)).

thinking point

Do the cases discussed in this section not suggest that the courts have tilted the balance too far in favour of Article 8 ECHR at the expense of Article 10?

76

 3.6 # Defences

Apart from pleading consent by the claimant or else arguing that the information is already in the public domain, the principal defence to an action for breach of confidence is that disclosure is 'in the public interest'. Some commentators treat disclosure in the public interest as going to the issue of whether the information is protectable. The better view is that public interest is a defence to be raised in order to justify what would otherwise be the wrongful use of secret information which has been imparted in confidence. This is because disclosure in the public interest is also a defence to copyright infringement and there have been several Court of Appeal decisions (notably *Hyde Park v Yelland* [2000] 3 WLR 215 and *Ashdown v Telegraph Group* [2001] 4 All ER 666) involving both breach of confidence and copyright infringement, where disclosure in the public interest was pleaded as a defence to both causes of action, and was dealt with as such by the court. 'In the public interest' is used in a similar way in the privacy cases: once it is established that the claimant had a reasonable expectation of privacy, then the court has to balance Articles 8 and 10 ECHR, ie it has to decide whether public interest overrides the claimant's rights.

cross reference
See section 9.5.4.

3.6.1 **Disclosure in the public interest: the basis of the defence**

Disclosure *in* the public interest (which is not the same as saying that something, such as the latest gossip about celebrities, is 'of public interest') means that the defendant is seeking to justify what has been done by reference to the interests of society as a whole. Disclosure is necessary in order for the rule of law to be upheld. 'There is no confidence in the disclosure of an iniquity' and 'no man can be made the confidant of a crime or fraud' are *dicta* often cited as the reason for the defence (see *Gartside v Outram* (1856) 26 LJ Ch 113 and *Initial Services Ltd v Putterill* [1968] 1 QB 396, CA, respectively). However, even though disclosure to public authorities may be justified (for example where there has been a breach of the law by the claimant) that may not entitle the defendant to tell the world at large. It may be more appropriate to inform the police or regulatory authorities (*Francome v Mirror Group Newspapers* [1984] 2 All ER 408; *Cream Holdings Ltd v Banerjee* [2004] 3 WLR 918).

3.6.2 **Public interest: the expansion of the defence**

The public interest defence, as originally set out in *Initial Services Ltd v Putterill*, was concerned with where there had been criminal conduct on the part of the claimant, or at least some other serious breach of the law (in *Initial* the employer's breach of competition law justified the 'whistle-blower' employee's conduct in revealing what had gone on). Since that decision, the defence has been raised in many cases, not always successfully. In *Lion Laboratories v Evans* [1984] 2 All ER 417 publication of the fact that a device (the 'Intoximeter') for breath-testing motorists for drink-driving was unreliable was justified because otherwise there might be wrongful convictions. In *Hellewell v Chief Constable of Derbyshire* [1995] 1 WLR 804, the public interest defence was held to justify the distribution by the police to shopkeepers of photographs of the claimant taken when he was in custody. Although the photographs were confidential, the police could make reasonable use of them for the purposes of crime prevention, detection and investigation, and they were being distributed to a limited number of shops who had been badly affected by crime.

By contrast, in *Hyde Park Residence v Yelland*, publication in a newspaper of stolen video stills rebutting the claim that Princess Diana was about to marry Dodi Al Fayed was not 'in the public interest' (it might have been 'of public interest') as the information could have been supplied without publishing photographs taken from the CCTV footage (copyright in which was owned by the claimant). In *Ashdown v Telegraph Group*, publication of diaries showing the extent of the Labour/Liberal Democrat negotiations during the 1997 General Election campaign was equally not justified as being 'in the public interest'. Again the information could have been made available without infringing the claimant's copyright. Further, the fact that key documents had been stolen from the claimant's safe did not lend credence to the defence. Last, of course, there was the division of judicial opinion in *Naomi Campbell v MGN* as to the extent to which 'in the public interest' allowed disclosure of the five key facts about the claimant's drug addiction, with the majority concluding that only two of the five should be made public in the interest of 'setting the record straight'.

More problematic than these cases is *A v B (a Company)* where Lord Woolf refused to restrain the publication of a footballer's marital infidelities on the basis that this was in the public interest. As a celebrity in the public eye, it was suggested, the claimant had forfeited his right to be let alone. We have already noted the implicit criticism of this thinking (and of Ouseley J's decision in *Theakston v MGN*) by the Court of Appeal in *Douglas v Hello! Ltd (No 2)*. Subsequent cases, no doubt influenced by the *Von Hannover (No 1)* ruling with its strict criteria, have been more dismissive of the public interest defence, including *McKennitt v Ash*, *HRH Prince of Wales v Associated Newspapers Ltd* and *Mosley*.

Public interest can be a two-edged sword. In *Volkswagen AG v Garcia and others* [2013] EWHC 1832 (Ch), the defendants wanted to publish an academic paper revealing the weaknesses in a computer chip used by the claimant and other car manufacturers in car immobilisers. One of the arguments they advanced was that there was a strong public interest in exposing the security flaws. Nevertheless, Birss J held that this was outweighed by the greater public interest in not facilitating car crime.

3.6.3 Public interest: government information

thinking point
Do the courts always distinguish clearly between 'in the public interest' and 'of public interest'?

In the context of Government information, the public interest defence operates in a slightly different way. In *A-G v Jonathan Cape Ltd* [1976] QB 752, the court refused to restrain the publication of the internal workings of the British Cabinet in a politician's diaries as there was no public interest justification for keeping it secret. Today, where a Crown servant pleads the public interest defence, the Crown must meet the additional burden placed on it by *Spycatcher*, namely that it must be shown not only that the information was confidential but also that it was in the public interest that it should *not* be published.

3.7 Remedies: particular problems

3.7.1 Injunctions

If a claimant is successful in an action for breach of confidence, it will normally want to restrain the defendant from making further use of the secret information. However, case law relating to the award of an injunction for breach of confidence is contradictory. It raises the question of the proper function of an injunction, and in particular whether such relief should be available once the information has become public knowledge. Where publication is the result of the *confider* making the information public, then no injunctive relief is available (*Mustad & Sons Ltd v Allcock & Dosen*). The position is less clear where the information becomes public either through the conduct of the confidant or through the conduct of a third party. Despite the equitable maxim that 'equity does nothing in vain', there are decisions where an injunction has been granted. This raises the question about the purpose of an injunction. Is it to protect the claimant or to punish the defendant?

In *Cranleigh Precision Engineering v Bryant* [1966] RPC 81, post-publication injunctive relief was not granted, the court applying the maxim that equity does nothing in vain. By contrast, in *Schering Chemicals v Falkman* the majority of the Court of Appeal were prepared to grant an injunction, despite the relevant information (about the side effects of the claimant's pharmaceutical) being known. Lord Denning's powerful dissent should be noted. Similarly, injunctive relief was granted in *Speedseal v Paddington* [1986] 1 All ER 91 (probably because of the nature of the defendant's conduct), and in *Spycatcher*. In the latter case, there is a distinct lack of clarity by the House of Lords as to whether Peter Wright, the former civil servant, could be enjoined from publishing his memoirs in the United Kingdom when they were readily available elsewhere. Their Lordships obviously felt some distaste in concluding that there was no point in issuing an injunction once the book had been published, as Peter Wright was profiting from his own wrong.

The role of injunctive relief was revisited by Arnold J in *Vestergaard Frandsen A/S v BestNet Europe Ltd* [2010] FSR 29. He concluded (at [76]) after a detailed review of earlier cases that the so-called 'springboard' doctrine does *not* enable the court to grant an injunction once information has ceased to be confidential and that *Speedseal v Paddington* was wrong. Publication of the confidential information brings the obligation of confidence to an end, regardless of whether this was by the confider, the confidant or a stranger.

cross reference
See section 3.4.1.

3.7.2 **Compensation**

The case law on compensation for breach of confidence is likewise contradictory. Where the claimant seeks an award of damages, it is necessary to distinguish between those cases where the confidential obligation arises as a result of a contract and those cases where it does not. Where the breach of confidence is also a breach of contract, damages are calculated under the normal contract rules, although in exceptional cases, it is possible to award an **account of profits**. The ability to award an account is illustrated by *AG v Blake*, where a former security services employee who had defected to the then Soviet Union had published his memoirs, from which he earned considerable royalties. His behaviour was held to be analogous to breach of a fiduciary obligation, for which an account would have been the normal remedy.

Where the parties are not in a contractual relationship, the question is whether damages are awarded under the Senior Courts Act 1981 (formerly the Supreme Court Act) s.50 (ie in lieu of or in addition to equitable relief) or whether they are awarded independently on a quasi-tortious basis. If the latter is the case, a further question is how are they to be calculated? One answer is in the case of *Seager v Copydex (No 2)* [1969] RPC 250. Here the Court of Appeal decided that the measure of damages was to be as in the tort of conversion, so that the claimant was to be awarded the retail selling price of each infringing item produced by the defendants. The calculation suggests that damages were awarded independently of the power in s.50. It might well be, however, that in using such a computation, Lord Denning was influenced by the fact that at the time conversion damages were available for breach of copyright under the Copyright Act 1956 s.18. This particular form of monetary relief has since been abolished, which would mean that if *Seager v Copydex (No 2)* is correct, breach of confidence would be the only area of intellectual property in which such a generous award is allowed. Further, any expansion of the tort of conversion to cover intangible personal property was rejected by a majority of the House of Lords (Lords Hoffmann, Walker and Brown) in *Douglas and Zeta-Jones v Hello! Ltd*. By contrast, in *Dowson & Mason v Potter* [1986] 2 All ER 418 the court awarded a reasonable licence fee, that is, the sum which the claimant would have charged for permission to use the information commercially, a calculation identical to that used in patent and copyright infringement actions and much more in keeping with the principles enunciated by Lord Wilberforce in *General Tire v Firestone* [1976] RPC 197 concerning damages for infringement of intellectual property rights and with the thinking of the Supreme Court of Canada in *Cadbury Schweppes Inc v FBI Foods Ltd*. That a reasonable licence fee is the correct measure has now been confirmed by the Court of Appeal in *Force India Formula One Team Ltd v Aerolab SRL* [2013] EWCA Civ 780.

cross reference
See section 2.3.2.1.

A particular problem may present itself in the newly emerging case law on privacy. In *Douglas v Hello! Ltd (No 2)* the Court of Appeal dismissed the claimant's appeal for damages to be increased from Lindsay J's award of £14,600 so as to accord with what might have been charged as a reasonable licence fee. Apart from the fact that their contract with their authorised publishers prohibited them from agreeing to any further exploitation of their wedding photographs, the difficulty which the court faced was that an interim injunction to prevent the invasion of their privacy should have been maintained but in fact had been wrongly discharged. Damages for this form of harm would have been inadequate. Once privacy is lost, it cannot be recaptured. The question remains, therefore, what form of monetary remedy should the claimants have been awarded for this newly created form of action? We may note that this particular issue was not the subject of appeal to the House of Lords, although Lord Walker (at [295]) expresses doubts about the correctness of awarding 'modest' damages.

The quantum of damages for invasion of privacy was revisited by Eady J in *Mosley v News Group Newspapers*. Noting that an infringement of privacy could never be effectively compensated by money, he decided that £60,000 should be awarded. There should be adequate financial remedy to acknowledge the infringement and to compensate for embarrassment and distress, even though what could be achieved through compensation was limited. However, there should be no award of exemplary or punitive damages (to deter others), but equally, just because some viewed the claimant's conduct with distaste was not a reason to reduce the award.

3.7.3 **Proprietary relief**

One final question is whether a constructive trust could also be available if the defendant has 'used' the information to make a personal gain. Although this idea was accepted in the Canadian case of *LAC Minerals v International Corona Ltd* (1989) 61 DLR (4th) 14, the Supreme Court of Canada in *Cadbury Schweppes Inc v FBI Foods Ltd* has subsequently declared that a proprietary remedy is not appropriate. Instead, the court should calculate damages on the basis of lost profits during the notional period of one year it would have taken the defendant to 'reverse engineer' the claimant's secret recipe for a drink. Similarly, the House of Lords in *AG v Blake* ruled that a constructive trust should not be imposed on the defendant's gains. There was no proprietary interest to protect. The lack of property right to support a constructive trust was repeated in *Douglas v Hello! Ltd (No 2)* (CA). However, as noted earlier, their Lordships in *Blake* did suggest that an account of profits should be available instead where the defendant had been in a fiduciary or quasi-fiduciary position. Such reasoning could therefore apply not just to Crown servants (as in *Blake*) but also to high-ranking employees, such as company directors. However, it should be remembered that *Blake* was an exceptional case: *Devenish Nutrition Ltd v Sanofi-Aventis SA* [2009] Ch 390.

Summary

This chapter has explained:

- how breach of confidence operates in a commercial context to protect secret information;
- the way in which the cases have developed the criteria for protection; and

- the interaction between breach of confidence and the Human Rights Act leading to separate protection against the misuse of personal information.

 # Reflective question

Using breach of confidence as a vehicle for creating a right of privacy was a big mistake. Discuss.

Annotated further reading

Aplin, T. 'The Development of the Action for Breach of Confidence in the post-HRA Era' [2007] *IPQ* 19
Provides a wide-ranging review of the case law.

Carty, H. 'The Common Law and the Quest for the IP Effect' [2007] *IPQ* 237
Considers in the light of the House of Lords in *Douglas v Hello!* whether breach of confidence could be expanded to provide wider protection for 'valuable intangibles' against misappropriation.

Carty, H. 'An Analysis of the Modern Action for Breach of Commercial Confidence: When is Protection Merited?' [2008] *IPQ* 416
Argues that the House of Lords in *Douglas v Hello!* missed the opportunity to state clearly a modern framework for liability.

Hunt, C. 'Rethinking Surreptitious Takings in the Law of Confidence' [2011] *IPQ* 66
Criticises the House of Lords' rulings in *Campbell* and *Douglas* for their lack of analysis of how an obligation of confidence can extend to a surreptitious taker.

Moreham, N.A. 'Privacy in the Common Law' (2005) 121 *LQR* 628
Analyses protection against the invasion of privacy in light of *Campbell v MGN*, considering in particular the desirable scope of 'private information' and the desirable extension of the action to cover non-information-based intrusions.

Morgan, J. 'Privacy, Confidence and Horizontal Effect: *"Hello" Trouble'* [2003] *CLJ* 443
A critique of the interlocutory decision in *Douglas v Hello!*

Mulheron, R. 'A Potential Framework for Privacy? A Reply to *Hello!'* (2006) 69 *MLR* 679
Considers the difficulties which arise from any judicial attempt to create a right of privacy and the criteria which ought to be deployed in creating a coherent tort of privacy.

Phillipson, G. 'Transforming Breach of Confidence? Towards a Common Law Right of Privacy under the Human Rights Act' (2003) 66 *MLR* 726
The seminal article on breach of confidence (referred to with approval by Lord Nicholls in *Campbell v MGN*) which explores the effect of the fusion of the Human Rights Act and breach of confidence.

Schreiber, A. 'Confidence Crisis, Privacy Phobia: Why Invasion of Privacy Should be Independently Recognised in English Law' [2006] *IPQ* 160
Argues that breach of confidence should not be extended to misuse of personal information and that Parliament should legislate to create a separate tort.

Sims, A. ' "A Shift in the Centre of Gravity": The Dangers of Protecting Privacy through Breach of Confidence' [2005] *IPQ* 27
Compares the differing approaches of United Kingdom and New Zealand courts in protecting privacy, arguing that it would be better to create a separate stand-alone tort rather than extend the action for breach of confidence.

Part 3

Patents

Introduction to patents

Learning objectives

Upon completion of this chapter, you should have acquired:

- an appreciation of the historical influences which have shaped present-day United Kingdom patent law;

- knowledge of the ways in which the Patents Act 1977 marked a radical departure from the previous law;

- an understanding (by way of background) of United Kingdom patent procedure;

- knowledge of the statutory rules concerning the ownership of United Kingdom patents; and

- a grasp of the key issues in patent cases.

Introduction

This chapter deals with a number of matters central to the chapters which follow, namely the historical context in which the law of patents has developed, the origins of current United Kingdom legislation and a guide to understanding the key issues likely to be raised in patent litigation. By way of background it will also explain the procedure to be followed when obtaining a United Kingdom patent and the statutory rules governing ownership.

4.1 Historical background

4.1.1 The history of patents

It is frequently stated that the origins of **patents** are obscure. The word 'patent' itself derives from the Latin phrase *literae patentes* meaning 'open letter'. It reflects the practice of the Crown in England from the Middle Ages onwards to **grant** monopolies to individuals by way of an open letter to which the Great Seal was affixed. The **United Kingdom Intellectual Property Office ('UKIPO')** itself says that the first recorded patent (for the making of stained-glass windows in Eton College) was granted in 1449, yet there is extensive academic literature (see Wyndham Hulme, 'The History of the Patent System under the Prerogative and at Common Law' (1896) 12 *LQR* 141) of patents being granted at least a century before. It has been suggested (see Seaborne Davis, 'Further Light on the Case of Monopolies' (1932) 48 *LQR* 394) that these ancient patents could be subdivided into four categories, namely those involving inventions as we might understand the term today, dispensations from statutory regulation, powers of supervision over particular trades, and personal trading monopolies over everyday items (such as vinegar or playing cards). Even the first category (inventions as such) could be subdivided into those where the **patentee** had themselves created some sort of technical advance and those where the patentee was merely the first person to introduce into the country technology already in use elsewhere. The principal reason for granting a monopoly over technology already known outside the kingdom was to encourage the importation of skilled labour and know-how in order to promote local manufacture. The national interest lay at the heart of most of the grants made by the Tudor monarchs: 'new' technology might relate to public works or weapons of war, it might help to make domestic industry more competitive or boost overseas trade, it might reduce unemployment or make a particular commodity cheaper.

The practice of granting patents has existed for many centuries and was by no means exclusive to England. Arguably, the Tudor practice was influenced by legislation elsewhere in Europe, for example, the Statute of Venice 1474.

The Statute of Venice

The Statute of Venice is considered to be one of the earliest to set out patent fundamentals. It reads:

> Be it enacted that, by the authority of this Council, every person who shall build any new and ingenious device in this City, not previously made in our Commonwealth, shall give

notice of it to the office of our General Welfare Board when it has been reduced to perfection so that it can be used and operated. It is forbidden to every other person in any of our territories and towns to make any further device conforming with and similar to said one, without the consent and licence of the author, for the term of 10 years. And if anybody builds it in violation hereof, the aforesaid author and inventor shall be entitled to have him summoned before any magistrate of this City, by which magistrate the said infringer shall be constrained to pay him hundred ducats; and the device shall be destroyed at once. It being, however, within the power and discretion of the Government, in its activities, to take and use any such device and instrument, with this condition however that no one but the author shall operate it.

We have among us men of great genius, apt to invent and discover ingenious devices; and in view of the grandeur and virtue of our City, more such men come to us every day from diverse parts. Now, if provision were made for the works and devices discovered by such persons, so that others who may see them could not build them and take the inventor's honor away, more men would then apply their genius, would discover, and would build devices of great utility and benefit to our commonwealth.

The first paragraph contains all the ingredients of a modern patent statute, namely the criteria for protection ('new and ingenious device...not previously made...when it has been reduced to perfection'), the need to register ('give notice'), the exclusive right conferred on the 'author', the prohibition on **infringement**, the penalties for infringing conduct, and power for the Government to make use of the invention. The second paragraph sets out the reasons why patents are desirable.

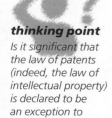

thinking point
Is it significant that the law of patents (indeed, the law of intellectual property) is declared to be an exception to the principle that all monopolies are bad?

Criticism of the overuse (and abuse) of patents by Elizabeth I led to legal challenges, such as that in *Darcy v Allin (the Case of Monopolies)* (1602) 11 Co Rep 84b, where (so we are told) the patent for playing cards was held contrary to law. Where, however, the monopoly resulted in the acquisition of new technology, the courts were prepared to uphold the grant as valid (*Clothworkers of Ipswich Case* (1615) Godbolt 252). The practice of James I in granting so-called 'odious monopolies' if anything, was worse than that of his predecessor. Resultant disquiet in Parliament led to the enactment of the Statute of Monopolies 1623. Section 1 declared all monopolies to be 'altogether contrary to the laws of this realm, and...void', but s.6 contained an exception for 'any manner of new manufacture'. Section 6 was, until 1977, the only substantive provision on patent law in the United Kingdom, and (surprisingly) is still in force today. The law of patents (and indeed intellectual property generally) is therefore built on a very limited exception to the principle that monopolies are bad.

4.1.2 **The development of United Kingdom patent law**

Like many areas of commercial law, the law of patents was shaped primarily by nineteenth-century events, and was a belated response to the Industrial Revolution. Apart from the concerns about the lack of efficiency in the patent system (satirised in Charles Dickens' *Poor Man's Tale of a Patent*), there was vigorous debate about whether there should be patents at all (see F. Machlup and E. Penrose, 'The Patent Controversy in the Nineteenth Century' (1950) 10 *J of Economic History* 1). Some (principally those who favoured free trade) called for their abolition, believing that they stifled innovation. Such economic objections to patent protection, prompted by but by no means entirely consistent with *laissez-faire* political philosophy, can be contrasted to the objections to patents in the sixteenth and seventeenth centuries, when patents were perceived as an undesirable use of the Crown prerogative. Ultimately, the anti-patent movement failed (despite the absence of patent laws in several neighbouring European states such as Switzerland) because, as Matthew Fisher has argued, (in 'Classical Economics and the Philosophy of the Patent System' [2005] *IPQ* 1) the abolitionists were unable to prove that there was no link between Britain's prosperity and the patent system.

Objections to the patent system as it stood at the start of the nineteenth century were threefold (see Dutton, *The Patent System and Inventive Activity during the Industrial Revolution 1750–1852*, Manchester University Press, 1984). First, there was cumbersome administrative machinery; second, patents were expensive to obtain (not least because it was necessary to obtain a separate grant for a patent in England, Scotland and Ireland); and last, the law was inefficient in protecting the rights of inventors. Legislative reform tended to be cautious and concerned with procedural improvements to the patent system, yet contained a shift in the basis of patent protection from Crown prerogative to Government administration (see Sherman and Bently *The Making of Modern Intellectual Property Law*, Cambridge University Press, 1999). Minor changes occurred in 1835 but the real impetus for reform was the Great Exhibition of 1851. Temporary legislation of that year led in turn to the passing of the Patent Law Amendment Act 1852. This established UKIPO (under the then name of the Commissioners for Patents). The effect of the Act of 1852, as Dutton explains, was that inventors were to be protected from the date of application rather than the date of grant; there was to be a single patent for the United Kingdom; and an index of patents was to be set up and available for public consultation. The last-mentioned feature marks the start of patents providing an information system for the scientific and engineering communities. Nevertheless, the role of the then Patent Office was limited to receiving and publishing patent applications. Whether or not a patent was granted was the decision of the Law Officers, not the Patent Office itself.

thinking point
Do you find it surprising that the legislative reforms up to the Patents Act 1977 contained no substantive principle?

Further significant changes occurred in the Patents, Designs and Marks Act 1883 (which provided for the Patent Office to **examine** applications and for the Patent Office seal to replace the Great Seal on the formal document of grant); the Patents Act 1902 (which extended the examination system to a limited consideration of whether the invention was new in the light of **prior art**); and the Patents Act 1949 (which provided an exhaustive list of statutory grounds of **invalidity**, and also established the posts of specialist patent judges in the Chancery Division). What is noteworthy, however, is that no patent legislation contained any statement of substantive principle. Until the passing of the Patents Act 1977, there was no definition of what was a patentable **invention**, and no statutory explanation of what amounted to infringing conduct. Guidance instead was found in the wording of s.6 of the Statute of Monopolies and in the formula of the Royal Grant. The revolutionary effect of the Patents Act 1977 in this regard is explained later.

4.2   The justifications for patent protection

4.2.1   Academic literature

We have already considered a number of justifications frequently advanced for the protection of intellectual property in general. Those relating specifically to patents can be traced back to nineteenth-century debates about reform. Machlup and Penrose and Fisher have identified four arguments deployed in support of maintaining some form of protection in response to those who wished to abolish the patent system entirely in the interests of free trade. These arguments are, first, a moral justification based on the assertion that there is a natural property right in ideas. Appropriation of ideas is therefore tantamount to stealing. The 'natural law' justification owed much to the writings of John Locke's labour theory, even though it is highly debatable whether Locke contemplated intangible property rights. The second argument is that justice and fairness demand that there should be a reward for services useful to society. Because reward for the inventor cannot be guaranteed if left to market forces, the state should intervene by creating a temporary monopoly for the patentee. The 'reward by monopoly theory' was greatly influenced by the writings of Adam Smith, John Stuart Mill and Jeremy Bentham. However, as Fisher points out, the theory is not without criticism. Applied logically, the inventor of a groundbreaking patent should receive greater protection than someone who thinks up a minor improvement to existing technology, yet the law draws no distinction between the two. Also, the theory takes no account of how the invention was created, whether by prolonged research, accident or genius. It is perhaps based on the romantic notion of the inventor as hero, imagery which does not accord with research and development carried out by large multi-national corporations. The third argument is that patents are necessary to secure economic development, hence the incentive of patent protection is necessary to ensure that inventions are made. The incentive theory assumes that industrial progress is desirable, that inventions are necessary for such progress, and that granting of patents is the most effective way of providing such incentives. All of these assumptions can, of course, be challenged. Nevertheless, the incentive argument is the one most frequently advanced. Last, there is the 'exchange for secrets' theory. The argument here is to the effect that if there were no patents, inventions would be kept secret, so disclosure by the inventor is the consideration for the grant of exclusivity. The patent is therefore a contract between the inventor and the state. In due course, the information in the patent becomes part of the store of human knowledge to be shared by all. Despite the attractions of this argument, the quality of patent specifications in the Victorian era was poor, and it is only in recent times that the patent information system lives up to the expectations of the exchange for secrets theory.

The assumption underlying all of these justifications is, of course, that patents are a good thing. Nevertheless, patents create legal monopolies which prevent competitors from entering the market. There are well-documented examples of the holders of key inventions (for example, James Watt's steam engine) using their monopoly power to prevent subsequent developments and thereby hindering technological change. That being so, how should the law strike a balance between innovation and competition? Is there an economic argument which could be deployed in striking such a balance? Needless to say, there is extensive USA literature on this aspect of patent theory. Of this we mention but one article, simply because it draws together a number of other leading articles and because it has been referred to by the House of Lords in *H Lundbeck A/S v Generics (UK) Ltd* [2009] RPC 407. Merges and Nelson (in 'On the Complex Economics of Patent Scope' (1990) 90 *Col L R* 839) point out that it is mistaken to assume that technical advance proceeds similarly in all industries, and that it is necessary to separate out discrete inventions (where the patent does not point the way to wide-ranging technical advances); 'cumulative' technologies (such as the aircraft or semi-conductor industries); chemical technologies (which have features of both of the previously mentioned categories); and 'science-based' technologies (for example, biotechnology) where technical advance is driven by developments in

cross reference
See section 1.4.

science outside the industry. They conclude that public policy ought to encourage inventive rivalry and not hinder it. Although rivalry can be inefficient, it will generate more rapid technical progress, whilst broad patents block progress. The answer lies, they argue, in the way in which courts interpret patent **claims** in the light of subsequent technological developments. Courts need to be sensitive to the nature of technical advances in particular industries, so that in a handful of cases it may be necessary to curtail broad patent claims, primarily those involving pioneering breakthroughs.

4.2.2 Case law

The justifications for patent protection are from time to time rehearsed in United Kingdom case law, sometimes as part of the conclusions to be reached on the facts of the case. Lord Oliver in *Re Asahi KKK's Patent* [1991] RPC 485 at p. 523 and the Court of Appeal in *Dranez Anstalt v Hayek* [2003] FSR 561 at [25] both refer in general terms to the incentive theory as the reason why patents are granted. Lord Hoffmann in *Biogen Inc v Medeva plc* [1997] RPC 1 at p. 51 appears to pay greater regard to the 'reward by monopoly theory'. He stated that the court should recognise the patentee's technical contribution whilst taking care not to stifle research, an argument which clearly had a bearing on the decision of the House to declare the patent in question invalid. Equally, in *H Lundbeck A/S v Generics (UK) Ltd* at [48], Lord Mance made explicit use of the argument by Merges and Nelson that the scope of patent protection should reflect its inventive contribution, only here the conclusion was that the patent was valid, perhaps because, in contrast to *Biogen*, this was a 'discrete' invention. Most recently, Lord Neuberger in *Eli Lilly and Company v Human Genome Sciences Inc* [2012] RPC 102 at [99] overturned the decision of the Court of Appeal that a patent for a protein discovered by 'bioinformatics' should not be granted because it would stultify research by others rather than encourage it. The purpose of the patent system, he said, was to provide a temporary monopoly as an incentive to innovation whilst at the same time facilitating the early dissemination of any such innovation.

thinking point
Which of the justifications for the patent system do you find most convincing in the twenty-first century?

4.3 Understanding the Patents Act 1977

4.3.1 The impact of international conventions

When it was introduced, the Patents Act 1977 was described as a 'culture shock' to United Kingdom patent lawyers. Previous legislative reforms were procedural only. The 1977 Act therefore dealt with the substantive law of patents for the first time. Its provisions are influenced by three major international documents, the Patent Co-operation Treaty 1970 ('**PCT**'), the European Patent Convention 1973 ('**EPC**') and the draft Community Patent Convention 1975 (now Regulation (EU) No 1257/2012 of the European Parliament and of the Council of 17 December 2012 implementing enhanced cooperation in the area of the creation of unitary patent protection [2012] OJ L 361/1) (the '**Unitary Patent**'). The Act was intended to give effect to the United Kingdom's obligations under each of these.

4.3.1.1 The PCT

The PCT, administered by **WIPO**, creates a procedural mechanism assisting the intending patentee who wishes to obtain protection in more than one state. At present, PCT membership is over 125 countries. A single application to a local, national or regional patent office (the 'receiving office') is subjected to an international **search** and **preliminary examination** by one of the International Searching Authorities. At present these number 14 (though more are to be added): Australia, Austria, Brazil, Canada, China, Finland, Japan, Korea, the Nordic Patent Institute, the Russian Federation, Spain, Sweden, the USA and the **EPO**. The international **search report** lists references to published patent documents and journal articles which might affect **patentability** and is accompanied by a written opinion on potential **novelty** and **inventive step**. Following the search, WIPO publishes the application. The preliminary examination gives the **applicant** the opportunity to amend the application in light of the search report and to raise arguments. After this an international preliminary report on patentability is issued. Thereafter, it is up to the applicant, armed with the search report and the preliminary report on patentability, to activate the national phase, in which the patent is examined by designated national or regional patent offices. If successful, a PCT application therefore becomes a series of national patents. Apart from the ability to make multiple filings, the chief advantage of the PCT system is that the applicant can delay the decision whether to proceed with the application in particular countries until armed with the search report, and is not required to file a translation of the patent documents into the local language until 30 months after the **priority date** of the patent (translation costs are significant in obtaining patent protection). It also means that the designated national or regional patent offices will take as their starting point for **substantive examination** the report prepared by the International Searching Authority.

4.3.1.2 The EPC

It must be remembered that the EPC is *not* an EU measure, but is an instrument of the Council of Europe. Membership of the Convention is open to any country belonging to the Council of Europe (there are currently nearly 40 members of the EPC), but patent applicants need not be citizens of these states. It provides for search, examination and grant of a **European patent** by the European Patent Office ('EPO'), so one application produces a bundle of parallel national patents. The EPC route accordingly bypasses local patent offices and is a regional system of centralised grant, in contrast to the PCT which is a centralised filing mechanism. However, once granted, European patents are treated as national patents, so that infringement and **revocation** actions are heard by local courts. Because the EPC does not provide for any supra-national court to rule on European patents once granted (its Boards of Appeals are merely internal judicial organs overseeing decisions in respect of the grant of patents), there is a serious risk of the courts of the Contracting States applying different standards in cases concerned with **validity** and infringement. The classic example of this danger of diversity is *Improver v Remington* [1990] FSR 181, where the United Kingdom Patents Court held that the **claimant's** EPILADY device had not been infringed, whilst sister courts in the Netherlands and Germany came to the opposite conclusion.

cross reference
See further
section 6.5.5.

The Administrative Council of the EPO convened a revision conference of the then 20 Contracting States in November 2000. Changes included amending Article 52 EPC (dealing with patentability) so that it complies with **TRIPs**, amending Article 53 (dealing with **exceptions to patentability**) so as to comply both with TRIPs and the EU Biotech Directive (Directive 98/44/EC of the European Parliament and of the Council of 6 July 1998 on the legal protection

cross reference
See further
chapter 5 for
the effect of the
changes.

of biotechnological inventions [1998] OJ L 213/13), and amending Article 54 so as to clarify the practice of allowing 'Swiss form claims' for second medical use. The other alteration was to Article 69 and the Protocol thereto so as to make clear that the scope of patent claims includes equivalent elements. The revised text of the EPC entered into force on 13 December 2007.

The Patents Act 2004 was the United Kingdom's ratification of the EPC 2000 changes. The implementation of these changes into domestic law (by amending ss.2 and 4 of the 1977 Act) was deferred until the revised EPC itself came into force, that is, on 13 December 2007. Those provisions in the 2004 Act modifying other aspects of domestic law came into force on 1 January 2005.

4.3.1.3 The Unitary Patent

The **EU Patent** (as it was called under the Lisbon Treaty) should have been implemented in the 1970s alongside the EPC as part of a twin-track approach to patents in Europe: whilst the EPC was intended to deal with the issuing of patents, the EU Patent was to ensure that the post-grant rights of patentees throughout the EU with regard to infringement, licensing, renewal and invalidity were harmonised. The intention was that there should be a unitary patent for the whole of the EU, as a special type of European patent granted by the EPO. Originally, this was to have been achieved by the Community Patent Convention 1975, but in view of the absence of any real progress in its ratification, the EU Commission decided in 2000 to restart the process by using a different legal instrument, namely a Council Regulation under what is now Article 352 of the **Treaty on the Functioning of the European Union ('TFEU')** (the implied powers provision). Again, negotiations stalled in 2004, one of the stumbling blocks being the translation of patent documents.

The ratification of the Lisbon Treaty in December 2009 should have enabled the process to be reactivated. Article 118 TFEU enables the creation of European intellectual property rights for the better functioning of the internal market, legislation being effected under the ordinary legislative procedure. Despite the hopes that Article 118 TFEU would enable the EU Patent to be achieved (in effect by the EU acceding to the EPC as a Contracting State and by the creation of an EU and European Patent Court system), the 2009 proposals were declared incompatible with the EU Treaties by the ECJ in March 2011. The response of the Council of Ministers was to proceed with 'enhanced cooperation' under Title III TFEU: 25 of the then 27 Member States agreed to proceed with Unitary Patent Protection (Spain and Italy refused). The net result, as explained in chapter 1, was the creation of two Regulations late in 2012 establishing unitary patent protection and dealing with the thorny issue of translation, together with the Agreement on the Unified Patent Court in January 2013. It remains to be seen whether the so-called Unitary Patent (which is not unitary at all) will succeed when all previous attempts have failed.

4.3.2 **The nature of the 1977 Act**

The 1977 Act is a hybrid creature. It introduced substantive provisions on patentability and **exclusions** therefrom (derived from the EPC) into domestic law, as well as a statutory definition of infringement derived from what became Article 7 of the stillborn EU Patent. The grounds of revocation in s.72 are different from those applying before. The Act also introduced, as a purely domestic measure, rules on the ownership of inventions made in the course of employment and a scheme of compensation for employee-inventors. The origins of these different provisions should be borne in mind when applying rules of interpretation.

4.3.3 **The importance of s.130(7)**

The fundamental provision in interpreting the 1977 Act is s.130(7). It declares that certain key sections (specifically those on patentability, infringement and revocation) are deemed to have the same effect in the United Kingdom as the corresponding provisions of the conventions discussed earlier have in other states to which those conventions apply. In plain English, United Kingdom courts are to have regard to how courts in other countries interpret the EPC. In particular, they should have regard to the decisions of the EPO Boards of Appeal with regard to patentability (see *Merrell Dow v Norton* [1996] RPC 76 at p. 82 *per* Lord Hoffmann; and *Bristol-Myers Squibb v Baker Norton Pharmaceuticals Inc* [1999] RPC 253 at pp. 272–3 *per* Jacob J). Notice should be taken of how German courts have dealt with the interpretation of patent claims: *Kirin-Amgen Inc v Hoechst Marion Roussel Ltd* [2005] 1 All ER 667 at [72–75] *per* Lord Hoffmann and *Conor Medsystems v Angiotech Pharmaceuticals Inc* [2008] RPC 716 at [3], again *per* Lord Hoffmann. German decisions should also be used to interpret s.60(2) Patents Act, based on what is now Article 8 of the draft EU Patent: *Grimme Maschinenfabrik GmBH v Scott* [2010] FSR 193 at [122] *per* Jacob LJ. Despite this, there are several examples where the EPO Boards of Appeal and United Kingdom courts have reached differing conclusions on the patentability of a particular invention. As patent law is fact sensitive, such divergence is largely attributable to differences in procedure and evidence: *H Lundbeck A/S v Generics (UK) Ltd* at [35] *per* Lord Walker; *Eli Lilly and Company v Human Genome Sciences Inc* [2010] RPC 429 at [6], [41] *per* Jacob LJ.

thinking point
In what ways can the Patents Act 1977 be described as a 'culture shock'?

4.4 **UKIPO procedure**

This brief explanation of how to obtain patent protection in the United Kingdom is intended as background information, an aid to understanding the context in which key issues of patent law arise. Procedure before the EPO is broadly similar, except that there is no prescribed time limit for completion of the application, and there is a right of post-grant **opposition**. In essence, there are five key stages in the United Kingdom procedure to obtain a domestic patent as shown in Diagram 4.1.

4.4.1 **Filing**

The documents necessary to support a patent application are set out in the Patents Act ss.14(1) and (2), namely the request for a grant, the appropriate fee, a **specification** containing a **description** of the invention, a claim or claims and any drawings referred to in the description or claims and an **abstract**. The last-mentioned document is a key component in the patent information system, and will be entered on the databases maintained by the major patent offices.

Diagram 4.1

Overview of United Kingdom patent application procedure

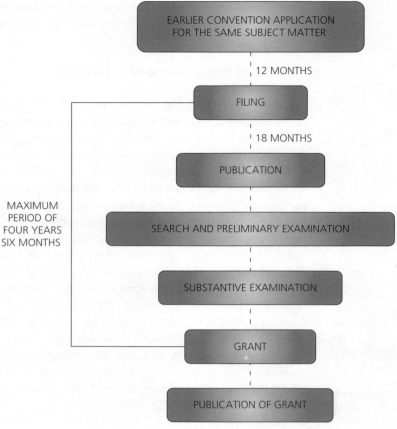

EARLIER CONVENTION APPLICATION FOR THE SAME SUBJECT MATTER

12 MONTHS

FILING

18 MONTHS

PUBLICATION

MAXIMUM PERIOD OF FOUR YEARS SIX MONTHS

SEARCH AND PRELIMINARY EXAMINATION

SUBSTANTIVE EXAMINATION

GRANT

PUBLICATION OF GRANT

Notes:

1 Filing date is the Priority Date for the purposes of validity unless there is an earlier Convention Application.

2 Filing Date determines the maximum duration (20 years) and the payment of annual renewal fees from Year 5 onwards.

The term 'specification' is the name for the patent document as a whole, but basically comprises two parts, the description of the invention and the claims. These require greater elaboration.

4.4.1.1 The description of the invention

The description is deemed to be addressed to the hypothetical creature through whose eyes issues of validity and infringement are judged in patent law, the '**skilled addressee**' or notional skilled technician (the phrase 'skilled addressee' is used throughout this book). This person is the equivalent of the 'reasonable man' in the law of negligence, and their attributes are discussed in greater detail later in the chapter. Section 14(3) Patents Act 1977 requires the specification to disclose the invention 'in a manner which is clear enough and complete enough for the invention to be performed by a person skilled in the art'. This is known as **sufficiency**. Sufficiency relates to the clarity of the description of the invention, not the claims.

cross reference
See section 4.6.2.

Lack of sufficiency is a ground of revocation under s.72(1)(c). For the present, examples of lack of sufficiency include *Monsanto Company v Merck & Co Inc* [2000] RPC 709 (there was no guarantee that the skilled addressee, carrying out the instructions in the description, would produce a class of pharmaceutical compounds which had the desired characteristics, namely anti-inflammatory drugs without particular side effects); and *Kimberly-Clark Worldwide Inc v Procter & Gamble Ltd*, unreported, Pumfrey J, 21 July 2000 (a patent for a new type of disposable nappy was insufficient because the skilled addressee, performing the various tests for absorbency set out in the description, would have arrived at contradictory results). Similarly, in *Novartis AG v Johnson & Johnson Medical Ltd* [2010] EWCA Civ 1039, it was held that the skilled addressee would not be able to carry out the invention without prolonged research: the patent claimed extended wear contact lenses by reference both to certain characteristics such as ophthalmic compatibility, corneal health and wearer comfort, and to physical parameters such as oxygen transmission and ion permeability. Achieving both sets of objectives was too much to expect. However, the House of Lords has stated that the requirement of sufficiency should not be overstated. In *Conor Medsystems v Angiotech Pharmaceuticals Inc* [2008] RPC 716 it said that disclosing *that* the invention works, and *how* to perform it, is different from explaining *why* it works. The latter is not required.

cross reference
Revocation of patents is discussed at 6.4.

4.4.1.2 The claims

Under s.14(5), the claim or claims are required to define the matter for which the applicant seeks protection, be clear and concise, be supported by the description, and relate to one invention or a group of inventions so linked as to form a single **inventive concept**. As a result of s.60 Patents Act 1977, claims may relate to a product (a thing) or a process (how to make something or use something or do something). A patent may have all **product claims**, or all **process claims**, or have a mixture of claims, for example a pharmaceutical patent may have claims both for a new compound and how to make it. The infringement provisions in the Patents Act also provide for protection in respect of products which are directly derived from process patents (see s.60(1)(c), based on Article 64(2) of the EPC), which removes the need for a separate category of 'product-by-process' patents. As Lord Hoffmann explained (at [90]) in *Kirin-Amgen Inc v Hoechst Marion Roussel Ltd*, this type of claim is relatively rare because the EPO is reluctant to accept it (and indeed has criticised the United Kingdom for being the only Contracting State to permit such a claim). The only time when a 'product-by-process' claim will be allowed is where the patent concerns a new substance whose difference from a known substance cannot be described in chemical or physical terms, in which case the process by which it is obtained is an important element of the invention.

Later in this chapter we consider the importance of claims both for validity and infringement.

4.4.1.3 The significance of the priority date

Under s.15, the **filing date** of the patent will be the date on which certain minimum formalities are satisfied. The filing date is to be treated as the '**priority date**' unless the application is based on an earlier Convention application. Under s.5, this will occur where the United Kingdom application is based on an earlier filing in respect of the same subject matter in another Contracting State of the **Paris Convention**. If this is the case, the priority date of the United Kingdom application is in effect backdated to the filing in the other **Convention country**. The priority date of a patent is of crucial importance, as it is the date on which the validity of the patent is assessed. Matter made available to the public before the priority date is known as the 'prior art' and the claims of the patent are compared with the prior art in order

cross reference
See section 1.5.1.1.

to determine whether the invention as set out in the claims meets the requirements of novelty and inventive step. The actual filing date, however, remains relevant in calculating the duration of protection of the patent (Patents Act 1977 s.25). If it transpires that the patent is not able to claim **priority** from an earlier Convention application (because, for example, it did not relate to the same subject matter) then the validity of the patent is assessed at the actual filing date, not the earlier priority date (*Biogen Inc v Medeva plc*).

4.4.2 **Publication**

Eighteen months after filing, the application is automatically published in the *Patents Journal*, early **publication** being a key feature of the EPC and hence the 1977 Act. If the patent contains information prejudicial to public safety, publication can be prohibited under ss.22 and 23. A patentee may decide to withdraw the application before it is published (for example, because it has done further tests on the invention and has realised that the initial application was flawed), in which case the information contained therein will remain undisclosed to the public and can be included in a later application, as long as, that is, a third party has not lawfully made the same information public in the meantime.

The date of publication is significant in relation to infringement, as once the patent has been granted, the patentee can sue for any acts of infringement committed between the publication date and the date of grant, subject to certain conditions (Patents Act 1977 s.69). Unlike EPO procedure, there is no system of opposition, but third parties can make **observations** to UKIPO under s.21.

Once a patent has been published, the remaining steps in the procedure must be initiated by the applicant. If they are not, the application is deemed to have been withdrawn. Whilst there is nothing to stop an applicant abandoning its application after publication, the point to remember is that the information contained in the application will have been made public and so cannot form the basis of a fresh application.

4.4.3 **Search and preliminary examination**

Under s.17(4), the patent examiner is required to make such investigation as is reasonably practicable and necessary to identify the documents needed for substantive examination to determine whether the invention is new and contains an inventive step. Under s.15A (inserted into the 1977 Act by the Regulatory Reform (Patents) Order 2004), the examiner shall determine whether the application complies with the formal requirements of the Act.

4.4.4 **Substantive examination**

Once the search and preliminary examination have been completed, under s.18 the patent application is examined as to whether it complies with the substantive requirements of novelty and inventive step in the light of the search report produced by UKIPO under s.17. Objections to the application are notified to the patentee by letter, and if these objections cannot be overcome (usually by **amendment**) then the applicant is entitled to a hearing, from which there is a right of appeal to the Patents Court.

4.4.5 Grant

If the application is successful, then upon payment of the correct fee the patent will be granted (s.18(4)). The grant must be made within a maximum period of four and a half years (54 months) from the priority date. The fact that the patent has been granted is published in the *Patents Journal* (s.24). It will last for a maximum of 20 years, calculated from the filing date of the application (s.25), but from the fifth year onwards, its continued existence is subject to the prompt payment of annual **renewal fees**, which increase with each year of the life of the patent.

4.4.6 Amendment

A patent applicant can always seek to amend the patent application during the course of its progress through the UKIPO procedure (see ss.17, 18 and 19). Similarly, a patent can be amended once it has been granted (see ss.27, 73 and 75). However, there are restrictions on amendment in s.76. In essence, the patentee cannot extend the description so as to disclose additional matter, and cannot expand the scope of protection in the claims. Any amendment which so broadens the patent is a ground of revocation under s.72(1)(d), and (e). Whether an amendment has such a broadening effect is determined through the eyes of the skilled addressee (see *Re Flexible Directional Indicators Application* [1994] RPC 207 as regards pre-grant amendments and *Bonzel v Intervention (No 3)* [1991] RPC 553 as regards post-grant amendments).

4.4.7 Summary

The interaction between the key dates in the timeline of a patent can be summarised by Diagram 4.2.

Diagram 4.2

The timeline of a UK patent

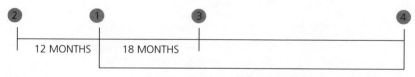

Notes:
1 Filing date: duration of term of protection (20 years) calculated from this date; validity of patent to be determined in the light of the prior art at this date (unless Convention priority claimed).
2 Priority date: UK application can be backdated (for purposes of validity only) to first filing date in respect of the same subject matter in another Contracting State of the Paris Convention or WTO (but duration still calculated from actual filing date).
3 Date of publication in the *Patents Journal*. Application may be withdrawn before this date without contents becoming part of the state of the art. If an infringement action is brought (once the patent has been granted), damages *may* be backdated to this date, in respect of infringing conduct committed between the date of publication and the date of grant, subject to the conditions in s.69 Patents Act. Publication is followed by the preliminary and substantive examination of the application, but only at the request of the applicant.
4 Date of grant: infringement action may only be brought after this date. Annual renewal fees become payable from the fifth anniversary onwards.

thinking point

Would the United Kingdom patent system be better if there were a system of opposition, as in the EPO?

4.5 Ownership of patents

4.5.1 Who is an inventor?

Before deciding who is entitled to the ownership of a particular invention (and hence able to sue for infringement and grant **licences**) it is first necessary to examine what is meant by the word 'inventor'. Section 7 Patents Act 1977 deals with the question of who is an inventor. Subsection (1) declares that any person may apply for a patent, but this is qualified by subsection (2) which provides that the patent may only be granted to the inventor or their successor.

The word 'inventor' is defined in s.7(3) as the 'actual deviser' of the invention. The phrase may be compared with that found in earlier legislation, namely 'the first and true inventor'. Cases decided under the old law had concluded that the inventor was the person who was the 'moving spirit' or inventive genius, rather than someone who put the invention into practical effect. Thus in *Re Smith's Patent* (1905) 22 RPC 57, an application to revoke the patent succeeded, the evidence being that the patentee had not been the inventor but one merely employed to prepare engineering drawings on behalf of the real creator. Similarly in *Re Homan's Patent* (1889) 6 RPC 104, the challenge by an opponent who alleged that he was the rightful inventor because he had made samples for the patentee was rejected by the court, on the basis that the opponent had not appreciated what it was that the patentee was trying to achieve until it was explained to him.

At the time the 1977 Act was introduced, it was argued that the phrase 'actual deviser' in s.7(3) meant a change in the law. Nevertheless, cases decided under the 1977 Act have adopted the same thinking as before. The inventor is the *natural* person who thinks up the inventive concept underlying the patent: *Staeng Ltd's Application* [1996] RPC 183, confirmed in *Henry Brothers (Magherafelt) Ltd v Ministry of Defence* [1999] RPC 442. By way of illustration, in *IDA Ltd v Southampton University* [2006] RPC 567, an article had appeared in *The Times* where one of the defendant's professors had set out his ideas about how to build a better cockroach trap. He was then contacted by one of the claimant's staff who had suggested how to improve the invention by using magnetic powder. It was held that it was the claimant's employee who had provided the inventive concept, the 'bright idea', and so they were entitled to the patent.

Where there is a dispute as to entitlement, UKIPO has jurisdiction to resolve the matter (see ss.8, 9 and 37 Patents Act 1977). At one time, the Court of Appeal took the view that the key word in these provisions was the word 'entitlement', as the sections concern in effect a property dispute. Accordingly, it said, someone who seeks to challenge entitlement to a patent has to show that there has been either a **breach of confidence** or a breach of contract: *Markem v Zipher* [2005] RPC 761. In *IDA Ltd v Southampton University* there was a breach of confidence in that the telephone call in which the claimant's employee had suggested the improvements to the cockroach trap was confidential, thus entitling the claimant to the patent. The House of Lords has since disagreed with this. In *Yeda Research & Development Co Ltd v Rhone-Poulenc Rorer* [2008] RPC 1 it said that the only question is 'who came up with the inventive concept?' (either solely or jointly). Questions of entitlement and novelty were to be kept separate and both *Markem* and *IDA* were overruled with regard to the approach to entitlement disputes.

Under s.72(1)(b) Patents Act 1977, the grant of a patent to the wrong person is also a ground of revocation but the ability to challenge for revocation on this ground is limited to co-inventors and has a strict time limit of two years from grant. The inventor is entitled to be mentioned in the patent even if he or she does not own it: s.13 Patents Act 1977.

4.5.2 Ownership of employee inventions

Having examined the criteria used by the courts to identify an inventor, we turn to look at the special statutory rules concerning employee-inventors. This is a topic where intellectual property law, contract law and employment law overlap. Each has its different values. The Patents Act 1977 provides a particular solution to the ownership of employee-inventions which is coloured by employment rights thinking. Once it has been decided who owns an invention, the employer or employee, the Act creates a scheme of compensation for employee-inventors. The details of the scheme will be considered. The unanswered question is whether the legislation lives up to aspirations of those who lobbied for reform.

4.5.2.1 The Pre-1977 law on ownership of employee inventions

Prior to the Patents Act 1977 there were no statutory rules on the ownership of inventions. The matter was governed entirely by a century or more of case law. The cases revealed that freedom of contract was the prevailing approach, and that the employer's superior economic bargaining power was rarely questioned. In essence, the employer would own an invention made by an employee either by virtue of a provision in the contract of employment or because the employee was deemed to hold the invention on trust for the employer. Such a trust would arise by virtue of the employee's fiduciary status or by virtue of his/her contractual duties.

With regard to the contractual solution, an employer had the economic power to insert a clause (called a 'pre-assignment clause') into the contract of employment stating that all inventions, whenever and wherever made, belonged to the employer. This practice was widely used but was eventually criticised for being in restraint of trade in *Electrolux v Hudson* [1977] FSR 312. Falconer J declared that a storekeeper who made improvements to a vacuum cleaner was beneficially entitled to the patent. It was not the employee's job to invent and the clause in his contract requiring him to hand over all inventions was unenforceable.

The use of the trust to determine ownership of inventions occurred in one of two situations. The court could treat a senior employee as having the status of a fiduciary, so that he or she would then be held to be a trustee of the invention (as happened to the managing director in *Worthington Pumping Engine Co v Moore* (1903) 20 RPC 41 and the senior researcher in *British Syphon Co v Homewood* [1956] 1 WLR 119). Alternatively, the court would examine the employment contract and conclude that as the employee was employed to invent, then he or she must be a trustee of the invention as the result of his or her duties: *Triplex Safety Glass Co v Scorah* [1938] Ch 211. It was, of course, open to the employer to draft the employment contract in such a way that the court could easily make such an inference.

The Patents Act 1949 conferred (in s.56) the power to resolve entitlement disputes. However, the restrictive interpretation accorded to the section by the House of Lords in *Sterling Engineering v Patchett* [1955] AC 534 at p. 543 meant that if by virtue of contract or trust the employer clearly owned the invention, then there was no dispute and the section could not be utilised.

4.5.2.2 The post-1977 law on ownership of employee inventions

As a result of the deliberations of the Banks Committee (*The British Patent System*) (1970) (Cmnd 4407) and the White Paper (*Patent Law Reform*) (1975) (Cmnd 6000), together with lobbying from trades unions, the Patents Act 1977 introduced what was then a new régime for employee inventions. The EPC has no influence here, as rules of ownership are a matter for domestic law. The effect of the 1977 Act can be summarised thus:

- it introduced a new (comprehensive) statutory test of ownership which is to the exclusion of anything which applied before;
- it introduced a scheme of compensation for employee inventors; and
- it rendered unenforceable certain terms in contracts of employment.

The statutory test of ownership

With regard to ownership of inventions, the key provision is s.39 Patents Act 1977. The following observations can be made about the wording of the provision:

- it displaces all the previous case law, due to the phrase 'notwithstanding anything in any rule of law';
- the 'default' position is found in s.39(2): in all cases except those that fall within s.39(1), the invention belongs to the employee; and
- the circumstances when the invention belongs to the employer under s.39(1) are precisely set out.

Section 39(1) contains two paragraphs which confer ownership on the employer. In para (a), the section stresses that the invention must be made in the course of the employee's duties (either normal duties or those specifically assigned to him); and that the circumstances in either case were such that *an* invention might reasonably be expected to result from the performance of his duties (emphasis supplied). The section utilises the phrase 'an invention' not 'the invention'. Consequently, the test is whether, as a result of the employee's duties, he or she is expected to invent, that is, *is the employee employed to invent*?

Two cases provide illustrations of this. In *Re Harris' Patent* [1985] RPC 19, Falconer J held that the patent belonged to the employee: as a salesman he was not expected to invent. In *Greater Glasgow Health Board's Application* [1996] RPC 207, Jacob J held that a junior doctor was not expected to invent, even though part of his time was spent teaching and researching in a university, his employer being a 'teaching hospital'. However, whether an employee is employed to invent is not a question to be answered only at the time the person is recruited.

A person's job description will necessarily evolve with time, and it is possible that someone not originally employed to invent can be found to be within s.39(1) as a result of how their job has developed, which requires an examination of all the surrounding circumstances: *LIFFE Administration and Management v Pinkava* [2007] RPC 667.

In para (b) (which is wider than para (a), *Staeng Ltd's Application*), the invention will belong to the employer where two cumulative conditions are satisfied. These are that (a) the inventor made it in the course of his employment duties; and (b) that when the invention was made, the nature of his responsibilities were such that he was under a special obligation to further the interests of the employer's undertaking. It is not entirely clear whether this provision enacts the thinking in *Worthington v Moore* and *British Syphon v Homewood*. The only decision on the provision to date is *Staeng Ltd's Application*. Here, UKIPO decided that the employee in question fell within s.39(1)(a), so that his employer was entitled to co-ownership of the invention with another company whose staff had played a part in the creative process. However, in addition, it concluded that the employee whose status was in dispute was also within the terms of s.39(1)(b) and so had a duty to further the interests of his employer. UKIPO took into account the wide-ranging nature of the employee's duties found in his job description (these included 'creative thinking') and his remuneration package, under which he received bonuses, and concluded that he was a director of the company in all but name.

Pre-assignment clauses

In relation to s.39, note should be made of the effect of s.42. The provision renders unenforceable any contractual provision which purports to diminish the employee's rights. The effect of this section means that an employer can no longer attempt to override the rules of ownership set out in s.39. The section therefore reflects the principle of protecting the employee against the unequal bargaining power of the employer.

4.5.3 **Compensation for employee inventions**

The Patents Act 1977 provides for two separate instances when an employee may be awarded compensation in respect of a successful patent of which they are the inventor but not the owner. The conditions imposed on the award of compensation are extremely restrictive and there is only one reported instance of an employee's claim being successful. Further, the conditions imposed by the Act are cumulative and it takes little imagination to work out that they may easily be circumvented.

4.5.3.1 Compensation where the employer owns the patent

Section 40(1) (as amended by the Patents Act 2004) deals with where the patent is owned by the employer as the result of the operation of s.39(1).

The cumulative conditions to be satisfied are:

- there must be an invention made by the employee which belongs to the employer;
- a patent for that invention has been granted;
- the patent, the invention or both, must be of outstanding benefit to the employer; and
- it is just that compensation should be awarded.

The second criterion is the most problematic. It requires that a patent must have been granted. This means that if a patent application is unsuccessful (for whatever reason) or if the patent, though successful, is revoked or if the employer decides not to file a patent application, then compensation cannot be claimed.

A restrictive interpretation has so far been accorded to the third requirement of 'outstanding benefit' under s.40(1). In *British Steel plc's Patent* [1992] RPC 117, it was held that there was no outstanding benefit where the savings in production costs, although totalling several hundred thousand pounds, amounted to 0.01 per cent of turnover. This suggests that the requirement of 'outstanding benefit' is harder to establish in the case of an employer with a large multi-million-pound business than where the employer runs a small enterprise. The wording of the section requires the benefit to the employer to be *the result* of the patent. There might be many other reasons why the employer's business is successful, for example the employer might acquire a lucrative contract in which the patent plays only a very small part (*GEC Avionics Ltd's Patent* [1992] RPC 107) or the company's success might be the result of a cordial relationship with a long-term customer (*Memco Med Ltd's Patent* [1992] RPC 403). However, outstanding benefit does not have to be proved over a lengthy period of business dealings: *Entertainment UK Ltd's Patent* [2002] RPC 291. Despite the stringency of the provision, compensation was awarded in *Kelly & Chiu v GE Healthcare Ltd* [2009] RPC 363 where the claimants were awarded £1 million and £500,000 respectively, representing 2 per cent and 1 per cent of the value of patents worth £50 million for a radioactive imaging agent, the key compound of which had been synthesised by the claimants.

4.5.3.2 Compensation where the employee owned the patent

The alternative compensation scheme provided by s.40(2) contemplates that the invention once belonged to the employee (because of the operation of s.39(2)) but no longer does so because the employee has handed it over to the employer or an associated company. The relevant criteria are:

- a patent must have been granted for an invention made and owned by the employee;
- he has since assigned it or granted an **exclusive licence** to the employer;
- the benefit from this is inadequate in relation to that derived by the employer; and
- it is just that additional compensation be awarded.

Again, these are cumulative requirements. Their precise nature means that compensation may not always be available, for example, if the invention is not patented or if (as a result of pressure from the employer) the employee grants a **non-exclusive licence** to the employer rather than assigning the patent or licensing it exclusively. There is no mechanism in the Act for dealing with such an anti-avoidance tactic on the part of the employer, just as there can be no redress if the employer deliberately decides not to seek patent protection. Further, the word 'inadequate' raises similar issues to its counterpart in s.40(1), 'outstanding benefit'.

4.5.3.3 Calculating compensation

The factors to be taken into account when calculating compensation under both s.40(1) and s.40(2) are in s.41. This states, in subsection (1), that an employee is to be given a 'fair share of the benefit' and in s.41(4), lists the factors to be taken into account, including the nature of the employee's duties, his remuneration and other advantages he derives from his employment, the effort and skill devoted to the invention, the efforts of other employees, and the contribution made by the employer. The narrow interpretation accorded under s.40 to the phrase 'outstanding benefit' suggests that courts are likely to treat the factors relevant to a 'fair share' in a similarly narrow fashion. In the one case which has so far applied s.41, *Kelly & Chiu v GE Healthcare Ltd*, Floyd J took into account the effect which the success of the *patent* had on the claimant's salaries and their subsequent employment and pensions, stating that this exerted 'downward pressure' on the award of compensation. Equally, although their research efforts had been considerable, so had the employer's, in particular further research carried out once the compound was synthesised, in developing the American market for the product, and in bearing the economic risk of the project. He added that an employee's 'fair share of the benefit' of a successful invention might lie anywhere in the range of 0 per cent to 33 per cent but, as already indicated, ultimately awarded a figure at the bottom end of this scale. In fact, the award amounted to 0.1 per cent of the defendant's turnover. One might ask, therefore, whether fairness is considered from the employer's or employee's perspective?

thinking point

Do the provisions in the Patents Act 1977 concerning employee inventions live up to the aspirations of those who lobbied for reform?

4.6 Key issues in patent cases

Many students find the law of patents challenging. They find the facts of patent cases difficult to understand (especially if they do not have a science background) and because of this, 'techno-fear' gets in the way. Despite these concerns, the law of patents itself is relatively straightforward, even more so when the key issues which have to be determined in patent litigation are understood. As a way of explaining these issues, we take a decided case by way of illustration. Having identified the steps taken by the court in resolving the dispute, we then examine some of the factors which affected the outcome. Such factors are germane to all patent cases.

The judgment we choose to examine is that in *Dyson Appliances Ltd v Hoover Ltd* [2001] RPC 473. It is structured in such a way that the issues are dealt with in a logical manner, as follows:

- the identification of the background of the invention (here it was that the vacuum cleaner industry assumed that vacuum cleaner bags *had* to be used to collect dirt but that these possessed certain disadvantages, such as loss of efficiency when the bag was full);

- the identification of the inventive concept (or 'epitome') of the invention (here it was the patentee's insight that vacuum cleaners could use a dual cyclone as a means of collecting large and small particles of dirt without the necessity of using a bag);

- the identification of the attributes of the skilled addressee of the patent, namely their qualifications and experience (here it was a graduate engineer with practical experience in the manufacture of vacuum cleaners);

- the identification of the **common general knowledge** which the skilled addressee possessed;

- the allocation of meaning to the claims in the light of the description and drawings. The court considered whether the patentee had used everyday English, or whether the patentee provided its own definitions of key words in the specification, or whether the meaning of key words in the specification had to be ascertained from specialist dictionaries. It also analysed each of the claims and identified the **integers** (or elements) of each one;

- the determination of infringement (the court made a comparison of *each* of the claims with the defendant's product); and

- the determination of the validity of the patent (the court made a comparison of *each* of the claims with the prior art).

Some of these points will now be elaborated further.

4.6.1 **The inventive concept**

One of the tasks a court dealing with a patent infringement action has to undertake is to decide what the patent is all about. This is usually referred to as 'identifying the inventive concept'. Some cases call it the 'epitome' of the invention (*Dyson Appliances Ltd v Hoover Ltd*), others describe the process as identifying the 'core' or 'kernel' or 'essence' of the invention (*H Lundbeck A/S v Generics (UK) Ltd per* Lord Walker at [30]). The inventive concept is not necessarily the same as the invention's technical contribution to the art, which is more concerned with the evaluation of its inventive concept. Thus in *Biogen Inc v Medeva plc*, the inventive concept was 'the idea of expressing unsequenced eukaryotic DNA in a prokaryotic [non-mammalian] host', described by Lord Hoffmann as a 'brilliant Napoleonic victory' in sequencing the genome for Hepatitis B. However, in terms of its technical contribution to the art it was not of lasting strategic value because within a couple of months the genome had been sequenced by others (*H Lundbeck A/S v Generics (UK) Ltd per* Lord Walker at [32–33], and *per* Lord Neuberger at [101]).

Identifying the inventive concept is done by construing the claims in the light of the description of the invention. When doing so the court should expressly or by implication take into account the problem which the patentee was trying to solve (*Biogen Inc v Medeva plc* at p. 45 *per* Lord Hoffmann). However, using the problem and solution test to identify the inventive concept is not always a straightforward matter.

case close-up

Wheatley (Davina) v Drillsafe Ltd [2001] RPC 133

There was a division of opinion as to the inventive concept of the patent in suit. The majority (Sedley and Mance LJJ) took a narrow view of the patent's inventive concept, regarding it as the use of a 'centre-less' drill cutter for drilling holes in underground petrol storage tanks without the need for the use of a pilot drill. The minority (Aldous LJ) took a broader view of the inventive concept. To him, what mattered was that the defendant's probe did not enter the tank (thereby avoiding the risk of sparks) which was the problem which the patent had sought to solve. As a consequence, he held that the defendant's device did infringe the patent, whilst the majority had concluded that there was no infringement. Aldous LJ therefore followed the advice of Lord Hoffmann in *Biogen v Medeva* in identifying the problem to be solved as part of the process of ascertaining the inventive concept. The case reveals that it is possible for the underlying inventive concept to be drawn broadly or narrowly by the court.

Another area of uncertainty is in relation to infringement: does the defendant have to take the inventive concept in order to be liable? In *Schütz (UK) Ltd v Werit UK Ltd* [2013] FSR 395, Lord Neuberger disagreed with both Floyd J (who thought that the answer was 'yes') and the Court of Appeal (who thought that the answer was 'no'). Lord Neuberger thought that the matter was more nuanced: whether the defendant had made an infringing product depended on the nature of the invention, the wording of the claims, and what the defendant had actually done. Here, what the defendant had done had been to supply a replacement component which was not the heart of the invention.

4.6.2 The skilled addressee and their common general knowledge

A patent specification is a unilateral statement by the patentee. The specification both describes the invention and demarcates the scope of the monopoly which the patentee wishes to claim as theirs. However, the patent specification does not exist in a vacuum: it is deemed to be addressed to a skilled person.

4.6.2.1 The role of the skilled addressee in patent law

The skilled addressee is a judicial construct, a legal fiction. He or she is not a real person, but a hypothetical creature through whose eyes various issues in patent law are determined. The reason for having such a person is to impart objectivity (*Lilly Icos Ltd v Pfizer Ltd* [2001] FSR 201 at [62]). The skilled addressee, armed with common general knowledge, is used in patent law to determine the following issues objectively:

- to construe the claims of the patent in the light of the description of the invention and any drawings contained in the patent specification;

- to determine whether an invention is new under s.2 Patents Act, ie whether the prior art contains enough information by way of enabling disclosure that the skilled addressee could have put the invention into effect before the priority date;

- to determine whether an invention possesses inventive step under s.3, that is, it was not obvious to the skilled addressee;

- to determine whether an invention is capable of industrial application under s.4, or whether the information which it contains is a purely theoretical possibility of exploitation;

- to determine whether the description of the invention is sufficient for the purposes of s.14(3);

- to determine whether an invention has been the subject of an impermissible amendment contrary to s.76, so that it is liable to revocation under either s.72(1)(d) or (e) for having extended the description or claims; and

- to determine whether an invention has been infringed by a product or process which is not literally within the wording of the claims.

It can thus be seen that the skilled addressee plays a crucial role with regard to the validity and infringement of patents, and that the identification of such a person is a task which has to be undertaken by any court dealing with patent litigation. Just like the task of deciding the inventive concept, the choice of the appropriate skilled addressee is a matter susceptible to the vagaries of judicial opinion. In *Dyson v Hoover*, the validity of the patent (which was upheld) was arguably affected by the court's decision that the skilled addressee did not have any practical experience in the use of cyclone technology.

It has been suggested by the Court of Appeal in *Schlumberger Holdings Ltd v Electromagnetic Geoservices AS* [2010] RPC 851 that in rare cases the skilled addressee might not be the same for all purposes: where the invention involves groundbreaking technology (so that the skilled addressee's knowledge is enhanced by reading the patent) a higher standard might be required for sufficiency than for **obviousness**. This is because the former is assessed post grant, whilst the latter is assessed at the priority date.

4.6.2.2 Characteristics of the skilled addressee

The qualifications and level of experience of the skilled addressee are for the court to determine in each case. These will vary depending on the field of technology with which the patent is concerned and how advanced the invention is. In the case of mechanical patents the skilled addressee is likely to be a graduate engineer in the relevant discipline with practical experience in the field in question (*Dyson Appliances Ltd v Hoover Ltd*). Where the patent involves genetic engineering, as in *Re Genentech's (Human Growth Hormone) Patent* [1989] RPC 613, the skilled addressee will be a team of postdoctoral researchers experienced in recombinant DNA. Where the patent involves hand-held devices for accessing the internet, the skilled addressee will have a Master's degree in computer science: *Research in Motion UK Ltd v Inpro Licensing Sarl* [2006] RPC 517. In the key case of *Catnic Components v Hill & Smith* [1982] RPC 185, Lord Diplock decided that a patent for a galvanised steel lintel used in cavity-walled buildings was addressed not to a graduate civil engineer, but to a building-site foreman, thereby providing a somewhat surprising addition to the reading matter of those who work in the construction industry. These examples should alert the reader to the fact that the choice of the skilled addressee is capable of being manipulated by the court to produce a desired outcome in a particular case, in the same way that the inventive concept can be viewed in different ways by the court.

cross reference
See further section 6.5.3.

Over the last century, the characteristics and abilities of the skilled addressee have been explained in some detail. One description is that in *Lilly Icos Ltd v Pfizer Ltd* [2001] FSR 201 at [62]:

> This is not a real person. He is a legal creation. He is supposed to offer an objective test of whether a particular development can be protected by a patent. He is deemed to have looked at and read publicly available documents and to know of public uses in the prior art. He understands all languages and dialects. He never misses the obvious nor stumbles on the inventive. He has no private idiosyncratic preferences or dislikes. He never thinks laterally. He differs from all real people in one or more of these characteristics.

It has also been suggested that the skilled addressee is 'half way between a mechanical idiot and a mechanical genius' (*Gillette Safety Razor v Anglo-American Trading* (1913) 30 RPC 465 at p. 481 *per* Lord Moulton) or perhaps 'a ventriloquist's dummy' (*Dyson Appliances Ltd v Hoover Ltd* [2002] RPC 465 *per* Sedley LJ at [88]). Such a person does not possess a spark of inventiveness (*per* Lord Reid in *Technograph v Mills & Rockley* [1972] RPC 346 at p. 355) but is sufficiently interested in his or her work to want to improve on the prior art (*per* Oliver LJ in *Windsurfing International v Tabur Marine* [1985] RPC 59 at pp. 69–71). The skilled addressee is expected to try experiments which appear to be technically rather than commercially worthwhile (*Hallen v Brabantia* [1991] RPC 195). Where the technical field is very advanced (such as biotechnology), the addressee is to be credited with sufficient time and the best available equipment to carry out the work (*Genentech Inc's Patent* [1989] RPC 147).

Other cases have described the skilled addressee as 'determined but prosaic' (*Koninklijke Philips Electronics NV v Princo Digital Disc GmbH* [2003] EWHC 1598 at [14]); and a 'nerd', 'if real, would be very boring' but 'not a complete android' (*per* Jacob LJ in *Rockwater Ltd v Technip France SA (formerly Coflexip SA)* [2004] RPC 919, CA at [6–15]). The skilled addressee will possess the prejudices of others working in that field of technology. In *Dyson Appliances Ltd v Hoover Ltd*, the vacuum cleaner industry accepted without question that vacuum cleaners without dust-collecting bags would not work. The court held that the skilled addressee would have such a 'mind set' when reading the claimant's patent.

Last, the skilled reader of the patent may be a team (*Valensi v British Radio Corporation* [1972] RPC 373 at p. 450; *Re Genentech's (Human Growth Hormone) Patent* [1989] RPC 613; *Schlumberger Holdings Ltd v Electromagnetic Geoservices AS*). Even if not in a team, the skilled addressee may well consult another for technical help in understanding the patent. As an example, see *Vericore Ltd v Vetrepharm Ltd*, [2003] EWHC 111 where the patent involved the use of chemicals to treat sea-lice in fish. It was said that the skilled addressee would be either a toxicologist or a fish health expert, and the one would consult the other.

Frequently the courts warn against assuming too high a level of qualifications and ability on the part of the skilled addressee. The skilled addressee is not to be equated with expert witnesses called by the claimant and defendant to assist the court. The former is meant to be the *average* technician in the area to which the patent relates. These latter individuals are usually specialists in their field.

4.6.2.3 Common general knowledge

The skilled addressee is deemed to come equipped with certain background information. This is called 'common general knowledge'. It may be observed that the phrase contains the words 'common' and 'general', words which indicate that such information is known by *all* those working in the particular sector to which the patent relates and is universal not specialist.

Again, there are numerous judicial descriptions of what the phrase 'common general knowledge' means. The leading explanation is by Sachs LJ in *General Tire v Firestone* [1972] RPC 457 at pp. 497, 500, where he described it as 'standard texts or material accepted without question by those in that line of work'. Common general knowledge, however, does not include prior patents.

Other descriptions of common general knowledge include 'a tool-box of knowledge' (*per* Aldous J in *Southco Inc v Dzus Fastener Europe Ltd* [1990] RPC 587 at p. 618); 'the technical background of the notional man skilled in the art' (*Raychem Corporation's Patent* [1998] RPC 31, [1999] RPC 497, CA); 'a good basis for further action' (*Wheatley (Davina) v Drillsafe Ltd* [2001] RPC 133, *per* Aldous LJ); and 'good background technical knowledge' (*Rockwater Ltd v Technip France SA (formerly Coflexip SA)* [2004] RPC 919 *per* Jacob LJ at [16–21]). Where the patent involves sophisticated technology, common general knowledge may be worldwide (*Re Genentech's (Human Growth Hormone) Patent* [1989] RPC 613).

Frequently the courts warn against assuming too high a level of common general knowledge. The fact that something is known to some or indeed recorded doesn't make it common general knowledge and the court should be sensitive to the fact that not all skilled readers will have equal access to information, particularly if the invention is not very complicated (*SEB SA* v De'Longhi SpA [2003] EWCA Civ 952). In *Beloit Technologies v Valmet Paper Machinery* [1997] RPC 489 at pp. 494–5 the Court of Appeal said this:

> It has never been easy to differentiate between common general knowledge and that which is known by some. It has become particularly difficult with the modern ability to circulate and retrieve information. Employees of some companies, with the use of libraries and patent departments, will become aware of information soon after it is published in a whole variety of documents; whereas others, without such advantages, may never do so until that information is accepted generally and put into practice. The notional skilled addressee is the ordinary man who may not have the advantages that some employees of large companies may have.

In other words, the knowledge which the skilled reader possesses should be both common and general to the *average* person in that field of technology.

4.6.3 **The importance of patent claims**

The claims of a patent fulfil a vital role. They are the patentee's attempt to demarcate the scope of the monopoly. By analogy with land law, a map will show the boundaries of an owner's fee simple estate. In the case of a patent, there is no diagrammatic method of showing the patentee's territory. Instead, this must be done in words.

One of the intriguing aspects of patent law is that claims will usually be drafted by a patent attorney (usually with a scientific or engineering background) on behalf of the patentee (though the patentee may choose to do this themselves, or else the patentee will employ its own in-house patent specialists to do the work for them). The claims will be drafted as a result of the client's instructions to the patent attorney (which presents opportunities for poor communication) and will be written with the objective of obtaining a successful grant from UKIPO. One thing which may surprise is that it is entirely down to the skill of the patent attorney how the claims can be drafted to avoid both the prior art *and* the exceptions and exclusions to patentability, in other words, form can prevail over substance. The other intriguing aspect of patent claims is that although they may be scrutinised by UKIPO (with possible amendment by the patentee in order to meet any objections) ultimately their worth will be decided in litigation to determine whether the claims are valid and/or have been infringed. This may happen up to 20 years after the claims were first written, and will entail a lawyer's 'detailed meticulous analysis' of the words used. Words intended to have a particular technical connotation may end up being given an entirely different meaning due to legal rather than scientific analysis.

cross reference
See further sections 5.3 and 5.4.

Patent claims are important in two particular respects. They are compared with the prior art in order to determine whether the patent is valid, and they are compared with the alleged infringement in order to determine whether the defendant's product or process falls within the territory marked out by the patentee's words.

All this flows from two key statutory provisions, namely ss.125 and 130(1) of the Patents Act 1977. The former incorporates Article 69 of the EPC together with the Protocol thereto into United Kingdom patent law, the latter contains the definition of 'patented invention', namely an invention for which a patent is granted. When combined, the two provisions link the words 'patent', 'invention' and 'patented invention' together, so that an invention and its scope is to be determined entirely by the wording of the claims. The claims are everything. They determine what is the invention in respect of which the patent has been granted and the scope of protection to be accorded to that invention. The same construction of the claims has to apply for *all* the purposes listed earlier in which the skilled addressee is used in patent law, which is why a court will attempt to construe the claims at a fairly early stage of its judgment. The claims are to be read purposively through the eyes of the skilled reader. The court should ask but one question: 'what would a person skilled in the art have understood the patentee to have used the language of the claim to mean?' (*Kirin-Amgen Inc v Hoechst Marion Roussel Ltd* at [34] *per* Lord Hoffmann).

 # Summary

This chapter has explained:

- the development of the use of patents and of patent law to protect inventiveness;

- the impact on domestic law of the United Kingdom's obligations under international, European and EU law;

- how entitlement to patents is determined; and

- the key issues in patent litigation and the tools used by a court in deciding them.

Reflective question

Despite the alleged use of objective criteria when deciding the key issues in patent cases, there are too many opportunities for a court to manipulate these in order to achieve a desired outcome. Discuss.

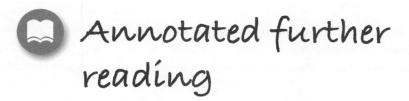 # Annotated further reading

Dutton, H.I. *The Patent System and Inventive Activity during the Industrial Revolution 1750–1852* (1984), Manchester University Press
Explores the legal and economic issues leading to the reform of the United Kingdom patent system during the nineteenth century.

Fisher, M. 'Classical Economics and the Philosophy of the Patent System' [2005] *IPQ* 1
Analyses the classical economic theories which are advanced to justify the law of patents and how these were utilised by the nineteenth-century reformers.

Fisher, M. 'The Tyranny of Words' [2007] *Common Law World Review* 262
Discusses the nature and importance of patent claims.

Fisher, M. 'The Case That Launched a Thousand Writs, or All That is Dross? Re-conceiving *Darcy v Allen: The Case of Monopolies*' [2010] *IPQ* 356
Argues that our understanding of *Darcy v Allen* is coloured by Coke CJ's account which was written long after the event and is incorrect.

Hulme, W. 'The History of the Patent System under the Prerogative and at Common Law' (1896) 12 *LQR* 141
An examination of the practice of granting patents before, during and after the Tudor monarchs.

Lemley, M. 'The Myth of the Sole Inventor' (2011–2012) 110 *Mich LR* 709
Argues that invention is a social not an individual phenomenon and that none of the current theoretical justifications for patent law, including the exchange for secrets theory, adequately explains it.

Machlup, F. and Penrose, E. 'The Patent Controversy in the Nineteenth Century' (1950) 10 *J of Economic History* 1
Explores the debates which took place as a result of the anti-patent movement.

MacLeod, C. and Nuvolari, A. 'Patents and Industrialisation: An Historical Overview of the British Case, 1624–1907', A Report to the Strategic Advisory Board for Intellectual Property Policy 2010 (available from the UKIPO website)
Considers whether the patent system had any effect on industrial development in Britain and the lessons from history for today's 'strong' intellectual property regimes.

Merges, R. and Nelson, R. 'On the Complex Economics of Patent Scope' (1990) 90 *Col L R* 839
Analyses how patent claims can be interpreted both at prosecution and infringement stages and then considers the economics of the patent system.

Seaborne Davis, D. 'Further Light on the Case of Monopolies' (1932) 48 *LQR* 394
A discussion of *Darcy v Allin* and the Elizabethan practice of granting monopolies to favourite courtiers.

Sherman, B. and Bently, L. *The Making of Modern Intellectual Property Law* (1999), Cambridge University Press
Explores the historical and economic factors which have influenced present-day intellectual property law.

Patentability

Learning objectives

Upon completion of this chapter, you should have acquired:

- an appreciation of the debate surrounding the requirement of 'an invention';

- knowledge of the way in which the exceptions to and exclusions from patentability are interpreted;

- knowledge of the way in which the positive criteria for patentability are applied; and

- an understanding of the impact which the EPC has had on United Kingdom patent law.

Introduction

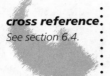
cross reference
See section 6.4.

The purpose of this chapter is to deal with the criteria for patentability. These are relevant both when deciding whether something is capable of patent protection, and, in the context of an infringement action, when a defendant seeks to revoke the claimant's patent for invalidity.

cross reference
See further
section 4.6.3.

5.1 Overview of the statutory requirements

The **patentability** of an **invention**, defined by Articles 52 to 57 of the European Patent Convention ('**EPC**'), (translated imperfectly into ss.1 to 4A Patents Act 1977) comprises five elements, three positive and two negative. They are that the invention possesses **novelty**, **inventive step** and **industrial applicability**; and does not consist of **excluded subject matter** or any of the **exceptions to patentability**. Novelty and inventive step require the invention, as set out in the **claims**, to be compared with the **prior art** and are regarded as the 'external' aspects of patentability. The requirements of industrial applicability, non-exclusion from protection and the avoidance of the exceptions from protection require the invention to be considered in the light of the policy which underpins the statutory provisions, and concern 'internal' **validity**. The factor common to all five elements of patentability is the significance of the claims. The combined effect of the Patents Act 1977 ss.125 and 130(1) means that the scope of a patented invention is determined from the wording of the claims. The claims have to be read purposively through the eyes of the **skilled addressee**. What must be appreciated is that the claims are for the **patentee** (or rather, his professional advisor) to draft. It is up to the patentee to word the claims in such a way that any obstacles posed by the prior art are avoided, and the internal elements of patentability are met. Successful **patents** depend as much on skilful wording as they do on creativity.

5.1.1 The impact of the EPC 2000

The revised version of the EPC came into force on 13 December 2007, as did the United Kingdom's implementation by means of the Patents Act 2004.

5.1.1.1 Changes to the EPC

Article 52(1) is amended to read 'European patents shall be granted for any inventions, in all fields of technology, provided that they are new, involve an inventive step and are susceptible of industrial application'. The presence of 'all fields of technology' echoes the wording of Article 27(1) **TRIPs**.

Articles 52(2) and (3) (dealing with excluded subject matter) are unchanged, but Article 52(4) is moved into Article 53, so that it becomes clear that methods of treatment are exceptions to patentability rather than exceptions to industrial applicability. Article 53 itself becomes the single provision dealing with the policy exceptions to patentability, namely inventions which are contrary to morality, those involving plant and animal varieties, and those concerned with methods of treatment.

Article 54 (novelty) has been amended, so that the provision on first medical use is now found in Article 54(4), whilst the new Article 54(5) sets out the principle of second medical use, thereby placing on a statutory basis the decision of the Enlarged Board of Appeal in *G 5/83 EISAI/Second medical indication* [1979–85] EPOR: B: 241.

5.1.1.2 Changes to the Patents Act 1977

There is no apparent implementation of the change to Article 52 EPC, so that the original wording of s.1 (the definition of 'patentable invention') remains unchanged. However, this may not be problematic, as United Kingdom courts are increasingly referring directly to the wording of the EPC rather than the text of the Act: *Aerotel Ltd v Telco Holdings Ltd/ Macrossan's Application* [2007] RPC 117.

The amendment whereby Article 52(4) EPC (the methods of treatment exception) became Article 53(c) is reflected in the simplification of s.4, which contains in subsection (1) the straight-forward definition of 'capable of industrial application'. Sections 4(2) and (3) are deleted. By way of replacement, s.4A(1) sets out Article 53(c). The exceptions to patenting methods of treatment are to be found in subsections (2), (3) and (4) (respectively, new substances used in such treatment, the first medical use of known substances, and the second medical use of known substances). The presence of s.4A(3) means that s.2(6) has been deleted.

The meaning of 'an invention'

The elements of a patentable invention are set out in s.1(1) Patents Act 1977, each element in turn being the subject of elaboration in subsequent sections. There is an apparent difference between United Kingdom and EPO case law as to whether there is a separate requirement of 'an invention' which must be satisfied before a patent can be **granted**. As Vaver comments (in 'Invention in Patent Law: a Review and a Modest Proposal' (2003) 11 *International Journal of Law and Information Technology* 286), although one can give a dictionary definition of invention, the parameters of the concept are not so precise. As a legal term of art, its meaning is not immutably fixed and will change over time.

5.2.1 'An invention': United Kingdom cases

There is little discussion in United Kingdom case law as to whether there is a separate requirement of 'an invention', probably because of the tacit assumption that if the criteria for patentability were met, then by definition there must be an invention. The opening words of s.1(1) ('that is to say') lend support to the conclusion that if all the other criteria for patentability are satisfied there must be an invention.

Three cases have debated whether there is a separate requirement of an invention and all (perhaps coincidentally) involved biotechnology. Whilst the policy issue of whether living matter should be patentable is not discussed, there are signs of judicial disquiet at having to accommodate the law to scientific developments which go beyond the traditional view of patents as involving mechanical or chemical advances.

In *Genentech Inc's Patent* [1989] RPC 147, the principal claims of the patent related to human tissue plasminogen activator ('t-PA'), a protein known to activate an enzyme which dissolved blood clots. **Revocation** of the patent was sought on various grounds, including lack of inventive step, lack of **sufficiency**, and that what was claimed was in effect a discovery not an invention. The Court of Appeal upheld the decision of Whitford J that the patent should be revoked. In relation to whether what was claimed was not an invention, Purchas and Mustill LJJ were prepared to state that the requirement of an invention was something which had to be disclosed by the claim before the remaining requirements of s.1(1) became relevant. The existence of an invention was a prerequisite to patentability.

A differently constituted Court of Appeal in *Chiron Corporation v Organon Teknika Ltd (No 12)* [1996] FSR 153 took a simpler view of the difference between an invention and a discovery. Morritt LJ pointed out that neither the Act nor the EPC contained a definition of the words 'discovery' or 'invention'. He relied on the words of Nicholls LJ in *Re Gale's Application* [1991] RPC 305 at p. 323:

> I turn now to section 1(2) of the Act. When considering these provisions, it is helpful to have in mind the principles of patent law . . . that an idea or discovery as such is not patentable. It is the practical application of an idea or discovery which leads to patentability. It leads to patentability even if, as frequently happens, the practical application of the discovery is inherent in the discovery itself or is obvious once the discovery has been made and stated.

The final case in the trilogy to debate whether 'an invention' is a separate requirement was *Biogen Inc v Medeva plc* [1997] RPC 1, although the views expressed were *obiter*. Two contrasting opinions were put forward by Lord Mustill and Lord Hoffmann. Taking the latter first (with whom Lords Goff, Browne-Wilkinson and Slynn agreed), Lord Hoffmann noted that the wording of s.1 might lead one to conclude that whether what was claimed was an invention should logically be decided as a preliminary issue. This, Lord Hoffmann considered, would be a mistake. The framers of the EPC had been unable to agree a definition of an invention, and were content that one should be omitted because they recognised that 'the question would almost invariably be academic'. The four conditions in s.1 not only restricted the class of inventions which could be patented, they also contained every element of the concept in ordinary speech. No one had been able to think of an example of something which satisfied all the conditions of s.1 but was not an invention. Lord Hoffmann thought that if, by working through the four criteria in s.1, one concluded that they were satisfied, that would be an end to the inquiry. 'There may one day be a case in which it is necessary to decide whether something which satisfies the conditions can be called an invention, but that question can wait until it arises.' The example given in *Genentech Inc's Patent* of something which was not an invention, namely water ('You cannot invent water, although you certainly can invent ways in which it may be distilled or synthesised') was unhelpful because most cases which came before the courts were far more difficult. 'Judges would therefore be well advised to put on one side their intuitive sense of what constitutes an invention until they have considered the questions of novelty, inventiveness and so forth.'

Lord Mustill, unsurprisingly, took a different view. Although agreeing with the outcome of the case, he did not concur with Lord Hoffmann that the separate identification of the invention was a waste of time. Although in most cases it would not be necessary to go beyond the four conditions in s.1, in some instances a close conceptual analysis of the nature of patentability would be appropriate. *Genentech Inc's Patent* had been such a case, where the claim was for a **product** existing in nature, rather than the mechanical or chemical inventions to which most of patent law relates. There could well be others in the future. Lord Mustill therefore indicated that the criterion of 'an invention' might, in some cases, require separate consideration. Such cases would inevitably involve biotechnology.

It is a matter of speculation whether biotechnology patents are singled out for special treatment because of their ethical implications or simply because they are based on something found in nature rather than something man-made. Either way, the conclusions of Lord Hoffmann need to be reconsidered in light of EPO case law.

5.2.2 'An invention': EPO cases

The initial attitude of the **EPO** can be seen in the Opposition Division's decision in *HOWARD FLOREY/Relaxin* [1995] EPOR 541, which adopted a similar approach to that of Lord Hoffmann in *Biogen*. However, current case law from the EPO Boards of Appeal regards 'an invention' as a separate requirement, a prerequisite for the **examination** with respect to novelty, inventive step and industrial application (*T 258/03 HITACHI/Auction method* [2004] EPOR 548 at [3.1]). Such conclusion flows from the original wording of Article 52(1) EPC, ('European patents shall be granted for any inventions *which are* susceptible of industrial application, *which are* new and *which involve* an inventive step', emphasis supplied) and from the amended wording ('European patents shall be granted for any inventions, in all fields of technology, *provided* that they are new, involve an inventive step and are susceptible of industrial application', again, emphasis supplied). Treating an invention as a separate requirement is reinforced by the wording of Articles 52(2) and (3), which declares that certain things are 'not to be regarded as inventions within the meaning of paragraph 1'.

The EPO's explanation of what is an invention is very broad. What matters is the presence of technical character (*T 931/95 PBS PARTNERSHIP/Controlling Pension Benefits System* [2002] EPOR 522). 'Technical character' means that there must be a physical entity or concrete product, man-made for a utilitarian purpose. Thus the use of pen and paper to write would qualify as 'an invention' according to the EPO in *HITACHI*, but that does not mean that such a device would meet the requirements of novelty and inventive step. Non-inventions, on the other hand, are those of an entirely abstract nature, for example theories or mathematical methods or economic calculations.

case close-up

T 154/04 DUNS LICENSING ASSOCIATES/Estimating Sales Activity [2007] EPOR 349

The EPO referred to the Conference of Contracting States which led to the revised version of Article 52(1) EPC. It was clear from this that 'technical character' was a mandatory requirement for any patentable invention. It must involve 'technical teaching'. Novelty and inventive step were separate, independent and relative criteria from the abstract requirement of an invention. Further, the list of excluded subject matter in Article 52(2), the common feature of which is the lack of technical character, should not be given too broad an interpretation. In passing, the EPO approved the views of Mustill LJ in *Re Genentech Inc's Patent*. However, it added that it (the EPO) had not developed any explicit definition of 'an invention' for good reason.

How does one decide whether something has 'technical character'? Early EPO cases stated that the invention must provide a technical contribution: *T 208/84 VICOM/Computer related invention* [1987] EPOR 74. However, the EPO in *PBS PARTNERSHIP* and in *DUNS LICENSING ASSOCIATES* expressly departed from this approach. Instead, it said, once it had been decided that something had technical character because it was a physical entity, technical contribution was relevant to the issue of whether the invention possessed inventive step. The move away from *VICOM* was reinforced by *HITACHI*, where the Board held that the first thing to do is to ask if the invention is excluded by Article 52(2) without any knowledge of the prior art. If the 'invention' possesses any technical means at all (for example, even something as simple as pen and paper), the next stage is to consider whether the invention was new, and if so, whether it was obvious, taking account of only those features which contributed to its technical character.

5.2.3 Impact of the EPO case law

thinking point
Is it possible to provide a workable definition of 'an invention' or is such an exercise a waste of time?

It remains to be seen whether United Kingdom cases will now follow the EPO in separating out the requirement of an invention. There are perhaps indications that this might happen in *H Lundbeck A/S v Generics (UK) Ltd* [2009] RPC 407 where Lord Neuberger (at [70]) appears to treat an invention as a discrete aspect of patentability. Further, in the same case, the issue of 'technical contribution' is treated as involving an evaluation of the **inventive concept**, that is, how far forward the invention has carried the state of the art, rather than part of the definition of 'an invention' (*per* Lord Walker at [30], Lord Neuberger at [101]).

5.3 Excluded subject matter

5.3.1 Overview of the exclusions from patentability

Section 1(2) Patents Act 1977 (based on Articles 52(2) and (3) EPC) contains a list of excluded subject matter. The EPO in *DUNS LICENSING ASSOCIATES* (at [8]), repeating its earlier views in *T 366/87 STERNHEIMER/Harmonic vibrations* [1989] EPOR 131, has stated that the common feature of the list is 'a substantial lack of technical character', following the classical notion of the difference between intellectual achievements in general and practical scientific applications. Further, in the same case (at [6]), the EPO appears to assume that all of the items on the list should receive the same treatment and should be narrowly construed.

United Kingdom decisions suggest that the list of excluded items is not a logical class at all and there are different policy reasons underlying each of the exclusions (*Re CFPH LLC's Application* [2006] RPC 259 at [21]), so that they should not be accorded the same treatment. In *Aerotel Ltd v Telco Holdings Ltd/Macrossan's Application* it was said that there is nothing in the EPC itself to indicate whether the list should be read widely or narrowly, and the list is expressed not as an exception but as positive categories of things not to be regarded as inventions. By contrast, in *Research in Motion v Inpro* [2006] RPC 517 at [187], Pumfrey J remarked that the exclusions should not be given too wide a scope. One must be astute not to defeat patents on the ground that the subject matter is forbidden by Article 52 EPC unless the invention lies in excluded subject matter as such.

More problematic than such differences of opinion is the interpretation given to the proviso to s.1(2). The wording of Article 52(3) EPC (on which the proviso is based) is easier to understand, that is, that 'patentability is only excluded *to the extent to which* the patent relates to such subject matter or activities *as such*' (emphasis supplied). The qualification 'as such' therefore needs to be read into each paragraph of the list of exclusions, considered in turn in the next section. When applying the proviso, it should be remembered that everything depends on the wording of the claims. It is the claims which define the subject matter of the invention (s.14(5) Patents Act 1977). This means that a patentee can word the **specification** in such a way that it avoids the various exclusions. There is nothing to stop a patentee from doing this.

5.3.2 **The meaning of 'as such'**

The interpretation of the phrase 'as such' was initially explained by the EPO in *VICOM*. It stated that the 'whole contents' approach should be adopted. The patent should be read as a whole to see if it achieved a technical advance, rather than ignoring those aspects which were excluded from protection and then assessing whether what remained was patentable. The emphasis should be on what the invention did, that is, whether it made a technical contribution to solving a problem. If the invention was merely a quicker way of performing a task which had been done previously by hand or by the human mind, then even if this resulted in increased efficiency it was not a patentable invention. Following *VICOM*, the United Kingdom Intellectual Property Office ('**UKIPO**') and Court of Appeal adopted the 'technical contribution' approach in determining whether inventions fell outside the list of exclusions found in s.1(2) Patents Act 1977: see *Merrill Lynch's Application* [1989] RPC 561, *Re Gale's Application* and *Re Fujitsu's Application* [1997] RPC 608.

The EPO has moved on from *VICOM*. The current approach is that of the *PBS PARTNERSHIP* and *HITACHI* decisions, where the Board of Appeal explained that once it has been determined that there is an 'invention', something having technical character, whether that invention falls within the list of exclusions is decided by asking if its technical contribution is obvious. The correct approach therefore is to see if there is an invention and *then* to ask whether it satisfies the requirement of patentability.

case close-up

Re CFPH LLC's Application [2006] RPC 259
. . . .

That United Kingdom case law was out of line with this changed EPO thinking was noted by the Patents Court in *CFPH LLC's Application*. The difference between the old and new approaches to 'an invention' was helpfully summarised by Peter Prescott QC as follows (at [44–45, 77]):

- the practice of UKIPO was to look at the claim and ask what was its technical contribution. If there was none, the application would be rejected. If there was some technical contribution over the prior art in the form of a new result, it would then be necessary to decide whether the application should be rejected on other grounds;

- the practice of the EPO, on the other hand, was to examine the claim and ask whether, without knowledge of the prior art, it had any technical features. If there were none, then the application would be rejected. If there were any technical features at all, the EPO then asked whether the invention was old or obvious, but in determining whether it is obvious, anything which is not a technical contribution is ignored;

The lack of accord between the United Kingdom and EPO approaches was commented on by the EPO in *DUNS LICENSING ASSOCIATES*. The Board of Appeal went out of its way to criticise the decision of the Court of Appeal in *Aerotel Ltd v Telco Holdings Ltd/Macrossan's Application*. In this case, Jacob LJ had set out a four-step formula for dealing with excluded subject matter, namely that first, one should properly construe the claim; next, one should identify the actual contribution; third, one should ask whether such contribution fell solely within the list of excluded subject matter; and last, one should check whether the actual or alleged contribution was actually technical in nature. It may be observed that there is overlap between these last two requirements.

Since *DUNS LICENSING ASSOCIATES* United Kingdom courts have struggled to accommodate the two conflicting approaches because of their obligation under s.130(7) Patents Act to achieve conformity with EPO case law (though in *Aerotel/Macrossan* Jacob LJ denied that EPO case law was settled). In *Astron Clinica Ltd & others v Comptroller General of Patents* [2008] RPC 339, Kitchen J stated that it was highly undesirable for there to be divergence between the United Kingdom and the EPO. It was not open to him to follow the *PBS PARTNERSHIP* and *HITACHI* cases, but it was possible to interpret *Aerotel/Macrossan* in such a way that it was consistent with the *IBM* decisions. He therefore felt able to hold that claims to computer programs were not necessarily excluded by Article 52(2) EPC. If claims to a method performed by running a suitably programmed computer or to a computer programmed to carry out the method were allowable (as under *PBS PARTNERSHIP*), then so too 'in principle' was a claim to the program itself. Such a claim, however, had to be drawn to reflect the features of the invention which would ensure the patentability of the method which the program was intended to carry out when it was run. Subsequent to the decision in *Astron*, UKIPO revised its Practice Note on excluded subject matter, in effect restoring its previous practice note issued after the *IBM* decisions.

In *Symbian Ltd v Comptroller-General of Patents* [2009] RPC 1 the Court of Appeal upheld Patten J's decision that the Patents Examiner had misapplied *Aerotel/Macrossan* when holding that a method for accessing data in a dynamic link library was excluded from patentability. The invention was patentable because it resulted in a faster and more reliable computer. Lord Neuberger felt that the court was not able to depart from *Aerotel/Macrossan* but that it was possible to effect a reconciliation between *Aerotel* and *DUNS*. He also warned against blindly following the structured approach in *Aerotel*. Each case needed to be decided on its facts. The court should treat an invention as unpatentable where its technical effect lay solely in excluded matter. Finally, in *AT&T Knowledge Ventures LP v Comptroller-General of Patents* [2009] FSR 743, Lewison J applied the ruling in *Aerotel/Macrossan* when concluding that a computer software invention (used to connect a device such as an MP3 player to a music download site by detecting the characteristics of the storage medium) was devoid of technical effect. It did not make a computer work in a new or different way: all it did was to send particular information to a potential supplier. It did not solve the problem of incompatibility between formats, rather it circumvented the problem by supplying information which minimised the chance of buying something useless, nor

cross reference
Discussed further at section 5.3.4.3.

did it result in an increase in the speed or reliability of the computer. It was no more than a computerised list of the characteristics of particular devices. Helpfully, Lewison J set out five signposts which would indicate that a program made a technical contribution, including its external effect, whether there was any impact on the architecture of the computer, whether the computer operated in a new way, whether it was more efficient, and whether the perceived problem was overcome rather than just obviated. The 'signposts' have since been considered and applied in other cases.

5.3.3 'As such': conclusions

Vaver has argued that the practice (as found in Article 52(2) EPC) of excluding fixed categories of things which cannot be patentable is 'unsound' except for those which, on any view, fall outside the concept of 'an invention'. He further argues that construing the exclusions narrowly, as the EPO does, and allowing the exclusions to be circumvented by clever claim drafting is also unsound. It would be far better, he says, to allow flexibility into the system so that patent offices could deny protection, as under the Statute of Monopolies, to 'generally inconvenient' patents. It is, of course, a matter of debate whether patent **applicants** would rather face a wide-ranging discretion to refuse protection or have a statutory régime which, although less than transparent, gives the professional advisor the opportunity for creative drafting.

thinking point

Which do you find easier to apply, when deciding whether something is excluded from protection 'as such', the approach of the EPO or the approach of the Court of Appeal? Would a definition of 'an invention' help to achieve better understanding of when something is not patentable?

5.3.4 The list of exclusions

5.3.4.1 Section 1(2)(a): Discoveries, scientific theories or mathematical methods

This group of exclusions can be categorised as abstract ideas. There is no applied technology. To this list there may be added by analogy economic calculations (*PBS PARTNERSHIP*). Such abstract ideas can be viewed as non-inventions (*HITACHI*). A common example of an exclusion falling within paragraph (a) is Einstein's theory of relativity.

There is, however, a fine dividing line between a patent which claims a discovery and one which claims its practical application. In *Chiron v Organon (No 12)*, the Court of Appeal held that although the identification of Hepatitis C amounted to a discovery, the patent was valid because what was claimed were testing kits which enabled doctors to identify whether someone had the disease. Another example can be found in the facts of *Biogen v Medeva* where the identification of the virus which caused Hepatitis B amounted to a discovery, but the process for its artificial replication was an invention, even though by the time the application was filed, that process was obvious.

5.3.4.2 Section 1(2)(b): Aesthetic creations

Aesthetic creations such as the plot of a play, a detective story or a piece of music cannot be the subject matter of a patent. The policy for this exclusion is that first, such items are best left to the law of **copyright**, and second, that to permit the patenting of such forms of creativity would confer too great a monopoly, preventing the circulation of cultural ideas (*Re CFPH LLC's Application*). An example of a rejected application falling under this paragraph is *ESP's Application* (1945) 62 RPC 87 which concerned architect's plans.

5.3.4.3 Section 1(2)(c): a scheme, rule or method for performing a mental act, playing a game or doing business, or a program for a computer

It can be observed that this group of exclusions covers a wide range of items, which frequently overlap, so that in respect of (for example) an internet gambling system, the objection could be that it is a means of performing a mental act (calculating the odds), doing business (arranging for debiting or crediting money to the gambler), or a specially written computer program to achieve those ends. Nevertheless, for convenience, we divide the list into three separate categories: performing mental acts, computer programs and means of doing business.

A further complication is that many of the cases involve what might be called 'hybrid' inventions, that is, they are part technical character and part exclusion. In consequence, they raise again the meaning of 'an invention' and the application of the phrase 'as such' when examining the patentee's claims. As if these challenges were not enough, the EPO and UKIPO have had to decide the relevant cases against the background of demands for the law to be changed. These calls for reform have been prompted partly by the advent of the TRIPs Agreement, Article 27(1) of which declares that 'patents shall be available for any inventions…in all fields of technology'. The other major catalyst for change has been the practice of the United States Patent and Trademark Office which has adopted a far more liberal attitude to the granting of software patents and business methods patents. Businesses who have successfully obtained US patents do not understand why similar protection is not available in Europe. However, both the EU and EPO have decided not to follow the US trend, so the cases can be viewed as an attempt to hold back the tide.

Performing a mental act

In relation to 'inventions' which involve methods of performing a mental act, two cases neatly demonstrate the point in *HITACHI* that merely to computerise something which was previously done in a person's head or on paper is not patentable. In *Raytheon's Application* [1993] RPC 427 patentability for an automated ship identification system was denied as the alleged invention merely mechanised a task previously done by the human eye, and in *Merrill Lynch's Application*, an automated dealing system was held to be no different from the previous manual method of trading in securities.

That this category overlaps with both the computer program exclusion and the business methods exclusion is illustrated by several cases. In *Re Shopalotto.com Ltd's Patent Application* [2006] RPC 293 the decision to deny patent protection for an online lottery was upheld and in *IGT v Comptroller General of Patents* [2007] EWHC 1341 (Ch) a means of controlling gaming machines was equally held to be unpatentable. In *Raytheon v Comptroller General of Patents* [2008] RPC 46 an inventory management system, which was denied patent protection, could be regarded both as a mental act or a way of organising business regardless of the computer automation involved. Last, in *Oneida Indian Nation v Comptroller General of Patents* [2007] EWHC 954 (Pat), a means of facilitating off-site gaming was held to fall within the Article 52(2) exclusions.

The mental act exclusion was further reviewed by Birss J in *Halliburton Energy Services Inc's Application* [2012] RPC 297, as a result of which UKIPO has amended its practice notice. Birss J stated that the exclusion was to be narrowly interpreted. In the instant case, a simulation process for designing a drill bit in a computer did not fall within any excluded subject matter and made a technical contribution to the art.

Computer programs

There is a widespread misconception that you cannot patent a computer program: you can, provided that the subject matter has technical character. Such technical character lies not in the simple operation of computers but in effects which go further than normal computer operations. Also, as indicated earlier, many of the cases involve methods of doing business or the presentation of information and so are liable to be rejected on grounds other than the computer program exclusion.

The exclusion for computer programs was based on a different policy consideration. At the time the EPC was being formulated, the assumption was that patent protection would prove too much of a burden for the software industry and would stifle innovation. In consequence, it was thought that protection would be better left to the law of copyright.

In *Aerotel/Macrossan*, the Court of Appeal helpfully sets out the various phases in the development of the EPO's case law. Once applications for computer-implemented inventions began to be made ('computer-implemented inventions' is the preferred terminology today), the EPO's initial approach was to ask whether the machine as programmed achieved a technical advance: see *VICOM* and *T 26/86 KOCH & STERZEL/X-ray apparatus* [1988] EPOR 72. Both of these cases explained the term 'technical advance' as meaning that some physical change was produced as a result of the operation of the programmed machine. The 'technical advance' argument was deployed in *Merrill Lynch's Application* where, as previously noted, the Court of Appeal held that an automated dealing system could not be patented as it was simply a way of dealing in stocks and shares. Likewise, in *Re Gale's Patent*, which involved a method of calculating square root stored on ROM, the Court of Appeal held that the instructions contained in the program did not embody a technical process which existed outside the computer, nor did they solve a technical problem lying within the computer. In *Re Fujitsu's Application*, a method of processing crystalline structures by computer was held unpatentable, Aldous LJ making specific reference to the *VICOM* decision whilst stressing the need for a technical contribution. One (rare) successful United Kingdom case was *Quantel v Spaceward Microsystems Ltd* [1990] RPC 83, where the patent involved a computerised video graphics system.

The second phase in EPO case law is to be found in *T 1173/97 IBM/Computer program product* [2000] EPOR 219 and *T 935/97 IBM/Computer program product II* [1999] EPOR 301. The Boards of Appeal declared that the purpose of Articles 52(2) and (3) EPC was not to exclude *all* programs from patentability. Instead, the computer programs exclusion was directed only to those programs which amounted to abstract creations lacking in technical character. Those that possessed technical character were patentable.

When does a computer program have a technical character? According to the EPO, just operating a computer is not enough. A program will be potentially patentable, however, (subject to novelty and inventive step) if it produces additional technical effects going beyond the normal physical interaction between hardware and software.

The third phase of the case law came in the controversial *PBS PARTNERSHIP* decision. This adopted the 'any hardware' approach, so that a method of controlling a pensions benefit program was rejected, but a suitably programmed computer was not excluded (although in fact the patent was refused on the ground that it lacked inventive step). Last, in *DUNS LICENSING ASSOCIATES*, the EPO abandoned the 'any hardware' test. If there is something which has technical character because it is a physical entity, then one should treat that as an invention. The prior art is relevant in deciding whether the invention is new and non-obvious, but is not relevant when considering excluded subject matter.

It had been hoped that the tensions between the EPO and United Kingdom courts about the patentability of computer programs would be resolved by the Enlarged Board of Appeal of the EPO in *G 3/08 PRESIDENT's REFERENCE*, but in May 2010 this was declared inadmissible.

Methods of doing business

In relation to the exclusion relating to methods of doing business, previously mentioned cases are relevant. However, there is a difference of approach between them, so it will be useful at this point to explore their respective facts and conclusions in more detail.

---

case close-up

T 931/95 PBS PARTNERSHIP/Controlling Pension Benefits System [2002] EPOR 522

. . . .

The application involved two distinct sets of claims. There were those claims which concerned a method of controlling a pensions benefit program by processing data about individual employees, and then working out their contributions, benefits and associated life insurance. Other claims in the patent related to the apparatus which controlled the system. The EPO treated the two sets of claims separately, holding that the method claims lacked technical effect but the apparatus claims were in principle patentable. Ultimately, however, it held the apparatus claims lacked inventive step because any software developer who knew the structure of the benefit system would have considered the claims obvious.

---

case close-up

T 258/03 HITACHI/Auction method [2004] EPOR 548

. . . .

HITACHI involved a computerised Dutch auction system, which claimed to overcome the technical deficiencies of previous systems by synchronising key information during the online bidding process. The same Technical Board of Appeal that had decided *PBS PARTNERSHIP* modified its approach. It held that both method claims and apparatus claims in principle were 'inventions' having technical effect. However, applying *PBS PARTNERSHIP* it concluded that both lacked inventive step. The solution to the prior problem which the patent claimed to provide was no more than a modification to the auction method. It was therefore a means of doing business.

A United Kingdom decision which makes the same points is *Re Shopalotto.com Ltd's Patent Application*. The patent related to a computer configured to provide a lottery playable via the internet. It had been rejected by UKIPO as being a scheme, rule or method for performing a mental act, playing a game or doing business, or a program for a computer, or the presentation of information. The applicant contended that the alleged invention fell within the practice of permitting the patenting of board games as set out in a then Patent Office ruling of 1926. Pumfrey J was highly critical of reliance on the Official Ruling, declaring that it could have no application to the 1977 Act. Agreeing with the comments in *CFPH LLC's Application* that the list of exclusions in s.1(2) was heterogeneous, Pumfrey J concluded that the physical underpinnings of the claims were to a general purpose computer, connected to the internet, and so squarely within the ambit of excluded subject matter.

thinking point
Do the criteria established in EPO case law provide clarity when deciding whether a computer program is patentable?

5.3.4.4 Section 1(2)(d): The presentation of information

Two United Kingdom cases illustrate the last exclusion in s.1(2). *Re Townsend's Application* [2004] EWHC 482 concerned an attempt to patent an advent calendar, which was rejected by Laddie J as it was simply a means of showing dates in December. Similarly, in *Re Crawford's Patent Application* [2006] RPC 345 the patent related to a display system for buses, indicating whether the bus was picking up or dropping off passengers. Kitchin J upheld the rejection of the application by UKIPO. The alleged invention did not contain any technical contribution but was simply the presentation of information.

5.4 Exceptions to patentability

5.4.1 Overview

In respect of the three exceptions in Article 53 EPC, the criteria for patentability are (in theory) met, but the right to obtain a patent is denied for policy reasons. Article 53 is derived from the wording of the Council of Europe's Strasbourg Convention on the Unification of Certain Points of Substantive Law on Patents for Invention 1963. Consequently, the wording of Article 53 was conceived at a time when the scientific advances achieved as a result of the discovery of the structure of DNA in 1953 could not possibly have been predicted. One question therefore is whether Article 53 is adequate to cope with the challenges of twenty-first-century science.

5.4.2 Impact of the Biotech Directive

In respect of two of the exceptions to patentability (patents contrary to morality and patents involving plant and animal varieties), Directive 98/44/EC of 6 July 1998 on the legal protection of biotechnological inventions [1998] OJ L 213/13 ('the Biotech Directive') has had a major impact. The original version of this was rejected by the European Parliament in March 1995. A revised version of the Directive, taking into account the ethical objections of the European Parliament was eventually agreed three years later. The Directive requires EU Member States to protect biotechnological inventions (Article 1) and declares that inventions which satisfy the criteria for patentability shall be patentable even if they concern a product consisting of biological material (as defined in Article 2) or a procedure whereby biological material is produced (Article 3(1)). Further, biological material which is isolated from its natural environment or which is the subject of a technical process is patentable even if it occurs in nature (Article 3(2)) or in the human body (Article 5(2)). There are a number of exclusions in Articles 4–6 of the Directive, reflecting concerns about the ethics of patenting living matter. The Directive was the subject of an unsuccessful challenge before the ECJ in Case C-377/98 *Kingdom of the Netherlands v European Parliament and Council of the European Union* [2001] ECR I-7079.

One aspect of the *Netherlands* case is that it explains the relationship between the Directive and the EPC, the former being an EU legislative measure, the latter being a Convention promulgated by the Council of Europe. The Opinion of AG Jacobs and the ruling of the ECJ reveal two things. First, the EPC Implementing Regulations were modified so as to incorporate the wording of Article 6 of the Directive. Second, when rejecting the challenge to the Directive (on the grounds that the Directive itself was contrary to public policy) the ECJ adopted the case law of the EPO. In effect there has been two-way traffic between the EU and the EPC on the availability of patent protection for living matter. Although each institution operates its own legal system, both systems now contain the same basic principles.

The public policy exceptions in Articles 53(a) and (b) to which the Biotech Directive is relevant (found respectively in s.1(3) and Sch. A2 Patents Act 1977) are closely related. It is possible for a patent to be challenged under both of these categories. For this reason, the same EPO cases are relevant to both exceptions. Both exceptions have so far been given a narrow interpretation, though that may change. The relationship between the Biotech Directive and the EPC can be seen in Diagram 5.1.

Diagram 5.1

The relationship between the Biotech Directive and the EPC

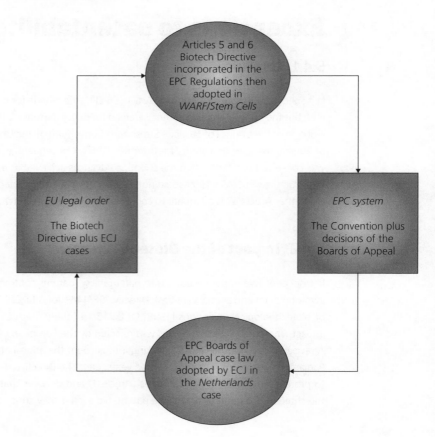

5.4.3 **Patents contrary to public policy**

One minor difficulty is that there are four separate provisions which individually prohibit the granting of patents on public policy grounds. They are: Article 53(a) EPC, as amended; s.1(3) Patents Act 1977, as amended; Article 6(1) of the Biotech Directive; and Article 27(2) of the TRIPs Agreement. The last-mentioned allows Contracting States, if they wish, to derogate from the principle in Article 27(1) that patents are to be granted for any inventions in all fields of technology, whilst the other three provisions contain mandatory wording ('patents *shall* not be granted' as opposed to 'members *may* exclude from patentability' (emphasis supplied)). That apart, all four provisions prohibit the granting of patents 'the *commercial* exploitation of which would be contrary to *ordre public* or morality' (emphasis supplied). What is prohibited is not the patent *per se*, rather it is the *use* to which the invention is put which matters. An example of this might be a patent which explains how to manufacture a new type of letter bomb (applications for inventions involving weapons will generally have their **publication** in the *Patents Journal* prohibited under s.22 Patents Act 1977 and may well be the subject of Crown use under s.55).

Specific instances of inventions which would be caught by the public policy exception can be found in Articles 5(1) and 6(2) of the Biotech Directive (incorporated into Sch. A2, para 3(a)–(e) Patents Act 1977). These include the human body at the various stages of its formation and development and the simple discovery of one of its elements, including the sequence or partial sequence of a gene; processes for cloning human beings; processes for modifying the germ line genetic identity of human beings; uses of human embryos for commercial purposes; and processes for modifying the genetic identity of animals which are likely to cause them suffering without any substantial medical benefit to man or animal. All are the result of the political pressures exerted by the European Parliament.

5.4.3.1 EPO case law

There has been no United Kingdom case law on s.1(3). In relation to Article 53(a) EPC, the EPO has adopted a robust attitude to attempts to challenge patents on grounds of morality. Its initial thinking was set out in *T 19/90 HARVARD/Onco Mouse* [1990] EPOR 4, [1990] EPOR 501 and [1991] EPOR 525, where the patent was for a transgenic mammal modified to grow cancer cells. After the patent's initial rejection (on the ground, subsequently found to be incorrect, that it claimed an animal variety) the Board of Appeal had remitted the case to the Examining Division, directing it to reconsider the ethical objections raised against the application. The Examining Division subsequently held that the Article 53(a) objection should be decided in favour of the applicant. Patent law, it was noted, does not give the proprietor a positive right to use the invention but rather a negative right to exclude others from using the invention for a limited period of time. It was up to the legislator to regulate the use of technical knowledge. The risks inherent in new technologies had to be weighed in terms of the harm which might be done to higher life forms. Here the three interests to be reconciled were the need to remedy widespread and dangerous diseases, the need to protect the environment against the uncontrolled dissemination of unwanted genes, and the need to avoid cruelty to animals. The last two considerations might justify treating the invention as immoral, but were outweighed by the significance of improved anti-cancer treatments, the fact that fewer animals would be needed when compared to conventional animal testing, and that no release of the animals into the environment was contemplated.

Article 53(a) was also one of the grounds of the **opposition** brought by Greenpeace against the grant of the patent in *T 356/93 PLANT GENETIC SYSTEMS/Glutamine synthetase inhibitors* [1995] EPOR 357. The aim of the invention was to develop plants and seeds which were resistant to a particular class of herbicide. This was achieved by integrating into their genome the DNA coding for a protein which neutralised the effect of the weed-killers. The patent contained both **process claims** (how the plant genome was modified) and **product claims** to the corresponding plant cells and eventual plants. Greenpeace's opposition was based on three interrelated arguments, namely that plants were part of the 'common heritage' of mankind and should be available to all without restrictions; that the Opposition Division had failed to carry out the balancing exercise required by *HARVARD*, underestimating the harm to the environment caused by the eventual release of herbicide-resistant plants; and that public opinion (which was against the patenting of genetically engineered plants because it was immoral) had been ignored. Each of these arguments was dismissed. Although the protection of the environment fell within the concept of *ordre public*, plant biotechnology could not be regarded as being any more contrary to morality than traditional selective breeding, and the subject matter of the patent did not concern activities which were wrong as such in the light of conventionally accepted standards of conduct of European culture. Revocation of a patent under Article 53(a) on the grounds of a serious threat to the environment should only occur if there was sufficient evidence of harm, which here had not been made out. The Board was sceptical of the value of opinion polls, which may not be truly reflective of society, especially if the questions are weighted, and felt that it did not have the authority to carry out those tasks which properly belonged to the regulatory authorities.

In *HOWARD FLOREY/Relaxin*, an opposition was brought, *inter alia*, under Article 53(a) by the Green Party in the European Parliament against the grant of the patent claiming the relaxin gene. Several arguments were deployed, namely that as the invention depended on the taking of tissue from a pregnant woman, it was contrary to human dignity to make use of the particular condition (pregnancy) to make a profit; that such conduct amounted to slavery and infringed the right to self-determination; and that the patenting of genes amounted to the patenting of life, which was immoral. Again, the opposition was dismissed. The Opposition Division stated that the function of Article 53(a) was to ensure that patents would not be granted for inventions which 'would be universally regarded as outrageous' and reiterated that the exception to patentability was to be narrowly construed. It pointed out that many useful products over the years have been produced from human tissue and that the instant case was no different in that consent had been freely given before removing the sample. In any case, once the first sample had been obtained, it could be synthetically reproduced *ad infinitum*, without the need to obtain further samples. The slavery argument was rebutted by pointing out the negative nature of the patent right, such that it did not confer any right to any particular human individuals, so that the right to self-determination was not affected. Finally, and curtly, the Opposition Division pointed out that the patent did not entail the patenting of life:

> It is worth pointing out that DNA is not 'life', but a chemical substance which carries genetic information and can be used as an intermediate in the production of proteins which may be medically useful. The patenting of a single human gene has nothing to do with the patenting of human life. Even if every gene in the human genome were cloned (and possibly patented), it would be impossible to reconstitute a human being from the sum of its genes.

The one decision which goes against this trend is that of the Enlarged Board of Appeal in *G 2/06 WARF/Stem Cells* [2009] EPOR 129. The patent contained a series of claims involving the use of human embryonic stem cells (hESCs). By combining Article 53(a) with the text of the Implementing Regulations derived from Article 6(2) of the Biotech Directive, the Board was able to hold that it was not possible to grant a patent for an invention which *necessarily* involved the use and destruction of human embryos from which the stem cells were derived. It was not the fact of the patenting itself which was contrary to *ordre public*, rather it was the *performing* of the invention which included a step which contravened that principle. However, it stressed that the decision did not affect the patentability in general of inventions relating to hESCs, but only those involving the destruction of embryos.

The use of hESCs has also been considered by the ECJ in Case C-34/10 *Oliver Brüstle v Greenpeace eV* [2011] ECR I-9821. The issue was whether the patent (involving a treatment for Parkinson's disease) was invalid under Article 6(2). The ECJ ruled that 'human embryo' must be understood in a wide sense, agreeing with the Advocate General that a fertilised egg must be regarded as a human embryo. Likewise, the prohibition in Article 6(2)(c) on the use of embryos for commercial purposes had to be given a wide meaning, regardless of whether or not the use of the embryo is referred to in the patent and regardless of how long ago the originating embryo was destroyed. The ruling thus goes far beyond that of the EPO in *WARF/Stem Cells* and has been much criticised, not least because it had the effect of undermining the European biotech industry. However, on its return to Germany the Federal Court upheld the patent in an amended form because of the presence of a disclaimer excluding the destruction of hESCs.

A further referral to the ECJ has now been made by the Patents Court in *International Stem Cell Corporation v Comptroller General of Patents* [2013] EWHC 807 (Ch), seeking clarification as to whether 'embryo' includes unfertilised human ova whose division and further development have been stimulated by parthenogenesis, and which, in contrast to fertilised ova, contain only pluripotent cells and are incapable of developing into human beings.

5.4.3.2 Conclusions

The inevitable outcome of the EPO decisions is that any challenge to a patent under Article 53(a) will only succeed in the most extreme case either where, as the Opposition Division in *HOWARD FLOREY* said, the invention is 'outrageous' or where the claims of the patent fall squarely within the text of the Implementing Regulations as in *WARF*. Further, the previously discussed cases display a subtle shift of emphasis. The initial requirement in *HARVARD* was that the Tribunal carry out a balancing exercise. However, in *PLANT GENETIC SYSTEMS* and *HOWARD FLOREY* the burden of proof is placed on the opponent of the patent to show that the invention is likely to cause serious harm. No regard is to be had to public opinion. That this attitude towards public opinion is now well entrenched is evidenced by the decision of the Opposition Division concerning the patenting of animals, *LELAND STANFORD/Modified Animal* [2002] EPOR 16. The case did not involve a genetically modified animal, instead, the animal had been subjected to xenotransplantation in order to provide a model for HIV infection. The Opposition Division said that so long as a claimed invention has a legitimate use, it is not the role of the EPO to act as a moral censor; it would be presumptuous for the EPO to interfere with the public debate. Simply because technology is perceived as controversial is not a bar to its patentability. The principle of balancing the benefits to society against harm to the animal is reiterated, but the onus is placed on those challenging the patent to adduce evidence of 'conclusively documented hazards'. Even then, it was not for the EPO to monitor such risks: that was for the regulatory authorities charged with overseeing research and medical practice. Patent law does not exist to regulate research.

thinking point

How convincing do you find the EPO's statement that patent law does not exist to regulate research?

5.4.4 **Animal and plant varieties and biological processes**

The exclusion in Article 53(b) EPC (found in Patents Act 1977 Sch. A2, para 3(f)) denies patent protection for any variety of animal or plant or any essentially biological process for the production of animals or plants, not being a microbiological or other technical process or the product of such a process (this wording may be compared with that of the Biotech Directive Article 4 and with TRIPS Article 27(3)(b)).

Under this exception, morality aside, the issue is whether it is possible to patent something found in nature. The exception raises yet again the difference between a discovery and its practical application. The traditional analysis is that there is a clear distinction, on the one hand, between something found in nature (which is not patentable) and, on the other, (a) a process for reproducing that substance in the laboratory; and (b) the synthetic equivalent of that substance resulting from the process. The two latter are patentable, subject to novelty and inventive step being satisfied: *per* Lord Wilberforce in *Re American Cyanamid (Dann's) Patent* [1971] RPC 425; and *American Cyanamid v Berk* [1976] RPC 231. This principle is now set out in Articles 3(2) and 5(2) of the Biotech Directive, both of which draw a contrast between the identification and isolation of living matter.

Article 53(b) contains four separate elements. As with the list of excluded subject matter in Article 52(2), whether a patent falls within the exception depends on the wording of the claims. The patentee is free to word the specification in such a way that the statutory exceptions are avoided.

5.4.4.1 Animal varieties

The first prohibition is against the patenting of animal varieties. The EPO has explained that there is a taxonomy (ie system of classification) implicit in the exclusion, namely, in descending order, animals in general, animal species, varieties within that species. Whether a patent relates to an animal variety depends on the wording of the claims. Hence a genetically engineered mouse is not an animal variety, but an animal species (rodents) and so potentially patentable: *HARVARD*. It does seem counter-intuitive to say that animal varieties cannot be patented but animals can, but the *HARVARD* reasoning was applied in *LELAND STANFORD*. Here, the Opposition Division repeated the point that claims directed to a taxonomic group higher than an animal variety are patentable, and further, that this is in accordance with Article 4(2) of the Biotech Directive ('inventions which concern plants or animals shall be patentable if the technical feasibility of the invention is *not confined* to a particular plant or animal variety') (emphasis supplied).

5.4.4.2 Plant varieties

The same thinking applies to the second element, **plant varieties**. However, unlike the animal variety exception, there is a specific reason why plant varieties cannot be patented, and that is because there is an alternative legal mechanism for protecting plant varieties, under the International Convention for the Protection of New Varieties of Plants 1961, as amended in 1991 (the 'UPOV Convention'). There is in place both a regional system of obtaining plant variety protection (Council Regulation (EC) 2100/94 of 27 July 1994 on Community Plant Variety Rights [1994] OJ L 227/1) and a national system (the Plant Varieties Act 1997).

As with animal varieties, the issue is to be decided by interpreting the claims. It must be determined whether the patentee has claimed plants generally or a specific plant variety. Only the latter will fall within the exception. Hence, in *T 320/87 LUBRIZOL/Hybrid plants* [1990] EPOR 173 it was held that hybrid plants and their seeds were not a 'plant variety' because they did not comply with the definition of a variety. In *PLANT GENETIC SYSTEMS* it was held that genetically modified tobacco plants which were herbicide resistant were not a plant variety. As with the prohibition on patenting animal varieties, the legislative provision contains an implicit taxonomy, whereby a plant variety is the lowest level of the classification system.

The EPO Enlarged Board of Appeal revisited the plant variety exclusion in *G 1/98 NOVARTIS/ Transgenic plant* [2000] EPOR 303. One of the questions referred to it was whether a claim which relates to plants but which does not identify specific varieties can obviate the prohibition on patenting plant varieties. The Board answered this by referring to the legislative history of Article 53(b) and stated that there was no indication that patent protection should not be available in respect of matter not covered by the UPOV Convention. The extent of the exclusion from patentability therefore matches the availability of plant variety protection. Whether a claim was in respect of a plant variety depended on its substance. Substance was to be determined by identifying the underlying invention and the breadth of its application. In the instant case, the invention could be carried out by modifying plants which might or might not be varieties. The genetic modification effected by the claimed process did not necessarily result in a plant variety, and so was not excluded. Further, a claim to a *process* for modifying plants could not be a claim to a plant variety. However, if a claim was in substance for a plant variety (which would be a product claim), it mattered not by what technical means that variety had been produced. Again, it may be noted that Article 4(2) of the Biotech Directive maintains the distinction between plants in general and plant varieties.

thinking point
Is the EPO's argument that there is a system of classification which means that only specific varieties of plants and animals cannot be patented logical?

5.4.4.3 Biological processes

The final prohibition is against patenting essentially biological processes. The exception contemplates the difference between technical intervention and traditional cross-breeding methods: the latter are not patentable. According to the EPO in *LUBRIZOL*, whether or not a process is 'essentially biological' has to be judged by the essence of the invention, taking into account the totality of human intervention and its impact on the result achieved. The presence of human intervention is not by itself sufficient to guarantee that the invention falls outside the exception. Human interference may mean that the process is not 'purely biological', but not actually contribute anything of substance to the invention. In the instant case, the human intervention was quite different from that used in classical breeders' processes and so was not essentially biological. Likewise in *HARVARD*, the EPO felt that the introduction of the oncogene sequence into the mouse cells did not involve an essentially biological process and in *PLANT GENETIC SYSTEMS* it was decided that the process as a whole did not fall within the Article 53(b) exclusion because the steps taken were 'essentially technical' and could not occur without human intervention.

By contrast, in *PLANT BIOSCIENCE/Broccoli* and *STATE OF ISRAEL/Tomatoes* [2011] EPOR 247, the Enlarged Board of Appeal concluded that a non-microbiological process for the production of plants which consisted of sexually crossing the whole genomes of plants and of subsequently selecting from them was in principle excluded from patentability as being 'essentially biological'. The process did not escape the exclusion of Article 53(b) EPC merely because it contained a technical step which assisted the performance of crossing and selecting plants.

5.4.4.4 Microbiological processes

The wording of Article 53(b) creates an exception to the exception, in that microbiological processes are deemed patentable. The only cases which have discussed the meaning of 'microbiological processes' are *PLANT GENETIC SYSTEMS* and *NOVARTIS*. In the former, the Board of Appeal chose to explain that the term microbiological 'qualifies technical activities in which direct use is made of micro-organisms'. In the latter, the EPO agreed that it was tempting to conclude that genetic modification was a microbiological process within the meaning of Article 53(b), but then added that the two were not identical. 'Microbiological processes', as used in Article 53(b), was synonymous with processes using micro-organisms which were different from the parts of living beings used for the genetic modification of plants. Genetically modified plants were not to be treated as the product of a microbiological process, because otherwise this would provide a back door means to protecting plant varieties, and give the producers of such plant varieties a privileged position relative to breeders of plant varieties resulting from traditional breeding.

5.4.4.5 Patenting biotechnology: the ethical debate

The role which ethics should play in the decision-making processes of patent offices has provoked considerable debate. Authors such as Crespi ('Biotechnology Patenting: the Wicked Animal Must Defend Itself' [1995] *EIPR* 431 and 'Patenting and Ethics—a Dubious Connection' (2003) 85 *JPTOS* 31) maintain that the patent system is ethically neutral. Further, many of the emotive arguments (Crespi calls them 'blood-curdling') demanding that patent offices take greater account of ethical principles confuse a number of points. Crespi maintains that the issues should be separated as follows:

- objections to patents themselves (reminiscent of the anti-patent debate of the nineteenth century);
- objections to patents for certain types of inventions, such as gene patents. In particular, the argument goes, 'genes are special' and should be treated differently from other substances because of their inalienable nature, as part of the 'heritage of mankind';
- objections to gene patents because genes are discoveries not inventions; and
- objections to gene patents because genes 'are essentially just information' and hence different from other chemical compounds.

As Crespi points out, all of these arguments can be refuted by a proper understanding of the technology, of patent law itself (for example, the difference between a discovery and an invention discussed earlier), and of the nature of the patent monopoly as a negative right to stop others.

By contrast, writers such as Drahos ('Biotechnology Patents, Markets and Morality' [1999] *EIPR* 441) contend that the creation, operation and interpretation of the patent system are linked to moral standards. The patent community (ie patent attorneys and administrators) take the view that morality has little to do with the grant of patents, inspired no doubt by the decision of the US Supreme Court in *Diamond v Chakrabarty* (1980) 447 US 303 to the effect that it was for Congress not the courts to decide on the ethics of patenting living matter. Nevertheless, the strength of pro-patenting attitudes, the increasing harmonisation of global patent law (driven by the demands of technology-exporting countries), and the fear of the major patent offices (the US, Japan and the EPO) that weakening the patent system will undermine economic growth and prosperity, must be balanced by taking into account the values and attitudes of society.

There is, in fact, a third argument which can be made (see Norman, 'Patenting Biotechnology: A Case of Legal Abstentionism?' [2002] *ELM* 278–88). This is to the effect that if the criteria for patentability are strictly applied (particularly inventive step, industrial applicability and sufficiency) then patent law itself is more than adequate to deal with the perceived threat of biotechnological inventions.

5.4.5 Methods of treatment

The methods of treatment exception comprises both surgery and therapy (whether on the human or animal body) and methods of diagnosis. The three alternative exclusions are cumulative, so that the claimed method must be neither a therapeutic nor a surgical nor a diagnostic one: *G 1/07 MEDI-PHYSICS/Treatment by surgery* [2010] EPOR 219.

The policy reason why methods of treatment cannot be patented is simply that medical or veterinary practitioners should not be hindered in the conduct of their professional practice by patent protection: *MEDI-PHYSICS*. Other jurisdictions may permit the patenting of methods of treatment, as the TRIPs Agreement allows Contracting States the option of whether or not to allow such patents. As an example, Australia permits the granting of such patents: *Anaesthetic Supplies Pty Ltd v Rescare Ltd* (1994) 122 ALR 141. The need to protect medical or veterinary practitioners from patent litigation can be met (as in the USA) by providing a specific defence to infringement rather than prohibiting the patenting of the particular method, as does the EPC.

5.4.5.1 United Kingdom case law

Cases decided under the Patents Act 1949 (which contained a similar exception) were full of contradictions. Thus, it was not possible to patent the use of sound waves as an anaesthetic (*Neva's Application* [1968] RPC 481), nor a system of abortion (*Upjohn (Kirton's) Application* [1976] RPC 324), nor a method of filling teeth (*Lee Pharmaceutical's Application* [1975] RPC 51). However, it was possible to patent a system of evaluating health screening tests (*Bio-digital's Application* [1973] RPC 668), contraception (*Schering's Application* [1971] RPC 337), and a method of making a wound dressing (*Nolan's Application* [1977] FSR 435).

It has been held under the 1977 Act that the phrase 'method of treatment' is to be given a wide interpretation, so that it would include a system of immunisation (*Unilever (Davis') Application* [1983] RPC 219). One extreme United Kingdom decision is *Re Stafford-Miller Ltd's Application* [1984] FSR 258, where the judge upheld a method of killing ectoparasites on humans as patentable, a patent application described as being 'on the absolute frontier of the law'.

5.4.5.2 EPO case law

Despite the normal rule of construction that exclusions should be narrowly interpreted, the EPO has interpreted the method of treatment exception broadly, because of its underlying policy: *MEDI-PHYSICS*. In *T 383/03 THE GENERAL HOSPITAL CORP/Hair removal method* [2005] EPOR 357 it was said that 'treatment' could be defined as any non-insignificant physical or psychic intervention performed directly by one human being (who need not be a medical practitioner) on a human being or animal using the means or methods of medical science.

Each of the elements in the exception has been given a wide definition. 'Therapy' was said in *T 58/87 SALMINEN/Pigs III* [1989] EPOR 125 to cover any non-surgical treatment which was designed to cure, alleviate, remove or lessen the symptoms of, or prevent or reduce the possibility of contracting any malfunction. In *T 81/84 RORER/Dysmenorrhoea* [1988] EPOR 297 the EPO declared that it was undesirable to distinguish between healing or cure and relief. Further, the treatment does not have to be administered personally by a doctor or vet (*T 116/85 WELLCOME/Pigs I* [1988] EPOR 1; *T 19/86 DUPHAR/Pigs II* [1989] EPOR 10) and indeed can be administered by the patient themselves (*T 964/99 CYGNUS/Device and method for sampling substances* [2002] EPOR 272).

Nevertheless, some early cases (namely *T 144/83 DU PONT/Appetite suppressant* [1987] EPOR 6 and *T 36/83 ROUSSEL-UCLAF/Thenoyl peroxide* [1987] EPOR 1) allowed claims for cosmetic treatment. The correctness of these decisions has been questioned. However, in *T 383/03 THE GENERAL HOSPITAL CORP/Hair removal method*, the EPO allowed a patent for removing hair by optical radiation on the ground that it resulted in an aesthetic improvement of the person even though excess hair can be a symptom of a disease. This case was itself doubted in *MEDI-PHYSICS*.

In relation to 'surgery', the EPO in *T 182/90 SEE-SHELL/Bloodflow* [1994] EPOR 320 pointed out that over the years the term has undergone a change in meaning, so that today surgery can be used for non-curative as well as curative treatment. Nevertheless, a broad meaning should be given, covering both non-invasive and invasive procedures and regardless of the mechanism of the intervention (ie whether this was mechanical, electrical, thermal or chemical). In *MEDI-PHYSICS*, the Enlarged Board of Appeal added that where the invention comprised a number of steps (as here, injecting a special gas into the heart so that a scanner could take clearer pictures of the patient's blood flow), the fact that just one of the steps involved a surgical procedure meant that the whole claim was caught by the Article 53(c) exclusion. The Board, however, declined to provide a definition of surgery which would once and for all delimit the exact boundaries of the concept.

The term 'diagnosis' was considered by the Enlarged Board of Appeal in *G 1/04 CYGNUS/ Diagnostic methods* [2006] EPOR 161. It said that if a claim included features relating to the diagnosis for curative purposes representing deductive decision-making as an intellectual exercise, the preceding steps taken in making such a diagnosis, and the specific interactions with the human or animal body which occur when carrying these out, it would be caught by the wording of Article 53(c). Further, whether a method was a diagnostic method did not depend on the presence of a medical or veterinary practitioner as long as there was some interaction with a human or animal body.

5.4.5.3 The exceptions to methods of treatment

Section 4A(2) Patents Act 1977 (repeating the wording of Article 53(c) EPC) provides in effect that any substance used in a method of treatment is patentable. The provision is therefore directed to new and inventive substances. This means that not just pharmaceutical products are patentable but so too is equipment which carries out treatment or diagnosis: *T 426/89 SIEMENS/Pacemaker* [1992] EPOR 149.

But what if there is a *known* substance which can be used in a method of treatment? Section 4A(3), based on Article 54(4) EPC 2000, provides that where a known substance (for example, egg shells) is used for the first time in a method of treatment (a 'first medical use'), it can be patented for use in that method of treatment even though the substance itself is not new. Novelty is 'borrowed' from its new use, even though the use itself (the method of treatment) cannot be patented. The wording of the claims, however, must be such that the monopoly is limited to the particular use to which the known substance is to be put (ie it must be a purpose-limited product claim).

EPO case law extended this to cover second and subsequent medical uses (provided such uses were new and inventive): *G5/83 EISAI/Second medical indication*. The case has now been put on a statutory basis by Article 54(5) EPC 2000, reflected in s.4A(4) Patents Act 1977. Although United Kingdom courts were initially reluctant to recognise the principle (see *Wyeth/Schering's Applications* [1985] RPC 545), it is now accepted. An example of a successful second medical use patent is that in *American Home Products Corp v Novartis Pharmaceuticals UK Ltd* [2001] RPC 159, where the substance rapamycin, used initially as an anti-fungal agent, was found to be beneficial in transplant surgery. The patent for this unexpected second therapeutic use was upheld. By contrast, where a naturally occurring substance (such as taxol, derived from the yew tree, which is used in treating cancer) had been the subject of a patent, it was not possible to obtain a further patent after research had identified its optimum dosage, as this was simply a clarification of the preferred method of treatment: *Bristol-Myers Squibb Company v Baker Norton Pharmaceuticals Inc* [2001] RPC 1. However, both the Court of Appeal and the Enlarged Board of the EPO have since stated that there is nothing in principle to stop the patenting of a dosage régime where this was new and not directed to a method of treatment: *Actavis UK Ltd v Merck & Co Inc* [2009] 1 WLR 1186; *G 2/08 ABBOTT RESPIRATORY/ Dosage régime* [2010] EPOR 262. Thus the new use need not be the treatment of a different disease (*ABBOTT RESPIRATORY* at [5.10.3]).

Where the principle in *EISAI* is to be utilised, it used to be the law that the specification had to contain so-called 'Swiss form' claims, namely 'use of X for the manufacture of a medicament for treatment of Y'. The latest revisions to the EPC remove that requirement, so that it will now be possible to have a claim which reads 'Substance X for use in treatment of disease Y' (see the Explanatory Notes to the Patents Act 2004 and the observations of the Enlarged Board of Appeal in *ABBOTT RESPIRATORY*). Again, this is a purpose-limited product claim.

5.4.6 **Conclusions**

To summarise this complex area of patent law, the following propositions can be made:

- methods of treatment are not patentable under Article 53(c) EPC, s.4A(1) Patents Act 1977, for public policy reasons;
- new substances or equipment used in such treatments are patentable (Article 53(c), s.4A(2));
- known substances having a first medical use are patentable under EPC Article 54(4), s.4A(3) Patents Act, novelty being found in the new use (this would be have to be in the form of a purpose-limited product claim, eg 'substance x for use as a treatment for y'); and
- known substances having a second medical use are patentable under EPC Article 54(5), s.4A(4) Patents Act, novelty residing in the subsequent (unexpected) therapeutic use (this would have to be again as a purpose-limited product claim).

thinking point
Is the availability of patent protection for the first and second medical use of a known substance logical?

5.5 Novelty

5.5.1 Overview of the statutory provisions

The requirement of **novelty** is set out in s.2 Patents Act 1977, based on Article 54 EPC. Section 2(1) contains the fundamental statement of principle that an invention shall be taken to be new if it does not form part of the state of the art. Section 2(2) explains what is meant by 'state of the art', that is, all matter which has at any time before the **priority date** of the invention been made available to the public, whether in the United Kingdom or elsewhere.

The key word in both subsections is the word 'invention'. An invention is a piece of information (*per* Lord Hoffmann in *Merrell Dow v Norton* [1996] RPC 76 at p. 86), so that making matter available to the public under s.2(2) requires the communication (or disclosure) of information. The **disclosure** contemplated by s.2(2) corresponds with the requirement of disclosure by the patentee for the purposes of sufficiency under s.14(3) Patents Act 1977. Such disclosures are sometimes referred to in the cases as 'the teaching' of the prior art and 'the teaching' of the patent respectively.

cross reference
See section 4.4.1.1.

Two other provisions in s.2 require elaboration. Section 2(3) is intended to deal with the problem of 'double patenting', ie where two rival patentees are in a race to the patent office door, as occurred, albeit with differing outcomes, in *Re Asahi KKK's Patent* [1991] RPC 485 and *Synthon BV v Smithkline Beecham plc* [2006] RPC 323. The point to remember when reading s.2(3) is that the United Kingdom and European patent systems are based on the principle of first to file, rather than first to invent, as was the case in the USA. Section 2(3) provides that the state of the art includes information contained in an earlier filed but later published patent, provided that the relevant information is in both the filed and published version of the first patent, and that the first patent has a priority date before that of the second patent. This is illustrated in Diagram 5.2:

Diagram 5.2

Patents Act 1977 s.2(3)

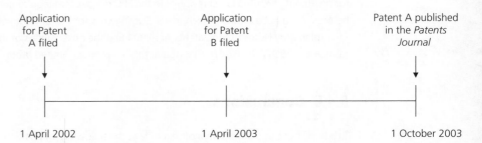

Application for Patent A filed	Application for Patent B filed	Patent A published in the *Patents Journal*
1 April 2002	1 April 2003	1 October 2003

Note: Information in Patent A, although unknown when Patent B is filed, becomes part of the prior art when published, as the information is deemed to be available to the public as of the filing date of Patent A.

The net result is that the applicant for the second patent may find that their invention lacks novelty because of the contents of another patent application which was unknown at the time of filing.

Next, s.2(4) (based on EPC Article 55) contains an exception in respect of two categories of communication, but only if these occurred during the period of six months before the priority date of the patent. These are: information disclosed in **breach of confidence**; and display of the invention at an international exhibition. Provided the requirements of the section are met, the novelty of the patent is preserved.

5.5.2 Overview of the issues

Anticipation is one of the key technical words of patent law. It means that the **prior art** matches exactly the subject matter (ie the claims) of the later invention so as to render it not new. Anticipation occurs where the prior art contains an **enabling disclosure**. This composite phrase comprises two separate issues which must be dealt with sequentially, namely disclosure and enablement: *Synthon BV v Smithkline Beecham plc, per* Lord Hoffmann at [19–33] and Lord Walker at [58]. Consequently, when considering whether a patent passes the test of novelty, what has to be decided is:

- whether the information was accessible (potentially rather than actually) by any member of the public (even one person) without any fetter of confidentiality; and if so
- whether that information contained an enabling disclosure such that the skilled addressee, armed with the prior art, could perform the invention without undue burden.

cross reference
See section 4.6.2.

What amounts to the prior art requires an understanding of how information can be made available. Information is usually supplied through documents, but it can be obtained by the supply of goods, the use of an item, or its demonstration. In every case, however, the question to be asked is what would the skilled addressee understand from that information? As with other areas of patent law, novelty is determined objectively from the viewpoint of the skilled addressee, possessed of the appropriate qualifications, practical experience and **common general knowledge**. Whether the prior art contains an enabling disclosure depends on a comparison through the eyes of the skilled addressee of each claim of the patent with *each individual* item of prior art. Separate pieces of prior art cannot be taken together for the purpose of anticipation unless they clearly cross-refer to each other. If the item of prior art does not contain *all* the elements (or **integers**) of a claim, then the claim is valid for novelty but may still be subject to attack for lack of inventive step. The importance of the patent's claims should be noted: it is the claims which are individually compared with the prior art. It is possible for one or more claims in a patent to be struck down for lack of novelty, but for other claims to survive (although they may lack validity for other reasons).

5.5.3 Impact of the 1977 Act

In relation to the definition of the 'state of the art' in s.2(2), the 1977 Act changed the previous law in two respects.

5.5.3.1 Worldwide novelty

Under the 1949 Act, only information available in the United Kingdom was taken into account whereas now information from anywhere in the world is relevant. Section 2(2) contains the phrase 'in the United Kingdom *or elsewhere*' (emphasis supplied). There is therefore a change from relative to absolute novelty.

5.5.3.2 Prior use

Under the 1949 Act, information made available through publication had to contain an enabling disclosure whilst information made available through **prior use** did not. As a result, any uninformed prior use of an invention, whether by the patentee or a third party, could destroy novelty. There was a policy reason why any use in public (even if it conveyed no information) would destroy novelty. 'From earliest times it had been taken for granted that...it was intended to declare unlawful the grant of any patent which would put it into the power of the grantee to prevent any other trader from doing whatever he had done before in the course of his trade' (*per* Lord Diplock in *Bristol-Myers Co (Johnson's) Application* [1975] RPC 127 at p. 157). An example of the harshness of the old law is *Gore v Kimal* [1988] RPC 137. Samples of PTFE tape had been supplied to customers. The patent in question related to the *process* of making the substance, and it was impossible from analysis of the tape to work out what that process was. Nevertheless, Whitford J held that by entering commercial transactions before the patent was filed, the patentees had disqualified themselves from protection.

By contrast, the 1977 Act simply requires that the information be 'made available to the public', the phrase used in the 1949 Act to define publication. The result is that under the 1977 Act *all* forms of prior art must contain an enabling disclosure: *Re Asahi KKK's Patent* (HL), confirming a trio of first instance decisions, *Genentech Inc's (Human Growth Hormone) Patent* [1989] RPC 613, *Pall v Bedford Hydraulics* [1990] FSR 329 and *Quantel v Spaceward Microsystems*. The policy point adverted to by Lord Diplock in *Bristol-Myers Co (Johnson's) Application* is now dealt with by the defence to patent infringement of prior use found in s.64 Patents Act 1977.

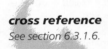

cross reference
See section 6.3.1.6.

As a result of this change, cases decided under earlier legislation on anticipation by prior use should be treated with caution as their outcome might be different today (see to this effect the remarks of Aldous J in *PLG Research Ltd v Ardon* [1993] FSR 197 at p. 225). The thinking in *Asahi* is entirely consistent with the case law of the EPO. In *G 1/92 Availability to the Public* [1993] EPOR 241, the Enlarged Board of Appeal noted that Article 54(2) EPC does not make any distinction between the different means by which information is made available to the public, so that information deriving from use is governed by the same conditions as information disclosed by oral or written **description**. The Board went on to say that an essential purpose of the prior art's teaching is to enable the person skilled in the art to manufacture or use a given product by applying such teaching. Where such teaching results from a product put on the market, if it is possible for that person to discover the composition or the internal structure of the product *and to reproduce it without undue burden* (original emphasis), then both the product and its composition or internal structure become part of the state of the art.

5.5.4 The meaning of 'the public'

The meaning of 'the public' in s.2 was explained by Aldous J in *PLG Research Ltd v Ardon* at p. 226 as follows:

> Section 2 uses the words 'made available to the public'...to form part of the state of the art, the information given by the use must have been made available to *at least one member of the public who was free in law and equity to use it.* (emphasis supplied)

This statement makes clear two things, that 'the public' can consist of just one person; and the key distinguishing characteristic of the recipient of the information is that they must not be bound by confidentiality. Hence, information which is confidential cannot destroy novelty. An example is the EPO case *T 245/88 UNION CARBIDE/Atmospheric Vaporizer* [1991] EPOR 373: novelty was held not to have been destroyed where an invention located on private property (a shipyard) was viewed through a fence. Further, even if the invention had been publicly available, the EPO was not convinced that the skilled addressee would have been able to see all the relevant details, in other words, there had not been an enabling disclosure. Another example of confidentiality protecting novelty is *Re Gallay* [1959] RPC 141, where a duty of secrecy was implied as a contract term in the case of a joint venture. However, in *Re Dalrymple* [1957] RPC 449, the large number of members in a trade association meant that the fact the word 'confidential' was stamped on the front of a document circulated to all had no effect.

cross reference
See chapter 3.

5.5.5 **Anticipation by prior use**

Prior use of a later claimed invention may be by a third party of whom the patentee is unaware. This occurred in *Fomento v Mentmore* [1956] RPC 87, where an improved type of ballpoint pen was used by a Canadian visitor to a village shop in England; and in *Windsurfing International Inc v Tabur Marine* [1985] RPC 59, where a 12-year-old boy built and sailed his home-made sailboard some years before the **claimant** filed its United Kingdom patent. Equally, the prior use may be by a competitor, as happened in *Bristol-Myers Co (Johnson's) Application* where the opponents to the patent application had accidentally discovered the same substance, ampicillin, in their laboratories, but being unaware of its properties had put the substance to one side. Finally, of course, the prior use may be by the patentee themselves. We have already encountered the decision in *Gore v Kimal*, where samples were supplied to customers before the patent was filed. Similarly, if the patented device is demonstrated in public, this will destroy novelty: *Wheatley's Application* [1985] RPC 91. But what if the disclosure occurs not in a public place but on private premises where members of the public (albeit unskilled people) are present and can examine the device if they wished? In *Folding Attic Stairs Ltd v The Loft Stairs Company Ltd* [2009] FSR 887, Peter Prescott QC thought that it was the *place* of disclosure which mattered, so that there is a significant difference between public and private premises. The visitors to the factory would not have appreciated what they had seen, but even if they had, this would not have anticipated claim 1 of the patent which was for the manufacturing process.

5.5.6 **Anticipation through documents**

Documentary prior art will include earlier patents, such as occurred in the two House of Lords, decisions of *Re Asahi KKK's Patent* and *Merrell Dow v Norton*. The only issue in both cases was whether the description of the substance in an earlier patent amounted to an enabling disclosure. In *Asahi*, it was held that the mere identification of a particular substance (a polypeptide) did not teach the skilled addressee how to replicate it in the laboratory. By contrast, in *Merrell Dow* the earlier patent gave instructions which, if followed by the skilled addressee, would have led inevitably to the production of the later-claimed substance.

Documentary prior art may also include photographs (*Van der Lely v Bamfords Ltd* [1963] RPC 61); sales leaflets (*Monsanto (Brignac's) Application* [1971] RPC 153); books and magazines as long as they *could* have been read by a member of the public (*Lang v Gisbourne* (1862) 31 Beav 133, *Bristol Myers Application* [1969] RPC 146) even if no one actually did so; and information in a library as long as the public have access to it (*Harris v Rothwell* (1887) 35 Ch D 416). A company's private research library may not be accessible by the public, so that documents stored there do not amount to prior art: *Re Tecalemit* [1967] FSR 387, *Re Bakelite* [1967] FSR 582.

5.5.7 The test for enablement

case close-up

General Tire v Firestone [1972] RPC 457

The test for enabling disclosure is to be found in *General Tire v Firestone* [1972] RPC 457 which is generally endorsed by modern cases as being the correct statement on anticipation, even though in that case the Court of Appeal was only dealing with anticipation through documentary disclosure. Sachs LJ put forward a number of *interchangeable* tests which can be used in order to decide whether there has been anticipation. First, he suggested, the court should ask the question 'would the prior use infringe if carried out today?' (referred to as 'the infringement test'). The second question to be posed is whether 'the claimed subject matter is derivable directly and unambiguously from the [prior] publication?' The third test is to enquire whether 'the earlier material point[ed] inevitably to the later invention?' Another useful aspect of Sachs LJ's judgment is that he draws a distinction between a 'signpost' and a 'flag-post' contained (metaphorically speaking) in the prior art. A 'signpost' (that is, a general indication which points out one of the possible ways to achieve the later invention) will not suffice to destroy novelty; only if the prior art 'plants the flag' at the precise spot claimed by the patentee will there be anticipation.

Interestingly, the House of Lords, although endorsing *General Tire v Firestone* on two separate occasions, has changed its mind about which of the above three tests is to be preferred (without explicitly distinguishing or overruling its own earlier decision). In *Merrell Dow v Norton*, Lord Hoffmann (at p. 86), when discussing anticipation by use, indicated that the infringement test should be avoided:

> The 1977 Act therefore introduced a substantial qualification into the old principle that a patent cannot be used to stop someone doing what he has done before. If the previous use was secret or uninformative, then subject to section 64, it can. Likewise, a gap has opened up between the tests for infringement and anticipation. Acts done secretly or without knowledge of the relevant facts, which would amount to infringement after the grant of the patent, will not count as anticipations before.

case close-up

Merrell Dow v Norton [1996] RPC 76

The claimant had previously obtained patent protection for terfenadine, a substance used to treat hay fever. It was later (unexpectedly) discovered that the human body converted terfenadine into an acid metabolite (ie the product of a metabolic reaction) and so a second patent was obtained for the acid metabolite. Their Lordships held that the clinical trials conducted by the patentee before the second patent was filed did not anticipate it, because there was no way that patients knew what was going on inside their bodies once the pharmaceutical was swallowed. There was no public information which would enable anyone to work the invention. However, the second patent *was* anticipated by the information contained in the first patent, because 'the terfenadine specification teaches that the ingestion of terfenadine will produce a chemical reaction in the body and for the purposes of working the invention in this form, this is a sufficient description of the making of the acid metabolite. Under the description the acid metabolite was part of the state of the art' (*per* Lord Hoffmann at p. 91).

In *Synthon BV v Smithkline Beecham plc*, however, Lord Hoffmann (at [22]) adopted the infringement test from *General Tire*, although he was dealing specifically with documentary disclosure by a prior patent in the context of s.2(3) Patents Act 1977, rather than anticipation by use as in *Merrell Dow*. The decision is clouded by the fact that the earlier patent contained incorrect information. At first instance Jacob J (with whom the Court of Appeal had disagreed) felt that the skilled addressee, armed with common general knowledge, would have done further experiments to achieve the correct results and so make the substance claimed in the second patent. In restoring Jacob J's decision, Lord Hoffmann quoted from Lord Westbury in *Hills v Evans* (1862) 31 LJ Ch 457:

> the antecedent statement must be such that a person of ordinary knowledge of the subject would at once perceive, understand and be able practically to apply the discovery without the necessity for making further experiments and gaining further information before the information can be made useful. If something remains to be ascertained which is necessary for the useful application of the discovery, that affords sufficient room for another valid patent.

Lord Hoffmann went on to state that the requirements of disclosure and enablement must be kept distinct (which is incontrovertible) but then declared that the *General Tire* infringement test was the appropriate one to be used to determine whether there had been disclosure, when arguably it, and the other authorities relied on by Lord Hoffmann, were all concerned with the issue of enablement. To make matters worse, Lord Hoffmann does not say why he had changed his mind since *Merrell Dow* about the suitability of the infringement test, and even summarises his own conclusions in the latter case incorrectly. The net result of the two cases, however, is that a gap appears to have opened up between the treatment of anticipation by use and anticipation by disclosure, even though both statute and EPO case law treat them identically.

Several cases neatly illustrate the need for an enabling disclosure in the case of prior use. All show the key issue is whether the skilled addressee, had they been present when the information was made public, could have implemented the invention.

thinking point
Is it possible to reconcile Lord Hoffmann's views in Merrell Dow v Norton with his speech in Synthon?

case close-up

Lux Traffic Controls v Pike Signals [1993] RPC 107

The clearest illustration of the role of the skilled addressee is found in *Lux Traffic Controls v Pike Signals* [1993] RPC 107. Traffic lights containing a new infrared detector were tested in a public place. It was held that even though there was no evidence that anyone had examined the inside of the device, had the skilled addressee been present at the trial, it would have been possible for such a person to deduce from their observations how the device worked without having to examine the 'black box' containing the electronics.

By contrast, in *Pall v Bedford Hydraulics* samples of microporous filters were supplied for testing which were incapable of analysis so there was no enabling disclosure (the case forms a useful contrast with *Gore v Kimal* as to the differences between the pre- and post-1977 law on prior use). Likewise, in *Quantel v Spaceward Microsystems*, the demonstration of a video graphics system at a trade fair was held not to destroy novelty as those present were not able to get close enough to the device to observe how it worked.

5.5.8 **Novelty of purpose**

The ability to obtain a patent for the first and second medical use of a pharmaceutical substance was explained earlier. The EPO has further extended this principle to novelty of purpose in non-medical fields in its decision in *G 2/88 MOBIL III/Friction reducing additive* [1990] EPOR 73 which concerned a new use for a substance previously used as a rust inhibitor. The Enlarged Board of Appeal declared that if the new use of the substance had not been made available, then it mattered not that it might have been inherent in its previous use. United Kingdom courts have reluctantly accepted the principle (see *Merrell Dow v Norton* and *Bristol-Myers Squibb Company v Baker Norton Pharmaceuticals Inc*), the reluctance stemming from the 'intuitive response' (*per* Lord Hoffmann in *Merrell Dow*) that you cannot patent something which has been done before, even if no one knew that it had been done. To take advantage of the *MOBIL III* principle, the claims have to be worded so as to limit the patentee's monopoly to the particular new use of the known substance.

cross reference
See section 5.4.5.3.

140

5.5.9 **The link with inventive step**

The test of enabling disclosure is very precise, so that if an individual item of prior art does not contain *all* the elements (integers) of the later claimed invention, then the invention is valid for novelty. It is then necessary to consider separately and sequentially whether the invention meets the requirement of inventive step. It is here that Sachs LJ's metaphor in *General Tire* is very handy. If the prior art contains a signpost, pointing in the general direction of the invention, that does not suffice for anticipation. It may well, however, give the skilled addressee sufficient information to make the invention obvious.

5.6 **Inventive step**

5.6.1 **Inventive step: general principles**

The next positive element of patentability is that there must be an inventive step, or rather, the invention must not be obvious. It is found in s.3 Patents Act 1977, derived from Article 56

EPC. Inventive step is to be considered *after* novelty has been decided, and involves different issues. Something may be new but not involve any contribution to the state of the art. Whilst novelty is concerned with whether the invention is *quantitatively* different from what has gone before (so that a small difference between the invention and the prior art means that it is new), inventive step is concerned with whether it is *qualitatively* different. Novelty and inventive step therefore need to be kept distinct.

Inventiveness is a question of fact to be decided objectively and without hindsight. Thus in *Lilly Icos Ltd v Pfizer Ltd* [2002] EWCA Civ 1, the patent for VIAGRA was little more than putting into practice the recommendations and suggestions already found in the prior art. It may be difficult to avoid hindsight where the patent relates to an everyday item and the inventive step is small (see for example *SEB SA v De'Longhi SpA* [2003] EWCA Civ 952, which concerned deep fat fryers), but nevertheless, the court must ensure that hindsight is not used, particularly where the patent is challenged some years after grant.

Many cases assert that the word 'obvious' requires no further explanation, but then proceed to offer synonyms, such as 'very plain' (*General Tire v Firestone*), 'so easy that any fool could do it' (*Edison Bell v Smith* (1894) 11 RPC 389 at p. 398), 'routine development work' (*Lucas v Gaedor* [1978] RPC 297 at p. 377), or 'workshop adjustment' (*Cincinnati Grinders v BSA Tools* (1931) 48 RPC 33 at p. 75). By contrast, it is said, an inventive step involves 'a flash of insight' (*Unilever plc v Chefaro Proprietaries Ltd* [1994] RPC 567 at p. 584), an 'intellectual jump' (*Biogen v Medeva*), or a 'significant advance' (*Schlumberger Holdings Ltd v Electromagnetic Geoservices AS* [2010] RPC 851 at [93]).

5.6.2 Inventive step: the United Kingdom test

For many years, the test for inventive step was that established by Oliver LJ in *Windsurfing International v Tabur Marine* [1985] RPC 59 at p. 73. The test provided a structured approach for determining whether an invention was or was not obvious. Case law was littered with judicial pronouncements on the importance of sticking to such an approach (for example the House of Lords in *Sabaf SpA v MFI Furniture Centres Ltd* [2005] RPC 209).

case close-up

Pozzoli SpA v BDMO SA [2007] FSR 872

The *Windsurfing* test has now been re-stated and re-ordered by Jacob LJ in the Court of Appeal in *Pozzoli SpA v BDMO SA* [2007] FSR 872. He stated that the court should:

- identify the notional person skilled in the art and their common general knowledge;
- identify the inventive concept of the claim in question, or if that cannot readily be done, construe it. The inventive concept is usually called 'the epitome' or 'essence' of the invention. It is to be extracted from the wording of the claims, bearing in mind the problem which the patent attempted to solve, and hence is subject to the vagaries of judicial opinion (consider the majority and minority views of the inventive concept in *Wheatley (Davina) v Drillsafe Ltd* [2001] RPC 133);
- identify the differences between the matter cited as forming part of the state of the art and the inventive concept; and

thinking point
Does the Pozzoli
*test actually help to
decide whether an
invention possesses
an inventive step?*

Occasionally, it is possible to discern a different approach in cases involving biotechnology. An example is the judgment of Mustill LJ in *Genentech Inc's Application* where he suggested that the court should imagine the hypothetical skilled addressee, up to date with the prior art and looking towards the goal to be achieved; then ask by what routes it would have been possible to reach the goal; then ask what obstacles were in the way and how they could have been overcome; and finally decide whether this would have required pertinacity, sound technique, trial and error or a spark of imagination. It may be observed that the *Genentech* test involves an element of hindsight, which probably explains why it has not been generally adopted.

5.6.3 Inventive step: the EPO approach

The test adopted by the EPO in deciding whether an invention possesses inventive step has many similarities with United Kingdom law, but there are subtle differences. Both systems deploy the skilled addressee as the person through whose eyes the matter is determined, such person being imbued with the common general knowledge of the relevant technical field and possessing the prejudices of others working in that area. Both systems stress the objective nature of the exercise and the need to avoid using hindsight. The apparent difference between them lies in the use of the problem and solution approach by the EPO. It has stated that this consists of:

- the identification of the closest prior art;
- assessing the technical results achieved by the invention when compared with such art;
- defining the technical problem to be solved as the object of the invention; and
- examining whether or not a skilled person, having regard to the state of the art, would have suggested the technical features for obtaining those results.

The fourth stage does not entail asking whether the skilled person *could* have carried out the invention (this involves hindsight), but whether he *would have done so* in the hope of solving the problem or in the expectation of finding a technical improvement.

However, it should not be assumed that there is a huge difference between the two systems. The *Pozzoli* test requires the court to identify the inventive concept of the patent. This should be done, according to Lord Hoffmann in *Biogen v Medeva*, by taking account of the problem which the patentee was attempting to solve. Ultimately, therefore, the differences may be more apparent than real.

5.6.4 The test is objective not subjective

Inventive step is a 'jury question' (that is, a question of fact) to be determined by the court objectively, using the standard of the skilled addressee (*Dow Corning's Application* [1969] RPC

544 at pp. 560, 561; *Technograph v Mills & Rockley* [1969] RPC 395 at p. 407 (CA)). Inventive step is therefore determined without reference to the inventor. It doesn't matter how the inventor achieved success, whether by accident, hard work, intuition or creativity: *Allmanna Svenska Electriska A/B v Burntisland Shipping Co* (1952) 69 RPC 63 at p. 70. What the inventor actually did is therefore irrelevant: *Nichia Corp v Argos Ltd* [2007] FSR 895.

5.6.5 The meaning of 'prior art' for the purpose of inventive step

The *Pozzoli* test requires the court to compare the prior art with the invention. A question which remains unresolved is whether the prior art is the same for inventiveness as it is for novelty. The approach of the EPO is to compare the invention with the nearest prior art. United Kingdom cases have not been so clear. Initially, it was said that all prior art should be considered (*Woven Plastic Products v British Ropes* [1970] FSR 47). However, the later cases of *Technograph v Mills & Rockley* [1972] RPC 346 (HL) and *General Tire v Firestone* both held that the concept of the 'diligent researcher' should be used, so that the invention was to be compared with items of prior art which such a person would discover. Most recently, it has been said that 'obscure' prior art should be ignored (*Beloit Technologies v Valmet Paper Machinery* [1995] RPC 705, [1997] RPC 489). Nevertheless, in *Windsurfing* itself (which after all is the basis of *Pozzoli*), the Court of Appeal held that all prior art should be considered.

5.6.6 The prior art: 'mosaicing'

In contrast to novelty, where each item of prior art has to be considered in isolation, it is possible to combine different items of prior art when arguing that an invention is obvious. This process is called 'mosaicing'. Despite this colourful language, it is unusual for a court to hold that separate, unrelated pieces of prior art can be combined when attacking a patent under s.3, because it has to be shown that the skilled reader would think it obvious to mosaic, remembering that the skilled addressee has no inventive capacity. One example of where the court decided that the skilled addressee would combine separate items of prior art is *Dow Chemicals (Mildner's) Patent* [1975] RPC 165, where the patent involved a means of covering an electrical cable with a plastic jacket bonded to a metal shield. The Court of Appeal held that it was permissible to combine separate documents about electrical cables and adhesives. A recent case which has also discussed the practice of mosaicing is *SEB SA v De'Longhi SpA* which concerned a patent for deep fat fryers. The Court of Appeal refused to disturb the conclusions of Pumfrey J that the skilled addressee, working in the field of small domestic appliances, would have combined common general knowledge about the use of metals and plastics in the manufacture of such appliances, the use of an air-filled gap as an insulator, and the use of insulating rings in toasters, coffee makers and irons.

A related issue is where an invention is said to consist of a combination of existing technology. The very act of putting together two or more known features may of itself involve an inventive step especially where the skilled addressee has only basic skills and qualifications in the relevant field and has a technical prejudice against changing accepted technology. However, there will only be a 'collocation' (as it is known) if the invention, considered as a whole, consists of a single inventive concept where the combination of known elements produces a synergy. If each element performs its own function independently of the other, then there is not one invention but two, and each part must be considered on its own in the light of the prior art: *Sabaf SpA v MFI Furniture Centres Ltd*, applying EPO Guidelines and the earlier United Kingdom case of *British Celanese Ltd v Courtaulds Ltd* (1935) 52 RPC 171. An example of a combination of known elements which is not inventive (because it does not amount to a collocation) is the putting together of a mincing machine and a filling machine to produce a sausage-making machine.

5.6.7 Inventive step: secondary issues

Sometimes subsidiary arguments are raised by a patentee to support the contention that a patent possesses an inventive step. They usually come into play when one is considering the question 'if it is obvious, why was it not done before?' (*Schlumberger* at [77]). These secondary issues, attractive as they are, are peripheral to the objective assessment under the *Pozzoli* test: *Beloit Technologies v Valmet Paper Machinery*. Secondary issues are also recognised by the EPO, which likewise treats them as subsidiary to the problem and solution test.

The first of these arguments concerns the length of time taken to develop the invention. Thus in *Re Beecham's (Amoxycillin) Application* [1980] RPC 261 the fact that it took six years to develop the next generation of antibiotics in a highly competitive field convinced the court that the patent possessed an inventive step. By contrast, in *Genentech Inc's Patent* the Court of Appeal was not convinced that the time taken to develop a treatment for an illness by means of genetic engineering demonstrated inventiveness: it was simply a question of throwing time and money at the problem.

Another subsidiary argument which can be advanced by the patentee to demonstrate inventiveness is that the patent has proved to be highly successful (*Rotocrop v Genbourne* [1982] FSR 241). Commercial success, however, may be attributable to other factors, such as fashion (*Wildey v Freeman* (1931) 48 RPC 405 which involved a patent for an electric comb) or a successful advertising campaign (*Haskell Golf Ball Co v Hutchinson* (1906) 23 RPC 301 which involved a patent for an improved golf ball). However, if something is inventive, it is not a counter-argument to say that it is simple, as simplicity itself may be evidence of inventiveness: *Haberman v Jackel International Ltd* [1999] FSR 683.

case close-up

Haberman v Jackel International Ltd [1999] FSR 683

Laddie J put forward a number of factors to be considered by the court when determining inventive step:

- What was the problem which the patented development addressed?
- How long had that problem existed?
- How significant was the problem seen to be?
- How widely known was the problem and how many were likely to be seeking a solution?
- What prior art would have been likely to be known to all or most of those who would have been expected to be involved in finding a solution?

- What other solutions were put forward in the period leading up to the publication of the patentee's development?

- To what extent were there factors which would have held back the exploitation of the solution even if it was technically obvious?

- How well has the patentee's development been received?

- To what extent can it be shown that the whole or much of the commercial success is due to the technical merits of the development, ie because it solves the problem?

Significantly, the list takes as its starting point the problem and solution approach. The list was approved by Jacob LJ in *Schlumberger*.

5.7 The requirement of industrial application

5.7.1 The statutory requirement

The last positive element of patentability (found in s.4(1) Patents Act 1977, derived from Article 57 EPC) is that the invention must be capable of industrial application (Article 57 uses the term 'susceptible' rather than 'capable'). 'Industrial application' means that the invention can be made or used in any kind of industry, including agriculture.

The requirement can be equated with the phrase 'any manner of new manufacture within the Statute of Monopolies' in s.101 of the Patents Act 1949. Under previous legislation, case law had held originally that there had to be the production, improvement or preservation of a 'vendible product' (*GEC's Application* (1943) 60 RPC 1), a somewhat narrow concept which assumed the presence of something tangible. The meaning of 'vendible product' was gradually expanded by subsequent cases until it meant that the invention had to produce some economic advantage, that is have a useful effect: see *NRDC's Application* [1961] RPC 134 (which involved the application of a herbicide) and *Swift & Co's Application* [1962] RPC 37 (which involved a process of tenderising meat by injecting an animal before slaughter). Under the 1977 Act, it has been held that s.4 simply requires that the invention must not be something which is useless for any known purpose, in other words the issue is whether the subject matter of the patent is 'useful': *Chiron v Organon (No 12)* [1996] FSR 153. Such definition resembles the 'utility' requirement in USA patent law. The EPO has held that cosmetic salons and beauty parlours fall within the meaning of Article 57 (see *DU PONT/Appetite suppressant* and *ROUSSEL-UCLAF/Thenoyl peroxide*), stating that 'industry' implies that an activity is carried out continuously, independently and for financial gain.

5.7.2 Case law

Objections to patents under s.4(1) are rare, but two cases illustrate the role of the provision. In *Re Duckett's Patent Application* [2005] EWHC 3140, Kitchin J upheld the decision of the

UKIPO to reject the application. The invention related to a propulsion system (ie an engine) involving an electric system and a hydraulic system. Because the invention went against the well-established laws of nature (it appeared to create something out of nothing and so breached the principle of conservation of energy) it was not capable of industrial application. In *Blacklight Power Inc v Comptroller General of Patents* [2009] RPC 173 the patent examiner had held that a plasma reactor based on an allegedly new species of hydrogen (christened by the applicant 'the hydrino') which was supposed to exist in a lower energy state than recognised by the standard laws of physics was not capable of industrial application because it was inconsistent with generally accepted theories. However, Floyd J allowed the appeal and remitted the case because the examiner had applied too stringent a test: what should have been asked was whether the applicant had a reasonable prospect of showing that his theory was valid, rather than asking whether it was more probable than not that the theory was true.

5.7.3 A particular problem with biotech patents

The requirement of utility may also prove to be a means of challenging biotech patents in the light of the decision of the EPO Opposition Division in *ICOS CORPORATION/Transmembrane receptor* [2002] OJ EPO 293. Revoking the patent on the grounds of lack of inventiveness, lack of utility, and lack of sufficiency, the EPO seems to have taken the same approach to lack of inventiveness as the Court of Appeal in *Genentech Inc's Patent*, that is, the identification of the relevant genetic sequence was no more than the result of routine procedure which would have been followed by a skilled person in the light of prior art. In relation to utility, the patentee had successfully crossed the boundary between discovery and invention in that they had isolated the particular amino acid sequence. However, the potential uses of the invention were speculative. The patentee had merely 'brainstormed' about how the invention *might* be used. This was not sufficient under Article 57: the practical applications of the invention had to be clearly spelled out.

The treatment of speculative patents was considered by the Supreme Court in *Eli Lilly and Company v Human Genome Sciences Inc* [2012] RPC 102. Lord Neuberger concluded that Kitchin J and the Court of Appeal had applied EPO case law too strictly. Summarising that law (at [107]) he stated that the substance in question was part of a wider family of proteins which were known to have certain effects useful in the control of tumours and which were of interest to the pharmaceutical industry. The invention therefore satisfied Article 57.

thinking point

Consider the relationship between the justifications for patent protection, the objection that something is a mere discovery, and the objection that the patent is not capable of industrial application because it is speculative.

Summary

This chapter has explained:

- the concept of 'an invention' and the statutory list of things which are deemed not to be one;

- the public policy exceptions to patentability; and

- the positive patentability requirements of novelty, inventive step and industrial applicability.

Reflective question

It is time for the law of patents to take into account ethical concerns.
Discuss.

Annotated further reading

Crespi, S. 'Biotechnology Patenting: the Wicked Animal Must Defend Itself' [1995] *EIPR* 431
Explores the arguments concerning whether ethical objections should be taken into account when granting patents.

Crespi, S. 'Patenting and Ethics—a Dubious Connection' (2003) 85 *JPTOS* 31
Revisits the arguments concerning gene patents and ethical concerns.

Drahos, P. 'Biotechnology Patents, Markets and Morality' [1999] *EIPR* 441
Argues that it is vital for patent professionals to take ethical concerns into account.

Norman, H.E. 'Patenting Biotechnology: A Case of Legal Abstentionism?' [2002] *ELM* 278–88
Argues that the concerns about granting biotech patents can be overcome if the patentability criteria are rigorously applied.

O'Sullivan, E. 'Is Article 53(a) EPC Still of Narrow Interpretation?' [2012] *JIPLP* 680

Considers whether the decisions in *WARF/Stem Cells* and *Brüstle v Greenpeace* indicate that Article 53 might be given a broader interpretation in the future.

Parker, S. and England, P. 'Where Now for Stem Cell Patents?' [2012] *JIPLP* 738:

Reviews the decisions in *WARF/Stem Cells* and *Brüstle v Greenpeace*.

Vaver, D. 'Invention in Patent Law: A Review and a Modest Proposal' (2003) 11 *International Journal of Law and Information Technology* 286

Compares statutory provisions dealing with what are 'patentable inventions' in the light of their historical origins and considers whether it is best to define 'an invention' and to prescribe what cannot be patented.

Warren-Jones, A. 'Morally Regulating Innovation: What is "Commercial Exploitation"?' [2008] *IPQ* 193

Considers the meaning of 'commercial exploitation' in relation to biotech patents, concluding that there is a lack of consensus and that Member States will need further guidance.

Infringement of patents

Learning objectives

Upon completion of this chapter, you should have acquired:

- an understanding of the issues raised in a patent infringement action;

- knowledge of the conduct which can infringe a patent under s.60 Patents Act;

- knowledge of the defences and counterclaims which a defendant to a patent infringement action may raise;

- an understanding of the challenge facing a court in interpreting patent claims to see if the defendant's conduct actually falls within the scope of the patentee's monopoly; and

- an appreciation of the role of the Protocol to Article 69 EPC in determining the scope of the patent monopoly.

Introduction

- To the uninitiated, a report of a patent infringement case may seem daunting to read. We therefore provide, by way of introduction, an overview of the issues likely to occur in any patent case, before considering the key points of infringement in law and fact, defences and counterclaims, and the requirement properly to construe the claims of the patent.

6.1 Overview of the issues in a patent infringement action

6.1.1 Patent infringement: practical issues

cross reference
See chapter 2.

Intellectual property actions are assigned by the Senior Courts Act 1981 (previously the Supreme Court Act) to the Patents Court, with an alternative forum being the Intellectual Property Enterprise Court (formerly the Patents County Court). A **claimant** therefore has to decide which of these two courts to use. A further issue (depending on the facts) may be choice of defendant. As a matter of common sense, suing the person or undertaking who made an infringing version of the patented **product** or used the **patented process** would seem the most obvious thing to do, but infringing conduct in respect of **patents** can occur in a number of different ways, so that there can be liability for acts preparatory to **infringement** and for dealing subsequently in infringing products. Further, because infringing conduct must be committed within the territory of the United Kingdom, if the principal act of infringement (that is, manufacture) occurred in another jurisdiction, then it may be necessary to identify other defendants who are within the United Kingdom.

6.1.2 The elements of the case

It may be useful at this stage to separate out the issues normally raised in a patent infringement action. The **patentee** will have to show two things, namely that one or more infringing acts have been committed within the United Kingdom (to borrow from the criminal law, it must be shown that the *actus reus* of infringement has occurred); and, in addition, that the defendant's conduct falls within the scope of protection afforded to the patent, ie within the literal or purposive meaning of the **claims**. These two issues are sometimes called 'infringement in law' and 'infringement in fact'.

By way of response, the defendant to a patent infringement action can raise a number of different arguments. It can deny that the claimant has established the elements of the infringement action by showing that no infringing conduct has been committed, or even if it has, that the defendant's product or process is not within the meaning of the claims. Alternatively, it may be argued that the patent is no longer in force (because the annual **renewal fees** have not been paid), that the claimant has not the standing to sue (because an **assignment** or an exclusive licence has not been recorded on the register), or that one or more of the statutory or case law defences to patent infringement apply. Last, the defendant can counterclaim that the patent is **invalid** and should be **revoked**.

Seeking to attack the **validity** of any registered intellectual property right is regarded as a standard tactic to adopt (and one which increases the cost of intellectual property litigation). In some jurisdictions separate tribunals deal with infringement and validity. For example, in Germany, patent litigation is conducted before District Courts (*Landgerichte*) but patents can only be annulled by the Federal Patent Court. By contrast, United Kingdom courts can deal with a claim to infringement and a request to revoke the right in the same action, therefore any claimant contemplating patent infringement litigation has to be sure (so far as possible) that the patent is safe from counter-attack. The aggressive nature of intellectual property litigation should never be underestimated.

6.1.3 **Possible outcomes**

The claims of any patent play a pivotal role. In relation to patent litigation, the Civil Procedure Rules Part 63 and Practice Direction 63 require a claimant to identify *which* claims have been infringed and how. Likewise, a party seeking a declaration that a patent is invalid must set out clearly the grounds of challenge, which must relate to individual claims. Consequently there are a number of different possible outcomes to a patent infringement action, namely:

- one or more claims are valid and infringed;
- one or more claims are valid but not infringed;
- one or more claims are invalid but had they been valid would have been infringed;
- one or more claims are invalid but had they been valid would not have been infringed.

Further, some claims may be valid whilst others are invalid, and only some claims may have been infringed but not others, so that the above permutations can be multiplied to include partially valid/partially invalid and partially infringed patents! Individual claims in a patent must therefore be treated separately.

thinking point

Does the fact that a court can deal with both infringement and validity at the same time, when coupled with the CPR requirement to identify which claims have been infringed and which are invalid, lead to unnecessary complexity in patent litigation?

6.2 **Categories of infringing acts**

The Patents Act 1977 had a significant effect in relation to patent infringement. It was the first time that any United Kingdom statute had contained a definition of infringing conduct. Previously what amounted to a trespass upon the patentee's monopoly was inferred from the wording of the Royal Grant, which conferred on the patentee the right to 'make, use, exercise and vend the said invention . . . [to] have and enjoy the whole profit and advantage of the said invention . . . and . . . [to] have and enjoy the sole use and exercise and the full benefit of the said invention'. Nevertheless, whether before or after the date of the 1977 Act, it has always been clear that patent infringement had to involve some sort of commercial activity: *British United Shoe Machinery Co v Simon Collier* (1910) 27 RPC 567 at p. 572. An example of what amounts to taking 'the whole profit and advantage of the invention' is *Smith Kline & French Laboratories v Douglas Pharmaceuticals* [1991] FSR 522. The New Zealand Court of Appeal held there was infringement when the defendant imported a sample of the claimant's patented drug CIMETIDINE into New Zealand for the sole purpose of obtaining a product **licence**, which would have enabled the defendant to market the drug once the patent had expired (New Zealand law corresponded to the Patents Act 1949). It was use of the **invention** resulting in a commercial advantage.

6.2.1 **Direct infringement**

6.2.1.1 The origins of s.60

The Patents Act 1977 s.60(1) sets out what conduct is a direct infringement of a patent. At the time of drafting, the wording was based on what was then Article 29 of the Community Patent Convention 1975. In due course this became Article 7 of the draft EU Patent Regulation 2009 although there is no such provision in the **Unitary Patent**. Even though the Convention and Regulation were never implemented, they should always be referred to when attempting to resolve any ambiguity with regard to the wording of the Patents Act: *Smith, Kline & French v Harbottle* [1980] RPC 363. In dealing with the statutory provisions on infringing conduct, defences and **revocation**, we will explain the meaning of the United Kingdom legislation by referring to the wording of the final (2009) version of the stillborn **EU Patent**, but it should be remembered that the Community Patent Convention 1975 was the basis of all the infringement provisions in the Patents Act 1977.

cross reference
See further section 4.3.1.3.

6.2.1.2 The scope of s.60(1)

Both s.60(1) and Article 7 of the EU Patent draw a clear distinction between patents for products and patents for processes. Whether a patent relates to a product (a thing) or a process (how to make something or use something or do something) depends entirely on the wording of the claims. A patent may have all **product claims**, or all **process claims**, or a mixture of both. Under para (a), in respect of product patents, infringing conduct consists of making, disposing, offering to dispose of, using or importing the product or keeping the product for disposal or otherwise. Under para (b), in relation to process patents, there are just two infringing acts, using the process or offering it for use. Section 60(1)(b) includes a requirement of knowledge. However, the wording of the EU Patent makes clear that such knowledge is only to be proved in respect of the act of 'offering for use', but not 'using' the process. The actual wording of Article 7(b) demonstrates the point:

> The EU patent shall confer on its proprietor the right to prevent all third parties not having his/her consent . . . from using a process which is the subject-matter of the patent or, when the third party knows, or it is obvious in the circumstances, that the use of the process is prohibited without the consent of the proprietor of the patent, from offering the process for use within the EU.

The knowledge required under s.60(1)(b) is that use of the process which has been offered to another would infringe. This suggests that the defendant has to have information about the patent in order to know that use of the process by another will infringe. The test is objective, because of the words 'obvious to a reasonable person in the circumstances'. By analogy to similar wording in s.22 CDPA 1988, the defendant's conduct is likely to be compared with that of the reasonable trader in that area of commerce: *LA Gear v Hi-Tec Sports plc* [1992] FSR 121. The inference must be that companies which seek patent protection for their own inventions or who exploit patents as part of their business are expected to familiarise themselves with patented inventions in their line of business by conducting regular searches of the United Kingdom patent database: *Tamglass Ltd Oy v Luoyang North Glass Technology Co Ltd* [2006] FSR 608. Ignorance of the claimant's patent is unlikely to provide an excuse in such circumstances.

Finally, under s.60(1)(c), there are further infringing acts in respect of process patents, namely disposing of, offering to dispose of, using or importing any product obtained directly by means of that process, or keeping any such product whether for disposal or otherwise. It has been held by the House of Lords that the infringement provisions in the Patents Act, together with Article 64(2) **EPC**, provide for protection in respect of products which are directly derived from process patents, which removes the need for a separate category of 'product-by-process' patents. As Lord Hoffmann explained in *Kirin-Amgen Inc v Hoechst Marion Roussel Ltd* [2005] 1 All ER 667 at [90], this type of claim is relatively rare because the **EPO** is reluctant to accept it. The only time when a 'product-by-process' claim will be allowed is where the patent concerns a new substance whose difference from a known substance cannot be described in chemical or physical terms, in which case the process by which it is obtained is an important element of the invention.

As a statutory tort, liability under s.60(1) is strict. Apart from infringement by offering a process for use, the defendant's state of mind is irrelevant as regards liability (*Proctor v Bennis* (1887) 4 RPC 333) although it may have an effect on the award of **damages** or an account of profits. The strict nature of liability for direct patent infringement was stressed by Lord Hoffmann in *Merrell Dow v Norton* [1996] RPC 76 at p. 92. However, one issue which remains to be resolved is whether liability can be strict in relation to inventions which claim a new use of an old product, in accordance with the EPO's decision in *G 2/88 MOBIL III/Friction Reducing Additive* [1990] EPOR 73.

A practical point to remember is that under s.69, based on Article 11 of the EU Patent, a patent infringement action cannot be brought until the patent has been granted. However, once an action is brought, the claim for damages can, provided certain conditions are met, be backdated to the **publication** of the patent application, thereby compensating for acts of infringement committed between the date of publication and the date of **grant**. Publication of a patent application is therefore notice to the world that the invention is the property of the claimant. Section 69 Patents Act 1977 is presented diagrammatically in Diagram 6.1.

Diagram 6.1

Patents Act 1977 s.69

Filing Date	Date of Publication	Date of Grant
←——— Period A ———→	←——— Period B ———→	
1 April 2005	1 October 2006	1 October 2009

Note: Any acts of infringement committed in Period A are not actionable. Damages may be awarded for any acts of infringement committed during Period B, *but* there must be no difference between the patent as published and the patent as granted *and* proceedings can only be started once the patent is granted.

Three other observations can be made about the wording of s.60(1). It requires, first, that the infringing conduct be done without the patentee's consent. Permission to exploit the patent is therefore a complete defence to patent infringement. Next, the section requires that the infringing conduct be committed within the United Kingdom (*Menashe Business Mercantile Ltd v William Hill Organisation Ltd* [2003] RPC 575). Because of the territorial nature of the patent right, conduct occurring in another territory will not infringe a United Kingdom patent. The patentee may well have parallel patent protection in that other jurisdiction, but even so, that will be of no assistance to any United Kingdom litigation. Action against an infringer must be brought in the state which granted the patent right: *Coin Controls Ltd v Suzo International (UK) Ltd* [1997] 3 All ER 45. Lastly, the section requires that the infringing conduct be done 'whilst the patent is in force'. This simply means that the annual renewal fees must have been paid.

6.2.1.3 Key words and phrases

Several key words and phrases in s.60(1) require further elaboration. As explained earlier, where there is any doubt about the meaning of a particular word or phrase, or uncertainty as to whether it changes the previous law, reference should be made to the relevant recitals and wording of the EU Patent: *Smith, Kline & French v Harbottle*.

'Making' and 'Disposing'

At first glance, the word 'makes' appears to need no explanation. However, as the Supreme Court observed in *Schütz (UK) Ltd v Werit UK Ltd* [2013] FSR 395, it does not have a precise meaning; whether an activity amounts to 'making' is a question of fact and degree. Where, as here, the defendant supplied replacement plastic bottles to fit the patented cages of the claimant's intermediate bulk carriers, because the bottles were a subsidiary part of the patented item, there was no infringement.

The word 'disposes' must be understood as involving some sort of commercial dealing. Thus in *United Telephone Co v Sharples* (1885) 2 RPC 28 the purchase of patented equipment was accompanied by a statement that it was intended for export. This was held to be infringement even though the defendant in fact intended the equipment to be used in experiments by school pupils. Similarly, in *British Motor Syndicate v Taylor* (1900) 17 RPC 723, proof of intention to export was held to amount to a disposal.

'Offering to dispose'

The word 'offers' in s.60(1) should not be interpreted in the sense used by the law of contract. In *Dunlop Tyre Co v British & Colonial Motor Co* (1901) 18 RPC 313, the display of the product at an exhibition was held to be an offer, and in *Gerber Garment Technology v Lectra Systems* [1995] RPC 383 it was held that including pictures of the patented equipment in a catalogue amounted to an offer. In particular, (at pp. 411–12) Jacob J stressed that the words 'offer to dispose of' in s.60(1)(a) were not intended to reflect the English law of contract but should be construed purposively to have the effect intended by Article 7 of the EU Patent. Sending details of machinery which infringed a United Kingdom patent by fax to a prospective purchaser has also been held to amount to an offer: *Tamglass Ltd Oy v Luoyang North Glass Technology Co Ltd*.

'Using'

'Use' was considered by the court in *British United Shoe Machinery Co v Simon Collier* to be something more than the mere possession of machine parts which, when assembled, would have infringed the patent, at least in the absence of evidence that it had ever been assembled. The inference must be that 'use' requires some sort of activity over and above possession. The decision should, however, be treated with a degree of caution because today the conduct of the *Collier* case would probably amount to 'keeping'. A more modern example of 'using' comes from the decision in *Merrell Dow v Norton*, where Lord Hoffmann indicated that but for the private use defence, patients who swallowed terfenadine might have committed such an infringing act.

'Keeping for disposal'

The word 'keeps' is a new form of liability. In *Hoffmann-La Roche v Harris* [1977] FSR 200 it was held that the word should be treated as requiring some sort of commercial activity which deprives the patentee of the benefit of the invention. The defendant had imported three batches of a patented drug and had argued that there was no liability for 'keeping' because one batch was for export, one for experimental use, and one was for supply to a compulsory **licensee**. The court held that all three batches infringed. There was possession of the patented product with the intention to trade so as to secure a profit, therefore it mattered not whether the ultimate customer was at home or abroad. Oliver J, however, in *Smith, Kline & French v Harbottle* made clear that 'keeps' is not to extend to the activities of a mere warehouse-keeper or carrier. Referring to the language of Article 7 of the EU Patent (where the equivalent word is 'stocks') he decided that the intention of the legislature was to impose liability for stocking a product with a view to commercial supply, rather than mere possession in the course of one's own business.

'Directly'

The word 'directly' appears in s.60(1)(c) which creates liability for the infringement of a process patent by dealing in products obtained directly from that process, and also in Article 64(2) EPC. The meaning of the word was considered in *Pioneer Electronics Capital Inc v Warner Music Manufacturing Europe GmbH* [1997] RPC 757. The patent was for the processes used to create a master disc as a preliminary to pressing mass-produced compact discs. The defendant denied that its compact discs infringed the patent, as the completed discs were not identical to the master, having undergone three further stages of manufacture and being made of different material. In agreeing with the defendant, the Court of Appeal made extensive reference to German case law on which Article 64(2) was said to have been based, observing that the courts of the Netherlands, Switzerland, Denmark and Austria had also adopted the same approach. The test to be applied was whether the end product retained the essential characteristics of the patented process, in other words, was there 'a loss of identity' between the process and the end product?

6.2.2 Indirect infringement

Besides conferring on a patentee the right to sue those who make and deal in patented products, those who use or offer for use patented processes, and those who deal in the direct products of such processes, the Patents Act 1977 also imposes liability on those who assist the primary infringer. Section 60(2) (based on Article 8 of the EU Patent) declares that supplying the means relating to an essential element of the invention in order to put the invention into effect amounts to indirect infringement. There is an exception in s.60(3) whereby there is no liability if what has been supplied is a staple commercial product, unless the supply or offer of the staple commercial product is made for the purpose of inducing the person supplied to commit an infringing act falling within s.60(1). 'Staple commercial product' was explained in *Nestec SA v Dualit Ltd* [2013] EWHC 923 (Pat) at [182] as being something which is supplied commercially for a variety of uses, of the kind which is needed every day and can be generally obtained, such as nails, screws, bolts and wire. In the instant case, the defendant's coffee capsules had no other use than to fit a limited range of portionised coffee machines.

According to the Court of Appeal in *Grimme Maschinenfabrik GmBH v Scott* [2010] FSR 193, s.60(2) introduces a new form of liability into United Kingdom law and should not be called '**contributory infringement**' as liability does not depend on there having been primary infringement.

The following observations can be made about s.60(2) and (3).

First, the conduct in question (the supply of the essential means) must occur within the United Kingdom (just like any act of direct infringement). It involves behaviour whereby something tangible ('means') is provided or offered to the primary infringer. Second, that tangible something must be an essential element of the invention. Whether something is an essential element will depend on the court's interpretation of the teaching of the patent (*Nestec v Dualit*), as s.60 must be read against the background of s.125, which declares that an invention shall be taken to be as set out in the claims (*Menashe Business Mercantile Ltd v William Hill Organisation Ltd*). Next, the result of the infringing conduct must be that it puts the invention into effect. Quite simply, this means that it makes the invention work. Finally, the provision requires knowledge on the part of the defendant. In contrast to s.60(1)(b), this is not knowledge of the patent, rather it is knowledge that what has been supplied will make the invention work, implying that the defendant has some sort of appreciation of the technology concerned. However, and just like s.60(1)(b), such knowledge is to be determined objectively, as the provision contains the phrase 'or it is obvious to a reasonable person in the circumstances that those means are suitable for putting, and are and intended to put, the invention into effect'. Again, therefore, the defendant's behaviour will be measured against the yardstick of the reasonable trader in that area of commerce.

cross reference
*See further
section 5.5.7.*

6.2.2.1 Two examples of contributory infringement

case close-up

Merrell Dow v Norton [1996] RPC 76

One example of where the defendant was alleged to have committed contributory infringement is *Merrell Dow v Norton*. Here the patentee had discovered that the subject matter of its first patent, terfenadine, when swallowed by a patient, was turned into an acid metabolite by the patient's liver. Accordingly, a second patent for the acid metabolite was obtained. The patentee then sued the defendant, another pharmaceutical company, under s.60(2). The argument was that by supplying terfenadine to patients (the original terfenadine patent had by now expired) the defendant was supplying the means essential for them to make the acid metabolite in their bodies, this being the substance claimed by the second patent. Despite the fact that the patients themselves had not committed infringement (because of the private use defence in s.60(5)(a)), the defendant would still have been liable (because of the specific wording of s.60(6)) for providing something which put the invention, the subject matter of the second patent, into effect, had it not successfully sought the revocation of the second patent on the ground of **anticipation**.

case close-up

Menashe Business Mercantile Ltd v William Hill Organisation Ltd [2003] RPC 575

· ·

A second example of contributory infringement can be found in *Menashe Business Mercantile Ltd v William Hill Organisation Ltd*. The patent was for a gaming system, involving a host computer, a terminal computer, a communication means between them and a program for operating the terminal computer. The defendant bookmaker had supplied its customers with a program on CD-ROM which effectively turned their home computers into the terminal required in the patentee's system and enabled them to participate in online gaming. The defendant denied infringement because its host computer was located outside the United Kingdom. The Court of Appeal held that the defendant was liable under s.60(2). It had supplied the CDs which were suitable for putting the invention, ie the gaming apparatus, into effect, because punters could use the gaming system in the United Kingdom.

thinking point

Consider the impact which EU law has had on the way in which a patent can be infringed when compared with the position under the Statute of Monopolies.

6.2.3 Choice of defendant: s.60 in action

It will have become apparent from our discussion of s.60 Patents Act 1977 that patent infringement may be committed before, during and after manufacture. We set this out diagrammatically in Diagram 6.2:

Diagram 6.2

Timeline of a patent infringement

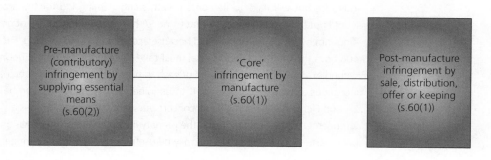

Pre-manufacture (contributory) infringement by supplying essential means (s.60(2))

'Core' infringement by manufacture (s.60(1))

Post-manufacture infringement by sale, distribution, offer or keeping (s.60(1))

Whilst at first glance the principal defendant ought to be someone who makes an infringing product or uses an infringing process, there may well be liability for others who supply essential ingredients or those who deal in the infringing product subsequently. Choice of defendant ultimately is one for the patentee to make, on the advice of lawyers, but two simple examples will illustrate the breadth of the provisions in the Act.

6.2.3.1 Example 1: manufacture within the United Kingdom

Imagine that a pharmaceutical company, Omnifarm plc, owns a United Kingdom product patent for a new antibiotic, Cuprocillin. The product has two key ingredients, copper sulphate (a chemical known for many years and which is readily available) and vandalite, a relatively new compound which is difficult to make. Omnifarm has discovered that Fleming Ltd has made the identical drug without permission and has then supplied the drug to GenPharm Ltd, a wholesaler. GenPharm Ltd has in turn supplied Cuprocillin to Shoes plc, a chain of chemists' shops, and Mercia Hospital. Fleming Ltd obtained its supplies of copper sulphate from April and its supplies of vandalite from June, who is the only United Kingdom manufacturer of the ingredient. The hospital has been administering the drug to its patients.

Potentially, Fleming Ltd, GenPharm Ltd, Shoes plc, the hospital, April and June could all be defendants to infringement proceedings. Fleming Ltd is, of course, the prime target, having made the patented product. As regards those liable for post-manufacture acts of infringement, GenPharm Ltd and Shoes plc have kept the product and have also disposed of it. Further, Shoes plc can be said to have offered to dispose of the product if it is on display in its shops, even if it has not actually sold any. The hospital could be alleged to have infringed by using the product in the treatment of its patients, although the patients themselves (who might equally be said to have infringed by using the product) will have the defence of private use. April and June may have committed contributory infringement by supplying Fleming Ltd with the essential means of putting the invention into effect. April, however, is likely to have the defence of having supplied a staple commercial product. Vandalite, however, would not be a staple commercial product, although Omnifarm plc will have to show that June had the requisite knowledge for contributory infringement. As she is the only United Kingdom manufacturer of the ingredient, meeting the objective standard of s.60(2) should not be a problem.

6.2.3.2 Example 2: manufacture outside the United Kingdom

An alternative scenario might be that Cuprocillin has been made in France by Curie SA and then imported into the United Kingdom by Fleming Ltd for supply to the other parties as in our first example. In this case the act of manufacture will not have been committed within the jurisdiction. Unless Omnifarm plc has a French patent, it can do nothing to stop manufacture in France but will have to be content with suing Fleming Ltd for the act of importation. It would not be possible to allege that Curie SA has 'offered to dispose of goods' in the United Kingdom by supplying Fleming Ltd because according to *Kalman v PCL Packaging* [1982] FSR 406 both the offer and the disposal must take place in the United Kingdom. However, in the second example, should the claimant wish to pursue Curie SA as the originator of the infringing goods, it may be possible for it to be joined as defendant if it can be proved that Curie SA and Fleming Ltd had acted in concert pursuant to a 'common design' which resulted in infringement. The argument that the primary infringer and a United Kingdom importer have been parties to a common design may be useful where a primary infringer is located outside the United Kingdom, but a company based within the jurisdiction arranges for them to make the infringing product. However, the mere supply of infringing goods to a United Kingdom purchaser is not enough for this type of liability. 'Each person must make the infringing acts his own': *Sabaf SpA v Meneghetti* [2003] RPC 264 at [58].

6.2.3.3 Adding other defendants

The Court of Appeal has held in *Unilever v Gillette* [1989] RPC 583 that it is possible to join a United Kingdom company's foreign parent company as a co-defendant if the two have acted in concert, although financial and voting control on their own are not enough (*Unilever v Chefaro Proprietaries Ltd* [1994] FSR 135). The court added (following the House of Lords' decision in relation to **copyright** infringement in *CBS v Amstrad* [1988] AC 1013) that where someone *procures* the infringement of a patent, this leads to liability as a joint tortfeasor with the *specific* primary infringer of the patent, although there can be no separate liability for *generally* inciting the commission of patent infringement. Finally, *Evans v Spritebrand* [1985] FSR 267, although a copyright infringement case, is generally taken to be authority for the proposition that a director can be personally liable for acts of patent infringement carried out by the company if he (or she) has personally and deliberately participated in the carrying out of the infringing acts. Such personal liability would result in the director becoming a joint tortfeasor with the company.

6.2.3.4 Conclusion

Omnifarm plc will have to decide whether it is worthwhile suing all of these parties. Clearly, it will be most efficient to stop the source of manufacture of the infringing product, so where this occurs in the United Kingdom, Fleming Ltd is likely to be the first defendant to any infringement action. Where manufacture occurs abroad, then it is the importer who is likely to be sued first, with the manufacturer remaining out of reach unless it is possible to prove a common design. One thing which Omnifarm will need to consider is whether in terms of good public relations it is wise to sue a major wholesaler, a major retailer and a hospital for patent infringement. It will also need to reflect on whether any potential defendant is worth suing, ie do they have the ability to pay damages.

6.3 Statutory and case law defences

The most obvious response to an action for patent infringement is for the defendant to say 'but I didn't infringe'. Such a denial may entail several quite separate arguments: a plea that no infringing act within the wording of s.60(1) has been committed; that what has been done is not within the monopoly claimed by the claimant's patent (which will require the court to construe the patent); or that the defendant is protected by one or more of the various exceptions and defences provided by case law and statute. Any such defence should be clearly distinguished from the alternative strategy of counterclaiming that the patent is invalid and liable to be revoked. Revocation and construction are considered later in the chapter. The statutory and case law exceptions to infringement will now be considered in turn. The majority of these defences presuppose that infringing conduct has in fact been committed, but that the defendant should be exonerated in the interests of fairness.

6.3.1 **Defences derived from EU law**

The Patents Act 1977 sets out a number of defences to patent infringement. Some of these were previously known in United Kingdom law, but are given a statutory basis for the first time. These defences were found in Articles 9 to 12 of the EU Patent, are concerned to strike a fair balance between the patentee and third parties, but apply only in specific circumstances.

6.3.1.1 Private not commercial purposes

Section 60(5)(a) provides that an act done for private not commercial purposes is not infringement. Aldous J in *Smith, Kline & French v Evans* [1989] FSR 513 suggested that the test is subjective. 'Private' should be contrasted with 'public' and thus means something done for one's personal use rather than something done secretly. This is, however, subject to the overriding requirement that the conduct in question must not be done for a commercial purpose. Aldous J added that experiments done in order to conduct legal proceedings (for example, challenging the validity of a patent) fall within the scope of the defence.

6.3.1.2 Experimental purposes

Section 60(5)(b) provides that an act done for experimental purposes *relating to the subject matter of the invention* is likewise not to be treated as infringement. This is a long-established exception, first recognised in *Frearson v Loe* (1878) 9 Ch D 48 at p. 66 where it was said that 'patent rights were never granted to prevent persons of ingenuity exercising their talents in a fair way'. Hence, the manufacture of patented articles without a licence simply for the purpose of *bona fide* experiments does not give rise to liability. By contrast, in *Monsanto v Stauffer Chemical* [1985] RPC 515, field trials of a herbicide conducted with a view to obtaining safety clearance from two non-statutory, non-regulatory bodies (the Pesticides Safety Precaution Scheme and the Agricultural Chemicals Advisory Scheme) were held outside the exemption, the defendant's case probably not being helped by the fact that it had also proposed trials by a Government Department, the Forestry Commission and various water authorities.

As Aldous J pointed out in *Smith, Kline & French v Evans*, the wording of s.60(5)(b) requires the experiments to be done for purposes 'relating to the subject matter of the invention'. Such subject matter has to be determined by the claims of the patent. In *Smith, Kline & French v Evans* itself, this meant that experiments carried out on goods which were the subject matter of one patent with a view to challenging a separate but related patent were not protected by this defence. Similarly, in *Corevalve Inc v Edwards Lifesciences AG* [2009] FSR 367, Peter Prescott QC pointed out that s.60(5)(b) Patents Act does not allow the patented invention to be used for experimental acts relating to a different invention. Here the defendant's device for an artificial heart valve was different. Applying *Monsanto v Stauffer* and the German decision in *Klinische Versuche (Clinical Trials) I* [1997] RPC 623, where, as here, the defendant had mixed purposes (developing confidence in its product by the professionals who would use it, building up technical data through the use of its device in hospitals, and generating revenue) it was necessary to determine what was the preponderant purpose. It could not be said that data gathering was the predominant purpose so, had the defendant's device infringed, the experimental use defence would not have been available.

6.3.1.3 Extemporaneous preparation of prescriptions

Section 60(5)(c) enables the extemporaneous preparation in a pharmacy of a medicine prescribed by a doctor or dentist to be exempt from liability, for the obvious policy reason of protecting health-care professionals in the conduct of their practice.

6.3.1.4 Vehicles, ships and aircraft temporarily or accidentally within the territory of the United Kingdom

Sections 60(5)(d), (e) and (f) exempt from liability the use of a patented product or process which forms part of any vehicle, ship or aircraft temporarily or accidentally within the United Kingdom jurisdiction. The word 'temporarily' was considered by the Court of Appeal in *Stena Rederi Aktiebolag v Irish Ferries Ltd* [2003] RPC 681, a case which concerned a ferry travelling between Eire and the United Kingdom. It was said that 'temporarily' meant 'for a limited period of time'. The frequency, persistency and regularity of the visits were irrelevant.

6.3.1.5 Farmer's privilege

Sections 60(5)(g) and (h) were inserted into the Patents Act 1977 as part of the United Kingdom's implementation of Directive 98/44/EC of the European Parliament and of the Council of 6 July 1998 on the legal protection of biotechnological inventions [1998] OJ L 213/13. The defences apply where there is use by a farmer of the product of his harvest for propagation or multiplication by him on his own holding of previously purchased plant propagating material, or where there is use by a farmer of an animal or animal reproductive material for agricultural purposes following a sale by the patentee to the farmer of breeding stock or other animal reproductive material. The defence assumes that the farmer has legitimately acquired a patented animal or plant from the patentee. It only operates where the farmer uses the next generation of plants or animals for his own farming activities and not where the farmer undertakes further commercialisation of such items.

6.3.1.6 Prior use

The defence of **prior use** is set out in s.64 Patents Act 1977, as amended by the CDPA 1988 Sch. 5 para 17. The equivalent provision in the EU Patent is Article 12.

The wording of s.64 is precise. The use in question must be in the United Kingdom and must have been started before the **priority date** of the patent. Further, the defendant must act in good faith. If these conditions are met, then where the defendant does an act which would infringe the patent were it in force, or makes effective and serious preparation to do such an act, then they have the right to continue to do such an act. Any product which is the subject of the prior use can be disposed of without liability. However, the right is personal to the defendant, who may not license another to perform the act of prior use.

Section 64 was accorded a very narrow interpretation by the Court of Appeal in *Lubrizol Corp v Esso Petroleum Ltd* [1998] RPC 727, building on the earlier decision in *Helitune Ltd v Stewart Hughes Ltd* [1991] FSR 171. The defendant had, before the priority date of the claimant's patent, manufactured a batch of the patented substance in the United States (ie outside the United Kingdom) and had imported some samples into the United Kingdom so that it could be tested by potential customers. It was held that the key feature of s.64 was the word 'act' rather than the prior existence of the infringing product. The act here was one of importation, not manufacture. The defendant could have continued to import the substance, but was not at liberty to commence making the infringing product. Further, although it had held internal discussions about setting up a manufacturing plant in the United Kingdom before the priority date, no decision had been taken about the location of the plant, so there had not been 'effective and serious preparations' to make the product.

cross reference
See section 5.5.

The role of s.64 in permitting the defendant to continue what would otherwise be infringing conduct has to be understood in the context of s.2 and the way it changed the law on **novelty**. Section 64 contemplates that the prior use in question was not such as to amount to an **enabling disclosure**, otherwise the patent would be invalidated (*Merrell Dow v Norton*). The section therefore applies only to conduct which is uninformed use.

6.3.2 **Case law defences**

In addition to the statutory defences outlined in the previous section, there are a number of other arguments to which a defendant may have recourse.

6.3.2.1 Exhaustion of rights

At one time, the Patents Act 1977 contained a provision, s.60(4), setting out the defence of **exhaustion of rights**, a defence relevant to the infringing act of importation and any subsequent dealings in the imported goods. The section was never activated (being dependent on the implementation of the EU Patent) and was deleted by the Patents Act 2004. However, the lack of activation can be considered academic. The jurisprudence of the European Court of Justice on the meaning of Articles 34 and 36 of the **Treaty on the Functioning of the European Union ('TFEU')** has established when a patentee can or cannot object to the importation of goods which technically infringe the patent. Because of the supremacy of EU law, the case law of the Court must prevail over any rule, statutory or otherwise, of domestic law (Case 106/77 *Simmenthal v Italian Finance Ministry* [1978] ECR 629, Case C-213/89 *Factortame Ltd v Secretary of State for Transport* [1990] ECR I-2433), so the defence will still be available in the appropriate circumstances, that is, where a patented product has been imported into the United Kingdom. The Unitary Patent contains, in Article 6, the standard exhaustion of rights provision.

The defence of exhaustion of rights will be examined in detail in the context of **trade mark** infringement in chapter 16, but for the purpose of its role in a patent infringement action, the case law can be summarised as follows.

The difference between infringing and parallel imports

The crucial question to be determined in any case is whether the imports to which the patentee objects are **infringing imports** or **parallel imports**.

Infringing imports are those which originated from an unconnected third party, such as a competitor or (more usually) someone seeking to make pirated copies of the patentee's goods. Such was the scenario in Case 24/67 *Parke Davis v Probel* [1968] ECR 55, where the claimants were relying on their Dutch pharmaceutical patent to prevent the importation into the Netherlands of goods made in Italy. The case was, however, argued on the basis of the competition law provisions (Articles 101 and 102 TFEU) owing to the lengthy transitional period accorded to Article 34 TFEU. The ruling of the ECJ was therefore concerned with whether the ownership of a patent placed the patentee in a dominant position which was abused by its seeking to prevent the importation of goods from another Member State (the answer to this was 'no'). Nevertheless, the outcome of *Parke Davis* would be the same today if it were decided under the free movement of goods provision in the TFEU. The derogation in Article 36 TFEU which permits Member States to restrict the free movement of goods in order to protect '**industrial and commercial property**' will always enable a patentee to keep infringing imports out of its territory. This is because the 'specific subject matter' of the patent right is the right to put the goods into circulation for the first time anywhere in the **EEA** and this subject matter is harmed if the patentee is unable to object to the importation of what are essentially counterfeit goods (see Case C-317/91 *Deutsche Renault AG v Audi AG* [1993] ECR I-6227, a case on the rights of the trade mark owner but equally applicable to patents).

However, where the goods are parallel imports (that is, goods first marketed in another EEA Contracting State which can be traced back to the patentee in some way, whether through a parent/subsidiary relationship, a licence, or a chain of contracts), then Article 36 TFEU gives way to Article 34. The principle of the free movement of goods prevails over the interests of the intellectual property owner. Thus, according to Case 15/74 *Centrafarm BV v Sterling Drug* [1974] ECR 1147, the patentee in Member State A (in this case the Netherlands) could not use its patent right to prevent the importation of goods put in circulation in the EU by a subsidiary company in Member State B (the United Kingdom), as the sale of the goods in the United Kingdom by the subsidiary was deemed to exhaust the patentee's rights. The parallel importer was thus free to exploit price differentials between the two Member States, thereby introducing an element of price competition for the patentee in the latter's own territory.

The issue of consent to marketing

In determining whether exhaustion has occurred, the key factor is whether the patentee (either personally or through a subsidiary or licensee) consented to the sale of the patented product somewhere in the EEA, not whether the Member State where this first sale occurred granted the patentee protection. In Case 187/80 *Merck v Stephar* [1981] ECR 2063, the ECJ held that the patentee could not use its patent rights in the Netherlands to prevent the importation from Italy of drugs which it had marketed there. The fact that at the time Italy did not grant patent protection for pharmaceuticals was irrelevant, as the patentee had deliberately chosen to market the goods somewhere in the EU and so had to take the consequences. The facts of the case were the opposite of those in *Parke Davis* (the goods in *Merck* had originated with the patentee, rather than having been made by a counterfeiter) and were mirrored in Cases C-267/95 *Merck v Primecrown* and C-268/95 *Beecham v Europharm* [1996] ECR I-6285. Here the patentees were trying to rely on their United Kingdom patents to prevent the importation of goods from Spain and Portugal. The ECJ declared that the fact that the Member States of export did not (at the time) grant patent protection for pharmaceuticals was irrelevant. The patentees had chosen to market their products in those countries regardless of any return on their investment. This consent to marketing exhausted any rights they might have had in the United Kingdom.

Consent to marketing is assessed on a factual basis, so that where the patentee has been forced to grant a **compulsory licence** in Member State A, that does *not* exhaust its rights, and the patent can be relied on to prevent importation into Member State B of goods made by another undertaking under the compulsory licence: Case 19/84 *Pharmon v Hoechst* [1985] ECR 2281.

6.3.2.2 Licence to repair

It used to be said that someone who purchased a patented article had the right to repair that article, as long as the repair was not so extensive that it resulted in a new article being made. The principle was established in *Sirdar v Wallington* (1907) 24 RPC 539, and an example of the application of the defence can be found in *Solar Thompson v Barton* [1977] RPC 537. Here, the claimant had supplied a conveyor system to a factory. The system contained pulleys with special rubber linings which were the subject matter of a patent belonging to the claimant. When the linings wore out, the factory owner arranged for the defendant to make some replacements. The Court of Appeal held that the purchaser of the equipment had an implied licence to repair it, and that such licence included the right to have the repairs carried out by a third party.

The extent of the so-called 'defence' was considered by the House of Lords in *United Wire Ltd v Screen Repair Services (Scotland) Ltd* [2000] 4 All ER 353. The patents related to mesh screens used in sifting machines deployed in the oil exploration industry. The screens were used to remove solids from drilling fluid and had a relatively short life, the mesh lasting from a few hours to a few days. The frames to which the mesh screens were bonded were often still serviceable. The defendants carried on a screen repair business. They cleaned and recoated the frame made by the claimant, and fitted new meshes. The defendants argued, *inter alia*, that the repaired screens did not fall within the wording of any of the claims of the patents but, if they did, their acts were merely non-infringing repairs because the patentee had impliedly licensed anyone who acquired a screen assembly to prolong its life by repair. The House of Lords considered that the sale of a patented article could not confer an implied licence to make another. Instead, the repair of a patented product was by definition an act which did not amount to making it. Repair was one of the concepts (like modifying or adapting) which shared a boundary with 'making' but did not trespass on its territory. The notion of an implied licence to repair distracted attention from the question raised by s.60(1)(a) of the Patents Act 1977, namely whether the defendant had *made* the patented product. The owner's right to repair was not an independent right conferred on him by an express or implied licence, rather it was a residual right, forming part of the right to do whatever did not amount to making the product. *United Wire Screen*, however, was later distinguished by the Supreme Court in *Schütz (UK) Ltd v Werit UK Ltd*: here the defendant's conduct in replacing a part which easily wore out was not 'making'. The implication must be that the implied licence defence can still be raised.

6.3.2.3 That the infringement is 'not novel'

The last case law defence neatly illustrates the 'culture' of United Kingdom patent law, in that it involves the intersection of infringement and validity, and the fact that both issues depend on the interpretation of the claims of the patent. The defence is called 'the *Gillette* defence' after the case which first established it, *Gillette Safety Razor Co v Anglo-American Trading Co* (1913) 30 RPC 465. Close examination of the case shows that this is not so much a defence, rather it is a way of pleading which places the patentee (in the words of Lord Moulton) 'on the horns of a dilemma'.

case close-up

Gillette Safety Razor Co v Anglo-American Trading Co (1913) 30 RPC 465

The patent was for improvements to the safety razor, the main feature being that a thin flexible razor blade was clamped in a curved holder by the handle, the effect of the clamp being to make the blade rigid. The alleged infringement by the defendant consisted of a similar razor, the blade of which was flat. The defendant pointed out the existence of a prior American patent which involved the use of the handle acting as a clamp to hold the razor blade. He then argued that either he had not infringed (because what he had produced, a flat razor blade, was not within the claims which referred only to curved blades) or that what he had done was not novel because the only difference between his razor and the earlier patent was that his razor had a thinner blade, which could still be fitted to the handle of the American razor. Lord Moulton found for the defendant, and welcomed the method of arguing the case because it could save time and trouble. The defendant had to succeed either on invalidity or non-infringement. If the claims of the patent were interpreted widely, so as to catch what the defendant had done, the patent would be invalid because it was anticipated by the **prior art**. On the other hand, if the claimant argued for a narrow construction of the patent so as to avoid the prior art, the defendant's conduct would fall outside the monopoly claimed. The patentee could not have it both ways.

The 'heads I win, tails you lose' effect is sometimes known as the 'squeeze' argument. The effect of the *Gillette* defence can be shown diagrammatically: see Diagram 6.3.

Diagram 6.3

'The Gillette *defence'*

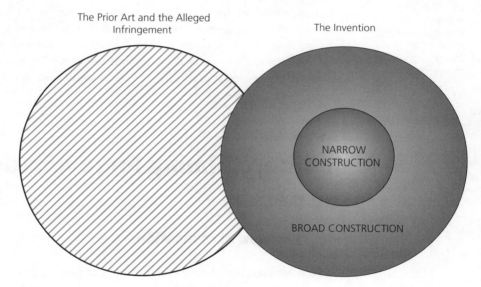

The Prior Art and the Alleged Infringement

The Invention

NARROW CONSTRUCTION

BROAD CONSTRUCTION

Notes:

If a narrow construction is adopted, the patent is valid but not infringed.

If a broad construction is adopted, the patent covers the alleged infringement but equally is invalidated by the prior art.

The exact limit of the *Gillette* defence needs to be understood. This was explained by Lord Evershed MR in *Page v Brent Toy Products* (1950) 67 RPC 4 at p. 11. He stated that *Gillette* is not a separate defence. Rather it is a convenient brief form of raising by way of the pleadings the whole of the defendant's case, but only where the defendant is able to raise as alternatives the pleas of non-infringement and **invalidity**. In the instant case, the *Gillette* argument was not available because under the law in force at the time, the patent for children's building blocks could not be challenged as the novelty-destroying prior art was to be found in a previous patent **specification** more than 50 years old.

6.3.3 **Restriction on the availability of damages**

Section 62 of the Patents Act 1977, rather than providing the alleged infringer with a true defence, restricts the patentee's right to claim damages in three circumstances. Under s.62(1), damages (and also an **account of profits**) are not available against the innocent defendant, but as pointed out by Lloyd Jacob J in *Wilbec v Dawes* [1966] RPC 513, the onus is on the defendant to prove such innocence objectively. The wording of the section includes the phrase 'he was not aware and had no reasonable grounds for supposing that a patent existed' and so the defendant will be judged by the standard of others in that industry (*LA Gear v Hi-Tec Sports plc*). In this case the defence of innocence failed anyway, as the defendant's attention had been drawn to the patent application in earlier correspondence. Section 62(1) goes on to provide, in effect, that in order to ensure knowledge on the part of the defendant, it is not enough merely to mark the goods 'patented': the patent number should also be given.

Section 62(2) confers on the court the discretion to refuse to award damages in respect of any acts of infringement committed during the period when the patentee had failed to pay the annual renewal fees. Finally, there is a discretion in s.62(3) to refuse the award of damages in respect of infringing acts committed before the patent specification was amended, unless the court is satisfied that the original patent specification was drafted in good faith and with reasonable skill and knowledge. The provision therefore contemplates that the defendant has sought revocation of the patent as a counterclaim to infringement, in response to which the patentee has applied to amend it in order to avoid a conflict with the prior art. It also assumes that the defect in the patent is curable by **amendment** and that the infringement action succeeded.

thinking point
Do the various statutory and case law defences strike an adequate balance between the needs of the patentee and those of third parties?

166

6.4

Counterclaiming for revocation of the patent

6.4.1 **Overview of revocation**

In addition to raising one of more of the statutory or case law defences outlined earlier, a defendant to a patent infringement action may attempt instead to have the patent declared invalid. Tactically speaking, having the patent revoked is by far the most effective response as its retrospective removal from the register means that there is nothing to infringe. Nevertheless, the onus will be on the defendant to substantiate the counterclaim. The patentee can of course resist the application to revoke by seeking to show the patent is valid, but equally can seek to amend the patent so as to overcome the objections. The deployment of expert evidence by both parties of necessity increases the cost and complexity of patent litigation. Revocation may be total or partial (so the court may delete some claims whilst leaving others).

cross reference
See further section 2.5.

Section 74 Patents Act 1977 sets out when a patent may be challenged. The validity of the patent may be put in issue in infringement proceedings, in a **threats action** under s.70, in proceedings for a declaration of non-infringement under s.71, in revocation proceedings before the court or **Comptroller** under s.72, or in any dispute as to Crown use. The Comptroller also has power to revoke of his own initiative under s.73. There is no requirement of standing, so that any person can apply: *Cairnstores Ltd v AB Hassle* [2002] FSR 95. The applicant need not have a commercial interest in pursuing such action: *TNS Group Holdings Ltd v Nielsen Media Research Inc* [2009] FSR 873.

6.4.2 **Grounds for revocation**

The grounds for revocation are to be found in s.72(1) Patents Act 1977, as amended by the CDPA 1988 Sch. 5. The equivalent provision in the EU Patent is Article 28. The five grounds are that (a) what has been granted is not a patentable invention under s.1; (b) the patent has been granted to the wrong person under s.7; (c) the **description** of the invention is **insufficient** for the purposes of s.14; (d) there has been an impermissible amendment which broadens the description of the invention; and (e) there has been an impermissible amendment which has extended the scope of the claims. Section 72 is a self-contained provision which excludes any consideration of the previous law or any other objection to the patent, owing to the presence of the phrase 'but only on' in the opening words of the provision: *Genentech Inc's Patent* [1989] RPC 147; *Mentor v Hollister* [1991] FSR 557.

The grounds of revocation most likely to be encountered are lack of **patentability** (which raises all the issues found in s.1 Patents Act 1977, particularly novelty and **inventive step**) and **insufficiency**. Two of the grounds of revocation require further discussion.

6.4.2.1 Grant to the wrong person

Despite the apparent breadth of wording of s.72(1)(b), the ability to revoke a patent on the basis of wrongful entitlement is considerably curtailed. Section 72(2) provides that the application to revoke can only be made by a person who is themselves entitled to be granted the patent (that is, a co-inventor or the inventor's employer) and further, that such an application must be brought within two years of the date of grant of the patent. Section 72(1)(b) should be seen as part of a family of measures dealing with entitlement disputes, in particular ss.8 and 37 Patents Act 1977. In *Yeda Research & Development Co Ltd v Rhone-Poulenc Rorer* [2008] RPC 1 the House of Lords said that the only question under these two provisions is 'who came up with the inventive concept?' (either solely or jointly). Questions of entitlement and novelty were to be kept separate, so that the earlier decisions in *Markem v Zipher* [2005] RPC 761 and *IDA Ltd v Southampton University* [2006] RPC 567 which had held that there had to be a **breach of confidence** or a breach of contract should be overruled. The same reasoning must logically apply to s.72.

6.4.2.2 Insufficiency

One debate which has occurred concerns the precise relationship between revocation for insufficiency and s.14. It was initially uncertain whether s.72(1)(c) empowered the court to act only where the description of the invention was unclear, or whether the power extended to where the claims of the patent were broader than the description (under the 1949 Act, this was called lack of support or unfair basis, a ground of revocation no longer expressly stated in the current statute). In other words, can s.72(1)(c) be used to strike down overly broad claims?

The initial response of the Court of Appeal in *Chiron v Organon (No 12)* [1996] FSR 153 was to say that s.72(1)(c) was confined to revocation for lack of clarity in the description. If the claims in the patent were too broad, that is, the monopoly contained within them exceeded the description of the invention, that was a matter for the **United Kingdom Intellectual Property Office ('UKIPO')** to deal with at the application stage, but if it did not, then there could not be a subsequent challenge to the breadth of the claims. However, the House of Lords in *Biogen v Medeva* [1997] RPC 1 took a different approach, saying that if the patentee had claimed protection for matter not set out in the description, then that could be challenged after grant by third parties under s.72(1)(c). That led some judges and writers to suggest that there were in fact two types of insufficiency, namely 'classical' insufficiency (failure to explain the invention to the **skilled addressee**) and '*Biogen*' insufficiency (failure of the claims to match the description). The matter was initially resolved by Aldous LJ in *Kirin-Amgen Inc and others v Hoechst Marion Roussel Ltd and others* [2003] RPC 31, at [71] where he said:

> [the specification must enable the invention to be performed] to the full extent of the monopoly claimed. If the invention discloses a principle capable of general application, the claims may be in correspondingly general terms. The patentee need not show that he has proved its application in every individual instance. On the other hand, if the claims include a number of discrete methods or products, the patentee must enable the invention to be performed in respect of each of them.

Since then, the matter has been revisited by the House of Lords in *H Lundbeck A/S v Generics (UK) Ltd* [2009] RPC 407. Lord Neuberger at [93] (with whom Lord Walker agreed) analysed what Lord Hoffmann had said in *Biogen*. The issue was not whether the claimed invention could deliver the goods, but whether the claims covered other ways in which they might be delivered, ways which owed nothing to the teaching of the patent or any principle it disclosed. In *Biogen*, the disputed claim was very unusual because the molecule was identified partly by the way in which it had been made and partly by what it did. The patent disclosed one way in which the DNA fragments could produce Hepatitis B antigens but the claim covered other ways. The decision to revoke the patent in *Biogen* for insufficiency was entirely in accord with what the EPO had said in *T 409/91 EXXON/Fuel Oils* [1994] EPOR 149. The patent in the instant case was entirely different from the 'very unusual' nature of that in *Biogen*, as it was a 'straightforward' claim to a single chemical product.

In other words, the ability to revoke a patent for overly broad claims depends on whether the claims correspond with the description. A general description can have general claims; but detailed claims require a correspondingly detailed description. Much depends, of course, on the identity of the skilled addressee and what is held to be within their **common general knowledge**.

Where a defendant raises both lack of inventive step and insufficiency as grounds of revocation there is another type of 'squeeze' argument to trap the patentee. If it is alleged that the invention is obvious because the skilled addressee would as a matter of course be able to reach the same point as the invention by relying on the prior art and/or their common general knowledge, then the patentee may respond by saying that the prior art did not contain enough of a signpost (as suggested by Sachs LJ in *General Tire v Firestone* [1972] RPC 457) to guide the reader of the patent. The defendant's rejoinder could then well be that if the prior art did not contain enough information to point the way to the later invention, then the patentee has assumed too much knowledge on the part of the skilled addressee who would be unable to perform the invention from the description found in the specification: *Schering-Plough Ltd v Norbrook Laboratories Ltd* [2006] FSR 302.

thinking point

Is there really a separate ground of challenge known as Biogen *insufficiency*? If so, how does it fit in with the justifications for patent protection and the requirement that an invention must be capable of **industrial application**?

6.5 The scope of the patentee's monopoly

6.5.1 The problem identified: variants

As indicated at the start of this chapter, a key part of the claimant's case is to show that what the defendant has done falls within the wording of the claims of the patent. In other words, the defendant has trespassed on the 'territory' marked out by the claims. However, a defendant will rarely commit what is called 'textual' infringement by producing something that is an 'exact match' of the invention. Rather, there will be differences between the alleged infringing product or process and what is set out in the wording of the claims. These differences are called '**variants**'.

When faced with such variants, the task before the court involves two stages. First, it is necessary to construe the patent by allocating a meaning to the claims. Interpreting words is a notoriously subjective activity and may be further complicated if the defendant is arguing that the patent is invalid because of prior art. The same interpretation of the claims applies for both validity and infringement: the patentee cannot have it both ways. Much will depend on the sort of words used by the claimant (or rather, the patent attorney who drafted the claims) in asserting what was considered to be unique about the invention. Are those words general and descriptive, or specific and technical? In respect of words with specific meanings, has the patentee provided their own definition, or does such definition have to be gleaned from a dictionary? A further factor is that the specification is addressed to the hypothetical skilled addressee, whose identity and attributes will be determined by the court. The patent specification will have been drafted, in all probability, by someone who by training is a scientist or engineer, not a lawyer. It will then be subjected to minute examination by lawyers in the Chancery Division of the High Court. Opportunities for strange results abound.

Once a meaning has been allocated to the claims, the second stage of the inquiry is to decide whether the alleged infringement falls within the scope of the claimant's invention. The claimant will seek to convince the court that it does, the defendant will, of course, try to argue that it does not.

6.5.2 The law on patent claim interpretation before 1982

It is often said that the traditional approach to the allocation of meaning to patent claims under United Kingdom law was literal interpretation. Claims (rather like a map in a conveyance of land) were treated as marking the outer limit of the patentee's protection. They were treated as 'fence-posts'. This flows from a somewhat well-worn statement by Lord Russell in *EMI v Lissen* (1939) 56 RPC 23 at p. 39 to the effect that 'what is not claimed is disclaimed'. However, the court would not apply a strict literal interpretation where this would produce a manifestly foolish result or deprive the patentee of all protection: *Henricksen v Tallon* [1965] RPC 434.

Whether variants infringed *used* to be determined by the 'pith and marrow doctrine' or the doctrine of 'mechanical equivalents'. In order to infringe the defendant must have taken the 'pith and marrow' of the invention by incorporating all the essential **integers** in the alleged infringement (an integer is an element of a claim). If such integers, being the 'substance' of the invention, were present, it did not matter if other, non-essential, integers had 'mechanical equivalents' substituted for them. The 'pith and marrow' doctrine can be traced to the judgments of Parker J in *Marconi v British Radio Telegraph & Telephone Co* (1911) 28 RPC 181 at p. 217 and Lord Evershed in *Birmingham Sound Reproductions v Collaro* [1956] RPC 232 at p. 245.

Cases applying the 'pith and marrow' doctrine reveal that deciding what amounts to the 'substance' of any given invention is fraught with difficulty. Two brief illustrations will suffice. In *Van der Lely v Bamfords* [1963] RPC 61, the patent concerned a mechanical hay rake with rear wheels which could be 'de-mounted' (that is, realigned with the front axle of the hay rake) so as to enable the machine to perform two functions, hay-raking and hay-gathering. The defendant's hay rake had demountable front wheels, which enabled it to do exactly the same tasks. By a majority of 4:1, the House of Lords held that there was no infringement. The phrase 'hindmost wheels' in the claim did not cover 'front' wheels. It was up to the patentee to claim the appropriate protection. If the patentee had not said clearly was what was intended then the consequences must be accepted. Only Lord Reid argued for the application of common sense, stating that there was infringement because the defendant's machine worked in the same way. In *Rodi & Wienenberger v Showell* [1969] RPC 367, the patent concerned an expandable watch-strap with 'U' shaped links. The defendant's watch-strap had 'C' shaped links (if you turn a 'U' through 90 degrees it becomes a 'C'!) Again, the House of Lords held that there was no infringement because the defendant's product was not within the wording of the claims. This time the majority was 3:2, and again, Lord Reid, in the minority, argued that patent claims should not be treated as if they were addressed to conveyancers. Rather, he said, they were addressed to persons skilled in the relevant art and should not be subjected to meticulous verbal analysis.

6.5.3 **Purposive construction**

In 1982, the House of Lords appeared to make a radical departure from its earlier approach as a result of the 'purposive construction' test introduced by Lord Diplock in *Catnic Components v Hill & Smith* [1982] RPC 185. The patent related to galvanised steel lintels placed over doors and windows in buildings with cavity walls. The claim stated that the back-plate of the lintel had to be 'vertical'. The defendants' lintel (admittedly copied from the patentees' brochure) had a back-plate which was at a slight angle to the vertical. This made it less efficient although it still performed the same engineering function (load bearing). The simple issue for the House of Lords was whether the word 'vertical' was to be treated as a precise requirement or not. Their Lordships decided that it was not, instead it meant 'substantially vertical'. Such liberal treatment of a word which to a civil engineer would have an exact meaning was no doubt helped by the choice of a building site foreman as the hypothetical skilled addressee of the patent.

Lord Diplock (giving the only speech) stated (without the citation of authority) that a patent specification should be given a 'purposive' construction, rather than 'a purely literal one derived from applying to it the kind of meticulous verbal analysis in which lawyers are too often tempted by their training to indulge', a phrase already used by Lord Reid in *Rodi & Wienenberger v Showell*. Lord Diplock then set out what became known as the '*Catnic* question'. Because of its importance, we set out the relevant extract in full.

case close-up

Catnic Components v Hill & Smith [1982] RPC 185

Lord Diplock's *Catnic* question reads as follows:

> The question in each case is: whether persons with practical knowledge and experience of the kind of work in which the invention was intended to be used, would understand that strict compliance with a particular descriptive word or phrase appearing in a claim was intended by the patentee to be an essential requirement of the invention so that any variant would fall outside the monopoly claimed, even though it could have no material effect upon the way the invention worked.
>
> The question, of course, does not arise where the variant would in fact have a material effect upon the way the invention worked. Nor does it arise unless at the date of publication of the specification it would be obvious to the informed reader that this was so. Where it is not obvious, in the light of the then-existing knowledge, the reader is entitled to assume that the patentee thought at the time of the specification that he had good reason for limiting his monopoly so strictly and had intended to do so, even though subsequent work by him or others in the field of the invention might show the limitation to have been unnecessary. It is to be answered in the negative only when it would be apparent to any reader skilled in the art that a particular descriptive word or phrase used in a claim cannot have been intended by a patentee, who was also skilled in the art, to exclude minor variants which, to the knowledge of both him and the readers to whom the patent was addressed, could have no material effect upon the way in which the invention worked.

thinking point

How 'revolutionary' was Lord Diplock's speech in Catnic?

Despite being hailed at the time as a 'revolutionary' approach to claim interpretation, Lord Diplock's speech contains arguments which are remarkably similar to those advanced by the minority in *Van der Lely v Bamfords* and in *Rodi & Wienenberger v Showell*. Nevertheless, it has been held by the Court of Appeal that the *Catnic* 'purposive construction' test replaced the 'pith and marrow' doctrine: *Codex v Racal-Milgo* [1983] RPC 369.

6.5.4 **The impact of the EPC 1973**

The *Catnic* decision involved a patent granted under the Patents Act 1949 and so was essentially a product of the 'common law of patents'. Was it relevant to patents granted under the 1977 Act? Two provisions in the current legislation should be noted, both derived from the EPC. First, s.125(1) (based on EPC Article 69) declares that an invention is to be as stated in the claims (interpreted in the light of the description which will precede them in the patent specification, together with any drawings) and the extent of the protection conferred by a patent shall be determined accordingly. Second, s.125(3) replicates the wording of the Protocol to Article 69 EPC. Because it is so central to the cases which follow, we set out the original wording of the Protocol in full.

case close-up

Protocol to Article 69 EPC 1973

The Protocol to Article 69 EPC 1973 reads as follows:

> Article 69 should not be interpreted in the sense that the extent of the protection conferred by a **European patent** is to be understood as that defined by the strict, literal, meaning of the wording used in the claims, the description and drawings being employed only for the purpose of resolving ambiguity found in the claims. Neither should it be interpreted in the sense that the claims serve only as a guideline and that the actual protection conferred may extend to what, from a consideration of the description by a person skilled in the art, the patentee has contemplated. On the contrary, it is to be interpreted as defining a position between these extremes which combines a fair protection for the patentee with a reasonable degree of certainty for third parties.

As Sherman has explained ('Patent Claim Interpretation: The Impact of the Protocol on Interpretation' (1991) 54 *MLR* 499), when the EPC was drafted, it was realised that although the process of granting European patents had been centralised, once granted such patents would be at the mercy of idiosyncratic interpretations, caricatured as ranging from the United Kingdom 'fence-post' approach described earlier, to treating the claims merely as guidelines, which was said to be the case in Germany and the Netherlands. There would be no point in having a centrally granted patent if its treatment varied from state to state. Fear of divergency led to the attachment of the Protocol in an attempt to ensure uniformity. Sherman questions whether something designed as a compromise at a diplomatic level could achieve internal change in a national legal system. Was the Protocol simply a statement of aspirations?

6.5.5 *Catnic* reformulated

The first case to consider the impact of the Protocol in United Kingdom law was *Improver v Remington* [1990] FSR 181. The patent involved a hair-removing device in which a coiled helical spring was spun lengthwise by an electric motor, so that as the windings of the spring opened and closed they acted like high-speed tweezers. The defendant's rival device used a bent rubber rod with slits in it instead of the looped spring, but otherwise worked in the same way. As the rod was a variant, the question was deceptively simple. Did it infringe?

The difficulty with the case was that the Court of Appeal, in earlier interlocutory proceedings (*Improver v Remington* [1989] RPC 69) had declared (without explanation) that Lord Diplock's purposive construction test in *Catnic* was the appropriate test for patents granted under the 1977 Act. In the substantive hearing, Hoffmann J (as he then was) was bound by that finding.

Accordingly, he took Lord Diplock's question from *Catnic* and reworked it into a more complex three-stage test.

case close-up

Improver v Remington [1990] FSR 181

Hoffmann J said this:

If the issue was whether a feature embodied in an alleged infringement which fell outside the primary, literal or acontextual meaning of a descriptive word or phrase in the claim ('a variant') was nevertheless within its language as properly interpreted, the court should ask itself the following three questions:

(1) Does the variant have a material effect upon the way the invention works? If yes, the variant is outside the claim. If no -

(2) Would this (ie that the variant had no material effect) have been obvious at the date of publication of the patent to a reader skilled in the art? If no, the variant is outside the claim. If yes -

(3) Would the reader skilled in the art nevertheless have understood from the language of the claim that the patentee intended that strict compliance with the primary meaning was an essential requirement of the invention? If yes, the variant is outside the claim.

If Hoffmann J's statement is compared with that of Lord Diplock, the *Catnic* question itself becomes the third question, placed after a discussion on the effect of the variant and the skilled addressee's perception of the variant, matters which Lord Diplock treats as subsidiary issues to be looked at later. The restructuring of *Catnic* into three sequential inquiries has the effect of placing greater emphasis on the wording of the claim, harking back to the days of *EMI v Lissen*. Hoffmann J explained that the first two questions are questions of fact, and are to be used to provide the factual background against which the specification must be construed. He then stated that it is the third question which raises the matter of construction. Lord Diplock's formulation made it clear that the answers to the first two questions are not conclusive. Even though the variant made no material difference and this would have been obvious at the time, the skilled addressee may decide that the patentee for some reason was confining the claim to a specific meaning. In conclusion, Hoffmann J held that the defendant's device did not infringe, because although the variant did not have a material effect on the way the invention worked, and although it would have been obvious to a skilled addressee that a rubber rod would have the same desired attributes as a looped spring, the wording of the claim was so precise that only the use of a looped spring would infringe.

6.5.6 Application of the *Catnic/Improver* Questions

From the time of the *Improver v Remington* decision until 2004, United Kingdom courts generally applied what became known as the *Catnic/Improver* questions to determine whether a variant infringed. An example is *Daily v Berchet* [1992] FSR 533 where the invention concerned a baby walker. The device had a safety feature, namely an automatic breaking arrangement, so that when downward pressure was exerted on the frame (for example, when the child used the frame to lift itself off the ground) brake pads were applied to the rims of the rear wheels, thus preventing the walker from moving forward. The approach of the Court of Appeal was to take Claim 1 of the patent, and fragment it into its essential integers or features, in many ways not unlike the technique used in the old 'pith and marrow' cases. The resultant emphasis placed on the phrase 'in association with the rear wheels' as a key feature of the invention led inevitably to a finding of non-infringement because the defendant's walking frame (for invalids) had a braking system which applied friction to the ground to stop forward movement, rather than applying pressure to the wheels.

Other examples of the use of the *Catnic/Improver* questions include *Electrolux v Black & Decker* [1996] FSR 595 (where the patent for an electric hover mower which used a fan blade to suck up the grass cuttings was not infringed by a rival mower where the fan did not have such an effect) and *American Home Products Corp v Novartis Pharmaceuticals UK Ltd* [2001] RPC 1 where a patent employing 'Swiss form claims' for the second medical use of the substance rapamycin was held not to be infringed by the manufacture of a derivative substance. The wording of the claim was so precise that the skilled addressee would assume that only rapamycin and not any second or third generation version of it would be protected.

thinking point

Why should a case decided under the Patents Act 1949 provide the correct test to determine the scope of protection of patent claims in the era of the EPC? Does the reformulation of the Catnic *question in* Improver v Remington *lay too much stress on the literal wording of the claims?*

6.5.7 **Dissent**

There was only one United Kingdom decision that questioned the correctness of the *Catnic/Improver* questions, namely *PLG Research Ltd v Ardon* [1995] RPC 287. Millett LJ argued that it was preferable to follow the approach at the time of the German courts to claim interpretation (the German approach has since changed). He stated that they used a modified version of the *Improver* questions. The first two questions were identical (namely, as a question of fact, whether the variant worked in the same way as the invention and if so, whether this would have been obvious to the skilled addressee). However, the third question was replaced by an alternative which asked what variants the skilled reader would contemplate as falling within the claims.

PLG v Ardon was immediately criticised (and Millett LJ's remarks were stated to be *obiter*) by Aldous J in *Assidoman Multipack v The Mead Corporation* [1995] RPC 321. It was then repeatedly stated by the Court of Appeal (for example, in *Beloit v Valmet* [1997] RPC 489 and *Kastner v Rizla* [1995] RPC 585) that reliance on the *Improver* questions provided the correct, structured approach to determine patent claim interpretation.

6.5.8 **Rebranding *Catnic/Improver* as 'the Protocol questions'**

The *Catnic/Improver* questions were renamed 'the Protocol questions' in *Wheatley (Davina) v Drillsafe Ltd* [2001] RPC 133. There is a division of opinion in the Court of Appeal as to whether there had been infringement in this case. The differences between the majority and the minority in *Wheatley v Drillsafe* lie in the way in which the court approached the issue of **inventive concept.** The majority took a narrower view of the patent's inventive concept, regarding it as the use of a 'centre-less' drill cutter for drilling holes in underground petrol storage tanks without the need for the use of a pilot drill. The minority (Aldous LJ) adopted a broader view of the inventive concept: what mattered was that the defendant's probe did not enter the tank (thereby avoiding the risk of sparks) which was the problem which the patent had sought to solve. Aldous LJ therefore followed the advice of Lord Hoffmann in *Biogen v Medeva* in identifying the problem to be solved as part of the process of identifying the inventive concept. The case reveals that it is possible for the underlying inventive concept to be drawn broadly or narrowly by the court. This means that different answers will be obtained to the Protocol questions in each instance.

With regard to the Protocol questions themselves, *Wheatley v Drillsafe* explained that they were intended simply to assist with purposive construction of the claims. Question 1 envisaged that the claim had an ambit wider than its literal meaning, so as to give fair protection to the patentee, but subject to the safeguard for third parties when taken in conjunction with Question 2. Question 3 also provided a fair result for the patentee, namely the avoidance of an unintended meaning, whilst protecting third parties by emphasising the purpose of the words.

6.5.9 **When *Catnic/Improver* was ignored**

Not every case utilised the three-stage test advocated by Hoffmann J in *Improver v Remington*. The court dispensed with the questions in *Warheit v Olympia Tools Ltd* [2003] FSR 95, where the invention was very simple and there was literal infringement. Equally, in cases dealing with pharmaceutical patents, it was said that the Protocol questions, though providing a structured approach, were not always appropriate and that the Protocol itself simply required the third question to be put, ie what did the skilled addressee think the patentee intended: *Pharmacia Corp v Merck & Co Inc* [2002] RPC 775 (CA) and *Merck & Co Inc v Generics (UK) Ltd* [2004] RPC 607.

6.5.10 *Kirin-Amgen*

In *Kirin-Amgen Inc v Hoechst Marion Roussel Ltd*, the issue of claim interpretation was revisited by Lord Hoffmann. The patent involved the production of erythropoietin ('EPO') by recombinant DNA technology, EPO being a protein which regulates the production of red blood cells. The defendant had developed another way of making EPO which the patentee alleged infringed two claims of the patent. The House of Lords agreed with the Court of Appeal that the patent had not been infringed.

Lord Hoffmann (giving the only speech) made clear that the scope of protection of a patent is determined by the claims. Anything which extends protection outside the claims is expressly prohibited. There is therefore nothing in European patent law which equates to the US 'doctrine of equivalents'. When deciding whether a variant infringes, there is only one question to be asked. 'What would a person skilled in the art have understood the patentee to have used the language of the claim to mean?' Everything else, including the Protocol questions themselves, was only guidance to a judge trying to answer that question. Further, the Protocol questions could be unhelpful, because, for example, in an area of rapid change (such as recombinant DNA technology) it cannot be assumed that the skilled addressee would know a variant would work in the same way.

6.5.10.1 A return to *Catnic*?

Lord Hoffmann in *Kirin-Amgen* added that the Protocol is concerned with the construction of Article 69, not the construction of claims. The Protocol says that literalism should be avoided, but otherwise says that one should not go outside the claims. Accordingly, fair protection for the patentee together with certainty for third parties are both catered for by asking 'what is the full extent of the monopoly which the person skilled in the art would think he was intending to claim'? As a result, the original *Catnic* question was in full accord with the Protocol. Contradicting his own statement in *Improver v Remington*, Lord Hoffmann declared that purposive construction *does* depend on context. Strict compliance is appropriate where 'figures, measurements, angles and the like are given'. The Protocol questions were therefore difficult, if not impossible, to apply where the language used was very exact, and were not a substitute for trying to understand what the person skilled in the art would have understood the patentee to mean by the language of the claims. Lord Hoffmann appears to be saying that where the patent involves sophisticated technology, of necessity the language of the claims will have to be precise (otherwise there might be a risk of '*Biogen* insufficiency'), so that the Protocol questions do not assist the court. The only issue is to ask what the skilled addressee understood the patentee to mean. This appears to mark a complete return to Lord Diplock's question in *Catnic* and an abandonment of the three-stage test in *Improver v Remington*. It also has the effect of conferring narrower protection on what might otherwise be regarded as 'leading edge' inventions.

6.5.11 EPC 2000: revision of the Protocol

The 2000 amendments to the EPC included a revision to the Protocol to Article 69. The amended Protocol consists of two Articles. Article 1 reproduces the current version of the wording, except that 'patentee' is replaced by 'patent proprietor'. Article 2 is new: it provides that 'For the purpose of determining the scope of protection conferred by a European patent, due account shall be taken of any element which is equivalent to an element specified in the claims'. One may speculate as to whether this will lead, in due course, to a European doctrine of equivalents (which Lord Hoffmann in *Kirin-Amgen* at [44] vehemently denied existed) or whether resort to the skilled addressee and their perception of the wording of the claims will ensure that little change actually occurs. Fisher (in 'New Protocol, Same Old Story? Patent Claim Construction in 2007; Looking Back with a View to the Future' [2008] *IPQ* 133) argues that German courts have acknowledged that there remains a difference between their style of interpretation of patent claims and that found in the United Kingdom. This difference is due, he says, to the German concern to reward the patentee, whilst United Kingdom courts focus on the patent as incentive rather than reward. However, United Kingdom courts are adamant that there is now conformity throughout the EPC Contracting States with regard to patent claim interpretation so that nothing further remains to be done: see Lord Hoffmann in *Kirin-Amgen* at [75]. The German and United Kingdom views cannot both be right.

6.5.12 Post-*Kirin*

Since the House of Lords decision in *Kirin-Amgen*, a number of cases have attempted to provide a concise summary of the principles of patent claim construction.

The scope of the patentee's monopoly

177

case close-up

Virgin Atlantic Airways Ltd v Premium Aircraft Interiors UK Ltd [2010] FSR 396

A summary of the effect of *Kirin-Amgen* can be found in *Virgin Atlantic Airways Ltd v Premium Aircraft Interiors UK Ltd* where Jacob LJ at [5] stated as follows:

- the first overarching principle is that contained in Article 69 EPC;

- Article 69 says that the extent of protection is determined by the claims. It goes on to say that the description and drawings shall be used to interpret the claims. In short, the claims are to be construed in context;

- it follows that the claims are to be construed purposively—the inventor's purpose being ascertained from the description and drawings;

- it further follows that the claims must not be construed as if they stood alone—the drawings and description only being used to resolve any ambiguity. Purpose is vital to the construction of claims;

- when ascertaining the inventor's purpose, it must be remembered that he may have several purposes depending on the level of generality of his invention. Typically, for instance, an inventor may have one, generally more than one, specific embodiment as well as a generalised concept. But there is no presumption that the patentee necessarily intended the widest possible meaning consistent with his purpose be given to the words that he used: purpose and meaning are different;

- thus purpose is not the be-all and end-all. One is still at the end of the day concerned with the meaning of the language used. Hence the other extreme of the Protocol—a mere guideline—is also ruled out by Article 69 itself. It is the terms of the claims which delineate the patentee's territory;

- it follows that if the patentee has included what is obviously a deliberate limitation in his claims, it must have a meaning. One cannot disregard obviously intentional elements;

- it also follows that where a patentee has used a word or phrase which, acontextually, might have a particular meaning (narrow or wide) it does not necessarily have that meaning in context;

- it further follows that there is no general 'doctrine of equivalents';

- on the other hand purposive construction can lead to the conclusion that a technically trivial or minor difference between an element of a claim and the corresponding element of the alleged infringement nonetheless falls within the meaning of the element when read purposively. This is not because there is a doctrine of equivalents: it is because that is the fair way to read the claim in context; and

- finally purposive construction leads one to eschew the kind of meticulous verbal analysis which lawyers are too often tempted by their training to indulge.

One can see from this summary that despite the requirement to strike a middle path between fair protection for the patentee and certainty for third parties, there is considerable emphasis on the wording of the claim. There is also reiteration of the view (despite the EPC 2000 changes) that there is no general 'doctrine of equivalents'.

6.5.13 Examples of the application of the *Kirin-Amgen* test

Following the decision of the House of Lords in *Kirin-Amgen*, it is becoming clear that the choice of the skilled addressee, as well as the context of the patent (ie how sophisticated it is) and the precision of language used by the patentee, can all have a crucial bearing on how claims are interpreted. A number of cases illustrate the interrelationship of these factors in patent claim interpretation, although ultimately it all comes back to the *Kirin-Amgen* question: what would a person skilled in the art have understood the patentee to have used the language of the claim to mean?

Our starting point is *Corus UK Ltd v Qual-Chem Ltd* [2008] EWCA Civ 1177 where it was held that the use of the word 'tailored' in a patent for an improvement to a process for the manufacture of steel would be understood by the skilled reader to mean 'so chosen to have the desired effect'. It did not mean that there had to be a precise means in the apparatus of adjusting the gas pressure. The context of the patent was significant. The characteristics of the skilled addressee made a difference in *Ancon Ltd v ACS Stainless Steel Fixings Ltd* [2009] EWCA Civ 498, where it was held that the words 'elliptical cone shape' in a patent concerned with bolts used in fixing metal building structures should not be interpreted by a geometer but by a practical designer and manufacturer of fixings for buildings. Lord Diplock's use of a building site foreman as the addressee of the *Catnic* patent might have had something to do with the case.

The unsophisticated nature of the invention played a part in the decision in *Boegli-Gravures SA v Darsail-ASP Ltd* [2009] EWHC 2690 (Pat). The patent involved a system for embossing packaging foils between two rollers with 'pyramidal teeth' to produce an optical effect. Arnold J held the words 'pyramidal teeth' were being used in a figurative sense to denote something roughly shaped like a pyramid rather than a precise geometric shape. By contrast, the invention in *Occlutech GmbH v Aga Medical Corporation* [2010] EWCA Civ 702 was more sophisticated and hence the skilled addressee was more highly qualified. Nevertheless, the case illustrates nicely the difference between the use of words which are precise and those which have a more generalised meaning. The patent involved a device for insertion into a blood vessel or similar, the device being stated to be 'dumbbell-shaped' and with clamps at the ends. It was held not to be infringed by a rival device with a similar shape (having a pinched central section) which had its ends fixed by welding. Although the shape could be described as being like a dumbbell and so was within the wording of the claim, the use of the word 'clamp' in the context of surgical devices indicated a degree of precision.

Last, Lord Hoffmann's remarks in *Kirin-Amgen* about the implication of using 'figures, measurements, angles and the like' are illustrated by *Zeno Corporation v BSM-Bionic Solutions Management* [2009] EWHC 1829 (Pat). Here, the patent was for a hand-held unit 'for' the thermal treatment of insect bites, where the device was to have a maximum temperature in a range from 50 to 65° C, preferably 55 to 60° C, and was to be held in place 'for a time interval ranging from 2 to 12 seconds, preferably 3 to 6 seconds'. Lewison J held that there was no

infringement by a device used for the thermal treatment of acne which used a lower temperature and was held in place for a longer period of time. The temperature range and time inter-
vals were held to be precise measurements, and there was no evidence that the defendant's
device would have any beneficial effect in the treatment of insect bites.

thinking point

Do you think that Lord Hoffmann's test in Kirin-Amgen *does fulfil the requirements
of the Protocol to Article 69? Does the current case law on patent claim
interpretation provide for certainty and predictability?*

Summary

This chapter has explained:

- what amounts to infringing conduct of a patent;

- the defences and counterclaims which a defendant has raised; and

- the problems faced when trying to decide whether what the defendant has produced falls
  within the language of the claims.

Reflective question

Any attempt to amend the Protocol to Article 69 of the European Patent Convention by insert-
ing a reference to obvious equivalents is a complete waste of time. It will not make United
Kingdom courts change their minds about the interpretation of patent claims.

Discuss.

Annotated further reading

Fisher, M. 'New Protocol, Same Old Story? Patent Claim Construction in 2007; Looking Back
with a View to the Future' [2008] *IPQ* 133
Considers whether the EPC 2000 amendments to Article 69 will actually have any effect.

Fisher, M. 'A Case-study in Literalism: Dissecting the English Approach to Patent Claim Construction in the Light of *Occlutech v Aga Medical*' [2011] *IPQ* 283

Argues that the current prevailing attitude of the courts favours a literal interpretation of the claims, reinforced by an over-reliance on dictionary definitions.

Sherman, B. 'Patent Claim Interpretation: The Impact of the Protocol on Interpretation' (1991) 54 *MLR* 499

Explains the origin of the Protocol to Article 69 EPC and assesses its likely impact in harmonising national attitudes to patent claim interpretation.

Turner, J. 'Purposive Construction: Seven Reasons Why Catnic is Wrong' [1999] *EIPR* 531

A highly critical analysis of Lord Diplock's speech in *Catnic*.

Part 4

Copyright and related rights

An introduction to copyright

Learning objectives

Upon completion of this chapter, you should have acquired:

- an understanding of historical factors which have shaped present-day United Kingdom copyright law;

- an appreciation of the range of external influences which have prompted domestic legislation;

- knowledge of the arguments usually advanced to justify copyright protection;

- knowledge of the principal features of copyright and how copyright differs from other forms of intellectual property; and

- an appreciation of the key distinction between an idea and its expression.

Introduction

We discuss in this chapter a number of issues which permeate any study of copyright law, and which are therefore of importance in the chapters which follow.

Like any legal subject, copyright law is a product of its history. We therefore provide a brief account of how United Kingdom copyright law has developed from the mid-sixteenth century. The purpose of giving an account of the history of United Kingdom copyright law is to highlight two recurring themes (the belated reaction of the law to changing technology and the effect of external influences on domestic law) and, further, to suggest that any discussion of copyright law should not be separated from an appreciation of its theoretical justifications.

Burkitt points out (in 'Copyrighting Culture—The History and Cultural Specificity of the Western Model of Copyright' [2001] *IPQ* 146) that copyright law cannot be divorced from its historical origins. However, he says, it is wrong to assume that there is a single, unified historical account of copyright's development. Even within the so-called 'Western' model of copyright, at least four different philosophical approaches can be detected (in England, the USA, France and Germany). The values inherent in these diverse legal systems have been imposed on other cultures, for example, those which are a product of imperialist China or of Aboriginal Australia, regardless of the fact that these other systems may have no notion of individually owned intellectual property rights.

Bearing in mind Burkitt's argument about differing cultural traditions, we consider next philosophical arguments advanced by United Kingdom judges and writers as reasons for copyright protection. This is to help the reader to reflect, when dealing with the material in later chapters, whether the current law lives up to its theoretical justifications. As an introduction to this reflective process, we compare and contrast copyright law with other forms of intellectual property to demonstrate the surprising breadth of protection given to the right owner despite the fact that copyright protection arises automatically and, in many instances, as the result of a minimum expenditure of effort. Such broad protection is at odds with the reasons given as to why we have a law of copyright. Many writers argue that copyright needs to be reined in so as to accord with its justifications, but we pose the question whether it is ever possible to turn back the legal clock.

The chapter concludes with another key issue in copyright law, namely the difference between an idea and its expression. Copyright law, it is frequently stated, does not protect ideas but the form in which they are expressed. Such distinction is easy to state, but difficult to apply, and copyright cases abound with, on the one hand, examples where the courts appear to have come close to protecting mere ideas and, equally, where they appear to have failed to protect the creator's expression.

History

7.1.1 The supposed origins of copyright law

It is alleged that the first ever 'case' involving **copyright** occurred in Ireland in the sixth century. The missionary St Columba was accused of plagiarism, having visited a particular monastery where he surreptitiously borrowed a rare book in order to copy it. Complaint was made to the High King of Meath, Diarmuid, by the owner of the original book who demanded that the copy be handed over. In giving judgment in favour of the book's owner, the King took inspiration from traditional Irish law, which was to the effect that any calf found wandering belonged to its mother, wherever the cow might be kept. His ruling was 'As to every Cow its Calf, so to every Book its Copy', a statement which is said to be the foundation of modern copyright law. When reading this pronouncement, it should be remembered that books at that time were made of vellum, that is, cow hide.

7.1.2 The advent of printing

A recurring theme of copyright law is that it responds belatedly to changing technology. The advent of the printing press in the late fifteenth century meant that books no longer had to be copied laboriously by hand, a skill previously practised by a few 'scriptors' in monasteries (witness the story of St Columba). This labour-intensive and slow method of reproduction had severely limited the availability of books. The ability to reproduce text mechanically not only overcame this problem but also meant that the ideas and information contained in such printed matter became readily available to the public. Predictably, the reaction of the Tudor monarchs (specifically, Queen Mary) was to use the Royal Prerogative to grant a charter to the Stationers' Company, just as Queen Elizabeth I later granted patents to her favourite courtiers. The Company, as a craft guild, had supervisory powers over its members, so that before a book could be printed a **licence** had first to be obtained. Licences were only granted to company members, who accordingly had the exclusive right to print and distribute books. The Company's powers included those to search out and destroy any books contrary to law. Viewed from today's perspective, the Crown used the Company as a means of controlling printing so as to censor materials thought to be contrary to the interests of the established church or the state.

cross reference
See section 4.1.1.

The system of licensing books was maintained throughout the Civil War (despite the abolition of the Star Chamber) and was reinstated after the Restoration by the Licensing Act 1662. In due course, however, the legislation lapsed, leaving the Company to regulate the publishing trade as best it could through its rules of membership. By now, however, the ability to copy books easily (and hence cheaply) was causing concern in the book trade. There was intensive lobbying for legislation to deal with the perceived problem of piracy, but it should be noted that most of the pressure came from the publishers themselves, that is, entrepreneurs, rather than disgruntled **authors**, the creators.

7.1.3 The Statute of Anne

The Copyright Act 1709 (the 'Statute of Anne', said to be the first copyright legislation anywhere in the world) conferred on authors 'the sole right and liberty of printing books' for a term of 14 years from first publication, with a further period of 14 years being available if the author were still alive at the end of the first term of protection. For books already printed at the date of the Act (10 April 1710) the duration of protection was 21 years. The chosen periods of protection were similar to those available for **patents** under the Statute of Monopolies 1623. Authors were able to assign their rights to others, and booksellers and printers were declared to fall within the meaning of the authors' 'assigns'. The Statute was entitled 'An Act for the Encouragement of Learning, by Vesting the Copies of Printed Books in the Authors or Purchasers of such Copies', and its Preamble declared that the statute was 'for the encouragement of learned men to compose and write useful books'. In reality, however, the reference to authors was a token gesture, an excuse to restore to publishers the protection they had previously enjoyed.

cross reference
See section 4.1.1.

7.1.3.1 Debate: the scope of the Statute of Anne

In the eighteenth century, as the periods of protection given under the 1709 Act began to expire, a debate ensued as to the relationship between copyright granted under the Act and the author's assumed common law protection. Did the Act create a new authorial copyright or did it simply declare a right which already existed at common law? As Burkitt points out, the debate coincided with the rise of authors as autonomous professionals rather than scribes dependent on the patronage of the ruling class. Once again, it was the booksellers who argued that authors had literary property in their work, justified by Lockean labour theory. This literary property, it was said, belonged to the author at common law; the author was free to assign this to a publisher, and moreover such right existed indefinitely at common law. Equally, however, there were those who argued that literature was simply a collection of ideas, too transient and fleeting to be protected as property. Once an idea was made public, because no one had exclusive control over it, it could not be viewed as belonging to anyone.

7.1.3.2 The debate resolved

Two key cases considered these arguments, *Millar v Taylor* (1769) 98 ER 201, and *Donaldson v Beckett* (1774) 1 ER 837. Both cases concerned a book of poetry, *The Seasons*, written by one James Thompson, the copyright in which had been owned by Millar. On the expiry of the period of protection under the Statute of Anne, Taylor printed and sold 1,000 copies of the book. In *Millar v Taylor*, the Court of King's Bench upheld Millar's claim for loss of profit, holding that common law copyright had not been taken away by the Statute. Willes J, in the majority, avoided using Lockean arguments, preferring instead theories of 'natural justice' and equity. Literature should be encouraged and the author should be entitled to the fruits of his labour. Lord Mansfield, too, relied on equitable notions of fairness and the moral rights of the author. Only Yates J dissented, arguing (at p. 233) that 'nothing can be an object of property which is not capable of sole and exclusive enjoyment'.

cross reference
See section 1.4.1.

Subsequently, Millar's executors sold the copyright in *The Seasons* to Beckett, who, relying on the judgment in *Millar v Taylor*, successfully obtained an **injunction** against Donaldson for printing and distributing further copies of Thomson's works. Donaldson appealed to the House of Lords, who referred the matter to the 12 common law judges for an opinion. By a majority, the judges in *Donaldson v Beckett* held that there was a common law copyright in published works, but by an even narrower majority they ruled that the Statute took away that right. The limited term of protection under the Statute removed the perpetual common law right upon publication.

7.1.3.3 Comment

Two comments about *Donaldson v Becket* need to be made. First, as Deazley argues (in 'The Myth of Copyright at Common Law [2003] *CLJ* 106), analysis of the case reveals that its ruling is misunderstood and that it denied the existence of any common law copyright. Nevertheless, Parliament appears to have assumed that the case did leave intact the author's perpetual common law copyright in unpublished works, as this right was declared to be abolished by the Copyright Act 1911. Second, as Burkitt observes, the discussion in *Donaldson v Beckett*, in contrast to that in *Millar v Taylor*, appears to favour the economic view of copyright rather than the aesthetic. Although the judges express concerns about the dangers of creating a perpetual monopoly, the net effect of the case is the 'commodification of literature'.

7.1.4 Piecemeal legislative developments

The developments which occurred after *Donaldson v Beckett* reflect the reactionary nature of copyright law, always attempting to catch up with changes in business and technology. An illustration is *Bach v Longman* (1777) 2 Cowp 623 where the court felt constrained to give a wide meaning to the word 'books' in the Statute of Anne so as to include sheet music. In the main, however, the changes were legislative in nature and involved one or more of three possible reforms, namely introducing new categories of **work** to the copyright régime, adding to the scope of protection given to the right holder by entitling them to object to new forms of infringing conduct, or extending the term of protection.

Examples of the way in which new categories of work were added included the protection conferred on engravings in 1734 and 1766, on sculptures in 1798, and on paintings, drawings and photographs in 1862. Examples of the extension of the scope of protection to include infringing conduct other than copying was the addition of the right to control performances of dramatic works in 1833 and of musical works in 1842. The duration of protection was increased to 28 years or the author's life, whichever was longer, in 1814, and to 42 years or the author's life plus seven years, whichever was longer, in 1842. It was not until the Copyright Act 1911 (enacted in response to the **Berne Convention**) that the standardised period of the author's life plus 50 years was introduced. The same Act also put copyright in unpublished works on a statutory footing, abolishing common law copyright in the process, and repealed many of its myriad predecessors, bringing all forms of copyright work under the umbrella of a single statute.

7.1.5 External influences

Changes to copyright law from the latter part of the nineteenth century onwards reflect the way in which trade became increasingly international. At first, British authors received no protection in other countries, nor, indeed did foreign nationals qualify for protection in the United Kingdom (*Jefferys v Boosey* (1854) 4 HLC 415). In consequence, there was nothing to stop a publisher in another country from making copies of a book written by a British author and then importing these copies into this country, often undercutting the price of the 'authorised' version of the work. The initial response of the Government was to introduce laws empowering the customs authorities to seize these pirated works, and to extend copyright law to British dominions. Subsequently, a series of bilateral treaties with other countries was negotiated, conferring reciprocal protection on each state's nationals.

7.1.5.1 The Berne Convention

Nevertheless, pressure grew for an international solution to the problem. The protagonists were divided into two camps, those states (like France) who wanted a universal law of copyright which emphasised the author's natural right of property, and those states (like the United Kingdom) who wanted a more pragmatic solution so as to reflect the fact that not all countries were major producers of copyright works, but instead were consumers of such products, and that there was no uniform view as to the nature of the author's entitlement. The Berne Convention for the Protection of Literary and Artistic Works 1886 (signed by 10 states and subsequently the subject of five major revisions) reflected, Burkitt suggests, the pragmatic approach. It established minimum rather than absolute standards for the protection of copyright. Its key ingredient is the principle of **national treatment**. An author of one Contracting State is entitled to the same protection in another Contracting State as the authors of the latter receive. When added to the fundamental principle that Contracting States may not impose any formality such as registration as a precondition of protection, the Convention appears to provide a simple solution. However, it is important not to expect too much of the principle of national treatment. Because the Berne Convention lays down minimum standards, there can be differences in detail between the laws of Contracting States as to the types of work protected, the scope of protection, and the duration of protection. 'National treatment' does not guarantee that an author from France will receive the same treatment under United Kingdom law as he or she is entitled to in France, rather it means that the French author will receive the same treatment as a British author can expect.

Although one of the founding signatories of the Berne Convention, the United Kingdom did not incorporate the Convention into domestic law until the Copyright Act 1911, the impetus for change coming from the 1908 version of the Convention. Later revisions to the Berne Convention (in 1928, 1948, 1967 and 1971) prompted further legislative reforms, specifically the Copyright Act 1956 ('the 1956 Act') and the Copyright, Designs and Patents Act 1988 ('CDPA').

7.1.5.2 Other conventions

The Berne Convention is not the only international agreement which has affected the content of domestic law. The **Rome Convention** on the Protection of Performers, Producers of Phonograms and Broadcasting Organisations 1961 (the so-called 'neighbouring rights' convention) has had a major effect, although it must be said that United Kingdom law protected sound recordings and broadcasts before the advent of the Convention. Its particular effect has been with regard to the rights of performers to control the recording of their performances.

cross reference
See further
section 10.2.

The United Kingdom initially fulfilled this obligation by means of the criminal law, set out in the Performers' Protection Acts 1958–1972, but as a result of case law intervention during the 1980s, civil redress for bootleg recordings was created by Part II of the CDPA. Further protection for performers has been added to Part II of the Act as a result of EU Directives. However, the most recent expansion (the creation of moral rights for performers) has come not from the EU but from the **WIPO** Performers and Phonograms Treaty 1996 ('WPPT'). Like its companion, the WIPO Copyright Treaty 1996 ('WCT') which seeks to enhance the protection afforded to copyright owners under the Berne Convention in the digital environment, the WPPT attempts to add to the Rome Convention rights in like manner.

7.1.5.3 European Union legislation

The three major legislative reforms to United Kingdom copyright law in the twentieth century (the Acts of 1911, 1956 and 1988) can each be attributed to the United Kingdom's obligations under the Berne Convention (of which there are now well over 160 signatories). In the last two decades, however, the driving force for the reform of domestic copyright law has been the EU, with no fewer than 11 Directives requiring alteration to United Kingdom copyright legislation. The EU legislative programme was initiated by two key discussion documents, the Green Paper on Copyright and the Challenge of Technology (COM (88) 172 final of 7 June 1988) and Commission Communication on the Working Programme of the Commission in the field of copyright and neighbouring rights (COM (90) 584 final of 17 January 1991).

For convenience, the Directives can be grouped together as follows. First, there are those which deal with the impact of digital technology, namely the Semiconductor Directive (Council Directive 87/54/EEC of 16 December 1986 on the legal protection of topographies of semiconductor products [1987] OJ L 24/36); the Computer Programs Directive (Council Directive 91/250/EEC of 14 May 1991 on the legal protection of computer programs [1991] OJ L 122/42 now codified as Directive 2009/24/EC of the European Parliament and of the Council of 23 April 2009 [2009] OJ L 111/16); the Database Directive (Directive 96/9/EC of 11 March 1996 on the legal protection of databases [1996] OJ L 77/20); and the Information Society Directive (Directive 2001/29/EC of the European Parliament and of the Council of 22 May 2001 on the harmonisation of certain aspects of copyright and related rights in the information society [2001] OJ L 167/10). It is the fourth of these which has had the most wide-ranging effect on the general principles of copyright law (particularly with regard to the issues of **originality**, **infringement** and defences to infringement) and on **neighbouring rights** such as those of performers, based as it is on the WCT and the WPPT.

cross reference
The Information Society Directive is considered throughout chapters 8, 9 and 10.

Next, there are those which deal with the relationship between copyright and broadcasting, namely the 'Television without Frontiers' Directive (Council Directive 89/552/EEC of 3 October 1989 on the co-ordination of certain provisions concerning the pursuit of television broadcasting activities [1989] OJ L 298/23); and the Copyright Broadcasting Directive (Council Directive 93/83/EEC of 27 September 1993 on the co-ordination of certain rules concerning copyright and neighbouring rights applicable to satellite broadcasting and cable re-transmission [1993] OJ L 246/15).

cross reference
See further section 10.1.8.

Third, there is one which deals specifically with the rights of artists when an original work of art is resold, the Droit de Suite Directive (Directive 2001/84/EC of the European Parliament and of the Council of 27 September 2001 on the resale right for the benefit of the author of an original work of art of [2001] OJ L 272/32).

Last, there are those whose impact has been on the law of copyright generally, namely the Rental Rights Directive (Council Directive 92/100/EEC of 19 November 1992 on rental right and lending right and on certain rights related to copyright in the field of intellectual property [1992] OJ L 346/61, now codified as Directive 2006/115/EC of the European Parliament and of the Council of 12 December 2006 [2006] OJ L 376/28); the Copyright Term Directive (Council Directive 93/98/EC of 29 October 1993 harmonising the term of copyright protection [1993] OJ L 290/9, now codified as Directive 2006/116/EC of the European Parliament and of the

Council of 12 December 2006 [2006] OJ L 372/12, amended in relation to sound recordings and performances by Directive 2011/77/EU of the European Parliament and of the Council of 27 September 2011 [2011] OJ L 265/1); and the Enforcement Directive (Directive 2004/48/EC of the European Parliament and of the Council of 29 April 2004 on the enforcement of intellectual property rights [2004] OJ L 157/45). Awaiting implementation into United Kingdom law by October 2014 is Directive 2012/28/EU of the European Parliament and of the Council of 25 October 2012 on certain permitted uses of orphan works [2012] OJ L 299/5.

cross reference
See further chapter 2.

7.1.5.4 External influences: conclusions

The preceding account has attempted to show how the framers of United Kingdom copyright legislation no longer have much freedom of choice with regard to the types of right which are recognised, the scope and duration of protection, and the defences available to an infringer. The nineteenth-century ideal of a universal law of copyright is still a long way off. It is also a matter of debate whether the avalanche of change has been too much, so that copyright has been debased.

thinking point

Review the key phases in the development of United Kingdom copyright law outlined in the previous paragraphs. Then consider whether today's legislative responses could learn anything from the past.

7.1.6 **Future reforms**

The importance of ideas to the United Kingdom economy has prompted a number of Government-initiated reviews. The *Gowers Review* (hereafter, 'Gowers') was published in December 2006. It was asked to consider whether the intellectual property system was 'fit for purpose' in the 'era of globalisation, digitisation and increasing economic specialisation' and gave a qualified 'yes' as an answer. Gowers identified three areas in which United Kingdom law could be improved, namely strengthening enforcement, reducing costs of obtaining and protecting rights, and improving the balance of intellectual property rights to allow individuals, businesses and institutions to use content in ways consistent with the digital age. Although its 54 recommendations cover the whole spectrum of intellectual property rights, the majority are concerned with copyright law. Subsequently, the Hargreaves Review of Intellectual Property and Growth (hereafter 'Hargreaves'), published in May 2011, made 10 recommendations, including changes to copyright exceptions, designs and enforcement. Changes to copyright exceptions have been effected by statutory instrument, whilst the revisions to design law are made by the Intellectual Property Act 2014. To the disinterested observer, such modifications appear to be on the fringes of copyright law. It is taken as read that the underlying assumptions of the copyright system remain valid in the digital era, a supposition with which not all would agree.

cross reference
The changes to copyright exceptions are explained at section 9.5; the revisions to design law in chapter 11.

7.2 The justification for copyright protection

A number of theories can be advanced to support why we have intellectual property protection. Not all intellectual property rights can be vindicated under each theory, but most theories can be manipulated in order to explain why copyright protection is needed. Most of the advocates of the various theories rely on assertion rather than empirical evidence.

7.2.1 The justifications summarised

cross reference
*See further
section 1.4.1.*

To recap some of the theories, these include utilitarianism (which argues that authors should be given a limited monopoly either as an incentive to create or as a reward for having created something which enriches society), the labour (or natural law) theory (which argues that the product of a person's intellect belongs to them in like manner as any tangible artefact they have created out of 'the commons'), and the Hegelian theory that intellectual creations are an extension of the author's personality and should therefore be accorded property rights.

These arguments were summarised by Sir Hugh Laddie (in 'Copyright: Over-strength, Over-regulated, Over-rated' [1996] *EIPR* 253) as the 'three sacred principles' which underpin copyright law. His principles were: that one should not steal what belongs to another (which assumes that ideas are property, a point considered further later); that a person should be entitled to own the product of the intellect just as much as they might own a piece of furniture they have carved from a tree (the labour or desert theory, much influenced by the writings of John Locke); and that it is in society's interests to reward those who are inventive, or to encourage creativity, as this will in the long term improve everyone's standard of living. Sir Hugh further argued that these sacred principles do not justify the current width of copyright legislation. In particular, he highlighted the unwarranted expansion of copyright to provide three-dimensional protection for two-dimensional artistic works; the availability of **additional damages**; the extension to the term of protection; the low test of originality coupled with the ease of creation; the availability of criminal sanctions; and the narrow nature of the United Kingdom's fair dealing defence when compared with the fair use defence in the United States.

Landes and Posner (in 'An Economic Analysis of Copyright Law' (1989) 18 *Journal of Legal Studies* 325) consider in detail the economics of copyright as an incentive to create. They argue that the need for copyright protection has increased over time as modern technology has reduced the time needed to make copies as well as enabling more perfect copies to be made. Further, various rules of copyright can be regarded as attempts to promote economic efficiency by balancing the consequences of enhanced protection against the need to encourage greater creativity. By contrast, Breyer (in 'The Uneasy Case for Copyright: A Study of Copyright in Books, Photocopies and Computer Programs' (1970) 84 *Harv LR* 281) argues that extensions to copyright protection are both unnecessary and harmful. Having reviewed both the moral rights and incentive theories, he questions whether it is necessary to attribute property rights to creativity. Further, he states that the non-economic goals served by copyright law are not an adequate justification for the copyright system, as other arrangements could be made to protect an author's dignitary rights. It must be stressed that both of these seminal pieces were written before the advent of the digital age, which has reduced to almost zero the cost of making perfect copies of a work. More recently, Rahmatian (in 'Copyright and Commodification' [2005] *EIPR* 371) has argued that to suppose that the world would be a better place if copyright were not treated as a property right and if creativity were not treated as a commodity ignores the real issue. The problem, he says, is that lawmakers, under pressure from the international entertainment industry, forget that there is a need for restrictions on the power which flows from the proprietary nature of copyright.

7.2.2 **Theory versus reality**

The justifications for copyright can be measured against the rules of United Kingdom copyright law. In many instances there is a conflict between the theory and what statute and case law say. For example, if copyright law is justified under utilitarianism, why does the period of protection now last until 70 years after the author's death, so that those who benefit are the author's successors? If copyright law is justified under Locke's labour theory, why is the threshold for copyright protection set so low that items like professional directories (*Waterlow v Rose* [1995] FSR 207) and lists of television programmes (*Independent Television Publications v Time Out* [1984] FSR 64) are protected? If Hegelian personality theory is the justification, why does United Kingdom law treat copyright as an economic right which can be bought and sold like any other commodity, with freedom of contract the guiding principle, rather than treating it as a dignitary right unique to its author?

Sir Hugh Laddie accepted that copyright itself can be justified, but his concern is its over-expansion. As Vaver (in 'Rejuvenating Copyright' (1996) 75 *Can BR* 69) points out, there are many detractors who argue that copyright itself should no longer be recognised, perhaps influenced by the fact that, economically speaking, copyright is dominated by large corporations (such as Microsoft, Sony or Walt Disney) rather than individual creators. He says that it is its very attractiveness which threatens it as an institution: 'everyone wants their activity protected under copyright because it is by far the best game in town'. Whilst not arguing for copyright's abolition, Vaver suggests that it is time to re-evaluate the activities which society wishes to encourage, what degree of incentive should be offered as encouragement, and who should benefit from that incentive.

cross reference
*See further
section 8.2.*

Gervais suggests (in 'The Compatibility of the Skill and Labour Originality Standard with the Berne Convention and the TRIPs Agreement' [2004] *EIPR* 75) that the real problem lies in the approach of common law countries to the meaning of the word '**original**', a key requirement for protection. If 'original' were to be interpreted to mean the author's intellectual creativity, rather than 'not copied', this would accord with the intention of the drafters of the Berne Convention and bring the United Kingdom into line with civil law jurisdictions. It would also have the benefit of leaving those cases where the defendant misappropriates the **claimant**'s investment to be dealt with under **unfair competition** law, rather than devaluing copyright.

thinking point
Three of the previously mentioned writers (Laddie, Vaver and Gervais) all appear to agree that copyright needs rethinking and should be formulated so as to match more closely its perceived justifications. Do you think that it is possible to turn back the clock in the way they suggest?

7.3 Copyright compared with other intellectual property rights

7.3.1 Ease of creation

cross reference
See further chapter 8.

The existence of copyright protection does not depend on registration. Indeed, it is a condition of Article 5(2) of the Berne Convention that its Contracting States must not impose any formal requirements for the 'enjoyment and exercise of these rights'. Copyright in a work therefore arises automatically and instantaneously, upon the act of creation, provided certain simple conditions are satisfied. The key criteria are that the work must be original, it must be recorded in a material form and the author or the work must qualify for United Kingdom protection by being 'connected' in some way to a Contracting State of the Berne Convention, the **Universal Copyright Convention ('UCC')** or the **World Trade Organization ('WTO')**.

7.3.2 Scope of protection

It might be assumed that if an intellectual property right can easily be created, the protection conferred on its owner must be relatively limited. The contrary is the case. On the one hand, copyright is not a true monopoly right in the same sense as patents or **registered designs**, so that proof of independent creation is always a defence to an infringement action—indeed, it is the corollary of the requirement of originality. However, the breadth of copyright can be judged from the fact that it protects the right-holder not just against the copying of the work by another, but against issuing tangible copies of the work (by sale or rental), performing the work in public, communicating the work to the public by intangible means (by broadcasting it or uploading it onto a website), and adapting the work. These five forms of conduct are known as 'restricted acts' and are categorised as primary infringement. It is not necessary for the whole of the work to be copied, as liability arises should a 'substantial part' be taken, 'substantial' being assessed qualitatively not quantitatively (*Hawkes & Son v Paramount Film Services* [1934] Ch 593). The exact percentage taken does not matter. Further, copying can be indirect as well as direct and the copier does not even have to copy the source work consciously (*Francis Day & Hunter v Bron* [1963] Ch 587). Innocence is therefore not a defence to the acts of primary infringement, although it may affect the award of **damages** (CDPA s.97). Not only is the primary infringer liable for taking the work, but liability can be imposed for secondary infringement, so that anyone who subsequently deals knowingly in infringing copies in the course of trade may be sued.

However, and in sharp contrast to patents, designs and **trade marks**, copyright infringement (at least under current United Kingdom law) does *not* have to be done for profit. There is liability for infringement committed in the home. Whilst it might be thought that domestic infringers are not worth pursuing (which makes copyright law appear ridiculous), there are increasing examples of right-holders suing those who regularly commit infringement in the home, for example by downloading music or films: *Polydor Ltd v Brown* [2005] EWHC 3191 (Ch).

One other aspect of the breadth of the copyright infringement action should be mentioned, which is that someone who authorises the commission of an infringing act is just as much an infringer as someone who copies or who sells infringing copies. The word 'authorises' has been held to encompass not just conduct whereby the defendant 'sanctions, countenances or approves' the behaviour of another, but also where the defendant exhibits 'indifference from which authorisation may be inferred': *Moorhouse v University of New South Wales* [1976] RPC 151. The significance of authorisation is likely to increase in the era of the internet, as it has been held that the act of authorisation need not be committed in the United Kingdom as long as the act of primary infringement is (*ABKCO Music v Music Collection International* [1995] RPC 657). The implications of the *ABKCO* decisions for websites which enable United Kingdom visitors to download music and films should be considered.

A further difference exists between copyright and registrable forms of intellectual property protection. Patents, trade marks and designs can be declared invalid for failing to comply with the relevant statutory requirements, and trade marks may also be revoked for mismanagement, in particular for non-use. In contrast, copyright, once established, cannot be declared invalid, although a court may hold that the work in question is incapable of enforcement on grounds of public policy: *Glyn v Western Feature Film Co* [1916] 1 Ch 261.

7.3.3 Involvement of the criminal law

A challenge which faces both copyright and trade mark owners is how to combat commercial piracy. Both the CDPA and the Trade Marks Act 1994 ('TMA') (in, respectively, ss.107 and 92) impose criminal sanctions where an act of infringement is committed by way of trade. Such liability is not confined to counterfeiters, but applies equally to the copyright owner's business competitors (*Thames & Hudson v Design & Artists Copyright Society* [1995] FSR 153). The maximum penalties, police search and seizure powers, and the ability of the court to order forfeiture of seized items were rationalised by the Copyright, etc and Trade Marks (Offences and Enforcement) Act 2002 and the penalties were increased by the Digital Economy Act 2010. The 2002 Act did not, however, make any changes to the type of behaviour prohibited by the 1988 and 1994 Acts. Enforcement of ss.107 CDPA and 92 TMA is delegated to Local Authority Trading Standards Departments, with confiscation orders available to the magistrates' court under the Criminal Justice Act 1988 (Confiscation Orders) Order 1995. Trading Standards Departments have increased powers as a result of s.107A of the CDPA having been brought into force on 6 April 2007 by the Criminal Justice and Public Order Act 1994 (Commencement no 14) Order 2007.

A more universal concern is the impact of counterfeiting. In its report of June 2008, *The Economic Impact of Counterfeiting and Piracy*, the OECD estimated that in 2005 the trade in counterfeit and pirated products could have been worth $200 billion. Likewise, the EU Commission reported late in 2005 that there had been a 1,000 per cent increase in counterfeit seizures made by EU customs authorities between 1998 and 2004. Counterfeiting is no longer confined to luxury brands but to medicines, car parts and foodstuffs, with the obvious implications for consumer safety. EU law accordingly enables the intellectual property owner to call on the assistance of the customs authorities in the fight against counterfeiting by means of Regulation (EU) 608/2013 of the European Parliament and of the Council of 12 June 2013 concerning customs enforcement of intellectual property rights [2013] OJ L 181/15. The intellectual property owner can notify customs authorities who have power to prevent the importation of suspect goods at the point of entry. The goods in question are liable to forfeiture and destruction.

7.3.4 No liability for use

Traditionally, there has always been one significant limitation on the scope of copyright protection. The purchaser of a legitimate copy of a work is free to use it in whatever way they choose. Thus, someone who buys a book, besides being at liberty to read it, can use it to light a fire, tear out the pages, prop up the leg of a table with it, or do any other sort of conduct, provided that what has been done is not within the list of 'restricted acts' which are the prerogative of the copyright owner.

The advent of digital technology means that the purchaser's freedom to use a copyright article needs re-evaluating. To give one simple example, in order to use computer software, the program must be copied into the computer's memory. Whilst a licence to do so may readily be implied in the case of someone who buys a legitimate copy of software, the purchaser of a pirated copy will not be so protected and so will infringe each time they use the software, even if such use is for a legitimate purpose such as word-processing a letter or an essay. Further, whilst s.28A CDPA provides the defence of making a temporary copy of any work as part of a technological process for a lawful purpose, such defence does not apply to computer software.

7.3.5 Fragmentary nature

Mention must be made of one particular characteristic of copyright. Unlike patents and trade marks, copyright is not a unitary right, but a collection of a number of different rights. It has a fragmentary nature. This can be demonstrated by two examples.

First, each type of copyright work can, as a result of the list of 'restricted acts' found in s.16 CDPA, be reproduced in a multiplicity of ways. If this is combined with the way in which copyright protection arises automatically in every Contracting State of the Berne Convention, Universal Copyright Convention and WTO, the owner of a copyright work will have (quite literally) thousands of rights which exist worldwide.

Example 1

The trilogy *The Lord of the Rings* was written by J.R.R. Tolkein, who died in 1973. His literary executor (his son Christopher) has, by virtue of s.16 CDPA, the right to control the following until the end of 2043:

- the 'reproduction' of the trilogy (indeed, each part of the trilogy) 'in any material form';
- the first sale of each copy of the books, together with the rental of any copies;
- any public performance of the books, such as a reading or recitation;
- their communication by intangible means, whether by broadcast or by the internet;
- their adaptation, for example if they are turned into plays, or converted into pictorial form, or translated.

Consequently, there are hardback rights, paperback rights, serialisation rights, talking book rights, dramatisation rights, film rights, radio and television broadcast rights and the right to control the translation of the books into any language (consider how many languages there are worldwide). These rights exist not just in the United Kingdom, but in each state which is a signatory to the Berne Convention, the Universal Copyright Convention or the WTO (well over 160 countries worldwide). Each one of these rights can be **assigned** or **licensed** to third parties, either collectively or individually.

It will be appreciated that copyright's fragmentary nature combined with the lack of registration and the lengthy duration of protection makes the task of identifying who owns which right very complicated.

The second illustration of the fragmentary nature of copyright highlights the way in which one individual tangible product, for example a film DVD, may consist of a large number of individual copyrights. Some of these rights will flow from the copyright in another 'source' work, others will be independent of it, but the owners of each of these rights will need to give their permission before the film itself can be made, exhibited in public, communicated to the public, or copies of it sold or hired to the public.

Example 2

Consider, as an example, the novel *Death in Venice* written by Thomas Mann (1875–1955) which was first published in 1912. The novel was originally in German, but was translated into English by, amongst others, H.T. Lowe-Porter and Stanley Appelbaum. Visconti's 1971 film, *Death in Venice*, is based on the novel and has music by Gustav Mahler as its soundtrack. A film will have screenplay (the story) and dialogue, as well as music, costumes and sets. All of these could be copyright works in their own right, but equally they might be derived from earlier works. Thus the screenplay and dialogue of *Death in Venice* might be derived directly or indirectly from the original novel, or from an English translation of that novel (or indeed a translation of the novel in another language).

thinking point

From the previous example given, identify everyone who might have owned prior copyrights and who therefore would have had to give their consent to the making and subsequent exhibition of the film Death in Venice.

7.3.6 **Duration**

cross reference
See further section 8.5.

For most categories of work listed in s.1 of the CDPA, the simple rule of thumb is that protection lasts for a period of the author's life plus 70 years; indeed, this rule is applicable throughout the whole of the EU. Despite the ease of creation, copyright lasts far longer than either patent or design protection, and as previously explained, is not liable to **revocation** or **invalidity** proceedings.

However, there is a further complication awaiting the copyright lawyer in practice. The provisions of the CDPA apply only to works created after its operative date (1 August 1989). As regards works created before that date, the principle found in Sch. 1 to the Act is that copyright will continue to subsist in an 'existing' work *after* commencement only if it subsisted therein *before* commencement (the so-called 'gateway' provision). In practice, therefore, it will be necessary to refer to the old law in respect of works created before 1989. The wording of previous copyright legislation will be relevant in deciding whether the work was of a type which was capable of protection, whether the author of the work qualified for protection (indeed, what the relevant definition of 'author' was at the time the work was created), and what the duration of the work originally was.

Example 3

Consider a novel written in 1910, where, because the author died in 1950, copyright will remain in force until 2020. The novel will have to meet the criteria for protection set out, not in the 1956 Act, nor even in the 1911 Act, but in the Copyright Act 1842, because of the general principle that whether a work attracts United Kingdom copyright depends on *the law in force when the work was made*. Therefore even though such a novel should continue to be protected under the CDPA, it will have to meet the criteria in legislation well over 150 years old!

One final complication should be noted concerning duration. Since 1989, there have been considerable revisions to the CDPA as the result of various EU Directives. Such changes have created new categories of works, extended the duration of protection, and/or created new rights for existing works. The transitional provisions set out in United Kingdom implementing legislation are complex and will not generally be dealt with in this book.

Once the copyright in a work has expired, then that work passes into what is called the 'public domain' and is therefore free for everyone to use. However, this simple statement requires qualification. Many successful copyright works are often the subject of continuous revision or updating by their owners. Each time a new version of the work emerges, provided enough effort has gone into the revision, a fresh copyright will arise. A good example of this is the Mickey Mouse cartoon character, whose appearance over the decades has been subtly altered. Another example is where a very old piece of music, which never was in copyright, is the subject of extensive research and revision so as to make it capable of performance today. The creator of the modern 'performing edition' of the music is entitled to copyright in that version: *Sawkins v Hyperion Records* [2005] 1 WLR 3281. A final example is where a work long out of copyright (if indeed it ever had protection) is incorporated into another copyright work. So, were a new edition of Shakespeare's plays to be printed, although the plays themselves have never been protected by copyright, the publisher may have copyright in the typographical arrangement of the words on the printed page under s.8 CDPA. The publisher can therefore object to the copying of that layout even though the content of the book itself is not protected.

thinking point
Do the characteristics of copyright fit in with its theoretical justifications?

The idea/expression divide

One of the fundamental tenets of copyright law is that copyright does not exist to protect ideas, but rather the form in which they are expressed: *Donoghue v Allied Newspapers* [1938] Ch 106 at p. 109. This deceptively simple statement conceals what is perhaps the greatest challenge facing the student of copyright: how to draw the dividing line between an idea and its expression.

7.4.1 Idea versus expression: legislation

As Spence and Endicott point out ('Vagueness in the Scope of Copyright' (2005) 121 *LQR* 657) the CDPA itself gives little indication of this challenge. Section 1(1) merely declares that 'copyright is a *property* right which subsists…in the following descriptions of *work*' whilst s.2(1) states that the owner of the copyright in *a work of any description* has the *exclusive right* to do the acts…*restricted by the copyright* in a work of that description. Article 9(2) of the **TRIPs** Agreement, however, makes the clear distinction between ideas and expression. It should be remembered (as Gervais points out) that the TRIPs Agreement itself, in Article 9(1), expressly incorporates both the provisions of the Berne Convention and the background discussions which are used to interpret its key provisions.

7.4.2 Idea versus expression: case law

Several cases can be used to illustrate the distinction between an idea and its expression. In *Green v Broadcasting Corp of New Zealand* [1989] 2 All ER 1056 the Privy Council held that there was no copyright infringement where the defendant copied the format for a television talent show: all that had been taken was the mere idea. Nevertheless, close reading of the case reveals that the claimant could quite easily have identified key elements in each programme, such as the running order, catchphrases and other stage business which might (with careful pleading) have been claimed as a dramatic work. Similarly, in *Norowzian v Arks Ltd (No 2)* [2000] FSR 363 the defendant advertising agency, in creating a television advert called *Anticipation* for GUINNESS, had borrowed the claimant's idea of editing a film by a technique known as 'jump cutting' so that the actor appeared to make movements which were physically impossible. It was held that there had been no copying of the claimant's dramatic work, nor of his original film (called *Joy*). Although decided on the narrow point that there had been no taking of the claimant's work, it could be argued that what had been taken was the idea of how to edit the film in a particular way, not any particular copyright work. Nevertheless, it could be argued that the claimant's 'creativity' lay in the editing technique as much as in his film. Copyright law seems here unable to offer protection.

Despite these two illustrations, there are many examples in the cases of where the courts appear to be conferring protection on ideas themselves.

case close-up

Elanco v Mandops [1980] RPC 213

The claimant's patent for a weed-killer had expired so the defendant was, quite properly, entitled to make its own version of the product. In order to sell the weed-killer, it had to produce an appropriate instruction leaflet. Having changed the first version of its leaflet on the claimant's insistence so as to avoid copyright infringement, the defendant was successfully sued for having reproduced the wording in its second leaflet, even though this had been carefully redrafted in order to avoid taking the wording of the claimant's instructions. As the leaflet consisted principally of factual information (usually regarded as falling below the threshold for copyright protection), it is tempting to conclude that the Court of Appeal (in contrast to the Privy Council in *Green*) was protecting the underlying idea, not its expression. The net effect of the case was, of course, to extend the period of protection over the claimant's product, even though the original patent had expired.

7.4.3 Idea versus expression: can the line be clearly drawn?

The most recent illustration of the difference between taking the ideas in another's work and taking the expression is *Baigent and Lee v Random House Group Ltd* [2007] FSR 579.

Summary

199

case close-up

Baigent and Lee v Random House Group Ltd [2007] FSR 579

The authors of a book, *The Holy Blood and The Holy Grail*, sued the publishers of Dan Brown's bestselling novel, *The Da Vinci Code*, alleging copyright infringement by copying the 'central theme' of their work (the defendants, ironically, were the publishers of the claimants' own book, prompting speculation that the litigation was no more than a publicity stunt). Upholding the decision of Peter Smith J, the Court of Appeal held that although there had been copying (evidenced by points of similarity between the two works) what had been taken fell on the wrong side of the dividing line between ideas and their expression. The claimants' alleged 'central theme' (that descendants of Christ had married into the French royal family in the fifth century) was not the 'structure or architecture' of their book (which would have been capable of protection). Instead, the 'central theme' amounted to no more than a series of generalised propositions, at too high a level of abstraction to qualify for copyright protection. It was not the product of skill and labour by the claimants. Lloyd LJ (with whom Mummery LJ expressly agreed) declared (at [5]) that copyright does not subsist in ideas. It protects the expression of ideas, not the ideas themselves. Unhelpfully, perhaps, he then added that no clear principle 'is or could be laid down . . . to tell whether what is sought to be protected is on the ideas side of the dividing line, or on the expression side'.

The net result of the case is to confirm the idea/expression divide but to offer little guidance as to how it should be applied in any particular case.

thinking point

Throughout copyright law (particularly in infringement cases) you will find references to 'the idea/expression dichotomy'. Do you agree with Lloyd LJ in Baigent *that it is not possible to state the distinction in such a way that it can be applied consistently in all cases?*

Summary

This chapter has explained:

- the history of copyright law in the United Kingdom and the external influences which have shaped its content;

- the theoretical justifications for copyright and the extent to which they accord with the current law; and

- the principal characteristics of copyright, including the crucial difference between protecting an idea and protecting the expression of that idea.

? Reflective questions

Has copyright protection expanded so far that protection can no longer be justified? If so, would it not be better to abolish copyright altogether?

Annotated further reading

Breyer, S. 'The Uneasy Case for Copyright: A Study of Copyright in Books, Photocopies and Computer Programs' (1970) 84 *Harv LR* 281

Reconsiders the traditional justifications for copyright protection (namely moral rights and economic inducement), argues that neither is adequate and suggests that the case for copyright expansion is weak.

Burkitt, D. 'Copyrighting Culture—The History and Cultural Specificity of the Western Model of Copyright' [2001] *IPQ* 146

Reviews the different philosophical and cultural attitudes which coloured the development of early copyright law in England, the USA, France and Germany and considers their impact on the copyright law in countries such as China and Australia.

Deazley, R. 'The Myth of Copyright at Common Law' [2003] *CLJ* 106

Argues that the decision of the House of Lords in *Donaldson v Beckett* has been consistently misunderstood and gives an analysis of all the speeches in the case.

Gervais, D. 'The Compatibility of the Skill and Labour Originality Standard with the Berne Convention and the TRIPs Agreement' [2004] *EIPR* 75

Considers whether the TRIPs Agreement requires Contracting States to adhere to a higher standard of originality contemplated by the Berne Convention than is the case today in many common law jurisdictions.

Laddie, H. 'Copyright: Over-strength, Over-regulated, Over-rated' [1996] *EIPR* 253

Claims that the current scope of copyright protection is too great so that the balance is tilted too far in favour of the copyright owner.

Landes, W. and Posner, R. 'An Economic Analysis of Copyright Law' (1989) 18 *Journal of Legal Studies* 325

The seminal economic analysis of copyright protection which argues that the law can be explained as a means for promoting efficient allocation of resources.

Rahmatian, A. 'Copyright and Commodification' [2005] *EIPR* 371

Considers the relationship between copyright and creativity and whether it is correct to confer property rights on creativity.

Spence, M. and Endicott, T. 'Vagueness in the Scope of Copyright' (2005) 121 *LQR* 657

Argues that while vagueness in the scope of copyright protection is not of itself a bad thing, the purposes of copyright protection should be spelled out more clearly by the courts when deciding cases.

Vaver, D. 'Rejuvenating Copyright' (1996) 75 *Can BR* 69

Argues that the expansion of copyright has produced an incoherent system, and that copyright law needs a moral centre if it is to be respected.

Subsistence of copyright

Learning objectives

Upon completion of this chapter, you should have acquired:

- knowledge of the eight categories of work to which copyright protection is accorded under United Kingdom law;

- understanding of the way in which each category of work is defined in both legislation and case law;

- knowledge of the fundamental requirement of originality and the problems which it presents;

- knowledge of how copyright protection arises automatically once a work has been recorded in material form;

- an appreciation of the distinction between authorship and ownership and of the role which each concept plays in United Kingdom copyright law; and

- knowledge of the rules which govern the duration of copyright protection under present legislation.

Introduction

The starting point of this chapter is s.1 Copyright, Designs and Patents Act 1988 ('CDPA') which declares that copyright is a property right which subsists in eight different categories of 'work'. Chapter I of Part I CDPA provides further detail about each type of work. The statutory 'definitions' of each type of work, together with the sections dealing with authorship, ownership, qualification for protection (set out in Chapter IX of Part I, somewhat removed from the family of provisions dealing with other aspects of the existence of copyright), and duration, frequently lack clarity, or else appear to be a statement of the obvious. Fortunately (or perhaps, from the student's point of view, unfortunately) there is a wealth of case law which adds flesh to the statutory skeleton.

Section 172 CDPA

The lack of legislative clarity is compounded by the threefold effect of s.172 CDPA. First, the CDPA is stated to be both a restatement and amendment of the law of **copyright**, second, it is said that a provision in Part I which corresponds to a provision in previous legislation is not to be taken as departing from the previous law simply because of a change of expression and third, it is declared that decisions under the previous law may be referred to for the purpose of establishing whether a Part I provision departs from the previous law. This wording begs a number of questions: how can something be both a restatement and an amendment at one and the same time; how does one tell whether a change of expression is significant; and how can an earlier case help one to decide whether a later statute does change the law?

Section 1 CDPA conceals another challenge, in that it doesn't distinguish between what are in effect two different types of copyright. Literary, dramatic, musical and artistic works, besides having been protected under United Kingdom law for more than a century and a half, are regarded as being the intellectual product of a human **author** who has expended 'skill, labour and judgement' in their creation. We shall refer to this group as 'authorial' copyrights. On the other hand, sound recordings, broadcasts and the typographical arrangement of published editions arise as a result of the investment of capital by an enterprise (although this is not to deny that there will be human creativity involved). These we shall refer to as 'entrepreneurial' copyrights. Other countries within Europe regard the 'entrepreneurial' copyrights not as true copyright, but as so-called **neighbouring rights**, with a narrower scope of protection. Films, however, fall somewhere in between. United Kingdom law for many years regarded them as entrepreneurial copyrights, rewarding the investment by the production company by treating that enterprise as the author of the film. However, the **Berne Convention** and, more recently, European Union law, regard films as belonging in the 'authorial' category because of the creativity of the director.

Section 1 CDPA is a reflection of the common law tradition of requiring an alleged **work** to fit within recognised categories. Such an approach may have to be adjusted in due course in light of ECJ jurisprudence which avoids such classification and instead accords protection to any and every 'intellectual creation': Case C-5/08 *Infopaq International A/S v Danske Dagblades Forening* [2009] ECR I-6569 at [33–37] (*Infopaq*); Case C-393/09 *Bezpečnostní softwarová asociace—Svaz softwarové ochrany v Ministerstvo kultury* [2010] ECR I-13971 at [45–46].

This chapter will set out the criteria which must be satisfied before United Kingdom copyright protection will arise. The criteria can be summarised in a five-point plan, as follows:

- does the alleged 'work' fall within one of the recognised categories listed in s.1 CDPA;
- if so, does it possess **originality**;
- if so, have the conditions for the subsistence of copyright been met (these require the work to have been recorded in permanent form and for the work or its author to be qualified for protection by being 'connected' to the United Kingdom);
- who is the author of the work, and are they the owner of it; and
- is the work still within the period of protection or has copyright expired?

cross reference
See section 7.3.5.

One point to be remembered is the fragmentary nature of copyright. We gave an example of a film which, besides being a copyright work of itself, may contain other copyright works (the story, the dialogue, the music, the design of the costumes and so on). This characteristic of copyright is reminiscent of a Russian doll: remove one layer, and another appears; remove that and another one appears, and so on. Copyright is often multi-layered, and the rights in each layer may well belong to different people, have a different scope of protection, and last for different periods of time.

8.1 Categories of copyright work

8.1.1 Literary, dramatic and musical works

8.1.1.1 Literary works

Section 3(1) CDPA provides that a literary work is any work, other than a dramatic or musical work, which is written, spoken or sung. This phrase requires two comments. First, although it is relatively easy to distinguish words from music, where is the dividing line between a literary work and a dramatic work, as the words 'other than' (not present in the equivalent provision in the 1956 Act) suggest there is no overlap between the two? In the case of an opera, might the story be a dramatic work but the words of the songs literary works? The Act offers no guidance. Second, and again in contrast to its predecessor, the section contemplates copyright in the spoken word. As Phillips neatly illustrates (in 'Copyright in Spoken Words—Some Potential Problems' [1989] *EIPR* 231) the combined effect of ss. 3(2) and 3(3) means that words when spoken are inchoate copyright. Once fixed, they become literary works. The fixing (ie putting the words in permanent form) could be simultaneous, for example, by a sound recording, or belated, for example by someone writing the words down from memory some time after the event. MacQueen (in ' "My tongue is mine ain": Copyright, the Spoken Word and Privacy' (2005) 68 *MLR* 349) points out that there are a number of difficulties in according copyright to the spoken word. Are the words enough (in terms of quantity) to cross the minimum threshold for copyright to arise (for example, as the title of a song is incapable of being a copyright work, *Francis Day v Twentieth Century Fox* [1940] AC 112, could a simple sentence in a conversation

thinking point
In an age when media 'sound bites' are given such prominence, what are the implications of conferring copyright on the spoken word?

be copyright); are the words original; has there been adequate fixation; and in the case of an interview, could the interviewer be a **joint author** with the interviewee given the interactive nature of the event? We return to these points later.

cross reference
See section 8.2.3.3.

Returning to the statutory definition, s.3(1), as amended, adds that the term 'literary work' includes a table or compilation, other than a database; a computer program; preparatory design material for a computer program; and a **database**. With regard to the requirement that the work be 'written', s.178 CDPA (the general definition section for Part I) declares that 'writing' includes any form of notation or code, whether by hand or otherwise and regardless of the method by which, or medium in or on which, it is recorded, and that 'written' shall be construed accordingly.

Section 3 tells us nothing about what counts as a literary work. For this we turn to the cases. These illustrate perfectly the way in which United Kingdom law views copyright as an economic right governed by the maxim that 'what is worth copying is worth protecting'. The starting point of the case law is *University of London Press v University Tutorial Press* [1916] 2 Ch 601 in which Peterson J accorded protection to examination papers. He explained that 'literary work' did not require that the item possessed any sort of intellectual merit, rather, the phrase was analogous to the term 'printed matter' so that anything committed to paper was protected. The net effect is that a wide range of everyday items fall within the scope of copyright, for example, a five-letter code for sending messages (*Anderson & Co v Lieber Code Co* [1917] 2 KB 469), football pools coupons (*Ladbroke v William Hill* [1964] 1 WLR 273), greyhound race forecast cards (*Bookmakers Afternoon Greyhound Services v Wilf Gilbert* [1994] FSR 723), and lists of TV programmes (*Independent Television Publications v Time Out* [1984] FSR 64).

The low threshold for United Kingdom copyright protection begs the question of whether this gives the copyright owner too much power over factual information contained in a literary work. One response to the *ITP v Time Out* case was the enactment of the Broadcasting Act 1990 which provided for the **compulsory licensing** by broadcasting organisations to newspapers and other print media of TV programme listings. Another was the ECJ's decision in Cases C-241–242/91 P *RTE v Commission (Magill intervening)* [1995] ECR I-743. Here, the refusal of three broadcasting organisations in the 1980s (the BBC, ITV and RTE) to **license** Magill so that he could publish a multi-channel TV guide was held to be a breach of EU competition law. The Court did not deny that the organisations had copyright in their respective lists of programmes but did hold, in effect, that such copyright was secondary to the broadcasters' main product, television programmes, and that they were using their market power to stifle the publication of a new product for which there was public demand. One might speculate that the hidden message of the case was that the Court considered the threshold for copyright protection in the United Kingdom and Eire was too low, but did not have the jurisdiction to comment on the point.

The Court revisited the issue of when a refusal to license copyright can amount to an abuse of dominant position in Case C-418/01 *IMS Health GmbH v NDC Health GmbH* [2004] ECR I-5039. The case concerned IMS' alleged copyright in a database of regional sales information about pharmaceutical products and its refusal to license others. The ECJ declared that three conditions had to be satisfied before a refusal to license copyright was a breach of Article 102 of the **Treaty on the Functioning of the European Union (TFEU)**. First, the undertaking requesting the **licence** must intend to offer new products not offered by the copyright owner and for which there was a potential consumer demand; second, the refusal could not be justified by objective considerations; last, the refusal had to have the effect of eliminating all the copyright owner's competitors in that market. The case serves as an example of the interface between intellectual property law (particularly where the product is, in effect, information) and competition law, but raises the question of which is the best means of limiting the power of the right owner, the intellectual property régime itself or competition law.

There is, however, a minimum threshold below which the 'work' will not attract protection. Song titles are not protectable (*Francis Day v Twentieth Century Fox*) and the argument that an invented word **trade mark** should be treated as a literary work was rejected by the Court of Appeal in *Exxon Corporation v Exxon Insurance Consultants* [1982] RPC 69 because it did not provide 'information, instruction or pleasure of a literary kind' (*per* Stephenson LJ at p. 88). Factual information at the front of a diary was denied protection in *Cramp v Smythson* [1944] AC 329 because it was commonplace, and in *Navitaire Inc v EasyJet Airline Co* [2005] ECDR 160 (which relied on the reasoning in the *Exxon* case), individual command names in a computer program were held incapable of copyright protection as literary works.

One case which stood out of line was *Shetland Times v Jonathan Wills* [1997] FSR 604 where it was assumed for the purposes of granting interim relief that newspaper headlines were copyright works. In view of the ECJ's ruling in *Infopaq* and its application by the Court of Appeal in *Newspaper Licensing Agency v Meltwater Holding BV* [2012] RPC 1 (reversed on a different point by the Supreme Court in *Public Relations Consultants Association Ltd v Newspaper Licensing Agency Ltd* [2013] RPC 469), *Shetland Times* may not be the aberration it was once thought to be.

8.1.1.2 Dramatic works

The only assistance offered by s.3 CDPA is to declare that a dramatic work *includes* a work of dance or mime, so that it does not have to have words. Again, the inference from ss.3(2) and 3(3) (by analogy with the cases on spoken word copyright) must be that a dramatic work need not be written down as long as it is recorded in some medium (for example, film), even if the recording is unauthorised.

Turning to the cases for guidance, it seems that a dramatic work requires some sort of presentation or delivery (*Fuller v Blackpool Winter Gardens* [1895] 2 QB 429) or else it must be a work of action capable of being performed before an audience (*Norowzian v Arks Ltd* [2000] FSR 363). In the latter case, the Court of Appeal suggested, *obiter*, that a film could be a dramatic work, but arguably the court confused the underlying work with the medium in which it was recorded. Presumably, the performance must be by a human being, as it has been held that a video game cannot be categorised as a dramatic work: *Nova Productions Ltd v Mazooma Games Ltd* [2007] RPC 589.

Television game show formats (despite their enormous commercial value) were denied copyright protection as dramatic works in *Green v Broadcasting Corp of New Zealand* [1989] RPC 700. The last-mentioned case also reveals the conservative nature of United Kingdom copyright law, in that it assumes that a work (whether dramatic or some other category) must in some way be finite and complete. One of the reasons given in *Green* as to why the 'Opportunity Knocks' format was not protectable was that the content of the show changed with each edition. This narrow approach has implications for improvised plays and other ways in which the performing arts can be delivered.

8.1.1.3 Musical works

The CDPA s.3 defines a musical work as 'a work consisting of music, exclusive of any words or action intended to be sung, spoken, or performed with the music', rather a statement of the obvious. The definition in the 1911 Act (now repealed) talked about 'any combination of melody and harmony reduced to writing'. Again, however, this betrays the conservative assumptions which United Kingdom copyright law makes: could a period of silence be a musical work?

cross reference
See section 8.4.5.

From the wording of s.3(1) it is clear that in the case of a song, the words and music are separate copyright works and so may be owned by different people (although in some jurisdictions, a song is treated as a single copyright work with the lyricist and composer joint authors). However, as explained later, where the song is produced by collaboration between the lyricist and composer, it is now treated as a work of **co-authorship** for the sole purpose of determining the duration of protection. For musical works, the threshold for protection is very low. In *Lawson v Dundas* 12 June 1985, unreported, the four-note tune used as the 'ident' of Channel 4 was held to be a copyright work, and in *Bamgboye v Reed* [2004] EMLR 61, the addition of a drum accompaniment to a piece of music was sufficient to confer protection on the **claimant**. By contrast, in *Coffey v Warner/Chappell Music Ltd* [2005] FSR 747 the singer's vocal expression, pitch contour and syncopation were held not capable of being regarded as a copyright work, because they were not sufficiently separable from the remainder of the work to constitute a musical work in their own right. Again, because of the effect of ss.3(2) and 3(3), the music doesn't have to be formally written down at the outset: *Hadley v Kemp* [1999] EMLR 589.

case close-up

> ***Sawkins v Hyperion Records*** [2005] 1 WLR 3281
>
> These issues are brought together in the judgment of Mummery LJ in *Sawkins v Hyperion Records* [2005] 1 WLR 3281 at [53–56]. He begins by stating that according to 'ordinary usage' the essence of music is combining sounds for listening to. Music, he says, is not the same as mere noise. Although we think of music as an organised performance played from a musical score, the written score is not essential for the existence of the music or of copyright in it. One must distinguish the music from its fixation. However, the fixation, whether in a written score or on a record, is not in itself the music in which copyright subsists. Mummery LJ suggests that there is no reason why a recording of spontaneous singing, whistling or humming or improvisations of sounds with or without musical instruments should not be regarded as 'music' for copyright purposes. He also adds that it is wrong to single out the notes as uniquely significant for copyright purposes and to deny copyright to the other elements that make some contribution to the sound of the music when performed, such as directions for tempo, volume and other 'performance indicators'.

Mummery LJ therefore takes into account that a performance may be an integral part of a musical work, an attitude which contrasts with the outcome in the *Coffey* case discussed earlier and with the more 'traditional' views of Park J in *Hadley v Kemp* where it was assumed that the creation of music has to involve the writing down (or at least the recording) of the notes divorced from any input from the performers. *Hadley v Kemp* separates authorship from performance. Such separation means that the perception of music under United Kingdom copyright law is at odds with many popular forms such as jazz (which depends on improvisation) and rap (which relies on sampling). Again, in due course, the *Infopaq* decision may require a reassessment of these cases.

8.1.2 Artistic works

Section 4(1) CDPA provides the meaning of the phrase 'artistic work' and is divided into three paragraphs. It covers, first, graphic works, photographs, sculptures or collages, irrespective of their artistic quality; second, works of architecture; and finally, works of artistic craftsmanship. Further elaboration is provided in s.4(2) which explains that a 'graphic work' includes (a) any painting, drawing, diagram, map, chart or plan; and (b) any engraving, etching, lithograph, woodcut or similar work).

This indiscriminate list of items covers both two-dimensional and three-dimensional art forms, the latter comprising works of architecture (which according to s.4(2) CDPA can be either buildings or models for buildings), sculptures (which term includes any cast or model made for the purposes of sculpture), and works of artistic craftsmanship. In common with works falling under s.3, s.4 is conservative in its thinking as to what is an artistic work. Some of the 'installation' art found today doesn't easily fall within the statutory 'definition'. The statement in para (a) that the types of art listed do not have to possess artistic quality has the merit that the judiciary does not have to decide whether something deserves protection. On the other hand, the sparse definition of 'artistic work' does mean that some cases appear to have been decided on the basis of assumptions which may not accord with the expectations of the creator of the work in question.

As with s.3, we have to look to case law for elaboration, taking the key words and phrases in s.4 in turn.

8.1.2.1 Graphic works

Section 4(2) 'defines' graphic work by giving a list of various two-dimensional art forms. The first of these is a 'painting'. It has been suggested (in *Merchandising Corporation of America v Harpbond* [1983] FSR 32) that this involves 'representation or depiction by colours on a surface' which immediately begs two questions, 'could a blank canvas be a painting' and 'what do you mean by "surface" '? The *Harpbond* case answered the second by saying that someone's face could not be a 'surface' so that new stage make-up for the singer Adam Ant was not protected, the court also suggesting that the lack of permanence was fatal to copyright protection being granted.

cross reference
See further
chapter 11.

Of the remaining items in the list in s.4(2), the most important is probably the word 'drawing'. However, the commercial significance of this category of artistic works is much reduced because of the defence in s.51 CDPA which means that the right owner is unable to rely on copyright to prevent another from making **articles** to that design, but has instead to rely on **unregistered design right**. The case law on what is a 'drawing' reveals a very low threshold, so that mundane articles receive protection. In *Hutchison Personal Communications v Hook Advertising* [1995] FSR 365, a logo for a mobile phone network consisting of an inverted 'R' (which looked like a rabbit's head) was held to be a work, whilst in *Bernstein v Sidney Murray* [1981] RPC 303 rough fashion sketches were protected. Technical drawings are also included, so that drawings for machine parts (*British Northrop v Texteam Blackburn* [1974] RPC 57), circuit diagrams (*Anacon v Environmental Research Technology* [1994] FSR 659), and architect's plans (*Jones v London Borough of Tower Hamlets* [2001] RPC 407) have all been held to be copyright (architect's plans fall within para (a) of s.4(1), buildings fall within para (b)). Lastly, cartoons (such as 'Popeye') are 'artistic works' within the CDPA: *King Features Syndicate Inc v O & M Kleeman Ltd* [1941] AC 417.

It might be thought that the terms 'engraving' and 'etching' are concerned with types of pictorial representation, but two cases have given them wide meanings so that three-dimensional objects fall within their scope. In the New Zealand case of *Wham-O Manufacturing Co v Lincoln* [1985] RPC 127 it was held that plastic frisbees made by extrusion mouldings were engravings and the wooden models for the moulds were sculptures, and in *Hi-Tech Autoparts Ltd v Towergate Two Ltd* [2002] FSR 254 it was held that rubber car mats with grooves cut in them to help drainage were etchings. These two cases should be contrasted with the decisions on sculptures (discussed later).

8.1.2.2 Photographs

Section 4(2) CDPA explains that the word 'photograph' means 'a recording of light or other radiation on any medium on which an image is produced or from which an image may by any means be produced and which is not part of a film'. This definition, which draws a distinction between still and cinematic photography, is wide enough to cover all types of photographic activity, ranging from celluloid to X-ray to digital imagery. Nevertheless, the extent to which photographs *should* be protected by copyright has proved somewhat controversial. In *Graves' Case* (1869) LR 4 QB 715 it was held that a photograph of an engraving was itself an artistic work. The case has been criticised (on the ground that there was no originality) and also justified (on the basis that the technology of the time required a greater effort on the part of the photographer than do today's digital cameras, so that there was skill, labour and judgement).

case close-up

Antiquesportfolio.com Ltd v Rodney Fitch & Co Ltd [2001] FSR 345
. . . .

In *Antiquesportfolio.com Ltd v Rodney Fitch & Co Ltd* [2001] FSR 345 the principle that there is copyright in photographs, no matter how simple, was upheld. Skill, labour and judgement, said Neuberger J, may be found in three ways, either in the photographer's choice of subject matter, or in things like camera angle, lighting and so on, or by the photographer being in the right place at the right time. The one exception might be when a 'slavish imitation' is taken of a two-dimensional copyright work, for example by photocopying a drawing, although Neuberger J did not decide the point.

The thinking in *Antiques Portfolio* was applied by HHJ Birss QC in *Temple Island Collections Ltd v New English Teas Ltd* [2012] FSR 321 when he decided that a photograph of a red bus crossing Westminster Bridge was protected by copyright, the reasoning being reinforced by making reference to the ECJ's ruling in *Infopaq*. The ECJ relied on its own ruling in *Infopaq* when determining that a photograph can be copyright, provided it is the author's own intellectual creation: Case C-145/10 *Eva-Marie Painer v Standard Verlags GmbH*, 1 December 2011.

An entirely different matter, however, is the scope of protection afforded to photographic copyright. What should be remembered in relation to copyright in photographs is the basic rule that independent creation is always a defence to **infringement**. Just because you own copyright in a simple holiday snapshot of a famous building (for example, the Louvre Museum in Paris) does not prevent someone else taking a similar picture. However, as Lupton explains (in 'Photographs and the Concept of Originality in Copyright Law' [1988] *EIPR* 257) the outcome may be different if the first photograph to be taken has involved creative effort in the choice of scene, lighting, camera angle, exposure and so on. Were this to be the case, then its owner may be able to stop another person taking a similar photograph, at least where there is evidence that they had seen the first photograph and so had the opportunity to copy its composition. This argument was accepted in the *New English Teas* case.

A much misunderstood (and often inaccurately reported) case is *Bauman v Fussell* (1953) [1978] RPC 485. It concerned a photograph of a cockfight. The copyright owner subsequently attempted to sue for infringement in respect of a painting of the same scene. The decision of the Court of Appeal was *not* that there was no copyright in the photograph, but that there had been no substantial taking from it. Although the scene had been copied, the alleged infringer had not taken the key features of the picture. Usually, therefore, an action for the infringement of photographic copyright will have to be based on an exact reproduction, as happened in *Gabrin v Universal Music Operations Ltd*, [2004] ECDR 18, where a photograph of Elvis Costello had been taken for publicity purposes, and was subsequently turned into a poster publicising his concerts. Many years later, the poster was used to create the cover of a CD. Patten J held that in principle there had been indirect copying of the original photograph, a point strictly speaking *obiter*, as the action was defeated on the ground that the claimant had no title to sue.

8.1.2.3 Sculptures

The term 'sculpture' is stated by s.4(2) CDPA to include any cast or model made for the purposes of sculpture. Cases have discussed whether *any* three-dimensional object could be a sculpture or whether the word imports some sort of artistic requirement. In *J & S Davis v Wright* [1988] RPC 403 Whitford J held that dental impression trays were not sculptures (in part because they were not permanent) and in *Metix (UK) Ltd v G.H. Maughan (Plastics) Ltd* [1997] FSR 718 Laddie J decided that cartridges used to mix chemicals were not sculptures. In so holding, he accepted counsel's definition of a sculpture as 'a three-dimensional work made by an artist's hand'. This implies that functional three-dimensional articles should not be treated as artistic works but are best left to design right protection.

case close-up

Lucasfilm Ltd v Ainsworth [2012] 1 AC 208

. . . .

The policy of denying that functional three-dimensional articles are sculptures was made explicit by Mann J at first instance in *Lucasfilm Ltd v Ainsworth*, a case concerned with alleged copyright in the Stormtrooper helmets in the film *Star Wars*. Having reviewed the previous case law on 'sculptures', he discussed ([2009] FSR 103 at [118]) the proper meaning of the word. Considering the 'normal' (ie lay) sense of the word, he stated that not every three-dimensional object can be regarded as a sculpture. To hold otherwise would not be right. A sculpture should have, as part of its purpose, a visual appeal in the sense that it might be enjoyed for that purpose alone, whether or not it might have another purpose. The purpose was that of the creator, the 'artist's hand' referred to by Laddie J in *Metix*. An artist (in the realm of the visual arts) created something because it had visual appeal which was to be enjoyed as such. It had to have the intrinsic quality of being intended to be enjoyed as a visual thing. For that reason, items such as model soldiers had correctly been treated as sculptures, but the frisbee in *Wham-O* should not have been, nor should the moulds for the toasted sandwich maker in *Breville Europe plc v Thorn EMI Domestic Appliances Ltd* [1995] FSR 77. What mattered was whether the maker intended the object to have a visual appeal for its own sake. So, for example, a pile of bricks in an art gallery would amount to a sculpture, but a pile of bricks left outside a house by a builder would not. Mann J's decision that the helmets were not sculptures and his approach to the meaning of the word was endorsed by both the Court of Appeal and the Supreme Court.

8.1.2.4 Collages

cross reference
See section 8.3.2.

The case of *Creation Records v News Group Newspapers* [1997] EMLR 444 provides a useful link between the concept of a sculpture and that of a collage. It concerned a collection of items in a swimming pool to be photographed for the cover of the Oasis CD *Be Here Now*. The collection was held not to be a sculpture (again, the conservative assumptions made by copyright law are apparent) and although the assembly might amount to a collage, it did not obtain copyright because it was not permanent. The requirement of permanence is considered later.

8.1.2.5 Buildings

The word 'buildings' is stated by s.4(2) CDPA to include any fixed structure and a part of a building or fixed structure. It should not be assumed that copyright in works of architecture is confined to grandiose public buildings such as art galleries or cathedrals. In *Meikle v Maufe* [1941] 3 All ER 144, copyright was held to exist in showrooms on Tottenham Court Road, London, the infringement being by the building of an extension which matched the original facade and interior. In *Hay v Sloan* (1957) 12 DLR 2d 397 (a case concerned with suburban housing) the judge speculates as to how low the threshold for works of architecture might be, contemplating that even a crenellated pigsty might be a copyright work.

8.1.2.6 Works of artistic craftsmanship

The phrase 'artistic craftsmanship' is not defined in the CDPA, but as a composite concept it involves two elements, artistry and craftsmanship, both of which must be satisfied. The difficulty here is the lack of assistance from the cases.

As regards what is 'artistic', the consensus seems to be that it equates to 'eye appeal', something which looks nice.

case close-up

Hensher Ltd v Restawile Upholstery (Lancs) Ltd [1976] AC 64

As to who should decide whether an object meets that criterion, the House of Lords offered five different suggestions in *Hensher Ltd v Restawile Upholstery (Lancs) Ltd* [1976] AC 64, a case involving the design for a three-piece suite, admittedly at the lower end of the market. The suggestions range from the judge's opinion, to the intention of the maker, whether the article has been made by an artist, the opinion of an expert witness, or even public opinion. These comments should be seen as *obiter* for two reasons, namely the concession by counsel that the prototype for the furniture was a work of craftsmanship, and the finding that there was no copyright because the original prototype had been destroyed once production commenced. The lack of permanence is yet again the excuse for denying protection to a functional object.

The issue of who decides whether a particular work of craftsmanship is artistic was resolved in *Merlet v Mothercare plc* [1986] RPC 115 where the Court of Appeal confirmed that it is the intention of the creator which is paramount. Here, therefore, a baby cape was not a work of artistic craftsmanship because its designer intended it primarily to be a means of protecting the infant from the weather.

Further clarification of what is a work of artistic craftsmanship can be found in the case of *Vermaat v Boncrest Ltd* [2001] FSR 43. The court said that it had to be possible to say that the author was both a craftsman and an artist. A craftsman was a person who made something in a skilful way and who took justified pride in his workmanship. An artist was a person with creative ability who produced something with aesthetic appeal. Further, it was not necessary for the same person to conceive and execute the work, so that if two or more people combined to design and make an article, there was no reason why it should not be regarded as a work of artistic craftsmanship. Again, however, the finding in the case was that the work was not protected in copyright: although the articles (bedspreads) were a product of craftsmanship, they lacked artistry. An additional factor emerges at first instance in the decision in *Guild v Eskandar Ltd* [2001] FSR 38 (overturned on appeal on different grounds: [2003] FSR 23). Rimer J thought that where the original article (here, knitwear) had been made by machine it could not be a work of craftsmanship, so that protection (if any) was by means of design right under Part III CDPA. Whether an article has been made by hand or machine is therefore crucial. *Hensher* and *Boncrest* (together with Australian case law) were relied on by Mann J at first instance in *Lucasfilm* in deciding that the Stormtrooper helmets were not works of artistic craftsmanship, a conclusion confirmed on appeal.

A rare case in which a claim that a work was one of artistic craftsmanship succeeded was *Shelley Films v Rex Features* [1994] EMLR 134 which concerned the film costumes, sets and masks for *Frankenstein*.

thinking point
Does the way in which literary, dramatic, musical and artistic works are defined in the cases provide adequate protection for those involved in the creative arts?

8.1.3 **Films**

8.1.3.1 Historical background

Despite being added to the list of copyright works in the 1928 version of the Berne Convention, it was not until the Copyright Act 1956 that United Kingdom law gave express recognition to this category. Prior to the 1911 Act, films could only be protected as a series of photographs, but because of the wording of the Fine Arts Copyright Act 1862, copyright was lost on the first sale of the film. Under the 1911 Act, they could still be treated as photographs, or as original dramatic works or (when talking pictures arrived) as 'musical works reproduced by mechanical contrivances' but there was no separate copyright protection for films as such. Moreover, under the 1911 Act there were fewer 'connecting factors', so many USA films were not granted United Kingdom copyright because at the time, the USA did not belong to the Berne Convention (it only acceded to the Convention on 1 March 1989). The 1911 Act's treatment of films was preserved by the 1956 Act for those films made before its commencement date, such treatment being continued by the 1988 Act.

The 1956 Act's idiosyncratic treatment of films was to be found in s.13. The definition reflects the technology of the time, namely 'any sequence of visual images recorded on material of any description . . . capable . . . of being shown as a moving picture or of being recorded on other material . . .' which suggests a series of frames on celluloid. This did not cover video recordings which consist of electronic impulses recorded on tape or disc, so long before its replacement in 1989, the Act was out of date. The 1956 Act contained no requirement of originality: there was some debate as to whether this was a deliberate omission, but given that the Berne Convention requires originality in respect of all works falling within its scope, it can perhaps be considered an oversight.

With regard to whether United Kingdom copyright was to be accorded to a film, it all depended on whether the maker of the film was a '**qualified person**' during the making of the film or if it was first published in a **Convention country**. However, publication was defined as 'issuing copies to the public' and not 'exhibition to the public'. If one remembers that selling copies of films was not common during the early years of the 1956 Act, in practice the existence of protection depended solely on the status of the maker of the film. It should also be remembered that the membership of the Berne Convention was relatively small until the 1980s, so many films made outside the United Kingdom remained unprotected.

Ownership of film copyright vested in the maker, which under the 1956 Act meant the person by whom the arrangements for the film's creation were made, although this statement of principle was merely a starting point and often overridden by contractual arrangements.

The major drawback of the 1956 Act was its rule on duration. Copyright was to last 50 years from registration (basically only feature films in 35mm format designed to be projected one reel at a time were registrable under the Films Act 1960) or 50 years from publication. Consequently, in the case of many films, copyright never started to run (because they were neither registrable nor published, because copies of the film had not been sold) and so was, in effect, perpetual. The CDPA 1988 Sch. 1 deals with this problem by stating that copyright in such films will expire at the end of 50 years from the end of the calendar year in which that Act came into force (ie in 2039).

8.1.3.2 Current treatment

The current definition of 'film' is to be found in s.5B CDPA, as amended. A film means a recording on any medium from which a moving image may by any means be produced, wording which hopefully now is wide enough to cover any future technological changes. A film soundtrack receives dual protection, being treated both as part of the film and as a sound recording in its own right.

8.1.4 **Sound recordings**

8.1.4.1 Historical background

Prior to the 1911 Act there was no protection for sound recordings, and equally, the making of a recording was not an infringement of a musical work: *Boosey v Whight* [1900] 1 Ch 122. The 1911 Act, which (unusually) *was* retrospective in this regard, conferred protection for 'records, perforated rolls and other contrivances by means of which sounds may be mechanically reproduced', a reflection of the technology of the day. It was further decided in *Gramophone Co v Stephen Cawardine & Co* [1934] Ch 450 that there was copyright in a sound recording even if the musical work embodied in it was out of copyright, so that the owner of the copyright in the sound recording could control the public performance of it.

Under s.12 of the 1956 Act, 'sound recording' meant 'the aggregate of sounds embodied in and capable of being reproduced by means of a record of any description, other than a soundtrack associated with a film', in other words it was the *sounds* incorporated in a record, rather than the record itself, which were copyright. The section was therefore not limited to music. There was no requirement of originality. Copyright was to exist if the maker was a qualified person at the time the recording was made, or if the recording was first published in a Convention country. 'Publication' bore its usual meaning of 'issuing copies to the public'. Section 12 vested ownership in the maker of the recording, 'maker' being the person owning the original recording medium, rather than the person who made the arrangements for the creation of the work, yet another difference between the CDPA and its predecessor. Duration was to be 50 years from first publication.

8.1.4.2 Current treatment

Under the CDPA, 'sound recording' now means a recording of sounds, from which sounds may be reproduced, or a recording of the whole or part of a literary, dramatic or musical work, from which sounds reproducing the work or part may be produced, regardless of the medium on which the recording is made or the method by which the sounds are reproduced or produced (s.5A, as amended). Sound recordings are not limited to recordings of music but of any sound, and hopefully the definition is wide enough to cope with changing technology.

8.1.5 **Broadcasts**

8.1.5.1 Historical background

Prior to the 1956 Act, there was no protection for broadcasts, as they were considered too temporary to be capable of protection. The 1956 Act, in recognising copyright in broadcasts, did not have any retrospective effect, except for Sch. 7 which provided that where a pre-1956 programme was rebroadcast after the operative date of the Act it would attract a 50-year period of protection. Section 14 of the 1956 Act defined TV broadcasts as meaning 'visual images broadcast by way of television' and sound broadcasts as 'sounds broadcast otherwise than as part of a TV broadcast', so that TV did not have to be capable of being seen as a moving picture. 'Broadcast' meant 'emission through the atmosphere by wireless telegraphy', reflecting the technology of the time, so that cable transmission or retransmission was not included. There was no mention of originality, and for copyright to subsist, the broadcast had to be made from a place in the United Kingdom, in other words only the BBC and IBA could own United Kingdom broadcast copyright, although there were reciprocal arrangements for broadcasts from other countries. One point of debate was whether the broadcast had to be capable of being received by a significant section of the public, some writers arguing that this was implicit in the Act. Copyright was to last 50 years from the end of the calendar year in which the broadcast was first made, with no prolongation of the term in the case of repeated broadcasts.

8.1.5.2 Current treatment

The CDPA operates in the global telecommunications market. The Act has to be read in conjunction with the Broadcasting Acts 1990 and 1996 (the former deregulated broadcasting) as well as Council Directive 89/552/EEC of 3 October 1989 on the co-ordination of certain provisions concerning the pursuit of television broadcasting activities [1989] OJ L 298/23 (the 'Television without Frontiers Directive') and Council Directive 93/83/EEC of 27 September 1993 on the co-ordination of certain rules concerning copyright and neighbouring rights applicable to satellite broadcasting and cable re-transmission (the 'Copyright Broadcasting Directive') [1993] OJ L 246/15.

Under the CDPA s.6, as amended to take account of the Information Society Directive (Directive 2001/29/EC of the European Parliament and of the Council of 22 May 2001 on the harmonisation of certain aspects of copyright and related rights in the information society [2001] OJ L 167/10), the term broadcast means 'an electronic transmission of visual images, sounds or other information'. It must be either transmitted for simultaneous reception by members of the public being capable of being lawfully received by them, or else be transmitted at a time determined solely by the person making the transmission for presentation to members of the public. The definition therefore covers cable and wireless broadcasts, terrestrial and satellite, analogue and digital, as well as information such as teletext. It does not include any internet transmission unless this takes place simultaneously on the internet and by other means, or is a concurrent transmission of a live event, or is a transmission of recorded moving images or sounds forming part of a programme service offered by the person responsible for making the transmission, being a service in which programmes are transmitted at scheduled times determined by that person. This revised definition, which draws a clear distinction between a broadcast and the making of information, images and sounds available on the internet, reverses the decision in *Shetland Times v Jonathan Wills* which had assumed that a website was a broadcast.

8.1.6 **Typographical arrangements**

The one uniquely British category of copyright work (which is not found in any of the International Conventions) is set out in s.8 CDPA, namely protection for the published editions of literary, dramatic or musical works which do not reproduce the typographical arrangement of a previous edition. It was introduced in the 1956 Act as a result of lobbying by the publishing industry, concerned that their investment in typesetting new editions of books (whether or not those books were themselves copyright works) would be eroded by the ability to make a facsimile copy of the printed page. Given changes in technology, it is arguable that this category of work is an anachronism. Copyright under s.8 is separate from that (if any) in the work

itself and is conferred on *publishers* in respect of the layout *only* of printed editions of books, periodicals, plays and music (ie only works falling within s.3). A typeface (as opposed to the layout of the printed page) is protected as an artistic work.

Section 8 was scrutinised by the House of Lords in *Newspaper Licensing Agency Ltd v Marks & Spencer plc* [2003] AC 551. Relying on Australian authority, their Lordships held that in respect of newspapers, it is the whole edition, not individual articles, which is protected by s.8. Therefore, in photocopying press cuttings on 'lifestyle' issues for internal distribution the defendant had not infringed the s.8 right as it had not reproduced the whole published edition.

thinking point
Do the statutory definitions of each type of 'work' and the judicial interpretations enable the CDPA to cope with changing technology?

8.2

The requirement of originality

8.2.1 Meaning in relation to literary, dramatic, musical and artistic works

Section 1(1)(a) CDPA declares that copyright subsists in every *original* literary, dramatic, musical or artistic work. As Gervais puts it (in 'The Compatibility of the Skill and Labour Originality Standard with the Berne Convention and the TRIPs Agreement' [2004] *EIPR* 75) originality is at the very core of copyright. What may come as a surprise is the definition of originality under United Kingdom law.

In *University of London Press v University Tutorial Press* Peterson J (at p. 608) stated that the word means source not inventiveness. The only issue was whether the author had expended the minimum amount of skill, labour and judgement in the creation of the work. As Lord Pearce put it in *Ladbroke v William Hill* at p. 291 'the word "original" does not demand original or inventive thought, but only that the work should not be copied but should originate from the author'.

The minimalist definition of 'originality' conflicts, according to Gervais, with the intention of the makers of the Berne Convention who regarded the term as meaning 'creativity'. The thinking in the *University of London Press* (endorsed by the House of Lords in *Ladbroke v William Hill*) is attributable, he argues, to the fact that at the time there was no recognition of the tort of misappropriation. Had Peterson J been able to make use of a case such as *International News Service v Associated Press* (1918) 248 US 215, where the US Supreme Court protected the business investment in a news telegraphy service through the action for unfair competition, instead of defining originality in terms of the right to protect investment, he might have given it the true meaning of the author's intellectual endeavour. It is arguable that the ECJ's ruling in *Infopaq* will require a radical rethink of the requirement of originality: 'intellectual creativity' may be present in a very simple phrase but lacking in a list of items compiled by 'the sweat of the brow'.

8.2.2 Meaning in relation to films, sound recordings, broadcasts and published editions

In ss.1(1)(b) and (c) and in the wording of ss.5, 6 and 8 (which define sound recordings, films, broadcasts and published editions) the word 'original' does not appear. Instead each provision

Chapter 8 Subsistence of copyright

216

declares that the particular category of work does not attract copyright 'to the extent that it is a copy of' a previous sound recording, film, broadcast or published edition. This raises the question of whether these particular categories of works must be original.

Whilst it could be argued that the omission of the word 'original' might be significant, the requirement that the work be 'not copied' is entirely consistent with the *University of London Press* case. Further, it should be remembered that films fall within the scope of the Berne Convention and are therefore subject to the requirement of originality. In view of this, it would seem illogical to argue that films must be original, but the other forms of entrepreneurial copyright need not, given that they all share the same definition of originality.

8.2.3 Specific problems

Peterson J's definition of 'originality' in the *University of London Press* case has generated a number of specific problems.

8.2.3.1 Revisions by or with the consent of the author

The first aspect of originality which requires further discussion is where the author of a work (assuming that he or she is also the owner, or else has the owner's permission) revises the work. Does the updated version of the work attract fresh copyright? Unfortunately, there is no clear answer, the cases revealing that it is all a question of degree as to whether enough 'skill, labour and judgement' has been expended on the revision. The fact that it is a question of degree means, in effect, that it lies in the court's discretion whether to accord fresh copyright to the amended work. In *Interlego v Tyco* [1989] AC 217 the Privy Council held that minor adjustments to the engineering drawings for LEGO bricks were too minimal to result in fresh copyright protection being given. The case is complicated by the fact that the claimant was trying to avoid relying on **registered design** protection (which had by the date of the case expired and which was not capable of being extended) and the distaste which the court felt at the attempt to rely on copyright as an alternative is evident. By contrast, in *Cala Homes v Alfred McAlpine Homes East Ltd* [1995] FSR 818, Laddie J held that revisions made to an architect's plans for houses had been done with enough skill, labour and judgement to attract fresh copyright. It didn't matter that the alterations had been done by the claimant's employees at the direction of the original architect. Here, the conclusion that there was new copyright in the revised drawings may have been influenced by the finding that the defendant had flagrantly copied the plans.

8.2.3.2 Taking another's work

Where someone other than the original author undertakes what we call 'transformative activity' on the source work (though the term 'transformative use' has a unique meaning in USA copyright law and should not be confused with the issues arising under United Kingdom law), fresh copyright may arise in the later work. Again, this depends on how much skill, labour and judgement is invested by the second author, so that minor changes will not lead to the creation of a new work: *Brighton & Dubbeljoint Co Ltd v Jones* [2005] FSR 288.

Where the source work is no longer copyright, because the term of protection has expired or indeed, if it never had copyright protection in the first place, then the second author's efforts will result in there being copyright in the revised or edited work. A good example of this is *Sawkins v Hyperion Records* where the claimant was held to be the owner of copyright in a new 'performing' edition of ancient music. However, where the source work is still in copyright, it is necessary to distinguish whether the second work has copyright in its own right from whether it is an infringement of the first. In *ZYX Music v King* [1995] 3 All ER 1, Lightman J dismissed the defence that the claimant's copyright in the arrangement of an earlier hit song was unenforceable because it infringed the original version. An author who makes an arrangement of an existing copyright work has the right to enforce the copyright in the arrangement even whilst infringing that in the source work. The claimant was entitled to sue the company who had knowingly distributed a 'cover' version of its song despite being an infringer itself. We have illustrated the effect of 'transformative activity' on another's work in Diagram 8.1.

Diagram 8.1

'Secondary activity': both creation and infringement

(based on *ZYX Music v King*)

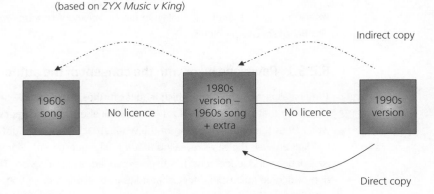

Notes:

1 The 1980s version is both an infringement of the 1960s song and a copyright work in its own right in respect of 'added matter'.

2 The 1990s version infringes both the 1980s version and the 1960s original song.

8.2.3.3 Compilations and collections

A compilation or collection of other works is itself a copyright work. This point was a key element in the House of Lords' decision in *Ladbroke v William Hill* and so is beyond debate. Further, it does not matter if the collection is of earlier works or of factual information: *Ravenscroft v Herbert* [1980] RPC 193. As with 'transformative activity' discussed in the previous paragraph, where the collection is of existing copyright works, it will infringe unless a licence from the owners of the previous works has first been obtained.

Whether the collection or compilation itself meets the requirement of originality depends on the amount of effort expended on its assembly. As ever, the threshold in United Kingdom law is low, amounting in some cases to no more than the 'sweat of the brow'. This is perhaps attributable to the fact that the early cases on collections (for example, *Macmillan & Co Ltd v Suresh Chunder Deb* (1890) ILR 17 Calc 951, concerning an anthology of poetry) were decided before there was an express statutory requirement of originality. Despite this, modern case law has continued to confer copyright protection on items such as professional directories even where these are assembled using factual information stored on a card-index: *Waterlow v Reed* [1992] FSR 409. The significance of conferring copyright protection on directories is illustrated by *Waterlow v Rose* [1995] FSR 207, where the Court of Appeal held that the owner of copyright was entitled to stop the defendant from *using* the directory in order to write to those listed in it asking them to complete a questionnaire so that it could collect its own data.

The correctness of conferring copyright on factual compilations has been debated in other jurisdictions, with varying outcomes. In the USA, a higher threshold of creativity was imposed by the Supreme Court in *Feist Publications v Rural Telephone Service Co* (1991) 111 Sup Ct 1282 so that the 'sweat of the brow' was not enough. The opposite conclusion was reached in Australia in *Desktop Marketing Systems Pty Ltd v Telstra Corporation Ltd* (2002) 192 ALR 433, a case which, like *Feist*, involved a telephone directory. The court held that in assessing whether a factual compilation is an original work, the labour and expense of collecting the information can be taken into account. Consequently, what the court called a 'whole of the universe' compilation was capable of attracting copyright. The Supreme Court of Canada took a different view in *CCH Canadian Ltd v Law Society of Upper Canada* SC [2004] 1 SCR 339 where it declared that the 'sweat of the brow' approach to originality was too low a standard. To be 'original', the work must originate from an author, not be copied from another work, and must be the product of an author's exercise of skill and judgement. The exercise of skill and judgement required to produce the work must not be so trivial that it could be characterised as a purely mechanical exercise.

Databases

The United Kingdom view of compilations and collections has to be reassessed in light of Council Directive 96/9 on the legal protection of databases [1996] OJ L 77/20, as implemented by The Copyright and Rights in Databases Regulations 1997 (SI 1997/3032). The Directive creates a two-tier system of protection for databases, dependent on whether or not intellectual activity was involved in their creation. A collection of information may therefore under United Kingdom law now attract one of three means of protection:

- a compilation protected by the law of copyright if it doesn't meet the definition of database in Article 1 of the Directive. Whether the 'sweat of the brow' effort in making the compilation will suffice (as in the past) must be open to doubt in view of *Infopaq*;

- a database (defined in Article 1 of the Directive as 'a collection of independent works, data or other materials arranged in a systematic or methodical way and individually accessible by electronic or other means') in which copyright exists by virtue of Article 3 of the Directive because it results from intellectual creation (the Directive is not limited to electronic databases); or

- a database (as defined in Article 1 of the Directive) in which the *sui generis* **database right** exists by virtue of Article 7 of the Directive because it has arisen as a result of substantial investment.

Interpretation of the database right

Article 3 of the Directive was considered by the ECJ in Case C-604/10 *Football Dataco Ltd v Yahoo! UK Ltd, Stan James (Abingdon) Ltd and others*, 1 March 2012 where it was said that copyright protection depends on whether the selection or arrangement of the data which it contains amounts to an original expression of the creative freedom of its author. Article 7 of the Directive was, in part, given a narrow interpretation by the ECJ in Case C-203/02 *British Horseracing Board v William Hill Organisation Ltd* [2004] ECR I-10415. The Court ruled that the 'substantial investment' which is required as a condition of protection must relate to obtaining and verifying data. The right-holder must have committed its resources to seeking out existing independent materials or to monitoring their accuracy. Just collecting facts and figures is not enough. Equally, with regard to how the *sui generis* database right is infringed, a 'substantial part evaluated qualitatively and quantitatively' (the test for infringement in the Directive) means that the volume of data taken by the defendant must be compared with both the total volume of the contents and the claimant's investment in obtaining, verifying or presenting those contents. However, the Court took a broader view of the restricted acts of 'extraction' and 'utilisation', so that the database owner could object to any unauthorised act of appropriation even if the contents had been made accessible to the public.

The views expressed in the *British Horseracing Board* case have been reiterated by the ECJ in Case C-304/07 *Directmedia GmbH v Albert-Ludwigs-Universität Freiburg* [2008] ECR I-7565 and Case C-545/07 *Apis-Hristovich EOOD v Lakorda AD* [2009] ECR I-1627. In the former case, concerning a database of poetry, the Court stated that whilst the database right does not prevent consultation of a database (which the owner may or may not restrict to those who have paid), transfer of material from the protected database to another database following an on-screen consultation can still amount to an 'extraction'. It was immaterial whether the extraction depended on a technical means such as downloading or photocopying, or whether there was manual recopying. Neither did it matter that the alleged infringer had omitted some of the items from the protected database whilst adding others, nor whether the extraction was to create another database, whether in competition with the original or not. In the second case, which concerned databases of Bulgarian legislation and case law, the ECJ pointed out that under the Directive, 'extraction' covered both permanent and temporary transfer (the difference between which depended simply on the duration of storage in another medium). It repeated that it didn't matter whether the extraction led to the creation of a new database, even if organisationally different from the protected database (so the alleged infringer's motives were immaterial) and that the fact that the two databases shared physical and technical characteristics could be evidence of extraction. Further, it didn't matter if the contents of the protected database were publicly accessible or consisted of official materials: the database right protects the investment in obtaining and verifying such data.

8.2.3.4 Reports of the spoken word

Section 3(1) CDPA contemplates that the spoken word can attract copyright protection once it is recorded, even if the recording is done by another person. This in turn raises the question of whether someone who makes a report of a speech can acquire copyright *in the report* as a separate work. If, for example, a celebrity is interviewed by a reporter, the interview is recorded using, say, an MP3 device, and the reporter then subsequently produces a written report of the interview containing not just extracts of the words spoken by the celebrity but his or her own comments and observations on the interview, a number of different copyrights can be identified. These are:

* the literary work consisting of words spoken by the celebrity, assuming these pass the minimum threshold for copyright protection, the celebrity owning the copyright as author unless it can be argued that the interview, being an interactive process, leads to joint authorship between the celebrity and journalist. Copyright will arise in the words spoken once the speech is recorded (s.3(2)) even if the recording is done by someone else (s.3(3) CDPA);
* the sound recording of the interview. Whilst the recording operates under s.3(2) to 'fix' the copyright in the spoken word, it will of itself be protected under s.5A CDPA; and

- the reporter's story of the interview, assuming that this last mentioned possesses sufficient originality through the expenditure of skill, labour and judgement to attract fresh copyright or else, under *Infopaq*, involves enough intellectual creativity (the so-called 'reporter's copyright', which is illustrated in Diagram 8.2).

Diagram 8.2

'Reporter's copyright': both copyright and infringement

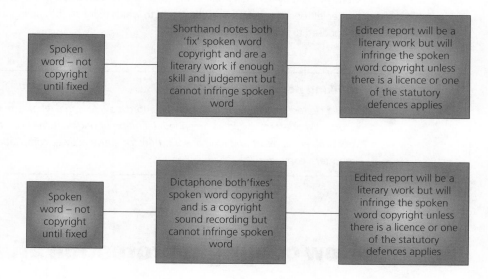

Spoken word – not copyright until fixed

Shorthand notes both 'fix' spoken word copyright and are a literary work if enough skill and judgement but cannot infringe spoken word

Edited report will be a literary work but will infringe the spoken word copyright unless there is a licence or one of the statutory defences applies

Spoken word – not copyright until fixed

Dictaphone both 'fixes' spoken word copyright and is a copyright sound recording but cannot infringe spoken word

Edited report will be a literary work but will infringe the spoken word copyright unless there is a licence or one of the statutory defences applies

cross reference
See section 9.5.3.1.

The use of the recording of the interview for the purposes of reporting current events would be governed by the defence in s.58 CDPA. Interestingly, the written report based on the recording would not be within the defence as it is not a 'direct' record, and theoretically infringes the spoken word copyright as an indirect copy (assuming substantial taking) although doubtless in most cases the celebrity is only too glad to receive the oxygen of publicity.

221

Two cases support this analysis of the combination of s.3(3) and the current requirement of originality in United Kingdom copyright law.

case close-up

Walter v Lane [1900] AC 539

A leading politician, Lord Rosebery, made a series of speeches during an election campaign, those speeches being written down in shorthand by a reporter from *The Times* where the speeches were subsequently published. The House of Lords held by a majority of 4:1 that the defendant had infringed the copyright in the reports by publishing a book containing the speeches.

For many years, *Walter v Lane* was the subject of considerable criticism, partly because Lord Rosebery himself took no part in the action and partly because at the time (the case was decided under the 1842 Act), originality was not an express requirement of protection, only being introduced by the Act of 1911. However, following the judgment of Browne Wilkinson J in *Express Newspapers v News (UK)* [1990] 3 All ER 376 (a case where the key facts occurred after the operative date of the CDPA) it seems that *Walter v Lane* is still good law. In the *Express Newspapers* case, involving a 'tit-for-tat' copying of so-called 'exclusive' interviews by rival tabloid newspapers, the defendant paper had interviewed Marina Ogilvy (a member of the Royal family), the interview (which had lasted some eight and a half hours) being edited subsequently by its reporter. Browne Wilkinson J held that in reproducing the text of the interview, the claimant had infringed the defendant's copyright. There was both copyright in the words spoken by Ms Ogilvy and in the reporter's edited version of the interview. However, a matter left open for debate was the extent to which there can be copyright in the news itself, as opposed to a report of the news.

thinking point

Would United Kingdom copyright law be improved if 'originality' meant 'intellectual effort'? What effect would an amended definition of originality have on the four problem areas of updating a work, transformative activity, compilations and 'reporter's copyright'?

8.3 How copyright protection arises

8.3.1 Absence of formalities

In order for there to be copyright in a work under United Kingdom law, two things need to be shown. These are that the work must be recorded in some medium (after all, as copyright exists to prevent copying, there must be something which can be copied in the first place) and that the work or its author is connected in some way with the United Kingdom.

That United Kingdom law does not impose any formal requirement such as registration for copyright to come into existence is entirely attributable to the wording of Article 5(2) of the Berne Convention. In contrast, Article III of the **Universal Copyright Convention ('UCC')** does impose the precondition that copies of a work must bear a copyright notice, consisting of the name of the author, the year of first publication and the copyright symbol (©) 'placed in such manner and location as to give reasonable notice of claim of copyright'. Although required only when seeking protection in a state which adheres to the UCC rather than Berne, the use of the copyright symbol to put the world on notice that copyright is being claimed has become common practice. In respect of sound recordings (phonograms), the **Rome Convention** imposes a similar requirement, the symbol in this case being ℗.

The non-lawyer often confuses the question of whether copyright exists with *proof* that it exists. It must be stressed that copyright comes into being the moment the work is made. Proof as to the identity of its creator and the date of its creation can easily be effected by posting a copy of the work (by recorded delivery) to a trusted person or organisation (for example a solicitor or bank). Needless to say, there are businesses who advertise that they can help aspiring authors or composers to 'register' their copyright (naturally, for a fee) by being the recipients of copies of the work.

8.3.2 Permanent form

The requirement that a work must be recorded likewise owes its origins to the Berne Convention, this time Article 2(2) which permits its Contracting States to stipulate that works shall not be protected 'unless they have been fixed in some material form'. The words 'fixed' and 'material' appear wide, but as discussed earlier in this chapter, United Kingdom law has traditionally taken a somewhat conservative view of how a work may be recorded, a view which may be far removed from those who are involved in the creative and performing arts. So, for example, under s.48(1) of the 1956 Act, literary and dramatic works were defined in such a way that there had to be some form of writing or notation. This begged the question whether a novel could be fixed using a sound recording or word processor rather than pen and paper, and whether an improvised play would count as a copyright work. In contrast, s.49(4) of the same Act stated that literary, dramatic and musical works were created 'when reduced to writing *or some other material form*', wording reflecting that of the Berne Convention. One debate under the old law was, therefore, whether s.49(4) prevailed over s.48(1), so that any form of fixation sufficed, or whether musical works (because they were not defined in s.48(1)) were the only category to get the benefit of the more liberal provision.

Turning to the CDPA, s.3(2) provides that copyright does not exist in a literary, dramatic or musical work unless the work is recorded 'in writing or otherwise'. Are the words 'or otherwise' to be interpreted narrowly or broadly, that is, does 'or otherwise' suggest something akin to pen and paper or does it cover any medium? The definition of 'writing' in s.178 does not help much, because it declares that it '*includes* any form of notation or code, whether by hand or otherwise, and regardless of the method by which, or medium in or on which it is recorded' (again, the presence of the phrase 'or otherwise' may be significant). The problem is compounded if one remembers the idiosyncratic provisions of s.172. Nevertheless, the conclusion in *Hadley v Kemp* was that the songs by Gary Kemp became copyright works when, following rehearsals, the group went into the recording studio to make a recording. In the era of MP3 players, to restrict copyright to an act of creation which relies on pen and paper does not make sense.

cross reference
See section 8.1.2.

Another comment which needs to be made about the requirement of fixation concerns artistic works. There have been a number of cases where the courts have denied protection to alleged artistic works on the ground that they were not permanent (as examples, consider the outcomes in *Hensher Ltd v Restawile Upholstery (Lancs) Ltd, Creation Records v News Group Newspapers, J & S Davis v Wright* and *Merchandising Corporation of America v Harpbond*). Yet each of the works in question was capable of being copied and in each case the defendant had reproduced the work, so they must, to quote the language of the Berne Convention, have been in 'material' form at some stage. Further, in *Metix (UK) Ltd v G.H. Maughan (Plastics) Ltd* at p. 721, Laddie J remarked *obiter* that a sculpture in ice would nevertheless be a copyright work. The requirement of permanence seems to be used in these decisions as a means of filtering out of copyright works which the judges consider do not deserve protection.

thinking points

Does the requirement of 'in writing or otherwise' as a precondition of copyright protection adequately reflect the diverse ways in which human beings can create 'works'? Does the insistence that a work be permanent accord with the policy that copyright law protects against the taking of an author's creative efforts?

8.3.3 Qualification for copyright protection: terminology and mechanics

The requirement that the work or the author must be 'connected to' the United Kingdom again flows from the provisions of the Berne Convention, subsequent Conventions such as the UCC and the Rome Convention adopting the same model. The Berne Convention states in Article 2(6) that the works covered by the Convention (literary, dramatic, musical and artistic works, and films) are to enjoy protection throughout all its Contracting States. The United Kingdom's obligation to confer copyright protection not just on its own authors and their works, but on those from other Berne Convention members is dealt with by Chapter IX of Part I CDPA (in ss.153 to 159). Two technical aspects of this group of provisions require further explanation.

First, the language of the CDPA must be understood. The Act refers to countries to which it 'extends' (broadly speaking, colonies and dependent territories) and to countries to which it is deemed to 'apply'. This latter category, for the sake of convenience, are referred to as 'Convention countries', that is, Contracting States of the Berne Convention or UCC (for literary, dramatic, musical and artistic works, and films), the Rome Convention (for sound recordings and broadcasts), or any member of the World Trade Organization (**WTO**). Second, the mechanism whereby the current membership of these Conventions is recognised in domestic law is by means of a statutory instrument, currently The Copyright and Performances (Application to Other Countries) Order 2013 (SI 2013/536). Such an Order is necessary because in accordance with the traditional United Kingdom approach to international treaties the Berne Convention (and its sister copyright treaties) do not have direct effect in domestic law unless and until incorporated by legislation. Because of the increasing number of adherents to the family of copyright conventions, the Government revises the Order on a regular basis.

8.3.4 Qualification for protection: literary, dramatic, musical and artistic works

The simple rule is that the author or the work must in some way be connected with the United Kingdom or a country to which the CDPA extends or to a country to which the Act applies. Whether a work created by a non-United Kingdom national attracts United Kingdom copyright depends on either the status of the author at a key point in time or the place where the work was first published.

8.3.4.1 Qualification by reference to the status of the author

If United Kingdom copyright is being claimed by reference to the status of the author, a distinction is drawn between whether the work is unpublished or published. In the case of unpublished works, it must be decided whether the author was a '**qualifying person**' when the work was *made*. In the case of published works, it must be decided whether the author was a 'qualifying person' at the time of *first publication* of the work. 'Qualifying person' means, under s.154, that the author was a citizen of or was domiciled in or was resident in the United Kingdom or a country to which the Act extends or a country to which the Act applies at the relevant date. 'Domicile' and 'residence' are not defined in the CDPA but are two separate concepts. Whilst the latter is a question of fact ('where does the author live?'), the former involves a mental element, ('which country does the author regard as home?').

Table 8.1 illustrates the 'connecting factor' in respect of unpublished works:

The author must have *at the time the work was made*:	The UK	A country to which the CDPA extends (ie a UK colony or dependency)	A Convention Country (ie a member of Berne, UCC or WTO)
Nationality of			
Domicile in			
Residence in			

A tick in any of the three right-hand columns will accord the work United Kingdom copyright. Table 8.2 illustrates the position in respect of published works:

The author must have *at the time the work was first published*:	The UK	A country to which the CDPA extends (ie a UK colony or dependency)	A Convention Country (ie a member of Berne, UCC or WTO)
Nationality of			
Domicile in			
Residence in			

Again, a tick in any of the three right-hand columns will accord the work United Kingdom copyright.

8.3.4.2 Qualification by reference to first publication of the work

If for some reason the author was not a qualifying person (for example, our author might be a national of Iran who has never left that country), the final way the work can obtain United Kingdom copyright (under ss.155 and 159) is by reference to the place it was first published. In effect, what needs to be shown was that the work was first published either in the United Kingdom or in an 'extension' country or in a Convention country.

8.3.4.3 Meaning of 'publication'

For the purposes of Chapter IX of Part I CDPA, 'publication' is defined in s.175. The definition is derived from Article 2*bis*(2) of the Berne Convention (the availability of copies must be such as to satisfy reasonable public demand and must be with the consent of the author). 'Reasonable public demand' is illustrated by *Francis Day & Hunter v Feldman & Co* [1914] 2 Ch 728 where it was held that putting copies of sheet music on display in a shop with six copies having been sold was a genuine publication. Section 175 goes on to list what does *not* count as publication, that list being derived from the same provision in the Berne Convention. Finally, s.155(3) gives one last chance to obtain United Kingdom copyright protection by providing that even if a work is first published in a non-Convention country it can still obtain protection if it is subsequently published in a Convention country within 30 days (this so-called 'simultaneous' publication rule is again a product of the Berne Convention). The application of the qualification rules for copyright is illustrated diagrammatically in Diagram 8.3.

Diagram 8.3

Application of the qualification rules for copyright

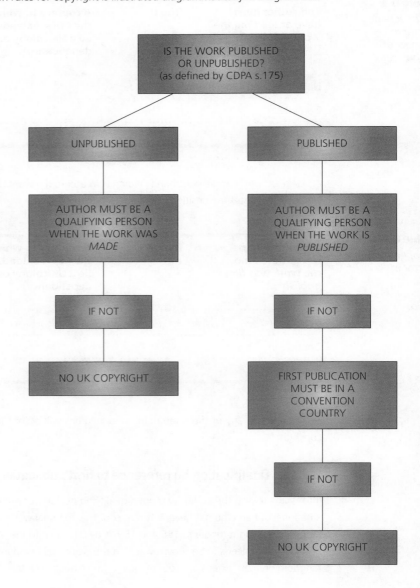

8.3.5 **Summary**

Whether a literary, dramatic, musical or artistic work obtains copyright protection under United Kingdom law depends on establishing that the work or its author are in some way 'connected' with the United Kingdom. Such connection can arise through the status of the author as a qualifying person (which can apply to both published and unpublished works) or by the work in question having been first published in a Contracting State of the Berne Convention or UCC or in a state belonging to the WTO.

8.3.6 Qualification for copyright protection: sound recordings, films, broadcasts and published editions

The principles outlined earlier for literary, dramatic, musical and artistic works apply in similar fashion to the other categories of copyright work, but with minor differences in detail. As regards the status of the author operating as the connecting factor, in the case of sound recordings, films and broadcasts United Kingdom copyright protection will arise if the author was a qualifying person at the time the work was made, whilst in the case of published editions, if the author was a qualifying person when the edition was first published (s.154). If the place of first publication is the connecting factor, then for sound recordings, films and published editions, it must be shown that the work was first published either in the United Kingdom or in an 'extension' country or in a Convention country (s.155). In the case of broadcasts, it must be shown that the place of first broadcast was either the United Kingdom or a Convention country (s.156). It should be remembered that although films fall within the scope of the Berne Convention, sound recordings and broadcasts are covered by the Rome Convention. The protection of published editions is not derived from any convention obligation and is therefore a product of domestic law only.

thinking point

*Given that the United Kingdom is obliged to comply with the requirement of **national treatment** under the Berne Convention, are the rules in Chapter IX, Part I of the CDPA as clear and straightforward as they might be?*

8.4 Authorship and ownership

8.4.1 Tangible and intangible rights

Because copyright is an intangible right, it is necessary to distinguish between the ownership of the medium in which a work is embodied from the ownership of the copyright itself, a point made in *Re Dickens* [1935] Ch 267 where it was held that the beneficiary under a will of unpublished manuscripts was not entitled to the copyright in them (though s.93 CDPA now provides for copyright in unpublished manuscripts to pass with a bequest of such papers).

8.4.2 Ownership of copyright

Section 11(1) CDPA provides that initial ownership of copyright vests in the 'author' of the work. This deceptively simply rule is merely a starting point in the process of identifying the owner. In United Kingdom law (in contrast to other jurisdictions) copyright is freely assignable.

In many sectors of the economy (for example in the media and entertainment industries) it is standard practice for there to be extensive (not to say complex) contractual arrangements dealing with copyright ownership.

cross reference
See section 4.5.2.2.

The only statutory exception to the basic rule is in s.11(2) which provides that literary, dramatic, musical and artistic works and films created in the course of employment belong to the author's employer, subject to any contractual arrangement to the contrary. There is no equivalent provision for the other types of work, yet one could imagine (say) a journalist making an electronic recording of an interview. Would the journalist be regarded under s.9 (discussed later) as the 'author' of the sound recording because, in the words of s.178, he or she has made the arrangements necessary for the making of the sound recording?

The wording of s.11(2) should be compared with that of s.39 Patents Act. 'In the course of employment' in the former provision is arguably a more flexible concept (and hence subject to a degree of judicial discretion) than the notion of 'normal duties...such that an invention might be expected' found in the latter. It is beyond the scope of this work to go into the vast number of employment law cases on whether a person is an employee and we shall confine ourselves to those decisions where ownership of copyright was at stake. In *Stevenson, Jordan & Harrison v MacDonald & Evans* (1952) 69 RPC 10 the Court of Appeal held that the copyright in a book written by an accountant belonged to his estate, not his employer, with the exception of one chapter which was based on a project which his firm, who were management consultants, had undertaken. He was not employed to deliver lectures or write books. By contrast, in *Beloff v Pressdram Ltd* [1973] RPC 765 it was held that an internal memorandum written by a journalist to her editor belonged to her employer, *The Observer*, not to her. She was employed as part of the business and her work was an integral part of that business.

One useful test as to whether a work is written in the course of employment is whether the employee could have been ordered to produce the work. In *Noah v Shuba* [1991] FSR 14, Mummery J held that a consultant epidemiologist who had, in his spare time, written a paper on good hygiene practices for tattoo parlours, was the owner of the copyright. Even though his secretary had typed the manuscript, he could not have been ordered to write the paper by his employers.

One common misconception concerns works that have been commissioned. By '**commission**' we mean that A asks B to write a book or a play or a piece of music or create an artistic work and agrees *unconditionally* to pay for the work in any event. In other words, it must be possible for A to sue B for breach of contract if he does not complete the work and for B to sue A for non-payment (*Gabrin v Universal Music Operations Ltd*). There is *no* rule in United Kingdom law that the person who commissions a work is the owner of copyright in it. The normal rule applies, ie that the author is the first owner.

There are, however, two ways in which a person who commissions a work can become the copyright owner. The first is to enter into an agreement complying with s.91 CDPA. This provides for the assignment of future copyright and requires a written agreement signed by the putative author of the work to hand over the work to another. If the conditions of the section are met, the copyright vests automatically in the **assignee** once the work is created. Second, a commission may give rise to a claim in equity, either for an **exclusive licence**, or for equitable title to the work. A court has the power to imply a suitable term to this effect into the contract to give effect to the parties' intentions but will only imply the absolute minimum necessary to make the contract work: *R Griggs Group Ltd and others v Evans and others* [2005] FSR 706.

Under the Copyright Act 1956 s.4 there was a rule that the commissioner of certain types of artistic works (photographs and portraits) was the copyright owner. This rule was abolished by the CDPA, but will continue to apply to such works created before its operative date. Section 104 CDPA assists the claimant in any copyright infringement action by creating a number of presumptions as to existence and ownership of copyright. The net effect is that the onus is on the defendant to disprove.

8.4.3 Who is an author?

As explained, identification of the 'author' of a work is the first step in identifying its ownership. But who is the author? Section 9 CDPA gives the answer, but again makes the distinction between authorial and entrepreneurial copyrights. In the case of literary, dramatic, musical and artistic works, it simply declares that the person who creates the work is the author. However, in relation to claims of **joint authorship**, deciding as a matter of fact what amounts to creative input is not always easy. Where a literary, dramatic, musical and artistic work is computer-generated, the author is the person making the arrangements 'necessary for the creation of the work'. As yet there is no guidance from case law as to where to draw the line between where a computer is merely a tool in the hands of a creative person and where it is the computer which generates the work, nor is there any guidance as to the meaning of 'arrangements necessary for the creation of the work'.

In the case of entrepreneurial copyrights, there are significant differences in detail. In the case of a sound recording, the author is the producer (in contrast to the position under the 1956 Act), for films the author is deemed to be the principal director and the producer, whilst for broadcasts it is the person who makes the broadcast. For published editions, it is the publisher who is the author. Section 178 CDPA defines the producer of a sound recording or a film as the person who makes the necessary arrangements for its creation. Again it must be stressed that the CDPA merely provides a starting point, and that in many instances contractual arrangements will be used to determine the matter. In *Slater v Wimmer* [2012] EWPCC 7, HHJ Birss concluded that in the absence of a clearly worded agreement between the two parties, copyright in a film made by the claimant of the defendant sky-diving over Everest was determined by the statutory provisions: the defendant was producer (he had made the necessary financial arrangements), the claimant was director (he had creative control), and as joint authors each had infringed the other's rights by copying the film and communicating it to the public.

8.4.4 The difference between authorship and ownership

Having identified who is the author of a work, it is necessary to keep separate the roles of authorship and ownership in copyright law. The author may not be the owner. It is the *owner* who can sue for infringement and who has the ability to **assign** or license the right, in whole or in part (see CDPA s.96 and ss.90–93 respectively). Authorship, on the other hand, is relevant as to (a) whether the work attracts United Kingdom protection; (b) the calculation of the length of the term of copyright protection; and (c) the determination of whether **moral rights** have arisen. So for example, a work such as an instruction manual for a piece of equipment written in the course of employment will be owned by the employer (who may well be a company whose assets are subsequently transferred as part of a corporate acquisition) but the life of the human author will determine the duration of copyright protection for the work.

8.4.5 Joint authorship

Section 10 CDPA provides for there to be works of joint authorship. The definition of what is a work of joint authorship is very precise, ie it must *not* be possible to identify each author's respective contribution. So for example, a book written by two people in which one writes chapters 1, 3, 5 and 7 and the other writes chapters 2, 4, 6 and 8 will not be a work of joint authorship as each person's contributions can be identified. The rights of co-owners are set out in s.173(2) CDPA.

Further, case law (of which there has been a considerable amount over the last decade, no doubt prompted by the claimant's hope of receiving royalties from the exploitation of a successful work) has made clear that each alleged co-author 'must share responsibility for the form of expression' and make 'a significant and original contribution to the creation of the work', phrases which have become a judicial mantra when deciding a claim for joint authorship. However, deciding what amounts to creative input is not always easy.

Unsuccessful claims for a share of royalties arising from alleged joint authorship include *Lawson v Dundas* where Whitford J held that the claimant had contributed nothing towards the orchestral arrangement of the Channel 4 musical 'ident'; *Fylde Microsystems v Key Radio Systems Ltd* [1998] FSR 449, where simply correcting 'bugs' in software was insufficient to confer joint authorship; *Ray v Classic FM plc* [1998] FSR 622, where it was held that the claimant was the sole author of a database of classical music, although the court granted the defendant radio station an exclusive licence to use the database as an implied term of the contract; *Hadley v Kemp*, where Park J held that Gary Kemp was the sole author of the songs performed by the group Spandau Ballet as the compositions were complete before rehearsals began; and *Brighton & Dubbeljoint Co Ltd v Jones* where it was held that there was no joint ownership of a play because the changes made by the claimant to the script for a play were of the sort to be made by a director, and she did not have the final say as to whether these changes were to be accepted.

By contrast, in *Beggars Banquet v Carlton* [1993] EMLR 349 it was held that a film company and TV company were joint authors of a TV documentary about the death of a member of the audience at a 'rave' (though it is unclear exactly what the TV company had contributed to the work). In *Beckingham v Hodgens* [2003] EMLR 376 the Court of Appeal held that there was joint ownership of the tune 'Young at Heart' after the addition of a violin 'riff' by the claimant. Similar outcomes occurred in *Bamgboye v Reed*, where the claimant's contribution was the addition of drum accompaniment to a tune called 'Bouncing Flow' and in *Fisher v Brooker* [2009] 1 WLR 1764, where the House of Lords restored the original judgment of Blackburne J that the claimant was entitled to 40 per cent of the ownership of the 1967 hit *A Whiter Shade of Pale* as a result of having composed the distinctive organ solo. However, in both *Beckingham v Hodgens* and *Fisher v Brooker* it was possible to identify, respectively, the violin line and the organ line in each piece of music. Could it really be said that the contribution of each author was not distinct, as required by s.10? It could be, of course, that it was easier to make a finding of joint authorship despite the express wording of s.10, in view of the complexity of working out the parties' separate contributions had this not been the case.

thinking point
Are the cases on joint authorship correct?

The Copyright and Duration of Rights in Performances Regulations 2013 (SI 2013/1782), implementing Directive 2011/77/EU of the European Parliament and of the Council of 27 September 2011 [2011] OJ L 265/1, have amended s.10 CDPA by providing for there to be works of co-authorship. Such works arise where there is collaboration between the author of a musical work and the author of a literary work where the two are created in order to be used together, ie a song. The sole purpose of the amendment is to provide for a change in the calculation of the term of protection, explained in the next section.

8.5 Duration

8.5.1 Duration: overview

The term of protection for copyright is one area where EU law has had a significant impact on the CDPA. In common with similar legislation in other jurisdictions, such as Australia and the USA, the Copyright Term Directive has lengthened the duration of most categories of copyright work. In so doing, it sought to limit the benefit of the extended period of protection to works the authors of which are nationals of the **EEA** or the country of origin of which is the EEA. Section 15A CDPA gives a detailed definition of the term 'country of origin', determined primarily by the place of first publication, but if the work is unpublished, then by the nationality of the author.

The CDPA itself, in contrast to its predecessor, did much to standardise the term of protection, originally providing for a term of the author's life plus 50 years for literary, dramatic, musical and artistic works, 50 years from the making of the work in the case of films, sound recordings and broadcasts, and 25 years from creation in the case of published editions. However, this standardisation applied only to works created after the operative date of the Act (1 August 1989). With regard to existing works, there were a number of anomalous provisions concerned with duration in the 1956 Act. For example, a work unpublished at the death of its author remained in copyright until 50 years after its publication (meaning that if it was never published, then the period of protection was in effect perpetual) and as mentioned earlier, certain films also attracted indefinite protection. Schedule 1 CDPA deals with all of these anomalies by providing for the expiry of copyright after an appropriate period of time. It is beyond the scope of this work to deal with these arrangements. For the purposes of our discussions, it is assumed always that the work in question was created after the operative date of the CDPA.

8.5.2 Duration for literary, dramatic, musical and artistic works

Section 12 CDPA, as amended, now provides that the term of protection for literary, dramatic, musical and artistic works shall be the author's life plus 70 years, calculated from the end of the calendar year when the author died. In the case of works of joint authorship and, now, co-authorship, the calculation is based on the death of the last author to die. The overriding condition, however, is that the author must be an EEA national or the work's country of origin must be in the EEA. If this is not the case, then the term of protection is to be that laid down by the law of the country of origin.

The duration of protection applies regardless of the type of work found within ss.3 and 4, regardless of how much effort went into its creation, and regardless of whether the work is published or unpublished. There are, however, a number of exceptions. Thus, in the case of works of unknown authorship, the term is 70 years from creation or 70 years from making available to the public, provided that the making available happened within 70 years of creation; in the case of computer-generated works the period is 50 years from creation.

In implementing Article 10 of the Copyright Term Directive, The Duration of Copyright and Rights in Performances Regulations (SI 1995/3297) contained some complex transitional provisions. Regulations 16 and 17 drew a distinction between works made after the commencement of the Regulations (1 July 1995) which automatically got the benefit of the enhanced term of protection, works already in being (which were accorded 'extended copyright' by adding an extra 20 years at the end of the original term), and works the copyright in which had expired before 1995 which were accorded 'revived copyright'. The owner is given another 'bite of the cherry' for the balance of a 20-year period calculated from when copyright originally expired, the work thus passing from the public domain back into copyright. The condition to be satisfied before the 'extended' or 'revived' term of copyright applies is that the work must have been protected in at least one EEA Member State on 1 July 1995. The one EU Member State which is normally used for comparison is Germany, as the copyright term in that country was, prior to the Directive, the author's life plus 70 years. However, it should be remembered that the threshold for copyright protection in Germany has traditionally been higher than that in the United Kingdom. Whilst novels and orchestral symphonies would attract the benefit of the extended or revived term, photographs might not, because photographs were, in Germany, treated as 'neighbouring rights' and accorded a much shorter protection prior to the Directive. The Regulations do contain, in Regulation 23, certain savings for those who had entered into agreements or made copies of the relevant work before the commencement date.

The case of *Sweeney v Macmillan Publishers Ltd* [2002] RPC 651 provides a good illustration of the application of these transitional arrangements. It also shows how different versions of a novel can give rise to separate copyrights each of which had a different term of protection under the 1956 Act. The defendant brought out a 'Reader's Edition' of *Ulysses* by James Joyce, the book being based partially on the original unpublished version of the novel (which was still in copyright), but primarily on a later published edition, the copyright in which had expired but which was revived as a result of the Copyright Term Directive. It was held that the defendant infringed both versions of the novel. Although it had made enquiries of the copyright owner about republishing the expired copyright work, this did not amount to 'making arrangements' under Regulation 23. As the unpublished version was still in copyright, this was not subject to the transitional arrangements.

thinking point
If copyright law is meant to reflect the underlying policy of encouraging or rewarding creativity, is it right that the term of protection for literary, dramatic, musical and artistic works is the same regardless of the merits of the work? Why should a mobile phone ringtone get the same length of protection as a symphony?

8.5.3 Duration for films

The changes made to the term of protection for films reflects the way in which the EU regards films as 'authorial' rather than 'entrepreneurial' copyright. Under the old law, protection was for 50 years from the end of the calendar year in which the film was made, or, if it was released during this period, 50 years from the calendar year of release. Section 13B, as amended, provides for copyright to expire at the end of 70 years from the death of the survivor of the principal director, the author of the screenplay, the author of the dialogue, or the composer of music specially created for and used in the film. As ever, there is the condition that one of the authors of the film must be an EEA national or the country of origin of the film must be an EEA Contracting State. If this is not the case, the film is accorded the same term of copyright as in its country of origin. This provision does not accurately match the wording of Article 2(2) of the Copyright Term Directive which uses the phrase 'music specifically created for use in the . . . work'. Further, the United Kingdom has not implemented at all the wording of Article 3(3) of the same Directive which gives separate rights to the producer of a film, such rights to last 50 years from the creation of the film, or, if it was made available to the public during such time, 50 years from release. However, The Copyright and Related Rights Regulations 1996 (SI 1996/2967) did accord the producer the status of co-author of the film (by amending s.9 CDPA) and did, in their amendment of s.105 CDPA (presumptions) use the correct wording of Article 2(2) (*music specifically created . . .*).

8.5.4 Duration for sound recordings

The term of protection for sound recordings has been amended on a number of occasions, in order to implement the original version of the Copyright Term Directive, the Information Society Directive, and the latest amendment to the Copyright Term Directive (Directive 2011/77/EU of the European Parliament and of the Council of 27 September 2011 [2011] OJ L 265/1). Section 13A provides that copyright expires at the end of 50 years from the end of the calendar year in which the recording was made or if during that period it is published, 70 years from publication, or if during that period the recording is not published but is made available to the public by being played in public or communicated to the public, 70 years from being made available. Again, the requirement is that the author of the sound recording (the definition of which is provided by s.9 CDPA, explained earlier) must be an EEA national. If that is not the case, the duration of protection is to be that accorded in the author's own country.

8.5.5 Duration for broadcasts

The most straightforward period of protection (in terms of calculation) is for broadcasts. Section 14 CDPA, as amended, states that the term is 50 years from the end of the calendar year of first broadcast, provided that the author of the broadcast is an EEA national. If this is not the case then the length of protection is that provided in the author's own country. Copyright in repeats expires at the same time as copyright in the original broadcast.

8.5.6 **Duration for published editions**

The period of protection for published editions is unaffected by the Copyright Term Directive and therefore remains at 25 years from the end of the calendar year of first publication.

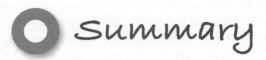

Summary

This chapter has explained:

- the various categories of copyright work recognised under the CDPA;

- the requirements of originality, fixation and qualification for protection; and

- how it is decided whether someone is an author of the work and how the duration of protection is determined.

Reflective question

By allowing copyright to be conferred when minimal skill, labour and judgement has been expended by the creator, United Kingdom law has lost sight of the reasons why intellectual property rights are justified.

Discuss.

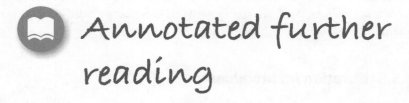

Annotated further reading

Brennan, D.J. and Christie, A. 'Spoken Words and Copyright Subsistence in Anglo-American Law' [2000] *IPQ* 309
Reviews the history of the protection of spoken word copyright and argues that the United Kingdom could, in accordance with the Berne Convention, permit there to be copyright in the spoken work without the need for permanent form.

Derclaye, E. '*Infopaq International A/S v Danske Dagblades Forening* (C-5/08): Wonderful or Worrisome? The Impact of the ECJ Ruling in *Infopaq* on UK Copyright Law' [2010] *EIPR* 247

Argues that the implications of *Infopaq* are much more wide-ranging than first thought.

Gervais, D.J. 'The Compatibility of the Skill and Labour Originality Standard with the Berne Convention and the TRIPs Agreement' [2004] *EIPR* 75

Considers whether the TRIPs Agreement requires Contracting States to adhere to a higher standard of originality contemplated by the Berne Convention than is the case today in many common law jurisdictions.

Lupton, K. 'Photographs and the Concept of Originality in Copyright Law' [1988] *EIPR* 257

Discusses the difficulties with granting copyright to photographs and argues that the Fine Arts Copyright Act 1862 provides some of the answers.

MacQueen, H. ' "My tongue is mine ain": Copyright, the Spoken Word and Privacy' (2005) 68 *MLR* 349

Considers some of the difficulties in according copyright to the spoken word and its relationship with privacy.

Phillips, J. 'Copyright in Spoken Words—Some Potential Problems' [1989] *EIPR* 231

Explores the implications of s.3 CDPA in relation to spoken word copyright and the fact that someone other than the author may fix the work in permanent form.

Rosati, E. 'Originality in a Work, or a Work of Originality: The Effects of the *Infopaq* Decision' [2011] *EIPR* 746

Argues that the *Infopaq* decision has the effect of harmonising the fundamental concept of originality.

Infringement of copyright

Learning objectives

Upon completion of this chapter, you should have acquired:

- an understanding of the arguments parties to a copyright infringement action are likely to raise;
- an appreciation of the nature of the action for copyright infringement;
- knowledge of the types of conduct which amount to primary infringement of copyright;
- knowledge of the types of conduct which amount to secondary infringement of copyright;
- understanding of the application of the principal defences known as 'fair dealing' in copyright; and
- knowledge of other major statutory and non-statutory defences to copyright infringement.

Introduction

cross reference

See respectively sections 7.2 and 7.4.

In this chapter, we build on issues previously discussed. We look at what the right-holder can do to prevent others exploiting the work. In discussing the scope of protection accorded to the copyright owner, we reconsider the justifications for copyright and the idea/expression divide in relation to the statutory requirement that the defendant must have taken a substantial part of the claimant's work.

cross reference

See chapter 8 for the requirements for United Kingdom copyright protection.

Because copyright protection does not depend on registration, there is no equivalent in copyright law of the counterclaim (usually raised in relation to registrable forms of intellectual property) to remove the right from the register. Instead, the existence of one or more of the key elements which must be satisfied before copyright arises may well be disputed by the defendant, so all the issues concerned with the subsistence of copyright must be kept in mind.

9.1 Issues in a copyright infringement action

As with any action to enforce an intellectual property right, it is important to identify the arguments which each party is likely to raise.

9.1.1 The claimant's case

The **claimant** will need to establish two things, first, that it is the owner or **exclusive licensee** of one or more rights in a '**work**' entitled to **copyright** protection under United Kingdom law. The fragmentary nature of copyright should be remembered. Thus a 'complex' work such as a film or broadcast may contain a number of other works, each one of which will in turn consist of a collection of rights. Each of these rights can be dealt with separately, and indeed may have been the subject of a series of transactions (that is, **assignment** or **licensing**) in the past (as an example see *Governors of the Hospital for Sick Children v Walt Disney* [1966] 2 All ER 321). Presumptions set out in ss.104 and 105 Copyright, Designs and Patents Act 1988 ('CDPA') assist the claimant in establishing the right to sue, the net effect being to put the onus of proof on the defendant to show that the claimant is not entitled.

cross reference

Discussed further at 17.3.2.1.

By s.101 CDPA, an exclusive licensee has the right to sue for **infringement** as if it were the owner of copyright.

The second item to be proved is that the defendant has committed one or more of the five restricted acts of primary infringement listed in s.16 CDPA, or else has authorised another to commit such an act. Whilst the acts of primary infringement (each one of which receives more detailed treatment in ss.17 to 21 CDPA) must be committed within the United Kingdom, authorising another to commit a restricted act can be committed outside the jurisdiction as long as the conduct so authorised has occurred within the United Kingdom (*ABKCO Music v Music Collection International* [1995] RPC 657). In addition, the claimant must demonstrate that the restricted act relates to the whole of the copyright work or a substantial part of it, although it does not matter whether the defendant took directly or indirectly from the claimant's work. Alternatively, the claimant may allege that the defendant has committed one or more of the acts of secondary infringement listed in ss.22 and 23 CDPA (in effect, the defendant has dealt commercially in infringing copies of the work), but in contrast to an allegation of primary infringement, the claimant will have to show both that the defendant had the requisite knowledge and that it was dealing in infringing copies.

9.1.2 **The defendant's case**

The arguments open to the defendant are as follows:

- to deny that the claimant is the owner or **licensee** of the copyright work, in other words, it is not entitled to sue. An example of this argument succeeding can be found in *Beloff v Pressdram Ltd* [1973] RPC 765 where the copyright work in question (an internal office memorandum) was held to belong not to the claimant but to her employer, as it had been written in the course of employment;

- to deny that the work in question is entitled to United Kingdom copyright protection. This denial raises a number of separate points. First, that what has been taken is not a work but a mere idea (*Baigent & Lee v Random House Group Ltd* [2007] FSR 579) or is everyday factual information (*Cramp v Smythson* [1944] AC 329) or else falls below the threshold of copyright protection (*Francis Day v Twentieth Century Fox* [1940] AC 112); second, that even if it is a work, it is not **original** (*Interlego v Tyco* [1989] AC 217); next, even if it is an original work, it has not been recorded in permanent form (*Creation Records v News Group Newspapers* [1997] EMLR 444); next, that the **author** of the work did not qualify for protection under United Kingdom law; or, lastly, that even if all the other elements for the subsistence of copyright were satisfied, the term of protection has expired. The defendant may raise one or more of these arguments in the alternative;

- in relation to primary infringement, to deny that any infringing conduct has been committed. One particular aspect of such denial is to plead that the defendant's work was independently created and therefore was not derived from that of the claimant. Alternatively, if infringing conduct is admitted, the defendant may deny that what was taken amounted to a substantial part of the work, or argue that what was taken was not the expression but the idea;

- in relation to secondary infringement, to deny that the infringing conduct has been committed, or if this is admitted, to deny that the defendant had the requisite knowledge and/ or that the articles dealt with by the defendant were infringing copies;

- last, if entitlement to sue, subsistence of copyright, and infringing conduct are all admitted, or are found by the court to be established, the defendant may seek to rely on one or more of the myriad statutory defences to copyright infringement set out in the CDPA, or else to plead one or more of the more general, non-statutory defences.

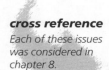

cross reference

Each of these issues was considered in chapter 8.

thinking point

Considering the preceding account of the issues in a copyright infringement action, whom would you rather represent, the claimant or the defendant?

The nature of copyright infringement

9.2.1 The difference between use and infringement

Copyright law has always drawn a distinction between the right of property in a tangible object in which a copyright work is embodied, and the intangible right of property in the copyright itself (*Re Dickens* [1935] Ch 267). Copyright infringement entails taking the work without the consent of its owner, rather than any dealing with the physical object. The consequence is that the lawful owner of the physical item (whether acquired by gift or purchase) is free to deal with it as they wish, as long as a restricted act is not committed. Thus the recipient of a letter from a celebrity, being the owner by way of gift of the piece of paper on which the letter is written, may sell that letter at auction, but the purchaser will not be able to publish extracts of the letter in a newspaper without the consent of the copyright owner. The purchaser of a book of modern poetry can study the poems, but cannot read them aloud at a poetry evening held at a local village hall. A computer user can view material from the internet on screen but may not print or save it to disc. This is because the acts of publishing the letter (ie reproducing it in the newspaper and then selling copies of the paper), performing the poetry in public, or saving a file to disc are all restricted acts which the copyright owner alone is entitled to enjoy or license.

The distinction between using the object embodying a work and taking the work itself has been eroded with the advent of digital technology. To give one example, in order to use a computer program, it must first be loaded into the computer's memory, an act of copying. Whilst such conduct is non-problematic for someone who has lawfully acquired a copy of the software (because of the defence found in s.50C CDPA), a person who has obtained a pirated copy will infringe the copyright in the software each and every time they use it. In contrast, the means whereby a computer stores internet material in a temporary cache to enable it to be viewed falls within the defence of making temporary copies in s.28A CDPA: *Public Relations Consultants Association Ltd v Newspaper Licensing Agency Ltd* [2013] RPC 469 at [31].

9.2.2 Copyright infringement as an interference with property

As a statutory tort, the commission of one or more of the primary acts of copyright infringement will give rise to strict liability. Copyright infringement is an interference with the right of property conferred on the copyright owner by s.1 CDPA, and so the state of mind of the infringer is irrelevant. The claimant does not have to prove that the defendant knew that copyright existed in the source work, nor that what was done amounted to infringement. Conversely, where the defendant simply takes the underlying idea of the claimant's work rather than the work itself, the fact that he knew that he was doing so makes no difference and the claimant's action will still fail (*Baigent & Lee v Random House Group Ltd*).

The principle that the infringer's state of mind is irrelevant is, however, qualified in two ways. Knowledge is crucial for liability for secondary infringement, and in relation to primary infringement, the innocence of the defendant that copyright existed (determined objectively) means that **damages** may not be awarded (s.97(1) CDPA), although this does not affect the award of any other remedy.

9.2.3 **Copyright infringement need not be for profit**

In contrast to **patents**, **designs** and **trade marks**, copyright is the one form of intellectual property where there can be liability for infringement committed in the home, at least under current United Kingdom law. Contrary to popular belief, copyright infringement does not have to be committed in the course of trade (indeed, copyright infringement which is committed commercially attracts both civil and criminal liability). Private and domestic use is not a *general* defence to copyright infringement (though many argue that it should be), but some defences in the CDPA (for example, the so-called 'time-shift' defence in s.70 and the proposed new defence in s.28B) do protect the private copyist as long as certain conditions are met. The common reaction to the fact that copying a protected work in the home gives rise to liability is that such a law is unenforceable and therefore stupid. Nevertheless, right owners (or industry associations representing their interests) are growing increasingly aggressive in their pursuit of home infringers (as an example, see *Polydor Ltd v Brown* [2005] EWHC 3191 (Ch)).

9.2.4 **Objective similarity and derivation**

The key feature of copyright infringement which distinguishes it from patents, trade marks and **registered designs** is that the claimant must show that there is a causal link between the copyright work and the alleged infringement. Therefore, independent creation will always be a defence to copyright infringement (*Kleeneze Ltd v DRG Ltd* [1984] FSR 399). This particular feature of copyright protection enables the defendant to put forward a number of different explanations as to how the alleged infringement came to resemble the claimant's work. The fact that the two works are similar may be a matter of coincidence, or it may be that the defendant's work was first in point of time so that the claimant might be the copyist. Equally, both works might be derived from a common source (*Roberton v Lewis* (1960) [1976] RPC 169, *Warwick Films v Eisinger* [1969] 1 Ch 508). Last, the defendant may simply try to convince the court that their work was independently created, with no 'borrowing' from the claimant's work. However, where the defendant had the opportunity to copy the source work or is assumed by the court to have known of the claimant's creation, a court may well be reluctant to accept such an argument.

The requirement that the claimant's work must be the source of the alleged infringement was summed up by Diplock LJ (as he then was) in *Francis Day & Hunter v Bron* [1963] Ch 587, where he stated that in order for a claim of copyright infringement to succeed, there must be objective similarity and derivation.

9.2.4.1 Objective similarity

The requirement of objective similarity requires the court to compare the source work with the alleged infringement. The purpose of such comparison is to enable the court to decide whether the similarities are more likely to be the result of 'copying rather than coincidence', taking into account whether the similarities are 'close, numerous and extensive' and disregarding similarities which consist of commonplace or unoriginal information, or general ideas (see Lord Millett in *Designers' Guild Ltd v Russell Williams (Textiles) Ltd* [2000] 1 WLR 2416 at [39]). Such comparison is carried out objectively and is of the work as a whole. Judges frequently warn against the dangers of making too detailed a comparison of minor elements, or of fragmenting the work into its constituent parts (*Baigent & Lee v Random House Group Ltd*, relying on *Ladbroke v William Hill* [1964] 1 WLR 273). Thus in *Francis Day & Hunter v Bron*, the Court of Appeal, when required to compare two popular songs, avoided a note-by-note analysis of the music but instead considered the overall impression the two works would have on the listener, in particular the first eight bars of each song.

The comparison may not only be of the expression used by the author of the source work, but also of that work's structure or 'architecture'. Hence, in *Corelli v Gray* (1913) 30 TLR 116 it was held that even though the language used by the claimant had not been copied, the taking of incidents and plots from the claimant's novel and turning them into a play amounted to infringement. Sargant J, at first instance ((1913) 29 TLR 570), emphasised that whilst copyright is not a true monopoly because proof of independent creation is always a valid defence, it does prevent the misappropriation of the first author's skill, labour and judgement. If the creator's efforts have been taken, it is no argument to say 'but I only took the concept'. However, protecting the structure or 'architecture' of a work in the name of preventing misappropriation of effort can at times come very close to protecting the underlying idea (*Baigent & Lee v Random House Group Ltd*).

9.2.4.2 Derivation

Derivation means that there must be a causal link between the claimant's and defendant's works. The claimant's work must be the *source* of the infringement. The length of the causal chain does not matter, because s.16 CDPA expressly protects against indirect taking, so that a copy of a copy of a copy of a copy of the source work will infringe.

case close-up

Solar Thomson v Barton [1977] RPC 537

A good example of derivation is the Court of Appeal's decision in *Solar Thomson v Barton* [1977] RPC 537. The claimant was the **patentee** for a system of conveyor belts which included pulleys with special rubber linings. When the linings wore out, the defendant, who helped to maintain machinery of one of the claimant's customers, made his own replacement linings, and when threatened with copyright infringement (the claimant asserting copyright in the drawings for the machinery) sent a pulley to a third party designer and asked them to design a replacement lining. The Court of Appeal held that because the instructions left the third party designer little choice, the replacement created by the third party was an infringement of the claimant's copyright drawings. Although the case today would be decided under unregistered design law rather than the law of copyright, it is a useful illustration both of how long the causal chain of derivation can be, and of liability for indirect copying.

9.2.4.3 Derivation: further examples

An example of direct rather than indirect derivation can be found in *LB (Plastics) v Swish Products* [1979] RPC 551. The claimant had designed a drawer system for self-assembly furniture. The

House of Lords agreed with Whitford J that there had been infringement because the defendant had seen the claimant's drawings for the furniture. Tellingly, Lord Wilberforce remarked (at p. 619) that where, as here, there are 'striking similarities' between the two works together with an 'opportunity to copy', then a finding of copyright infringement is a logical conclusion.

In contrast, in *Purefoy Engineering v Sykes Boxall* (1955) 72 RPC 89 there was no derivation where rival manufacturers each produced a catalogue of their own range of machine tools. Neither had copied from the other and the similarity of the two catalogues was coincidence. In *Warwick Films v Eisinger*, a film script was held not to have been copied from the claimant's book about the trials of Oscar Wilde, as the defendant film company had relied on the original court transcripts as the source for the screenplay.

9.2.4.4 Derivation: the test

Of the two elements identified by Diplock LJ, it must always be remembered that copyright is essentially concerned with derivation rather than with overall similarity (*per* Lord Millett in *Designers' Guild Ltd v Russell Williams (Textiles) Ltd* at [39–41]). One should avoid laying too much emphasis on overall similarity, otherwise there is the danger of treating copyright infringement as if it were **passing off**.

case close-up

Designers' Guild Ltd v Russell Williams (Textiles) Ltd [2000] 1 WLR 2416

Lord Millett explained the three-stage test for infringement, especially where there has been what is called 'altered copying'. The first step is the identification of those features of the defendant's work which the claimant alleges have been copied. The correct approach requires an overall comparison to be made. Next, if the claimant demonstrates similarities and shows that the defendant had the opportunity to copy, the burden of proof passes to the defendant to show that despite the similarities, these did not result from copying. Last, once it is established that the defendant's work incorporates features of the source work, it must be decided whether these features are a substantial part, assessed by reference to their importance to the source work, *not* their importance to the alleged infringement. Although Lord Millett was speaking in the context of artistic copyright (a design for curtain fabric), the test applies to any other category of copyright work where only part of the work is taken: *Baigent & Lee v Random House Group Ltd*.

9.2.5 **The requirement of substantial taking**

Section 16 CDPA, the 'umbrella' provision on primary infringement, states that the infringement may relate to the whole of the protected work or a substantial part of it. There are many cases which declare that what is 'substantial' is a matter of quality not quantity, so that the percentage of the claimant's work taken does not matter, the principal authority being *Ladbroke (Football) Ltd v William Hill (Football) Ltd*. Nevertheless, as Spence and Endicott remark (in 'Vagueness in the Scope of Copyright' (2005) 121 *LQR* 657) even the House of Lords in *Designers' Guild Ltd v Russell Williams (Textiles) Ltd* barely addresses the issue of substantiality, although Lords Hoffmann and Scott do state that what has to be considered, when deciding whether a substantial part of the claimant's work has been copied, is whether the infringer has taken the 'skill and labour' of the original author. Indeed, the protection of such skill and labour is declared by their Lordships to be the overall purpose of copyright law. However, in the instant case there was no attempt to explain what skill and labour had been expended by the claimant in creating the work. Spence and Endicott further argue that by not defining 'substantial' with greater precision, and by running together the issue of whether there has been copying with whether that copy is a substantial part of the original work, the House of Lords comes close to saying that 'what is worth copying is worth protecting'. The thinking in *Designers' Guild* also makes it harder to identify the dividing line between an idea and its expression, a fundamental issue of copyright set out in Article 9(2) of the **TRIPs Agreement**. Last, if the ECJ's ruling in Case C-5/08 *Infopaq International A/S v Danske Dagblades Forening* [2009] ECR I-6569 does prove significant with regard to the meaning of 'originality', the conclusion must be that 'substantial taking' will also need to be re-evaluated. In *SAS Institute Inc v World Programming Ltd* [2013] RPC 421, Arnold J, in applying the ruling of the ECJ (Case C-406/10, [2012] RPC 933) assumed that *Infopaq* was the right test, so that in order to infringe, the defendant must reproduce something which amounts to the intellectual expression of the author. Consequently, copying the language in which a computer program was written did not infringe (subsequently confirmed [2013] EWCA Civ 1482).

9.2.5.1 Substantial taking: illustrations

Cases illustrating the 'traditional' United Kingdom view that substantial taking looks to quality rather than quantity are *Hawkes & Son v Paramount Film Services* [1934] Ch 593, where a 30-second extract from the 'Colonel Bogey' march included in a news film of a public ceremony was held to infringe the music copyright; and *Spelling Goldberg v BPC Publications Ltd* [1981] RPC 280, where the use of one frame from one episode of the 'Starsky & Hutch' television series to make a poster amounted to substantial taking. In both of these decisions, what was taken was the creator's expression, in contrast to *Norowzian v Arks Ltd* [2000] FSR 363, where arguably what was taken was not the copyright work (a film) but the technique (jump cutting) used to create the expression.

Nevertheless, there are other decisions which blur the dividing line between copying the idea and copying the expression. In *Elanco v Mandops* [1980] RPC 213, the Court of Appeal held that the defendant had infringed the claimant's instruction leaflet for weed-killer. The defendants had already rewritten the leaflet at the claimant's insistence, and the leaflet had to contain essential factual information, so arguably what was being protected was not expression but the idea. Another borderline decision is that in *Geographia v Penguin* [1985] FSR 208. Here, the defendant's copying the colouring of maps was held to amount to taking insignificant features which didn't prejudice the copyright owner. But should the colours of a map showing political boundaries be treated as an idea (to add colour for clarity) or an expression? Finally, in *Johnstone Safety Co v Peter Cook International plc* [1990] FSR 161, it was held that the hexagonal base of a traffic cone, alleged to have been copied by the defendant, was a feature common to other designs for cones. It was a functional element of the cone, and anyway there had been no substantial taking. Although decided in the law of copyright, the case today would be decided under the principles of design right and it may well be that the court was influenced by the recently enacted provisions curtailing the use of copyright to protect functional articles. Again, the question to be asked is whether the shape of the base of a traffic cone is idea or expression.

9.2.6 Substantial taking: conclusion

How substantial taking is to be determined has been summarised as follows.

Baigent & Lee v Random House Group Ltd [2007] FSR 579

Mummery LJ in *Baigent & Lee v Random House Group Ltd* at [124] sets out the nature of the inquiry undertaken by the court in a copyright infringement action, an inquiry which, he says, should be carried out chronologically. First, there should be an analysis of the similarities between the alleged infringement and the original copyright work, because unless similarities exist, there is no arguable case of copying. Second, it should be asked what access, direct or indirect, did the author of the alleged infringing work have to the source work, because unless there is evidence from which access can be proved or inferred, the crucial causal connection between the two cannot be established. Third, did the author of the alleged infringement make some use of material derived by him, directly or indirectly, from the original work? Fourth, if the defendant contends that no such use is made, what is his explanation for the existence of similarities between the two works? Fifth, if use was made of the source work, did this amount to a 'substantial part' of it? Finally, what factors support the conclusion that what has been taken is a 'substantial part' of the original?

thinking point

In relation to the requirement of substantial taking, consider whether it is either desirable or possible for there to be clear judicial guidance on what is the 'substance' of a work. Would greater reliance on the justifications for copyright protection assist?

9.2.7 Liability for infringement by others

Copyright infringement has a broader reach than other forms of intellectual property rights, in that it imposes liability for the conduct of others. Naturally, as a statutory tort, the normal rules of vicarious liability for an employee's conduct will apply (*PRS v Mitchell & Booker* [1924] 1 KB 762) and the opportunities for employees to commit infringing conduct (for example by photocopying literary works or by downloading material from the internet) are numerous. For that reason, any responsible business should have a clearly stated policy warning employees of the implications of such conduct.

The most significant aspect of being liable for the conduct of others is to be found in s.16 CDPA. The section imposes liability should someone 'authorise' the commission of a restricted act, and according to *ABKCO Music v Music Collection International*, there can be liability where the act of authorisation is committed outside the United Kingdom as long as the restricted act (copying, issuing, performing, etc) occurs within the jurisdiction.

The limits of 'authorisation' need to be understood. In *Moorhouse v University of New South Wales* [1976] RPC 151 the High Court of Australia defined 'authorise' to mean 'sanction, countenance and approve' but added that authorisation also occurred where there were acts of indifference from which permission to infringe could be inferred. The University was therefore held to have authorised its students to commit infringement by photocopying because of the absence of suitable warning notices in the library. The significant facts of the decision should be noted. It involved the provision of copyright materials as well as the equipment necessary to make the copies. In other cases, claimants have failed to establish liability for authorisation because one or other of these key ingredients was absent. Thus in *CBS v Ames* [1981] 2 All ER 812, a record shop was held not to have authorised the copying of sound recordings when it had sold blank tapes and allowed its customers to hire the records. It had supplied the recording medium but not the recording equipment. In *Amstrad Consumer Electronics plc v British Phonographic Industry Ltd* [1986] FSR 159, the Court of Appeal held that to supply a double-headed cassette deck on its own was not enough to 'authorise', because the element of control over the users of such machines was lacking. Also, the manufacturer of the deck (which had sought a declaration that its advertisements for the machine were lawful) could not be said to have incited copyright infringement because the incitement was not directed to identifiable individuals, but to the public at large. However, the court added that the manufacturer's conduct might amount to 'inciting' the commission of a crime under what is now CDPA s.107. This last remark led one of the record companies who belonged to BPI to attempt to obtain an **injunction** against Amstrad for persistent breaches of the criminal law in *CBS Songs Ltd v Amstrad Consumer Electronics plc* [1988] AC 1013. The House of Lords distinguished between 'facilitating' infringement and 'authorising' it, adding that even if Amstrad had incited the commission of criminal conduct (which it had not because the advertisements were not directed at particular individuals), such criminal liability did not entitle record companies to obtain an injunction to restrain infringement under civil law. Lord Templeman (at p. 1060) thought the position was 'lamentable' because the record companies and their artists were powerless to stop the home taping of music.

cross reference
See section 9.3.3.

One minor form of secondary liability for the conduct of another is to be found in s.25(1) CDPA which deals with where a defendant permits a place of public entertainment to be used for a public performance. This should be understood in the context of the primary restricted act of performing a copyright work in public, and of the role of copyright collecting societies in licensing premises for the public performance of music and sound recordings, discussed later.

thinking point

Do you agree with the House of Lords in CBS v Amstrad *that the law of copyright is deficient if it does not assist the copyright owner to prevent the supply of equipment which facilitates copying? Is imposing a levy on such equipment the answer?*

9.3 Primary infringement

The framework provision for primary infringement is s.16 CDPA. Each of the five restricted acts listed therein receives individual treatment in the sections which follow. We consider these separate statutory provisions in turn. As is common throughout any discussion of copyright, attention to detail is important, because not all categories of works are covered by each section.

9.3.1 Copying: s.17

9.3.1.1 The meaning of 'copying'

cross reference
The relationship between s.17(3) and the defence in s.51 CDPA is considered at section 11.3.2.2.

This restricted act applies to every description of copyright work, and includes the making of temporary copies or copies which are incidental to some other use of the work (subject to the defence in s.28A). Section 17 deals with each category of work in turn. In relation to literary, dramatic, musical and artistic works, 'copying' is defined in s.17(2) to *mean* reproducing the work in any material form, including storing the work in any medium by electronic means. An additional form of copying in relation to artistic works only is provided by s.17(3), which declares that copying *includes* the making of a three-dimensional version of a two-dimensional work and vice versa. So, for example, making a toy based on a cartoon drawing or taking a photograph of a sculpture or of a work of architecture would fall within the provision. Section 17(4) declares that copying in relation to a film or broadcast *includes* making a photograph of the whole or part of an image forming part of the film or broadcast (thereby confirming the earlier Court of Appeal decision in *Spelling Goldberg v BPC Publications Ltd*). Finally, s.17(5) explains that copying a typographical arrangement *means* making a facsimile copy; in other words, the category of work covered by s.8 CDPA will only be infringed by activities such as photocopying or scanning. There must be a facsimile copy of the whole published edition and nothing less will suffice: *per* Lord Hoffmann in *Newspaper Licensing Agency Ltd v Marks & Spencer plc* [2003] 1 AC 551 at [20].

What amounts to copying a work will be coloured by the statutory definition of the work itself. Whilst copyright in a literary, dramatic, musical and artistic work will be infringed by its being reproduced in *any* material form, the definition of a sound recording (see s.5A) as 'a recording of sounds from which sounds may be reproduced' means that in order to infringe the copy must itself reproduce sounds, in other words a sound recording would not be infringed by someone writing down the sounds on paper. Similarly, a film, being 'a recording from which a moving image may be reproduced' will only be infringed by something which reproduces the recording of the moving image. Copyright in a recipe is not infringed by making a cake (*J & S Davis v Wright* [1988] RPC 403) though for a contradictory decision in relation to fabric design see *Moon v Thornber* [2012] EWPCC 37.

Copying can occur in several ways. The defendant may make an exact reproduction of the claimant's work, or may take only part of the work adding something of his or her own (in which case they will be both an infringer of what has been taken and the creator of the added matter), or may create a work which appears to be similar. However, one guiding principle is that the simpler the source work, the greater degree of copying is required. In *Kenrick v Lawrence* (1890) 25 QBD 99, a drawing of a hand explaining to voters how to vote was so simple that it could only be infringed by an exact copy. Likewise in *Guild v Eskandar Ltd* [2003] FSR 23, knitwear designs were held to be so basic that the defendant could easily escape liability by adding extra detail.

9.3.1.2 Indirect copying

As previously explained, s.16 CDPA provides for liability to be imposed whether the defendant takes from the claimant's work directly or indirectly. We have already considered *Solar*

Thomson v Barton as an illustration of indirect copying. Other examples include *Bernstein v Sydney Murray* [1981] RPC 303 where it was held that making garments which copied those sold by the claimant infringed the copyright in the claimant's drawings for those garments; and *Plix Products v Winstone* [1986] FSR 608 where the New Zealand Court of Appeal held that where the defendant had made containers in which Kiwi fruits could be transported by following the specifications and verbal instructions given by the New Zealand Kiwifruit Association, which in turn had based its standards on packaging designed by the claimant, the defendant had infringed the claimant's copyright drawings. More recently, in *Gabrin v Universal Music Operations Ltd* [2004] ECDR 18, Patten J held that the defendant recording company had infringed the claimant photographer's copyright when it had produced a CD cover based on a print which in turn had been based on the original photograph of Elvis Costello taken some 20 years earlier. In each of these cases, the causal link between the original work and the defendant's infringement was unbroken.

Because of the importance of understanding the concept of indirect copying, we set out an illustration in Diagram 9.1 below. Whilst the illustration shows indirect copying only one step away from the original (as in the *Gabrin* case), there is no reason in principle (subject to the requirement of substantial taking) how many steps removed from the original work the indirect copy may be.

Diagram 9.1

Indirect copying

(based on *Gabrin v Universal Music Operations Ltd*)

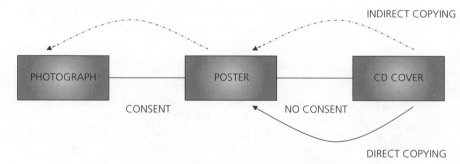

9.3.1.3 Subconscious copying

As liability for copyright infringement does not depend on the defendant's state of mind (*Baigent & Lee v Random House Group Ltd*) it is possible for a defendant to commit copyright infringement even though they are unaware that they are copying the claimant's work. Subconscious copying is an argument usually found in cases concerned with musical copyright, where the claimant will contend that the defendant must have heard the tune in question so that they became familiar with it and then unwittingly reproduced it later on. The allegation of subconscious copying failed in *Francis Day & Hunter v Bron*, where the court accepted that there was similarity but insufficient evidence of derivation. In *EMI Music Publishing v Papathanasiou* [1993] EMLR 306, Whitford J rejected the claim that the defendant (professionally known as Vangelis) had based his tune 'Chariots of Fire' on an earlier piece. The only similarity between the two tunes was one particular phrase, which was commonplace, and viewed overall the pieces were not alike. The most famous instance of subconscious copying is the US decision in *ABKCO Music Inc v Harrisongs Music Ltd* 722 F 2d 988 (2d Cir 1983) where it was held that George Harrison had subconsciously copied 'He's So Fine' when writing his hit 'My Sweet Lord'.

9.3.2 Distributing copies: s.18

Section 18 CDPA covers two aspects of the copyright owner's right of distribution. The principal provision deals with the right to issue tangible copies of the work by placing them in circulation within the **EEA**. Section 18A deals with the right to control the rental or lending of the work to the public. Whilst the former applies to all categories of work, the latter applies only to literary, dramatic, musical and artistic works (other than works of architecture and a work of applied art), films and sound recordings.

The principal provision, s.18, has been amended twice since its original enactment. Both in its original and amended form, it creates a new type of restricted act, as explained by Sterling (in 'Copyright, Designs and Patents Act 1988: the New Issuing Right' [1989] *EIPR* 283) and by Phillips & Bently (in 'Copyright Issues: the Mysteries of Section 18' [1999] *EIPR* 133). Previously there was liability for publishing a *work*. As explained by the House of Lords in *Infabrics v Jaytex Ltd* [1981] 1 All ER 1057, 'publishing' is a one-off occurrence—either a work is published or it is not. The consequence under the old law was that if a copyright owner wanted to object to dealings in further copies of the work which had not been approved, they had to establish liability for secondary infringement. The current situation is that there is liability for issuing *copies* of the work. Hence the copyright owner is given the ability to control the first sale of *each and every copy made*, a point confirmed by Laddie J in *Nelson v Rye & Cocteau Records* [1996] 2 All ER 186 at p. 208.

> **example**
>
> An author licenses a publisher to print 2,000 copies of a book but states that only 1,000 copies are to be distributed. The first 1,000 copies are quickly sold out. The publisher then sells the remaining 1,000 without seeking the author's permission. Under the old law, the work would have been regarded as 'published' so that the author had no right to object to the distribution of additional copies. Under s.18, this is infringement.

The current wording of s.18 is remarkable for its lack of clarity. Reference to the origin of the wording in the Rental Rights Directive (now codified as Directive 2006/115/EC of the European Parliament and of the Council of 12 December 2006 [2006] OJ L 376/28) reveals that the section is meant to incorporate the doctrine of intra-EU **exhaustion of rights**, so that whilst the copyright owner cannot object to the issuing of copies which have previously been put in circulation within the EEA, they can object to the issuing of copies which have previously been put in circulation outside the EEA. It has been confirmed by the ECJ in Case C-479/04 *Laserdisken ApS v Kulturministeriet* [2006] ECR I-8089 that Member States no longer have a discretion to maintain any doctrine of international exhaustion of rights in relation to copyright. Further, the separate rental right in copyright (s.18A) is a deliberate exception to the doctrine of exhaustion: Case C-61/97 *Egmont Films v Laserdisken* [1998] ECR I-5171.

The exact meaning of 'issue to the public' is, however, unclear. Consider as an example the normal chain of distribution of a book (from author to publisher to wholesaler to retailer to purchasing public) illustrated by Diagram 9.2 below. Is (as Philips & Bently discuss) the issuing right concerned with the *disposition* of the copies (ie once copies of a book have been supplied to a wholesaler the right is exhausted) or is issuing concerned with the *destination* of the copies (ie the right is only exhausted once copies are purchased by *the public*)? The answer to the question makes a crucial difference to the position of the retailer and should be compared with the law as it stood under the 1956 Act decision of *Infabrics v Jaytex*. If the issuing right is spent once a copy of the work has been *disposed* of to the first person in the chain of distribution, then any person further down the chain can deal with that copy without restriction. However, if the issuing right is only spent once it reaches its destination (ie the public), then a retailer will be liable for infringing the issuing right. As yet there is no guidance on this point, but reference to the exhaustion of rights case law concerning trade marks suggests that the key fact is whether the first person acquiring the goods has the power of disposal of them, that is, they have legal title (Case C-16/03 *Peak Holding AB v Axolin-Elinor AB* [2004] ECR I-11313). By analogy, this points to the disposition theory. In view of the legislative origins of s.18, the matter awaits resolution by the ECJ.

Diagram 9.2

Section 18 CDPA

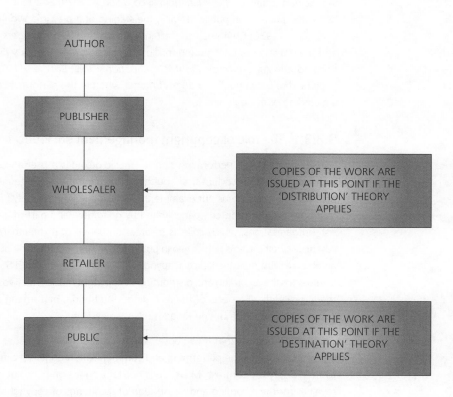

Finally, despite its obscure wording, s.18 changes the relationship between primary and secondary infringement. In contrast to what was said on the old law in *Infabrics v Jaytex*, it is now possible for a retailer to be made liable for primary infringement. Thus, if an author has not given permission for particular copies of the work to be distributed, or if the copies in question were first marketed outside the EEA, then the person who supplies them in the United Kingdom has committed a restricted act. This point appears not to have been understood by the United Kingdom Government, because there is a conflict between s.18 and the definition of infringing copy for the purposes of secondary infringement in s.27 (see later).

9.3.3 **Performing the work: s.19**

cross reference
See further
chapter 8.

Under s.19, the performance of a literary, dramatic or musical work in public is a restricted act, as is the playing or showing in public of a film, sound recording or broadcast. The performance right therefore does not apply to artistic works, a point which may surprise some of today's exponents of modern art, but which is entirely in keeping with the assumptions underlying the CDPA about the nature of creativity.

Section 19 contains a definition of 'performance' which includes the delivery of speeches and sermons, and any mode of acoustic and visual presentation. It does not, however, define what is 'in public', the meaning of which has to be found in case law. The early decision in *Duck v Bates* (1884) 13 QBD 843 provided a relatively narrow interpretation of the phrase, so that a performance of a play by hospital staff for patients was held to be in private. Modern case law makes clear that what matters is the relationship between the spectator of the performance and the copyright holder, not the relationship between the spectator and the person providing the performance: *PRS v Harlequin Record Shops* [1979] 2 All ER 828. Anything outside the domestic sphere is 'in public'. Hence, the staging of a play in a Women's Institute (*Jennings v Stephens* [1936] Ch 469), a concert in a private club (*PRS v Rangers Club* [1975] RPC 626), and the provision of background music in factories (*Ernest Turner v PRS* [1943] Ch 167) and shops (*South African Music Rights Organisation v Trust Butchers* [1978] 1 SA 1052) have all been held to be 'in public'. It doesn't matter whether the performance is live or by means of a recording or through a radio.

9.3.3.1 The role of copyright management societies

Management of the performing right in music provides a useful illustration of the role of copyright collecting societies, although such organisations are found across the spectrum of copyright. We take as our example the Performing Right Society ('PRS'), founded in 1914 as a non-profit-making company limited by guarantee and part of a worldwide network of sister organisations, which collects royalties on behalf of its members, primarily composers, whenever their music is performed in public or communicated to the public. PRS is now part of an alliance with the Mechanical Copyright Protection Society ('MCPS') whose task is to grant **licences** for the recording and distribution of copyright music. The two organisations between them deal with all aspects of the recording, distribution, performing and communication of copyright music in the United Kingdom.

The starting point is that a composer, songwriter or music publisher, on becoming a member of PRS, **assigns** the performing and communication rights set out in ss.19 and 20 CDPA to the Society (by contrast, MCPS does not take an assignment but acts as agent to collect royalties for the recording and distribution of recordings of copyright music under ss.17 and 18 CDPA). In the case of copyright music which is performed in public (whether live or via a recording or by means of a radio or television broadcast), PRS grants a blanket licence to the controller of the premises where the performance occurs. In the case of the communication of copyright music, it grants a specific licence to the organisation which is going to use the music in a radio or TV broadcast. In the blanket licence scheme, there are over 40 different tariffs depending on the nature of the business activity in which the music is used, ranging from cinemas to pubs to hairdressing salons to aircraft to ringtones for mobile phones. Premises are checked by inspectors to ensure that they have the appropriate licence. Failure to obtain a licence will result in PRS commencing proceedings against the owner of the premises for copyright infringement. Where music (whether live or recorded) is used in a broadcast, there is likewise a range of tariffs depending on how the music is going to be used, such as in radio and television advertisements, as background music for a play or documentary, as an 'ident' for a particular radio station, or in hospital or student radio broadcasts. Resulting royalties are divided between the members, who number about 50,000. Disputes about licensing schemes are dealt with by the Copyright Tribunal under s.149 and Sch. 6 CDPA.

thinking point
How aware do you think owners of premises are as to the implications of providing background music for visitors to those premises?

Other copyright management societies include the Copyright Licensing Agency ('CLA') (which deals with the photocopying of literary, dramatic, and musical works), the Newspaper Licensing Agency ('NLA') (managing the rights of newspapers and periodicals over both tangible and intangible media), the Design and Artists Copyright Society ('DACS') (controlling the use of artistic works), and Phonographic Performance Ltd ('PPL') (which licenses the public performance of sound recordings). A business, such as a hairdresser, which uses CDs to play background music to its customers, will therefore need both a PRS and PPL licence.

9.3.4 **Communicating the work to the public: s.20**

Section 20 CDPA, amended as a result of Article 3 of Directive 2001/29/EC of the European Parliament and of the Council of 22 May 2001 on the harmonisation of aspects of copyright and related rights in the information society [2001] OJ L 167/10 ('the Information Society Directive'), provides for the copyright owner's communication right. The Directive in turn was influenced by **WIPO's** Copyright Treaty 1996. In contrast to s.18 which deals with distribution of the work by tangible means (ie physical copies), s.20 is concerned with electronic, intangible means of distribution and therefore covers both broadcasting and the internet. It applies to all categories of copyright work with the exception of typographical arrangements of published editions. The revised wording of s.20 achieves the same result as *Shetland Times v Jonathan Wills* [1997] FSR 604, which treated websites as if they were broadcasts.

The communication right has been the subject of numerous references to the ECJ. In Case C-306/05 *Sociedad General de Autores y Editores España v Rafael Hoteles SA* [2006] ECR I-11519 it observed that the Directive did not define 'communication to the public' but that the phrase should be given a wide interpretation so as to give broad protection to authors. Whilst installing television sets in hotel rooms was not 'communication', using the sets to provide TV programmes to customers was. With regard to the meaning of 'the public', the Court said (at [40]) that what matters is that the transmission is to a public different from that targeted by the original act of communication, ie a new public. Similarly, in Cases C-403/08 and C-429/08 *Football Association Premier League Ltd and others* [2011] ECR I-9083, it said that 'communication to the public' requires the work to be transmitted to a new public, ie one not contemplated by the copyright owner at the time of the initial transmission. It did however make plain that the communication right is separate from the reproduction right, so that the defendant had infringed the communication right by screening football matches in her pub using a satellite decoder purchased in another EU State without the copyright owner's permission, however, the reproduction right had not been infringed because the copies of the broadcast stored in the decoder's cache were within the temporary copies defence, explained later.

The Court's emphasis on there being a new public means that s.20 covers not just those who indulge in unlicensed file sharing activities (*Polydor Ltd v Brown* [2005] EWHC 3191, *Dramatico Entertainment Ltd v BSB Ltd* [2012] RPC 665) but also those whose service enables viewers to catch up on free-to-air programmes they may have missed (Case C-607/11 *ITV Broadcasting Ltd v TV Catchup Ltd*, 7 March 2013).

9.3.5 Adaptation: s.21

The restricted act of adaptation applies to literary, dramatic and musical works only, and so is the one type of infringement which is not of general application. Further, the definition of 'adaptation' is much narrower than might be expected and will apply in very limited circumstances. 'Adaptation' is stated by s.21(3) to mean, in relation to a literary or dramatic work, its translation, turning a play into a book and vice versa, or turning the work into a pictorial format suitable for newspapers and magazines (but *not* turning a story or play into pictures to be published as a *book*). In relation to musical works it means arranging or transcribing the work. There are separate provisions dealing with the adaptation and translation of computer programs and databases. The section further provides that an adaptation is made when it is recorded in writing or otherwise. Once so recorded, it is also infringement to copy the adaptation, issue copies, perform it, and communicate it to the public (s.21(2) CDPA).

thinking point
Does the adaptation right in s.21 CDPA fulfil any useful purpose given the breadth of s.17?

Section 21 concludes by declaring that no inference is to be drawn as to what does or does not amount to copying a work. The dividing line between copying and adaptation is therefore left unclear, but in view of the narrow scope of s.21 and the breadth of s.17, a claimant is more likely to allege that the defendant has committed altered copying rather than adaptation.

9.4 Secondary infringement of copyright

9.4.1 Acts of secondary infringement

Liability for secondary infringement of copyright occurs when the defendant undertakes commercial dealings in infringing copies. The relevant conduct is set out in ss.22 and 23 CDPA. It comprises, in summary, importing (except for private and domestic use), possessing, selling, letting or hiring, offering for sale or hire, exhibiting in public and distributing. 'Commercial dealings' is not limited to those who trade in goods, so that in *Pensher Security Door Co Ltd v Sunderland City Council* [2000] RPC 249 a local authority was held liable for the installation of security doors in a council-owned block of flats when the doors infringed the claimant's design. The sections are therefore concerned with tangible copies only.

Sections 22 and 23 are subject to two preconditions which must be satisfied before the defendant can be held to have infringed. These are the requirement of knowledge, and the fact that the defendant must have been dealing in infringing copies.

9.4.2 The requirement of knowledge

Both of the previously mentioned provisions are qualified by the phrase 'which he knows or has reason to believe'. This imposes an objective standard, so that the defendant is to be judged by a reasonable person in that line of business: *LA Gear v Hi-Tec Sports plc* [1992] FSR 121; *Vermaat v Boncrest Ltd (No 2)* [2002] FSR 331. To ensure that a retailer is fixed with notice that they are dealing in suspect goods, the copyright owner can write, and the retailer is deemed to have the requisite knowledge 21 days after the date of the letter, as 21 days is a sufficient period of time for the defendant to make the necessary inquiries and to obtain legal advice: *Monsoon Ltd v India Imports of Rhode Island* [1993] FSR 486. To continue trading in the counterfeit goods after that will risk the award of additional **damages** for flagrant infringement under s.97 CDPA.

9.4.3 The definition of 'infringing copy'

The second requirement is that the defendant must have been dealing in infringing copies of the claimant's work. This may seem self-evident. However, the definition of 'infringing copy', set out in s.27 CDPA, is problematic in a number of ways:

- it fails to take into account the impact of s.18 which creates the distribution right;
- it is in conflict with the case law of the ECJ with regard to international exhaustion of rights; and
- the actual wording of the section gives rise to practical uncertainties.

9.4.3.1 The wording of s.27

One aspect of s.27 is straightforward. Section 27(2) declares that an article is an infringing copy if its making constituted an infringement. This means that where a work is copied by a counterfeiter (whether in the United Kingdom or any other country adhering to the **Berne Convention** or the **WTO**) the articles in question (for example, CDs or DVDs) will be infringing copies. Any person who subsequently deals in such copies, provided they have the requisite knowledge, will commit secondary infringement.

The real difficulty lies in the wording of s.27(3) which reproduces (though with alterations) similar provisions in the 1956 Act. It states that an article is also an infringing copy if it has been or is proposed to be imported into the United Kingdom and its making in the United Kingdom would have constituted an infringement of the copyright or a breach of an exclusive licence. This wording contains an artificial assumption, namely that had the imported article (made elsewhere) been made in the United Kingdom, its manufacture 'would have constituted an infringement'. Section 27(5) contains an exception to s.27(3) (in language not totally transparent) for those instances where the ECJ's case law on intra-EU exhaustion of rights applies.

9.4.3.2 The interpretation of the section

So how has the assumption (or hypothesis) in s.27(3) been interpreted? There are two possibilities. First, the court could assume that the articles were made in the United Kingdom by the person who *actually* made them in the country of export, which requires only one hypothesis, namely as to the place of the manufacture of the goods. Second, the court could assume that the articles were made in the United Kingdom by the person who imported them into the United Kingdom. This requires the making of two hypothetical assumptions, one as regards the identity of the maker and the other as regards the place of manufacture.

case close-up

CBS Ltd v Charmdale [1980] 2 All ER 807

....

The first interpretation was that adopted by Browne-Wilkinson J (as he then was) in *CBS Ltd v Charmdale* [1980] 2 All ER 807. Here the defendant had imported copies of sound recordings into the United Kingdom and was sued for secondary infringement by the subsidiary company (who was an exclusive licensee) of the copyright owner, CBS Inc. The records had been made in the USA by the parent company. Browne-Wilkinson J decided that the wording of the 1956 Act required the court to make but one hypothesis. Here the goods had been made by the copyright owner. Had that person made them in the United Kingdom rather than in the USA, they would not have been infringing copies. The defendant was not liable.

The second interpretation was applied by the New Zealand High Court in *Barson v Gilbert* [1985] FSR 489, the relevant New Zealand legislation being identical in substance to the 1956 Act. The justification for making a double hypothesis was that to hold otherwise would undermine the position of the exclusive licensee in New Zealand, who would be exposed to price competition from **parallel imports**.

The net effect of the two alternatives is that the *Charmdale* interpretation creates a doctrine of international exhaustion of rights (which renders s.27(5) redundant) because it is assumed that the actual maker of the goods made them in the United Kingdom. Articles obtained indirectly from the copyright owner can never amount to infringing copies. The *Barson v Gilbert* solution enables the copyright owner to keep parallel imports out of the United Kingdom unless the articles have originated in the EEA, in which case s.27(5) will apply to provide the importer with the defence of intra-EU exhaustion of rights.

9.4.3.3 Section 27(3): a conclusion

The inclusion of s.27(3) as an alternative definition of 'infringing copy' to that found in s.27(2) is erroneous (it must be emphasised that s.27(2) is entirely acceptable). Why did Parliament see fit to base the provision on sections found in the 1956 Act even though s.18 CDPA created the distribution right, which as we explained earlier, has built into it the EU policy that there should be no international exhaustion of rights? Further, Parliament added an alternative within s.27(3) itself, so that the imported article can either infringe copyright or breach an exclusive licence. This means that there may or may not be international exhaustion of rights, depending on whether the copyright owner has appointed an exclusive licensee for the United Kingdom. Unlike patents and trade marks, there is no means for a third party to find out whether an exclusive licensee has been appointed, as there is no register to consult. Is it logical to have the *Charmdale* rule applying where there is no licensee and *Barson v Gilbert* applying where there is? In any event, as the ECJ has stated in Case C-479/04 *Laserdisken ApS v Kulturministeriet*, Member States no longer have any discretion to maintain a policy of international exhaustion of rights in copyright. The presence or absence of an exclusive licensee is therefore irrelevant to the ability of the copyright owner to prevent non-EEA parallel imports.

thinking point

Draft a memorandum to the United Kingdom Government explaining why s.27(3) CDPA should be repealed.

9.5 Defences to copyright infringement

9.5.1 **Overview**

Discussion of the defences to copyright infringement immediately presents the student with three challenges. First, the defences are numerous: there are now well over 50 to be found in the CDPA, in addition to those available at common law, the list having been added to as a result of the Hargreaves Report. Second, the statutory defences are all fact-specific: by this we mean that they are only available to a defendant if the infringing conduct has occurred in a particular factual scenario. If the defendant's conduct does not fall within the parameters set out in the relevant section, the defence is not available. So, for example, prior to the Hargreaves' amendments, there was the defence of dealing with a work for the purposes of criticism or review in s.30(1) CDPA (now replaced with the defence of quotation). Although the words 'criticism' and 'review' were not to be interpreted too narrowly (*Pro Sieben Media AG v Carlton UK Television Ltd* [1999] 1 WLR 605), they did not cover taking the claimant's work for the purposes of a comparative advertisement which alleged that the defendant's magazine was better than the claimant's as this was not 'criticism or review' of the work (*IPC Media Ltd v News Group Newspapers Ltd* [2005] FSR 752). Finally, each of the statutory defences is hedged about with restrictions and conditions. Some defences apply to all categories of copyright work, but many apply only to some. Some defences require due acknowledgement to be made, others do not. Attention to detail becomes paramount.

The specificity of United Kingdom legislation should be contrasted with the approaches of other jurisdictions, such as the 'fair use' defence in §107 of the USA Copyright Act. Indeed, both the Berne Convention Article 9(2) and the **WIPO** Copyright Treaty 1996 Article 10(1) provide for what is commonly referred to as the 'three-step test', namely that any limitations or exceptions to the rights of authors (1) should be confined to certain special cases which (2) do not conflict with a normal exploitation of the work and which (3) do not unreasonably prejudice the legitimate interests of the author. The simplicity of such an approach should be compared with the complexity of domestic law. However, as Burrell points out (in 'Reining in Copyright Law: Is Fair Use the Answer' [2001] *IPQ* 361) it is too easy to blame Parliament for this state of affairs where the balance of copyright law seems tilted in favour of the right owner at the expense of the user. There is ample evidence, he suggests, that judges are more likely to favour the claimant rather than the defendant even where statute appears to confer on the court a measure of discretion.

9.5.2 **General statutory defences: fair dealing**

The comments made earlier about how copyright defences are fact-specific and subject to different preconditions can be illustrated by the following chart, Table 9.1. This sets out the principal general defences (which we shall deal with under the umbrella term of 'fair dealing'), and indicates which categories of work are covered by which defence and the requirements attached to each. For the sake of ease of understanding we have omitted some of the detail concerned with computer programs and databases.

Table 9.1

Copyright defences: categories of work(s) and requirements

Section	Factual situation	Category of work(s)	Condition(s)
28A	Making temporary copies.	All except computer programs, databases and broadcasts.	1. Must be transient or incidental; and 2. Must be an essential part of a technological process; and 3. Must not have any independent economic significance; and 4. Must be to enable the transmission of the work in a network or to enable a lawful use of the work.
28B	Private copying.	All categories.	1. Must be of a lawfully acquired, permanent copy; 2. Must be for the individual's private use for ends that are neither directly nor indirectly commercial; 3. Must not be transferred to another.
29(1)	Non-commercial research.	All categories.	Must be accompanied by a sufficient acknowledgement unless this is impossible for reasons of practicality.
29(1C)	Private study.	All categories.	1. Must be done by the researcher or student personally; 2. Must be a single copy.
29A	Data analysis for non-commercial research.	All categories.	Must be accompanied by a sufficient acknowledgement unless this is impossible for reasons of practicality.
30A	Quotation for purposes such as criticism or review.	Any work.	1. Must be accompanied by a sufficient acknowledgment; 2. Must have been lawfully made available to the public.
30(2)	Reporting current events.	Any work other than photographs.	Must be accompanied by a sufficient acknowledgement unless the reporting was by sound recording, film or broadcast where this would be impossible for reasons of practicality.
30B	Caricature, parody or pastiche.	All categories.	-
31	Incidental inclusion in an artistic work, sound recording, film or broadcast,	Any work, but a musical work, words spoken or sung with music, or a sound recording	-

Section	Factual situation	Category of work(s)	Condition(s)
	including issuing copies, performing or communicating the work containing the source material.	or broadcast containing such music or words is not to be regarded as incidentally included where the inclusion is deliberate.	

thinking point

Are the general defences set out in ss.28–31 CDPA logical in the way they apply to different categories of copyright work and in the conditions which must be fulfilled before they can be used?

9.5.2.1 Applying the fair dealing provisions

The leading case on the application of the provisions is *Pro Sieben Media AG v Carlton UK Television Ltd*. The Court of Appeal explained that two steps must be taken sequentially, namely a determination of whether the appropriate factual scenario (for example reporting current events or quotation) has been made out, and then, if it has, whether the defendant's dealing was fair. Both of these are to be determined objectively (through the eyes of the reasonable person) without regard to the defendant's opinions or intentions: *Pro Sieben*; *Hyde Park Residence Ltd v Yelland* [2000] 3 WLR 215.

Despite the clarity of *Pro Sieben*, one issue omitted from all the cases is a discussion of the policy underlying the application of the defences. Such policy, argues Griffiths (in 'Preserving Judicial Freedom of Movement—Interpreting Fair Dealing in Copyright Law' [2000] *IPQ* 164) could be that derogations from rights of property should be strictly construed or equally that freedom of expression should prevail. Instead, he says, what can be discerned from the cases is the pragmatic need to preserve judicial discretion. In contrast to Burrell (in 'Reining in Copyright Law: Is Fair Use the Answer' [2001] *IPQ* 361), Griffiths suggests that the majority of cases display a considerable degree of flexibility.

This is an area where the last decade has witnessed a marked increase in the volume of case law. It may be too soon to say which of these two views is correct.

Are the circumstances of the defence established?

Despite the statement in *Pro Sieben* that whether the relevant circumstances have been met is an objective test, it has been constantly stated that the key words such as 'current events' should be given a wide meaning. 'Any attempt to plot their precise boundaries is doomed to failure' *per* Robert Walker LJ in *Pro Sieben* at p. 614.

Therefore 'current events' includes not only political news but sport: *BBC v BSB* [1992] Ch 141. Whether the term extends to events which occurred more than one year ago is less clear, but it can cover commenting on media coverage generated by allegations made about past events: *Hyde Park Residence Ltd v Yelland*.

It is unclear whether the 'quotation' defence (which replaces 'criticism or review') will operate in the same way. The old defence included not just the work taken but another work or a performance of the work, as well as the work's underlying ideas or to its moral or social implications. In *Time Warner v Channel 4 Television* [1994] EMLR 1 the Court of Appeal accepted that a television programme criticising the copyright owner's decision to prohibit the exhibition and distribution of the film *A Clockwork Orange* could not be separated from criticism of the content of the film itself. In *Pro Sieben*, the same court held that the use of an extract from the claimant's television interview with Mandy Allwood, who was expecting octuplets, was an integral part of the defendant's criticism of the evils of 'cheque book journalism'.

case close-up

Fraser-Woodward Ltd v British Broadcasting Corporation & Brighter Pictures Ltd [2005] FSR 762

Mann J upheld the 'criticism or review' defence where a documentary series *Tabloid Tales*, made by the second defendant and broadcast by the BBC, had included images of newspaper articles containing the claimant's photographs. The images had been broadcast to support the programme's criticism of the 'cult of celebrity', seeking to show that some celebrities, such as Victoria Beckham, were adroit at manipulating the popular press.

case close-up

Football Association Premier League v Panini (UK) Ltd [2004] 1 WLR 1147, CA

The defence of 'incidental inclusion' was considered in *Football Association Premier League v Panini (UK) Ltd* [2004] 1 WLR 1147, CA. At first instance it was suggested that 'incidental' should mean casual, inessential, subordinate or merely background. Consequently the defence was not available to the defendant who had produced collectible stickers with pictures of football players which showed the claimant's logo as well as their club's badge. The appearance of the logo was an integral part of the photograph and so was not incidental. In upholding the appeal, the Court of Appeal said that 'incidental' and 'integral' were not necessarily opposites, and thought it more appropriate to ask why the work had been included in the infringement on both commercial and aesthetic grounds. Here it was important to the defendant's business that the pictures showed players wearing their club's shirt, so the use of the logo was not incidental. In any event, the defendant's product (albums to put the stickers in) was a literary not artistic work and so the defence did not apply (yet another example of the idiosyncrasies of the general defences in the CDPA). In contrast, in the *Fraser-Woodward* case it was held that in respect of the one photograph not covered by the criticism or review defence, the television programme had focused on the headline within which the photograph had been inserted by the newspaper. As the photograph had been there in the original newspaper page, its use in the programme was incidental.

The particular problem of parody

One of the most welcome revisions to copyright defences must be the introduction of fair dealing by way of parody. As Spence explains, (in 'Intellectual Property and the Problem of Parody' (1998) 114 *LQR* 594), there are numerous meanings of the term 'parody', not least because it can be used in countless ways, for example in political debate, in commerce, in advertising and to entertain. He suggests that in the context of intellectual property, it can be taken to mean, broadly speaking, 'the imitation of a text for the purpose of commenting, usually humorously, upon either that text or something else'. 'Target' parodies, he says, seek to comment on the text or its creator; 'weapon' parodies involve the use of that text to comment on something else. Spence puts forward two reasons why parody should receive special treatment namely 'transformative activity' and free speech. We considered 'transformative activity' in the context of originality, where it was noted that a person who takes another's work and adds to it using their own creative endeavour will have copyright in the addition even though they have infringed the source work (*ZYX Music v King* [1995] 3 All ER 1). However, while other jurisdictions such as the USA and Germany recognise transformative use as part of the fair use defence, under United Kingdom law such use does not receive special treatment. Free speech as a justification for parody is recognised in some countries (see Rütz, 'Parody: A Missed Opportunity' [2004] *IPQ* 284), particularly those with written constitutions. Up to now, United Kingdom law treated parody no differently from other types of transformative use. It was suggested by Younger J in *Glyn v Western Feature Film Co* [1916] 1 Ch 261 at p. 268 that a parody should not infringe if the parody itself amounted to an original work, but this appears to be the only decision where a parody was given special treatment and further, the principal argument in that case was whether the source work was debarred from copyright protection on grounds of public policy. Cases since have held that whether or not a parody infringes depends solely on the issue of substantial taking. Thus, in *Joy Music v Sunday Pictorial* [1960] 2 QB 60 (an example of weapon parody) there was no infringement of the copyright in song lyrics where the defendant's newspaper article proposed a new set of words commenting satirically on a speech by Prince Philip. The new words could be sung to the music of the original song, but the music itself was not reproduced: it was left to the reader's imagination to add the new words to the music. In *Schweppes v Wellingtons* [1984] FSR 210 (an example of target parody), Falconer J held that there had been substantial taking of the claimant's labels for tonic water bottles. The fact that the defendant was attempting to parody the style of the label in selling 'joke' products was neither here nor there. Likewise, in *Williamson v Pearson* [1987] FSR 97 the use of a well-known song in a television advert, albeit with altered lyrics, was held to be substantial taking of the musical work.

However, even though there is now a parody defence to copyright infringement, this will have no effect if at the same time the defendant commits trade mark infringement. In *Ate My Heart Inc v Mind Candy Music* [2011] EWHC 2741 interim relief was granted to restrain the release on YouTube of a song performed by a cartoon character 'Lady Goo Goo' which infringed the registered mark LADY GA GA by means of **dilution**. Humour, it seems has no part to play in trade mark law.

Assessing 'Fairness'

Once it is established that the defendant's conduct falls within the specific factual requirements of a particular defence, the court must then determine, objectively, whether the taking was fair. Lord Denning once remarked (in *Hubbard v Vosper* [1972] 2 QB 84 at p. 94) that what is 'fair' is a question of degree, adding that ultimately it is a matter of impression. Nevertheless, from the Court of Appeal's decision in *Pro Sieben* it is possible to identify a number of factors to be considered. None is conclusive, but all form part of the assessment of fairness. Depending on the circumstances of the case, some factors may weigh more heavily than others. The factors are the amount of the original work which is taken and the proportion which it forms of the defendant's work, the purpose of the use, the necessity of such use, whether the original work has already been published, and the motives of the copier.

Considering these in more detail, the amount taken is not conclusive one way or the other. In *Hubbard v Vosper*, Megaw LJ suggested that taking the whole of a short work might be fair in certain cases of criticism or review. In the *Time Warner* case, it was held that incorporating twelve and a half minutes of the film in a 30-minute television programme was acceptable. Whether the defendant's use competes with the claimant's exploitation of the work is another key factor. In *Sillitoe v McGraw Hill* [1983] FSR 545 the court concluded that the use made by the defendant of extracts of contemporary novels as part of its study guides was driven by the commercial imperative of making money. The defendant's motives equally can have a bearing: in *Associated Newspapers v News Group Newspapers* [1986] RPC 515 the only motive in publishing private correspondence of the Duke and Duchess of Windsor was to boost newspaper sales, whereas in *Pro Sieben* the court accepted that the defendant's motives had been to expose the evils of cheque-book journalism. However, even if the defendant is driven by a desire to expose an untruth, that will count for nothing if the information could have been communicated to the public by other means. In *Hyde Park v Yelland*, although the defendant newspaper editor was concerned to show the truth about the visit of Princess Diana to the Villa Windsor in Paris, it was not necessary to infringe the copyright in the CCTV security video by printing stills in *The Sun*: the information could have been conveyed by other means. The fact that the video had been unlawfully obtained (through a disgruntled former employee of the claimant) meant conclusively that the dealing was not fair.

Prior to the introduction of the Human Rights Act 1998 in October 2000, there was some debate that the Act would require courts in copyright infringement actions to have greater regard to Article 10 of the European Convention on Human Rights ('ECHR') (freedom of expression).

thinking point
Does the way in which 'fairness' is assessed in the 'fair dealing' defences produce certainty for those who wish to make lawful use of another's copyright work?

case close-up

Ashdown v Telegraph Group Ltd [2001] 4 All ER 666
. . . .

An early opportunity to test this hypothesis occurred in *Ashdown v Telegraph Group Ltd* [2001] 4 All ER 666, a case which conveniently combined the defences of fair dealing, in the **public interest**, and freedom of expression. The defendant newspaper group had obtained a copy of a confidential minute taken by the claimant in a previous meeting with the then Prime Minister which it published as part of a major article about the extent of the collaboration between the Liberal Democratic and Labour parties. This resulted in an action for breach of confidence and copyright infringement. The Court of Appeal accepted that when interpreting the CDPA, a court had to apply the Act in a manner which accommodates the right to freedom of expression. However, it then decided that the facts of the case did not give rise to 'one of those rare cases' where Article 10 ECHR 'trumped' copyright, and proceeded to apply the fair dealing defences in favour of the claimant. The reasons given for dismissing the defendant's reliance on s.30(2) were that the defendant's use competed commercially with the claimant's intended autobiography, it had been motivated by profit, the minute was previously unpublished, and the amount taken from the source work was disproportionate.

As Griffiths argues (in 'Copyright Law after Ashdown—Time to Deal Fairly with the Public' [2002] *IPQ* 240) the judgment is less than satisfactory in that it demonstrates an unwillingness to engage substantively with the requirements of Article 10. The factors to be taken into account when determining fairness were, he says, applied in a formulaic and inflexible manner.

9.5.3 Statutory defences: miscellaneous

thinking point
*Do you think
that the Court of
Appeal in* Ashdown
*genuinely took the
right to freedom
of expression fully
into account when
applying the fair
dealing defence to a
newspaper?*

The remaining defences in the CDPA can be subdivided according to whether they deal with the defendant's particular situation (for example the visually impaired, education, libraries, archives, public administration) or with particular works (for example computer programs, databases, designs, typefaces, works in electronic form). We select two of the latter category for further discussion.

9.5.3.1 Use of notes or recordings of spoken words

The defence found in s.58 CDPA should be seen as the obverse of the fact that copyright subsists in the spoken word. The section provides that where a record of spoken words is made, in writing or otherwise, for the purpose of reporting current events or broadcasting the whole or part of the work, it is not an infringement of any copyright in the words as a literary work to use the record or material taken from it for that purpose, provided the record is a direct record of the spoken word and the making of the record was not prohibited by the speaker, the use made of the record was not of a kind prohibited by the speaker before the record was made, and the use is by or with the authority of a person who is lawfully in possession of the record. This means, for example, that where a reporter electronically records a conversation with a celebrity or a politician, although the latter will own the copyright in the words spoken, the reporter will be at liberty to use the recording either for the purpose of reporting current events or to include in a broadcast. If, however, what is used is not a direct record (so if the notes or recording are copied the *copy* cannot be used) or if the recording is stolen, then the defence will not apply. It is, on the wording of the section, open to the interviewee to prohibit the making of the record. If (say) a reporter, despite the prohibition, persists in taking notes or making a recording, this would operate to 'fix' the copyright in the spoken word but the recording would be of no real value because it could not be exploited without infringing copyright.

cross reference
See section 8.2.3.4.

9.5.3.2 Time-shift

It is in relation to broadcasts that we find another example of where private and domestic use can be a defence to copyright infringement. Yet again, however, s.70 CDPA (as amended) is subject to a number of restrictions. It provides that the making of a recording of a broadcast *solely* for the purpose of enabling it to be viewed or listened to at a more convenient time does not infringe copyright in the broadcast nor any material comprised in it. The recording must be made on domestic premises (and hence not in a café or other commercial establishment—*Sony Music Entertainment (UK) Ltd v Easyinternetcafe Ltd* [2003] FSR 882) and there can only be one reason for the making of the recording. Hence someone who systematically records broadcasts of films so as to build up their own collection would not be within the defence. Further, s.70(2) provides that where a lawfully made recording is then sold or hired or offered for sale or hire or communicated to the public it then becomes an infringing copy. So again, if the home taper then makes the recording available on a file-sharing website (which would amount to 'communicating to the public'), they would no longer have the benefit of s.70.

9.5.4 **Statutory defences: in the public interest**

cross reference
See section 3.6.1.

In common with the law of breach of confidence, a defence that copyright infringement was justified 'in the public interest' may be pleaded. Indeed, most of the cases in which the defence has been raised involved both causes of action. There is a subtle difference between arguing that disclosure is 'in the public interest' and 'of public interest'. The need to know gossip and trivia do not justify an infringement of copyright.

The defence was first recognised (although it was rejected on the facts) in *Beloff v Pressdram*, where Ungoed-Thomas J (at p. 56) stated that the disclosure must be of 'matters, carried out or contemplated, in breach of the country's security, or in breach of law, including statutory duty, fraud, or otherwise destructive of the country or its people, including matters medically dangerous to the public; and doubtless other misdeed of similar gravity'. Since then, the law has moved on from this strict approach so that there is no longer a requirement that there must be a 'misdeed'. The best illustration of the defence in a copyright infringement action is to be found in *Lion Laboratories v Evans* [1984] 2 All ER 417 where the Court of Appeal accepted that the defendant ought to be able to reproduce the claimant's internal papers which revealed that its breathalyser was faulty. Had the defendant not been able to do so, there was a serious chance that large numbers of motorists would be wrongly convicted of drink-driving.

When the CDPA was enacted, the Government belatedly introduced a statutory provision codifying the public interest defence. Section 171(3) provides that 'nothing in this part affects any rule of law preventing or restricting the enforcement of copyright on grounds of public interest or otherwise'. As Burrell suggests (in 'Reining in Copyright Law: Is Fair Use the Answer' [2001] *IPQ* 361), at first glance this appears to amount to an express statutory recognition of the public interest defence.

thinking point
Do you think
that the Court
of Appeal in
Ashdown *genuinely
considered the
effect of the
Human Rights Act
when applying the
defence of 'in the
public interest'?*

However, in *Hyde Park Residence Ltd v Yelland*, the Court of Appeal adopted a different view, the majority holding that there was no defence of in the public interest and that all the section did was to restate the point that equitable remedies are discretionary. Burrell points out that in so doing, they ignored the legislative history of the provision as well as earlier case law and academic writing. A differently constituted Court of Appeal in *Ashdown v Telegraph Group Ltd* at [58] held that copyright could restrict freedom of expression so that a defence of in the public interest should be available, although it did not apply in the case. However, the public interest defence received a far narrower treatment in *Ashdown* than it did in *Lion Laboratories*, the court suggesting that it would apply only in 'very rare' circumstances. As Burrell says, the combined effect of *Yelland* and *Ashdown* has been to restrict a defence that Parliament intended to be much broader despite the coming into force of the Human Rights Act. Subsequent decisions, such as that in *HRH Prince of Wales v Associated Newspapers Ltd* [2007] 3 WLR 222, indicate that this approach is unlikely to change in the near future.

9.5.5 **Non-statutory defences**

9.5.5.1 Acquiescence

The general equitable defence of acquiescence may be raised in a copyright infringement action. However, its meaning is quite precise. In *Film Investors Overseas Services SA v Home Video Channel Ltd* Times, 2 December 1996, the court stressed that the claimant's conduct must amount to a misrepresentation, so that there is an intimation to the defendant, on which the defendant relies, that copyright will not be enforced. Consequently, mere delay in commencing proceedings is not acquiescence: *Farmers Build Ltd v Carier Bulk Handling Materials Ltd* [1999] RPC 461, CA.

---

case close-up

Fisher v Brooker [2009] 1 WLR 1764

The defence was considered by the House of Lords in *Fisher v Brooker* [2009] 1 WLR 1764 where Lord Neuberger (at [62–63]) remarked that he did not think that acquiescence added anything to two other equitable defences, namely laches and estoppel. Whichever of the three defences was deployed, the basic question was whether it would be unconscionable for the claimant to go back on his word. In the present case, this would only be met if the defendants could show that they had reasonably relied on the claimant not wanting to claim a share in the royalties of *A Whiter Shade of Pale*, that they had acted on this reliance, and that it would be unfairly to their detriment if the claimant was now permitted to enforce his rights. The three criteria had not been established. In any event, such equitable arguments were more appropriate to the question of equitable relief rather than a claim to a property right granted by statute.

9.5.5.2 Public policy

A defendant may choose to argue that the claimant's copyright should be unenforceable on the general principle (found throughout intellectual property) that it is contrary to public policy. Although there is no statutory basis for this defence, it was recognised as long ago as *Glyn v Western Feature Film Co*, where the court accepted the defendant's argument that the source of its film, the claimant's novel, did not deserve protection because it encouraged adultery.

When applying the public policy defence, it is important to distinguish between where the claimant's conduct is not deserving of protection from where the copyright work itself is disentitled to protection. This difference was endorsed by the House of Lords in *AG v Guardian Newspapers (No 2)* [1990] 1 AC 109 ('*Spycatcher*'). The point is neatly illustrated by *ZYX Music v King* where although the claimant was an infringer (by virtue of having reproduced an earlier pop hit) this did not prevent it from enforcing its own copyright in its arrangement against the defendant.

The principles which guide the court in applying the public policy defence were restated by the Court of Appeal in *Hyde Park Residence Ltd v Yelland and others*, relying on Lord Goff's opinion in *Spycatcher*. It said that the court will not enforce copyright if the work is immoral, scandalous, contrary to family life, contrary to public health or safety, or the administration of justice, or where it incites others to commit such harm. In keeping with the underlying policy that restrictions on a property right should be narrowly construed, these are strict criteria.

9.5.5.3 Implied licence

As consent is always a defence to any intellectual property infringement action, a defendant may attempt to argue that it had permission. However, the argument of implied licence rarely succeeds, as the court will only imply permission to commit a restricted act if this is necessary to make an *existing* agreement between the parties effective. The principles on which the court will act were set out in *R Griggs Group Ltd and others v Evans and others* [2005] FSR 706. As regards the implied licence defence, in *Banier v News Group Newspapers* [1997] FSR 812, the court declined to imply a licence to publish photographs which had already appeared in another newspaper, as the parties were not in a contractual relationship. Even where a licence has previously been granted, the court may be reluctant to make a finding of an implied licence if there has been a lengthy period of time since the earlier grant: *Gabrin v Universal Music Operations Ltd*.

9.5.5.4 Exhaustion of rights

cross reference
See further chapter 16.

The application of the exhaustion of rights defence (implicit in s.18 and s.27 CDPA) is far from straightforward. Normal principles will apply to the first sale within the EEA of tangible goods containing copyright material; and Member States do not have any power to continue to apply international exhaustion to non-EEA goods (Case C-479/04 *Laserdisken ApS v Kulturministeriet*). Where, however, copyright products are licensed, the rental right in such goods can never be exhausted (Case C-61/97 *Egmont Films v Laserdisken*); equally, other rights, such as the performance right, may not be exhaustible (Case 158/86 *Warner Bros v Christiansen* [1988] ECR 2605). More problematic is computer software: despite industry assumptions that the normal method of supply would be by way of licence, in Case C-128/11 *UsedSoft GmbH v Oracle International Corp*, 3 July 2012, the ECJ ruled that exhaustion applies not only where the software is supplied on a physical medium, but where it is distributed by means of downloads from a website.

Summary

This chapter has explained:

• the nature of copyright infringement as a statutory tort;

• the statutory provisions which deal with primary and secondary infringement; and

• the statutory and case law defences which may be available.

Reflective question

The case law interpreting the CDPA provisions on infringement of copyright and the defences thereto fails to strike a reasonable balance between the right-holder and those who wish to make use of the work.

Discuss.

Annotated further reading

Burrell, R. 'Reining in Copyright Law: Is Fair Use the Answer' [2001] *IPQ* 361
Argues that although it might be desirable in the interests of flexibility to adopt a more general 'fair use' defence, judicial practice has failed to take adequate account of the interests of the users of copyright material, so that without a change of attitude, relaxing legislative requirements would not have any effect.

Griffiths, J. 'Preserving Judicial Freedom of Movement—Interpreting Fair Dealing in Copyright Law' [2000] *IPQ* 164
Considers which principles ought to colour the interpretation of the fair dealing defences in the CDPA, but concludes that most cases have been characterised by judicial flexibility.

Griffiths, J. '*Copyright Law after Ashdown*—Time to Deal Fairly with the Public' [2002] *IPQ* 240
Considers the Court of Appeal's judgment in *Ashdown v Telegraph Group* and considers that despite the court's apparent acceptance of the Human Rights Act, its treatment of the fair dealing defences is weighted in favour of the copyright owner at the expense of the public interest.

Phillips, J. and Bently, L. 'Copyright Issues: the Mysteries of Section 18' [1999] *EIPR* 133
Considers the unresolved problems of s.18 CDPA and whether the disposition or destination theory should prevail.

Rütz, C. 'Parody: A Missed Opportunity' [2004] *IPQ* 284
Comments on how the United Kingdom's implementation of the Information Society Directive failed to take the opportunity to make parody a defence to copyright infringement.

Spence, M. 'Intellectual Property and the Problem of Parody' (1998) 114 *LQR* 594
Considers the various ways in which parody ought to receive special treatment in United Kingdom copyright law.

Spence, M. and Endicott, T. 'Vagueness in the Scope of Copyright' (2005) 121 *LQR* 657
Examines the seminal case of *Designers' Guild v Russell Williams Textiles* and considers whether it is desirable that key issues, such as substantial taking, should be left vague.

Sterling, J.A.L. 'Copyright, Designs and Patents Act 1988: the New Issuing Right' [1989] *EIPR* 283
Explains the differences between the former restricted act of 'publishing' a work and the issuing right in s.18 CDPA.

Moral rights and performers' rights

Learning objectives

Upon completion of this chapter, you should have acquired:

- an appreciation of how rights related to copyright exist in parallel to but separate from copyright;

- an appreciation of the fact that moral rights for authors do not fit well within a legal culture, such as the United Kingdom's, which traditionally views copyright as an economic right;

- knowledge of the moral rights accorded to authors by the CDPA 1988 and the limitations placed upon them;

- an understanding of how protection may be accorded to a performance of a work, as distinct from the work itself; and

- knowledge of the incremental protection which has been accorded to performers over the last two decades, largely as a result of EU legislation.

Introduction

This chapter completes the copyright picture by dealing with two related rights, namely moral rights and rights in performances. Each presents a different challenge. In the case of moral rights, there is an inherent conflict within United Kingdom law, namely how can a system which views copyright as an economic right accommodate rights concerned with authorial integrity. Even assuming that authorial rights can be made to work in such an alien environment, it is arguable that the myriad restrictions on moral rights found in the Copyright, Designs and Patents Act 1988 ('CDPA') make it at best a token gesture towards the United Kingdom's obligations under the Berne Convention for the Protection of Literary and Artistic Works 1886 ('the Berne Convention'). In the case of protecting performers' interests, we shall see that the rights created by the Rome Convention on the Protection of Performers, Producers of Phonograms and Broadcasting Organisations 1961 ('the Rome Convention') and by the WIPO Performers and Phonograms Treaty 1996 ('WPPT'), at face value very simple, have been woven into legislation of inordinate complexity.

What should be remembered is that one simple scenario can give rise to a number of copyrights, moral rights and performers' rights, each one of which may be owned by a different person and/or licensed to someone else.

example

Consider a concert given by a rock star accompanied by an orchestra and a troupe of dancers. The various rights which might exist are:

- subject to the new law on co-authored songs, the words and music of each song may have separate **copyright**, with the lyricist and composer being the authors and first owners of each respectively. Such copyrights will probably have been assigned to a music publishing or management company. Even if they have not, the right to control the public performance of the music will have been assigned to the Performing Right Society who will collect and administer the royalties for any public performance of the song;

- the person who made the orchestral arrangement of the music will have copyright in the arrangement. Again, such copyright will probably have been assigned to another;

- the person who created the choreography for the dancers will have copyright in this as a dramatic work;

- regardless of the ownership of the copyright in the various works in the previous list, their creators will each have the **moral rights** of paternity and integrity in the works they have created. Whilst such moral rights cannot be assigned during each author's lifetime, it is possible that these rights might have been lost through waiver when the copyrights mentioned earlier were assigned;

- the rock star, orchestra and dancers will each have rights in their respective performances. These rights consist of the non-property right to object to the making of any illicit recording of a performance, a property right to control the reproduction and distribution of permitted recordings of the performance, and a right to control the dissemination of the performance by electronic means. As with moral rights, the non-property right remains personal to the performer during their lifetime, but the property right can be assigned to another; and

- lastly, the rock star orchestra, and dancers will have the performers' moral rights of paternity and integrity. Again such rights cannot be assigned during the lifetime of each performer, but may be lost through waiver.

10.1 Moral rights

10.1.1 The concept of moral rights and their justification

cross reference
The new provisions on co-authored works are explained at section 8.4.5.

As Ginsburg observes (in 'Moral Rights in a Common Law System' [1990] *Ent LR* 121) the term 'moral rights', translated from the French *droit moral*, is not concerned with morality but with non-pecuniary interests, just as the French term *dommage moral* denotes non-economic loss in the law of tort. The notion of rights personal to the creator was identified by Lord Mansfield in *Millar v Taylor* (1769) 98 ER 201, who remarked that without protection, an **author** would not be the master of the use of his own name and would have no control over the correctness of his own work. Ginsburg argues that protection of moral rights is justified because the rights improve the climate in which authors and artists create their **works**. Knowing that they will receive credit for what they have created and that their work will survive in its intended form may be more important than pecuniary gain. The protection of moral rights, she says, sends a message that society cares about creation and about authorship. It also provides the public with information about who created a work and helps avoid deception by preventing wrongful attribution of authorship.

As Ricketson describes (in 'Moral Rights and the Droit de Suite: International Conditions and Australian Obligations' [1990] *Ent LR* 78), the recognition of moral rights can be traced back to France in the early nineteenth century. Subsequently Germany and other civil law members of the **Berne Convention** began to provide similar protection for authors, principally the rights of integrity, paternity and disclosure. Common law members of Berne tended not to grant moral rights, although piecemeal protection for authors was available through other means, such as the actions for defamation, **passing off** and breach of contract (for an example of breach of contract being used to prevent the derogatory treatment of a dramatic work, see *Frisby v BBC* [1967] Ch 932). Moral rights were first introduced into the Berne Convention by the Rome revision of 1928, although the text reflected a diplomatic compromise between those countries keen to enhance authorial rights and those who wanted the freedom to choose other means of protection outside copyright law.

The current provision on an author's moral rights is Article 6*bis* of the 1971 version of the Convention. It declares that independently of the author's economic rights, and even after the transfer of the same, the author shall have the right to claim authorship of the work and to object to any distortion, mutilation or other modification of, or other derogatory action in relation to the said work, which would be prejudicial to his honour or reputation. It also requires

Contracting States to ensure that these rights are to last at least until the expiry of the author's economic rights. As Ricketson observes, the obligation to keep moral rights independent of economic rights does not mean that the former should be treated as inalienable, ie incapable of assignment, although many countries choose to do so. Equally, there is nothing in Article 6*bis* to prevent Contracting States from allowing authors to **assign** or waive their moral rights just as they can assign or waive copyright.

10.1.2 The treatment of moral rights in other jurisdictions

It might be assumed that there are two models for treating moral rights, namely the civil law and common law systems. Not so. Dworkin (in 'The Moral Rights of the Author: Moral Rights and the Common Law Countries' (1994–1995) 19 *Colum-VLA Journal of Law & the Arts* 229) explains how the United Kingdom, United States, Australia and Canada have each, over the years, adopted different strategies in relation to authorial rights, with Canada being closest to the civil law model. Further, as Dietz explains (in 'The Moral Right of the Author: Moral Rights and the Civil Law Countries' (1994–1995) 19 *Colum-VLA Journal of Law & the Arts* 199) the approach of civil law countries is far from standardised. Philosophically, some countries (such as Germany) view moral rights as an integral part of copyright (the so-called monist view) whilst others (typically, France) treat moral rights and copyright as two separate entities, each with its own characteristics, particularly with regard to duration and alienability (the dualist view). There are further variations with regard to categories of moral rights, their duration, and whether they are capable of waiver. Types of moral rights which are recognised include not just the 'core' rights of paternity and integrity, but the divulgation (disclosure) right and the right to repent or withdraw the work. Duration of moral rights can be perpetual (as in France and Spain) or dictated by the length of the copyright term (as in Germany). Similarly, there is divergence as to whether moral rights can be waived, whether such waiver (if permitted) is subject to any test of reasonableness, and whether moral rights can be denied to particular categories of work, such as computer programs. It is not surprising that Dietz declares Article 6*bis* to be 'minimalist'.

thinking point
Would it be helpful if the Berne Convention spelled out with greater precision the contents of moral rights?

10.1.3 Moral rights in the United Kingdom

The CDPA 1988, in Part I, Chapter IV, formally introduced the moral rights of the author into United Kingdom law in fulfilment of Article 6*bis*. The two 'new' moral rights (the right of paternity and right of integrity) arise in respect of those categories of work covered by the Berne Convention (ie, literary, dramatic and musical works; artistic works; and films). Throughout the discussion which follows, we contrast the complexity of wording of the United Kingdom provisions with the simple language of the Berne Convention.

The other two Chapter IV rights are not the result of the Berne Convention. One (the right to object to a false attribution of authorship in the case of a literary, dramatic, musical and artistic work or a film) was present in the Copyright Act 1956. The other (the right of privacy in **commissioned** photographs and films) was inserted belatedly into the CDPA and was a necessary consequence of the change to rules on ownership of copyright in commissioned photographs. Whilst previously the person who commissioned a family photograph would own the copyright in it and thus be able to control its publication, s.9 CDPA now provides for the author of the work (ie the photographer) to be the first owner. Commissioning a work no longer gives rise to a right of ownership although a term as to equitable ownership of copyright or an exclusive licence to exploit it may be implied by the court into the contract of commission in order to give effect to the parties' expectations (*R Griggs Group Ltd and others v Evans and others* [2005] FSR 706).

A further right has now been added. It is debatable whether this is an economic right or a moral right, although Ricketson argues that it is economic in nature. This is the artist's resale right. Found initially in Article 14*ter* of the Berne Convention, it was introduced into EU law by the *Droit de Suite Directive* (Directive 2001/84/EC of the European Parliament and of the Council of 27 September 2001 on the resale right for the benefit of the author of an original work of art of [2001] OJ L 272/32, throughout this chapter, the 2001 Directive). This was implemented into United Kingdom law by The Artist's Resale Rights Regulations 2006 (SI 2006/346) (the 'Regulations').

We shall examine each of these rights individually, and then consider provisions which are common to them all.

10.1.4 The right of paternity or attribution

Under CDPA s.77, the author of a literary, dramatic, musical or artistic work or film has the right to be identified as its author. The right arises in circumstances which may be described as 'commercial dealings' with the work, although as ever with the CDPA, there are significant differences in detail between the different categories of work.

In the case of literary and dramatic works (other than words intended to be spoken or sung with music) and adaptations of such works, the author has the right to be identified whenever the work is published commercially, performed in public, communicated to the public (ie by being broadcast or placed on the internet), or when copies of a film or sound recording including the work are issued to the public (s.77(2)). In the case of a musical work (which includes for these purposes the words which are to be sung or spoken with music, and any adaptation of the work) the identification right arises whenever the work is published commercially, or when copies of a sound recording including the work are issued to the public, or when a film where the soundtrack includes the work is shown in public (s.77(3)). There are similar rights for artists (when a work is published commercially, exhibited or communicated to the public), for architects and for film directors (when the film is shown in public, communicated to the public or copies are issued to the public) (ss.77(4)–(6)).

'Identification' means that the author's name must appear on each copy of the work issued to the public, but if that is not appropriate, then it must be given in some other manner likely to bring his or her identity to the notice of the person acquiring a copy. In the case of a building, the architect should be identified 'by appropriate means visible to persons entering or approaching the building', and where a work is being performed or exhibited, identification must be in a manner likely to bring the author's identity to the attention of the audience. In each case, the identification must be clear and reasonably prominent.

There are some interesting anomalies in s.77, as Dworkin observes. In contrast to literary and dramatic works, there is no right to be identified as the composer of music when the musical work is performed or communicated to the public. Thus there is no obligation to identify the composer where music is provided in public premises, such as shopping malls, pubs and discothèques, regardless of whether the performance of the music is live or by means of a sound recording. Thus in the example at the start of the chapter, the composer of the songs has no right to be identified at the rock concert. Nor is there any requirement for broadcasting organisations to identify the creators of musical works. It was said during the Parliamentary debates that it would be far too inconvenient for broadcasters if they had to acknowledge the composer of every tune played on the radio or used as the theme tune of a television programme or included in a broadcast advertisement. By contrast, although an artist does not have the right to control the 'performance' of the artistic work under s.19 CDPA he or she does have the right to be named should the owner of the tangible copy decide to display the work in public.

However, before the right of paternity can arise, it has to be asserted. According to s.78(2), assertion can either be general or in relation to specific (restricted) acts. It *has* to be made in writing, either when the copyright is assigned to a third party, or by any other written instrument. No guidance is given in the Act as to what sort of wording suffices. To go back to the example at the start of the chapter, if the lyricist and composer have assigned the copyright in the words and music of the songs to a publishing or management company, their rights of paternity will only be operative if the assignment document contained a suitable clause asserting their rights. If no such clause was present, the right of paternity will be lost. Inequality of bargaining power may put creators in a weak position. It remains to be seen whether the case law on inequality of bargaining power in copyright transactions can be applied in the context of moral rights. As yet there are no cases in point.

cross reference
See section 17.4.2.

In the case of the public exhibition of an artistic work, s.78(3) provides for two methods of assertion. First, the assertion can be made when the artist parts with possession of the original by ensuring that their name appears on the work or its frame (the CDPA has a somewhat narrow view of what constitutes an artistic work). Second, the right can be asserted when the right to reproduce the work is licensed.

Section 78(4) provides that an assertion which is made under s.78(2) upon the assignment of copyright binds the **assignee** of copyright and anyone claiming through them, even if they did *not* have notice of the assertion, whereas a general assertion binds *only* those to whom notice of the assertion is brought. In relation to the public exhibition of artistic works, any third party acquiring the work is bound by an assertion made by the artist when parting with possession of the work, but where the reproduction right is licensed, the right binds the **licensee** and anyone receiving a copy of the work. The separate treatment accorded to artistic works in comparison with other categories of work together with the differing effects of assertions on third parties (exacerbated by the lack of any registration system) are typical of the complexities found in the CDPA.

The requirement to assert the right of paternity has been the subject of considerable criticism. First, as Ginsburg points out, the drafters of the CDPA appear to have misunderstood Article 6*bis* which simply states that 'the author shall have the right to claim authorship of the work'. Parliament has twisted a straightforward personal right into a complex commercial transaction. Further, such obligation to assert an author's basic right may well breach the requirement in Article 5*bis* that Contracting States may not impose any formality as a precondition for protection under the Convention.

To make matters worse, s.79 CDPA provides for a number of instances of when the right to be identified as author does not arise. Under s.79(2), certain categories of work, namely computer programs, typefaces and computer-generated works, are excepted. Under s.79(3),

272

cross reference

See section 9.5.2.

thinking point

Has the United Kingdom really fulfilled its obligations under the Berne Convention to give effect to the right of paternity?

works created in the course of employment do not receive protection if the employer consents to the relevant infringing act, and likewise, any work made for the purpose of reporting current events does not attract the right (s.79(5)) nor does the right apply where a literary, dramatic, musical or artistic work is published with the author's consent in a newspaper, magazine or other periodical or in a reference work (s.79(6)). Certain categories of author, therefore, particularly employees and journalists, receive harsh treatment. There are also exceptions for works which are Crown or Parliamentary copyright, or where the copyright was originally vested in an international organisation. Finally, under s.79(4), the right is excluded where a number of defences to copyright **infringement** apply, in particular those of fair dealing and incidental inclusion. Since these exceptions appear in the Berne Convention in relation to copyright rather than moral rights, one may only assume that Parliament was more concerned with the interests of copyright exploiters than with those of copyright creators.

10.1.5 **The right of integrity**

The author of a literary, dramatic, musical or artistic work or film has the right to object to its derogatory treatment (s.80). In contrast to the right of paternity, the right of integrity does not have to be asserted, but the framers of the CDPA have still managed to find ways of narrowing the protection accorded under the Berne Convention.

The problem lies in s.80(2) which defines both 'treatment' and 'derogatory'. 'Treatment' means any addition to, deletion from, alteration to, or adaptation of the work. However, it does not include the translation of a literary or dramatic work, nor the arrangement or transcription of a musical work if this involves no more than a change of key. It was said in the Parliamentary debates that translation and transposition preserve the basic integrity of a work, yet as Cornish observes (in 'Moral Rights under the 1988 Act' [1989] *EIPR* 449), of all the ways of misrepresenting an author's true worth, poor translation must be the most frequent occurrence. He also questions whether the exclusion in respect of the transposition of musical works can really be justified. These criticisms apart, s.80(2) is narrower than Berne in two regards: the words 'distortion, modification or mutilation' in Article 6*bis* are arguably wider than 'addition', 'deletion' and 'alteration' in s.80(2); and second, the latter omits the key phrase in Article 6*bis* 'other derogatory action *in relation to* the said work' (emphasis supplied). As Dworkin argues, this means that an artist could object if a portrait is defaced (such as by adding a moustache to the subject), but could not object if the portrait is placed in an unfavourable location in a gallery or included in a book of pornography or if it was destroyed or allowed to fall into disrepair.

According to s.80(2), 'derogatory' means that the treatment amounts to a distortion or mutilation of the work, or is otherwise prejudicial to the honour or reputation of the author or director. Again, the grammatical structure of s.80(2) should be compared with that of Article 6*bis*. The section appears to impose a double condition, first that there should be 'treatment' (or rather, mistreatment) of the work, and then that this treatment must be prejudicial to the author's honour.

A further difficulty is whether the requirement of prejudice should be decided subjectively or objectively. As Sprawson comments (in 'Moral Rights in the 21st Century: A Case for Bankruptcy' [2006] *Ent LR* 58) moral rights are personal in nature and a reflection of the personality of the creator. How could an objective assessment of what is derogatory be compatible with the nature of a personal right? Nevertheless, in what little United Kingdom case law there has been so far on the right of integrity, the courts have adopted an objective approach to the question of what is derogatory (rather like the test for what is defamatory) so that the author's hurt feelings are not taken into account. So, in *Tidy v Trustees of the Natural History Museum*, 29 March 1995, unreported, where the artist unsuccessfully objected to his posters of dinosaurs being turned into postcards, Rattee J decided the question of prejudice through the eyes of a reasonable person (though he didn't explain whether this was the reasonable artist or the reasonable member of the public). In *Pasterfield v Denham* [1999] FSR 168, revisions to a tourist information leaflet were held not to be derogatory. Similarly, in *Confetti Records v Warner Music UK Ltd* [2003] EMLR 790 Lewison J concluded that the addition of rap words to a song was not derogatory, but the court may have been hampered by the facts that the witnesses could not agree on the meaning of the words and the author did not object to what had been done. There are two cases where a claim for derogatory treatment has succeeded, namely *Delves-Broughton v House of Harlot Ltd* [2012] EWPCC 29 where the discussion of the issues was minimal, and *Morrison Leahy Music Ltd v Lightbond Ltd* [1993] EMLR 144. In the latter case, in awarding interim relief, Morritt J held that there was an arguable breach of s.80(2) CDPA. The creation of a medley of songs (in a sound recording to be called *Bad Boys Mega Mix*), the songs having been written by the second **claimant**, George Michael, took both the words and music out of their original context and so was prejudicial to the author's honour or reputation. These cases can be contrasted with the Canadian case of *Snow v The Eaton Centre Ltd* 70 CPR 2d 105 where the temporary festooning of Christmas decorations on sculptures of Canada geese hanging in a shopping mall amounted to a breach of the artist's right of integrity.

The circumstances when the right of integrity is infringed are listed in ss.80(3)–(6) CDPA, and as with the right of paternity, essentially involve commercial exploitation of the affected work. In the case of a literary, dramatic and musical work, under s.80(3) the infringing conduct must involve commercial publication, performance or communication of the work, or issuing copies to the public of a sound recording or film which includes a derogatory treatment of the work. In the case of artistic works, s.80(4) provides that infringement occurs when the work is published commercially, exhibited or communicated to the public, although for certain three-dimensional works (namely models for buildings, sculptures and works of artistic craftsmanship) there is liability when a graphic work or photograph containing the derogatory treatment is issued to the public. Such protection does not apply to works of architecture in the form of the building itself, although the architect may demand that where there is derogatory treatment his or her identification is removed from the building (s.80(5)). This means that the derogatory treatment of the building is not of itself actionable, and further, if the architect has not been identified under s.77, he or she has no redress. One may speculate why graphic representations of three-dimensional works do not receive protection against communication to the public, unlike two-dimensional works such as the photograph in dispute in *Delves-Broughton*. One can easily envisage a situation where a photograph of an artistic work which has been the subject of derogatory treatment (such as the sculptures of the geese in *Snow v The Eaton Centre*) is posted on a website, yet unlike literary, dramatic and musical works there is no redress for communicating intangible two-dimensional copies of the work, only issuing tangible copies. In the case of films, under s.80(6) the director can object where the film is shown in public, communicated to the public, or copies of it are issued to the public.

In contrast to the right of paternity, there is also liability for secondary infringement under s.83. This provision is worded in an almost identical fashion to s.23 CDPA. The author, artist

thinking point
Does the language of s.80(2) CDPA provide effective protection to creators who wish to object to the derogatory treatment of their works?

cross reference
See section 9.4.

or director can therefore object where there are commercial dealings in infringing copies of the work which has been the subject of derogatory treatment. By 'commercial dealings' is meant conduct such as possession in the course of a business, selling, hiring, public exhibition and distribution. Just as with secondary infringement of copyright, it must be proved that the defendant knew or had reason to believe that he was dealing in an infringing copy. The assessment of the defendant's knowledge will, as under s.23, be done through the eyes of the reasonable trader in his position: *LA Gear v Hi-Tec Sports plc* [1992] FSR 121; *Vermaat v Boncrest Ltd (No 2)* [2002] FSR 331.

As with the right of paternity, there are numerous exceptions and qualifications to the right, found respectively in ss.81 and 82. Just as with s.79, there is no protection for computer programs, computer-generated works, any work made for the purposes of reporting current events and works created for publication in newspapers, magazines, periodicals and reference works (CDPA ss.81(1)–(4)), so again journalists are denied protection. There is a further exception where the treatment of the work has been done in order to avoid the commission of an offence or by the BBC in order to prevent the work offending against 'good taste or decency' (s.81(6)). This last exception is subject to the requirement that where the author or director has been identified, then there must be a 'sufficient disclaimer'. Again, where the right of paternity has not been asserted under s.77, the requirement of the disclaimer will not apply. As yet, there is no guidance as to what is 'sufficient'.

thinking point
Has the United Kingdom truly fulfilled its obligations under the Berne Convention to give effect to the right of integrity?

Under s.82, the right of integrity is curtailed in certain cases. These are where ownership of the copyright in the work was vested in the author's or director's employer under s.11; or else was Crown or Parliamentary copyright; or else was vested in an international organisation; and the treatment of the work was done with the consent of the copyright owner, unless the author or director was identified at the time of the relevant act or had previously been identified in or on published copies of the work. As with s.81(6), a sufficient disclaimer removes liability. The effect of these provisions means that (just as with the right of paternity) employee-creators are vulnerable to the loss of the right of integrity. They are bound by their employer's consent (seemingly having no redress if they don't agree with what the employer has done), and have no protection at all where the right of paternity has not been asserted. As we have seen, inequality of bargaining power may mean that the author was not aware of the implications for the integrity right if the paternity right is not asserted.

10.1.6 **False attribution of authorship**

Under s.84, a person can object to the false attribution of authorship of a literary, dramatic, musical or artistic work or the false attribution of being the director of a film. The right also applies to any adaptation of the source work.

The right is infringed when copies of the work containing the false attribution are issued to the public, or in the case of an artistic work, where it is exhibited in public. There is also infringement where a literary, dramatic and musical work which has wrongly attributed authorship is performed in public or communicated to the public (ie it is broadcast or placed on a website) or, in the case of a film, it is shown in public or communicated to the public. Like the integrity right, there is liability for secondary infringement, that is, dealing in infringing copies in the course of a business with the appropriate knowledge.

Clark v Associated Newspapers [1998] 1 All ER 959

....

An example of s.84 in operation is *Clark v Associated Newspapers* [1998] 1 All ER 959, where the claimant (a politician and successful author) successfully alleged that a satirical column in the *London Evening Standard* entitled 'Alan Clark's Secret Election Diary' and, later, 'Alan Clark's Secret Political Diaries' would be assumed by readers to be his work. The defendant's indication that the column had been written by another, although in capital letters, would not be noticed by the average reader, who was, assumed the judge, a commuter 'skim reading' the newspaper during the journey home after work.

10.1.7 **Privacy in photographs and films**

As mentioned earlier, s.85 was added to the CDPA in the latter stages of its progress through Parliament. It creates a right of privacy in photographs and films which have been commissioned for private and domestic purposes. The commissioner of the photograph or film has the right to object to copies of the work being issued to the public, or the work being exhibited in public, or the work being communicated to the public (that is, by broadcast or via the internet). Liability is imposed not just on the person who commits such conduct, but on someone who authorises such conduct.

There are, however, a number of exceptions to the right of privacy, as a result of the application of a number of defences to copyright infringement. Of particular note are the defences of incidental inclusion and Parliamentary and judicial proceedings.

10.1.8 **The artist's resale right**

Recital 3 of the 2001 Directive (which the United Kingdom opposed) states that the purpose of the *droit de suite* is to ensure that artists share in the economic success of their original works of art, Recital 4 adding that the resale right is an integral part of copyright and is an essential prerogative for authors. The recitals continue with the declaration that the majority of Member States recognise the resale right and that harmonisation of laws is required in the interests of the internal market. One of the United Kingdom's concerns was that the Directive would have an adverse effect on the London art market, with the risk that business would be diverted to other countries, such as Switzerland or the USA, which do not have a resale right.

The Regulations which implement the Directive into United Kingdom law provide that the author of a work of art in which copyright subsists is to be paid a royalty on any sale of the work (provided the sale occurred after the date of the Regulations) which is a resale subsequent to the first transfer of ownership by the author. In other words, the resale right is triggered by any transaction subsequent to the first sale by the artist, whereby ownership of the tangible medium of the work of art is transferred to another. It is therefore irrelevant who owns the copyright, rather what matters is ownership of the physical object. The work must, however, be the subject of copyright protection. 'Work' means any work of graphic or plastic art such as a picture, collage, painting, drawing, engraving, print, lithograph, sculpture, tapestry, a ceramic, an item of glassware or a photograph. This should be compared

cross reference
See section 8.1.2.

with the somewhat narrower list of 'artistic works' in s.4 CDPA. The Regulations add that the right also applies to limited copies of the work provided these have been made by or with the authority of the author, although no definition is given of what is a 'limited copy'. Unlike the Berne Convention which extends the resale right to manuscripts, the 2001 Directive and the Regulations are limited to works of art.

In contrast to the moral rights set out in Part IV CDPA, any waiver of the right is to be of no effect. The Regulations further provide that the resale right cannot be assigned, whether during the artist's lifetime or by the artist's successors. The right can, however, be bequeathed under the artist's will or pass on their intestacy. Once inherited, the artist's heirs may also pass on the entitlement on their death. However, where the right has been bequeathed to a charity, it may be transferred to another charity, a provision obviously designed to assist museums and art galleries. The resale right is to last as long as copyright. However, when implementing the Directive the United Kingdom took advantage of the option set out in Article 8(2) of the 2001 Directive, so that the right is not available to the heirs of any artists dying before 1 January 2010. The United Kingdom notified the EU Commission on 18 December 2008 that it intended taking advantage of a further option set out in Article 8(3) by extending the period by which the resale right does not accrue to the artist's heirs for a further two years. This meant that until 1 January 2012 the right was only available to living artists.

A number of transactions are exempted from the right. It does not apply to the first transfer of ownership by the artist themselves, whether this is by sale, gift, or on death. Similarly, it does not apply to any resale within three years of the first transfer where the price was less than €10,000, nor does it apply to private sales, ie those where the seller, buyer or their agents are not art-market professionals. Lastly, the right does not apply to commercial sales (either by auction or private treaty) where the price was less than €1,000.

The right is available to artists who are '**qualifying individuals**', that is, **EEA** nationals or nationals of those countries listed in Sch. 2 of the Regulations. An artist's heirs (once they are entitled to the right after 2012) need not be qualifying individuals in order to enjoy the right, but if they are not qualifying, they are not able to transmit the right in turn when they die. In contrast to copyright, qualification for protection is based solely on nationality, so that the country of domicile or residence is irrelevant.

thinking point
Given that the resale right is personal to the artist, and cannot be waived or assigned, do you think it should be regarded as an economic right or a moral right?

The calculation of the royalty to be paid on resale is set out in detail in Sch. 1 of the Regulations. Payment of the royalty is the responsibility of the seller, who is jointly and severally liable with the seller's agent (if any) or failing that, the agent of the buyer, or, if there is no such agent, the buyer. The United Kingdom has decided that royalties should be managed for artists by collecting societies, the two currently involved being the Design and Artists Copyright Society and the Artists' Collecting Society.

10.1.9 Moral rights where there are joint authors

Section 88 deals with the rights of paternity, integrity, objection to false attribution and privacy where there are **joint authors**. The right of paternity means the right of *each* author to be identified, but each author must assert the right for themselves. Similarly, each joint author has the right to object to derogatory treatment. In the case of false attribution, an author can object to any false statement as to the authorship of the work of joint authorship and to the false attribution of joint authorship where it is a work of sole authorship. Likewise, the rights under s.85 belong to joint commissioners of the photograph or film. In each case, waiver by one joint author binds that person only and does not affect the rights of others.

10.1.10 Duration and property rights

The duration of moral rights is catered for by s.86. With the exception of the right found in s.84, the duration of moral rights is coterminous with the duration of copyright. The right to object to false attribution lasts for the lifetime of the person wrongly attributed as author and for 20 years after their death. As Stamatoudi observes (in 'Moral Rights of Authors in England: the Missing Emphasis on the Role of Creators' [1997] *IPQ* 478) the logic in providing a shorter period of protection to the right which is the converse of the paternity right is questionable, especially if regard is had to the justifications for moral rights.

Moral rights remain personal to the author and cannot be assigned, CDPA s.94. Upon the death of the author, in respect of the rights of paternity, integrity and privacy, s.95 creates a series of precise rules as to who inherits the rights. They are to pass primarily to the person to whom the rights in question were bequeathed by the author's will, but if none, then to the person to whom the copyright in the work was bequeathed, and should neither of these apply (ie there was no specific bequest in the will or the author died intestate), then the rights pass to the author's personal representatives. In all cases, however, the person inheriting the right is bound by any consent or waiver given by the author in their lifetime. However, any **damages** recovered for infringement of any of these moral rights after the author's death will not necessarily pass to the person who owns the rights. Section 95(6) declares that the damages devolve as part of the author's estate as if the right of action had subsisted immediately before his death. What this means is that even though an author might have bequeathed their moral rights to one person, or even where there is no bequest of moral rights, but a bequest of copyright which carries with it the author's moral rights by implication under s.95(1)(a) or (b), the named beneficiary will not get the damages. Instead, these will go, in all probability, to the author's residuary beneficiary. Permitting an author to bequeath their moral rights to a named individual but then not allowing that person to receive compensation should the rights be infringed defies logic.

The right to object to false attribution receives separate treatment from the other three moral rights. After the author's death it is actionable only by the author's personal representatives and so cannot be the subject matter of a specific bequest in a will, whether of moral rights or of copyright.

10.1.11 Remedies for the infringement of moral rights

Infringement of the rights of paternity, integrity, objection to false attribution and privacy is declared by s.103 CDPA to be actionable as a breach of statutory duty owed to the person entitled to the right. Such infringement is actionable by the author of the work, not any subsequent owner to whom the copyright might have been assigned: *Confetti Records v Warner Music UK Ltd*.

The usual remedy for breach of statutory duty will be damages, but as yet there is no guidance on how the calculation will be made. The author will have suffered no pecuniary loss, so one can envisage the defendant arguing for nominal damages to be awarded. How would it be

thinking point
Do you think that the provisions in the CDPA dealing with duration and transmission of moral rights are (a) clear and (b) logical?

possible to quantify hurt feelings? Further, the ability to award **additional damages**, set out in s.97 CDPA, is in that part of Chapter VI which is entitled 'Rights and Remedies of the Copyright Owner'. Given that s.103 has a separate heading 'Remedies for Infringement of Moral Rights', it is arguable that no power exists to award additional damages for flagrant infringement of moral rights.

Section 103(2) contains a further provision likely to diminish the author's rights. It provides that in the case of derogatory treatment, the court may, if it thinks it is an adequate remedy, grant an **injunction** prohibiting the doing of any act unless a disclaimer is made. The court is to approve the terms and the manner of the disclaimer, the purpose of which is to disassociate the author from the treatment of the work. This means that the infringing work can still be exploited commercially so that the defendant is in effect given a licence to commit derogatory treatment. What is unclear is how the disclaimer is to be brought to the attention of the public. As Stamatoudi comments, placing a disclaimer on the label of a sound recording will not inform those who hear the recording in a nightclub that the works contained in the recording have been the subject of derogatory treatment. It is also unclear whether injunctive relief under s.103(2) is in addition to or in substitution for damages.

10.1.12 Transitional arrangements

As befits the introduction of new rights in the CDPA, there are transitional provisions to be found in Sch. 1 to the Act.

There is to be no liability for anything done before the commencement date of the Act (1 August 1989). The rights of paternity and integrity are not to apply to any films made before that date, nor to any literary, dramatic, musical or artistic work of any author who died before that date. In other words, the Act applies retrospectively to works in copyright when it came into force, provided the author was alive at that date. The limitation with regard to films means that the United Kingdom courts will not have to deal with the thorny issue of whether the colourisation of old black and white films infringes the author's right of integrity.

10.1.13 Waiver and consent

Despite the fact that moral rights cannot be assigned during the author's lifetime, as both Dworkin and Cornish observe, the moral rights régime is emasculated by the fact that the author may either consent to conduct which would otherwise infringe, or may waive their rights.

Both consent and waiver are dealt with by s.87 CDPA. The section declares that any of the Chapter IV rights may be waived, provided that this is in writing and signed by the person giving up the right. Such waiver may be in relation to a specific work or groups of work or to works generally, whether existing or future. If made in favour of the copyright owner, the waiver extends to that person's licensees and successors in title unless there is a statement to the contrary. However, s.87(4) compounds the problem considerably by declaring that the section is not to be taken as excluding the operation of the general law of contract or estoppel in relation to an informal waiver. Therefore, despite the earlier statement that a waiver must be in writing, an author may find that due to conduct amounting to estoppel, his or her moral rights have been lost. We have already noted how in many instances, the right of integrity only survives if the right of paternity has been asserted. The combination of the conditions in ss.81 and 82 with s.87(4) presents yet further traps for the vulnerable author. It is a matter of speculation whether the case law on inequality of bargaining power could be extended to lack of assertion, consent or waiver in the case of moral rights.

10.1.14 Conclusion

Ginsburg argues that the CDPA is a poor model for common law countries to adopt when protecting moral rights. It leaves creators in a worse position then they were before. In particular, she says, s.78 which requires the right of paternity to be asserted, derives from a 'perverse' interpretation of Article 6*bis* and may be in breach of the Berne Convention obligation that no formality may be imposed. Further, the number of exceptions both to the right of paternity and the right of integrity, the application of the fair dealing defences, and the fact that moral rights can be waived lead one to conclude that the provisions are half-hearted, perhaps because their drafters seem to have lacked real conviction as to the desirability of moral rights. A plausible explanation may be that Parliament was primarily concerned to preserve the interests of those who exploit copyright works rather than pro-tect the interests of creators.

thinking point

The provisions in the CDPA dealing with moral rights are modified by others which provide for consent (whether by the author or his or her employer), waiver, disclaimer by the infringer, or failure to assert. Are any of these restrictions on an author's fundamental rights justified by the economic interests of others?

10.2 Rights in performances

10.2.1 The nature of performers' rights

It used to be said that there could be no copyright in a performance (as opposed to the work performed) because a performance was too fleeting and lacked the requisite permanence to be a work (see Lord Denning in *Ex parte Island Records* [1978] Ch 122). The underlying assumption was that a performance could only occur before a live audience in a theatre or concert hall, and that once delivered, all that remained was the recollection of the audience. This narrow view, separating the work from its presentation, should be contrasted with the opinion of Mummery LJ in *Sawkins v Hyperion Records* [2005] 1 WLR 3281 that a perfor-mance may be an integral part of a musical work. In any event, developing technology over the last century (initially analogue, but latterly digital) has led to performances being captured with increasing ease in a variety of media, such as sound recordings, films and broadcasts. In turn, such media themselves are capable of digital manipulation and transmission worldwide. As an example, consider the millions of videos captured on mobile phones and posted on YouTube. However, just as the protection of moral rights sends a message that society values

cross reference
See section 8.1.1.3.

the creativity of authors, surely a performer's efforts (whether they be an actor, dancer or musician) can be justified by the same arguments. Protection of the rights of the performer is vital.

10.2.2 **The Rome and WPPT Conventions**

Article 7 of the **Rome Convention** obliges Contracting States to protect performers by giving them the right to prevent any unauthorised broadcast or communication to the public of the performance, any unauthorised fixation of the performance, and the reproduction of any fixation of the performance. A 'performer' is defined by Article 3 to mean an actor, singer, musician, dancer or other person who acts, sings, delivers, declaims, plays in, or otherwise performs literary or artistic works. Article 19 declares, however, that once a performer has consented to the incorporation of their performance in a visual or audio-visual fixation, Article 7 is to have no further application. The Convention therefore assumes that the performer's principal concern is with the unauthorised broadcast or sound recording of the performance. It should be remembered that the wording of the Convention will have been influenced by the technology of its day. It has not been revised since.

However, the Rome Convention has been supplemented by the WPPT. Article 2 contains a slightly broader definition of 'performer' in that it adds the activity of interpretation to the conduct expected of a performer and includes 'expressions of folklore' within the list of works to be performed. It then expands the protection conferred on performers by granting them, in Articles 5 to 9, moral and economic rights. The latter entitle the performer to control the broadcasting and fixation of unfixed performances, and the reproduction, distribution and rental of copies of sound recordings of their performances. In addition, under Article 15, performers are to enjoy the right to equitable remuneration for the direct or indirect use of sound recordings published for commercial purposes or for any communication to the public, Article 15(4) making clear that 'communication to the public' includes posting on the internet.

10.2.3 **Pre-1988 United Kingdom law**

Prior to the CDPA, the Rome Convention was implemented by the Performers Protection Acts 1958–1972 ('PPA'). The PPA imposed criminal liability for making a film or recording of a performance without the performer's written consent; selling, hiring, distributing by way of trade any such films or records; using such a film or recording for the purposes of public performance; and making an unauthorised broadcast of the performance. Interestingly, the PPA gave performers protection against unauthorised filming, in contrast to the Rome Convention. The PPA required proof of knowledge on the part of the defendant, both as to the commission of the act itself and as to the lack of written consent from the performer. Liability was subject to the defence that the recording was for private and domestic use. The defence failed in *Helliwell v Piggott-Sims* [1980] FSR 582 where the defendant had made a number of recordings of rock concerts for the specific purpose of exchanging them with other enthusiasts.

The *Helliwell* case provides a nice illustration of the phenomenon which led to pressure for change. This was the problem of 'bootleg' recordings of concerts and other live performances. As explained by Lord Denning in *Ex parte Island Records*, modern technology enables a member of the audience at a concert to make an unauthorised recording of the performance, and then manufacture and distribute multiple copies of that recording. The making of the recording amounts, of course, to copyright **infringement** under s.17 CDPA, being a reproduction in any material form of the words and music performed at the concert, so that the copyright owner (and indeed any copyright management society responsible for collecting royalties for the reproduction right) has redress against the bootlegger and anyone dealing in infringing copies: *Carlin Music Corporation v Collins* [1979] FSR 548. However, the economic interests of the performers and those of any recording company with whom they might have had an exclusive recording contract are also being undermined by the activities of bootleggers.

The issue which therefore confronted the court in *Ex parte Island Records* and later cases was whether breach of legislation which imposed criminal penalties for bootleg recordings could give rise to protection in civil law for the performers and their recording companies. Under the principles of general law established in *Gouriet v Union of Post Office Workers* [1978] AC 435 and *CBS v Amstrad* [1988] AC 1013, breach of a criminal statute will not give rise to a claim by the 'victim' in civil law unless either the claimant was a member of a class whom the Act in question was intended to protect (so that there would be a claim at common law for breach of statutory duty) or the claimant suffered injury to a private right or incurred special damage (both giving rise to a claim in equity). Could the performers and their recording companies bring themselves within either of these categories?

Whether a performer could bring a claim at common law for breach of statutory duty depended on their being able to show that the legislation in question was passed to protect a particular class of persons, that they were a member of that class, and that the penalty found in the Act was imposed for failure to perform a defined duty (*Cutler v Wandsworth Stadium* [1948] KB 291). Despite the view of the majority of the Court of Appeal in *Ex parte Island Records* and of Harman J in *Shelley v Cunane* [1983] FSR 391 (a case concerning bootleg recordings of Pink Floyd) that the PPA was the wrong sort of Act to give rise to an action for breach of statutory duty, following the *obiter* comments of Lord Diplock in *Lonrho v Shell Petroleum* [1982] AC 173, it began to be accepted that such a claim was allowable against bootleggers. So in the first instance cases of *Ekland v Skripglow Ltd* [1982] FSR 431 and *Silly Wizard Ltd v Shaughnessy* [1984] FSR 163 the performers in each case were allowed to claim against the bootlegger. However, in the former case the claimant and defendant were in a contractual relationship, the terms of which had been breached by the defendant, and in the latter case the performer was also the owner of the copyright in the music being performed, so that there were special factors favouring the performer.

case close-up

> ### *Rickless v United Artists* [1988] QB 40
>
> The definitive Court of Appeal decision came in *Rickless v United Artists* [1988] QB 40 where it was held, upholding Hobhouse J at first instance, that Peter Sellers' estate could object to the making of another 'Pink Panther' film from discarded 'out-takes'. In confirming the award of $1 million damages, Browne-Wilkinson VC observed that uncertainties about the action remained, particularly whether protection survived the death of the performer and how long the right was to last.

As to whether recording companies could claim in equity because of damage to their economic interests in the exclusive recording contract with performers, the case law went in the opposite direction. Initially, in *Ex parte Island Records*, the Court of Appeal thought there should be a remedy. This, however, was doubted in *Lonrho v Shell Petroleum* and *Shelley v Cunane* and ultimately rejected by the Court of Appeal in *RCA v Pollard* [1983] Ch 135, a case concerned with bootleg recordings of Elvis Presley to which Presley's estate had not been joined as party. The court concluded that the bootleg recordings didn't destroy the exclusive recording contract with the performer, they merely made the contract less valuable. There was therefore no special damage.

10.2.4 The CDPA Part II: overview

Part II CDPA can in one sense be viewed as a culmination of the case law discussed in the preceding paragraphs. It gave effect to the thinking of the Court of Appeal in *Rickless v United Artists* by conferring civil law protection on performers; and overturned the decision in *RCA v Pollard* by giving rights to those recording companies which have exclusive recording contracts with performers.

However, Part II has since been amended four times in order to take account of obligations imposed on the United Kingdom as an EU Member State. These obligations flow from, first, the Rental Rights Directive (Council Directive 92/100/EEC of 19 November 1992 on rental right and lending right and on certain rights related to copyright in the field of intellectual property [1992] OJ L 346/61, now codified as Directive 2006/115/EC of the European Parliament and of the Council of 12 December 2006 [2006] OJ L 376/28); second, the Information Society Directive (Directive 2001/29/EC of the European Parliament and of the Council of 22 May 2001 on the harmonisation of certain aspects of copyright and related rights in the information society [2001] OJ L 167/10); third, Directive 2011/77/EU of the European Parliament and of the Council of 27 September 2011 [2011] OJ L 265/1) which amends the consolidated version of the Copyright Term Directive (Directive 2006/116/EC of the European Parliament and of the Council of 12 December 2006 [2006] OJ L 372/12); and last, the WPPT. In the case of the WPPT, the EU is a signatory to the Convention. It has not yet produced a Directive on moral rights for performers, but Recital 19 to the Information Society Directive makes clear that it regards Member States as bound by all the obligations of the WPPT. As a result, the United Kingdom Government took the view that the WPPT was in effect an EU Treaty, so that moral rights for performers could be introduced by secondary legislation under the European Communities Act 1972. As Simon observes (in 'The Introduction of Performers' Moral Rights' [2006] *EIPR* 552, 600) the resulting The Performances (Moral Rights etc) Regulations 2006 (SI 2006/18) were produced very speedily at the expense of Parliamentary scrutiny. Simon suggests that the use of secondary legislation was prompted by a desire for Parliamentary expediency together with fear of action by the EU for non-implementation of the WPPT.

thinking point
Was the United Kingdom Government correct to implement the WPPT without waiting for an EU Directive?

When passing The Performances (Moral Rights etc) Regulations 2006, the United Kingdom Government took the opportunity to restructure Part II of the CDPA into Chapters dealing with economic rights of performers (this category being divided into non-property and property rights) and their moral rights. For the sake of convenience, however, we deal with these rights in the historical order in which they were created, namely non-property rights (the original rights created by Part II CDPA), property rights (derived from the Rental Rights Directive), rights in respect of the internet (flowing from the Information Society Directive), and moral rights (the result of obligations under the WPPT).

10.2.5 The CDPA Part II: general matters

Before looking at these four aspects of performers' protection in turn, we must consider Chapter 1 of Part II. It consists of just two sections, ss.180 and 181 which contain, respectively, some (but not all) key definitions and the requirements for qualification for protection. Section 180(1) has been described as a 'chatty introduction' to what follows (*Experience Hendrix LLC v Purple Haze Records Ltd* [2007] FSR 769 at [24] *per* Jacob LJ). The section declares that economic rights and moral rights are to be conferred on performers. Rights are also to be conferred on persons who have exclusive recording contracts with performers when illicit recordings of performances are made without the performers' consent. We may note the change of terminology, with the term 'illicit recording' being substituted for Lord Denning's more colourful 'bootleg recording'. The term 'illicit recording' is itself defined by s.197 CDPA as meaning the recording of the whole or any substantial of a performance which is made otherwise than for private purposes without the consent of the performer. It is irrelevant where the recording is made. 'Exclusive recording contract' is defined by s.185 to mean a contract between a performer and another person under which that person is entitled to the exclusion of all others (including the performer) to make recordings of the performance with a view to commercial exploitation.

thinking point

Is the definition of 'performance' in s.180(2) CDPA as clear as it might be?

Section 180(2) provides the definitions of 'performance' and 'recording'. The former means a dramatic performance, a musical performance, a reading or recitation of a literary work or a performance of a variety act or similar presentation. Section 211 provides that 'literary work' is to have the same meaning as in Part I CDPA. That being so, does this mean that the literary work must be 'fixed', in which case Part II cannot apply to improvised performances? The wording of both the Rome Convention and the WPPT imply that the work being performed must be susceptible of copyright protection, although it is unclear whether they apply to works in the public domain, such as a Shakespeare play or Beethoven symphony. As Simon explains, academic opinion is divided as to whether there must be some pre-existing script for Part II protection to arise.

A further difficulty is that the subsection adds that the performance must be 'a live performance given by one or more individuals'. 'Live' is not defined in the CDPA but it might be assumed that it requires the performance to be before an audience rather than in a film or recording studio. If this were so, *Rickless v United Artists* would have a different outcome today (leaving on one side the breach of contract aspect of the case), as Peter Sellers' performances were in a film studio rather than in a theatre. Nevertheless, Vinelott J in *Bassey v Icon Entertainment plc* [1995] EMLR 596 held that a studio performance fell within Part II CDPA so that the singer had redress when copies of a recording which she had vetoed were issued without her consent.

Section 180(2) defines 'recording' as a film or sound recording of the performance, whether this is made directly from the performance itself, made from a broadcast of the performance, or made directly or indirectly from another recording of the performance. We may note that like the PPA, Part II CDPA is broader than the Rome Convention in protecting the performer against the filming of the performance as well as by an unauthorised sound recording.

cross reference

See section 8.3.3.

Section 181 sets out the precondition that in order to attract protection, the performance must be a **qualifying performance**, ie it must be given by a **qualifying individual** or take place in a **qualifying country**. Further detail is provided by s.206, which operates in a similar fashion to s.153 CDPA with regard to qualification for protection for copyright works. A 'qualifying individual' is someone who is a national of or resident in the United Kingdom, a Member State of the EU, or a country designated by Order in Council as giving reciprocal protection. As with Part I CDPA, the Copyright and Performances (Application to Other Countries) Order 2013 (SI 2013/536) lists the relevant countries, which are basically signatories to the Rome Convention. If the performer is not a qualifying individual, then protection may be claimed where the performance occurred in a qualifying country, that is, the UK, a Member State of the EU or a signatory to the Rome Convention. In order for the company with an exclusive recording contract to receive protection, it too must be a **qualifying person**, ie it must be incorporated in the United Kingdom or another qualifying country, and it must have a substantial business activity in such territory (CDPA ss.185(2) and 206(1)).

10.2.6 **Performers' non-property rights**

The non-property rights of the performer are set out in ss.182, 183 and 184 CDPA. The first of these sections gives a performer the right to object to the making of an illicit recording of a performance, the broadcasting of a performance, or the making of an illicit recording from a broadcast of the performance (such as where someone makes a recording of a live broadcast with the intention of selling copies of the recording). Under s.183, the **performer's rights** are infringed if the illicit recording is shown or played in public or communicated to the public (that is, posted on the internet), and under s.184, the performer's rights are also infringed by importation or other commercial dealings, such as sale or hire of copies of the illicit recording.

In parallel to the performer's rights with regard to illicit recordings, ss.186, 187 and 188 create rights for those recording companies which have exclusive recording contracts with the performer. Thus the recording company can object to the making of an illicit recording of the performance (s.186), to the showing or playing in public of that recording or the communication to the public of that recording (s.187), and the importation of or other commercial dealings in copies of the illicit recording (s.188). However, the rights of the recording company are not independent, because where the performer consents to the making of the recording, that consent binds the recording company (ss.186(1), 187(1), 188(1) and 193(2)). The performer's consent may be given in relation to a specific performance, a specific description of performances (for example, all those given on a particular concert tour or given in a particular country), or performances generally, in all cases whether past or future (CDPA s.193(1)) and will also bind anyone who inherits the performer's non-property right (s.193(3)).

The right to object to illicit recordings of performances is retrospective, ie it applies to performances occurring before 1 August 1989: s.180(3) CDPA. Furthermore, it doesn't matter that the performance took place in a country which at the time was not a qualifying country if that country subsequently joins the EU or the Rome Convention.

---

case close-up

Experience Hendrix LLC v Purple Haze Records Ltd [2005] EMLR 417

. . . .

Hart J held that the fact an illicit recording had been made of a Jimmy Hendrix concert in Sweden at a time when Sweden was not an EU Member State was irrelevant. If performances in the United Kingdom were given retrospective treatment by s.180(3), it would be illogical not to give protection to performances taking place elsewhere.

In a separate case involving the same parties, the Court of Appeal held that it was also irrelevant that the performer had died before the CDPA came into force. The right of a performer's successors to object to illicit recordings was recognised in *Rickless v United Artists* and Parliament had originally provided that the rights should last for 50 years after the date of the performance, the rights surviving for the benefit of the performer's estate: *Experience Hendrix LLC v Purple Haze Records Ltd* [2007] FSR 769, CA.

Section 189 provides for a number defences ('permitted acts') which can be raised where there has been a breach of the performer's economic rights (both non-property and property). The list of the 25 separate defences is set out in Sch. 2 CDPA. They mirror many of the defences to copyright infringement found in Part I Chapter III CDPA. As might be expected, the defences are set out in detailed fashion and are subject to numerous qualifications and conditions.

The duration of rights in performances is dealt with by s.191, amended by the *Copyright and Duration of Rights in Performances Regulations 2013* (SI 2013/1782) ('the 2013 Regulations') so as to implement Directive 2011/77/EU of the European Parliament and of the Council of 27 September 2011 [2011] OJ L 265/1. The Directive was the EU's response to numerous calls from the 'pop' stars of the 1950s and 1960s for the term of protection for sound recordings and performances to be extended. Section 191 accordingly provides for the right to expire 50 years from the performance or if, during that period, a recording of the performance (other than a sound recording) is released ('release' here meaning 'published, played or shown in public, or communicated to the public'), 50 years from release, or if a sound recording is released, 70 years from that release. No account is to be taken of any unauthorised release. If the performer is not an EEA national, the right is to have the same duration as in the performer's own country.

The new provisions concerning the duration of performers' rights are retrospective. The 2013 Regulations accordingly contain complex transitional provisions which are beyond the scope of this work.

Section 192A CDPA declares that the performer's non-property rights cannot be assigned, in other words, like moral rights, they remain personal to the performer. They can, however, pass on death, either to the person to whom such rights were bequeathed, or, if there is no such bequest, to the performer's personal representatives. As with moral rights, s.192A(5) provides that any damages recovered by the personal representatives for an infringement of the rights after the performer's death devolve as part of his/her estate, that is, they go to the residuary beneficiary and not to the person to whom the right was bequeathed. Section 192B likewise provides that the recording company's rights to object to illicit recordings are not assignable or transmissible.

The CDPA provides in s.194 that breach of the performer's non-property right is actionable as a breach of statutory duty, the same remedy as is provided for infringement of moral rights. This should be contrasted with the remedies provided for infringement of the performer's property rights, explained later. One might speculate as to how damages under s.194 might be calculated, although it should be remembered that the sum awarded ($1 million) in *Rickless v United Artists* was considerable. There are, however, the additional remedies of delivery up and seizure of illicit recordings set out in ss.195 and 196, whilst ss.198 to 204 deal with criminal penalties to be imposed on those who make, deal with, or use illicit recordings.

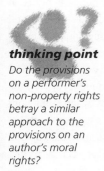

thinking point
Do the provisions on a performer's non-property rights betray a similar approach to the provisions on an author's moral rights?

10.2.7 **Performers' property rights**

Part II CDPA was amended in 1996 in order to give effect to the Rental Rights Directive. The Directive anticipated the effect of the WPPT by conferring copyright-type rights on performers to control the exploitation of *legitimate* copies of their performances.

cross reference
See section 9.3.1.

Section 182A begins by creating the performer's reproduction right, that is, the right to control the making of copies of a qualifying performance. Like s.17 CDPA, it provides that the copy can be direct or indirect and can be of the whole or a substantial part of the performance. It includes the making of transient (ie temporary) copies or those which are incidental to some other use of the recording.

cross reference
*See section 9.3.2
and Diagram 9.2.*

Sections 182B and 182C provide for rights analogous to those found in ss.18 and 18A CDPA, namely the distribution right and the rental and lending right. As with copyright, the distribution right is the right to control the issuing of copies to the public of the recording and the section contains the principle of **exhaustion of rights**, so that the distribution right is 'spent' where copies are put on the market within the EEA but not where they are first put in circulation outside the EEA. Just as with s.18, there is no guidance yet about the point at which copies are issued *to the public*. It is, however, clear, that 'issuing' requires the transfer of ownership or possession: Case C-456/06 *Peek & Cloppenburg KG v Cassina SpA* [2008] ECR I-2731. The rental right in s.182C is similarly concerned with the supply of tangible copies of the performance. 'Rental' means that copies are made available for use on terms that the copies will or may be returned for a direct or indirect economic advantage, whereas 'lending', which must be by an establishment which is accessible to the public (ie a library), does not involve a commercial advantage to that establishment. Rental and lending do not involve making the copies available for performance, playing in public, communication to the public, for reference use, or inter-library transactions. The separate rental right in copyright (s.18A) is a deliberate exception to the doctrine of exhaustion (Case C-61/97 *Egmont Films v Laserdisken* [1998] ECR I-5171) and one must assume that the same applies to the rental right in a performance.

Last, s.182D gives the performer the right to demand equitable remuneration when a commercially published sound recording of a qualifying performance is played or communicated to the public (whether by being broadcast or posted on the internet). The right to remuneration cannot be assigned except to a copyright collecting society but on the death of the performer is treated as his or her personal property. Likewise, the right cannot be restricted by contractual provisions. In the case of dispute about the amount of equitable remuneration, the matter is to be decided by the Copyright Tribunal.

The reproduction, issuing and rental rights are declared by s.191A to be property rights. In consequence, they receive the same treatment as copyright, so that they can be assigned and licensed (s.191B), with **exclusive licensees** being granted the same procedural rights as exclusive licensees of copyright (s.191D). Also like copyright, there can be an assignment of future rights (s.191C). The performer's property right passes on death in the usual way, and in parallel to copyright law (CDPA s.93), where a will bequeaths an unpublished sound recording, the performer's right passes under that bequest. In the case of an assignment of the rental right in a sound recording or film to the producer thereof, the performer retains the right to equitable remuneration, which can only be assigned to a copyright collecting society. According to *Bourne v Davis* [2006] EWHC 1567, where there is more than one performer, each performer has individual rights which they can control, so that one member of a group cannot assign

cross reference
See section 8.5.4.

thinking point
Is the different
treatment accorded
to the performer's
non-property and
property rights with
regard to ownership
and infringement
justified?

the property rights of the others. The 2013 Regulations add, in s.191HA, that the performer has the right to terminate an assignment of the reproduction, distribution and communication rights or the performer's property rights in a sound recording of a performance where the producer of that recording has, at the end of 50 years, failed to issue sufficient quantities of the recording or failed to make it available to the public by electronic transmission. The 50-year period is calculated from the first publication or making available to the public of the sound recording. Termination of the assignment has the effect of triggering the expiry of the copyright in the sound recording, thus leaving the producer, as owner of the copyright in the sound recording, without an enforceable right.

In the case of the infringement of the performer's property right, ss.191I and J confer remedies which are identical to those given to a copyright owner by ss.96 and 97 CDPA, that is, damages, injunctions, an **account of profits** and additional damages. The generosity of this provision should be contrasted with s.194 which treats infringement of the performer's non-property right as a breach of statutory duty. One can only assume that additional damages will not be available against a bootlegger.

10.2.8 Performers' rights in respect of the internet

As part of the range of property rights accorded to a performer, the 2003 amendments to the CDPA (implementing the Information Society Directive) introduced the right found in s.182CA, namely the right to control the making available to the public of recordings of a qualifying performance. The section makes clear that the right refers specifically to communication via the internet ('by electronic transmission in such a way that members of the public may access the recording from a place and at a time individually chosen by them'). For this reason, there are specific provisions in s.191JA enabling the award of injunctions against internet service providers who have actual knowledge that another person is using the service to infringe a performer's property right.

The communication right is treated in exactly the same manner as the other property rights of the performer explained in the previous section with regard to ownership and infringement.

10.2.9 Performers' moral rights

Under the WPPT, the protection for a performer's moral rights is limited to live aural performances. This means that visual performances are not protected, although the word 'aural' suggests that the right is not limited to music and so would apply to the aural part of a dramatic performance. Be that as it may, the CDPA is not so constrained. Because of the wording of Chapter 1 of Part II, the definition of 'performance' in s.180(2) must apply to all sections dealing with a performer's rights, so the CDPA is wider than the WPPT.

Section 205C creates the paternity right for a performer. There is the right to be identified whenever anyone produces or puts on a qualifying performance in public, broadcasts a live qualifying performance, communicates to the public a sound recording of a qualifying performance, or issues copies of such a recording to the public. The manner of identification depends on the circumstances of the performance, ie whether it is a performance in public, a broadcast of the same, a sound recording which is communicated to the public, or copies of a sound recording which are issued. However, in the case of a performance by a group, it is sufficient if the group is identified. 'Group' means two or more performers who have a particular name by which they may be collectively identified.

Like the author's moral right of paternity, the performer's right must also be asserted. Section 205D is worded in almost identical fashion to s.78, except of course that it does not replicate the special provisions about artistic works. The effect of assertion on third parties is the same.

There are eight exceptions to the paternity right set out in s.205E. The right does not apply where it is not reasonably practicable to identify the performer (would this apply to a large symphony orchestra?), nor does it apply to any performance given for the purpose of reporting current events or advertising goods or services. Certain of the defences in Sch. 2 which apply to a performer's property rights apply also to the right of paternity, namely news reporting, incidental inclusion, examinations, judicial proceedings and Royal Commissions.

The right to object to derogatory treatment (the integrity right) is set out in s.205F. Whilst this does not have to be asserted, the manner in which it can be infringed is narrower than the paternity right. The performer may only object if the performance is broadcast live or is played in public or communicated to the public by means of a sound recording 'with any distortion, mutilation or other modification that is prejudicial to the reputation of the performer'. It will be appreciated that this wording is even narrower than the equivalent for the author's right of integrity in s.80. Given the case law on s.80, it is likely that an objective test will be applied. Section 205F, in contrast to s.205C, does not contain any special treatment for groups. As with the author's right of integrity, there is secondary liability for dealing in sound recordings which infringe the integrity right (s.205H).

The exceptions to the integrity right are narrower than those to the paternity right. They include performances given for the purpose of reporting current events, and alterations to a performance which are part of 'normal editorial practice', a phrase likely to produce litigation. Where the alteration is to avoid the commission of an offence or made by the BBC to avoid the inclusion of offensive material in a broadcast, and the performer has been identified, there is no infringement of the right only where there is an adequate disclaimer. The conclusion must be that if the right of paternity has not been asserted, then there is no need for the disclaimer.

The duration of the moral rights is coterminous with the performer's economic rights, so that the governing factor is the date of the performance. Just as with an author's moral rights, a performer's moral rights can be waived or be the subject of consent, s.205J being worded in an identical manner to s.87. The performer's moral rights are personal to the performer and cannot be assigned (s.205L), but they can be transmitted on death. Section 205M mirrors the wording of s.95, so that the performer may bequeath their moral rights to a named individual, but failing that the moral rights pass to the person who has been bequeathed the performer's property rights, and failing that they pass to the performer's personal representatives. Section 205M(5) contains an identical provision to s.95(5), explained earlier, so that where there is an action for infringement of the performer's moral rights after their death, the damages are dealt with as part of the performer's general estate.

The remedies for infringement of moral rights are set out in s.205N. Infringement is actionable as a breach of statutory duty. In the case of infringement by derogatory treatment, the court is able to grant an injunction on terms which permit the infringer to continue with their conduct provided there is an appropriate disclaimer. As mentioned in the discussion of s.103(2) earlier, this means that the infringing work can still be exploited commercially so that the defendant

thinking point
Do the provisions of the CDPA with regard to performers' moral rights adequately fulfil the United Kingdom's obligations under the WPPT?

is in effect given a licence to commit derogatory treatment. Equally, it is not clear how the disclaimer is to be made known to the audience of the broadcast or those who hear the sound recording being played.

Unlike the performer's non-property rights, the performer's moral rights are not retrospective. The provisions in the CDPA apply only to performances occurring after 1 February 2006.

 # Summary

This chapter has explained:

- the relationship between copyright, moral rights and rights in performances;
- the way in which an author's moral rights have been introduced into United Kingdom law by the CDPA; and
- the incremental protection which has been accorded to performers following a series of amendments to the CDPA.

 # Reflective question

The implementation of moral rights and rights in performances in United Kingdom law leaves a lot to be desired.

Discuss.

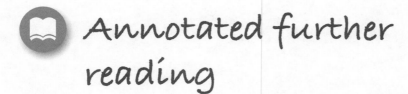 # Annotated further reading

Cornish, W. 'Moral Rights under the 1988 Act' [1989] *EIPR* 449
An overview of the introduction of moral rights by the CDPA.

Dietz, A. 'The Moral Right of the Author: Moral Rights and the Civil Law Countries' (1994–1995) 19 *Colum-VLA Journal of Law & the Arts* 199
A survey of the protection of moral rights in various civil law countries.

Dworkin, G. 'The Moral Rights of the Author: Moral Rights and the Common Law Countries' (1994–1995) 19 *Colum-VLA Journal of Law & the Arts* 229

An overview of the common law treatment of moral rights, with particular emphasis on the CDPA.

Ginsburg, J. 'Moral Rights in a Common Law System' [1990] *Ent LR* 121

A powerful critique of the half-hearted adoption of moral rights by the USA and United Kingdom.

Ricketson, S. 'Moral Rights and the Droit de Suite: International Conditions and Australian Obligations' [1990] *Ent LR* 78

An account of the obligations imposed by the Berne Convention and how common law countries like Australia have struggled to accommodate these.

Simon, I. 'The Introduction of Performers' Moral Rights' [2006] *EIPR* 552, 600

A very detailed analysis of the introduction of moral rights for performers as a result of the United Kingdom's implementation of the WIPO Performances and Phonograms Treaty 1996, arguing that the method of implementation and the slavish following of the authors' moral rights régime has led to stunted rights for performers.

Sprawson, R. 'Moral Rights in the 21st Century: A Case for Bankruptcy' [2006] *Ent LR* 58

A concise critique of the introduction of moral rights for performers.

Stamatoudi, I. 'Moral Rights of Authors in England: the Missing Emphasis on the Role of Creators' [1997] *IPQ* 478

A comparison of the treatment of moral rights in France, Germany and the United Kingdom.

Waisman, A. 'Rethinking the Moral Right to Integrity' [2008] *IPQ* 268

Argues that the right of integrity would be better understood by clarifying the distinction between modifying the work and modifying its support (ie the physical medium).

Part 5

Designs

Designs

Learning objectives

Upon completion of this chapter, you should have acquired:

- an appreciation of the choices available to a designer who wishes to acquire protection for the appearance of an article under United Kingdom and EU law;

- knowledge of the United Kingdom registered designs system and how it mirrors the designs régime of EU law;

- knowledge of how copyright may be used to protect the appearance of a three-dimensional object and how the CDPA curtails such use of copyright;

- understanding of the definition of unregistered design right and the various exclusions from protection under United Kingdom law;

- knowledge of the conditions to be satisfied for United Kingdom design right to subsist and how these differ from the conditions for copyright protection; and

- an understanding of the scope of protection accorded to the design right holder under United Kingdom law.

Introduction

This chapter deals with the three principal means available under United Kingdom law to protect the appearance of a product, namely registration, unregistered design right and copyright. EU-wide protection is also available, leaving the designer to choose between five different régimes. The unanswered question must be 'why is it necessary to have such complexity'?

11.1 Overview of the issues

11.1.1 The nature of design protection

Design law exists to protect the *appearance* of articles rather than the articles themselves. It is concerned with *how things look*. The underlying idea behind the law on designs is that it involves two distinct elements: an article or product (which under the law as it now stands, need not be mass-produced) and some added ingredient, a design feature, which enhances the appearance of the article. It is the design feature, the added matter, which receives legal protection, not the product itself (unless, of course, the product qualifies in its own right for **patent** protection). To give a simple example, a bottle would be the article. If the bottle is made in the shape of a human torso (such as the perfume bottles produced by Jean Paul Gaultier), it is the body shape which is protectable under the law of designs (and, incidentally, also under **trade mark** law).

The structure of United Kingdom design law makes a number of unquestioned (and sometime unjustified) assumptions about what makes a good design and how good designs should best be protected. Articles the appearance of which have a greater visual impact on the user are regarded as more deserving of protection than functional items. The former qualify for registration, the latter do not, although there is a second, lower tier of **copyright**-type protection for designs not having such visual impact. As a result of the law's assumptions, the duration of protection is longer for **registered designs**, the owner is given a monopoly-type right so that independent creation is not a defence, and the counter-arguments available to a defendant in an **infringement** action are fewer and far narrower. Nevertheless, as with all registrable rights, there is the ever-present risk that the registration may be declared invalid after a challenge by a third party, thus leaving the designer with nothing. Second tier protection for non-registered designs is shorter, narrower and offers greater scope to the defendant to argue that there has been no infringement. Such protection is, however, instantaneous and free.

The underlying assumptions made by the framers of current legislation can be challenged in several ways. For example, the creator of a good design may not *want* to seek protection through registration or may be prevented from technical reasons from so doing, therefore many meritorious designs end up in the second tier of protection. Separating out the visual impact of a design from its other qualities, such as the usefulness of the product, how sturdy it is, the materials from which it is made, or its price, is not always easy. A consumer may buy a piece of furniture for how it looks, but equally for one or more other reasons. To assume that only designs which look nice should qualify for registration overlooks the argument that other aspects of good design should be rewarded.

11.1.2 **The justifications for design right protection**

Designs have attracted far less debate as to the rationale for their protection than other areas of intellectual property law. The theories which underpin design law can, however, be categorised in a familiar way. Design law exists either to prevent misappropriation (the stealing of another person's efforts) or to encourage investment in better design for the good of society as a whole (ie the utilitarian theory). These arguments (often intertwined) have been advanced by both the United Kingdom Government and the EU Commission. The former stated that 'some protection should be available to give the manufacturer who has spent money on the design the opportunity to benefit from his investment, thus providing an incentive to further investment' (White Paper on *Intellectual Property and Innovation* 1986 (Cmnd 9712) para 3.21). The latter has declared (in Recital 7 to the EU Design Regulation (Council Regulation (EC) No 6/2002 of 12 December 2001 on Community designs [2002] OJ L 3/1), throughout this chapter 'the Regulation') that 'enhanced protection for industrial design not only promotes the contribution of individual designers to the sum of Community excellence in the field, but also encourages innovation and development of new products and investment in their production'.

thinking point
Would design law benefit if there were a clearer articulation of the reasons why good design should be encouraged?

11.1.3 **Policy**

Over the last 50 years, United Kingdom Government policy has fluctuated between, on the one hand, insisting that the designer can only obtain protection by registration and, on the other, permitting the designer to choose between registration under the Registered Designs Act 1949, as amended, (throughout this chapter, RDA) and reliance on copyright (or an equivalent copyright-type right).

Immediately prior to the introduction of the CDPA 1988, a designer could choose to register the appearance of their design at the Designs Registry (part of the **United Kingdom Intellectual Property Office, UKIPO**) or else argue that the original article was, in itself, an artistic **work**, such as a sculpture or work of artistic craftsmanship. More problematic, however, was where the design started out as a drawing. The designer in such a case was able, prior to 1989, to rely on the copyright in that drawing to prevent any unauthorised direct or indirect three-dimensional copy of that drawing (*LB (Plastics) v Swish Products* [1979] RPC 551). As a result of the decision of the House of Lords in *British Leyland v Armstrong Patents* [1986] AC 577, which criticised the **claimant's** reliance on copyright to prevent the manufacture of spare parts for its cars, provisions were introduced in the CDPA 1988 which curtail the ability of a designer to rely on the copyright in such 'design documents'. By way of replacement, there is a copyright-right type right, the **unregistered design right**, although some residual copyright protection is still available for articles which amount to artistic works in their own right. The United Kingdom unregistered design right is unique, having criteria entirely different from those applicable in the United Kingdom registered designs and the EU registered and unregistered designs systems.

thinking point
Given the availability of EU unregistered design right, is there any point in having a separate domestic system of unregistered protection?

11.1.4 Legal choices available to the designer

A designer who wishes to obtain protection for the appearance of an article has a complex and bewildering choice. The solution best suited to the designer's needs will depend on a number of commercial factors, including the nature of the product, how competitive that sector of the designs industry is, in which countries the product is likely to be marketed, and how long it is expected to be of commercial value (many designs are driven by short-term fashion considerations). Legally speaking, the debate centres on whether the effort of acquiring registered protection (with its consequent monopoly-type right and longer term) outweighs the instant, cost-free, but shorter duration of unregistered, copyright-type protection. The latter, of course, has the downside that the claimant must show copying in order to succeed in an **infringement** action, so that independent creation will always be a defence. Copying, it must be repeated, does not have to be shown for registered design right infringement: *The Procter & Gamble Company v Reckitt Benckiser (UK) Ltd* [2008] FSR 208.

11.1.4.1 Choosing registration

If the designer decides to register the design, they will have to choose between domestic registration or registration throughout Europe (or indeed, throughout the world).

As regards domestic law, the registered designs system has much in common with patents (indeed, until 1949 patents and designs were dealt with in the same Act). The RDA was rewritten in 2001 to take account of the EU Designs Directive (Directive 98/71/EC of the European Parliament and of the Council of 13 October 1998 on the legal protection of designs, [1998] OJ L 289/28, 'the Directive'), so that the current criteria for protection differ from their predecessors.

At the same time as amending national design laws, the EU, by means of the Regulation, introduced a pan-European system for protecting designs. The EU registered design right provides protection in all Member States by means of a single registration, obtainable from the **Office for Harmonisation in the Internal Market (Trade Marks and Designs) ('OHIM')** in Alicante. The criteria for national and EU protection of registered designs, found respectively in the Directive and Regulation, are therefore identical.

Should our designer decide that registration is appropriate the initial choice is between national or EU protection. As the criteria for protection are identical in both systems, which one to pursue comes down to the commercial considerations outlined earlier. A further practical complication is that in September 2007 the EU acceded to the Hague Agreement concerning the international registration of industrial designs. Like the **Madrid Agreement** for the International Registration of Trade Marks 1891, this operates as a procedural shortcut for the designer so that a single application filed with **WIPO** leads to protection throughout the Contracting States of the Agreement. The link between the EU design and the Hague Agreement became operative on 1 January 2008.

11.1.4.2 Choosing unregistered protection

For the designer unable or unwilling to seek registered protection, the choice lies between United Kingdom unregistered design right, EU unregistered design right or, in certain circumstances, United Kingdom copyright.

United Kingdom unregistered design right, set out in Part III CDPA, was the Government's response to the perceived abuse of copyright to control the market in spare parts. The criteria for protection are essentially derived from the concept of copyright and its requirement of **originality** (s.213(4) CDPA). In contrast, the EU unregistered design right (set out in the Regulation) has criteria which mirror those for registered designs (Article 4). However, here the period of protection is far shorter (three years as opposed to a maximum of 25 years), protection arises immediately the design is published within the EU (Article 11), and liability for infringement depends on proof of copying (Article 19). It is possible for a claimant to rely on both United Kingdom and EU unregistered design right in the same article even though the criteria for protection differ (*Landor & Hawa International Ltd v Azure Designs Ltd* [2007] FSR 181; *Bailey v Haynes* [2007] FSR 199; *Kohler Mira Ltd v Bristan Group Ltd* [2013] EWPCC 2).

Finally, in limited circumstances, explained later, a designer can rely on artistic copyright under s.4 CDPA to protect the appearance of an article. Such protection is mutually exclusive with United Kingdom unregistered design right (CDPA s.236).

We consider in this chapter the principal routes to securing protection for a design under domestic law. It is beyond the scope of this work to consider the alternative EU system, but it should be remembered that the domestic law on registered designs is a mirror-image of the protection available from OHIM.

By way of illustration, the designer's choice can be summarised diagrammatically: see Diagram 11.1.

11.2 The United Kingdom registration system

Because the current law on registered designs has been in place for a relatively short period of time, there is as yet little domestic case law to explain the key words and phrases in the legislation. However, the criteria for protection and infringement are identical under both the RDA and the Regulation, so reference will be made to EU registered and unregistered design cases. These include decisions by the Invalidity Division of OHIM, the courts of other EU Member States dealing with the enforcement of the **EU design** right, and United Kingdom tribunals.

11.2.1 Procedure

The introduction of the 'one-stop shop' of the EU registered designs system resulted in a decline in **applicants** using the domestic system (British designers in any event had made less use of registration than their counterparts in France and Germany). In response, the United Kingdom Government, as part of its deregulation strategy, simplified domestic procedure by means of The Regulatory Reform (Registered Designs) Order 2006 (SI 2006/1974) and The Registered Designs Rules 2006 (SI 2006/1975), both of which came into force in October 2006. The procedure (which in essence is the same as the procedure before OHIM) entails just three basic steps:

Diagram 11.1

Choices open to a designer

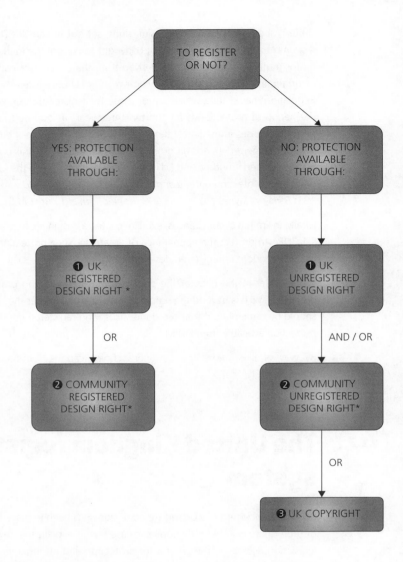

TO REGISTER OR NOT?

YES: PROTECTION AVAILABLE THROUGH:

NO: PROTECTION AVAILABLE THROUGH:

❶ UK REGISTERED DESIGN RIGHT *

❶ UK UNREGISTERED DESIGN RIGHT

OR

AND / OR

❷ COMMUNITY REGISTERED DESIGN RIGHT*

❷ COMMUNITY UNREGISTERED DESIGN RIGHT*

OR

❸ UK COPYRIGHT

* EACH OF THESE HAS THE SAME CRITERIA FOR PROTECTION

- filing the application, which now can relate to more than one design, rather than one single design, as before. OHIM statistics show that the majority of EU design applications relate to multiple designs, so designers are clearly taking advantage of the increased flexibility of the new law. As with patents, a design application may claim Convention priority from an earlier national filing. The validity of the design will be assessed by reference to the available prior art at the **filing date**, or, if Convention priority is claimed, at the **priority date**;

- examination for compliance with formalities; and

- grant and **publication**.

The application form must show clearly what is the design to be protected (photographs and/ or drawings showing the article from various angles are the normal means) and to indicate the products in which the design will be incorporated or to which it will be applied. In common with the EU system, there is no longer any **examination** by the Designs Registry to determine whether the design is new and has individual character (the two positive requirements for a valid design) so that it is left to third parties to challenge the design for lack of these requirements in subsequent **invalidity** or infringement proceedings. It is for this reason that the decisions of the Invalidity Division of OHIM are likely to play a crucial role in the development of case law.

All designs are now published upon grant (the previous system was voluntary and some designs were withheld from publication) although an applicant has the option to request delayed publication and grant for up to 12 months so that, for example, registration can be timed to coincide with the launch of the new product. During that one-year period, it may be possible for the proprietor to rely on any EU unregistered design right as a further means of protection, provided the criteria in Article 4 of the Regulation have been met.

Once granted, a registered design lasts for five years but can be renewed on four further occasions, giving a maximum term of protection of 25 years. Again, as part of the Government's deregulation strategy, it is now easier for the **registered proprietor** to have a lapsed design restored to the register where there has been a failure to pay the **renewal fees** on time.

11.2.2 **The informed user**

The intellectual property landscape is populated with hypothetical persons through whose eyes key issues of fact are determined. In the case of patents, this person is the notional **skilled addressee**. In the case of trade marks, it is the average consumer who is used to decide issues of registrability and infringement. For registered designs, the Directive and Regulation have created a new persona, that of the **informed user**. However, the informed user is *not* the same as the skilled addressee of patent law (otherwise the legislation would refer to the 'informed designer') yet they are more discriminating than the average consumer of trade mark law. This is because they have more extensive knowledge of the relevant design field, being aware of other similar designs, and appreciate the nature of the product, the relevant industrial sector, and the freedom of the designer in developing the design (*The Procter & Gamble Company v Reckitt Benckiser (UK) Ltd*, *per* Jacob LJ at [16], [25]). The informed user thus appears to be an amalgam of the skilled addressee and the average consumer. An example of someone who might typify an informed user (at least in the case of consumer goods) would be a wholesale buyer for a large retail chain (see Headdon, 'Community Design Right Infringement: An Emerging Consensus or a Difference Overall Impression' [2007] *EIPR* 336).

The characteristics of the informed user were set out by HHJ Fysh QC in *Woodhouse UK plc v Architectural Lighting Systems* [2006] RPC 1 at [49–50]. Explaining that this fictional character is used to determine issues of validity and infringement, such decisions are made on the basis of an overall impression, which is, of course, a *visual* impression. Such person is a *user* of the design, and moreover, a regular user, and is neither a manufacturer nor the person in the street. He or she does not possess an 'archival mind' but, having an average memory, is aware of 'what's about in the market' and 'what has been about in the recent past'. He or she has an awareness of product trend and availability, and some knowledge of basic technical considerations. However, as registered design right is concerned with the appearance of articles, the focus is on the appearance of the article, not manufacturing technology.

HHJ Fysh's thinking has since been followed by the Court of Appeal in *The Procter & Gamble Company v Reckitt Benckiser (UK) Ltd* and is in accord with the views of the ECJ.

---

case close-up

Case C-281/10P *PepsiCo Inc v Grupo Promer Mon Graphic SA and OHIM* [2011] ECR I-10153

PepsiCo appealed against the decision that its design for promotional items for games (known as 'pogs', 'rappers' or 'tazos') was invalid because of Grupo Promer's prior national registration. The ECJ upheld the decision that the designer's freedom of choice was severely constricted, so the small differences between the two designs were insignificant and did not produce a different overall impression on the informed user. As to the identity of the informed user, the ECJ said (at [53]) that the concept lay somewhere between the average consumer in trade marks and the sectoral expert. This person was particularly observant because of their personal experience or extensive knowledge. Here the informed user would have been a child between the ages of 5 and 10 (someone who played pogs) or a marketing manager in a company that made goods promoted by pogs.

thinking point

Will the characteristics of the 'informed user' provide sufficient certainty and objectivity in deciding registered design cases, or is this another concept which the court can manipulate to achieve a desired outcome?

11.2.3 **Criteria for protection**

11.2.3.1 Definition of 'design'

Under the RDA s.1(2), 'design' means 'the appearance of the whole or a part of a product resulting from the features of, in particular, the lines, contours, colours, shape, texture or materials of the product or its ornamentation'. 'Product' (according to s.1(3)) means 'any industrial or handicraft item other than a computer program; and, in particular, includes packaging, get-up, graphic symbols, typographic type-faces and parts intended to be assembled into a complex product'. 'Complex product' (also defined in s.1(3)) means 'a product which is composed of at least two replaceable component parts permitting disassembly and reassembly'.

The combined definition of 'design' and 'product' in the current law differs from that which applied under the original version of the RDA ('features of shape, configuration, pattern or ornament applied to an article by any industrial process being features which in the finished article appeal to and are judged by the eye'). The differences can be summarised thus:

- it is now possible to obtain protection for part of a product as well as the whole item;
- internal features are now capable of registration;
- there is no longer a requirement of 'eye appeal', instead the design must produce a 'different overall impression' on the informed user;

- previously designs had to be mass produced (because of the phrase 'by any industrial process'), but now handicraft items can be registered (which makes the name accorded by some writers, 'industrial designs', something of a misnomer);

- features of the product other than shape or ornament have been added to the definition, so that texture, materials and colour can now be claimed;

- graphic symbols are expressly mentioned as being part of a product, which means that logos are capable of protection both as designs and trade marks. The canny trade mark owner may well consider registering the logo as a design, in part for the simplicity of the procedure, but also for the 25-year period of protection which this would give. J.J.I. Peris suggests (in 'Registered Community Design: The First Two-Year Balance from an Insider's Perspective' [2006] *EIPR* 146) that graphic symbols used as icons in computer menus are registrable.

11.2.3.2 The positive criteria for protection

cross reference
See sections 5.5 and 5.6.

The amended RDA in s.1B has two positive criteria which a design must satisfy in order to be registrable, namely **novelty** and **individual character**. These requirements are separate and should be applied sequentially, like novelty and **inventive step** in patents. Both involve comparing the design with the prior art, which, like the prior art in patent law, is potentially worldwide.

The requirement of novelty was present under the old law, but today has a different meaning, the new definition being similar to that found in patent law. Novelty now means that a design is new if no identical design or no design whose features differ only in immaterial details has been made available to the public before the relevant date (RDA s.1B(2)). 'Making available' bears the patent meaning of published (whether following registration or otherwise), exhibited, used in trade, or otherwise disclosed anywhere in the world (RDA s.1B(5)). However, the requirement of novelty for registered designs is qualified in two respects.

First, and in contrast to patents, such novelty is relative rather than absolute. Section 1B(6) provides that a design is treated as not having been made available if the event in question (publication, exhibition, etc) could not reasonably have become known in the normal course of business to the relevant design circles in the **EEA**. Unlike a patent, a registered design will not be invalidated by the existence of some obscure prior art (*Green Lane Products Ltd v PMS International Group Ltd* [2008] FSR 1). As Peris explains (in the context of decisions by OHIM's Invalidity Division) the concept of relative novelty involves a two-stage argument. It is for the party challenging the design to show that there exists prior art which renders the design not new. The burden then shifts to the registered proprietor to show that such prior art could not reasonably have become known to the relevant design circles, and if (for whatever reason) the proprietor fails to do so then the design is invalid for lack of novelty. So far, OHIM's Invalidity Division has concluded that publication of an earlier design for an inter-dental brush in the Japanese Patent Office Journal would be known to those in the relevant design circle (*Sunstar Suisse SA v Dentaid SL*, OHIM Ref ICD 000000420, 20 June 2005) and that the inclusion of a design for a convector heater in a commercial catalogue available in Hong Kong would likewise have been known to those concerned in that design field (*Comercial Opera SA v Cata Electrodomesticos SL*, OHIM Ref ICD 000000131, 2 July 2004). Similarly, when considering whether an unregistered EU design was novel, the Landsgericht, Frankfurt, concluded that a design for an abdominal muscle trainer had been invalidated because of distribution of the same device in the United States prior to its launch in Europe: *Thane International Group's Application* [2006] ECDR 71.

However, as Lewison J pointed out in *Green Lane Products Ltd v PMS International Group Ltd*, it is far from clear as to what is meant by the 'sector concerned' in RDA s.1B(6). Is it the sector in which the registered design falls or is it the sector in which the prior art falls? The problem is neatly illustrated by the facts of *Green Lane* itself, where the claimant's EU registration for spiky laundry balls was challenged by the maker of spiky balls used in body massage. Lewison J concluded (and was upheld on appeal, *Green Lane Products Ltd v PMS International Group Ltd* [2008] FSR 701) that the 'sector concerned' meant the sector relating to the prior art. A design which was old and well known in one sector should not be registrable for a product in any other sector. Such a conclusion was essential in order to achieve consistency with the provisions on the EU unregistered design right, where, provided the design is new, its duration is calculated under Article 11 of the Regulation from when the design is first launched in Europe. First launch anywhere else destroys novelty. Just as the registered design right gives a monopoly over any kind of goods, 'it makes complete sense that the prior art available for attacking novelty should also extend to all kinds of goods, subject only to the limited exception of prior art obscure even in the sector from which it comes' (*per* Jacob LJ in *Green Lane Products Ltd v PMS International Group Ltd* (CA) at [79]).

The second qualification to the requirement of novelty is that there is no 'making available' where the disclosure was in breach of confidence or if the disclosure was by the designer within the 12 months' 'grace period' calculated from the filing or priority date (RDA s.1B(5)). The fact that a design will not be treated as having been made available to the public where it was disclosed in **breach of confidence** emphasises the practical importance of designs being kept secret prior to the design application being filed. Nevertheless, the presence of a 'grace period' does, according to Recital 20 of the Regulation, give the designer the ability to test the design in the marketplace without endangering the novelty or individual character of the design.

If it is concluded that the design is new, the next issue to consider is whether it has individual character, taking into account the degree of freedom which the designer had. Just as with novelty, 'individual character' involves a comparison between the prior art and the registered design, again through the eyes of the informed user, in order to see whether the design produces a different overall impression. Whilst the comparison for novelty is precise (the prior art must be *identical* to the registered design, or, if it differs, it must do so only in *immaterial detail*), the comparison for individual character is broader and more imprecise, leaving the court 'with a considerable margin for judgment' (*per* Jacob LJ in the Court of Appeal in *The Procter & Gamble Company v Reckitt Benckiser (UK) Ltd* at [34]). The differences in the comparisons to be made are analogous to the differences between novelty and inventive step in the law of patents.

Reference to Recital 13 of the Directive (relevant to Article 5 of the Directive on which RDA s.1B(3) and (4) is based) indicates that the registered design is to be compared with the 'existing design corpus' (ie 'what's about in the market' and 'what has been about in the recent past' to quote HHJ Fysh in *Woodhouse*), taking into account the nature of the product and the relevant industrial sector.

> ### case close-up
>
> **The Procter & Gamble Company v Reckitt Benckiser (UK) Ltd** [2008] FSR 208
>
> . . . .
>
> The Court of Appeal, in discussing the equivalent provision in the Regulation (Recital 14), has observed that these criteria have not been carried over into the text of the actual Articles of the Directive and Regulation but should nevertheless be taken into account when interpreting the substantive provisions. Another phrase not carried over into the Articles from the Recitals is the phrase 'clearly differs'. As Jacob LJ explains (at [18]), only if the 'overall impression' 'clearly differs' from that of the 'existing design corpus' will the design have individual character. In *Procter & Gamble*, there was little doubt that the claimant's design for an air-freshener aerosol had individual character, as it had received a number of industry awards.

> ### case close-up
>
> **LengD'Or SA v Crown Confectionery Co Ltd** (OHIM Ref ICD 000000370, 23 February 2005)
>
> . . . .
>
> An example of the nature of the exercise to be carried out by the tribunal when assessing individual character can be found in the OHIM decision in *LengD'Or SA v Crown Confectionery Co Ltd* (OHIM Ref ICD 000000370, 23 February 2005) where the design consisted of a shape for biscuits and was challenged on the grounds that it was the same as a previously registered three-dimensional **EU trade mark**, also for biscuits. OHIM concluded, first, that the design was novel as there were significant differences between it and the EU trade mark, one having rounded loops, the other having pointed loops. Second, because one involved six loops and the other eight loops the impression on the informed user was quite different.

11.2.3.3 The negative criteria for protection

The RDA excludes two types of design features from protection. It also provides for certain categories of design to be incapable of registration, and prohibits the registration of designs which conflict with earlier rights.

The exclusions from protection are set out in s.1C(1) and (2) and comprise features 'solely dictated by the product's technical function' and 'must fit' features, although this latter exclusion is declared not to prevent the protection of modular systems. 'Must fit' is a somewhat imprecise summary, and the exact wording of s.1C(2) should be remembered: 'features of appearance of a product which must necessarily be reproduced in their exact form and dimensions so as to permit the product in which the design is incorporated . . . to be mechanically connected to, or placed in, around or against another so that either product may perform its function'. As yet there is no case law on s.1C(2), but the interpretation given to the exclusion in s.1C(1) together with that of the parallel provision in s.213(3)(b)(i) CDPA suggest that it will have a narrow scope.

The exclusion for features dictated by the product's technical function looks at first glance to be similar to the exclusion for functional features found in the original version of the RDA.

Landor & Hawa International Ltd v Azure Designs Ltd [2007] FSR 181

The Court of Appeal in *Landor & Hawa International Ltd v Azure Designs Ltd*, when considering the identical exclusion under the EU unregistered design right, referred not to earlier case law but to Recital 10 of the Regulation as a guide to interpretation. The Court agreed with HHJ Fysh at first instance that the key issue was whether the *appearance* of the design was 'driven without option' by function, so that here the piping and zips on an expanding suitcase fell outside the exclusion because there were 'capricious' elements to the design. In so doing it declared that the broad interpretation given to the words in the old version of the RDA, 'dictated by the function which the article...has to perform', by Lord Pearson in the House of Lords in *Amp Inc v Utilux Products Ltd* [1972] RPC 103 at p. 124 should not apply here. Lord Pearson had concluded that the old exclusion applied if the shape was 'attributable to or caused by or prompted by function', which had the effect of making many designs unregistrable. Lord Pearson, said the Court of Appeal in *Landor*, was interpreting a British statute not a European provision. It also rejected the defendant's argument that the exclusion should be interpreted in the same way as the exclusion from registration as a trade mark of a shape necessary to achieve a technical result. The Advocate General in Case C-299/99 *Philips Electronics BV v Remington Consumer Products* [2002] ECR I-5475 had stated that the two exclusions should be interpreted differently. Whilst the shape of the goods might be denied trade mark protection if it was *attributable* to achieving a technical result, the level of functionality had to be far greater in the case of designs. The design feature had not only to be necessary but essential before it could be excluded from protection. Thus the exclusion for functional features is to be given a far narrower scope than was the case under the old RDA and under the current law of trade marks.

thinking point
Do the positive and negative criteria for protection effectively balance the interests of the designer with the needs of third parties?

The RDA in s.1D prohibits the registration of designs contrary to public policy or morality and Sch. A1 prohibits the registration of designs incorporating specially protected emblems, such as the coat of arms of the Royal family, the flags of other countries, and the Olympic symbol (similar exclusions are found in the Trade Marks Act 1994). Also prohibited from registration by implication are those designs which conflict with earlier EU or United Kingdom registered designs or trade marks, or earlier copyrights, as conflict with such an earlier right is a ground of invalidity under ss.11ZA and 11ZB.

11.2.4 **Ownership**

The rules on ownership are similar to those prevailing under the previous version of the RDA and are a mirror image of those which apply to the unregistered design right. In summary, s.2 RDA declares that the design belongs to the designer, except where it was made in the course of employment, in which case it is owned by the designer's employer. All references to **commissioned** designs have been removed by the Intellectual Property Act 2014 so as to ensure consistency with EU law which did not recognise the entitlement of a commissioner: Case C-32/08 *Fundación Española para la Innovación de la Artesanía (FEAI) v Cul de Sac Espacio Creativo SL and Acierta Product & Position SA*, [2009] ECR I-5611.

One significant change between the old RDA and the new version concerns the ability to challenge the validity of the design registration where it has been granted to the wrong person. Under the pre-2001 law, any person could seek to have a design declared invalid for having been granted to someone not entitled (see *Woodhouse UK plc v Architectural Lighting Systems*), whereas under the revised RDA only the person properly entitled to the design can challenge its wrongful grant: *Watson v Zap Ltd* [2007] ECDR 209.

11.2.5 **Infringement**

cross reference
See section 6.2.

Section 7(1) RDA declares that registration gives the exclusive right to use the design and any design which does not produce on the informed user a different overall impression. As with patents, this phrase incorporates two key issues, the nature of infringing conduct and the scope of protection accorded to the registered design.

As regards infringing conduct, 'use' is stated in s.7(2) to comprise making, offering, putting on the market, importing, exporting or using a product in which the design is incorporated or to which it is applied, or stocking such a product for those purposes. The list is almost identical to the infringement provisions found in s.60(1) Patents Act 1977. It may be observed that the scope of protection accorded to the owner is not limited to the articles for which the design was registered, but extends to any article to which the design is applied by the infringer because of the use of the indefinite article 'a'. Headdon gives the example of a new design for a saucepan which is then applied to a completely different product such as a hat.

thinking point
How easy is it to prove that the alleged infringement creates the same overall impression as the protected design?

With regard to the scope of protection, this involves a comparison being made between the registered design and the alleged infringement to see if the latter produces a different overall impression. If the impression is the same, then there is infringement, if the impression is different, there is not. The nature of the comparison is similar to that carried out in the context of validity, when the registered design is compared with the prior art to see if it creates a different overall impression. However, according to the Court of Appeal in *The Procter & Gamble Company v Reckitt Benckiser (UK) Ltd*, there is one difference between validity and infringement, because of the wording of the Recitals to the Directive and Regulation. Whilst in relation to validity, there must 'clearly' be a difference between the prior art and the registered design, for infringement the test is simply whether there is a different overall impression.

The nature of the exercise means that it is difficult to be precise about the level of generality used in the comparison—after all, what is an 'overall' impression? This is likely to produce a number of apparently conflicting decisions. In *Procter & Gamble* itself, the Court of Appeal disagreed with Lewison J as to whether the defendant's fresh air spray produced a different overall impression on the informed user than the claimant's 'Febreze' spray, ultimately holding that it did, so that there was no infringement. The court was no doubt influenced by the design accolades showered on the claimant's product and the criticisms which had been made of the defendant's. The comparison is likely to be more difficult to make where the infringing product is different from the articles covered by the design registration. To return to Headdon's illustration, how close does the design for the hat have to be before it creates a similar overall impression to the saucepan on the informed user? And who, in this case, is the informed user: a wholesale buyer of saucepans or a wholesale buyer of hats?

cross reference
See section 6.3.

The defences to infringement (set out in s.7A RDA) include consent, private and domestic use, experimental use, reproduction for educational purposes, use of equipment on aircraft and ships temporarily within the United Kingdom, the importation of spare parts for the repair of such aircraft and ships, the carrying out of such repairs, **exhaustion of rights**, and the use of components to repair a complex product. Again, these defences are very similar to those found in s.60(5) Patents Act 1977. The Intellectual Property Act 2014 adds the further defence of **prior use**, in wording similar to that found in s.64 Patents Act 1977.

11.2.6 **Invalidity**

As a result of the Directive, there are now comprehensive provisions as to when a registered design may be declared invalid, which are set out in s.11ZA RDA. Lack of substantive examination means that **revocation** actions are likely to be more frequent.

The grounds of invalidity are, first, that the design in question does not satisfy the definition of design in s.1(2), that it is not new or does not have individual character, that it is dictated by technical function, that it consists of a specially protected emblem, or that it is contrary to public policy. An application to have the design declared invalid on any of these grounds may be brought by *any* person. Other grounds of invalidity are that the registered proprietor is not entitled to the design, or that the design is similar to an earlier registered EU or United Kingdom design, or that it infringes an earlier registered trade mark, or that it infringes an earlier copyright. In the case of these further grounds of invalidity, the application may only be brought by the owner of the relevant earlier right (*Watson v Zap Ltd*).

11.2.7 **Summary**

The Directive and Regulation have had a significant impact upon the scope of registered design protection under domestic law. The definition of what amounts to a design is much broader and includes parts of products and their internal features. A registrable design need no longer have eye appeal, but must merely create a different overall impression from what was previously available. The product in question does not have to be made by an industrial process. The positive criteria of novelty and individual character are to be assessed through the eyes of the hypothetical 'informed user'. The scope of the infringement action has also been widened.

United Kingdom copyright as an alternative means of protection

11.3.1 **Relevant provisions of Part I CDPA**

For many creative industries, particularly those which need to respond quickly to changing fashions (for example, jewellery) the bureaucracy inherent in the registered design system (even in its simplified form) is an anathema. One form of instant protection which might appeal to a designer in such an industry is copyright.

Section 4 CDPA protects two- and three-dimensional artistic works. As regards two-dimensional works, under s.4(1)(a) there is copyright protection for graphic works, *irrespective of artistic quality*. The phrase 'graphic works' is stated by the section to include drawings. The threshold for protection is low, indeed it has been suggested (in *British Northrop v Texteam Blackburn* [1974] RPC 57, a case in which it was held that drawings for parts of machinery were copyright) that 'anything which goes beyond a single line on a piece of paper is a drawing'. 'Graphic work' also includes engravings and etchings. It should not be assumed that these are necessarily two-dimensional. In *Wham-O Manufacturing Co v Lincoln* [1985] RPC 127, plastic frisbees were treated as engravings, and in *Hi Tech Autoparts v Towergate Two Ltd (No 1)* [2002] FSR 254, car mats were treated as etchings.

As regards three-dimensional works, s.4 refers to sculptures and works of artistic craftsmanship. Some cases have given 'sculpture' a wide meaning, but more recently it has been defined (*obiter*) as 'a three-dimensional work made by an artist's hand' (*per* Laddie J in *Metix (UK) Ltd v G.H. Maughan (Plastics) Ltd* [1997] FSR 718). This suggests functional articles should not be treated as sculptures under the CDPA.

case close-up

Lucasfilm Ltd v Ainsworth [2012] 1 AC 208

Laddie J's approach was adopted by Mann J in *Lucasfilm Ltd v Ainsworth* ([2009] FSR 103 at [118]). He reviewed the previous case law on what is a sculpture. Considering the 'normal' (ie lay) sense of the word, he stated that not every three-dimensional object should be regarded as a sculpture. To hold otherwise would not be right. Rather, a sculpture should have, as part of its purpose, a visual appeal in the sense that it might be enjoyed for that purpose alone, whether or not it might have another purpose as well. The purpose was that of the creator, the 'artist's hand'. An artist (in the realm of the visual arts) created something because it had visual appeal which was to be enjoyed as such. It had to have the intrinsic quality of being intended to be enjoyed as a visual thing. Items such as model soldiers had correctly been treated as sculptures, but the frisbee in *Wham-O* should not have been, nor should the plates for moulding toasted sandwiches in *Breville Europe plc v Thorn EMI Domestic Appliances Ltd* [1995] FSR 77. What mattered was whether the maker intended the object to have a visual appeal for its own sake. So, for example, a pile of bricks in an art gallery would amount to a sculpture, but a pile of bricks left outside a house by a builder would not. This approach to the meaning of 'sculpture' was subsequently endorsed by the Court of Appeal and the Supreme Court.

More problematic is the composite phrase 'a work of artistic craftsmanship'. Two elements must be present in an object before it will receive protection under s.4(1)(c): it must possess artistry, which for present purposes can be assumed to equate to 'eye appeal', and it must be made by a craftsman, who is a person who makes something in a skilful way and who takes justified pride in his workmanship (*Vermaat v Boncrest Ltd* [2001] FSR 43). Therefore, if the article is made by machine, it will not count as a work of craftsmanship (*Guild v Eskandar Ltd* [2001] FSR 38). 'Eye appeal' is to be decided by the intention of the maker (*Hensher v Restawile* [1976] AC 64; *Merlet v Mothercare plc* [1986] RPC 115) so that if an article is designed with a particular function in mind it will not qualify for protection under s.4(1)(c). In *Merlet*, the claimant's baby cape was designed for the purpose of keeping a baby dry, so that this overrode any visual appeal in the garment. In *Lucasfilm*, Mann J (again, confirmed on appeal) decided that the Stormtrooper helmets for the film *Star Wars* were not works of artistic craftsmanship, concluding (at [131]) that 'for a work to be regarded as one of artistic craftsmanship it must be possible fairly to say that the author was both a craftsman and an artist. A craftsman is a person who makes something in a skilful way and takes justified pride in their workmanship. An artist is a person with creative ability who produces something which has aesthetic appeal.'

The significance of relying on copyright protection is that under s.17(3) CDPA, a two-dimensional artistic work is 'reproduced in any material form' by being converted into a three-dimensional form and vice versa. Consequently, if the design process starts off with the creation of a drawing, such as a fashion sketch (*Bernstein v Sidney Murray* [1981] RPC 303) or diagrams for self-assembly furniture (*LB (Plastics) v Swish Products* [1979] RPC 551), then where the defendant copies the claimant's article, they will infringe the copyright in the drawing even if they never saw the source work. Indirect copying suffices under s.16 CDPA. Copyright has the advantage of giving the designer instant protection but, in contrast to the registered design system, the claimant will need to prove that the defendant copied the claimant's work (or at least had the opportunity to copy). The claimant must demonstrate derivation and substantial taking in accordance with the test set out by Lord Millett in *Designers' Guild Ltd v Russell Williams (Textiles) Ltd* [2000] 1 WLR 2416.

cross reference
See section 9.2.4.4.

11.3.2 Statutory provisions curtailing copyright

11.3.2.1 The Copyright Act 1956

Because the policy of the CDPA was heavily influenced by case law decided under its predecessor, we set out, by way of historical explanation, the ways in which the designer's right to rely on copyright were curtailed under the 1956 Act.

The 1956 Act contained two provisions which attempted to restrict the use of copyright to protect the appearance of functional articles, both of which operated as a defence to an infringement action. First there was the so-called 'non-expert defence' in s.9(8) which has to be understood in the context of the rule that a two-dimensional artistic work (such as an engineering drawing) can be infringed by a three-dimensional article which directly or indirectly copies the drawing (as in *Bernstein v Sidney Murray* and *LB (Plastics) v Swish Products*). The subsection provided that the copyright in the drawing was not infringed if the defendant's article did not appear, to persons who were not experts in the relevant design field, to be a reproduction of the claimant's artistic work. The defence was successfully raised in *Merlet v Mothercare plc* where it was held that the non-expert, viewing the defendant's baby cape, would not be able to tell that it was derived from the claimant's cutting pattern for the garment. Section 9(8) was abolished immediately the CDPA came into effect.

Second, s.10 (in its original form) excluded from copyright protection any design which was or could have been registered under the RDA, a reflection of Government policy at the time that the protection of designs ought to be by registration alone. However, the provision was interpreted as meaning that designs which were not registrable (because they lacked eye appeal) fell outside s.10 and so were covered by the law of copyright: *Dorling v Honnor Marine* [1964] RPC 160. The net result was that if a designer chose not to register a design which possessed eye appeal they got no protection whatsoever, whereas a drawing for a functional article, such as a piece of machinery, being incapable of registration, *was* protected under copyright. The designer could therefore sue those who copied the article, an outcome described as 'bizarre' by the *Report of the Whitford Committee on Copyright and Designs Law 1977* (Cmnd 6732).

Section 10 was amended (in a somewhat idiosyncratic fashion) by the Design Copyright Act 1968. The legislation (hastily enacted by means of a Private Member's Bill) was intended to cater for those industries where speed of protection mattered (such as toys and jewellery). It provided that in the case of registrable designs, there would be copyright protection (so that the designer was not obliged to go through the bureaucracy of registration) but such protection was to last for a period of 15 years only (matching the then maximum period of design registration), calculated from the date of first marketing. The designer of an article with eye appeal could therefore choose to register *or* to rely on copyright.

The amended s.10 was interpreted by the House of Lords to have the same scope as the original s.10. It applied only to designs capable of registration, so that those ineligible for protection under the RDA (for example, simple engineering drawings for exhaust pipes for cars) still got the full benefit of 'ordinary' copyright: *British Leyland v Armstrong Patents*. However, in the light of concerns expressed in contemporaneous investigations conducted by the then Monopolies and Mergers Commission about the power of car manufacturers to control the market for spare parts, the House of Lords conjured up a special defence (borrowed from land law) to prevent the abusive exploitation of copyright. In the case of consumer goods which were going to need repair, the manufacturer of replacement parts could rely on the defence of 'non-derogation from grant'. As the owner of the copyright drawing had chosen to market the product, they could not object to the repair of it, nor to the making of parts used in that repair. The invention of such a defence (almost out of thin air) created uncertainty and was subsequently criticised and given a narrow scope by the Privy Council in *Canon KK v Green Cartridge Co (Hong Kong) Ltd* [1997] AC 728.

11.3.2.2 The CDPA

Like its predecessor, the CDPA restricts the rights of the copyright owner when seeking to protect the design of an article. The restriction operates as a defence in a copyright infringement action where the claimant alleges that the defendant has made an article which copies, directly or indirectly, the claimant's artistic work.

Section 51

The policy iterated in the *British Leyland* case, namely that it is an abuse of copyright protection to rely on an artistic work to prevent others from making articles based on that work, is to be found in s.51 CDPA. It should not be assumed, however, that the section is a direct enactment of the decision in *British Leyland*: *Mars UK Ltd v Teknowledge Ltd* [2000] FSR 138. Section 51(1) declares that it is not an infringement of any copyright in a design document or model recording a design for anything other than an artistic work to make an article to the design. Section 51(3) defines 'design' as 'the shape or configuration (whether internal or external) of the whole or part of an article, other than surface decoration' and 'design document' as 'any record of a design, whether in the form of a drawing, a written description, a photograph, data stored in a computer or otherwise', wording repeated in Part III CDPA dealing with the unregistered design right. The definition of 'design document' is therefore wide enough to cover any medium in which the designer's efforts are recorded and is not confined to 'drawings' in the conventional sense: *Mackie Designs Inc v Behringer Specialised Studio Equipment (UK) Ltd* [1999] RPC 717 at p. 720 *per* Pumfrey J.

The wording of s.51(1) is not easy to understand and any commentary on it is best broken down into a series of propositions, as follows:

First, the section does *not* say that copyright does not subsist in a design document for an article. Rather it declares that the copyright existing in a design document *is not infringed* where *an article is made to that design* (it should be remembered that the section is placed in the Chapter of Part I CDPA dealing with defences to copyright infringement). A designer will therefore have copyright in the design document. Such copyright will be infringed if a third party merely copies the document in two-dimensional form, for example, by photocopying it. The designer is prevented from suing for copyright infringement only in one very specific situation, namely where the third party copies the design document directly or indirectly *in order to make articles*. In such a situation, the designer is forced to rely on the protection offered by the unregistered design right in Part III CDPA.

Second, the key word in s.51(1) is the word 'for'. The question to be asked when applying the provision is whether the claimant is relying on a design document *for* an article. If the document is not *for* an article (for example, if an artist creates a painting of a chair, the painting will not be a design document *for* the chair but *of* the chair), the section does not apply. If a third party then makes a chair based on that shown in the painting, this will fall outside the defence and so will be dealt with under the normal rules on copyright infringement.

Last, it must be determined whether the article to be made from the design document is an artistic work in its own right. If it is (for example, if it is a sculpture, or a work of artistic craftsmanship) then again, s.51(1) has no application and the full force of copyright law is available to the designer. If, however, the article is not an artistic work in its own right, then the designer cannot bring a copyright infringement action against a third party who has made articles derived from the design document. Instead they must rely on the unregistered design right.

The key to understanding s.51(1) can be illustrated by the flow chart in Diagram 11.2.

Case Law on s.51

Several cases illustrate the application of s.51. A case where the s.51 defence succeeded is *Jo Y Jo Ltd v Matalan Retail Ltd* [2000] ECDR 178 where Rattee J accepted the defendant's argument that the claimant's drawings for ladies' cardigans were design documents for articles and therefore protected only by design right not copyright. More controversially, Laddie J in *BBC Worldwide Ltd v Pally Screen Printing Ltd* [1998] FSR 665 held that the defendant's use of pictures of the 'Telly Tubbies' on T-shirts fell within s.51. It could be argued that the designs were being used as two-dimensional decoration *on* articles, but this was an application for summary judgment and the report shows that the judge was clearly irritated by the claimant's handling of its case. By contrast, in *Flashing Badge Co Ltd v Groves* [2007] ECDR 308, Rimer J held that artwork applied to the face of novelty badges was protected by copyright rather than design right and so s.51 did not apply. Whilst the badges themselves were articles, and so caught by the defence, what the defendant had copied was the artistic work applied to the surface of the badge. The most recent case to apply the s.51 defence is *Lucasfilm v Ainsworth*: having concluded that the Stormtrooper helmets were neither sculptures nor works of artistic craftsmanship, Mann J (and the appellate courts) had no hesitation in concluding that the action for copyright infringement was barred.

11.3.3 **Summary**

The effect of s.51 CDPA is to draw a distinction between designs for the shape or configuration of functional articles and designs for articles which are artistic works in their own right,

Diagram 11.2

The application of s.51 CDPA

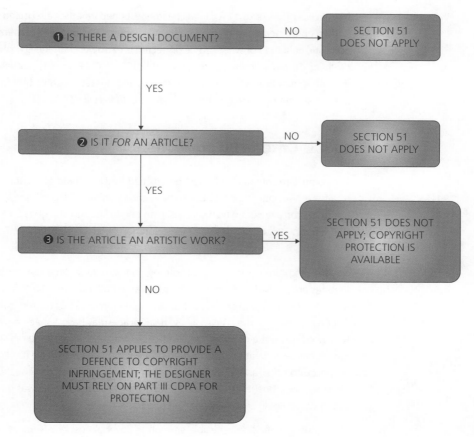

❶ IS THERE A DESIGN DOCUMENT? → NO → SECTION 51 DOES NOT APPLY

YES ↓

❷ IS IT *FOR* AN ARTICLE? → NO → SECTION 51 DOES NOT APPLY

YES ↓

❸ IS THE ARTICLE AN ARTISTIC WORK? → YES → SECTION 51 DOES NOT APPLY; COPYRIGHT PROTECTION IS AVAILABLE

NO ↓

SECTION 51 APPLIES TO PROVIDE A DEFENCE TO COPYRIGHT INFRINGEMENT; THE DESIGNER MUST RELY ON PART III CDPA FOR PROTECTION

such as sculptures and works of artistic craftsmanship. The latter, to the extent that no protection is sought under the RDA, as amended, obtain full copyright protection, the previous limitation of copyright term to 25 years from first marketing where such articles were the subject of mass production having been abolished by s.74 Enterprise and Regulatory Reform Act 2013. The former, although copyright works, cannot be enforced against a defendant who makes articles based on the design and so the designer must rely on the unregistered design right.

 11.4

United Kingdom unregistered design right

The United Kingdom unregistered design right is an offspring of United Kingdom copyright. Nevertheless, a detailed comparison shows that there are significant differences between the two. For convenience we set out at the end of this chapter a table of comparisons (Table 11.2). Further, in view of the divergences between United Kingdom unregistered design right on the one hand, and the RDA, Regulation and Directive on the other, we provide a further chart comparing the key features of the domestic unregistered designs régime with those derived from EU law (see Table 11.1). It has been questioned whether the United Kingdom still needs its own unregistered design right on top of that provided by the Regulation, particularly as the domestic definition of what can be protected is narrower than the EU counterpart: *Lambretta Clothing Co Ltd v Teddy Smith (UK) Ltd* [2005] RPC 88 at [41] *per* Jacob LJ. Despite this, the Intellectual Property Act 2014 has endorsed the retention of the domestic unregistered designs system by making minor amendments to Part III CDPA.

11.4.1 Criteria for protection

The composite criteria which must be satisfied for United Kingdom unregistered design right to arise are set out in s.213 CDPA. The section begins by declaring that unregistered design right is a property right which subsists in an original design and goes on to provide in s.213(2) that 'design' means 'the shape or configuration (internal or external) of the whole or part of an article'.

This wording contains the usual dichotomy, namely a three-dimensional object to which design features are applied. In *Farmer Build Ltd v Carier Bulk Handling Materials Ltd* [1999] RPC 461 at p. 483, Mummery LJ observed that the legislation does not confer protection on the article but on the *shape* of the article. An everyday article may have a shape or configuration applied to it which gives it a different appearance. Further, just as with the registered system, design right is concerned with the protection of the design not the article itself, so that if the design is applied to other articles there will be infringement. In *Electronic Techniques (Anglia) Ltd v Critchley Components Ltd* [1997] FSR 401 at p. 418 the example was given of a handle for a spoon which could equally be applied to a fork.

The statutory definition is flexible enough to cover almost any element of an article, so that, as Laddie J observed in *Ocular Sciences Ltd v Aspect Vision Care Ltd* [1997] RPC 289 at p. 422, in the case of a teapot the design could relate to the whole pot, the lid, the spout, the handle, the shape of the interior and so on. There is no need for the design to have artistic merit or eye appeal; it may not be visible during normal use of the article and it may (possibly) even be invisible to the naked eye. There is nothing to stop protection being conferred on simple shapes as long as the design satisfies the other criteria in s.213. In *Sales v Stromberg* [2006] FSR 89 the claimant, who was a practitioner of complementary medicine, designed two pendants in the shape of a double and triple spiral which were to hold imploded water, said to have a beneficial effect on the wearer. It was held that as a matter of principle, a simple geometric shape was capable of being protected as a design.

11.4.1.1 Positive aspects of the definition

Two elements in ss.213(1) and (2) require further elaboration, namely 'article' and 'shape or configuration'.

Article

The starting point is the word 'article'. This, as indicated earlier, means that the section is concerned with something which is three-dimensional, although as Jacob LJ pointed out in *Lambretta Clothing Co Ltd v Teddy Smith (UK) Ltd*, even something which is perceived as being 'flat' or two-dimensional (such as a sheet of paper) can be an article. Examples of 'articles' include cases for mobile phones (*Parker v Tidball* [1997] FSR 680) and contact lenses (*Ocular Sciences Ltd v Aspect Vision Care Ltd*). Even kitchen units can be articles although the whole fitted kitchen will not be: *Mark Wilkinson Furniture v Woodcraft Designs Radcliffe Ltd* [1998] FSR 63.

Shape or configuration

The word 'shape', it is said, suggests outward appearance or external form. More problematic is the word 'configuration'. In *Mackie Designs Inc v Behringer Specialised Studio Equipment (UK) Ltd* Pumfrey J thought that the word meant 'the relative arrangement of the various parts of an article to each other'. In *Scholes Windows Ltd v Magnet Ltd*, [2002] FSR 172 at [37] (a case concerned with replacement windows), Mummery LJ thought that the definition of design did not incorporate the nature or purpose of the article itself, nor its material structure. Hence the fact that the replacement windows were made of u-PVC rather than wood had no bearing on whether they qualified for protection. Nevertheless, it has been suggested that the properties of the material from which the article is made may contribute to its configuration. In *Block v Bath Aqua Glass Ltd* (Decision O/128/06, 22 May 2006), the UKIPO held that the juxtaposition of two or more differently coloured pieces of transparent glass was part of the configuration of some jewellery.

Originality

Just as with copyright, the key element in the definition is the requirement of originality. According to s.213(4), 'original' means '[not] **commonplace** in the design field in question at the time of its creation'. Despite this specific wording, the Court of Appeal departed from the language of the CDPA in *Farmer Build Ltd v Carier Bulk Handling Materials Ltd* and declared that 'original' bears the normal copyright meaning of 'not copied', so that the 'not commonplace' requirement is to be considered *separately and subsequently* to proof of originality (see also *Magmatic Ltd v PMS International Ltd* [2013] EWHC 1925). Consequently, even if the design is not copied, it may still lack protection for being 'commonplace'. The court added that given the already restrictive nature of design right, 'commonplace' should be interpreted narrowly. It is for the claimant to prove originality, but it is for the defendant to show that the design is commonplace in the United Kingdom. The phrase 'not commonplace' was suggested by Laddie J in *Ocular Sciences Ltd v Aspect Vision Care Ltd* to mean 'trite, trivial, common-or-garden, hackneyed, or of the type which would excite no peculiar attention in those in the relevant art'.

The nature of the comparative exercise undertaken when deciding whether a design is commonplace was explained by Mummery LJ in *Farmer Build Ltd v Carier Bulk Handling Materials Ltd*. The starting point is to identify the design field in question. In *Farmer Build* it was said that this should not be drawn too narrowly, whilst Jacob LJ in *Lambretta Clothing Co Ltd v Teddy Smith (UK) Ltd* (at [45]) stated that a reasonably broad approach was called for. In *Farmer Build* the design field was stated to be slurry separators (the subject matter of the claimant's design) rather than agricultural equipment but in *Scholes Windows*, the design field was declared to be not replacement u-PVC windows, but replacement *Victorian* u-PVC windows. By contrast, in *Rolawn Ltd v Turfmech Machinery Ltd* [2008] RPC 663, a case concerning a design for a wide area mower, Mann J concluded that the relevant design field was not mowers but agricultural machinery in general. It will thus be apparent that the court's choice of design field may well affect the outcome of the case.

thinking point
Does the wording of s.213(2) CDPA assist in determining what can be the subject matter of unregistered design right under United Kingdom law?

thinking point
Is the way in which the courts determine the relevant design field when deciding whether a design is commonplace always consistent?

The next step in the *Farmer Build* test is to compare the claimant's design with similar articles in the same field of design made by other unconnected persons (ie what is already 'out there'), taking into account (with the help of expert evidence) similarities and differences, but making the comparison objectively. The defendant's design is not considered at this stage of the comparison. Case law has decided that 'commonplace' is limited geographically to what is known to designers in the United Kingdom, but there is no temporal limitation, so that old designs can be taken into account: *Dyson Ltd v Qualtex* [2006] RPC 769. However, the Intellectual Property Act 2014 amends s.213(4) by specifying that 'commonplace' applies to **qualifying countries** as defined in s.217(4). It is possible for design right to exist in a combination of features which individually are commonplace but when amalgamated are significantly different to what is in the design field: *Ultraframe UK Ltd v Clayton and others* [2003] RPC 435 at p. 457. Similarly, the overall design for an article may not be commonplace, even though individual features are: *Rolawn Ltd v Turfmech Machinery Ltd*.

11.4.1.2 Negative aspects of the definition: exclusions

According to *Ultraframe UK Ltd v Clayton and others* [2003] RPC 435 at p. 457 the correct approach is to subtract from the design those features which fall within the exclusions, then apply the 'not commonplace' test to what is left in order to identify the relevant design. For ease of understanding we have already considered the meaning of 'not commonplace' as part of the positive aspect of originality, but the advice of the court in *Ultraframe* should be remembered. Further, as *Copinger & Skone-James on Copyright* (16th edn) points out (at 13.55), these exclusions only operate to exclude design right from the types of features listed in s.213(3), so that where the design comprises a number of features, some of which fall within these exclusions and some which do not, this does not mean that design right cannot subsist in the design as a whole. It simply means that design right cannot be claimed in those excluded features *on their own*. For that reason, a claimant in an infringement action is required to identify with precision those elements of the design in which protection is sought: *A. Fulton Company Ltd v Grant Barnett & Company Ltd* [2001] RPC 257.

A method or principle of construction

According to Copinger (at 13.56), the purpose of the exclusion in s.213(3)(a) is 'to ensure that designers cannot create an effective monopoly over articles made in a particular way'. Despite this, it has been given a narrow interpretation by the Court of Appeal in *Landor & Hawa International Ltd v Azure Designs Ltd*. The exclusion does not apply merely because a design serves a functional purpose, and will only operate where it can be shown that the purpose in question cannot be achieved in any other way. The 'method of construction' exclusion was applied by Mann J in *Rolawn Ltd v Turfmech Machinery Ltd* to deny protection to the folding arms of the mower and to the placing of the fuel tank over the rear wheels of the device. Another example of where the exclusion operated to deny protection was *Bailey v Haynes* [2007] FSR 199 which concerned the design for a micromesh bait bag for carp fishing.

It has been held that s.213(3)(a) will cover choice of materials. Hence in *Christopher Tasker's Design Right References* [2001] RPC 39 the use of aluminium in sliding wardrobe doors was not protectable, and in *Farmer Build* the choice of laminated rubber to line the roller in the claimant's slurry separator was not protected even though the shape of the roller itself was. The exclusion will also deny protection to how the article is made. So in *Parker v Tidball*, the stitching on the inside of a mobile phone case was treated as a method of construction. However, where the stitching is on the outside of an article and so decorative rather than structural, it may receive protection as part of the 'shape or configuration' of the article: *A. Fulton Company Ltd v Grant Barnett & Company Ltd*.

'Must fit' and 'must match'

The underlying policy for the two exclusions set out in s.213(3)(b) is derived from the decision of the House of Lords in *British Leyland v Armstrong* discussed earlier. It has the objective of leaving the manufacturers of spare parts free to compete by making articles which are compatible with the design. The exclusion doesn't apply to other forms of copyright such as software or databases (*Mars UK Ltd v Teknowledge Ltd*). Further, the 'must fit' and 'must match' exclusions are not as broad as the 'spare parts' defence in *British Leyland v Armstrong*, as it was not Parliament's intention to deprive the designer of all protection in relation to spare parts, but only certain aspects of them: *Dyson Ltd v Qualtex*. The same case pointed out that the phrases 'must fit' and 'must match' are a somewhat imprecise shorthand for the wording of s.213(3)(b). Copinger (at [13.68]) gives an example of a design which might fall within both of these exclusions: the cap of a fountain pen might be caught by both the must fit and must match exclusion but the clip on the cap would not be.

The 'must fit' exclusion ('features of shape or configuration which enable the article to be connected to, or placed in, around or against, another article so that either article may perform its function') is primarily concerned with the 'interface' between two articles or 'things': *Ultraframe UK Ltd v Clayton* and *Dyson Ltd v Qualtex*. Some cases have considered that parts of the human body are an 'article' for this purpose, so that in *Ocular Sciences Ltd v Aspect Vision Care Ltd* the need for a contact lens to fit the eyeball was held to fall within the 'must fit' exclusion and in *Parker v Tidball*, the shape of a mobile phone was dictated by the need to fit comfortably within the user's hand.

But how precise does the 'fit' have to be? In *Amoena (UK) Ltd and Another v Trulife Ltd*, 25 May 1995, unreported, it was held that the shape of a breast prosthesis was influenced but not dictated by the shape of a bra and would have fitted a number of different bras. The exclusion did not therefore apply. The court added that the s.213(3)(b) exclusion is concerned with 'a much more precise correspondence between two articles'. Likewise, in *A. Fulton Company Ltd v Grant Barnett & Company Ltd* the court considered the need for a case to fit over a folding umbrella. Park J remarked that it would be unacceptable to construe the provision as meaning that any article which is shaped so as to cover or contain another article cannot qualify for design right. He pointed out the very precise language of the provision. It does not provide that design right cannot subsist in *an article* if it can be placed in, around, or against another article, rather it provides that design right cannot subsist in *features of shape or configuration which enable the article to be so placed*.

A further problem of interpretation has been noted by Copinger. Is the exclusion concerned with how the component parts of a composite article fit externally to *another* article, as was the case with a child's safety barrier in *Baby Dan AS v Brevi SRL* [1999] FSR 377, or is it concerned with how the components of an article fit together: *Electronic Techniques (Anglia) Ltd v Critchley Components Ltd*? Copinger argues that the approach of *Critchley* is to be preferred to that of *Baby Dan* and gives some useful examples (see 13.62) of the 'must fit' exclusion, including parts of a table lamp which would be denied protection, such as the electric socket, the fitting for the bulb, and how the lampshade is attached.

The 'must match' exclusion ('features of shape which are dependent upon the appearance of another article of which the article is intended by the designer to form an integral part') was examined in the context of Part III CDPA in *Dyson Ltd v Qualtex*. Both Mann J and the Court of Appeal relied on the registered design case of *Ford Motor Company Ltd's Design Applications* [1995] RPC 167 which concerned the identically worded exclusion found in the pre-2001 version of the RDA. *Ford* had held that in relation to the design for a car, body panels, doors, bonnet, grille, boot, bumper, instrument panel, spoiler and windscreen were all *dependent* on the appearance of the car as a composite article. However, the steering wheel, wing mirrors, wheels, wheel covers and seats were not. The key word in s.213(3)(ii)(b), according to *Dyson* (at [64]), is the word 'dependent'. The question to be asked in each case is whether the overall appearance of the article (a car) would be radically different if the replacement part (for example a door) were not the shape it is. However, the Court of Appeal added that 'design dependency' did not extend to where the replacement part was made to look like the original because of consumer preference. As Amanda Michaels explains (in 'The End of the Road for "Pattern Spare" Parts?' [2006] *EIPR* 396) this narrow interpretation enabled the claimant to sue for infringement in respect of vacuum cleaner replacement parts the appearance of which was not totally dependent on that of the original article.

Surface decoration

The final exclusion in s.213(3) is 'surface decoration'. In *Mark Wilkinson Furniture v Woodcraft Designs Radcliffe Ltd* it was explained that surface decoration can be two-dimensional (for example a drawing or a painting) or three-dimensional (grooves or beading), though in the case of the latter it is a question of degree when the decoration such as carving becomes 'an aspect' of the shape of the item and hence protectable. An illustration of the last-mentioned point can be found in *Dyson v Qualtex*, where it was held that grooves on the vacuum cleaner's suction wand were not surface decoration but part of the shape of the article as their function was to give a better grip.

Surface decoration may be protected in its own right as an artistic work under s.4 CDPA, but in some cases may not. The choice of colours for a garment was held not to be an aspect of the shape or configuration of the garment in *Lambretta Clothing Co Ltd v Teddy Smith (UK) Ltd* and being surface decoration, was excluded from protection by s.213(3). Further, there was nothing in s.4 CDPA which could afford the designer any protection in the instant case. The court added that 'surface decoration' applied both where the surface was covered by a thin layer and where the decoration ran right through the article (such as the fabric of a garment). The outcome in *Lambretta* was the subject of comment by the Court of Appeal in *Dyson Ltd v Qualtex*, where Jacob LJ explained that normally copyright protection is the converse of design right exclusion in the case of surface decoration, but that *Lambretta* concerned the protection of colour which is not protectable under either United Kingdom copyright or United Kingdom unregistered design right (but is under the EU unregistered design right provisions). Further support for this argument can be found in *Flashing Badge Co Ltd v Groves* where the court distinguished between the shape of novelty badges and the artwork applied to their surface, the latter being protected under copyright.

thinking point

Do the exclusions from design right protection in s.213(3) CDPA strike a reasonable balance between protecting the investment of the designer and giving others the freedom to compete?

11.4.2 **Subsistence of design right**

cross reference
See section 8.3.

The rules on when design right protection arises may usefully be compared with those for copyright as there is one similarity but two major differences.

11.4.2.1 Permanent form

The requirement that the design must be in permanent form (CDPA s.213(6)) is like that for copyright, the Act providing that the recording of the design can either be in a design document or in an article made to that design.

11.4.2.2 Ownership

Our first contrast with the rules on the subsistence of copyright occurs in relation to the ownership of the design. These rules, which are intertwined with those on qualification for protection, must be applied in strict sequence and permit no flexibility. The combined effect of CDPA ss.214 and 215 is that the designer is treated as the creator (ie the **author**). Further, the designer is also (as under copyright) treated as the first owner *unless* there is:

- a contract of employment, in which case the employer will be first owner; or if not, then,
- the person who first marketed the design in a qualifying country is first owner, provided that person is a qualifying person.

Whilst an employer will own the copyright in the case of works created in the course of employment, there is no equivalent in copyright law of the person who first markets goods becoming the owner of the right.

317

11.4.2.3 Qualification for protection

The complex rules on ownership of design right have their counterpart in ss.213 and 218 to 220 CDPA which set out how a design qualifies for United Kingdom design right protection. The narrow scope of these provisions should be contrasted with the breadth of the copyright rules for qualification for protection.

Under s.213(5), the designer, or his employer must be a **qualifying person**, or else first marketing must be by a qualifying person within a qualifying country. If one turns to ss.218 to 220, it becomes apparent that these sections must be applied in a precise order. If the design was not created in the course of employment, then the designer must be a qualifying person (s.218). However, if the design was created in the course of employment, the employer must be a qualifying person. Finally, if neither of these applies, then the first marketing must occur in a qualifying country and be by a qualifying person.

thinking point
Given that unregistered design right is meant to be the 'offspring' of copyright, are the different rules on subsistence justified?

The precise order of ss.218–220 CDPA is exacerbated by the extremely narrow definitions of 'qualifying person' and 'qualifying country', both of which should be contrasted with their equivalent meanings under copyright. A 'qualifying person' must be a citizen of or *habitual* resident in the United Kingdom or an EEA Contracting State or a state listed in the relevant statutory instrument (the Designs (Convention Countries) Order (SI 1994/3219), as amended) or a company incorporated in or having substantial business activity in the United Kingdom or an EEA Contracting State or a state listed in the Order. Because unregistered design right is not covered by the **WTO TRIPs Agreement**, nor by the **Paris Convention**, the list of countries in the Designs (Convention Countries) Order is very short and basically confined to those which provide reciprocal protection for United Kingdom nationals. The net effect is that non-European designers are denied protection: *Mackie Designs Inc v Behringer Specialised Studio Equipment (UK) Ltd*.

The effect of the provisions on qualification for and ownership of unregistered design right in United Kingdom law can be illustrated diagrammatically: see Diagram 11.3.

Diagram 11.3

Subsistence and ownership of unregistered design rights

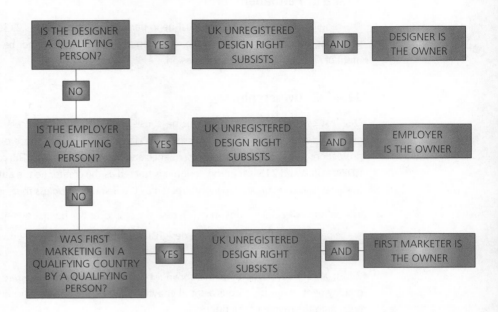

11.4.3 **Duration of design right protection**

The final contrast to be made between design right and copyright is the length of the term of protection. Section 216 CDPA states that the basic term is 15 years from the end of the year in which the design was first recorded or the end of the year in which the design was first manufactured, whichever is first. However, if marketing occurs anywhere in the world within five years of that date, the duration of protection is reduced to 10 years from first marketing. Further, the design right is subject to **licences of right** in the last five years of protection, which means that any potential infringer is able instead to demand a **licence** from the owner, the terms of such licence being settled by the UKIPO (CDPA s.237). In reality, the true term of protection is five years from when articles made to the design were first marketed, a period only marginally longer than the three-year term granted to EU unregistered designs.

11.4.4 **Infringement**

Infringement of United Kingdom unregistered design right has much in common with copyright infringement, yet in two key respects is somewhat narrower.

11.4.4.1 Similarities

Just like copyright infringement, the essence of design right infringement is derivation so that independent creation will always be a defence: *Ocular Sciences Ltd v Aspect Vision Care*

Ltd. Likewise, the rights accorded to the owner are subdivided into primary (CDPA s.226) and secondary infringement, with the latter (CDPA s.227) encompassing the usual dealings in infringing copies and requiring the requisite knowledge on the part of the defendant. Broadly speaking, the remedies for design right infringement mirror those for copyright infringement, except that there is no equivalent to the 'self-help' ability to seize infringing copies and there is no criminal liability for design right infringement. The defendant's innocence, whilst not negating liability, can affect the award of **damages**, so that an innocent primary infringer cannot be made to pay damages, and in the case of innocent secondary infringement, damages are limited to the amount of a reasonable royalty (CDPA s.233). Where there is an infringement action in the last five years of the right, the infringer can undertake to take a licence of right (CDPA ss.237–239).

11.4.4.2 Differences

There are, however, three key differences between copyright and design right infringement. First, there is only one restricted act of primary infringement in s.226, namely reproducing, directly or indirectly, articles to that design for commercial purposes or making a design document for the purpose of enabling such articles to be made. Primary infringement therefore has to involve copying for profit. There is no liability for issuing copies of the design, nor for communicating the design to the public. Second, the test for liability differs from that for copyright.

> **case close-up**
>
> **C & H Engineering v F Klucznik** [1992] FSR 421
>
> The reason for this difference was explained by Aldous J in *C & H Engineering v F Klucznik* [1992] FSR 421 at p. 428 where he stated that the wording of s.226 required the defendant 'to produce articles exactly or substantially to that design'. Therefore, assuming that there has been copying, the comparison to be made is between the design document and the alleged infringement to see whether, viewed through the eyes of the person to whom the design is directed, the infringing article is made exactly or substantially to that design. In contrast, therefore, to the test for copyright infringement set out by Lord Millett in *Designers' Guild Ltd v Russell Williams (Textiles) Ltd* at [39–41], what matters is overall similarity rather than substantial taking.

thinking point

Are the differences between United Kingdom copyright and United Kingdom design right with regard to the test for infringement justified?

Some decisions did adopt a different approach from that in *Klucznik*, in particular *Mark Wilkinson Furniture v Woodcraft Designs Radcliffe Ltd* and *Mackie Designs Inc v Behringer Specialised Studio Equipment (UK) Ltd*. Both chose to follow the *Designers' Guild* test by requiring there to be substantial taking. However, the matter would appear to be beyond doubt now as the Court of Appeal has confirmed that because of the difference in wording between CDPA s.16 and CDPA s.226, *Klucznik* is the correct test for design right infringement: *L Woolley Jewellers Ltd v A & A Jewellery Ltd* [2003] FSR 255.

The Intellectual Property Act 2014 has added new defences of private acts, experiments and teaching; and use on ships and aircraft temporarily within the jurisdiction; so as to reflect certain copyright and RDA exceptions.

cross reference
See section 9.2.4.

cross reference
See further chapter 2.

The final difference is that unlike copyright, but like other forms of **industrial property** (patents, trade marks and designs) there is a remedy for groundless threats to sue for design right infringement (CDPA s.253), as illustrated by *Quads4Kids v Campbell* [2006] EWHC 2482.

Summary

This chapter has explained:

- the choices available to a designer under United Kingdom law;

- the key features of the registered designs system;

- the extent to which copyright can be used to protect the appearance of an article; and

- United Kingdom unregistered design right.

Reflective question

The United Kingdom unregistered design right has proved to lack clarity, indeed it is unnecessarily complex. By contrast, the EU designs régime offers far better protection. For this reason, it would be best to abolish the former so that designers can rely on the latter.

Discuss.

Annotated further reading

Bently, L. and Coulthard, A. 'From the Commonplace to the Interface: Five Cases on Unregistered Design Right' [1997] *EIPR* 401
Reviews some of the early decisions on United Kingdom unregistered design right.

Bird, R. 'Registered Community Design: Early Decisions of OHIM Invalidity Division' [2006] *EIPR* 297
Reviews those cases which have so far given guidance as to the likely interpretation of the Regulation.

Garnett et al (ed) *Copinger & Skone-James on Copyright* (16th edn), ch 13

This practitioner reference work contains a comprehensive account of United Kingdom and EU unregistered design right, with useful examples of how the statutory provisions might apply to everyday articles.

Headdon, T. 'Community Design Right Infringement: an Emerging Consensus or a Difference Overall Impression' [2007] *EIPR* 336

Analyses some of the early infringement cases decided by national courts under the Regulation.

Michaels, A. 'The End of the Road for "Pattern Spare" Parts?' [2006] *EIPR* 396

Analyses the Court of Appeal's decision in *Dyson v Qualtex*.

Peris, J.J.I. 'Registered Community Design: The First Two-Year Balance from an Insider's Perspective' [2006] *EIPR* 146

Analyses the statistical data for the first two years' operation of OHIM and considers how the Invalidity Division and Board of Appeal have interpreted key words and phrases in the Regulation (the author is a member of OHIM's Invalidity Division and hence is best placed to give an overview of OHIM's case law).

Table 11.1

Table of comparisons: United Kingdom registered and unregistered designs compared

	UK registered designs	UK unregistered design right
Subject matter	A product or part of a product	An article or part of an article
Definition	The appearance of the whole or a part of a product resulting from the features of the lines, contours, colours, shape, texture or materials of the product or its ornamentation (RDA s.1(2))	The shape or configuration (whether internal or external) of the whole or part of an article (CDPA s.213(2))
Essential requirements	Novelty and individual character (RDA s.1B)	Original and not commonplace (CDPA s.213(4))
Exclusions	Shapes dictated by technical function and 'must fit' features (RDA s.1C) Designs contrary to public policy (RDA s.1D) Designs consisting of specially protected emblems (RDA Sch.A1) Designs conflicting with earlier rights (RDA s.11ZA)	A method of construction 'Must fit' features 'Must match' features Surface decoration(CDPA s.213(3))
Qualification for protection	The applicant must be the person claiming to be the owner of the design (RDA s.2)	The designer or employer must be a national of or habitually resident or incorporated in the UK, the EEA, or a designated country or first marketing must occur in a qualifying country (CDPA ss.217–220 plus SI 1994/3219)
Ownership	The designer or the designer's employer (RDA s.2)	The designer or the designer's employer or the first person to market articles in a qualifying country (CDPA s.215)
Duration	25 years from the date of filing providing the five-yearly renewal fees are paid (RDA s.8)	15 years from first recordal in a design document, but if marketed anywhere in the world within the first five years, then 10 years from first marketing, with licences of right available during the last five years (CDPA s.216)
Infringement	The exclusive right to use the design, ie making, offering, putting on the market, importing, exporting or using a product in which the design is incorporated or stocking such a product (RDA s.7)	Reproducing, directly or indirectly, articles to the design for commercial purposes (CDPA s.226) (primary infringement) and importing, possessing, selling, hiring, offering, infringing articles with knowledge in the course of a business (CDPA s.227) (secondary infringement)
Defences to infringement	Private and non-commercial use, experimental use, reproduction for teaching purposes, use on ships or aircraft temporarily within the UK, intra-EU exhaustion of rights, repair of a complex product (RDA s.7A)	Private and non-commercial use, experimental use, reproduction for teaching purposes, use on ships or aircraft temporarily within the UK (CDPA s.224A and s.224B)

Table 11.2

Table of comparisons: copyright and unregistered designs compared

	Copyright	Unregistered design right
Definition	Graphic work, photograph, sculpture, collage, work of architecture, work of artistic craftsmanship (CDPA s.4)	The shape or configuration (whether internal or external) of the whole or part of an article (CDPA s.213(2))
Essential requirement	Original (CDPA s.1(1))	Original and not commonplace (CDPA s.213(4))
Form	Recorded in permanent form (case law)	Recorded in a design document or an article must have been made to the design (CDPA s.213(6))
Qualification for protection	The author must be a national of, domiciled in, or resident in the UK, a country to which the Act extends, or a country to which the Act applies (ie a Berne, UCC or WTO Contracting State) at the relevant time or else the work must first be published in the UK, a country to which the Act extends, or a country to which the act applies (ie a Berne, UCC or WTO Contracting State) (CDPA ss.153–159)	The designer or employer must be a national of or habitually resident or incorporated in the UK, the EEA, or a designated country or first marketing must have been in a qualifying country (CDPA ss.217–220 plus SI 1994/3219).
Ownership	The author is first owner, unless the work was created in the course of employment, in which case the employer is the owner (CDPA s.11)	The designer or employer or the first person to market articles in a qualifying country (CDPA s.215)
Duration	Author's life plus 70 years (CDPA s.12)	15 years from first recordal in a design document, but if marketed anywhere in the world within the first five years, then 10 years from first marketing, with licences of right available during the last five years (CDPA s.216)
Primary infringement	Copying, issuing copies, communicating the work (CDPA ss.17, 18 and 20)	Reproducing, directly or indirectly, articles to the design for commercial purposes (CDPA s.226)
Secondary infringement	Importing, possessing, selling, hiring, offering, exhibiting infringing articles with knowledge in the course of a business (CDPA ss.22 and 23)	Importing, possessing, selling, hiring, offering, infringing articles with knowledge in the course of a business (CDPA s.227)

Part 6

Trade marks

Introduction to trade marks

Learning objectives

Upon completion of this chapter, you should have acquired:

- knowledge of the ways trade marks were used in the past;
- knowledge of the way trade mark law developed in the United Kingdom;
- an appreciation of the differences between trade marks and other forms of intellectual property;
- an understanding of the various functions which trade marks perform and of judicial attitudes towards those functions; and
- an understanding of the impact which EU law has had on the law of registered trade marks in the United Kingdom.

Introduction

The purpose of this chapter is to deal with themes which recur throughout the chapters which follow, dealing with passing off, and with trade mark registrability, infringement and exhaustion of rights. We consider the historical uses of trade marks, showing how, in some ways, little has changed about how trade marks form a bridge between the manufacturer and consumer of goods. The development of trade mark law is set out, with the objective of emphasising the cultural change which has occurred since 1994 in United Kingdom trade mark law as a result of EU reforms.

Next, we compare and contrast trade marks with other forms of intellectual property. This comparison will show that trade marks do not always fit in with the assumptions which underlie intellectual property protection. They do not reward creativity nor provide an incentive to innovate. Instead, their justification lies in the economics of the consumer society. Many (for example, Naomi Klein) would argue that the rise of consumerism has led to an overvaluation of trade marks, with the rights of the trade mark owner prevailing over the interests of the consumer and of society itself.

We also examine the commercial functions fulfilled by trade marks in the age of the consumer, with the objective of showing the dilemma inherent in trade mark law. If trade mark function is simply to tell the consumer about the commercial origin of the goods, this has a restrictive effect on the ability to register trade marks, and to protect them through the action for infringement. If, however, trade mark protection is enhanced to reflect the selling power of brands as image carriers, then they become barriers to entry and impede competition.

thinking point
Do you think that trade marks, as image carriers, are overvalued?

328

12.1 The history of trade marks

12.1.1 Ancient use of trade marks

The use of **trade marks** developed long before their legal protection. It is not possible to pinpoint accurately when the concept of ownership first evolved, nor when mankind first began to trade by bartering or selling goods, but it is reasonable to assume that the use of a symbol or sign to designate either ownership or commercial origin must have developed contemporaneously with these events. Ancient cave paintings in France show how trade marks were first used to claim ownership of cattle by the practice of burning (or branding) the hides of the animals with a symbol, the term 'brand name' today being a relic of this ancient custom. The use of a trade mark to designate the trade origin of goods goes back furthest in ancient China, where marks are thought to have been placed on pottery as long ago as 3000 BC. A good deal of information is available about ancient pottery, because it lasts almost indefinitely. Excavations from ancient Egypt, Asia Minor, India and Crete have all revealed potters' marks, and indeed marks used by other crafts, notably goldsmiths, ironsmiths and brickmakers.

Nevertheless, it is Greek and Roman antiquities which are most revealing of the historical background of trade marks. In Greece, vases, jars and pottery objects were marked in various ways, for example, amphorae used to export wine were marked with the name of the maker, the place of origin, and an official mark, the latter presumably signifying fitness to drink. Thousands of Roman trade marks have been catalogued, particularly those used on clay lamps. Roman goods were exported throughout the Roman Empire and their remains have been found in numerous countries across Europe and beyond. Even bread found in the ruins of Pompeii was found to bear the maker's stamp.

12.1.2 Medieval use of trade marks

Use of trade marks in the Middle Ages falls again into these two broad categories, namely marks to show ownership and merchants' marks. Schechter (in his seminal work, *Historical Foundations of Trade Mark Law*, Columbia University Press, New York, 1925) describes these as proprietary and production marks.

12.1.2.1 Proprietary marks

The use of the proprietary mark on goods (ie branding them as a means of showing ownership) can be considered similar to the adoption of heraldic devices. The practical significance of such branding becomes clear when it is remembered the frequency with which goods might be affected by piracy or shipwreck. Where goods had been so lost in transit, the seller or original owner could reclaim them, if they were later recovered, by proving that they bore his mark. Throughout the trading cities of Northern Europe, laws were passed enabling merchants to get back lost or stolen goods upon proof of entitlement to their mark. In England, Stat. 27 Ed III Chap 13 (1353) facilitated the recovery of goods in this manner, the statute being invoked as late as *Hamilton v Davis* (1771) 5 Burr 2732. Here, Lord Mansfield held that the **claimant** was entitled to recover certain hogsheads of tallow, lost en route from Ireland to Liverpool, from the defendant, even though it couldn't be established how the defendant had acquired the goods.

12.1.2.2 Production marks

When considering the use of production marks, two things need to be remembered, first the overwhelming power of the Craft Guilds, and the fact that the public bought goods direct from the maker. Not only in England, but throughout continental Europe, virtually all industry up until the fifteenth century was organised in towns and cities by the Guilds, who, in return for the grant of a monopoly over a particular product, saw it as their function to preserve high standards of quality. Goods were marked so that poor workmanship could be identified and punished. Consequently, as a form of consumer protection, there were numerous national, local and Guild regulations providing for the compulsory marking of goods, and setting out criminal penalties for breach. Examples include breadmakers, brewers, weavers and, of course, gold and silversmiths.

12.1.3 The rise of the age of the consumer

How then did the trade mark evolve from the production mark, designed to create collective **goodwill** for the Guild, to the asset mark of today, creating individual goodwill for the trader in question? Again, the answer lies in trading conditions. So long as goods were bought by the consumer dealing directly and face to face with the craftsman there was no need for a trade mark as an indication of origin (although one was needed as a guarantee of quality). Trading in the Middle Ages was by and large very localised, with consumers and craftsmen living in the same community, although as Schechter explains, cloth and cutlery were two trades which from a relatively early date were located in only a handful of towns, so that the resulting goods had, of necessity, to be transported over long distances to reach consumers. Moreover, with the craftsman usually having his place of business in the same vicinity as others of the same type and being closely controlled by his Guild, it was difficult for him to acquire any individual goodwill or indulge in any real form of competition, whether fair or unfair. It is only when goods of a durable nature are transported that the trade mark as a mark of origin acquires any significance.

The decisive event, therefore, which changes trade marks from what Schechter calls liability marks to asset marks, is the Industrial Revolution. Once technology enables goods to be mass produced in a mill or factory, and then transported to cities many miles away, the producer and consumer are separated. The maker's mark therefore has a different role to fulfil. It is needed to identify the source from which satisfactory goods have come. Nevertheless, the explosion in the use and exploitation of trade marks does not really happen until the latter part of the twentieth century. What matters is the way in which retailing habits change, from selling goods in small, personalised outlets (the local shop), to selling in sophisticated, multi-national hypermarkets offering thousands of competing brands of prepackaged, 'designer' goods from around the world. The advent of internet shopping is likely to have a further impact on the role of the trade mark.

thinking point
How does the use of trade marks today compare with their use in previous times?

12.2 The development of United Kingdom trade mark law

12.2.1 Trade mark law before 1875

Aldous LJ in *Marks & Spencer plc and others v One in a Million Ltd* [1998] 4 All ER 476 tells us that the first ever reported trade mark case is *Southern v How* (1618) Popham 143. Close examination of the case (which has five different reports) shows that it has nothing whatsoever to do with the law of trade marks, being an agency dispute. As Schechter tells us, the only link with trade marks lies in an irrelevant remark by the judge, Doderidge J, in which he recalls a case heard many years earlier about the counterfeiting of a trader's mark. Reported trade mark cases do not actually appear until the nineteenth century, and then, as one would expect of that time, they fall into two groups, those decided at common law and those decided in equity.

12.2.1.1 Common law cases

At common law, the protection of trade marks evolved from the action on the case for deceit. It took a few attempts before the principle was clearly established. So, for example, in *Sykes v Sykes* (1824) 3 B & C 543, the court held that it was important that the defendant placed his imitation of the claimant's mark on goods which were of inferior quality, whilst in *Blofeld v Payne* (1833) 4 B & Ad 409 the court said that what mattered was the defendant's fraudulent intent rather than the quality of the goods. Similarly, in *Crawshay v Thompson* (1842) 4 Man & G 358 the court stressed that if the defendant had acted innocently, there could be no liability even if the mark he had placed on his goods was confusingly similar to that of the claimant. What mattered, therefore, was not the quality of the goods, nor the effect of the statement on the consumer, but whether the defendant *intended* fraudulently to supplant the claimant.

12.2.1.2 Cases in equity

It took a little while for the Court of Chancery to catch up with the courts of common law. In *Blanchard v Hill* (1742) 2 Atk 484, Lord Hardwicke refused to grant an **injunction** to restrain the defendant from placing the claimant's trade mark on playing cards for the simple reason that to give protection would create an unfair monopoly. Freedom to trade was likewise used as the reason for denying equitable relief by Lord Eldon in *Cruttwell v Lye* (1810) 17 Ves 335. However, it was eventually recognised that the 'get up' of a business could be protected in *Knott v Morgan* (1836) 2 Keen 213, where Lord Langdale MR restrained the defendant from using the same words, colour scheme and lettering on his omnibuses as were already used by the claimant in his rival enterprise.

A significant shift in thinking occurred in *Millington v Fox* (1838) 3 My & Cr 338, where Lord Cottenham granted an injunction on the ground simply that a trade mark was 'property', treating it as conferring the same rights on its owner as entitlement to a piece of land. Use of the mark by another amounted to trespass. The defendant's state of mind was irrelevant. It was sufficient that the claimant's mark had been reproduced on the defendant's steel bars.

Thereafter, Chancery cases fall into two groups. There are those where it was held that likelihood of deception was a precondition to equitable relief and there are those which treated trade marks as property. An example of where the Court of Chancery followed the common law and insisted on deception is *Perry v Trufitt* (1842) 6 Beav 66. However, this case and others like it (such as *Croft v Day* (1843) 7 Beav 84 and *Burgess v Burgess* (1853) 3 De G, M & G 896) tell us that equity differed from the common law in its approach to deception, concentrating not on the defendant's state of mind but on the *effect* of the false statement on the consumer. An example of the property approach is *Hall v Barrows* (1863) 4 De G, J & S 150, where the Lord Chancellor, Lord Westbury, treated trade marks as analogous to **patents** and copyright for the purposes of **infringement**.

12.2.2 Trade mark law after 1875

After 1875, the developments are legislative rather than judicial. There were two key events in that year.

First, the Judicature Acts 1873–5 reorganised the court structure, creating a single High Court of Judicature. Within that, the Chancery Division was to have responsibility, *inter alia*, for patents, **copyright** and trade marks. The Acts also declared that where there was a conflict between the rules of common law and equity, equity was to prevail. In the case of protection of trade marks, the House of Lords, in *Reddaway v Banham* [1896] AC 199 and *Spalding v Gamage* (1915) 32 RPC 273, based its statements of principle for the tort of **passing off** firmly on the thinking in *Perry v Trufitt*, stressing the importance of the effect of the defendant's false

cross reference
See further chapter 13.

statement on the mind of the purchaser. Both cases deny that trade marks, at common law, are a species of property in their own right. Instead, the right of property which is protected is the goodwill of the claimant's business.

Second, there was the Trade Marks Registration Act 1875. As its name indicates, this introduced (after much lobbying by business) the first system of registration of trade marks. Thereafter, the scheme of protection for trade marks in the United Kingdom is divided into two, namely the registration system, and the tort of passing off for unregistered (or 'common law') trade marks. The 1875 Act can be regarded as primarily procedural in its effect (that is, it provided a system of registration but did not change the underlying case law concept of a trade mark) and was followed by a string of subsequent Acts (10 in total). The most important of these were the Trade Marks Act 1905 (which provided a statutory definition of a trade mark for the first time) and the Trade Marks Act 1938 (which provided for marks to be capable of **assignment** separately from the goodwill of the business and for marks to be **licensed**).

12.2.3 **Reform of the 1938 Act**

Reform of the Trade Marks Act 1938 was considered in detail by the Mathys Committee in 1974 (*British Trade Mark Law and Practice* Cmnd 5601), but the only change recommended by that Committee which was implemented was the introduction of the registration of service marks as a result of the combined effect of Trade Marks (Amendment) Act 1984 and the Patents, Designs and Marks Act 1986. Even this reform was horrendously complicated, with two separate versions of the 1938 Act existing side-by-side, one dealing with marks for goods and one dealing with marks for services.

The Government White Paper *Reform of Trade Marks Law* (Cm 1203) in September 1990 identified a number of reasons why the trade mark system was in urgent need of reform:

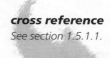

cross reference
See section 1.5.1.1.

- the 1938 Act was horribly out of date and having two parallel versions made it unwieldy, in addition to which it was written in language which judges had frequently criticised for being obscure. The fact that the 1938 Act was stated to be a consolidating measure meant recourse to earlier legislation or even pre-1875 case law, surely not appropriate at the end of the twentieth century;

- the United Kingdom had to fulfil its obligations to **WIPO** by ratifying the latest (1967) version of the **Paris Convention** for the Protection of Industrial Property 1883 and by joining the Protocol Relating to the **Madrid Agreement** Concerning the International Registration of Marks 1989;

- most important, however, were the United Kingdom's EU obligations which required it to implement the First Trade Marks Directive (Council Directive 89/104/EEC of 21 December 1988 on the approximation of the laws of Member States relating to trade marks [1989] OJ L 40/1) ('the Directive') (now codified as Directive 2008/95/EC of the European Parliament and of the Council of 22 October 2008 [2008] OJ L 299/25) and to provide for formal links between the United Kingdom Trade Mark Registry and the **Office for Harmonisation in the Internal Market (Trade Marks and Designs) ('OHIM')**, the body responsible for running the **EU trade mark system** under the Community Trademark Regulation (Council Regulation (EC) 40/94 of 20 December 1993 [1994] OJ L 11/1, now codified as Council Regulation (EC) No 207/2009 of 26 February 2009 on the Community trade mark [2009] OJ L 78/1) ('the Regulation').

The net result of the White Paper was the Trade Marks Act 1994 ('TMA'). Given the pressures for reform, one might assume that the Act would revolutionise the law of trade marks. Unsurprisingly, United Kingdom judges have, in many instances, continued to cling to principles developed under previous Acts. If anything, the driving force for change has been provided by European institutions.

12.2.4 Conclusion: the historical legacy

The preceding historical account shows several things. First, the way in which trade marks are *used* has, in some ways, changed little, even though trading conditions today are far removed from those of previous times. Although medieval use was primarily to guarantee quality, use since the Industrial Revolution has been to tell the consumer about the origin of the goods. Trade marks have always been messengers. They are the communications link between the manufacturer and ultimate consumer (not necessarily the purchaser) of the goods.

The legal history of trade marks shows that the principles articulated in the early cases continue to influence today's law. There is the perennial concern that trade marks create unfair monopolies. Further, the perception of early cases that the key to the protection of trade marks was the effect of the defendant's false statement on the consumer rather than the right of property in the mark remains today. It is bound up in the judicial concern not to create monopolies. In turn, it raises one of the underlying debates in the law of trade marks, namely whether trade mark law exists to protect consumers or the trade mark owner. If the answer is that the law protects the owner of the mark, how then is the balance to be struck between protecting brands and ensuring free competition?

thinking point

Given the pressures for reform, and the importance of brands to the consumer economy, is it surprising that the 1994 Act was the first major piece of trade mark legislation for over 50 years?

12.3 The nature of trade marks

12.3.1 Key characteristics

12.3.1.1 Exclusivity

Like other forms of intellectual property, the TMA declares (in s.9) that registration of a trade mark confers exclusive rights on its owner. Thus as with patents and copyright, trade marks confer negative rights to stop others (*Inter Lotto (UK) Ltd v Camelot Group plc* [2003] 3 All ER 191).

12.3.1.2 Proprietary nature

The TMA further states in ss.2 and 27 (in contrast to the historical debate) that registered trade marks and indeed, pending applications for trade marks, are property rights. The conclusion has to be, therefore, that unregistered marks do not possess the characteristics of property, but all registered marks do. For unregistered 'common law' marks protected by passing off, the property right resides in the goodwill of the business in which the mark has been used.

But are trade marks really proprietary in nature? Certainly, registered marks *look* like any other form of intangible, personal property. They can be bought and sold, permission can be granted to others to use them, they can be mortgaged, and a value can be placed on them (indeed, successful brand owners declare the value of trade marks in a company's balance sheet, sometimes as a means of deterring a takeover bid).

However, the entry of a trade mark on the register does not mean that its existence is guaranteed. As with any other form of registrable right, the Registry does not guarantee the **validity** of a trade mark (TMA s.70) and it is possible to apply to have a trade mark declared **invalid** under s.47 because at the time of registration it didn't comply with the Act. Further, and more significantly, a trade mark can be **revoked** for mismanagement under s.46. 'Mismanagement' basically comprises three things: that the proprietor has failed to use the mark for a given period of time (if you don't use it you lose it) or the proprietor has allowed the mark to become generic or the proprietor's conduct has caused the mark to become deceptive. As English property law does not have any concept of abandonment, the ability to revoke a trade mark suggests that as a property right it doesn't quite fit the standard model.

12.3.1.3 Monopolistic nature

Starting with *Blanchard v Hill*, there are numerous cases where judges have denied a trade mark protection on the ground that to do so would create an 'unfair monopoly'. Modern examples of such a 'knee-jerk' reaction include the House of Lords in *Re COCA COLA Trade Marks* [1986] RPC 421, where Lord Templeman asserted, without reasoning, that a bottle could not be a trade mark because of the anti-competitive effect of granting registration to a shape. Another example is the judgment of Jacob J in *British Sugar plc v James Robertson & Sons Ltd* [1996] RPC 281. Although his thoughts were no doubt coloured by the fact that the claimant's mark TREAT was highly descriptive of their product (a sweet topping) and therefore invalid, his remarks about powerful businesses seeking to close off large parts of the English language by registering undeserving trade marks are indicative of a negative attitude.

So are the judges correct in their assertions? The term 'monopoly' is used by economists to indicate that an undertaking is the only source of supply for a commodity. This is not the case with trade marks. Just because NIKE is registered for footwear doesn't mean that other companies can't make and sell trainers. They can do so as long as they adopt a different brand name for their product. If the name CROCODILE is registered for shoes, that does not prevent a television company from making a documentary about crocodiles. Perhaps it is the ease with which a trade mark can be created together with its potential duration which produces this adverse reaction.

12.3.2 Comparison with other forms of intellectual property

12.3.2.1 Overlap

Trade marks do overlap with other forms of intellectual property protection, particularly copyright and designs. For example, it is now possible to register the shape of a product as a trade mark. That shape might be a sculpture for the purposes of copyright law, or it might be a design, whether registered or unregistered. A trade mark which consists of a picture might also be a copyright **work**. In *R Griggs Group Ltd and others v Evans and others* [2005] FSR 706 it was held that artwork which combined the two previous logos for DOC MARTENS boots was a copyright work, but because it had been created so as to enable the new trade mark to be registered, there was an implied term in the contract to the effect that the artist would assign ownership of the copyright to the trade mark owner. Further, it is now possible to register a musical tune as a trade mark: Case C-283/01 *Shield Mark BV v Joost Kist* [2003] ECR I-14313. Unless the musical work is out of copyright (as it was in *Shield Mark*, where the tune was *Für Elise* by Beethoven) then there will have to be an assignment ensuring that title to the copyright is vested in the trade mark owner.

cross reference
See section 8.2.1.

However, such dual protection is not always available. Even though time and effort have been spent in creating a trade mark, this does not equate to 'skill, labour and judgement' for the purposes of copyright law, so that an invented word trade mark will not qualify as a literary work under s.3 of the CDPA.

case close-up

Exxon Corporation v Exxon Insurance Consultants International [1981] 3 All ER 241

The Court of Appeal held that the invented word EXXON, adopted by the claimant as its new corporate name and trade mark, did not qualify for copyright protection, even though several million dollars had been spent researching the new brand. The company was therefore unable to stop an unrelated organisation from adopting the same name. The case, were it to be decided today, might have a different outcome because of the broader scope of protection given to registered marks under ss.5 and 10 TMA.

12.3.2.2 Differences

Ease of creation

cross reference
See section 8.1.1.

The popular perception of copyright is that it requires the expenditure of creative effort by the author or artist (a perception which does not necessarily accord with the law). Most patents today result from huge investment in research. By contrast, almost anyone can think up a trade mark. The courts have accepted that the level of creativity can be very low (Case C-329/02 P *SAT.1 SatellitenFernsehen GmbH v OHIM (SAT.2)* [2004] ECR I-8317). Even a colour can be a trade mark. That being so, perhaps the judges are correct to speak of unfair monopolies.

Limited protection

cross reference
See section 15.3.2.

However, unlike patents and designs (which are absolute monopolies) but like copyright, the scope of protection for the trade mark owner is limited. Once a trade mark is registered, its proprietor can object to the use of the identical or similar **sign** in relation to identical, similar or dissimilar goods or services. Protection is absolute in the case of an identical sign used in relation to identical goods. However, where there is only similarity, the owner must prove that there is a likelihood of confusion on the part of consumers. Where there is no likelihood of confusion, or where the goods are dissimilar, then the owner has to show that the mark has a reputation and that the conduct of the defendant is an attempt to take unfair advantage of or cause detriment to the distinctive character or repute of the mark. Moreover, for each category of protection, it is necessary to show not only that the trade mark has been used in the course of trade, but also that it has been used 'in relation' to goods and services, and that such use affects the interests of the trade mark owner: Case C-206/01 *Arsenal Football Club v Matthew Reed* [2002] ECR I-10273. The requirement of 'trade mark use' therefore acts as a limit on the trade mark owner's monopoly.

Justification

It is in relation to why we recognise intellectual property that the biggest difference between trade marks on the one hand, and patents, designs and copyright on the other, is apparent. Patents, designs and copyright are susceptible to a number of different justifications. The trouble is that whether one believes in John Locke's labour theory, in Benthamite utilitarianism, in rewards and incentives, or the personality of the author, none works for trade marks.

cross reference
See section 1.4.

Instead, arguments in support of trade marks lie in economic theories about the importance of consumer choice. As Landes & Posner explain (in 'Trademark Law: An Economic Perspective' (1987) 30 *Journal of Law & Economics* 265), trade marks are best justified by the hypothesis that the law is trying to promote economic efficiency. Trade marks reduce consumer search costs (imagine, they say, having to ask for a jar of instant coffee without having a brand name available). Further, the protection accorded to trade marks encourages manufacturers to maintain quality, so that satisfied customers will return time and time again to buy their favourite product. Trade marks therefore promote competition.

However, although trade marks have the beneficial effect of helping consumers choose what to buy, there is a negative aspect to this. Trade marks create barriers to entry. Imagine a company wishes to launch a new brand of instant coffee. The advertising expenditure in bringing this product to the attention of customers already loyal to KENCO or NESCAFÉ would run into millions (in 1991 the then United Kingdom Monopolies and Mergers Commission estimated that it would cost £5 million to launch a new brand of coffee). Powerful brands therefore can be a disincentive to competitors.

Duration

Ironically, despite the ease of creation, and different theoretical basis, trade marks, unlike patents, designs and copyright, do not have a finite duration. Provided the owner pays the **renewal fees** promptly every 10 years, and provided there is no risk of a third party bringing a **revocation** action under TMA s.46, a trade mark could potentially last for ever. Trade Mark No 1 (the first ever to be registered under the 1875 Act) is the BASS RED TRIANGLE mark for beer. It is still in force today.

thinking point
Do the differences between trade marks and other categories of intellectual property rights mean that we should be less ready to brand them as 'unfair monopolies'?

12.4 Trade mark functions

In 1927, Frank Schechter, in his article 'The Rational Basis of Trade Mark Protection' (1927) 40 *Harv LR* 813, argued forcefully that the true function of a trade mark was 'to create and retain custom'. He further suggested that to require a claimant to show likelihood of confusion amongst consumers was too narrow a form of protection, and that the rationale of trade mark law demanded that they be protected against **dilution**, what he referred to as the gradual 'whittling away' of the mark's distinctive character.

In this section, we consider the commercial functions performed by trade marks, with the objective of deciding whether there has been legal recognition of those functions and whether Schechter's hypothesis has actually been achieved. Five possible functions can be identified.

12.4.1 **Origin function**

From the early nineteenth century, United Kingdom judges have assumed that the only function which a trade mark fulfils is to indicate to the consumer the commercial origin of the goods. But does it matter if the consumer does not know the precise identity of the business which launched the goods in the first place? According to Lindley LJ in *Powell v Birmingham Vinegar Brewery Co. Ltd* (1896) 13 RPC 235 at p. 250, a customer can be misled and can mistake one trader's goods for another even though they don't know the identity of either. The trader whose mark is imitated is 'just as much injured in his trade as if his name was known as well as his mark'. Similarly, Warrington LJ in *McDowell's Application* (1926) 43 RPC 313 at p. 337 declared that if it was shown that consumers had been misled by the defendant's mark, it didn't matter whether they did or did not know the precise source of the goods.

The Trade Marks Act 1938, in s.68, defined a trade mark as 'a mark used or proposed to be used in relation to goods for the purpose of indicating . . . a connection in the course of trade between the goods and . . . [the] proprietor'. The definition permeated all aspects of that Act, and was shown in due course to have two particularly restrictive effects.

cross reference
See further chapter 14.

First, it meant that celebrities (or rather, the successors of deceased celebrities) could not register the name of that person, because the name did not indicate the origin of the goods. In *ELVIS PRESLEY Trade Marks* [1999] RPC 567, the Court of Appeal upheld an **opposition** to the application to register the names 'Elvis' and 'Elvis Presley' on the grounds that a consumer, on seeing a bar of 'Elvis' soap would not think that it was a particular brand of soap, coming from a particular manufacturer, but that it commemorated the singer. The court did not seem concerned that to deny registrability would allow others to make free use of the ELVIS name, nor did it take into account the public perception of merchandising. It did, however, decide that the late singer's signature could be registered as a trade mark. Unfortunately, the *ELVIS PRESLEY* case, decided under the 1938 Act, appears to have been carried over into the present legislation. In both *DIANA, PRINCESS OF WALES Trade Mark* [2001] ETMR 254 and *JANE AUSTEN Trade Mark* [2000] RPC 879, the names of the two deceased individuals were held not capable of registration because they did not indicate origin, and were accordingly devoid of distinctive character under TMA s.3(1)(b). The matter has not yet been referred to the ECJ, and there must be some doubt as to whether the *ELVIS PRESLEY* decision's attitude to celebrities' names accords with the Directive's policy on registrability.

Second, the origin function, strictly applied, had significant implications for the protection accorded to the trade mark owner against infringers. In *Arsenal Football Club v Matthew Reed* [2001] RPC 922, Laddie J held that the defendant, who had sold unauthorised football merchandise from his stall, had not committed trade mark infringement. Fans, on seeing the famous Gunners' logo would not think that the scarves and T-shirts originated with the Club.

Instead, they were simply badges of allegiance. Laddie J did, however, refer the case to the ECJ, who approached the matter in an entirely different manner. In Case C-206/01 *Arsenal Football Club v Matthew Reed* [2002] ECR I-10273, the Court declared that 'the essential function of a trade mark was to guarantee the identity of origin of the marked goods or services to the consumer or end user by enabling him, without any possibility of confusion, to distinguish the goods or services from others which have another origin'. It added that the trade mark must offer a guarantee that all the goods or services bearing it have been manufactured or supplied under the control of a single undertaking responsible for their quality. Clearly, here, the defendant's clothing had not been approved by the Club, and so the guarantee offered by the trade mark was false. There had therefore been infringement. The ECJ made clear that the trade mark owner had to be protected against those who wished to take unfair advantage of the trade mark. Hence, the trade mark owner's rights, set out in the Directive and the TMA, were there to enable the owner to protect his specific interests. On the return from Luxembourg, Laddie J ([2003] 1 CMLR 382) refused to apply the ECJ's ruling, however, the Court of Appeal ([2003] RPC 696) accepted it.

cross reference
See section 15.3.2.5.

To put the matter another way, under *Arsenal*, the protection accorded to the mark reflects its functions, which in turn reflect the interests of the owner. The issue of trade mark infringement is approached from the viewpoint of the owner of the mark, not the consumer of the goods. Consequently, 'origin function' has a wider meaning under the TMA than it did under the 1938 Act, being concerned with the interests of the consumer in the quality of the goods and the interests of the proprietor in protecting the investment in the trade mark against freeriding. However, the ECJ appears to have retreated somewhat from its pro-trade mark owner views in *Arsenal*.

12.4.2 **Product differentiation function**

TMA s.1(1), based on Article 2 of the Directive, expresses the function of trade marks in a different way. It states that a trade mark means 'any sign ... which is capable of distinguishing the goods or services of one undertaking from those of other undertakings'. It might be thought that this is simply a modern reformulation of the origin function, but the ECJ appears to be saying otherwise. In Case C-299/99 *Philips Electronics BV v Remington Consumer Products* [2002] ECR I-5475, at [47–50] it asked whether the mark enabled the consumer to choose one product from another, confident that the goods had originated from one particular business which was responsible for their quality. In other words, this function reflects the economic role of trade marks (advocated by Landes & Posner) in promoting consumer choice and lowering consumer search costs.

That the product differentiation function is not the same as the origin function is supported by the way in which the ECJ has developed the notion of the average consumer as the arbiter of a range of matters under the Directive. Just as the notional **skilled addressee** is used to impart objectivity in the law of patents, so the average consumer is deployed to decide a number of issues in trade mark law. These include whether a sign has the potential to be a trade mark under Article 2, whether it falls foul of any of the **Absolute Grounds** for Refusal in Article 3, and whether it conflicts with another mark, in the context either of the **Relative Grounds** for Refusal or in the context of infringement proceedings. The consumer is also used to decide issues of revocation, in particular whether the trade mark has been allowed to become deceptive or generic. The notional consumer therefore holds a pivotal role.

12.4.3 Guarantee function

When we speak of a trade mark acting as a guarantee, the word 'guarantee' is not used necessarily in the contractual sense. Instead, we mean that the mark tells the consumer that the goods they are about to buy have the same quality as previously purchased items. 'Guarantee' therefore indicates consistency.

case close-up

Spalding v Gamage (1915) 32 RPC 273

The House of Lords in *Spalding v Gamage*, a passing off case, recognised the guarantee function of trade marks. Here the defendant had purchased a consignment of the claimant's footballs but advertised them as being of first class quality when in fact they were seconds. It was held that this misrepresentation harmed the goodwill of the claimant's business. Consumers, used to buying high quality products, would be put off from purchasing any more because of their bad experience.

Another example of the guarantee function being recognised in a passing off case is *United Biscuits (UK) Ltd v Asda Stores Ltd* [1997] RPC 513. Robert Walker J held that by deliberately copying the appearance of the wrappers in which the claimant's PENGUIN biscuits were sold, the defendant supermarket made its customers believe that its own PUFFIN biscuits had been made by the claimant and would therefore be of similar quality.

The ECJ has recognised the importance of a trade mark guaranteeing the consistency of a product in several cases dealing with the **parallel importation** of goods.

case close-up

Case C-10/89 *SA CNL-Sucal NV v Hag GF AG* [1990] ECR I-3711

Consumer expectations played a major part in its decision in Case C-10/89 *SA CNL-Sucal NV v Hag GF AG* [1990] ECR I-3711 ('*Hag II*'). As a result of government intervention after World War II, there were two versions of CAFÉ HAG decaffeinated coffee available to European consumers, one made by the original trade mark owner in Germany, the other by a company which had acquired the trade mark registration in Belgium. The ECJ thought it relevant that purchasers would be confused by the different quality and taste of the rival products. As a result, the original German owner of the mark could sue its Belgian rival owner for infringement. The fact that historically the two trade mark registrations in Belgium and Germany had been owned by the same enterprise was irrelevant.

Case C-143/00 *Boehringer Ingelheim v Swingward Ltd and Dowelhurst* [2002] ECR I-3759 shows how consumer preferences can play a part when medicines imported from another EU Member State are then reboxed or relabelled so that their instructions are available in the local language. The ECJ stated that consumers rely on the trade mark as a means of ensuring that (legitimate) goods have not been interfered with by the importer. The trade mark therefore guarantees the safety of the goods. In Case C-59/08 *Copad SA v Christian Dior Couture SA* [2009] ECR I-3421 the Court considered that the sale of luxury goods by a **licensee** to third parties which were not part of a selective distribution network might affect *the quality of the goods themselves*, thereby entitling the trade mark owner to sue the licensee for trade mark infringement under Article 8 of the Directive and negativing consent to first marketing for the purpose of the doctrine of **exhaustion of rights**. In Schechter's words, the trade mark helps to retain business.

The ruling of the ECJ in *Arsenal v Reed* also mentions the role of the trade mark in guaranteeing consistency. This guarantee, according to the Court, is an aspect of the product differentiation function found in Article 2 of the Directive.

A parallel can be drawn here between the modern role of trade marks and how they were used in medieval times. In the era of the Craft Guilds, trade marks told purchasers that goods were of a certain standard. The same is true today. There is therefore a consumer protection aspect to trade marks just as there was previously.

12.4.4 **Advertising function**

The core of Schechter's hypothesis is that the advertising function of a trade mark must be protected. He declares that 'the mark sells the goods'. Therefore, its selling power must be protected against those who wish to take unfair advantage of its reputation. In the case of successful brands, there will be many who wish to 'free-ride' on the strength of the mark.

Close examination of the ECJ's ruling in *Arsenal v Reed* indicates that the Court agrees. The ECJ stated that 'for that guarantee of origin, which constitutes the essential function of a trade mark, to be ensured, the proprietor must be protected against competitors wishing to take unfair advantage of the status and reputation of the trade mark by selling products illegally bearing it'. Although the statement is integrated into the Court's declaration that trade marks guarantee the consistency and origin of the goods, its use of the phrase 'unfair advantage' is significant.

Further, Schechter's hypothesis is part of United Kingdom law in another respect. The TMA, implementing two optional provisions in the Directive, contains in ss.5(3) and 10(3) a specific form of protection for trade marks which have a reputation. They confer on a trade mark's owner the ability either to oppose the registration of or to prevent the use in trade of an identical or similar mark which seeks to take unfair advantage of or cause detriment to the distinctive character or repute of the earlier mark. Arguably (though some would disagree) the two subsections introduce the doctrine of dilution into United Kingdom law. Dilution (as a form of harm to a trade mark with a reputation) has long been recognised in USA and Benelux trade mark law. The doctrine states that a mark with a reputation can be harmed in a number of ways. First, the mark can be 'watered down' by use on non-competing goods. Over a period of time it will lose its distinctive quality. To paraphrase Schechter, if the use of ROLLS ROYCE on lipsticks, hamburgers or steam shovels is not prevented, then the ROLLS ROYCE trade mark for cars will be undermined. Another form of harm is that a mark with a reputation can be tarnished if it is used on non-competing goods which have an unsavoury or unwholesome connotation.

case close-up

CLAERYN/KLAREIN (1976) 7 IIC 420

The best known example of tarnishing as a form of dilution is the leading Benelux Court of Justice decision of *CLAERYN/KLAREIN* (1976) 7 IIC 420. Here, the owner of the CLAERYN trade mark for Dutch gin was able to prevent Colgate using KLAREIN for a toilet cleaning liquid. Both marks were pronounced in an identical manner in Dutch. The court thought that consumers would not wish to be reminded of bleach when drinking a glass of high quality gin.

Last, a competitor may 'free-ride' on a mark with a reputation by using an identical or similar mark as a means of gaining quick access to the market.

At first, United Kingdom courts failed to understand the elements of TMA ss.5(3) and 10(3). In *Baywatch Production Co Inc v The Home Video Channel* [1997] FSR 2, it was held that proof of likelihood of confusion was required and that viewers of the BAYWATCH television series would not be misled by a soft-porn programme, BABEWATCH, shown on cable television. The meaning of the two subsections was explained by the ECJ in Case C-251/95 *Sabel BV v Puma AG* [1997] ECR I-6191. It stated that likelihood of confusion is not required, as the provisions pursue a different objective, namely that of protecting marks with a reputation.

case close-up

Case C-487/07 *L'Oréal SA v Bellure NV* [2009] ECR I-5185

The Court confirmed its ruling in *Sabel v Puma* in the later decision of Case C-487/07 *L'Oréal SA v Bellure NV* [2009] ECR I-5185. It clarified that the owner of such a mark is protected (provided all the other elements of the provision are satisfied) against the three types of harm mentioned earlier, namely the 'whittling away' or 'blurring' of the mark's distinctive character, 'tarnishment' or 'degradation' where the mark is used by the third party in a way which reduces its power of attraction, and 'parasitism' or 'free-riding' where the third party seeks to exploit, without paying any financial compensation, the marketing effort expended by the proprietor in order to create and maintain the mark's image.

Sections 5(3) and 10(3) of the TMA (and the parent provisions in the Directive) leave the origin function far behind. It doesn't matter that the consumer is not confused. Instead, any case under these provisions will consider the investment made by the owner in the mark. The trade mark is treated as a valuable asset in its own right. It is to be protected against those who wish to misappropriate its selling power. Schechter calls this 'the commercial magnetism' of the mark. Such language also appears in the Opinion of AG Colomer in *Arsenal v Reed*. He states that the trade mark acquires a life of its own, making a statement about quality, reputation and even, in certain cases, a way of seeing life. Further, the messages it sends out are autonomous. A distinctive sign can indicate at the same time trade origin, the reputation of its proprietor, and the quality of the goods it represents. As Loughlan remarks, (in 'Trade Marks: Arguments in a Continuing Contest' [2005] *IPQ* 294) trade marks carry values, associations and relations from one sphere to another. Trade marks link the economy and culture by investing consumer products with social and symbolic values. The irony is, of course, that in some instances, trade marks no longer make a statement about the origin of the goods but about the aspirations of the purchaser. However, if the commercial magnetism of the trade mark is protected, there are implications not only for free competition but for freedom of speech. There is a danger that cultural icons, which should be free for all to use, become private property.

12.4.5 Investment function

The ECJ intimated that a trade mark may have yet further functions which can be protected by the infringement action in its ruling in *L'Oréal SA v Bellure NV*. At [58] it stated that besides the 'essential' origin function, there were others including guaranteeing the quality of the goods or services and those of communication, investment or advertising.

Whilst the Court did not elaborate further in its ruling in *L'Oréal SA v Bellure NV* on the communication and investment functions, it did discuss the investment function in Case C-323/09 *Interflora Inc v Marks & Spencer plc* [2011] ECR I-8625 at [60–62], where the claimant ultimately succeeded in preventing the defendant retailer from using the claimant's name as an internet adword on Google for its own flower delivery service (see *Interflora Inc v Marks & Spencer plc* [2013] EWHC 1291). Noting that trade marks are often 'instruments of commercial strategy...used to develop consumer loyalty', the ECJ explained that even though this 'investment function' overlapped with the advertising function, it was none the less distinct. When the use by a competitor of an identical sign for identical goods substantially interfered with the proprietor's use of its trade mark to acquire or preserve a reputation capable of attracting consumers and retaining their loyalty, the third party's use must be regarded as adversely affecting the trade mark's investment function.

cross reference
*See section
15.3.2.6.*

thinking point
*Which of the commercial functions performed by trade marks is the most
appropriate in the current age of the consumer? Are there any dangers in protecting
the 'commercial magnetism' of trade marks?*

12.5 The impact of EU law

12.5.1 The need for harmonisation

One of the fundamental principles of the **Treaty on the Functioning of the European Union ('TFEU')** (formerly the Treaty of Rome) is the establishment of the internal market, in which all the Member States are treated as a single territory for the purposes of the free movement of goods, services, persons and capital. Fairly early in the development of the common market (as it was originally called) it was realised that the territorial nature of intellectual property rights was an obstacle to achieving the goals of the EU. Not only do such rights enable their owners to prevent the importation of goods from one Member State to another, but different Member States have different standards of protection. What is regarded as a trade mark in one state might be incapable of registration in another.

From the early 1980s, the EU Commission adopted a 'twin-track' policy towards accommodating intellectual property rights into the internal market. Although Article 345 TFEU (formerly Article 295 EC) declares that national rules on property ownership are not to be affected by the Treaty (so that the grant of intellectual property rights is a matter left to Member States) the objective of achieving a 'level playing field' enabled the Commission to legislate for the standardisation of national rights and for the creation of pan-European unitary rights. The legal vehicles for these two solutions were, respectively, a Directive and a Regulation.

12.5.2 The Trade Marks Directive

The Directive is declared to be a partial harmonisation measure only. It seeks to standardise the 'core' of trade mark law, by setting out what can be a trade mark, what objections can be made to it when an application to register it is made, how the mark is to be compared with prior rights, and the protection conferred on its owner to stop third parties infringing it. The Directive also deals with revocation of trade marks, with the requirement to use a mark, and with the ability of the owner to license the mark.

In many ways, the most important part of the Directive is its Recitals. These set out the reasons behind the Directive and are often utilised by the ECJ in dealing with questions referred to it by national courts under Article 267 TFEU (formerly Article 234 EC). Of particular significance, using the numbering in the consolidated (2008) version of the Directive, are Recital 10, which declares that trade marks are to receive the same level of protection in all Member States, although states are free to confer greater protection if they so wish; and Recital 11, which includes a statement as to the function of trade marks and the criteria to be taken into account when deciding whether there is a likelihood of confusion.

thinking point
Have United Kingdom courts recognised fully the impact of EU legislation on United Kingdom trade mark law?

To those used to United Kingdom legislation, with its proliferation of detail, the language of the Directive may seem stark. It is, of course, a product of the civil law tradition, where legislation is couched in broad statements of principle, with the detail being supplied in court rulings. For this reason, the case law of the ECJ on its interpretation is extremely important for all substantive aspects of trade mark law. Not only does the Directive itself introduce new statutory principles into United Kingdom trade mark law, but case law has extended those principles even further. The revolution in trade mark law expected when the TMA was passed has come not from within the United Kingdom legal system, but from outside.

12.5.3 The EU Trade Mark Regulation

Trade mark **applicants** now have a choice when it comes to obtaining protection. They can either obtain national protection in the United Kingdom (and indeed in other individual Member States) by the filing of separate national applications or they can obtain an EU trade mark registration from OHIM. The EU trade mark is a unitary right, that is, it is effective throughout the whole of the EU. The unitary concept creates an 'all or nothing' system. If the trade mark is invalid (for example because it is descriptive or deceptive in one Member State or conflicts with a prior right in one Member State) it is invalid for the whole EU (though there are provisions allowing it to be converted into national registrations).

Whether to register locally or at OHIM is essentially a commercial choice, reflecting the nature of the applicant's business. Undertakings are not forced to obtain EU protection (even though logically this would be the only way to prevent the conflict between the territorial nature of intellectual property rights and the internal market). Instead the national and EU systems run side-by-side.

The substantive provisions of the Regulation (dealing with what can be a trade mark, what objections can be made to it in application proceedings, how it is to be compared with prior rights, and the scope of protection accorded to the owner) are substantially identical to the equivalent Articles in the Directive. Decisions from OHIM (which also deals with **EU designs**) can be appealed to the General Court and thence (on a point of law only) to the ECJ. Therefore, in the context of trade mark law, the ECJ has parallel jurisdiction, namely to act as the ultimate appellate body to decisions of OHIM, and to provide preliminary rulings on the interpretation of the Directive to national courts. The resultant case law, dealing as it does with two substantially identical EU measures, is therefore entirely interchangeable.

12.5.4 **Interpretation of the TMA**

When asked to interpret a Directive, the ECJ, in keeping with the civil law tradition, will adopt the teleological style of interpretation, that is, it will consider the legislation in the light of its objectives, making use of working papers and discussions which preceded its enactment. Because of the influence of the Directive on the content of the TMA (in essence it lowers the test for registrability and broadens the scope of protection conferred on the owner), the meaning of the TMA can no longer be determined by the Chancery Division, the Court of Appeal or the Supreme Court. The ECJ is the only body which can give a conclusive ruling on its meaning. At national level, the Directive must be used as an aid to interpreting the TMA. Words and phrases which have their counterparts in earlier law must bear the meaning allocated to them by the ECJ, rather than that which developed in United Kingdom case law during the previous 100 years.

12.5.5 **Future developments**

In March 2013, the EU Commission published proposals for a revision of the Regulation and a 'recast' Directive. It has stated that it hopes the changes will be agreed in the Spring of 2014 and come into force two years later. Where appropriate in Chapters 14, 15 and 16 we indicate where the wording of the Directive is likely to change and how this might affect domestic law.

Summary

This chapter has explained:

- the use of trade marks over the centuries;

- the origins of United Kingdom trade mark law;

- the commercial functions which trade marks fulfil and how such functions are regarded by the courts; and

- the way in which EU reforms have impacted on domestic trade mark law.

Reflective question

If we abandon the origin function as the proper rationale for trade mark protection, then the modern trade mark will become a powerful means to suppress fair competition. Discuss.

Annotated further reading

Davis, J. 'Locating the Average Consumer: His Judicial Origins, Intellectual Influences and Current Role in European Trade Mark Law' [2005] *IPQ* 183
Examines the way in which the ECJ has developed the average consumer as the arbiter of key issues under the Directive and Regulation.

Gangjee, D.S. 'Property in Brands' LSE Law, Society and Economy Working Papers 8/2013 (available from www.lse.ac.uk/collections/law/wps/wps.htm)
Traces the emergence of a new *res* within European trade mark law due to the ECJ's recognition of functions other than the origin function.

Klein, N. *No Logo* (2000), London: Harper Collins
A critique of the power of brands.

Landes, W. and Posner, R. 'Trademark Law: An Economic Perspective' (1987) 30 *Journal of Law & Economics* 265
Explores the economic justification for trade mark protection.

Loughlan, P. 'Trade Marks: Arguments in a Continuing Contest' [2005] *IPQ* 294
Explores the arguments for and against strong protection for trade marks, taking into account the cultural and social reasons for allowing public access to trade signs.

Schechter, F.I. *Historical Foundations of Trade Mark Law* (1925), New York: Columbia University Press
A comprehensive account of the use of trade marks throughout Europe up to the nineteenth century.

Schechter, F.I. 'The Rational Basis of Trade Mark Protection' (1927) 40 *Harv LR* 813
Argues for the protection of the selling power of brands through the doctrine of dilution.

Passing off

Learning objectives

Upon completion of this chapter, you should have acquired:

- an understanding of the flexible, sometimes unpredictable nature of passing off as the means to protect unregistered trade marks;
- knowledge of the key elements which must be proved in order to succeed in a passing off action;
- knowledge of the defences which can be raised;
- an understanding of the various ways in which the tort of passing off can be committed;
- knowledge of the protection accorded to well-known marks under the Paris Convention; and
- an appreciation of the ways in which passing off may (or may not) develop in the future.

Introduction

In the United Kingdom, there is no obligation to register a trade mark. Protection has always been available at common law for marks in use, by means of the action for passing off. In consequence, a trade mark owner has the freedom to choose whether to register their mark, or whether to rely on common law protection. Indeed s.2 of the Trade Marks Act 1994 ('TMA') declares that nothing in the Act affects the law of passing off.

13.1 Preliminary matters

13.1.1 The relationship between passing off and the law of registered trade marks

It may seem odd to discuss the law of **passing off** before the law of registered **trade marks** is considered in detail. Nevertheless, we believe that there are good reasons to examine passing off at this stage. These reasons are:

13.1.1.1 Passing off and trade mark function

cross reference
See section 12.4.

We have seen how a number of different commercial functions are effected by trade marks. They tell the consumer about where the goods come from, they enable the consumer to choose between competing brands, they guarantee the consistency of quality of the goods, and they act as the means to create **goodwill**. All of these functions are reflected, in various ways, in the case law on passing off. However, as a result of the key ingredients of the tort, the origin function has come to dominate. This may prove to be something of a straightjacket should it be thought appropriate to develop passing off in the future; alternatively, it could be seen as a way to ensure that the power of the brand owner is kept within reasonable bounds.

13.1.1.2 Passing off and trade mark registrability

Prior to the TMA, passing off was the means to protect unregistrable marks. It acted to 'fill the gaps' in the registration system. Colour schemes, shapes and the appearance of products ('get-up') were not capable of registration before 1994 but could, in appropriate circumstances, be protectable as common law trade marks. The TMA enables a far greater range of subject matter to be capable of registration, so it might be thought that passing off is now of less value. Nevertheless, some of the concepts used in passing off have been transposed into the law of registration. For example, proving acquired distinctiveness for the purposes of the proviso to TMA s.3(1) has many characteristics of proving reputation as part of passing off; establishing a likelihood of confusion in **opposition** proceedings under the **Relative Grounds** for refusal is similar to the element of misrepresentation in passing off; and the protection of marks with a reputation, again in opposition proceedings, has much in common with the way that passing off has protected strong common law marks against **dilution**.

13.1.1.3 Passing off and trade mark infringement

In the same way, many passing off notions have been transferred into the law of trade mark **infringement**. Establishing likelihood of confusion for the purposes of TMA s.10(2) has much in common with passing off; and again, the infringement action to protect marks with a reputation shares features with passing off. Passing off, however, has a further role. It is usually pleaded in the alternative when a **claimant** brings an action for trade mark infringement. Should there be a successful counterclaim that the trade mark is **invalid** or should be **revoked** for mismanagement, then at least the claimant has something to fall back on (see *United Biscuits (UK) Ltd v Asda Stores Ltd* [1997] RPC 513 for an example of where the passing off claim became crucial once the registered marks had been revoked for non-use).

13.1.1.4 Passing off in the future

It may be asked, if the law of registered trade marks has become more flexible and has appeared to adopt many of the attributes of passing off, does the passing off action have a future? We will discuss this issue in greater detail at the end of this chapter, but for the moment, the following comments can be made:

- the greater flexibility in the law of registered trade marks owes more to the driving force of the ECJ in offering guidance as to the meaning of key words and phrases in the Trade Marks Directive (Council Directive 89/104/EEC of 21 December 1988 on the approximation of the laws of Member States relating to trade marks [1989] OJ L 40/1, now codified as Directive 2008/95/EC of the European Parliament and of the Council of 22 October 2008 [2008] OJ L 299/25) rather than any express incorporation of the values of passing off;

- passing off will always have a role to play for the trader who chooses not to register their mark (or who cannot register it, for whatever reason);

- the policy question which has to be answered is whether it is appropriate for passing off to expand. If it is concluded that passing off should develop further, then the elements which at present have to be proved to succeed in a passing off action will need to be reconsidered.

13.1.2 **The nature of passing off**

thinking point

Do you agree with Lord Diplock that the law should be flexible and be able to respond to unfair business practices, or is certainty preferable?

In *Erven Warnink BV v Townend & Sons* [1979] AC 731 at p. 730 Lord Diplock remarked that passing off was a 'protean tort'. By this he meant that passing off was a flexible form of action, one that could and should respond to changing business practices. Indeed, Lord Diplock argued forcefully in the case that passing off must develop into the action for **unfair competition**. Other judges have not been so liberal in their approach, most notably Lord Scarman in *Cadbury-Schweppes v Pub Squash Co* [1981] RPC 429.

The term 'protean' to describe passing off is appropriate in another sense. It suggests that the tort is difficult to pin down. The elusive nature of the tort is attributable to two things. First, it is entirely a product of case law. In consequence, it is always possible to find decisions which appear not to fit in with first principle or which contradict other cases. For this reason, constructing a logical justification for the tort is extremely difficult. Whilst most cases appear to treat passing off as a means of consumer protection, there are others which have granted a business protection against conduct which amounts to misappropriation, the theft of something of value which is nevertheless intangible. In other words, passing off in these cases is protecting the trader's investment rather than the consumer.

thinking point
Would it help
if there were
a clear judicial
pronouncement as
to the rationale for
passing off?

Second, in passing off it is for the claimant to prove each of the three ingredients of the tort. These elements are interdependent, so that strength in one area can offset a weaker case in another. However, what really matters is the quality of the evidence which the claimant adduces. The reason why so many cases fail is down to the claimant's inability to prove a key ingredient of the action. From the point of view of evidence, passing off is much more onerous than a claim for trade mark infringement. This may help to answer the question 'why register'?

13.2 The elements of passing off

13.2.1 The definition of passing off

Most cases today rely on one leading definition (or perhaps, description) of passing off.

case close-up

> **Reckitt & Colman v Borden (JIF LEMON)** [1990] 1 WLR 491
> . . . .
> Lord Oliver in *Reckitt & Colman Products Ltd v Borden Inc* [1990] 1 WLR 491 (the *JIF Lemon* case) set out what has come to be called 'the classic trinity'. He stated that first, a trader must establish that he has a goodwill or reputation attached to the goods or services which he or she supplies; second, the trader must demonstrate that the defendant has made a misrepresentation (whether intentional or not) leading or likely to lead the public to believe that the goods or services offered by the defendant are the goods or services of the claimant; and last, the trader must demonstrate that he or she has suffered or is likely to suffer damage by reason of the erroneous belief caused by the defendant's misrepresentation. The three elements are interdependent, and each element is a question of fact. It is up to the claimant to convince the court as to the existence of each one.

349

13.2.2 Reputation

13.2.2.1 What is reputation?

In one sense, reputation can be considered the equivalent of factual distinctiveness in the law of registered trade marks. Whether the claimant has reputation (or goodwill) is a question of fact, and hence entirely dependent on evidence showing that consumers recognise the **sign** as indicating origin. This is sometimes referred to in the cases as acquiring 'secondary meaning'. By 'sign' we mean a name, colour, shape or anything else which sends the consumer a message about the commercial origin of the goods. Almost any sign (but not every sign) is capable of protection through passing off.

It doesn't matter that the sign does not qualify for registration as a trade mark. It might be unregistrable because as a word it describes the quality of the goods (like the phrase 'camel hair belting' in *Reddaway v Banham* [1896] AC 199) or it is a word indicating geographical origin (like the name 'Stone Ale' in *Montgomery v Thompson* [1891] AC 217 or 'Yorkshire Relish' in *Powell v Birmingham Vinegar Brewery Co* (1896) 13 RPC 235) or because as a container it indicates the nature of the product inside (as in *JIF Lemon* itself). As long as there is proof of factual distinctiveness, the sign will be capable of protection in passing off. However, where the sign has *not* been used to indicate commercial origin, but instead has designated a particular type or model of product, then this does not suffice. An example of this is *Burberrys v Cording* (1909) 26 RPC 693 where the claimant had used the name 'Slip On' for a particular type of raincoat. Also, the court may not be convinced that the sign can be described separately from the goods in which the claimant trades, and so is not regarded as a trade mark at common law. In *Cadbury v Ulmer* [1988] FSR 385 protection was denied for the shape of the FLAKE chocolate bar simply because it was the product itself which the claimant was trying to protect. Alternatively, the sign might not be visible to the consumer when the goods are purchased, like the BLUE TACK pads in *Bostick v Sellotape* [1994] RPC 556.

13.2.2.2 Reputation and goodwill

Reputation cannot exist in isolation. It must be attached to a particular business. Reputation depends on the claimant being a trader (and not just a private individual), so that the claimant must have a business interest to protect (*OXFORD BLUE Trade Mark*, Registry, 23 March 2004). This business interest is usually called goodwill. 'Goodwill', as a type of intangible property, is not easy to define, even though it can be transferred and is capable of being valued for the purpose of a company's balance sheet. It has been described (in a tax case) as 'the attractive force which brings in custom' and 'that which distinguishes an old business from a new' (*per* Lord McNaghten in *CIR v Muller & Co's Margarine Ltd* [1901] AC 217). As Lord Diplock explained in *Star Industrial Co v Yap Kwee Kor* [1976] FSR 217 at p. 269, a passing off action is a remedy for the invasion of a right of property, not in the mark, name or get-up improperly used, but in the business or goodwill in which it has been used. Goodwill, as the subject of proprietary rights, is incapable of subsisting by itself. It has no independent existence apart from the business to which it is attached.

13.2.2.3 Limitations on goodwill

Goodwill (or reputation) is limited, both in time and geographically. It is also divisible, so that if business is carried on in several countries, a separate goodwill attaches to it in each. As regards its geographical scope, for our purposes this will normally be within the United Kingdom (or part of it). The existence of goodwill in the United Kingdom depends on there being customers in this country who are not members of a special class, in other words, they must be members of the general public (*per* the Court of Appeal in *Anheuser-Busch Inc v Budejovicky Budvar NP* [1984] FSR 413).

As regards the duration of goodwill, it may survive after a business ceases to trade, but only for a limited period. How long goodwill can survive after a business closes is a question of fact (*Ad-Lib Club v Granville* [1971] FSR 1). If the claimant has no intention of re-opening the business, then that points to the conclusion that goodwill has entirely disappeared (*Star Industrial Co v Yap Kwee Kor*; *Foster v Brooks* [2013] EWPCC 18). Another trader is then free to adopt the same or similar sign to the one used by the defunct business. By contrast, in *Jules Rimet Cup Ltd v The Football Association Ltd* [2008] FSR 254 the court accepted that the FA had never given up the intention to use the cartoon character 'World Cup Willie' (used to promote the 1966 World Cup), so that the symbol's goodwill survived 40 years.

13.2.2.4 Length of use to establish goodwill

It should not be assumed the claimant has to demonstrate many years' use of the sign in order to prove the existence of goodwill, provided that the remaining ingredients of passing off are present. In *Stannard v Reay* [1967] RPC 589, three weeks' use of the name 'Mr Chippy' for a mobile fish'n'chip van sufficed. Despite such a short period of use, the claimant obtained an **injunction** to prevent the defendant from operating a rival van under the identical name. However, the claimant was helped by the fact that his business had operated in a clearly defined location (the Isle of Wight) and there was evidence of damage to that business, as there had been a marked loss of sales as soon as the defendant began trading.

13.2.2.5 Exclusive reputation

The basic rule is that the reputation has to be exclusive to the claimant. However, in a number of cases, there may be two or more undertakings sharing that reputation. This may come about, first, where two companies independently of each other start using the same sign at more or less the same time. Where this coincidence happens, each will acquire a separate reputation and neither can stop the other from using the name in question. An example of this is *Anheuser-Busch Inc v Budejovicky Budvar NP* [2000] RPC 906, where BUDWEISER was the trade mark of two rival companies, one American and one Czech. The net outcome was that the two companies were forced to co-exist, neither having a right of priority over the other. Second, it is possible for two businesses to acquire their reputation from a common source. A case within this unusual category is *Sir Robert McAlpine Ltd v Alfred McAlpine plc* [2004] RPC 711 where the two companies were originally part of the same family business which had been divided along geographical lines. In such cases, each undertaking, it was held, had to ensure that they did not cause customers to mistake one firm for the other. Each co-owner was under a duty not to 'erode the exclusivity of the other's name'.

13.2.2.6 Shared reputation

The most frequent example of shared reputation has occurred in a family of cases, each one of which concerns the protection of a product which has special qualities. The product will originate from a specific geographical area which because of its climate or terrain imparts the particular quality to the product, or else the product is made to a unique recipe. Any of the businesses which make the product share the reputation, and can, therefore, sue a third party for passing off.

The cases on shared reputation have so far all concerned drinks or foodstuffs. Thus it has been held that champagne can only come from the Champagne district of France and has to be made by a unique method. There is no such thing as 'Spanish Champagne' (*Bollinger v Costa Brava Wine Co* [1961] RPC 116) and to call a drink made from pear juice 'Champagne perry' is a misrepresentation (*Bulmer v Bollinger* [1978] RPC 79). Further, calling a sparkling elderflower drink 'Elderflower Champagne' will dilute the unique quality of the Champagne name, even if customers are not confused: *Taittinger v Allbev* [1993] 2 CMLR 741. Similarly, the name 'sherry' is reserved for a fortified wine produced in the Jerez region of Spain, so that there cannot be a product called 'British Sherry' (*Vine Products v MacKenzie* [1969] RPC 1). Scotch whisky is similarly protected, and must originate from Scotland (*Walker v Ost* [1970] RPC 489). The protection afforded to advocaat in *Erven Warnink v Townend & Sons Ltd* was somewhat different, as here what mattered was not the place of production, but the precise recipe and particular ingredients. In *Diageo North America Inc v Intercontinental Brands (ICB) Ltd* [2010] EWCA Civ 920, it was held that this category of passing off was not limited to products perceived as being of a superior quality: to hold otherwise would deny protection to the claimant's goodwill. Here, selling an alcoholic drink under the name VODKAT without clear labelling to indicate that it was not vodka misled the public, particularly as the get-up of the claimant's leading brand of vodka (SMIRNOFF) had been copied. And in *Fage UK Ltd v Chobani UK Ltd* [2014] EWCA Civ 5 protection was given to Greek yoghurt, so that similar products created by the use of thickening agents rather than by straining could not be labelled with the protected name.

---

case close-up

Chocosuisse Union des Fabricants Suisses de Chocolat v Cadbury Ltd [1999]
RPC 826

. . . .

The case which can be considered the most extreme of the shared reputation cases (and one relied on in the *Diageo* case) is *Chocosuisse Union des Fabricants Suisses de Chocolat v Cadbury Ltd* [1999] RPC 826. Its outcome was dependent on the specific finding of fact that the use of the name 'Swiss Chocolate' had led United Kingdom customers to expect a particular quality. The Court of Appeal found that the defendant had committed passing off by selling its product under the name 'Swiss Chalet'. However, Chadwick LJ highlighted some of the difficulties presented by this category of passing off. For example, how extensive must the trade of the claimant be in order for them to share in the goodwill? Here, it was held that the first claimant, a trade association, could not sue as it did not have any United Kingdom goodwill to protect, although the second and third claimants, as manufacturers within the class, could. How should an individual trader prove that they are a member of the class? How long do they have to be in the class before they can sue? Where (as here) the product is not subject to any regulatory control, how is the class to be defined and how exact does the recipe have to be (many of the other passing off cases involving unique products are subject to detailed national and/or EU rules which set out where and how the product can be made). Last, in the case of an unregulated product, can the members of the class change the recipe? It will be clear from this discussion that much of the detail remains to be worked out with regard to this type of passing off.

13.2.3 **Misrepresentation**

13.2.3.1 The meaning of misrepresentation

thinking point
Is the Chocosuisse case consistent with previous case law on the protection of special products?

The second of Lord Oliver's 'classic trinity' is misrepresentation. As Lord Parker in *Spalding v Gamage* (1915) 32 RPC 273 at p. 284 explained, a false statement is the basis of the action. That false statement can be made expressly, though express misrepresentation is rare. More usually, the misrepresentation is implied, by the imitation of the claimant's sign. From this, we can see that the false statement can be by words or conduct.

Further detail on the requirement of misrepresentation is given by Lord Diplock in *Erven Warnink BV v Townend & Sons*. He stated that the misrepresentation must be made by a trader in the course of trade, to the defendant's prospective customers or ultimate consumers. It must be calculated to injure the business of another, and it must cause actual damage to the claimant's goodwill or be likely to do so. By 'calculated', Lord Diplock added, the misrepresentation must be likely to cause confusion (that is, 'on the balance of probabilities'). However, somewhat unhelpfully, Lord Diplock added that just because all the elements listed by him were satisfied did not mean that passing off had been established.

13.2.3.2 The effect of the misrepresentation

The crucial issue, however, is what effect the false statement has on the minds of the claimant's customers. According to the cases, the misrepresentation must lead customers to make an association with the claimant. It must make them think that this was 'something for which the [claimant] was responsible' (see the remarks of Goff and Buckley LJJ in *Bulmer v Bollinger*). So, for example, in *Associated Newspapers v Insert Media* [1991] FSR 380, the Court of Appeal held that where the defendant inserted advertising leaflets without permission inside magazines published by the claimant, the public would assume that the material had been approved or authorised by the claimant. In *United Biscuits (UK) Ltd v Asda Stores Ltd*, Robert Walker J held, when confronted by the defendant's lookalike PUFFIN biscuits (the wrappers of which had been deliberately designed to evoke those for the PENGUIN biscuits made by the claimants), customers would think that the supermarket had asked the claimant to make the biscuits for it, when it had not.

The effect of the misrepresentation on the mind of the consumer must, therefore, produce confusion as to the trade origin of the defendant's product (if passing off is to develop, the requirement of origin confusion would prove to be a major restriction on expansion). Quite simply, if the consumer is not confused about the source of the defendant's product, there can be no liability for passing off. Two major cases make this point.

The elements of passing off

case close-up

Hodgkinson & Corby v Wards Mobility Service [1995] FSR 169
....

The claimant alleged that by reproducing the shape of its cushions (used by healthcare professionals when nursing the chronically ill), the defendant had committed passing off. It was held that upon seeing the cushion, the relevant consumer would not have been confused into thinking that the cushions were made by the claimant. In the absence of origin confusion there could be no passing off.

case close-up

Harrods v Harrodian School [1996] RPC 697
....

The defendant had set up a preparatory school on the site of a sports club previously owned by the famous department store. The majority of the Court of Appeal held that although customers might 'call to mind' the name of the claimant when confronted by the name of the school, they would not be misled into thinking that the store had endorsed or approved the school. We may note the powerful dissenting judgment of Sir Michael Kerr. He remarked that although the basic ingredients of passing off were well established, their application to individual cases 'remained elusive'. He thought that the public, on seeing the defendant's name, would assume that the claimant was in some way 'mixed up' with the school. Further, the extensive reputation of the claimant had to be taken into account when deciding confusion. The deliberate choice of name by the defendant amounted to misappropriation. The damage inflicted in this case was the blurring or erosion of the distinctiveness of the name in question.

thinking point

In the light of Lord Diplock's comments in the Advocaat *case about the role of passing off, which do you find more convincing in the* Harrods *case, the majority or minority view?*

13.2.3.3 Proof of confusion

A further problem is how does the claimant satisfy the court that there is a likelihood of confusion? Unlike their German counterparts, United Kingdom courts are sceptical about the worth of survey evidence (see *Dalgety Spiller Foods v Food Brokers* [1994] FSR 505). They would rather have witnesses who will come to court to give evidence in person. An example is *Neutrogena v Golden Ltd t/a Laboratoires Garnier* [1996] RPC 473 where the claimant's solicitor e-mailed her staff to see how many had been confused by the defendant's television advert for shower gel, those replying then being asked to explain to the court how they had been misled by the defendant. Such evidence clearly had an impact on the result of the case.

13.2.3.4 The recipient of the misrepresentation

The defendant's false statement must, according to Lord Diplock, be made to the customer. But who is this person and what is their level of intelligence? One misconception is that the test is that of the 'moron in a hurry'. Reference to the origin of the phrase (in *Morning Star Co-operative Society Ltd v Express Newspapers Ltd* [1979] FSR 113) reveals that the judge remarked that '*even* the moron in a hurry' would not confuse the defendant's newspaper *The Daily Star* with *The Morning Star* published by the claimant, which implies that the average consumer is somewhat smarter than suggested. In the law of registered trade marks the notional consumer is deemed to be reasonably well informed, reasonably observant, and circumspect (Case C-342/97 *Lloyd Schuhfabrik Meyer & Co GmbH v Klijsen Handel BV* [1999] ECR I-3819). There is no reason why a similar standard should not be appropriate in passing off.

thinking point
Should the average consumer from the law of registered trade marks be used as the standard in passing off?

13.2.4 **Damage**

In the third element of the 'classic trinity', the claimant must establish that there has been or will be damage. Such damage must harm the goodwill of the claimant's business. It must be more than minimal, but need not be actual. A threat of damage will suffice provided all the other elements of passing off are established, but proof of damage will make passing off easier to establish.

13.2.4.1 Harm to goodwill: loss of custom

As Carty explains, (in 'Heads of Damage in Passing Off' [1996] *EIPR* 487) damage on its own is not enough, otherwise passing off becomes a tort of unfair competition. The damage must be *to* the claimant's goodwill. Because passing off exists to prevent origin confusion, diversion of custom as a result of the defendant's misrepresentation will cause a loss of sales revenue for the claimant. This is the normal form of harm and is illustrated by the facts of *Stannard v Reay*.

Customer confusion may also have other unexpected consequences. In *Neutrogena v Golden Ltd t/a Laboratoires Garnier*, the defendant's NEUTRALIA shower gel had been advertised on television in a way that some viewers found distasteful. A number of complainants, however, confused the defendant's products with the claimant's NEUTROGENA skin-care range. The court found that harm had been caused to the claimant's goodwill. Even in *Erven Warnink BV v Townend & Sons*, where the misrepresentation consisted of product misdescription rather than the creation of origin confusion, the damage consisted of lost sales of the genuine ADVOCAAT.

13.2.4.2 Other forms of harm

It is in this area of damage that the passing off cases appear most inconsistent. Forms of harm have been recognised which do not accord with the concept of origin confusion. The cases may be individually explicable because of the way in which evidence of harm was presented, but that does not make them any easier to reconcile with first principles. It is perhaps a case of the tail wagging the dog.

One particular category of harm identified by Carty is devaluation of reputation. This occurred in *Spalding v Gamage* where the defendant had sold footballs that had been made by the claimant, but described them in advertisements as being of first class quality when in fact they had been disposed of as faulty stock. There was thus no origin confusion (the balls were, after all, made by the claimant) but the harm done to goodwill was apparent. Another example of devaluation can be found in *Annabel's (Berkeley Square) v Schock* [1972] RPC 838, where a high-class London nightclub, Annabel's, successfully restrained the defendant from carrying on the business of an escort agency under the name Annabel's Escort Agency. The public's perception that escort agencies were in some way 'not nice' meant that, as Carty puts it, the claimant might be 'tarred with the same brush', should the public confuse the two. A more extreme case is *Rolls Royce Motors v Dodd* [1981] FSR 519, where Megarry J accepted that the claimant had suffered damage to the image of its product (luxury cars) by the defendant's having affixed the Rolls Royce badge to his home-built racing car powered by an aeroplane engine. The problem with this particular case is that it ignores the fact that the defendant wasn't actually trading in cars, and so didn't meet Lord Diplock's criteria for misrepresentation in passing off.

Another form of harm which has been recognised, according to Carty, is loss of control. The argument here is that the defendant's conduct will reduce the claimant's ability to expand their business into new areas at some date in the future, or else will deter potential **licensees** from coming forward. The former aspect was recognised in *Lego System AB v Lego M Lemelstrich* [1983] FSR 155 where the claimant toy manufacturer successfully sued a company which made plastic irrigation equipment. Falconer J accepted the argument that one day Lego might wish to expand into other types of plastic product.

case close-up

Irvine v Talksport Radio [2002] 2 All ER 414

The effect of the defendant's conduct on future licensees was a key ingredient in Laddie J's decision in *Irvine v Talksport Radio* [2002] 2 All ER 414. Here, the defendant had 'doctored' a digital image of the claimant so that he appeared to be listening to one of their radio broadcasts rather than using his mobile phone. The claimant had proved that he had an established goodwill in merchandising his image, so the conclusion had to be that if the defendant's conduct was not restrained, others would try to 'cash in' on the claimant's image without paying royalties.

The form of harm which Carty argues is hardest to reconcile with origin confusion is dilution. The ability of the owner of a strong trade mark to use passing off to prevent others selling dissimilar goods was recognised in *Eastman Photographic Materials Co v John Griffiths Cycle Co* (1898) 15 RPC 105, where the use of KODAK, already well known for cameras, was enjoined in respect of bicycles. In *Taittinger v Allbev*, the Court of Appeal recognised that the value of the name 'Champagne' would be weakened were it to be used in relation to a fruit-flavoured drink, even though there was little evidence of consumer confusion. Peter Gibson LJ remarked that 'blurring or erosion of the uniqueness that now attaches to the word champagne' was the harm being done and Mann LJ accepted that the claimant's case rested on the premise 'that the word champagne has an exclusiveness which is impaired if it is used in relation to a product...which is neither champagne nor associated with or connected to the businesses which produce champagne'. Carty argues that *Taittinger* involved no misrepresentation and no harm to goodwill. The decision, she says, 'refashions passing off by the back door'. Further difficulties are presented by *Harrods v Harrodian School*. Although the majority found that there was no actionable misrepresentation, Sir Michael Kerr adopted in full the thinking in *Taittinger*. Millett and Beldam LJJ do not deal adequately with all the arguments in *Taittinger*, and so, according to Carty, dilution remains as a form of harm protected by passing off.

thinking point
Does the Court of Appeal decision in Taittinger v Allbev *depart so radically from the previous cases on product misdescription?*

13.3 Defences to passing off

13.3.1 General defences

The normal way in which a defendant will resist a passing off action is to challenge whether the claimant has actually established each of the three ingredients of the tort. The claimant cannot succeed if one or more of the 'classic trinity' is missing. In each instance, however, as mentioned earlier, much may depend on the quality of evidence produced by the claimant to prove the 'classic trinity'.

So, for example, the claimant may not have convinced the court that the particular sign has acquired a secondary meaning, as in *Cadbury v Ulmer* where the court was not satisfied that the shape of its chocolate bar had come to indicate trade origin. Alternatively, the claimant may have failed to show that there has been a material misrepresentation, as was the case in *Harrods v Harrodian School*. Even if there was a material misrepresentation, there might be insufficient evidence of customer confusion. This was the reason why the Court of Appeal in *Bulmer v Bollinger* did not find in favour of the Champagne houses who sought to show that customers might be misled if BABYCHAM was sold as 'the genuine Champagne perry'. Incidentally, the case provides a neat illustration of judicial prejudices. The assumptions made by the court as to who was the typical consumer of champagne and who drank BABYCHAM would no doubt today be regarded as politically incorrect. Finally, there may be failure to prove damage to goodwill. A key issue in *Cadbury-Schweppes v Pub Squash Co* was the inability of the claimant to show that there had been a loss of sales following the launch of the defendant's lemonade. It should be remembered, though, that the Privy Council in this case adopted a very orthodox view of passing off and refused to accept other forms of harm, such as the misappropriation of the imagery used in the claimant's television adverts.

13.3.2 No common field of activity

cross reference
See chapter 18.

The defence of 'no common field of activity' is one which is sometimes pleaded. It means that the claimant and defendant are not in the same line of business. The requirement that claimant and defendant be competitors does not appear in Lord Oliver's 'definition' in *JIF Lemon*, so does the defence actually exist? Certainly, in the past, there have been a number of cases which recognised the defence. All of these involved the practice of character merchandising. The high point of the defence is the decision in *McCulloch v May* (1947) 65 RPC 58, where it was held that a children's radio presenter could not stop a cereal manufacturer from using his name to sell the product. With one notable exception (*Mirage Studios v Counter-Feat Clothing* [1991] FSR 145) United Kingdom courts have been unreceptive to the notion of protecting fame through passing off. This unwillingness to accord protection is perhaps one reason why the defence is only to be found in the merchandising cases.

thinking point
How do the three interdependent elements of Lord Oliver's 'classic trinity' fit together to create the tort of passing off? Is any one element more important than the others?

The best explanation of the 'defence' is to be found in *Annabel's (Berkeley Square) v Schock*, where the court pointed out that it is more difficult for a claimant to establish a likelihood of confusion if the parties are not in direct competition. In other words, 'no common field of activity' is not a defence as such, but rather is one aspect of whether the misrepresentation by the defendant is likely to deceive the public into thinking the celebrity has endorsed the product.

More recently, the Court of Appeal in *Harrods v Harrodian School* saw fit to say that the requirement of a common field of activity did not form part of the formula for passing off. Equally, Laddie J in *Irvine v Talksport Radio* was dismissive of the need to show that the parties were in competition, preferring instead to focus on the harm to the claimant's goodwill. We have already noted how the loss of potential licensees was a key factor in proving harm to goodwill.

13.4 Varieties of the tort

Passing off can be committed in an infinite variety of ways. We set out here examples of these, grouped together for convenience under two main headings. The headings derive from a point made by Lord Diplock in *Erven Warnink BV v Townend & Sons* where he described passing off as being subdivided into two categories. He called these 'orthodox' and 'extended' passing off. The latter category includes those cases which concern product misdescription, or else harm to goodwill other than through origin confusion. The context in which Lord Diplock made those remarks was, of course, his policy statement that passing off ought to expand to deal with any sort of unfair trading practices. Some have since doubted whether this subdivision actually exists, but we use it here as a means of organising the case law.

The illustrations of the tort should be considered always in light of Lord Oliver's 'classic trinity', the three interdependent factors which go to make up passing off. In essence, we are here concerned with the different ways in which the defendant can misrepresent to a customer that 'this is something for which the claimant was responsible'.

13.4.1 Orthodox passing off

The following may be considered as examples of 'orthodox' passing off:

13.4.1.1 Names

A well-established illustration of passing off is where the claimant's name is used as the name of the defendant's business. The name taken by the defendant can be that of an individual (*Biba Group Ltd v Biba Boutique* [1980] RPC 413); that of a company (*Harrods Ltd v R Harrod Ltd* (1924) 41 RPC 74); or the claimant's trading name (*Brestian v Try* [1958] RPC 161). Where the claimant has traded under a descriptive name, then the scope of protection will be quite narrow, and the defendant can avoid liability by choosing a slightly different name: *Office Cleaning Services Ltd v Westminster Window & General Cleaners Ltd* (1946) 63 RPC 39.

The protection of trading names appears to have been extended by analogy to telephone numbers in *Law Society v Griffiths* [1995] RPC 16. Here the defendant was held to have committed passing off by choosing a telephone number for his accident helpline which was only one digit different from that of the claimant's helpline. The misrepresentation occurred as a result of the defendant's silence in not correcting customers' assumptions that they had contacted the claimant for legal advice.

One question which is often asked is whether passing off can actually prevent a trader using their own name. The answer would seem to be 'yes'. If claimant and defendant have the same name, then the onus is on the defendant to *ensure* that customers are not misled: *Boswell-Wilkie Circus v Brian Boswell Circus* [1986] FSR 479.

case close-up

I N Newman Ltd v Adlem [2005] EWCA Civ 741
....

An illustration of this harsh rule can be seen in *I N Newman Ltd v Adlem* [2005] EWCA Civ 741. Here, the defendant had sold his business as a funeral director to the claimant's predecessor in business, but then set up a new business using his own name, which he also registered as a trade mark. Overturning the first instance decision, a majority of the Court of Appeal held that the goodwill of the original business had been transferred to the claimant. Accordingly, by trading in his own name the defendant had failed to do enough to ensure that customers would not be misled. Passing off was therefore established, and the defendant's trade mark registration was invalid under s.47(2) TMA.

The net effect is that the 'own name' defence in passing off is far narrower than the equivalent defence in trade mark infringement and there appears to be no decided case in passing off where the defence has succeeded: *Reed Executive plc v Reed Business Information Ltd* [2004] RPC 767.

13.4.1.2 Trade marks

The traditional use of passing off has always been to protect the claimant's unregistered trade mark. Whether the trade mark was descriptive or geographical was irrelevant, provided factual distinctiveness was established. If that factual distinctiveness was exceptionally powerful, then it was possible to prevent the use of the name on dissimilar goods: see *Eastman Photographic Materials Co v John Griffiths Cycle Co* and *Lego System AB v Lego M Lemelstrich*.

13.4.1.3 Get-up of the product

However, perhaps the most significant group of cases in 'orthodox' passing off (before the 1994 reforms) shows how the claimant could protect the get-up of their goods. By 'get-up' we mean the shape of packaging and of containers, the use of colour schemes, the layout of and typeface used on labels, indeed *any* aspect of the goods' *appearance* which helps the consumer to identify trade origin. This is sometimes referred to as 'trade dress'.

Examples of cases falling within this group include *William Edge & Sons v Niccolls* [1911] AC 693 where the House of Lords conferred common law protection on the packaging of 'dolly blue' whitening for laundry which had been sold in little muslin bags with a stick attached, so that it had the appearance of a doll. In *Combe International v Scholl (UK) Ltd* [1980] RPC 1 the appearance of the product was the special packaging used on 'odour-eater' insoles. In *United Biscuits (UK) Ltd v Asda Stores Ltd*, as we have already seen, what was protected was the style of the wrappers on PENGUIN chocolate biscuits, even though the brand name used by the defendant on its biscuits (PUFFIN) was held not to be confusingly similar. The case is a rare example of passing off being successfully used to deal with a problem debated (somewhat inconclusively) and then ignored by Parliament when implementing the Directive and recently raised as an issue for possible reform by the 2006 *Gowers Review of Intellectual Property* at para 5.82, namely how to provide brand owners with protection against supermarket 'own-brand lookalikes' (a matter likely to be resolved by the recast EU Trade Marks Directive).

cross reference
See section 1.2.1.

Containers for liquids are another typical instance of passing off being used to protect get-up. Cases include *John Haig v Forth Blending* (1953) 70 RPC 259 where the shape of the dimple whisky bottle was held to have acquired secondary meaning, and, of course, *JIF Lemon* itself, where the appearance of a plastic lemon for lemon juice (described by Lord Oliver as resembling a hand grenade) was held to have acquired '100% factual distinctiveness'. The fact that the claimants obtained their evidence of distinctiveness on Shrove Tuesday (when customers who don't normally buy fresh lemons were buying the claimant's product to put on their pancakes) might have had something to do with the successful outcome!

Consumers do not usually see colours and shapes as trade marks. In consequence, they need to be 'educated' that the sign does indicate origin, so far more factual distinctiveness needs to be proved. Relevant to this is the nature of the sign itself. So, as regards colours, the 'garish' scheme of purple and green pharmaceutical capsules was protected in *Hoffmann-La Roche v DDSA* [1972] RPC 1 but the 'very ordinary' pale blue colour of tablets in *Roche Products v Berk Pharmaceuticals* [1973] RPC 473 was not. The descriptive nature of the sign (green and yellow for cans of lemonade) may help to explain the result of *Cadbury-Schweppes v Pub Squash Co* where, it will be remembered, the Privy Council thought it significant that there was no evidence of confusion, which in turn was attributable to the lack of distinctiveness. This again highlights the interdependence of the ingredients in Lord Oliver's 'classic trinity'.

13.4.1.4 Effect of the TMA

Since 1994, the law of registered trade marks has changed dramatically and such revolution is bound to have an impact on passing off, as follows:

- the test for registrability is considerably broader than before. The key word in the definition of trade mark in TMA s.1 is 'sign'. The ECJ has interpreted this to mean anything which sends a message to any of the senses, so that in principle colours, sounds and smells can

cross reference
See sections 14.3
and 14.4.

cross reference
See section 12.4.

Cross reference
See section 15.3.3.

thinking point
Does 'orthodox'
passing off have
a role after the
TMA 1994?

all be registered as trade marks. The shape of products and their packaging are specifically mentioned as types of registered marks. The implication must be that those passing off cases giving protection to trade dress will decline in importance;

- some of the 'get-up' cases will need to be reconsidered in light of the ECJ's comments about trade mark function in Case C-206/01 *Arsenal Football Club v Matthew Reed* [2002] ECR I-10273. The dismissal of the claim for passing off in *Cadbury v Ulmer* on the ground that the appearance of the FLAKE bar did not have 'trade mark significance' is at odds with the comments of AG Colomer about the role of trade marks in the modern consumer era. The rejection of the claim in *Bostick v Sellotape* because the product was not visible at point of sale likewise contradicts what the ECJ said that the perception of the mark by the end user is as important as the views of the actual purchaser;

- the scope of protection accorded to the owner of a registered trade mark has been extended. Under previous law, protection was limited to the goods of the registration. Today, the owner can sue for infringement where the registered mark is used on identical, similar or dissimilar goods. Consequently, cases like *Eastman Photographic Materials Co v John Griffiths Cycle Co* and *Lego System AB v Lego M Lemelstrich* appear to be redundant. The TMA ss.5(3) and 10(3) introduce protection against dilution. If passing off is restricted by its definition to origin confusion, what does it add (if anything) to the law of registered trade marks?

13.4.2 **Extended passing off**

'Extended' passing off involves a misrepresentation which does not cause origin confusion, but results in some other form of harm to the claimant's goodwill. The cases can be grouped together as follows:

13.4.2.1 False suggestion of superior quality

This particular form of 'extended' passing off has long been recognised. In *Spalding v Gamage*, the defendant advertised the claimant's goods as being first class when in fact they were defective and had been disposed of as scrap. The House of Lords held that although the defendant had sold genuine goods, the false statement as to their quality caused harm to the claimant. Such harm was not caused by origin confusion, but by customers ceasing to buy the claimant's goods because they believed they had declined in quality. Another example of this type of passing off is *Wilts United Dairies v Thomas Robinson* [1958] RPC 94, where the tins of the claimant's condensed milk sold by the defendant were past their 'sell by' date. Similarly, in *Sodastream Ltd v Thorn Cascade Ltd* [1982] RPC 457 there was held to have been passing off when the defendant supplied refilled gas canisters for the claimant's fizzy drinks machines.

13.4.2.2 Geographical origin

cross reference
See section
13.2.2.6.

We have considered how the names of unique products had been protected, products such as champagne, sherry, advocaat, Swiss chocolate and Greek yoghurt. Whilst this category of passing off, which deals with product misdescription rather than origin confusion, is well established, the uncertainties surrounding the precise limits of the case law were discussed in *Chocosuisse Union des Fabricants Suisses de Chocolat v Cadbury Ltd*.

A further difficulty is that there is an overlap between this category of passing off and two other forms of intellectual property protection. First, TMA ss.49 and 50 provide, respectively, for the registration of **collective** and **certification trade marks**. The function of a collective mark is to indicate who is entitled to use the mark (normally, members of a trade association which owns the mark) whereas the function of a certification mark is to indicate that goods or services comply with certain objective standards (concerning, for example, material, safety or quality) which are laid down by regulation. An example of a certification mark is the 'wool mark' used on garment fabric, or the British Standards 'Kite Mark'. Second, there is EC Regulation 2081/92 [1992] OJ L 208/1, repealed and replaced by Council Regulation (EC) No 510/2006 of 20 March 2006 [2006] OJ L 93/12, on the protection of geographical indications and designations of origin for agricultural products and foodstuffs. This enables producers of regional products to register the name of the place where the product originates with the EU Commission in Brussels. Such protection is not, however, as powerful as might first be assumed. Much depends on the wording of the regulations in the country of origin. So, for example, in Case C-108/01 *Consorzio del Prosciutto di Parma v Asda Stores Ltd* [2003] ECR I-5121, the ECJ accepted that although the name 'Parma ham' was protected under EU law, the Italian regulations governing its use were not capable of having direct effect throughout the EU. In consequence, the trade association which oversaw the application of the name was unable to stop the defendant from selling pre-sliced, prepackaged Parma ham in the United Kingdom, even though Italian law required otherwise.

13.4.2.3 Advertising campaigns

A possible use of 'extended' passing off is to prevent the defendant from taking the idea underlying the claimant's advertising campaign. What is being taken is not any **copyright** material, such as words or music, but the misappropriation of the *concept* of the advert. It will be remembered that the Privy Council did not accept such an argument in *Cadbury-Schweppes v Pub Squash Co* despite clear evidence that the defendant had set out deliberately to copy the sporting theme of the claimant's advert for lemonade. However, other cases have tentatively suggested that passing off might be used in this way, at least where the defendant deliberately sought to take advantage of another's successful campaign. The suggestions can be found in *RHM Foods v Bovril Ltd* [1983] RPC 275 and *Elida Gibbs v Colgate-Palmolive* [1983] FSR 95, although both involved applications for interim relief. The cases do not, of course, fit in with the decision in *Pub Squash*.

13.4.2.4 Comparative advertising

Can comparative advertising amount to passing off? Normally, the answer is 'no', because if the defendant compares two products side-by-side there cannot be origin confusion: *Bulmer v Bollinger*. If the comparison is not explicit, but rather, implied (ie the defendant refers to the claimant's product in an indirect way) this may amount to passing off. In *McDonald's Hamburgers Ltd v Burgerking (UK) Ltd* [1986] FSR 45 the defendant launched an advertising campaign on the London underground which used the phrase 'It's Not Just Big, Mac'. Whitford J held that by so referring to the claimant's 'flagship' product the defendant had committed passing off.

Kimberley Clark v Fort Sterling [1997] FSR 877

The defendant launched a new range of toilet tissue, NOUVELLE, with a special promotional offer which declared that if customers were not satisfied, they could exchange it for ANDREX, which was made by the claimant. Laddie J held that on seeing the defendant's packaging, consumers would assume that the claimant had approved the offer or that NOUVELLE was actually made by the claimant. The average shopper would not stop to read a disclaimer in very small print which acknowledged that ANDREX was the claimant's trade mark.

thinking point
Is it possible to fit both 'orthodox' and 'extended' passing off into Lord Oliver's formula in JIF Lemon?

13.4.2.5 Reverse passing off

As might be supposed, 'reverse' or inverse passing off involves a false statement which is the exact opposite of that which is usually found in passing off. In 'orthodox' passing off, the defendant misleads customers by stating that his/her goods are those of the claimant. In 'reverse' passing off, the defendant misleads by saying that the claimant's product is made by the defendant. An example of such conduct occurred in *Bristol Conservatories v Conservatories Custom Built* [1989] RPC 455, where customers were shown a catalogue of the claimant's products but were led to believe that the goods had been made by the defendant.

13.5 The foreign claimant and the protection of well-known marks under the Paris Convention

13.5.1 The foreign claimant rule

The first part of Lord Oliver's 'classic trinity' requires the claimant to have a reputation or goodwill in the United Kingdom. How does this apply to an overseas company which does business in the United Kingdom? What has to be proved before it can bring a passing off action?

The starting point is to identify what sort of activity is being conducted in the United Kingdom. This could range from having business premises within the United Kingdom (such as a factory or an office), to having a facility to process orders for goods or bookings for services, to having customers within the jurisdiction who might have bought one of the claimant's products when on holiday or on a business trip overseas. Finally, the firm might have a reputation in the United Kingdom, but otherwise no other business presence. Which of these satisfies the requirement of goodwill? What is certain is that the need to show goodwill is satisfied if there are business premises. The presence of a manufacturing facility or similar will therefore suffice. An extreme example is *Sheraton Corporation v Sheraton Motels* [1964] RPC 202, a decision which has been doubted by some. The decision was to the effect that the ability to receive hotel bookings amounted to United Kingdom goodwill, even though the claimants did not at the time have any hotels in the United Kingdom. Similarly, in *Hotel Cipriani Srl v Cipriani (Grosvenor*

Street) Ltd [2010] RPC 485, the Court of Appeal confirmed that the claimant hotel group had United Kingdom goodwill because customers either made direct bookings with the group or instructed travel agents to do the same.

However, we live in a shrinking world. Surely the presence of customers alone should suffice? A resounding rejection of this proposition occurred in *Alain Bernadin v Pavilion Properties Ltd* [1967] RPC 581, where it was said that a foreign claimant must have both business presence *and* customers in the United Kingdom before being able to sue for passing off. The narrow approach is remarkable, given the old case of *Panhard Levassor SA v Panhard-Levassor Motor Co Ltd* [1901] 2 Ch 513, where the court restrained the use of the name of a French car company by the defendant, even though the claimant's only business 'presence' was the existence of several English customers who had in the past purchased the claimant's cars.

Two decisions have since set the record straight as regards what will suffice for local goodwill. The Court of Appeal in *Anheuser-Busch Inc v Budejovicky Budvar NP* (1984) declared that the minimum necessary to enable an overseas undertaking to sue for passing off is the presence of customers in the United Kingdom who can be misled by the defendant's misrepresentations. The court did say, however, that those customers had to be members of the public, not visiting foreign nationals such as members of the American armed forces. As a result, the claim for passing off failed because at the time, the claimant's trade mark *BUDWEISER* for beer was not known to the general public, having been supplied only to US forces personnel stationed temporarily within the United Kingdom. It has since been held that the two companies involved in this case, one American and one Czech, have concurrent rights to the *BUDWEISER* mark: *Anheuser-Busch Inc v Budejovicky Budvar NP* (2000). A more liberal approach still can be discerned in the judgment of Browne Wilkinson VC in *Peter Waterman Ltd v CBS* (*THE HIT FACTORY*) [1993] EMLR 27. He rejected the claimant's attempt to sue for passing off, holding that it had failed to demonstrate that the nickname accorded to its business had acquired distinctiveness. However, he went on to observe that any misrepresentation made to customers in England is an interference with that goodwill wherever it was situated. Although the defendant was based in New York, its recording studio was known to those in the entertainment industry in London and it therefore had sufficient use of the name in the United Kingdom to acquire goodwill.

These *obiter* comments by Browne Wilkinson VC echo the conclusions of Graham J in *Maxim's Ltd v Dye* [1977] 1 WLR 1155. In a far-thinking judgment, he held that the owners of Maxim's restaurant in Paris could obtain an injunction simply because the name was 'known' to the public as a result of 'spill over' advertising in films, television or magazines. In other words, he took a 'global' approach to the existence of goodwill. This accords with how the matter is dealt with in other common law jurisdictions. In Australia, for example, it has been held that reputation alone is sufficient to enable a foreign litigant to sue for passing off: *Conagra Inc v McCain Foods (Aust) Pty Ltd* (1992) 106 ALR 465.

13.5.2 **The impact of TMA s.56**

The presence of TMA s.56 necessitates a review of the previously discussed case law on what amounts to protectable goodwill in the case of a foreign claimant. The section implements the United Kingdom's obligations under Article 6*bis* of the **Paris Convention** for the Protection of Industrial Property 1883. It provides that the proprietor of a **well-known mark** is entitled to obtain an injunction to prevent the use or registration of a trade mark which is identical or similar to his mark, in relation to identical or similar goods or services, where the use of the same is likely to cause confusion. The section, however, does not enable the award of **damages**: *Hotel Cipriani Srl v Cipriani (Grosvenor Street) Ltd*. The purpose of s.56 is to enable overseas trade mark owners, who have neither registration nor use of their mark in the United Kingdom, to prevent others misappropriating it providing that they can establish that their mark is well known. Individuals or organisations domiciled in the United Kingdom cannot rely on this provision, again because of the wording of the Paris Convention: *Jules Rimet Cup Ltd v The Football Association Ltd* at [73]. The section implies that sufficient 'knowledge' of the mark is enough, a more relaxed test than proving that the claimant has protectable goodwill.

13.5.3 The meaning of 'well-known mark' under the Paris Convention

The question prompted by TMA s.56 is 'what is a well-known mark'? An answer can be found in *LE MANS Trade Mark Application*, Appointed Person, 8 November 2004. Here, the organisers of the 24-hour motor race opposed an application by a garage proprietor to register the name LE MANS for his garage business. Richard Arnold, QC, referred to the *Joint Recommendation Concerning Provisions on the Protection of Well Known Marks* adopted by **WIPO** in September 1999. This document listed the factors which ought to be taken into account by a court or registry when deciding whether a mark is well known for the purposes of Article 6*bis* of the Paris Convention. The criteria include the degree of recognition of the mark; how much and for how long it has been used; the amount of advertising and publicity accorded to the mark, and for how long such advertisements have been running; the geographical 'reach' of the mark; whether it possesses inherent or acquired distinctiveness; the degree of exclusivity enjoyed by the mark and the extent of use of the same or similar marks by third parties; the nature of the goods or services provided under the mark, and how those goods and services reach the public; whether the reputation of the mark symbolises quality goods; and the extent of the commercial value attributed to the mark. In the instant case the opponents clearly met these criteria.

thinking point
Does the 'foreign claimant' rule in passing off accord with current trends of globalisation, or is it simply a consequence of the requirement of goodwill?

The question which therefore remains, in the light of the remarks of Browne Wilkinson VC in *Peter Waterman Ltd v CBS (THE HIT FACTORY)* and Graham J in *Maxim's Ltd v Dye*, is whether s.56 requires Lord Oliver's classic trinity to be completely rewritten.

13.6

The future of passing off

Since the introduction of a system of registering trade marks in 1875, passing off has often been regarded as the means of 'filling in the gaps' in trade mark law. The 1994 reforms have considerably broadened the law of registered trade marks. This increase in scope applies to both registrability and infringement. Further, the judicial recognition of the functions which trade marks perform has been liberalised by the ECJ's decision in *Arsenal v Reed*. If registered trade marks are no longer restricted by origin function, where does that leave passing off, with its insistence that the defendant's misrepresentation must produce a likelihood of confusion on the part of the consumer?

Our discussion of passing off has shown how the case law has a pendulum effect. There are times when the courts are adventurous and want to expand passing off so that it becomes a tort of unfair competition. As illustrations of this, the judgments in *Vine Products v MacKenzie* and *Erven Warnink BV v Townend & Sons* specifically mention the need for passing off to be flexible and respond to changes in business practices. Both of these cases involve passing off by product misdescription, and both argue for the need for protection against unfair competition. Equally, the Court of Appeal in *Taittinger v Allbev* saw no need for there to be customer confusion, instead conferring protection against dilution. This suggests that passing off doesn't just protect goodwill, but the unique selling power of the brand name itself. Indeed, it has been suggested that passing off *ought* to be regarded as unfair competition by Aldous LJ in two cases, *BT plc v One in a Million* [1999] FSR 1 at p. 18 and *Arsenal Football Club v Matthew Reed* [2003] RPC 696 at [70]. For some commentators such as Carty, however, this is stretching passing off too far, so that it is in danger of losing sight of its rationale.

In contrast, there are just as many instances of when the courts are restrictive in their thinking. One prime example is *Cadbury-Schweppes v Pub Squash Co* where the Privy Council expressly refused to countenance any expansion of the tort beyond the traditional confines of origin confusion, despite there being clear evidence that the defendant had deliberately sought to 'free-ride' on the claimant's success. The certainty from having precise rules was preferable to flexibility. Similarly, the majority of the Court of Appeal in *Harrods v Harrodian School* held that in the absence of proven confusion there could be no liability. Another case reaching the same conclusion is *Hodgkinson & Corby v Wards Mobility Service*, where Jacob J remarked that there 'is no tort of copying. There is no tort of taking another man's market or customers. Neither the market nor the customers are the plaintiff's to own.'

Jacob LJ (as he had become) later observed in *L'Oréal SA v Bellure NV* [2008] RPC 196 at [141] that:

> the basic economic rule is that competition is not only lawful but a mainspring of the economy. The legislator has recognised that there should be exceptions. It has laid down the rules for these: the laws of patents, trade marks, copyrights, and designs have all been fashioned for the purpose. Each of them have rules for their existence and (save for trade marks) set time periods for existence. Each has their own justification. It is not for the judges to step in and legislate into existence new categories of intellectual property rights. And if they were to do so they would be entering wholly uncertain territory.

thinking point

In an era of emerging new technologies, is it preferable to have specific intellectual property rights which are clearly defined, or should the law be flexible enough to respond to changing business practices?

If we had a crystal ball, what might it tell us about the future of passing off? In simple terms, the question is one of policy. *Should* passing off develop into a form of protection against unfair competition, or should it remain as a strictly defined, alternative means of protection to registered trade marks? During the last decade and a half, the Government has resisted three separate attempts to introduce a law of unfair competition by means of legislation, although the *Gowers Review* has identified the need to protect brand owners against supermarket imitations. It seems unlikely that the judiciary will provide the means for change (especially in view of the expansion of registered trade marks). Academic opinion is divided.

13.6.1 In favour of unfair competition

The principal argument in favour of passing off being developed into a general tort of unfair competition is that the United Kingdom has an obligation under the Paris Convention to provide such a form of redress. Such a cause of action would, in an era when copying is all too easy, provide protection for an individual's creative endeavours, and would add flexibility. The relevant arguments can be found in A. Horton and A. Robertson, 'Does the UK or the EC Need an Unfair Competition Law?' [1995] *EIPR* 568.

13.6.2 Against unfair competition

The arguments against having a general tort of unfair competition are perhaps stronger. Spence argues (see 'Passing Off and the Misappropriation of Valuable Intangibles' (1996) 112 *LQR* 472) that there is no theoretical justification for unfair competition. He further contends that the action would be too general to provide any guidance for judges. As Parliament has already legislated to provide specific forms of protection, it would be wrong to go outside those boundaries (see *Victoria Park Racing v Taylor* (1937) 58 CLR 479 at p. 509 (*per* Dixon J) (Australian HC) and *Moorgate Tobacco v Philip Morris* [1985] RPC 291 at pp. 236–40 (*per* Deane J) (Australian HC)). If additional protection is required, then there should be *sui generis* legislation to deal with particular problems. Carty argues (in 'Dilution and Passing Off: Cause for Concern' (1996) 112 *LQR* 632) that the introduction of an action for unfair competition would lead to unnecessary judicial interference in the marketplace. There is also the perennial argument about opening the litigation floodgates.

Summary

This chapter has explained:

- the elements which go to make up the tort of passing off, which is the common law means of protecting trade marks;

- the 'protean' nature of the tort, both with regard to its potential to develop into a broader means of redress against unfair competition, and the numerous inconsistencies and contradictions which are to be found in the cases; and

- the likely impact of the Trade Marks Act 1994 on the tort and how it might change in the future.

Reflective question

The tort of passing off has no effective role to play in the modern intellectual property régime. Discuss.

Annotated further reading

Carty, H. 'Dilution and Passing Off: Cause for Concern' (1996) 112 *LQR* 632
Argues that a tort of unfair competition would be bad for business.

Carty, H. 'Heads of Damage in Passing Off' [1996] *EIPR* 487
Argues that *Taittinger v Allbev* is wrong to recognise dilution as a form of harm to goodwill in passing off.

Carty, H. 'Passing Off: Frameworks of Liability Debated' [2012] *IPQ* 106
Argues that passing off should remain firmly based in Lord Oliver's 'classic trinity'.

Davis, J. 'Why the United Kingdom Should Have a Law against Misappropriation' [2012] *CLJ* 561
Argues that trends in passing off show that remedies for misappropriation are necessary to protect investment in the attractiveness of brands.

Horton, A. and Robertson, A. 'Does the UK or the EC Need an Unfair Competition Law?' [1995] *EIPR* 568
Argues for the introduction of a general tort of unfair competition.

Spence, M. 'Passing Off and the Misappropriation of Valuable Intangibles' (1996) 112 *LQR* 472
Argues that general torts, such as misappropriation or unfair competition, are not justified theoretically and would not assist judges to decide cases.

Registration of trade marks

Learning objectives

Upon completion of this chapter, you should have acquired:

- background knowledge of Trade Marks Registry Procedure;

- an appreciation of the role of the average consumer in determining issues of registrability;

- knowledge of the three elements which form the definition of 'trade mark';

- an understanding of the different policy reasons which underlie the Absolute Grounds for Refusal of Registration, and how the Grounds have been interpreted;

- an understanding of the 'triad of protection' conferred on a senior trade mark by the Relative Grounds for Refusal; and

- an appreciation of the impact of the case law of the European Court of Justice.

Introduction

:
:
:
:
:
:
:
:
:
:
:
:
Whether a trade mark can be registered appears at first glance to be deceptively simple. The sign in question must satisfy the definition of 'trade mark', and it must not be prohibited by any of the Absolute or Relative Grounds of Refusal, all of these issues being judged through the eyes of the average consumer. Nevertheless, there is a huge body of case law to be digested. Furthermore, such case law reveals that there are tensions between the pre-1994 attitude of United Kingdom courts towards trade marks and the more liberal views of EU tribunals.

Overview of the issues

Whether a **trade mark** is capable of registration depends on three requirements. First, whether the subject matter of the application satisfies the definition of 'trade mark' in s.1 of the Trade Marks Act 1994 ('TMA'), second whether there are any objections to the application under the **Absolute Grounds** for Refusal in s.3, and last, whether there are any prior rights which could prevent registration under the **Relative Grounds** for Refusal in s.5. These three aspects of registrability will be considered in sequence.

14.1.1 The incoming tide of European law

The registrability of trade marks is a subject where the First Trade Marks Directive (Council Directive 89/104/EEC of 21 December 1988 on the approximation of the laws of Member States relating to trade marks [1989] OJ L 40/1, now codified as Directive 2008/95/EC of the European Parliament and of the Council of 22 October 2008 [2008] OJ L 299/25) ('the Directive') and the consequent interpretation of the Directive by the European Court of Justice has had a radical impact on United Kingdom domestic trade mark law. The torrent of references by national courts under Article 267 of the **Treaty on the Functioning of the European Union ('TFEU')** (reviewed by Peter Turner-Kerr in 'EU Intellectual Property Law: Recent Case Developments' [2004] *IPQ* 448) has produced definitive guidance on the meaning of almost every aspect of the definition of a trade mark and its suitability for registration. Another, complementary, body of case law (where the ECJ acts as the appellate body for decisions of the General Court in reviewing decisions of the Boards of Appeal of **OHIM**) has also emerged under the Community Trademark Regulation (Council Regulation (EC) 40/94 of 20 December 1993 [1994] OJ L 11/1, now codified as Council Regulation (EC) No 207/2009 of 26 February 2009 on the Community trade mark [2009] OJ L 78/1) ('the Regulation'). Because the wording of the substantive Articles in the Directive and Regulation is virtually identical, the two bodies of case law are interchangeable.

Examination of United Kingdom cases shows that the judiciary has taken time to appreciate the impact of the 'Europeanisation' of trade mark law. At times, they have appeared reluctant to abandon the legacy of the Trade Marks Act 1938. Many decisions in the early days of the TMA made use of reasoning derived from pre-1994 cases (as examples, see the discussion of the phrase 'capable of distinguishing' by the Court of Appeal in *Philips Electronics NV v Remington Consumer Products* [1999] RPC 809 and in *Bach Flower Remedies Ltd v Healing Herbs* [2000] RPC 513, and the assessment of 'likelihood of confusion' in *British Sugar plc v James Robertson & Sons Ltd* [1996] RPC 281). Adaptation to the brave new world of the Directive has undoubtedly been helped by the way in which the United Kingdom Trade Marks Registry ('the Registry') has frequently revised the *Trade Marks Registry Works Manual* (available online from the **UKIPO** website) in the light of ECJ rulings. The remarks of Lord Denning in *Bulmer v Bollinger* [1974] Ch 401 about the incoming tide have never seemed so apposite.

14.1.2 **Theoretical issues**

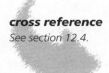

cross reference
See section 12.4.

We have previously examined the functions performed by trade marks. We noted how the origin function dominated United Kingdom trade mark law under the 1938 Act, and proved to be a straightjacket when deciding issues of registrability and **infringement**. The product differentiation function (enabling the consumer to choose between competing brands), the guarantee function, the advertising and investment function have all been recognised in case law. As a result of the decision of the ECJ in Case C-206/01 *Arsenal Football Club v Matthew Reed* [2002] ECR I-10273, trade mark function has the potential to go far beyond that of simply indicating origin. The theoretical debate underpins much of the case law on registrability.

14.1.3 **The importance of the average consumer**

Just as key issues in the law of **patents** are determined through the eyes of the notional **skilled addressee**, a judicial construct, so trade mark law depends heavily on the perception of the reasonable consumer. Article 2 of the Directive states that a trade mark must be capable of distinguishing the goods or services of one undertaking from those of another. In plain English, trade marks help consumers to choose and therefore act as messengers between the manufacturer of a product and the end user. The reasonable consumer (a hypothetical being) is the arbiter of registrability.

14.1.3.1 The characteristics of the average consumer

thinking point
Does the choice of the average consumer as the person to decide issues of registrability of trade marks really guarantee consistency and objectivity?

The ECJ first gave guidance as to the characteristics of the average consumer in Case C-342/97 *Lloyd Schuhfabrik Meyer & Co KG v Klijsen Handel BV* [1999] ECR I-3819 at [26]. It said that the average consumer is deemed to be reasonably well informed and reasonably observant and circumspect. However, their level of attention will vary depending on what sort of product is being purchased. Thus, someone spending £300 on a food mixer will pay greater attention and be less likely to be confused between competing brands than (say) someone pushing a trolley round a supermarket (*Whirlpool Corporation v Kenwood Ltd* [2010] RPC 51). Equally, someone buying a car (Case C-361/04 P *Ruiz-Picasso v OHIM* [2006] ECR I-643) or a mobile phone (Case C-16/06P *Les Editions Albert Réné Sarl v OHIM* [2008] ECR 10053) pays greater attention to detail.

14.2

An outline of procedure at the United Kingdom Trade Marks Registry

By way of background information, we consider next Registry procedure. This is dealt with in outline only: further detail is available from the UKIPO website. As a result of The Trade Marks (Relative Grounds) Order 2007 (SI 2007/1976), Registry procedure was significantly amended with effect from 1 October 2007. TMA s.7 (dealing with honest concurrent use) was repealed and s.8 brought into force, thus partially aligning United Kingdom practice with that of OHIM. In essence, the procedure can be broken down into six steps, as illustrated in Diagram 14.1.

Diagram 14.1

United Kingdom trade mark application procedure

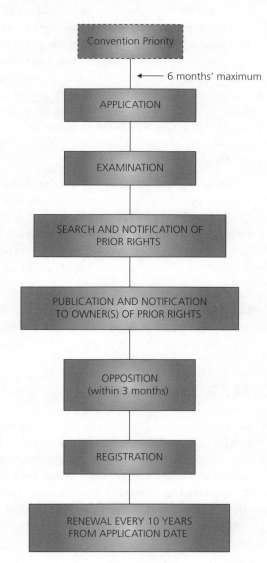

14.2.1 Filing

The starting point is for the **applicant** to complete Form TM3, available from the Registry website. Before doing so, the prudent applicant would undertake a search of the register to identify whether there are any prior rights which might conflict with the intended mark.

Besides choice of the mark itself, the principal decision will be as to the list of goods and services for which the mark is to be registered, as trade marks are registered in respect of specific items (s.32(2)(c)). There are 34 classes of goods and 11 classes of services listed in **WIPO's Nice Agreement** for the International Classification of Goods and Services 1957 (incorporated into United Kingdom law by means of Sch. 4 of the Trade Marks (Amendment) Rules 2001). The classes group related products together, for example Class 3 contains cleaning substances and Class 5 medical preparations. It is possible to make multi-class applications. However, many of the classes are very wide. The ECJ in Case C-307/10 *Chartered Institute of Patent Attorneys v Registrar of Trade Marks* [2012] ETMR 783 has stated that the list of goods and/or services must be 'identified with sufficient clarity and precision to enable the competent authorities and economic operators to determine the extent of protection conferred by the mark'. Wide and vague **specifications** will not be allowed (see UKIPO's Practice Amendment Notice PAN 3/13). In any case, it is not good practice to apply for a wider range of products than is actually needed. Any person can apply to **revoke** a trade mark for non-use under TMA s.46, the underlying policy being that the Register should be a true reflection of business. To 'stockpile' marks or to register marks for goods which are unlikely to be needed is contrary to such policy: *Imperial Group v Philip Morris* [1982] FSR 72.

cross reference
See section 1.5.1.1.

As with any right governed by the **Paris Convention** for the Protection of Industrial Property 1883, it is possible to claim Convention **priority** when filing a trade mark (s.36), thus backdating the trade mark to an earlier filing in another **Convention country**. The period by which the application can be so backdated is six months. However, in contrast to patents, where the 'race to the patent office' door is crucial, claiming priority is not so significant for trade marks and only a small percentage of applications take advantage of the right.

If all the paperwork is correct, the trade mark application is accorded a **filing date**. Should the application succeed, it is this date which will become the date of registration and therefore used to calculate the duration of protection. It is also the date at which the trade mark will be compared with earlier rights under the Relative Grounds provision.

14.2.2 Examination

Once the application has been made, it will be examined (s.37). **Examination** basically covers two things, formal compliance with the TMA (ie is the paperwork in order) and compliance with s.3 (Absolute Grounds). Objections (if there are any) are normally dealt with by correspondence. The TMA does not expressly give the applicant a right to a hearing, but such right can be inferred from a number of provisions, for example s.37(3). Appeals from the Examiner's decision are normally dealt with by a judicial officer, the Appointed Person, under s.76, or by the Patents Court.

14.2.3 **Search and examination report**

One impact of the 2007 changes is that there is no longer any examination of the application under the Relative Grounds for Refusal. Instead, the Registry conducts a search of earlier registered rights and notifies the results to the applicant, but will do no more than this. It is up to the applicant to decide whether to amend the **statement of goods** so as to avoid conflict, to withdraw the application, or to continue with it. The applicant has two months within which to respond to the examination report. If nothing is heard, the Registry assumes that the applicant wishes to continue.

14.2.4 **Publication and notification**

If there are no objections, or they are overcome, the mark is accepted. It is then **advertised** in the *Trade Marks Journal*, a weekly publication now available online. When publication occurs, the Registry informs the owners of any United Kingdom registered marks identified in the examination report. It also notifies the owners of any relevant Community or internationally registered trade marks but only if they have 'opted-in' to the notification procedure. The applicant has no right to a hearing about the Registry's intention to notify, nor can such a decision be appealed.

14.2.5 **Opposition**

Third parties have a fixed period from the date of publication within which to file an **opposition** to the application. The initial period is two months, but this can be extended on request by one further month. The request for the extension can only be made online. Thereafter, no further extension of time is possible.

The grounds of opposition fall into the same categories as objections by the Registrar, namely that the subject matter of the application does not meet the definition of 'trade mark' or that it is prohibited by the Absolute Grounds. Any third party can raise such objections and it doesn't matter whether or not the same matters were considered during examination of the application. However, there is one further objection which can only be raised by the owner of an earlier right, namely that the application should be rejected under the Relative Grounds for refusal because it conflicts with this earlier right.

As with the Registrar's objections, opposition can be dealt with by paperwork or by means of a hearing, with appeal to the Appointed Person or the court.

An alternative to filing an opposition is for a third party to make written **observations** to the Registrar under s.38(3). Although the person making the observations does not become a party to any proceedings, the Registry can re-open the case. Further, the observations will be entered on the file and will thus be available to any third party who subsequently tries to challenge the mark for lack of **validity**.

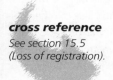

cross reference
*See section 15.5
(Loss of registration).*

Should the opponent lose the opposition, the applicant should not assume that this is the end of the matter, as the owner of the earlier right has five years within which to bring **invalidity** proceedings under TMA s.47(2).

14.2.6 **Registration**

If no opposition is filed, or if any opposition is overcome, the mark is registered for an initial period of 10 years. The period of registration is calculated from the filing date. Registration is only *prima facie* evidence that the mark is valid (s.72). It can always be challenged for lack of validity by any third party under s.47(1) (Absolute Grounds) and by the owner of the earlier right under s.47(2) (Relative Grounds) within five years. The effect of s.72 is to place the burden of proving invalidity on the third party. Should the mark be removed from the Register as a result of invalidity proceedings, the disgruntled owner has no redress, as s.70 declares that the Registrar does not warrant the validity of the registration of any mark.

A trade mark registration can be renewed every 10 years and is therefore capable of indefinite duration, subject to any challenge for revocation or invalidity.

thinking point
Do the 2007 changes to Trade Marks Registry procedure offer effective protection to third parties?

(14.3) **The meaning of 'mark'**

14.3.1 **The statutory provisions**

The definition of 'trade mark' is set out in TMA s.1, derived from Article 2 of the Directive. Section 1 is not a precise implementation. Whilst the Directive declares that 'a trade mark *may consist of* any **sign** capable of being represented graphically, particularly words, including personal names, designs, letters, numerals, the shape of goods or of their packaging, provided that such signs are capable of distinguishing the goods or services or one undertaking from those of other undertakings', the TMA begins with the phrase 'a trade mark *means* any sign capable of being represented graphically which is capable of distinguishing goods or services of one undertaking from those of other undertakings'. Arguably, the word 'means' is narrower than the phrase 'may consist of', and reflects the tendency of United Kingdom legislation to rely on exact definitions rather than general statements of principle. 'May consist of' is a phrase which indicates potential. Whether the thing applied for actually *is* a trade mark is determined under s.3. Section 1, however flawed its wording, should be seen as a very low threshold.

Both provisions list (non-exhaustively) the things which can be a trade mark. The inclusion of shapes (ie three-dimensional marks as opposed to 'designs' which are two-dimensional pictures) has the effect of reversing the House of Lords' decision in *Re COCA COLA Trade Marks* [1986] RPC 421. Here it was decided that a bottle could not be a trade mark 'because it would create an unfair monopoly', even though it is possible to protect the shapes of goods through the action in **passing off**.

Three particular decisions of the ECJ give insight as to the purpose of Article 2 of the Directive and are an aid to interpreting s.1. The Court has said that Article 2 simply sets out the minimum requirements for registrability (Case C-404/02 *Nichols plc v Registrar of Trade Marks* [2004] ECR I-8499, *per* AG Colomer at [32]) and that the list of subject matter is not exhaustive (Case C-283/01 *Shield Mark BV v Joost Kist* [2003] ECR I-14313, *per* AG Colomer at [22]). Most importantly (and, in contrast to the test under s.3, the Absolute Grounds), the policy of Article 2 is simply to define the *types* of sign of which a trade mark may consist without regard to the list of goods or services for which the applicant seeks protection (Case

cross reference
See section
13.4.1.3.

C-363/99 *Koninklijke KPN Nederland NV v Benelux-Merkenbureau (POSTKANTOOR)* [2004] ECR I-1619). In other words, the test under s.1 is to be carried out in the abstract. The views of the ECJ as to the scope of Article 2 are, of course, conclusive: because of this, the differences in wording between s.1 and Article 2 in the end don't matter.

Section 1 consists of three ingredients, the requirement of 'a sign', the need to represent such sign graphically, and for the sign to be 'capable of distinguishing'.

14.3.2 **Sign**

The choice of the word 'sign' is deliberately broad. According to Jacob J in *Philips Electronics NV v Remington Consumer Products* [1998] RPC 283 at p. 298 a 'sign' is 'anything which conveys information'. Most people think of a trade mark as being a word (a brand name such as KLEENEX), and indeed the same judge remarked in *British Sugar plc v James Robertson & Sons Ltd* [1996] RPC 281 at p. 305 a word is 'plainly included within the meaning of sign'. The ECJ has gone much further, stressing the policy of the Directive in encouraging registration. In Case C-273/00 *Sieckmann v Deutsches Patent- und Markenamt* [2002] ECR I-11737, AG Colomer (at [20–21]) commented that human beings receive messages with the help of all their senses, so that a message which can be understood by any of the five senses could be a trade mark. Further, in Case C-283/01 *Shield Mark BV v Joost Kist* [2003] ECR I-14313, AG Colomer (at [30]) repeated the point that trade marks do not have to be visual messages. However, in Case C-321/03 *Dyson Ltd v Registrar of Trade Marks* [2007] ECR I-687 the Court ruled that a transparent dust collecting bin for a vacuum cleaner was a concept not a sign.

Such an adventurous attitude is in contrast to United Kingdom law under the Trade Marks Act 1938. For many years there was a debate as to whether a product could be a trade mark of itself, or whether the trade mark had to be able to be described separately from the goods (see the narrow views of the Court of Appeal in *Re James's Trade Mark* (1886) 33 Ch D 392). More recently, in *Interlego AG's Trade Mark Applications* [1998] RPC 69 (a case decided under the pre-1994 law) it was held that the appearance of the lego brick could not be a trade mark for lego bricks, because the mark could not be described separately from the goods. However, a trade mark could cover the whole surface of the goods. In *Smith, Kline & French Laboratories Ltd v Sterling Winthrop Group Ltd* [1976] RPC 511, the House of Lords held that the two-tone colour scheme of pharmaceutical capsules was registrable. However, the product was the cold-cure contents of the capsule, and the trade mark was applied to (and therefore separate from) the goods.

A further debate in pre-1994 law was whether the trade mark had to be visible at point of sale. In *Unilever's Application* [1980] FSR 286 the court rejected an application to register the red and white stripes in the applicant's toothpaste because the mark could not be seen by the purchaser when buying the goods. This decision should be re-evaluated in light of the ECJ's ruling in *Arsenal Football Club v Matthew Reed*, where the Court stated that the perception of the end user of the goods should be considered as well as that of the initial buyer. By way of postscript, two further attempts to obtain protection for the red and white stripes of SIGNAL toothpaste also failed. In *Re Unilever plc's Application* [1984] RPC 155 the application consisted of a picture of the tube with a 'slug' of striped toothpaste being squeezed onto the brush. This, said the court, was simply a picture of the product itself and could not be registered. In *Unilever Ltd's Trade Mark (Striped Toothpaste No 2)* [1987] RPC 13, Hoffmann J (as he then was) rejected another application for two reasons, first, the stripes were functional not decorative (they indicated the two components, dentifrice and mouth freshener and so described the goods) and second, other traders might want to use the colour scheme.

14.3.3 **Capable of graphic representation**

Form TM3 contains an 8cm by 8cm space within which the applicant must enter the proposed mark. Where this is a word or a two-dimensional picture, the requirement is non-problematic. Reference to the broad meaning accorded to the word 'sign' reminds us, however, that anything which conveys a message to any of the senses is potentially registrable. Case law has shown that anything other than a word or picture (for example, shapes, colours and all sensory marks) face difficulty with the requirement of graphic representation.

case close-up

Case C-273/00 *Sieckmann v Deutsches Patent- und Markenamt* [2002] ECR I-11737

The purpose of graphic representation was explained by the ECJ in *Sieckmann*. The Court said that 'graphic representation' required the mark to be shown visually to enable it to be identified precisely. The sound operation of the registration system demanded this, first so that the scope of protection was clear, and second to make the Register accessible for all the key players, that is, the state (as manager of the Register) and other traders. Consequently, the representation had to be 'clear, precise, self-contained, easily accessible, intelligible, durable and objective'. However, having said that, in principle, a smell could be registered as a trade mark (because it sent a message to the consumer), the ECJ declared that the three methods proposed by the German trade mark registry for graphically representing the smell of cinnamon, namely a chemical formula (which in fact would only have revealed the substance not its smell), a written description, or a sample, did not meet the above-mentioned criteria. The Court was constrained by the form of the Article 267 TFEU reference which had asked a series of closed questions rather than seeking general advice as to how a smell might be represented.

In the light of *Sieckmann*, the earlier decision by the Board of Appeal of OHIM in *Vennootschap Onder Firma Senta Aromatic Marketing's Application* (Case R 156/1998–2) [1999] ETMR 429 that the smell of freshly cut grass for tennis balls was registrable must now be regarded as totally unsafe. Nevertheless, the clarity of the *Sieckmann* criteria appears to elude many applicants. In Case T-305/04 *Eden SARL v OHIM* [2005] ECR II-4705 the application was for a trade mark described as 'the smell of ripe strawberries' in respect of cleaning preparations, stationery, leather goods and clothing. The application form merely showed a picture of a strawberry, accompanied by the words 'the smell of ripe strawberries'. The General Court upheld the decision of OHIM that this was not a valid graphic representation of the trade mark.

thinking point
Was the ECJ in Sieckmann *correct to say that a smell could in principle be a trade mark and then reject the proposed methods of graphic representation? How could a smell be shown on the Register in such a way as to meet the* Sieckmann *criteria?*

14.3.3.1 Further ECJ cases

The ECJ itself has relied on the *Sieckmann* criteria on three further occasions. Sound marks were the subject of *Shield Mark* where the Court said that tunes were capable of graphic representation (through the use of musical notation) but other sound marks not so, as a description in words, a spectrogram, or a sound recording, were not sufficient. Because of the way the case was referred by the Benelux authorities, the ECJ did not have to consider whether sound marks were objectionable under the Absolute Grounds, nor how they might be dealt with in an infringement action. Colour marks were considered in Case C-104/01 *Libertel Groep BV v Benelux-Merkenbureau* [2003] ECR I-3793. Here the ECJ declared that in principle, single colours could potentially be trade marks and were to be represented graphically by the use of an internationally recognised method of identification, such as the Pantone system. In Case C-49/02 *Heidelberger Bauchemie GmbH v Deutsches Patent- und Markenamt* [2004] ECR I-6129, the ECJ said that where the mark consists of more than one colour, the representation must also include a systematic arrangement associating the colours in a predetermined and uniform way. The recast Directive will require the mark 'to be represented in a manner which enables the competent authorities and the public to determine the precise subject of the protection afforded to its proprietor'.

14.3.3.2 United Kingdom cases

United Kingdom decisions display a similar attitude towards the graphic representation of non-standard marks: precision is the key. With regard to smell marks, in *John Lewis of Hungerford Ltd's Trade Mark Application* [2001] RPC 575 it was held not enough merely to use words to describe a smell (again, cinnamon). The depiction of colours as trade marks was the subject matter in *Ty Nant Spring Water Ltd's Trade Mark Application* [2000] RPC 55, where it was held that to identify a colour (cobalt blue used on mineral water bottles) by its refractive index was not sufficiently ascertainable. And in *Swizzels Matlow Ltd's Trade Mark Application* [1998] RPC 244, the attempt to register a shape trade mark by writing on Form TM3 'a chewy sweet on a stick' failed. It remains a mystery why the applicant thought that these words explained clearly what the shape was and why it didn't put a drawing or photograph of the product in the space provided. A more complex reason for refusing the application occurred in *Société des Produits Nestlé SA v Cadbury UK Ltd* [2013] EWCA Civ 1174: although the applicant had identified the colour purple for its chocolate products by the appropriate Pantone reference, the application form stated that the mark would be the 'predominant' colour on the packaging which the Court of Appeal thought introduced an element of uncertainty. In *J W Spear & Sons Ltd and Mattel Inc v Zynga Inc* [2013] EWCA Civ 1175, an attempt to register 'an infinite number of permutations' of the size, lettering, numbering and colour of SCRABBLE tiles was held invalid: what was depicted was neither a sign nor did it comply with *Sieckmann* with regard to graphic representation.

14.3.4 Capable of distinguishing

In contrast to the United Kingdom courts (whose grappling with 'capable of distinguishing' is discussed later in the context of Absolute Grounds) the ECJ has adopted straightforward thinking about the meaning of the phrase.

case close-up

Case C-299/99 *Philips Electronics BV v Remington Consumer Products* [2002] ECR I-5475

In Case C-299/99 *Philips Electronics BV v Remington Consumer Products* [2002] ECR I-5475, at [47–50] the ECJ pointed out that Article 2 was concerned with the function of a trade mark. Did the mark enable the consumer to choose one product from another, confident that the goods had originated from one particular business which was responsible for their quality? Further, said the Court, Article 2 treats all categories of trade mark the same. Particular types of mark (for example, shapes, as in the *Philips* case itself) were to be subjected to the same test, namely did the sign guarantee the origin of the product?

The presence of the word 'capable' in Article 2, together with the ECJ's use of the word 'enable' in its ruling in *Philips v Remington* is significant. When combined with the Court's pronouncements on how Article 2 should be applied in *Nichols* and *POSTKANTOOR*, it becomes clear that the only question is whether the particular category of sign (for example, a colour, a shape, a smell or a sound) has the potential to act as a trade mark. In other words, *could* this sign help a consumer to choose between competing products (whether *in fact* it actually does so is a matter for determination under the Absolute Grounds)? So, in *Shield Mark*, AG Colomer (at [20]) says that sounds can *in principle* be trade marks (emphasis supplied). The same approach has been used by OHIM and the General Court under the Regulation. In Case T-316/00 *Viking Umwelttechnik GmbH v OHIM* [2002] ECR II-3715 at [23–24], the General Court emphasised that there was a distinction between whether signs of a particular category (here, colours) could in principle be trade marks and whether they actually were so.

14.3.5 Summary

The definition of 'trade mark' in s.1 of the TMA consists of three elements. The case law of the ECJ explains that the Directive was intended to encourage registration, and that the three elements are to be assessed in the abstract, that is, without reference to the goods or services of the application. The key question is whether what has been applied for has the potential to send a message to consumers to help them choose between competing brands. The only element of the definition likely to be problematic (in relation to colours, shapes and sensory marks) is the requirement of graphic representation.

14.4 Absolute grounds for refusal of registration

14.4.1 Overview of the legislation

The Absolute Grounds for refusal are found in TMA s.3, based on Article 3 of the Directive. The section lists objections to registrability based on the mark's own characteristics. The mark possesses some innate quality which prevents registration. In contrast to its predecessor (which required an applicant to show that the mark applied for was positively entitled to registration), the TMA contains a number of negative objections. Provided the 'sign' has passed the very nominal test in s.1, it is assumed registrable unless the Registry (or an opponent) can show that it falls within one or more of the Absolute Grounds in s.3. The onus of proof is therefore on the Registrar not the applicant. Another difference between the TMA and its predecessor is that there is no residual discretion conferred on the Registry. The list in s.3 is finite.

14.4.1.1 Policy

In providing guidance for national courts on the meaning of Article 3, the ECJ has gone out of its way to state the underlying policy for each of the Absolute Grounds. Whilst United Kingdom courts have tended to declare a blanket rule that particular signs must be left free for other traders, the ECJ has been more specific and has provided a justification for each of the objections.

14.4.1.2 The relationship between s.1 and s.3

A point that many have found puzzling is how to fit together the phrase 'capable of distinguishing' in s.1 with 'devoid of distinctive character' in s.3(1)(b). However, it now seems settled that the relationship between s.1 and s.3 is the difference between the *potential* of the sign to distinguish, considered in the abstract, and whether it does *actually* do so, either inherently or factually (see *Philips Electronics NV v Remington Consumer Products per* Jacob J at p. 289). This approach has been endorsed by the General Court and ECJ. The latter has said that even though the 'sign', considered in the abstract, has the potential to function as a trade mark under s.1, it must still be assessed concretely under s.3 to see whether it actually does so, or whether there is an objection to it (*POSTKANTOOR*).

14.4.1.3 The test to be applied

The common factor throughout ECJ case law on Absolute Grounds is the 'concrete test'. This means that the mark applied for is examined with reference to the goods and services of the application through the eyes of the relevant consumer *(POSTKANTOOR)*. This is in contrast to Article 2, where the mark is considered in the abstract, on its own, and *without* reference to the goods. The effect of the concrete test is to concentrate on the consumer's perception of the mark and the messages it sends.

14.4.1.4 The structure of s.3

Overall examination of s.3 shows that there is one general subsection (s.3(1)) which applies to all types of trade marks, no matter what they are. Section 3(1) is subject to a proviso, concerned with acquired (or factual) distinctiveness which does not apply to the remaining subsections. Subsections 3(2) to 3(6) apply to specific cases only. So, only three-dimensional shape marks fall within s.3(2). Section 3(3)(a) and (b) deal respectively with marks which are contrary to public policy or are deceptive, and s.3(4) and (5) deal respectively with marks which are contrary to any provision of United Kingdom or EU law, or which consist of or contain any specially protected emblems, such as coats of arms, state flag or the Olympic symbol. Finally, s.3(6) deals with applications made in bad faith. Each of the later subsections is more specific

thinking point
Is the relationship between Articles 2 and 3 of the Directive sufficiently clear?

A further point is that each of the Absolute Grounds is separate. An applicant might succeed in arguing that one of the grounds does not apply, but still be caught out by another.

14.4.2 Absolute Grounds: the general provision

Section 3(1) consists of four separate paragraphs. However, para (a) is distinct from the other three, for two reasons. First, it contains the word 'sign' whilst the others use the phrase 'trade mark'. Second, the proviso to subsection (1) applies to paras (b), (c) and (d), but not to para (a).

case close-up

Case C-265/00 *Campina Melkunie BV v Benelux-Merkenbureau (BIOMILD)* [2004] ECR I-1699

. . . .

With regard to paras (b), (c) and (d), the ECJ has said (in Case C-265/00 *Campina Melkunie BV v Benelux-Merkenbureau (BIOMILD)* [2004] ECR I-1699) that each is independent of the others, although they overlap. A mark could fall within one but not the other two, or it could fall within all three. Whichever is the case, this does not matter, as the mark will be denied registration if it is caught by one of the objections alone. Each paragraph must be interpreted in the light of its underlying policy. Further, each paragraph has a different policy (Case C-329/02 P *SAT.1 SatellitenFernsehen GmbH v OHIM (SAT.2)* [2004] ECR I-8317).

14.4.2.1 Section 3(1)(a): signs not satisfying s.1

Section 3(1)(a) declares that signs not satisfying s.1 shall not be registered; in other words, if something is either not a 'sign' or incapable of graphic representation or incapable of distinguishing it will fall within para (a).

case close-up

Case C-383/99 P *Procter & Gamble Company v OHIM (BABY DRY)* [2001] ECR I-6251

. . . .

The status of s.3(1)(a) was considered by AG Jacobs in Case C-383/99 P *Procter & Gamble Company v OHIM (BABY DRY)* [2001] ECR I-6251, where he declared (at [63–70]) that Article 7(1)(a) of the Regulation (the equivalent of Article 3(1)(a) of the Directive) was tautologous, a repetition of the definition of 'trade mark'.

The Court of Appeal has since accepted the view that s.3(1)(a) is not a separate ground of refusal if there is no objection under s.1 or the remainder of s.3: *West (t/a Eastenders) v Fuller Smith & Turner plc* [2003] FSR 816. The previous Court of Appeal pronouncement in *Bach Flower Remedies Ltd v Healing Herbs* should therefore be treated as unsafe. Case law decided by OHIM under the Regulation reveals that Article 7(1)(a) is never referred to as a ground of objection. Further, in *Philips v Remington*, the ECJ confirmed that if a mark is factually distinctive, there is not a separate objection that it is incapable of distinguishing. This rather obscure pronouncement was caused by one of the questions referred by the Court of Appeal, which was reluctant to surrender the residual discretion conferred by the 1938 Act to reject a trade mark application even if it did comply with the requirements for registration. In other words, the Court of Appeal was using 'capable of distinguishing' as a ground to object to trade mark applications which, intuitively, it didn't like even though they appeared to satisfy the criteria in the TMA.

14.4.2.2 Section 3(1)(b): marks devoid of distinctive character

Section 3(1)(b) prohibits the registration of trade marks that are devoid of any distinctive character. According to Jacob J in *British Sugar* (at p. 306), the phrase 'requires consideration of the mark on its own, assuming no use. Is it the sort of word (or other sign) which cannot do the job of distinguishing without first educating the public that it is a trade mark?' In other words, is the mark inherently distinctive? Does it say to the consumer (who has no prior experience of the product) 'I am a trade mark'? The General Court in Case T-305/02 *Nestlé Waters France v OHIM* [2003] ECR II-5207 explained it another way. Does the trade mark help the consumer make a repeat purchase if they liked the goods, or avoid them if they had a bad experience?

The policy underlying s.3(1)(b)

The policy of s.3(1)(b) was first set out in *Libertel*, where the Benelux court asked about the registrability of the colour orange for telephone equipment and services. The ECJ said that the public interest was aimed at the need not to restrict unduly the availability of *colours* for other traders in the same field of business (the Court did not refer to 'trade marks' generally). However, in *Nichols* and *SAT.2* the ECJ modified its thinking. It said that para (b) does not have the policy of requiring certain signs to be left free for other traders (which should be compared with the policy underlying s.3(1)(c)). Instead, the public interest cannot be separated from the essential function of a trade mark. The policy underlying para (b) is solely concerned with whether the sign in question acts as a trade mark. In *SAT.2*, the ECJ further observed that para (b) does not require much creativity or imagination by the creator of the mark. It is enough that the trade mark enables consumers to identify the origin of the product. In respect of word marks and picture marks, therefore, the test would seem fairly easy to satisfy. This is not necessarily so in the case of colours, shapes and sensory marks (non-standard marks), even though the Court has said that the section draws no distinction between different categories of trade mark (Cases C-53/01, 54/01 & 55/01 *Linde AG, Winward Industries Inc & Rado Uhren AG v Deutsches Patent- und Markenamt* [2003] ECR-I 3161). This is because consumers perceive non-standard marks as part of the product itself.

The test to be applied

The test to be applied under para (b) is the concrete test, confirmed by the ECJ in *Philips v Remington* at [63]. The mark is considered in relation to the list of goods and services on Form TM3 through the eyes of the reasonably attentive consumer. Does such a person regard the sign as a trade mark, taking into account all the relevant circumstances, remembering that the average consumer will make an overall assessment of the mark? The concrete test, dependent as it is upon consumer perception, helps to explain why, even though s.3(1)(b) is to be applied in an identical manner to all types of mark, certain signs (shapes, colours, sounds and smells) are more likely to be found lacking in inherent distinctiveness. For example, in *Viking v OHIM*, it was held that a grey-green colour scheme on garden tools would be viewed by customers as relating to the finish of the product rather than indicating origin.

There is now an extensive body of case law from the ECJ and General Court demonstrating the application of the concrete test to decide whether a mark lacks distinctive character.

case close-up

Case C-404/02 *Nichols plc v Registrar of Trade Marks* [2004] ECR I-8499

In *Nichols*, the ECJ was asked by the United Kingdom Patents Court how surnames should be treated. Former practice in the United Kingdom had been to check in the phone book to see how often the name occurred, and if there was more than a certain number of entries, to deny registrability because other traders might want to use the mark. The ECJ simply said that it depended on consumer perception: did the average purchaser regard the name as a trade mark for the particular goods (in this instance, vending machines)?

Shape marks have fared less well under s.3(1)(b), simply because the average consumer does not normally think that the shape of goods indicates origin. Thus, a cigar shape for chocolate bars was not registrable (Cases T-324/01 and T-110/02 *Axion SA & Christian Belce v OHIM* [2003] ECR II-1897). The same principle applies to colours (*Libertel* and *Viking*) and surface decoration applied to the goods (Case T-36/01 *Glaverbel v OHIM* [2002] ECR II-3887).

Trade marks, however, may be composite creations. They may consist of a combination of words and numerals, shapes and colours, words and pictures. The individual elements taken separately may each lack distinctive character. However, the court will not break the mark down into its component parts (sometimes called 'salami slicing'), but will instead make an overall assessment, because that is what the consumer would do. The combination itself may therefore be distinctive *(SAT.2)*. There have been a considerable number of cases before the ECJ on appeal from OHIM concerning the appearance of detergent tablets. In each case the Court has consistently applied the concrete test and asked how the average consumer would see the mark. Unless the applicant seeks to rely on the proviso to show evidence of factual distinctiveness, the consumer does not see the combined colour and shape as indicating the origin of goods: Cases C-468/01 P to C-472/01 P and C-473 and 474/01 P *Procter & Gamble Co v OHIM* [2004] ECR I-5141.

For some time now, there has been a trend of trying to register slogans as trade marks. These slogans (sometimes called 'strap lines') are used in conjunction with the main brand name. The approach of United Kingdom courts used to be that a slogan was an invitation to try the product and therefore could not be a trade mark (*HAVE A BREAK Trade Mark* [1993] RPC 217). The only pre-1994 example of a registrable slogan was *I CAN't BELIEVE IT's YOGURT Trade Mark* [1992] RPC 533, where it was accepted that the slogan had been used as the only brand name on the goods. By contrast, the ECJ has applied the concrete test to slogan marks. It has said that there is no need for a slogan to be particularly creative, but that normally the consumer would not regard a strap line as indicating origin (Case C-64/02 P *OHIM v Erpo Möbelwerk GmbH* ('*The Principle of Comfort*') [2004] ECR I-10031). It is up to the applicant to show factual distinctiveness under the proviso. In Case C-353/03 *Société des Produits Nestlé SA v Mars UK Ltd* [2005] ECR I-6135, and in contrast to the views of the Court of Appeal, the ECJ ruled that it didn't matter that the slogan had been used in conjunction with another trade mark, because even a secondary mark could, in appropriate circumstances, acquire factual distinctiveness in its own right.

A final point is that where the trade mark has been applied for in respect of multiple classes of goods, the Registry is required to consider the application of s.3(1)(b) (and indeed the rest of s.3(1)) to each item listed: *POSTKANTOOR*; and Case C-239/05 *BVBA Management Training en Consultancy v Benelux-Merkenbureau* [2007] ECR I-1455. The net result is that the mark may be inherently distinctive of some goods or services but not of others. In Case T-173/00 *KWS Saat v OHIM* [2002] ECR II-3843, the colour orange was held inherently distinctive of consultancy services but not so for seeds nor the equipment used to sow them.

14.4.2.3 Section 3(1)(c): descriptive signs

In essence, s.3(1)(c) prohibits the registration of trade marks consisting exclusively of descriptive signs. The presence of the word 'exclusively' suggests that a narrow interpretation of the provision could be adopted, but the case law of the ECJ has shown otherwise.

What is a descriptive sign?

Section 3(1)(c) prohibits the registration of 'signs or indications' which 'designate the kind, quality, quantity, intended purpose, value...or other characteristics of goods or services'. It therefore covers not just words which describe the goods, but other types of signs (for example colours, like the red and white stripes in *Unilever's Application* indicating ingredients). Similarly, the section prohibits the registration of words which describe 'other characteristics' of the goods. In Case C-498/01 P *OHIM v Zapf Creation AG (NEW BORN BABY)* [2004] ECR I-11349 the term 'new born baby' described the characteristics of dolls. Where a word has several possible meanings, it suffices if one of those describes the characteristics of the goods: Case C-191/01 P *OHIM v Wm Wrigley Junior Co (DOUBLEMINT)* [2003] ECR I-12447.

New words

But what if the trade mark consists of a new, made-up word, the component parts of which are descriptive (what the ECJ calls a 'neologism')? The Court has said (in *BIOMILD* and *POSTKANTOOR*) that the mark must be looked at as a whole to see if it conveys a descriptive meaning. It will be denied registration 'unless the mark as a whole creates, both aurally and visually, an impression far removed from that produced by a simple combination'. An example of an unsuccessful neologism is *FROOT LOOPS Trade Mark* [1998] RPC 240, where the mark was rejected because when spoken it directly described the goods (breakfast cereals). It sounded like 'fruit loops'. Conversely, 'UltraPlus' was registrable because it was an unusual combination of words. Even though taken individually the component parts were descriptive, the overall mark was not the normal way that consumers would refer to microwave ovenware: Case T-360/00 *Dart Industries Inc v OHIM* [2002] ECR II-3867.

Geographical names

Section 3(1)(c) also bars the registration of geographical names. The meaning of 'geographical name' was explained by the ECJ in Cases C-108/97 and 109/97 *Windsurfing Chiemsee Produktions und Vertriebs GmbH v Boots und Segelzubehor Walter Huber* [1999] ECR I-2779 at [31–35]. It means that consumers currently associate the name with the place where the goods come from. The place can be the source of the goods either now or in the future. Consequently, a 'fanciful' geographical name (such as 'North Pole' for bananas) can always be registered because consumers are unlikely to believe that those goods originate from that location. Equally registrable are names of places which consumers do not (and are unlikely to) associate with the goods. In Case T-379/03 *Peek & Cloppenburg KG v OHIM* [2005] ECR

II-4633, the General Court, on appeal from OHIM, held that although there was a town called 'Cloppenburg', German consumers did not associate the name with the production of goods and/or services. It was therefore not a 'geographical name'.

The underlying policy

The public interest underlying s.3(1)(c) has been stated in a restrictive fashion by the ECJ, in *DOUBLEMINT* (at [29–32]) and *POSTKANTOOR* (at [54–55]). The ECJ declared that the Directive pursues an aim that descriptive signs can be freely used by all. Because of the phrase 'may serve' in the Directive, descriptive signs must be left free for other traders, whether they want to use them today, or whether they *might* want to use them in the future. This is, however, not an absolute rule because of the presence of the proviso as to acquired distinctiveness (*Windsurfing Chiemsee*).

The test

Even though the underlying policy is stricter, s.3(1)(c) is applied in the same manner as s.3(1)(b). The concrete test is used to decide what information about the goods or services is conveyed to the average consumer by the proposed trade mark, in other words, how would the consumer refer to such goods? Where the mark consists of a number of elements, it is to be considered as a whole.

thinking point

Is it right that the policy underlying s.3(1)(b) differs from that underlying s.3(1)(c)?

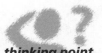

thinking point

Can the decision of the ECJ in BABY DRY be reconciled with what was said in DOUBLEMINT?

---

case close-up

Case C-383/99 P *Procter & Gamble Company v OHIM (BABY DRY)* [2001] ECR I-6251

. . . .

A controversial decision is *BABY DRY*. On appeal from OHIM, the ECJ held that the mark (a combination of two known words) was 'syntactically unusual' because the normal way in English of referring to the characteristics of babies' nappies would have been to refer to a 'dry baby'. The case should now be treated with caution for two reasons. First, the ECJ did not mention the policy of preventing the registration of descriptive marks, in contrast to its earlier ruling in *Windsurfing Chiemsee* and its later statements in *DOUBLEMINT* and *POSTKANTOOR*. Second, in *DOUBLEMINT* itself, the Court made plain (at [32]) that an application will be refused under s.3(1)(c) if at least one of the possible meanings of the mark describes the goods.

Foreign descriptive words

---

case close-up

Case C-421/04 *Matratzen Concord AG v Hukla Germany SA* [2006] ECR I-2303

. . . .

An illustration of the concrete test in relation to foreign descriptive words is Case C-421/04 *Matratzen Concord AG v Hukla Germany SA* [2006] ECR I-2303. A Spanish court had sought guidance as to whether a word which was descriptive of the goods (mattresses) in German was registrable in Spain. The evidence was that most Spanish people did not know the meaning of the word 'matratzen' ('mattress' in German) and so would not view it as descriptive of the goods. The ECJ ruled that where a word which is descriptive of the characteristics of the goods in the language of Member State B (Germany) is sought to be registered in Member State A (Spain), it should not be refused registration unless consumers in Member State A are capable of identifying the meaning of the (foreign) word. In other words, the Court adopted the mantle of the average Spanish consumer to decide what information was conveyed about the product by the mark.

Controversially, the recast Directive will reverse the *Matratzen* ruling so that a mark must be rejected where it would be descriptive if translated into any official language of the Member States. This has attracted considerable criticism.

14.4.2.4 Section 3(1)(d)

There are two separate limbs to s.3(1)(d). A mark will be refused registration if it has become customary, either in the current language, or in the *bona fide* and established practices of the trade. The wording of the provision is not concerned with whether the word (or whatever) is common, but whether it is customary *in the trade*, that is, whether it is being used by other traders in the relevant product, or indeed, whether it is used by customers to refer to that product. In *Wm Wrigley Jr Co's Application (LIGHT GREEN)* [1999] ETMR 214, an application to register the colour light green for confectionery was refused as the mark was already widely used by other sweet manufacturers. The United Kingdom Trade Marks Registry has offered further examples of marks which can be considered customary (ie generic), such as star devices for brandy or 'Red Lion' for public house services.

Underlying policy

The public interest of para (d) is, according to the ECJ, the same as under para (c), that is, it protects the interests of other traders (Case C-517/99 *Merz & Krell GmbH & Co v Deutsches Patent- und Markenamt*, (*BRAVO*) [2001] ECR I-6959). However, the ECJ, in clarifying the overlap between the two paragraphs, stated that the use of the mark does not have to be descriptive of the goods. Section 3(1)(d) does differ from s.3(1)(c) in that it deals with signs which are actually in use in trade, rather than signs which other traders *might* want to use.

The test

As with all aspects of s.3, the test is the same, namely the concrete test. The sign is considered in relation to the products listed on Form TM3 through the eyes of the notional consumer: Case C-371/02 *Björnekulla Fruktindustrier AB v Procordia Food AB* [2004] ECR I-5791 (a case on the parallel ground of revocation found in s.46(1)(c)). As the Appointed Person explained in *STASH Trade Mark*, 3 September 2004, there must be clear evidence that by the application date the mark is used by third parties to such an extent that it has become customary (that is, 'usual') in the trade for the relevant goods or services. In *STASH* itself, evidence of two uses of the mark by third parties before the application date did not amount to customary use. Much will depend on the nature of the market. The amount of use required will be far less where the products are specialised than where they are bought by members of the public.

14.4.2.5 The proviso to s.3(1)

The proviso to s.3(1) makes clear that marks which are caught by paras (b), (c) and (d) can still be registered where the applicant can show acquired distinctiveness. This is a major exception to these three objections: *Windsurfing Chiemsee*. The proviso is nicely explained by the Appointed Person in *AD2000 Trade Mark* [1997] RPC 168 as the difference between nature and nurture. A mark which began life by being inherently non-distinctive, descriptive or generic can still be registered if after use the relevant customers come to regard it as indicating origin. Such use must be before the application date.

Cases C-108/97 and 109/97 *Windsurfing Chiemsee Produktions und Vertriebs GmbH v Boots und Segelzubehor Walter Huber* [1999] ECR I-2779

The factors to be taken into account when deciding whether a 'significant proportion' of relevant consumers recognise the mark were listed by the ECJ in *Windsurfing Chiemsee* at [45–51]. The Court explained that there should be an overall assessment of the evidence, taking into account the nature of the sign in question. A 'weak' trade mark, such as a shape, colour or highly descriptive name will require far greater evidence of use, although there is no objection to the fact that the mark may have been used alongside another brand name or as part of the get-up of the product: *Société des Produits Nestlé SA v Mars UK Ltd*. The other factors are the market share held by the mark, how intensive, widespread and long-standing the use of it has been, the amount invested in advertising, and what proportion of consumers recognise the mark (although the ECJ stressed that there was no fixed percentage—it all depends on the facts). Other evidence can come from those in the same line of business, as the Court said that supporting statements from chambers of commerce and other trade associations were relevant to determining acquired distinctiveness.

The challenge of complying with the *Windsurfing* criteria is shown by Case T-16/02 *Audi AG v OHIM* [2003] ECR II-5167. It was held that the applicant had failed to satisfy the test simply by filing evidence of how many cars it had sold or exported under the name TDI, because the volume of sales by itself did not prove that consumers viewed it as a trade mark.

thinking point
Does the proviso to s.3(1) not mean that the interests of other traders can be overridden?

Use to support a claim of acquired distinctiveness under the TMA must be within the United Kingdom. This poses interesting questions when the mark is used on a website which is not targeted at United Kingdom customers (see *800-FLOWERS Trade Mark* [2002] FSR 191). In view of the discussion about trade mark function in *Arsenal Football Club v Matthew Reed*, such use might include promotional use.

14.4.3 **Absolute Grounds: specific provisions**

The remaining subsections of s.3 are specific in their application. However, because of the independent nature of the Absolute Grounds, even if an applicant manages to convince the Registry that the mark is unobjectionable under these other provisions, it is still possible for the application to fail under s.3(1).

14.4.3.1 Shape marks

Shapes (that is, three-dimensional objects) are specifically mentioned in s.1 as examples of trade marks. There is a separate set of Absolute Grounds which apply *only* to shape marks in s.3(2) although shape marks themselves are subject to the full list of objections in s.3. The ECJ has held, in *Linde*, that s.3(2) is an independent ground of objection and should be applied first, *before* s.3(1). In consequence, if an application is rejected under s.3(2), evidence of acquired distinctiveness will be of no assistance (*Philips v Remington*). Even if the shape does not fall within any of the specific prohibitions in s.3(2), it still needs to be considered under s.3(1) to see if it is distinctive, descriptive or common to the trade.

The most usual objection under s.3(1) to shape marks is that they are devoid of distinctive character. Thus in Case C-238/06P *Develey Holding GmbH v OHIM* [2007] ECR I-9375 protection was denied to the rather ordinary appearance of a squeezable sauce bottle. Very unusual shapes may, exceptionally, be inherently distinctive; examples include Case T-128/01 *DaimlerChrysler Corporation v OHIM* [2003] ECR II-701 (a car radiator grille) and Case T-460/05 *Bang & Olufsen A/S v OHIM* [2007] ECR II-4207 (the shape of a loudspeaker). Overcoming the objections under s.3(1) by proof of acquired distinctiveness will not be easy. Sufficient evidence of use (complying with the *Windsurfing Chiemsee* criteria) must be produced to show that consumers recognise the shape as indicating origin. Consumers do not do this readily: *Bongrain's Application* [2005] RPC 306.

Section 3(2), it must be repeated, applies only to three-dimensional marks, not two-dimensional picture marks: *Re August Storck KG's Trade Mark Application*, Appointed Person, 9 October 2007.

The origin of s.3(2)

The three paragraphs of s.3(2) can be summed up as comprising natural shapes, technical shapes and aesthetic shapes. It is generally agreed that the wording is derived from the Benelux Uniform Trade Mark Act 1971. Strowel (in 'Benelux: A Guide to the Validity of Three-dimensional Trade Marks in Europe' [1995] *EIPR* 154) gives decided examples under that legislation of the three types of prohibited shapes. For natural shapes, he suggests an egg box, an umbrella or a carrier bag, and gives the lego brick as an example of a technical shape. With regard to aesthetic shapes, there have been Benelux cases involving a set of miniature china houses or a children's bath in the shape of a scallop shell. However, Strowel argues that this exclusion does not bar the registration of shapes added to foodstuffs such as chocolate, ice cream, crisps or drink bottles. It is, he says, necessary to ask *why* the consumer bought the goods. The shape is not the prime reason for the purchase. Even if the goods cost more because of the trade mark, this is not the 'substantial' value required by the wording of the Directive. Strowel also argues that s.3(2) is a derogation from the very broad definition of 'trade mark' in s.1 and so should be interpreted narrowly.

The policy underlying s.3(2)

The public interest underlying s.3(2) has been set out by the ECJ. In *Philips v Remington*, relying on its earlier statement in *Windsurfing Chiemsee* about the policy of s.3(1)(c), the Court said that shapes falling within the wording of the provision had to be left free for all other traders to use. It would seem, therefore, that the policy of s.3(2) is not about avoiding overlap with patents and **design**s, but ensuring competitors' freedom of choice.

The scope of the shape exclusions

Shape objections have been considered by the ECJ in a number of cases. In *Philips v Remington*, contrary to the arguments advanced by Strowel, the Court gave a relatively broad interpretation of the technical shapes exclusion, rejecting the argument that it was irrelevant that the same result could be achieved by other means. The word 'necessary' in s.3(2)(b) was interpreted to mean 'attributable'. It added to this in Case C-48/09 P *Lego Juris A/S v OHIM* [2010] ECR I-8403 where guidance was given as to how the essential characteristics of a shape are to be determined. For once, the consumer's views are not paramount. In Case T-508/08 *Bang & Olufsen v OHIM* [2011] ECR II-6975, the General Court considered the aesthetic shapes exclusion. Building on existing jurisprudence, it said that the policy of s.3(2)(c) is the same as that of s.3(2)(b) and that the views of the consumer are not conclusive. Further, if a particular shape became a unique selling point of the product (here, the sculpture-like shape of a loudspeaker), then it was caught by the prohibition.

No case has yet been referred to the ECJ on natural shapes.

thinking point

Is the conclusion of the ECJ in Philips v Remington *about the meaning of s.3(2)(b) consistent with the argument that s.3(2) is a derogation from the policy of s.1 and should be construed narrowly?*

14.4.3.2 Marks contrary to public policy

Section 3(3)(a) prohibits the registration of marks contrary to public policy or morality. There are similar prohibitions against granting protection to offensive subject matter in patent and design law.

case close-up

Re Ghazilian's Trade Mark Application [2001] RPC 654

The leading decision is *Re Ghazilian's Trade Mark Application* [2001] RPC 654. The case explains that what matters is not whether a section of the public considers the trade mark distasteful, but whether it would cause outrage, and so be likely significantly to undermine current religious, family or social values. Again, we may note the role of the consumer, as the censure must be amongst an identifiable section of the public. Each case must be decided on its own facts, so a higher degree of outrage amongst a small section of the community may well suffice.

Ghazilian has been applied on several occasions, including 'standupifyouhatemanu.com', Trade Marks Registry, 20 November 2002, where the attempt to register the name of a website as a trade mark was refused as being likely to incite football hooliganism. In *Basic Trade Mark SA's Trade Mark Application (JESUS)* [2005] RPC 611 the choice of the name JESUS was held likely to cause offence to a significant section of the public. By contrast, in *Woodman v French Connection UK Ltd*, Registry, 20 December 2005, an attempt to have the mark FCUK declared invalid as being contrary to s.3(3)(a) failed. Although there had been complaints to the Advertising Standards Authority that the mark was too close to a particular expletive, there was no evidence to suggest that FCUK-branded goods had themselves caused outrage. Any offence that had been caused had not been as a result of the use of the mark itself, but rather by the context in which an individual trader had chosen to use the letters in promotional material.

14.4.3.3 Deceptive marks

Section 3(3)(b) prohibits the registration of trade marks which are deceptive to the public, for example as to the nature of the goods. Here, the legislation places the applicant in a dilemma. The easiest route will be to choose a known word as a means of selling goods. However, there is a fine line between descriptiveness and deceptiveness. As explained in *ORLWOOLA Trade*

Mark (1909) 26 RPC 683, 850, (and it is important to remember how the mark would have been spoken) if the goods are as described by the known word (here the goods were textiles) the mark is unregistrable because it is totally descriptive. If the goods do not possess those properties, the mark is deceptive. The assessment of deceptiveness under s.3(3)(b) is effected through the eyes of the reasonably well-informed, observant yet circumspect consumer who is used to 'hype' (*Kraft Jacobs Suchard Ltd's Application (KENCO THE REAL COFFEE EXPERTS)* [2001] ETMR 585).

case close-up

Case C-259/04 *Emanuel v Continental Shelf 128 Ltd* [2006] ECR I-3089
. . . .

The ECJ has provided guidance on deceptive marks. In Case C-259/04 *Emanuel v Continental Shelf 128 Ltd* [2006] ECR I-3089, the applicant for revocation was a famous fashion designer whose reputation increased dramatically when she created the wedding dress for the Princess of Wales in 1981. A trade mark consisting of her name and a logo was registered in 1994. As a result of financial difficulties, she had assigned her business to a company in 1996, becoming an employee of the business. Thereafter, there were successive transfers of the business which ultimately was owned by the defendant. In the meantime, the applicant had resigned. The defendant's predecessor had applied to register further marks consisting of the applicant's name. She opposed these applications under s.3(3)(b) and sought revocation of the earlier mark under s.46(1)(d) on the ground that it had become deceptive as to the origin of the goods. The ECJ ruled that the word 'deceive' in Article 3 referred to the intrinsic characteristics of the trade mark. The sign must objectively deceive the public by virtue of its qualities. Where the trade mark was a person's name and had been **assigned** as part of the business, it did not deceive the public even if it created the mistaken impression that that person took part in the creation of the goods for which the mark was used.

14.4.3.4 Marks contrary to law and specially protected emblems

Sections 3(4) and (5) can be considered together. Respectively, they prohibit the registration of trade marks which are contrary to United Kingdom or EU law and trade marks consisting of or containing specially protected emblems. Section 3(4) includes trade marks which breach United Kingdom legislation such as the Trade Descriptions Act 1968, the Plant Varieties Act 1997, the Hallmarking Act 1973 or the London Olympic Games and Paralympic Games Act 2006. EU secondary legislation includes EC Regulation 510/2006 on the protection of geographical indications and designations of origin for agricultural products and foodstuffs ([2006] OJ L 93/12). This enables geographical names to be registered where the area produces food or drink with unique properties (for example 'Stilton' for cheese).

Section 3(5) is amplified by s.4, which deals in detail with such matters as the Royal Coats of Arms, words indicating royal patronage, national flags and the flags and emblems of international organisations. An illustration is *COMBINED ARMED FORCES FEDERATION Trade Mark*, Registry, 24 July 2009, where it was held that a combination of the Union Flag, the words of the applicant organisation, and a crown would lead the average consumer to think that the user of the mark had royal patronage or mislead them into believing that it was an organ of the state.

14.4.3.5 Marks obtained in bad faith

Last, s.3(6) prohibits the registration of a trade mark to the extent that the application was made in bad faith. 'Bad faith' was considered by the Court of Appeal in *Harrison v Teton Valley Trading Co (CHINA WHITE)* [2004] 1 WLR 2577. It said that the objection is only available in limited circumstances, where the applicant's conduct amounts to dishonesty or where the applicant's conduct falls short of the standards of acceptable commercial behaviour observed by reasonable and experienced men in the area in question. The test involves a mixture of the subjective and objective: there must be a realisation by the applicant that what he was doing would be regarded by honest people as in bad faith. According to the Court of Appeal, this requires an inquiry into what the applicant knew, and whether a reasonable person would think the conduct was wrong. However, it is not necessary to show that the applicant thought that what he was doing was dishonest: *AJIT WEEKLY Trade Mark* [2006] RPC 633, Appointed Person.

'Bad faith' has been considered by the ECJ in Case C-529/07 *Chocoladefabriken Lindt & Sprüngli AG v Franz Hauswirth GmbH* [2009] ECR I-4893. Although the Advocate General, Eleanor Sharpston, provided a comprehensive review of the meaning of the phrase, the Court's ruling gives little clear guidance. The Court simply lists the factors to be taken into account and leaves the matter to be determined by the national court.

thinking point
Are the policy grounds underlying the various parts of Article 3 consistent? If not, does it matter?

An example of bad faith is attempting to register a mark knowing that it belongs to someone else (*MICKEY DEES (NIGHTCLUB) Trade Mark* [1998] RPC 359). However, there is no bad faith where there is a degree of uncertainty as to entitlement: *Gromax Plasticulture Ltd v Don & Low Nonwovens Ltd* [1999] RPC 367. Applying for a two-dimensional mark when it will be used in a three-dimensional form is not, without more, evidence of bad faith: *Robert McBride Ltd's Application* [2005] ETMR 990.

14.5 Relative grounds for refusal of registration

14.5.1 Overview of relative grounds

Whilst Absolute Grounds are concerned with an analysis of a proposed mark's innate qualities, Relative Grounds involve a comparison of the mark with prior rights, with what is already 'out there'. If the mark conflicts with an earlier mark (whether registered or unregistered) or an earlier **copyright** or design, then the application will be rejected. Such an objection can be overcome by obtaining the consent of the owner of the earlier right under s.5(5) of the TMA. The principal provisions in the TMA dealing with Relative Grounds (ss.5(1), 5(2) and 5(3)) are a mirror image of ss. 10(1), 10(2) and 10(3) setting out the owner's rights in infringement.

Judge Bornkamm (in 'Harmonising Trade Mark Law in Europe: the Stephen Stewart Memorial Lecture' [1999] *IPQ* 283) calls these two sets of provisions (derived respectively from Articles 4 and 5 of the Directive) the 'triad of protection'. Both s.5 and s.10 cover three distinct situations, in the case of Relative Grounds when comparing the earlier right and the mark applied for; and in the case of infringement, the registered mark and the infringing sign. These comprise in essence: double identity between the marks and their respective goods and services; identity and/or similarity between the marks and their goods and services in circumstances where there is a likelihood of confusion; and cases where the senior mark has a reputation which deserves protection against those wishing to take unfair advantage of its distinctive character. The case law of the ECJ on the interpretation of Articles 4 and 5 is completely interchangeable. Just as with the Absolute Grounds, the average consumer is the person through whose eyes the facts are decided.

The triad of protection can be explained in another way, as set out in Diagram 14.2. There is the absolute 'core' of protection when there is identity between the marks and their products; an outer, more flexible 'core' of protection dependent on similarity and confusion; and an outer rim of protection available only for those marks with a reputation. There is, however, a clear difference between the inner two zones and the outer zone. The former accord with the traditional role of the trade mark in protecting against consumer confusion, the latter is essentially concerned with protecting the owner of the mark against misappropriation. Whichever zone of protection is in issue, however, there must be either identity or similarity of marks. There is no protection against a dissimilar trade mark.

Diagram 14.2

Relative grounds: the 'triad of protection'

SECTION 10(3): PROTECTION FOR MARKS WITH A REPUTATION - DEPENDS ON WHETHER THERE IS DETRIMENT OR UNFAIR ADVANTAGE.

SECTION 5(2): SIMILARITY PLUS CONFUSION - DEPENDS ON THE GLOBAL APPRECIATION TEST.

SECTION 5(1): 'DOUBLE IDENTITY' ABSOLUTE (CORE) PROTECTION

14.5.2 The list of prior rights

The lengthy list of prior rights results from a combination of s.6 and s.5(4) TMA. It comprises earlier registered marks which have effect in the United Kingdom (whether they are on the domestic, EU or international registers); earlier pending applications for national, EU or international registrations, provided they mature to registration; subsequent EU registrations claiming seniority from earlier United Kingdom or international registrations; well-known trade marks entitled to protection under the Paris Convention; recently lapsed registrations; earlier used but unregistered marks (provided they are capable of protection under passing off); and earlier copyrights, or registered or unregistered designs. Of these, the most important are earlier registered marks.

14.5.3 **Applying the provisions**

Each of ss.5(1), 5(2) and 5(3) (forming the 'triad of protection') has specific criteria. They must be applied systematically in sequence: *Reed Executive plc v Reed Business Information Ltd* [2004] RPC 767. If the application does not fall within s.5(1) (because there is absence of identity in either the mark or the goods) you go to s.5(2). If there is no similarity of goods, or if there is an absence of confusion, you go to s.5(3).

14.5.4 **Double identity**

Section 5(1) provides that a trade mark shall not be registered if it is identical to an earlier mark and is in respect of the identical goods and services. There is no need to prove confusion. It is assumed that there will be consumer confusion in cases of total identity: Case C-2/00 *Hölterhoff v Ulrich Freiesleben* [2002] ECR I-4187.

14.5.4.1 Deciding identity

When deciding whether there is identity for the purposes of s.5(1), the register entry for the senior mark is crucial. So, the statement of goods on the applicant's Form TM3 is compared with those for which the senior mark is *actually* registered. If the goods are not identical, the case falls under s.5(2) (*British Sugar*). Likewise, the junior mark as it appears on Form TM3 is compared with how the senior mark is shown on the register: *Philips v Remington* (at p. 312). Where the senior mark is a word, what is registered is the word itself, so the type of lettering is irrelevant: *Bravado Merchandising v Mainstream Publishing* [1996] FSR 205.

14.5.4.2 The test for identity of marks

case close-up

Case C-291/00 *LTJ Diffusion SA v Sadas Vertbaudet SA* [2003] ECR I-2799
. . . .

The test for an identical mark was explained by the ECJ in Case C-291/00 *LTJ Diffusion SA v Sadas Vertbaudet SA* [2003] ECR I-2799 at [50–54]. The Court said that because protection is absolute under s.5(1) and s.10(1), 'identity' must be strictly interpreted. The two marks must be the same in all respects. The mark applied for must reproduce, without any modification, all the elements of the senior mark. The Court added that the comparison (an overall one) is made through the eyes of the well-informed, reasonably observant and circumspect consumer. The consumer will rarely have the opportunity to compare the two marks side by side so that insignificant differences may go unnoticed (this last point is sometimes referred to as the 'doctrine of imperfect recollection'). The consumer's circumstances may mean that the test is not as absolute as might be supposed.

The ECJ did not elaborate on what it meant by 'insignificant differences'. On the facts of the case itself, the addition of a dot over the mark was thought to be insignificant. But what if the mark applied for is ORIGINS when the senior mark is ORIGIN, or HUGGAR when the senior mark is HUGGER? Would the average consumer notice the difference?

14.5.4.3 Where the senior mark is contained in the junior mark

Where the senior mark is contained within the junior mark (that is, surrounded by additional words or pictorial matter rather than where the junior mark has more letters), for example, the senior mark is REED and the junior mark is REED ELSEVIER, how is the comparison to be made? In *Reed Executive plc v Reed Business Information Ltd* the Court of Appeal thought it important to decide whether the surrounding matter had trade mark significance (ie did it send the consumer a 'trade mark message'). If it did, then the marks were to be examined to see if they were similar. If it did not, the surrounding non-trade mark matter could be ignored, and the marks would be treated as identical. In the *Reed* case, it was held that ELSEVIER had trade mark significance, so what had to be compared was REED with REED ELSEVIER.

> **thinking point**
>
> *Is the ECJ's guidance in* LTJ *as to how identity of marks is to be decided sufficiently clear? How can the test be absolute yet permit insignificant differences to be ignored?*

14.5.5 **Similarity coupled with confusion**

Section 5(2) prohibits the registration of a mark which is identical or similar to an earlier registered mark and which is to be for similar or identical goods and services, provided there exists a likelihood of confusion on the part of the public, 'which includes a likelihood of association'.

14.5.5.1 The scope of s.5(2)

Section 5(2) covers a total of 10 permutations, which we set out in Table 14.1:

Table 14.1

Section 5(2) permutations

A mark applied for in respect of goods will be prevented from achieving registration by the presence on the Register of:	A mark applied for in respect of services will be prevented from achieving registration by the presence on the Register of:
an identical mark in relation to similar goods	an identical mark in relation to similar services
an identical mark in relation to similar services	an identical mark in relation to similar goods
a similar mark in relation to identical goods	a similar mark in relation to identical services
a similar mark in relation to similar goods	a similar mark in relation to similar services
a similar mark in relation to similar services	a similar mark in relation to similar goods

However, whatever the combination is, the overarching requirement is that there must be a likelihood of confusion.

14.5.5.2 Types of confusion

Section 5(2) demands that there must be a likelihood of confusion 'which includes a likelihood of association'. Case law has identified three types of confusion. First, there may be direct confusion, where the consumer confuses one product with another. Second, there may be indirect confusion, where the consumer thinks that the goods come from an economically linked undertaking or that the trade mark owner has expanded their business. Last, there may be 'mere' association. The consumer 'calls the trade mark to mind' but is not misled about the origin of the goods. This is sometimes referred to as 'non-origin confusion'.

14.5.5.3 The problem of 'likelihood of association'

The origin of the phrase 'likelihood of association' in the Directive is said to be the Uniform Benelux Trade Marks Act 1971. An example of a case under that legislation is *MONOPOLY v ANTI-MONOPOLY* [1978] BIE 39 and 43. Here it was held that to call a board game 'Anti-Monopoly' would not confuse customers. However, it would make them think of 'Monopoly' and would therefore injure (by **dilution**) the reputation of the senior mark.

The United Kingdom approach

The interpretation of s.10(2) (and by implication s.5(2)) was examined by Laddie J in *Wagamama Ltd v City Centre Restaurants* [1995] FSR 713. He applied normal rules of statutory interpretation, and held that 'likelihood of association' was included within the notion of 'likelihood of confusion'. Laddie J rejected all arguments (referring to them as 'Chinese whispers') that the Benelux meaning of association should be incorporated into United Kingdom law. To do so would enhance the trade mark right far too much.

The ECJ's approach

case close-up

> **Case C-251/95 *Sabel BV v Puma AG*** [1997] ECR I-6191
>
> The ECJ first examined the meaning of 'likelihood of confusion' in Case C-251/95 *Sabel BV v Puma AG* [1997] ECR I-6191. Up to a point, the Court agrees with *Wagamama* (but it should be remembered that the ECJ is not in a hierarchical relationship with national courts). However, the ECJ went much further than *Wagamama* in its treatment of 'likelihood of association'. It declared that association was not an alternative to confusion but 'serves to define its scope' (at [18]). In other words, although 'calling the trade mark to mind' does not amount to confusion (Case C-425/98 *Marca Mode CV v Adidas AG and Adidas Benelux BV* [2000] ECR I-4861), the thought processes of the average consumer, and the associations which that person makes when seeing the junior mark, play a part in proving confusion. For the purposes of s.5(2), though, only direct and indirect confusion will suffice.

thinking point
How important is association under s.5(2)?

The role of association

Association is not totally irrelevant. It is involved in the way in which direct confusion is assessed, and helps to show indirect confusion. This is attributable to two things, namely Recital 11 to the Directive (as numbered in the consolidated version) and the ECJ's 'global appreciation' test used to determine the likelihood of confusion. Further, 'association' is crucial in the protection for marks with a reputation under s.5(3).

14.5.5.4 The application of s.5(2)

Recital 11 to the consolidated version of the Directive is the starting point in the application of s.5(2). It declares that the appreciation of confusion 'depends on numerous elements, in particular, the recognition of the trade mark on the market, of the association which can be made with the used or registered sign, the degree of similarity between the trade mark and the sign and between the goods or services identified'. The Recital mentions two elements of the consumer's comparison of the senior and junior marks, namely 'the recognition of the trade mark' and 'the association which can be made'. Whether or not there is a likelihood of confusion is a question of fact in every case. From *Sabel v Puma*, the issues in s.5(2) are dealt with in the following order:

Similarity of marks

As a precondition to the application of s.5(2), there must be at least *some* similarity between the senior and junior mark: Case 106/03 P *Vedial SA v OHIM* [2004] ECR I-9573 at [51], [54]. If there is no similarity, the senior mark has no protection.

The first task is to decide whether there is identity or similarity between the two marks, as s.5(2) covers both. Identity is decided using the test in *LTJ*. If the marks are not identical, are they similar? The ECJ's advice on how to determine similarity of marks was influenced by cases decided under the Benelux Uniform Trade Mark Law 1971, for example, *Union v Union Soleure*, 20 May 1983, Case A 82/5 [1984] BIE 137. In *Sabel v Puma* at [23] the Court said that similarity depends on an aural, visual and conceptual comparison based on the overall impression given by the marks bearing in mind their distinctive components. To put this another way, how are the words spoken, how do they appear on paper and what is their underlying idea? The ECJ in *Sabel* added that these issues are decided from the viewpoint of the average consumer, who is assumed to make an overall comparison without going into minute detail.

case close-up

> **Case T-112/06 *Inter-Ikea Systems BV v OHIM (IKEA/IDEA)*** [2008] ECR II-212
>
> A good illustration of the aural, visual and conceptual comparison which must be made and how each of the three elements is to be balanced against the other is Case T-112/06 *Inter-Ikea Systems BV v OHIM (IKEA/IDEA)* [2008] ECR II-212. The Court began by confirming that the average consumer here would be very attentive as furniture (the goods in question) would only be bought after a period of reflection. When comparing the marks visually, the Court noted that the junior mark had a very dominant figurative element, whilst the senior mark consisted of just a single word. There was only a low degree of aural similarity because even though the sequence of vowel sounds were the same, the consonants 'd' and 'k' were spoken very differently, using different parts of the mouth. Last, there was no conceptual similarity, since the word 'idea' was a word generally understood by the European public whilst 'ikea' was a neologism with no obvious meaning and therefore no associations. There was no similarity.

In *Lloyd* (at [22–23]) the Court expanded on its comment in *Sabel v Puma* about 'the distinctive components' of a mark. The national court had to make an overall assessment of ability of the senior mark to guarantee the origin of goods, including whether it was inherently distinctive and whether it had any descriptive element. In addition, other factors included the market share held by the mark, how intensively and widespread it had been used, how much its owner had spent on advertising, what percentage of consumers recognised it, and how other traders perceived it—in other words, the same list of factors as appears in *Windsurfing Chiemsee* for the purpose of deciding factual distinctiveness under the proviso to s.3(1).

An example of similar marks can be found in *Neutrogena v Golden Ltd t/a Laboratoires Garnier* [1996] RPC 473 where Jacob J held that NEUTRALIA was similar to NEUTROGENA. Both marks were for skin care products, and the prefix 'neutra' conveyed the idea to the average shopper that the goods were kind to the skin. The average supermarket shopper would ignore the second part of each word, and would certainly not make a detailed comparison between the two names.

What if the senior mark is included in the junior mark? We have already considered, in the context of s.5(1) how the Court of Appeal (in *Reed Executive plc v Reed Business Information Ltd*) compared REED with REED ELSEVIER.

case close-up

Case C-120/04 *Medion AG v Thomson Multimedia Sales* [2005] ECR I-8551

The ECJ offered advice on how LIFE (the senior mark) should be compared with THOMSON LIFE when both marks were used on electronic goods. It said that overall assessment of the two marks would make the notional consumer think that the owner of LIFE had expanded its business, leading to indirect confusion. It didn't matter that LIFE was not the dominant part of THOMSON LIFE. To require that the senior mark formed the dominant part of the junior mark would in effect deny protection to the senior mark.

Similarity of goods

Next, once it is shown that the marks are at least not dissimilar, the goods must be compared.

case close-up

Case C-39/97 *Canon KK v Metro-Goldwyn-Mayer Inc* [1998] ECR I-5507

The test is that established in Case C-39/97 *Canon KK v Metro-Goldwyn-Mayer Inc* [1998] ECR I-5507. The ECJ explained (at [23]) that all relevant factors must be taken into account, including the nature of the goods, the end users, the method of use and whether the goods are in competition with each other or are complementary. Whether the goods of both marks appear in the same class within the Nice Classification of Goods and Services 1957 is of no assistance, as the classification is there for administrative purposes. The *Canon* test depends entirely on the facts of each case.

The test in *Canon* is slightly different from the one adopted in *British Sugar*, where Jacob J reworked the criteria set out in *Jellinek's Application* (1946) 63 RPC 59 (a case decided under the 1938 Act). Though the tests are similar, the one in *British Sugar* is narrower as it asks whether the goods are in competition with each other (ie one could be substituted for the other), which is not the same as asking whether the goods are complementary. 'Complementary goods' (for example shoes and shoe polish) are an example of indirect confusion and shows that the ECJ's test is broader. Another issue mentioned in *British Sugar* which is not in the *Canon* test is where the respective goods might be located in a supermarket: given that different supermarkets do not have the same layout and that anyway, the layout is often changed to reflect 'special offers', this is surely not relevant to the issue of similarity.

The global appreciation test

According to *Sabel v Puma* and *Canon*, the final aspect of deciding whether there is a likelihood of confusion is to apply the 'global appreciation' test, in other words all the elements are considered together, or, as the ECJ said in *Canon*, there is an interdependence of factors. If the two marks are conceptually similar, and the senior mark has a particularly distinctive character, either inherently, or because of how much it has been used, there will be a greater likelihood of confusion. On the other hand, if (as in *Sabel* itself) the senior mark has hardly been used, and is one of many on the register with the same underlying idea (here, a wild cat) then the chances of confusion are far lower. Further, in *Canon*, the Court said that a lesser degree of similarity between the goods and services could be offset by a greater degree of similarity between the marks and vice versa. In that case, although the goods were not particularly similar (photographic equipment versus video cassettes), because the senior mark was inherently strong, had been extensively used and heavily promoted, and because the two marks were very close (CANON versus CANNON) there was a likelihood of confusion. As the Court put it in *Lloyd*, the strength of the senior mark may have the effect of making less similar goods similar, or the closeness of the goods may make the junior mark more similar to the senior mark.

The 'global appreciation' test is entirely different from that applied by United Kingdom courts in the early days of the 1994 TMA. In *British Sugar*, it was held that 'likelihood of confusion' was only to be considered *after* it had been established *sequentially* that the goods and the marks were similar. Only notional and fair use of both senior and junior marks was to be assumed; in other words, no account was taken of the circumstances surrounding the senior mark. This 'sterile' test (there was no interdependence of factors) was based on the decision *Smith Hayden & Co Ltd's Application* (1946) 63 RPC 71 under the 1938 Act. Since *Sabel* and *Canon*, the ECJ's more flexible approach has been assimilated into United Kingdom case law. An example can be found in *BALMORAL Trade Mark* [1999] RPC 297. In *Reed Executive plc v Reed Business Information Ltd*, the Court of Appeal accepted that in the case of a used trade mark, the circumstances surrounding such use must be taken into account when determining confusion.

thinking point
Does the global appreciation test provide certainty when dealing with likelihood of confusion?

14.5.6 Marks with a reputation

Section 5(3) contains the final part of Bornkamm's 'triad of protection'. It provides that an earlier registration of the identical or similar mark will prevent the registration of the junior mark where the earlier mark has acquired a reputation and the use of the later mark without due cause would take unfair advantage of or be detrimental to the distinctive character or repute of the earlier mark. The subsection was amended by The Trade Marks (Proof of Use) Regulations 2004 (SI 2004/946), prompted by the ECJ's rulings in Case C-292/00 *Davidoff & Cie SA and Zino Davidoff v Gofkid Ltd* [2003] ECR I-389 and Case C-408/01 *Adidas-Saloman AG and Adidas Benelux BV v Fitnessworld Trading Ltd* [2003] ECR I-12537. Although Article 4(4)(a) and Article 5(2) of the Directive (the origins, respectively of s.5(3) and s.10(3)) required the senior mark to be registered for *dissimilar* goods or services, the Court said that there would be a gap in the scheme of protection if the owner of a mark with a reputation could not object to a junior mark where the goods were similar, in circumstances where there was no likelihood of confusion. The 2004 amendment therefore deletes the references in ss.5(3) and 10(3) to dissimilar goods and services. It may be questioned why the United Kingdom Government saw fit to amend the TMA, as national laws are required to be interpreted in accordance with a parent EU Directive in any event (Case C-106/89 *Marleasing* [1990] ECR I-4135 at [8] and Case C-91/92 *Faccini Dori v Recreb* [1994] ECR I-3325 at [26]). The recast Directive spells out that it matters not whether the goods are identical, similar or not similar.

14.5.6.1 The elements of s.5(3)

The ECJ has stated that s.5(3) pursues a different objective from s.5(2) (*Sabel v Puma* at [20]; and Case C-252/07 *Intel Corporation Inc v CPM United Kingdom Ltd* [2008] ECR I-8823 at [50]). For this reason, its criteria are quite specific. The elements of the provision (all of which must be satisfied) are:

- the junior mark must be identical or similar to the senior mark (applying either *LTJ* or *Sabel v Puma* respectively to decide identity and similarity);
- the senior mark must have a reputation;
- the use by the junior mark must be without due cause; and
- the use by the junior mark must take unfair advantage of or be detrimental to the distinctive character or repute of the senior mark.

14.5.6.2 Similarity

When comparing the senior and junior marks under s.5(3), the ECJ has said (in Case C-252/07 *Intel Corporation Inc v CPM United Kingdom Ltd* at [41–42] and Case C-487/07 *L'Oréal SA v Bellure NV* [2009] ECR I-5185 at [36–37]) that the similarity must be such that the relevant section of the public makes a connection between the sign and the mark, that is to say, establishes a link between them without confusing them. However, the existence of such a link on its own is not sufficient: there must be injury to the mark. Whether there is a link (ie whether the consumer 'calls to mind' the senior mark) is to be assessed globally, taking into account the degree of similarity between the conflicting marks, the nature of the goods or services for which the conflicting marks were registered, including the degree of closeness or dissimilarity between those goods or services, and the relevant section of the public, the strength of the earlier mark's reputation, the degree of the earlier mark's distinctive character, whether inherent or acquired through use, and the existence of the likelihood of confusion on the part of the public.

14.5.6.3 Reputation

case close-up

Case C-375/97 *General Motors Corporation v Yplon SA* [1999] ECR I-5421

'Reputation' was explained by the ECJ in Case C-375/97 *General Motors Corporation v Yplon SA* [1999] ECR I-5421 as requiring the senior mark to be 'known' by a significant number of the relevant public (ie the consumers of the product concerned), although it added that it is not necessary to show that a given percentage recognise the mark. 'Known' involves a lower burden of proof than showing that the mark is 'famous' or even 'well-known'. The ECJ in *General Motors* went on to state the factors to be considered when determining reputation. The statement appears to be almost the same as the matters listed in *Windsurfing Chiemsee* when proving factual distinctiveness. These are: the market share held by the trade mark, the intensity, geographical extent and duration of its use, and the size of the investment made by the undertaking in promoting it.

14.5.6.4 Absence of due cause

The meaning of 'due cause' was considered in *Pfizer Ltd v Eurofood Link (UK) Ltd* [2001] FSR 17 and *Premier Brands UK Ltd v Typhoon Europe Ltd* [2000] FSR 767. Both cases state that it is for the owner of the junior mark to prove 'due cause', rather than for the owner of the senior mark to prove an absence of due cause (proving a negative is impossible). In *Premier Brands*, Neuberger J (as he then was) debated (*obiter*) whether 'absence of due cause' meant 'necessity' or 'bad faith', but on balance inclined to 'necessity'.

14.5.6.5 Harm to the senior mark

In Case C-252/07 *Intel Corporation Inc v CPM United Kingdom Ltd* at [27] and in Case C 487/07 *L'Oréal SA v Bellure NV* at [38], confirmed in Case C-323/09 *Interflora Inc v Marks & Spencer plc* [2011] ECR I-8625 at [73–74], the ECJ identified three types of harm which can be caused to the senior mark. Any one of these suffices, but in each case the question of harm must be assessed globally:

- detriment to the distinctive character of the mark ('whittling away' or 'blurring'): the mark's ability to identify the goods or services for which it is registered is weakened owing to the 'dispersion of identity';

- detriment to the repute of the mark ('tarnishment' or 'degradation'): the goods or services for which the identical or similar sign is used are perceived by the public in such a way that the trade mark's power of attraction is reduced, particularly where the third party's goods or services possess a characteristic or quality which is liable to have a negative impact on the image of the mark; and

- taking unfair advantage ('parasitism' or 'free-riding'): the third party seeks by their use of the senior mark to ride on its coat-tails in order to benefit from the power of attraction, the reputation and prestige of the mark and to exploit, without paying any financial compensation, the marketing effort expended by the proprietor in order to create and maintain the mark's image.

For the first two categories of harm, the effect must be to make the consumer change their economic behaviour: *Intel* at [77]. However, as Gangjee and Burrell point out (in 'Because You're Worth It: L'Oréal and the Prohibition on Free Riding' (2010) 73 *MLR* 282), the ECJ in *L'Oréal* treats free riding as actionable *per se*.

14.5.6.6 Case law on s.5(3)

A number of United Kingdom cases have considered s.5(3).

Oasis Stores Ltd's Trade Mark Application [1998] RPC 631
. . . .

The principal decision is that of the Appointed Person in *Oasis Stores Ltd's Trade Mark Application* [1998] RPC 631. An opposition to the registration of EVEREADY for condoms was unsuccessfully opposed by the owner of EVER READY for batteries. It was said that the section is not intended to provide sweeping protection for any mark with a reputation. Whether there is protection is a matter of degree depending on all the circumstances. The gist of the action is 'cross-pollination' between the **claimant's** and defendant's trade marks. The factors which the court should take into account include the inherent distinctiveness of the earlier trade mark, the extent of its reputation, the range of goods or services for which the reputation is enjoyed, the uniqueness of the senior mark in the market, whether the respective goods or services, even though dissimilar, are in some way related or likely to be sold through the same outlets, and whether the senior mark will be any less distinctive than it was before or whether its reputation is likely to be damaged or tarnished in some material way.

thinking point
Is there a hidden danger in s.5(3) in that it offers protection against misappropriation rather than against origin confusion?

Examples of successful oppositions under s.5(3) include *C A Sheimer (M) Sdn Bhd's Trade Mark Application (VISA)* [2000] RPC 484 (VISA for credit cards tarnished by the registration of an identical mark for condoms); *Inlima SL's Application for a Three Dimensional Trade Mark* [2000] RPC 661 (the Adidas 'three stripe' mark for sports goods harmed if the applicant was allowed to register a bottle shaped like a football boot, etched with three stripes, for drinks, as sports goods manufacturers would not want to be associated with the evils of drink); and *Quorn Hunt v Marlow Foods Ltd* [2005] ETMR 105 (QUORN for vegetarian meat substitute would be tarnished by being associated with a hunting organisation). A key factor in the latter case was that on seeing the defendant's mark, consumers would change their economic behaviour, ie they would be put off from buying the opponent's goods.

14.5.7 Conflict with an earlier unregistered mark

cross reference
See further chapter 13.

Section 5(4)(a) implements an optional provision of the Directive. It allows the owner of a prior used but unregistered mark to oppose a later trade mark application. Oppositions under this subsection rarely succeed, because the opponent has to convince the Registry that a passing off action would succeed: *WILD CHILD Trade Mark* [1998] RPC 455. An example of an unsuccessful opposition is *OXFORD BLUE Trade Mark*, Registry, 23 March 2004, where Oxford University failed in its attempt to prevent the registration of OXFORD BLUE for cheese. The name OXFORD BLUE was recognised by the public as a sporting award, but the University had not done business under that name, and so had no **goodwill** capable of protection.

14.5.8 Conflict with an earlier copyright or design

The broader definition of trade mark in s.1 means that a trade mark might conflict with other types of intellectual property right. Section 5(4)(b) gives protection to the owner of an earlier copyright or design. There could be a clash between the trade mark and an earlier two-dimensional artistic work (see *KARO STEP Trade Mark* [1977] RPC 59) or between a shape trade mark and a three-dimensional artistic work, such as a sculpture or registered or unregistered design (*OSCAR Trade Mark* [1979] RPC 173). As music can be a trade mark (*Shield Mark*) there could now be a conflict between the owner of the copyright in the tune and a trade mark applicant.

14.5.9 Opposition based on a well-known mark

cross reference
See section 13.5.3.

The combination of TMA s.6(1)(c) and s.56 means that there is one further form of prior right which is protected in opposition proceedings, and that is a **well-known mark**. The criteria used to determine a well-known mark were set out in *LE MANS Trade Mark Application*, Appointed Person, 8 November 2004. A well-known mark can be the basis of a successful opposition under ss.5(1) and 5(2) but cannot be the basis of an opposition under s.5(3) because of the wording of the Paris Convention: Case T-150/04 *Mühlens GmbH v OHIM*, [2007] ECR II-2353. Individuals or organisations domiciled in the UK cannot rely on this provision, again because of the wording of the Paris Convention: *Jules Rimet Cup Ltd v The Football Association Ltd* [2008] FSR 254 at [73].

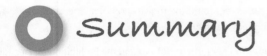

Summary

This chapter has explained:

- an outline of United Kingdom Trade Marks Registry procedure;

- the three elements which go to make up the definition of a 'trade mark' in s.1 TMA;

- the Absolute Grounds which can prevent registration, and how these have been interpreted by the ECJ; and

- the Relative Grounds which can prevent registration, and how the ECJ's case law has expanded the scope of protection for the registered trade mark owner.

? Reflective question

The choice of the reasonable consumer as the arbiter of registrability is uncertain and consequently unhelpful.

Discuss.

Annotated further reading

Bornkamm, J. 'Harmonising Trade Mark Law in Europe: the Stephen Stewart Memorial Lecture' [1999] *IPQ* 283

Explains the scope of protection accorded to the owner of a registered trade mark under Articles 4 and 5 of the Directive.

Davis, J. 'Locating the Average Consumer: His Judicial Origins, Intellectual Influences and Current Role in European Trade Mark Law' [2005] *IPQ* 183

Examines the way in which the ECJ has developed the average consumer as the arbiter of key issues under the Directive and Regulation.

Dawson, N. 'Bad Faith in European Trade Mark Law' [2011] *IPQ* 229

Argues that the doctrine of bad faith creates pressure for the convergence of unfair competition laws within the EU.

Firth, A., Gredley, E. and Maniatis, S. 'Shapes as Trade Marks: Public Policy, Functional Considerations and Consumer Perception' [2001] *EIPR* 86

Explains the underlying policy issues regarding the registration of shape trade marks and the role of the consumer in deciding registrability.

Gangjee, D. and Burrell, R. 'Because You're Worth It: *L'Oréal* and the Prohibition on Free Riding' (2010) 73 *MLR* 282

A critique of the ECJ's decision in *L'Oréal*.

Griffiths, A. 'Modernising Trade Mark Law and Promoting Economic Efficiency: an Evaluation of the *BABY DRY* Judgment and its Aftermath' [2003] *IPQ* 1

Considers the impact of *BABY DRY* in the light of the economic role fulfilled by trade marks.

Norman, H. 'Perfume, Whisky and Leaping Cats of Prey: A UK Perspective on Three Recent Trade Mark Cases before the European Court of Justice' [1998] *EIPR* 306

Explains how ECJ case law is moving the law of trade marks on beyond the traditional role of indicating origin.

Norman, H. '*Davidoff v Gofkid*: Dealing with the Logical Lapse Or Creating European Disharmony' [2003] *IPQ* 342

Explains how the ECJ broadened the scope of protection under Articles 4 and 5 for trade marks with a reputation.

Strowel, S. 'Benelux: A Guide to the Validity of Three-dimensional Trade Marks in Europe' [1995] *EIPR* 154

Explains the origins of s.3(2) of the TMA and argues for a narrow interpretation.

Turner-Kerr, P. 'EU Intellectual Property Law: Recent Case Developments' [2004] *IPQ* 448

Surveys many of the key cases on registrability under the Absolute and Relative Grounds.

Infringement of trade marks

Learning objectives

Upon completion of this chapter, you should have acquired:

- knowledge of the statutory provisions which govern the scope of the trade mark owner's right, together with those which provide counter-claims and defences to trade mark infringement;

- an understanding of the case law which has interpreted these provisions; and

- an appreciation of some of the theoretical and policy issues which underpin the case law.

Introduction

cross reference
See section 12.4.

The purpose of this chapter is to set out the rights of a trade mark owner (once the mark has been registered) to prevent others from making use of any sign which is the same as or similar to the registered mark in the course of trade.

Case law has reinforced the link between the scope of protection accorded to a registered mark and the commercial functions which trade marks perform. Further, there is considerable overlap between the Relative Grounds for refusal (which enable the registered proprietor to stop another later mark being entered on the Register) and the provisions on infringement (which enable the registered proprietor to stop another later mark being used). Another comparison which can be made is between the statutory rights conferred on the owner of a registered mark to stop infringers and the protection conferred at common law on the owner of an unregistered mark to prevent passing off.

cross reference
See chapter 13.

This is yet another area of trade mark law where European influence is very marked. The wording of the First Trade Marks Directive (Council Directive 89/104/EEC of 21 December 1988 on the approximation of the laws of Member States relating to trade marks [1989] OJ L 40/1, now codified as Directive 2008/95/EC of the European Parliament and of the Council of 22 October 2008 [2008] OJ L 299/25) ('the Directive') needs to be compared with that of the Trade Marks Act 1994 ('TMA'). As ever, only the ECJ can give a definitive interpretation of the wording of the legislation.

15.1 The issues

The issues which a **trade mark infringement** action raises can be conveniently divided into points which the **claimant** has to prove in order to succeed and those a defendant will wish to raise by way of response.

15.1.1 The claimant's arguments

A claimant who brings a trade mark infringement action will have to show two things: that an act of infringement has been committed (by analogy with the criminal law, think of this as the *actus reus* of infringement) and that such conduct falls within the scope of protection afforded to the registered mark. Just as in our discussion of **patent** infringement, the two issues can be considered as 'infringement in law' and 'infringement in fact'. Once these two points have been established, the court will normally find in favour of the claimant unless one or more of the counter-arguments raised by the defendant succeeds.

15.1.2 The defendant's arguments

The defendant to a trade mark infringement action has several possible counter-arguments:

- first, that there was no infringing conduct and/or that this did not fall within the scope of protection given to the registered mark; in other words, the claimant has failed to establish the key ingredients of the infringement action;

- even if all the ingredients of the infringement action have been proved, one or more of the statutory defences applies to exonerate the defendant. The availability of a particular defence will depend primarily on the facts of the case, as each defence has precise conditions which the defendant must meet in order to succeed; and

- last, that the trade mark should be removed from the Register, either under the **revocation** provisions (all of which are concerned with post-registration mismanagement of the trade mark by its proprietor) or under the **invalidity** provisions (which are to the effect that the mark was entered on the Register in error, being in breach of either the **Absolute** or **Relative Grounds**). The effects of revocation and a declaration of invalidity are different and from the defendant's point of view, the more effective argument is that the mark should be declared invalid.

Because of the risk of a successful counterclaim for revocation or invalidity, it is standard practice for a trade mark owner to plead **passing off** as an alternative cause of action. Even if the mark is removed from the Register, its use should confer some degree of protection at common law.

15.2 Categories of infringing acts

Two provisions in the TMA spell out types of infringing conduct. Section 10(4) (based on the wording of Article 5(3) of the Directive) sets out the acts of primary infringement, s.10(5) (a purely domestic provision) deals with **contributory infringement**. Sections 10(4) and (5) must be read subject to the requirement in s.9 that infringing conduct must be committed in the United Kingdom and be without the consent of the **registered proprietor**.

15.2.1 Acts of primary infringement

Under Article 5(3) of the Directive (repeated in s.10(4)), primary infringement consists of affixing the **sign** to goods or their packaging; offering or exposing goods for sale, putting them on the market, stocking them for those purposes under the sign, or offering or supplying services under the sign; importing or exporting goods under the sign; using the sign on business papers or advertising. The list covers the act of manufacture (placing the mark on goods) and post-manufacture conduct (distributing goods), and ancillary activities, such as advertising or stocking. Even if the defendant denies having used the claimant's mark when offering goods to the public over the internet, there may still be liability for 'stocking' the goods preparatory to putting them on the market: *Sony Computer Entertainment v Nuplayer Ltd* [2006] FSR 126. The list of conduct which amounts to use of a registered mark should not be regarded as exhaustive, owing to the presence of the phrase 'in particular' in Article 5(3).

One particular issue is whether the trade mark owner can stop goods which are in transit through the United Kingdom, destined for sale in a third country where there may not be protection for the mark. The ECJ (in Case C-281/05 *Montex Holdings Ltd v Diesel* [2006] ECR I-10881) has stated that the rights of the owner to intervene depend on there having been conduct which results in the goods being 'put on the market'. Consequently, goods have not been imported into the EU (and so have not been 'put on the market') where they have been placed in a transit warehouse for onward transmission to a non-EU state: Case C-405/03 *Class International BV v Colgate Palmolive* [2005] ECR I-8735. These two rulings were applied by the Court of Appeal in *Eli Lilly & Co v 8PM Chemist Ltd* [2008] FSR 313 so that the trade mark owner could not object to goods in transit. It didn't matter whether the goods were non-EU goods and on their way to another non-EU state (as in *Class*) or to a Member State where there was no IP protection (as in *Diesel*), being in transit through the territory of a Member State did not amount to an act of infringement as the goods were not being 'put on the market'. The recast Directive will reverse these cases, as well as clarifying the list of what amounts to infringing conduct.

15.2.2 Acts of secondary infringement

Section 10(5) supplements the Directive by creating contributory liability where the defendant has supplied material intended to be used for labelling or packaging, as a business paper, or for advertising the goods or services, in other words conduct preparatory to affixing the mark to the goods. For example, if a firm which makes and supplies cardboard boxes prints 'Intel Inside' on them and the boxes are then used by another firm as packaging for computers containing counterfeit chips, the supply of boxes would fall within s.10(5). The recast Directive will contain a similar provision.

15.2.2.1 The requirement of knowledge

Section 10(5) contains the phrase 'if when he applied the mark he knew or had reason to believe that the application of the mark was not duly authorised by the proprietor or a licensee'. The wording of this is almost identical to that found in ss.22 and 23 of the Copyright, Designs and Patents Act 1988 ('CDPA') which impose liability for secondary infringement by dealing in infringing copies of a work. In the **copyright** context this wording has been held to impose an objective standard, so that the defendant's state of mind is judged by that of the reasonable person in that line of business (*LA Gear v Hi-Tec Sports plc* [1992] FSR 121, *Vermaat & Powell v Boncrest (No 2)* [2002] FSR 331).

15.2.3 Non-graphic use

Whilst the 1938 Act, as amended, contemplated that infringing conduct could only be visual, under the TMA s.103(2) such conduct can be oral. If this were not the case, then there would be no protection against use of the mark on commercial radio or in sound recordings.

15.2.4 Use within the United Kingdom: websites

The requirement that the infringing conduct must be in the United Kingdom appears at first glance to be straightforward. The claimant needs to show that one of the acts listed in s.10(4)

thinking point
*Does the list of
infringing conduct
cover all ways in
which a trade mark
could be infringed in
the digital era?*

or (5) happened within the territory of the United Kingdom. But what is the position as regards use on a website? When will the inclusion of a United Kingdom registered trade mark in a website maintained in another jurisdiction amount to infringement in the United Kingdom? The answer depends on whether the website is 'targeted' at customers in the United Kingdom. If they can order goods on the site for delivery to an address in the United Kingdom and pay in sterling, then that is use 'in the United Kingdom': *Euromarket Designs Inc v Peters and Crate & Barrel Ltd* [2001] FSR 288; *L'Oréal SA v eBay International* [2009] RPC 693 at [402].

15.3   # The scope of trade mark protection

15.3.1   The impact of the Directive

If there has been infringing conduct within the United Kingdom, it must next be decided whether this falls within the mark's scope of protection. It is here that the Directive has had a significant impact on United Kingdom trade mark law, in two regards.

15.3.1.1   Breadth of protection

Under the 1938 Act, as amended, an infringement action could only be brought where the defendant used the infringing trade mark in relation *to the goods of the registration*. Hence, if the defendant used the claimant's trade mark on goods for which it was not registered, even if such goods were very similar, then the claimant had to seek redress under the law of passing off, something of a lottery. The Directive, by contrast, provides that the registered proprietor can object to use on identical, similar or even dissimilar goods.

15.3.1.2   Change of language

After the introduction of the TMA there was a debate as to whether, in order to infringe a registered trade mark, the use by the defendant of the alleged infringing sign had to be 'trade mark use'. Such debate was caused in part by the wording of TMA ss.9 and 10. Rather than copy the exact wording of Article 5 of the Directive, Parliament split the provision dealing with the rights of the trade mark owner between two separate sections, one (s.9) declaring the rights which exist in a registered mark, the other (s.10) providing a definition of when those rights are infringed, that is, setting out the scope of protection. This apparently unnecessary rearrangement of the infringement provision was explained during the passage of the Trade Marks Bill as being simply a matter of drafting technique (*Hansard*, 18 January 1994, col 24). The implications, however, proved to be far more significant.

Analysis of s.9 shows that it is narrower than Article 5. Instead of providing that 'the registered trade mark shall confer on the proprietor exclusive rights *therein*. The proprietor shall be entitled to prevent . . . ' (emphasis added), the TMA states that 'the proprietor of a registered trade mark has exclusive rights in the trade mark *which are infringed by use of the trade mark in the United Kingdom without his consent*' (again, emphasis supplied). The explanation for the alteration lies in the fact that s.9 simply copies the language of its predecessor, s.4 Trade

Marks Act 1938, as amended (which had been extensively criticised for being tortuous). This exercise in 'cutting and pasting' led to a debate as to whether, in order to infringe under the TMA, there has to be 'trade mark use'.

thinking point

Do you find the explanation as to why Article 5 of the Directive was divided between ss.9 and 10 TMA convincing? Does the wording of s.9 TMA correctly implement Article 5 of the Directive?

15.3.2 **The requirement of trade mark use**

15.3.2.1 The old law

Case law under s.4 of the 1938 Act had concluded that the section was limited by the definition of 'trade mark' in s.68 of the same Act, so that if a defendant used the claimant's trade mark for any purpose other than indicating the commercial origin of the goods, this was not trade mark infringement. This point is nicely illustrated by the decision in *Mars (GB) Ltd v Cadbury Ltd* ([1987] RPC 387) where Whitford J held that the registration of TREETS for confectionary was not infringed by the defendants' use of 'treat-size' on packets of miniature WISPA bars.

15.3.2.2 The policy debate

The question under the TMA is whether any use in commerce suffices for infringement or whether the requirement of 'use as a trade mark' is retained. This in turn begs the question of what is meant by 'trade mark use'. Is it use to indicate origin, or is it any use which undermines the wider functions of a trade mark, that is, 'anything which affects the legitimate interests of the trade mark owner or which affects the value of the mark by taking unfair advantage of its distinctive character or repute' (*per* the ECJ in Case C-10/89 *SA CNL-Sucal NV v Hag GF AG* [1990] ECR I-3711 at [14])? In other words, should trade mark law protect the registered proprietor against counterfeiting and confusion only, or should protection extend to any form of 'free-riding', that is, against any form of misappropriation of the value of the trade mark? Such policy debate is linked to the legally recognised functions which trade marks fulfil.

15.3.2.3 A problem of language

The policy choice has to be understood in the light of a difference between the 1938 Act and the TMA. The wording of ss.10(1), 10(2) and 10(3) refers to the defendant's infringing use of a '**sign**'. This is in contrast to the phrase 'trade mark' in s.9 and its predecessor, s.4 of the 1938 Act. 'Sign', found in TMA ss.2, 3 and 10, is a word with a very broad meaning, namely 'anything which conveys information' (*per* Jacob J in *Philips Electronics NV v Remington Consumer Products* [1998] RPC 283 at p. 298) or which sends a 'message' to any of the senses (*per* AG Colomer in Case C-273/00 *Sieckmann v Deutsches Patent- und Markenamt* [2002] ECR I-11737 at [20–21]). What is the effect of the word 'sign' on the requirement of 'trade mark use'?

15.3.2.4 Initial United Kingdom decisions

One possible interpretation of s.10 is that the word 'sign' merely indicates that use in commerce is all that is required. That was the view of Jacob J in *British Sugar v James Robertson* [1996] RPC 281, who thought that the wording of the section obviated the need to show trade mark use, and that s.9 was but a 'chatty introduction' to s.10. Jacob J disagreed with the outcome of an earlier case, *Bravado Merchandising v Mainstream Publishing* [1996] FSR 205, where Lord McClusky had accepted counsel's concession that trade mark use was a necessary component of the infringement action under the TMA. The Court of Appeal subsequently agreed with Jacob J (but only by way of *obiter*), stating that in order to infringe, trade mark use was not necessary (see *Philips Electronics NV v Remington Consumer Products* [1999] RPC 809 and *Marks & Spencer plc and others v One in a Million Ltd* [1998] 4 All ER 476).

The *British Sugar* approach has the advantage of reconciling 'trade mark' in s.9 with 'sign' in s.10. However, to state that all that is required is use in commerce ignores the functions performed by trade marks and runs the risk that trade marks are perceived as unfair monopolies.

15.3.2.5 ECJ guidance

case close-up

Case C-206/01 *Arsenal Football Club v Matthew Reed* [2002] ECR I-10273

The issue of trade mark use was considered by the ECJ in Case C-206/01 *Arsenal Football Club v Matthew Reed* [2002] ECR I-10273. The referral for a preliminary ruling under Article 267 of the **Treaty on the Functioning of the European Union ('TFEU')** (formerly Article 234 EC) was made by Laddie J ([2001] RPC 922) who had held that the defendant had not committed trade mark infringement by selling unauthorised merchandise to football fans, as the purchasers would not regard the name 'Arsenal' and the famous 'Gunners' logo as indicating commercial origin. Rather, each sign operated as a 'badge of allegiance' to the Club. There was therefore no 'trade mark use'. He also held that the defendant's use of the marks was not passing off, as there was no origin confusion on the part of the public. Laddie J's judgment should therefore be contrasted with that in *British Sugar*: the two cases reach opposite conclusions on the need for trade mark use. Further, Laddie J's thinking has the effect of confining the function of trade marks (whether registered or unregistered) to origin indication only.

The ECJ in its ruling made plain that use in commerce alone does *not* suffice for infringement. 'Trade mark use' is required. However, 'trade mark use' is given a much wider meaning than before. It means any use which affects the essential function of the trade mark, so that the trade mark owner is entitled to object to anyone who is seeking to take unfair advantage of the status and repute of the trade mark by selling products illegally bearing it. The decision therefore protects the wider function of a trade mark as a vehicle for 'creating and retaining custom'. In its reply, the ECJ made extensive reference to its earlier jurisprudence about the essential function of the trade mark and its role as guarantor of both commercial origin and the quality of the goods, stressing the importance of trade marks in achieving competition within the internal market. The exclusive rights conferred by the Directive (and hence the TMA) are to enable the trade mark proprietor to protect specific interests. These interests will be undermined if a third party's use of the sign is liable to affect the functions of the trade mark, in particular its essential function of guaranteeing to consumers the origin of the goods.

The *Arsenal* ruling was subsequently accepted as correct by the Court of Appeal despite Laddie J's refusal to apply it on the ground that the ECJ exceeded its jurisdiction, ([2003] 1 CMLR 382 (Laddie J), [2003] 2 CMLR 800 (CA)). The Court of Appeal repeated that when considering whether the defendant has trespassed on the scope of the claimant's registration, the question is no longer whether the defendant's use indicates the origin of the goods but whether that use undermines the essential function of the trade mark. In other words, is the use such that it takes unfair advantage of the status and repute of the trade mark? *Arsenal* appears to suggest that the court should examine the *defendant's* conduct rather than consider whether the *consumer* views the trade mark as indicating origin. It therefore introduces notions of **unfair competition** into the law of registered trade marks.

Since the *Arsenal* case, the ECJ has revisited the requirement of trade mark use and has stepped back from its earlier broad thinking.

case close-up

Case C-17/06 *Céline SARL v Céline SA* [2007] ECR I-7041

. . . .

The current view can be found in Case C-17/06 *Céline SARL v Céline SA* [2007] ECR I-7041 where the Court identified four conditions which must be satisfied before the trade mark right is infringed, the second one of which is self-explanatory:

* use must be in the course of trade;
* it must be without the consent of the proprietor of the mark;
* it must be in respect of goods or services; and
* it must affect or be liable to affect the functions of the trade mark, in particular its essential function of guaranteeing to consumers the origin of the goods or services.

Use in the course of trade

'In the course of trade' was considered by the General Court in Case T-195/00 *Travelex Global and Financial Services Ltd v Commission* [2003] ECR II-1677 in which it was held (relying on the earlier decision in *Arsenal Football Club v Matthew Reed*) that the Commission had not, when it adopted the official Euro symbol, used a sign which infringed the claimant's trade mark in the course of trade. This was because the adoption of the symbol was not 'use in the course of a commercial activity whereby goods and services are manufactured and supplied in a particular market'. A similar description was given in *RxWorks Ltd v Hunter* [2008] RPC 303 (a case which gives a useful summary of ECJ jurisprudence) as use 'in the course of a commercial activity with a view to gain and not as a private matter'. The same case points out that thanks to *Céline* and *Arsenal*, a trade mark can have significance beyond the point of sale, so it does not need to be visible when the goods are bought, and indeed can be 'embedded' in a product, such as a particular screen display in a computer or on a hidden part in a car engine.

example

Suppose that a famous trade mark is included within a painting, such as Manet's masterpiece *The Bar at the Folies-Bergère* showing a beer bottle with the Bass 'red triangle' mark on the label, or Andy Warhol's picture of a can of 'Campbell's' soup. Depicting the mark in such a manner would not be 'use in the course of trade' as it does not involve 'the manufacture and supply of goods in a particular market' (however, what would be the position if someone started selling postcards of the picture, or making T-shirts with the picture on the front?).

example

In *Electrocoin Automatics Ltd v Coinworld Ltd* [2005] FSR 79 it was held that the registration for OXO was not infringed by the appearance of the letters O, X and O on the display of a 'one-armed bandit' gaming machine. Again, although this was a commercial activity, it did not involve making and/or supplying goods.

Use 'in respect of' goods or services

This, the third of the *Céline* requirements, suggests that there must be degree of proximity between the mark and the goods. In *RxWorks Ltd v Hunter*, Daniel Alexander QC, sitting as a Deputy High Court Judge, pointed out the inconsistent language found in legislation and case law. Whilst the TMA requires there to be 'use in relation to goods and services' (yet another legacy from the 1938 Act), the Directive simply uses the word 'for' whilst the ECJ has talked about 'use in respect of'. He added that the ECJ appears to assume that 'in respect of' simply refers to the list of infringing conduct set out in Article 5(3) of the Directive, but that the ECJ has not yet been asked to rule on whether there was 'use in respect of' where the trade mark was 'embedded' in content-carrying media such as CDs or software.

Reference to other cases show that, on the one hand, incidental use of the trade mark will not infringe. In *Trebor Bassett Ltd v The Football Association* [1997] FSR 211, a **threats action** brought under TMA s.21 by the alleged infringer, it was held that the appearance of the 'three lions' logo in pictures of English football players appearing on collectable cards inserted in the claimant's sweet packets did not infringe the FA's registration. It was not 'in relation to goods', because the trade mark 'just appeared' (the case may usefully be contrasted with the defence of incidental use in copyright infringement). Equally, use by a *customer* when ordering goods (in contrast to use by the *retailer* when supplying them) will not amount to infringing use (Case C-2/00 *Hölterhoff v Ulrich Freiesleben* [2002] ECR I-4187). By contrast, using the mark on invoices for goods made in the United Kingdom to be shipped abroad is 'use in relation to' the goods (*Beautimatic International Ltd v Mitchell International Pharmaceuticals Ltd* [2000] FSR 267).

cross reference
See section 9.5.2.

Ultimately, whether a mark is used 'in relation to' or 'in respect of' goods depends on the facts. When a customer buys a DUALIT toaster from a John Lewis department store and carries it home in a shopping bag marked 'John Lewis', it cannot be said that the John Lewis mark is used 'in relation to' the toaster (*Daimler AG v Sany Group Co Ltd* [2009] EWHC 2581 (Ch) at [59]). As Jacob J remarked in *Euromarket Designs Inc v Peters and Crate & Barrel Ltd* at [57], only a trade mark lawyer would think that the 'Boots' trade mark had been used 'in relation to' films where a customer who had purchased a KODAK film at Boots took the film home in a Boots bag.

Consumer perception

The last element in the *Céline* list of requirements for infringement refers to the essential function of the trade mark guaranteeing to consumers the origin of the goods or services. The average consumer plays a key role in deciding issues of registrability, and it now appears that this person is also the arbiter of whether a trade mark has been infringed.

Case C-48/05 *Adam Opel AG v Autec* [2007] ECR I-1017

The question which the ECJ had to determine was whether the claimant's mark was infringed when it was used by the defendant on toy cars. The Court's response (at [23–25]) was to say that it all depended on what the consumer thought: did they see the mark as indicating that the toys had been made by the claimant, or did they think that the trade mark was simply part of the authentic appearance of the goods? If the consumer attached great importance to the fidelity of the model car to the original, this would not undermine the function of the trade mark. This is in contrast to the outcome in *Arsenal*, where the end user's perception was that the football club had guaranteed the origin of the merchandise.

In *RxWorks*, it was said that EU law focuses on asking 'what effect is the use likely to have' so that this was a means of controlling the trade mark owner's monopoly. The protection given to the trade mark owner is inversely proportional to the assumed abilities of the notional addressee. The less well informed and observant the average consumer was, the more such a person would assume that a sign intended to perform one function (indicating authenticity) performed another (indicating origin). Consequently, the expectations of the average consumer's ability must not be set too low. In the instant case, the claimant's mark 'vet.local' was buried in the workings of a computer system using the defendant's software, and would only be seen by system administrators. Such a person would not think that it denoted trade origin.

15.3.2.6 Conclusions on trade mark use

The issue of trade mark use is far from settled. The fourth *Céline* principle appears to mark a retreat from the broad approach of *Arsenal* and its application is always going to be a question of fact. Such questions will often be complex, involving consideration of the nature of the sign, its meaning, the context of use, and the scale of use. One only has to compare the different results in *Arsenal* and *Opel* to see how the context in which the mark is used can affect the outcome (were football fans any less perceptive than those who buy authentic model cars?)

Second, the digital era means that new ways of infringing are bound to emerge. Reference has already been made to where the mark is 'embedded', whether in computer software or other content-bearing media, where the use of the alleged infringing sign may not send a 'trade mark message'.

Last, there has been a significant number of ECJ cases involving the use of trade marks as 'adwords' on the internet, whereby a trader purchases a search engine keyword identical or similar to the claimant's mark so that when the user of a website types in the mark, a sponsored link is displayed which has nothing to do with the claimant's business. Is this 'trade mark use'? The various rulings distinguish between service operators (such as Google), marketplace operators (such as eBay), and the trade mark owner's competitors. The ECJ has said that whilst a service operator does not commit trade mark infringement when permitting a competitor to select the proprietor's mark as an adword (Case C-236/08 to C/238/09 *Google France v Louis Vuitton* [2010] ECR I-2417), a marketplace operator who makes use of Google's referencing service to acquire adwords which are then used to advertise its customer-sellers' products does infringe (*L'Oréal SA v eBay International* [2011] ECR I-6011). Competitors who, having

purchased adwords, use them to advertise their goods or services also infringe, at least where the reasonably circumspect internet user is unable to ascertain without difficulty whether the goods or services referred to by the advertisement originated from the proprietor of the trade mark or from an undertaking economically linked to it or, on the contrary, originated from a third party (Case C-558/08 *Portakabin Ltd v Primakabin BV* [2010] ECR I-6963). The use by a competitor is likely to affect adversely the origin function of the proprietor's mark, as well as its investment function (Case C-323/09 *Interflora Inc v Marks & Spencer plc* [2011] ECR I-8625).

15.3.3 **The application of the statutory provisions**

When considering the scope of protection accorded to the trade mark owner in an infringement action, it will become apparent that s.10, in its first three subsections, is a mirror image of the Relative Grounds for refusal in the first three subsections of s.5, what Bornkamm (in 'Harmonising Trade Mark Law in Europe: the Stephen Stewart Memorial Lecture' [1999] *IPQ* 283) calls the 'triad of protection'. The two provisions are, however, dissimilar in one respect. The difference is that s.5 refers to the junior application as a 'trade mark' whilst s.10 refers to the alleged infringement as a 'sign'. That apart, the case law on the two provisions is interchangeable, and the issues are determined from the viewpoint of the reasonably well-informed and reasonably observant and circumspect consumer (Case C-342/97 *Lloyd Schuhfabrik Meyer & Co KG v Klijsen Handel BV* [1999] ECR I-3819 at [26]).

cross reference
See section 14.5.

Bornkamm's 'triad of protection' can be illustrated another way: see Diagram 15.1. By way of reminder, there is the absolute 'core' of protection when there is identity between the marks and their products; an outer, more flexible 'core' of protection dependent on similarity and confusion; and an outer rim of protection available only for those marks with a reputation. There is, however, a difference between the inner two zones and the outer zone: the former accord with the traditional role of the trade mark in protecting against consumer confusion, the latter is concerned with protecting the owner of the mark against misappropriation.

Diagram 15.1

Trade mark infringement: the 'triad of protection'

Again, just as with s.5, s.10 requires a systematic, indeed sequential, application of the statutory provisions (*Reed Executive plc v Reed Business Information Ltd* [2004] RPC 767).

15.3.3.1 Double identity

Under s.10(1), use in the course of trade of the identical sign in relation to the identical goods or services will infringe the registered mark. No likelihood of confusion need be proved as it is assumed that there is such confusion where there is absolute identity: *Hölterhoff v Ulrich Freiesleben*.

When applying section 10(1), the comparison is between the *use* which the defendant has made of the sign and how the claimant's entry on the Register appears. How the claimant has actually used their mark is irrelevant. Hence, 'identical goods' entails a comparison between the defendant's product and the goods for which the claimant's mark is *actually* registered, so that if the goods are not identical, the case falls under s.10(2): *British Sugar v James Robertson*. Equally, 'identical sign' requires a comparison between the defendant's sign and the entry on the Register in respect of the claimant's mark: *Philips Electronics NV v Remington Consumer Products*.

cross reference

See section 14.5.4.1.

The test for deciding whether a sign is identical was explained by the ECJ in Case C-291/00 *LTJ Diffusion SA v Sadas Vertbaudet SA* [2003] ECR I-2799. It declared that identity must be strictly interpreted through the eyes of the relevant consumer, who rarely has the chance to make a direct comparison between the products and who may therefore have an imperfect recollection of the claimant's mark. Insignificant differences between the registered mark and the infringing sign may be ignored. An example of an insignificant difference would be a hyphen between two words: *IBM Corporation v Web-Sphere Ltd* [2004] FSR 796.

15.3.3.2 Similarity coupled with confusion

If there is not identity between the infringing sign and the registered mark, or if the goods upon which the infringing sign has been placed are not identical to the goods of the registration, one moves on to consider the next limb of protection, s.10(2). The provision can be summarised as requiring similarity coupled with a likelihood of confusion. The number of permutations in s.10(2) can be set out diagrammatically in Table 15.1 as follows:

Table 15.1

The requirement of similarity with likelihood of confusion: Section 10(2) permutations

A mark registered for goods will be infringed by the use in the course of trade of:	A mark registered for services will be infringed by the use in the course of trade of:
an identical sign in relation to similar goods	an identical sign in relation to similar services
an identical sign in relation to similar services	an identical sign in relation to similar goods
a similar sign in relation to identical goods	a similar sign in relation to identical services
a similar sign in relation to similar goods	a similar sign in relation to similar services
a similar sign in relation to similar services	a similar sign in relation to similar goods

cross reference

See section 14.5.5.

In each case, however, there must be a likelihood of confusion on the part of the public, which includes a likelihood of association. The meaning of 'likelihood of confusion', 'likelihood of association' and the case law of the ECJ which has interpreted Article 5(1)(b) of the Directive (the parent provision of s.10(2) TMA) have the same meaning as under the parallel provision in Article 4(1)(b) (s.5(2)). In essence:

- three types of confusion have been identified, namely direct confusion (confusing the products); indirect (thinking that the goods come from economically linked undertakings or that the trade mark owner has expanded their product line); and mere association ('calling to mind');

- 'association' can be traced historically to the Uniform Benelux Trade Marks Act 1971, but in the context of s.10(2) it must be regarded as a subset of confusion because of the grammatical structure of the provision (*Wagamama Ltd v City Centre Restaurants* [1995] FSR 713; Case C-251/95 *Sabel BV v Puma AG* [1997] ECR I-6191). However, association is not entirely irrelevant, as it 'serves to define [the] scope' of confusion (*Sabel BV v Puma AG* at [18]);

- when applying s.10(2) (Article 5(1)(b) of the Directive) the starting point is Recital 11 to the consolidated version of the Directive, which declares that the likelihood of confusion depends on numerous elements;

- when deciding whether the infringing sign is similar to the registered mark, the comparison is to be made aurally, visually and conceptually (*Sabel BV v Puma AG* at [23]), taking into account the factors listed in *Lloyd Schuhfabrik Meyer & Co GmbH v Klijsen Handel BV*. These include the greater or lesser capacity of the mark to identify the goods or services, the inherent characteristics of the mark, whether or not it contains a descriptive element, and the market share held by the mark; how intensive, geographically widespread and long-standing the use of the mark has been; the amount invested by the undertaking in promoting the mark; the proportion of the relevant section of the public which, because of the mark, identifies the goods or services as originating from a particular undertaking; and statements from chambers of commerce and industry or other trade and professional associations;

- when determining whether goods are similar, the test set out by the ECJ in Case C-39/97 *Canon KK v Metro-Goldwyn-Mayer Inc (formerly Pathé Communications Corp)* [1998] ECR I-5507 must be used, that is, all relevant factors must be taken into account, including the nature, the end users, the method of use and whether they are in competition with each other or are complementary. The fact that the claimant's and defendant's products are in the same class under the **Nice Agreement** for the International Classification of Goods and Services 1957 is irrelevant; and

- assuming that the conditions of similarity of marks and similarity of goods can be satisfied (Case 106/03 P *Vedial SA v OHIM* [2004] ECR I-9573), 'likelihood of confusion' requires a 'global appreciation' of all the issues, there being an 'interdependence of factors' such that a highly distinctive and extensively used mark will be given a wider penumbra of protection, and near-identity of goods may make not-so-similar marks appear similar (*Sabel BV v Puma AG*, *Canon*, and *Lloyd*). In other words, all the surrounding circumstances are to be taken into account (*Reed Executive plc v Reed Business Information Ltd*).

15.3.3.3 Marks with a reputation

When considering the final limb of the 'triad of protection', s.10(3) was amended by The Trade Marks (Proof of Use) Regulations 2004 (SI 2004/946) which deleted the reference to dissimilar goods in the subsection, just as was the case with s.5(3). The deletion (which has not been made to the Directive) was made in the United Kingdom to take account of the rulings of the ECJ in Case C-292/00 *Davidoff & Cie SA and Zino Davidoff v Gofkid Ltd* [2003] ECR I-389 and

Case C-408/01 *Adidas-Saloman AG and Adidas Benelux BV v Fitnessworld Trading Ltd* [2003] ECR I-12537 which were to the effect that there would be a gap in the scheme of protection if the owner of a mark with a reputation could prevent infringement by a junior sign if the goods were dissimilar but not if they were similar in cases where there was no likelihood of confusion. The recast Directive spells out that it matters not whether the goods are identical, similar or not similar.

cross reference
See section 14.5.6.

The rationale behind the protection of marks with a reputation (regardless of whether it equates to the doctrine of **dilution** found in other jurisdictions) can be restated thus, bearing in mind that the requirements of the provision are cumulative:

- the purpose of s.10(3) is distinct from that in s.10(2) and liability does not depend on there being a likelihood of confusion (*Sabel BV v Puma AG* at [20]; Case C-252/07 *Intel Corporation Inc v CPM United Kingdom Ltd* [2008] ECR I-8823 at [50]);

- there must be identity between the senior mark and the sign (assessed under the *LTJ* test) or at the least similarity (assessed under the test in *Sabel v Puma*). Where similarity is alleged, this must have the effect of making the consumer make a link to the senior mark, although the presence of such a link on its own is not enough as there must be resultant harm to the senior mark (Case C-252/07 *Intel Corporation Inc v CPM United Kingdom Ltd* at [41–42] and Case C 487/07 *L'Oréal SA v Bellure NV*, ECJ [2009] ECR I-5185 at [36–37]). Whether the consumer makes such a link is to be assessed globally, taking into account all the factors listed by the ECJ in *Intel*;

- the provision only applies to marks with a reputation, the meaning of which was explained by the ECJ in Case C-375/97 *General Motors Corporation v Yplon SA* [1999] ECR I-5421. 'Reputation' requires the mark to be 'known', which appears to be a lower standard than requiring the mark to be 'famous' or even 'well-known';

- use of the infringing sign must be 'without due cause', a phrase which probably means 'necessary' (*Premier Brands UK Ltd v Typhoon Europe Ltd* [2000] FSR 767), the onus being on the defendant to establish positively that they had good reason to use the mark;

- three types of harm can be caused to the senior mark, namely detriment to the distinctive character of the mark ('whittling away' or 'blurring'), detriment to the repute of the mark ('tarnishment' or 'degradation') and taking unfair advantage ('parasitism' or 'free-riding') (Case C-252/07 *Intel Corporation Inc v CPM United Kingdom Ltd* at [27] and Case C 487/07 *L'Oréal SA v Bellure NV* at [38]); and

- the section is not intended to provide sweeping protection for any mark with a reputation.

Whether there is protection is a matter of degree depending on all the circumstances. The gist of the action is 'cross-pollination' between the claimant's and defendant's trade marks: *Electrocoin Automatics Ltd v Coinworld Ltd*; *Oasis Stores Ltd's Trade Mark Application* [1998] RPC 631.

case close-up

Pfizer Ltd v Eurofood Link (UK) Ltd [2001] FSR 17
....

A good example of 'cross-pollination' can be found in *Pfizer Ltd v Eurofood Link (UK) Ltd* [2001] FSR 17 where the evidence clearly pointed to the defendant's having attempted to 'free-ride' on the success of the VIAGRA mark, not only by the choice of the name VIAGRENE for a drink which was claimed to have aphrodisiac properties, but by the choice of a blue lozenge-shaped logo for the website advertising the drink (VIAGRA tablets are made in the shape of a blue lozenge). The conduct amounted both to 'taking advantage' of the registered mark, and causing it 'detriment' by creating an association with something unwholesome.

By contrast, in *Premier Brands UK Ltd v Typhoon Europe Ltd* there was neither taking advantage of nor creating an unwelcome association with the mark TY.PHOO (registered for tea) when the defendant used TYPHOON for kitchenware. This was despite the claimant's strenuous assertions that its mark would be harmed because consumers might 'call to mind' a ferocious and damaging tropical storm. Equally, in *DaimlerChrysler AG v Alavi* [2001] RPC 813 the defendant had operated his Carnaby Street shop under the name MERC for many years and there was no evidence that he had attempted to make use of the reputation of the MERCEDES BENZ trade mark to sell his goods, nor that the cars' image had been tarnished as a result.

thinking point

When considering the criteria for infringement found respectively in TMA ss.10(1), 10(2) and 10(3), has the ECJ always provided clear guidance to enable lawyers to advise their clients as to the issues of identity of signs under s.10(1), similarity of signs and similarity of goods under s.10(2), and harm to marks with a reputation under s.10(3)?

417

 15.4 ## General defences to trade mark infringement

A defendant's principal argument will be to deny that there has been any infringing conduct, and/or that what has been done is not within the scope of protection given to the registered mark. There are, however, a number of statutory defences. Some flow from the definition of infringement itself, most are based on the Directive, but some are 'home grown'. The ECJ has repeatedly declared that Articles 5 to 7 of the Directive comprise a complete code of the trade mark owner's rights (Case C-414/99 *Zino Davidoff SA v A&G Imports Ltd,* Cases C-415/99 and C-416/99 *Levi Strauss & Co v Tesco Stores and Costco Wholesale UK Ltd* [2001] ECR I-8691) so it may be questioned whether the 'home-grown' defences are in breach of the Directive.

15.4.1 **Consent**

Implicit in the definition of infringement of any intellectual property right is that the conduct occurred without the consent of the proprietor. The phrase 'without his consent' occurs both in s.9 and Article 5 and is listed by the ECJ in *Céline* as the second of its requirements for infringement.

Such a defence is most likely to be raised in circumstances where the mark has been **licensed**. This was the background to the dispute in *Northern & Shell v Condé Nast* [1995] RPC 117, where the trade mark owner, relying on a minimum sales clause in a distribution agreement, appointed another **licensee** when the initial licensee did not meet its sales target. When sued for infringement by the original licensee, the second licensee successfully argued that it had used the trade mark with the consent of the proprietor.

15.4.2 **Non-trade mark use**

The argument that what the defendant has done is not trade mark use and so does not infringe is governed by the ECJ rulings in *Arsenal*, *Opel* and *Céline*. Not all use in commerce will infringe (*Travelex*). At one time it would have sufficed, in order to raise the defence, to argue that the mark had been used in a manner which did not indicate origin (*Mars v Cadbury*). Today, however, the question is broader, namely whether the defendant's use has affected the essential function of the trade mark, and in turn requires an examination of how the average consumer saw the use of the mark. All the surrounding circumstances will need to be considered.

15.4.2.1 Decorative use

Under the 1938 Act, decorative use of the mark (for example, putting the mark on a T-shirt) did not infringe because it did not indicate origin (*Unidoor Ltd v Marks & Spencer plc* [1988] RPC 275). Today, at least if the action is brought under s.10(3) where what matters is the association which the claimant's mark produces in the mind of the customer, even decorative use of a figurative sign may infringe. This was made clear by the ECJ in *Adidas-Saloman AG and Adidas Benelux BV v Fitnessworld Trading Ltd* (where the defendant had used a sign resembling the Adidas 'three stripes' mark to decorate clothing). The ECJ stated that the fact that a sign was viewed as an embellishment by the relevant section of the public was not, of itself, an obstacle to claiming infringement where the degree of similarity was such that the relevant section of the public established a link between the sign and the mark. So, in the case of decorative use of a figurative (ie picture) mark, such as the Adidas 'three stripes' mark, it all depends on how the public perceives the decoration: if it creates an association in the minds of the public it may infringe. The Court made the same point in Case C-102/07 *Adidas AG & Adidas Benelux BV v Marca Mode, C&A Nederland, H&M and Vendex* [2008] ECR I-2439, stating that there might be infringement under Article 5(1)(b) (if the customer was confused) or under Article 5(2) (if unfair advantage was taken of the claimant's mark).

15.4.3 **Use of another registered mark**

TMA s.11(1) is one of the provisions with as yet no counterpart in the Directive. It provides that use of another registered mark will not infringe. The section therefore contemplates that there will be two conflicting marks on the Register. This may have come about because the owner of the earlier mark did not file **opposition** proceedings, or such opposition proceedings failed. It is, of course, open to the owner of the senior mark, having sued for infringement and having been met by this defence, to seek to have the junior mark declared invalid under s.47, on the grounds that at the time of its registration, it breached the requirements of s.5. This will be subject to the time limits imposed by s.48.

The only qualification in s.11(1) is that the junior mark must have been used in the form in which it is registered. An example of where this was not the case (so that the defence failed) was *Neutrogena v Golden Ltd t/a Laboratoires Garnier* [1996] RPC 473, where the defendant's registered mark was NUTRALIA. However, what it had used was NEUTRALIA, which Jacob J held was not sufficiently similar to the registered mark (because of the different imagery created by the first syllables) for the defence to be available.

The recast Directive makes clear that the right to sue for infringement is subject to prior rights.

15.4.4 Protection for other traders

TMA s.11(2) (based on Article 6(1) of the Directive) contains three provisions which are all intended to safeguard the interests of other traders. The three defences are, however, qualified by a proviso which requires the court to consider whether the defendant's conduct, although technically within the wording of the defence, amounted to unfair competition.

15.4.4.1 Use of own name

Paragraph (a) permits the defendant to make use of his own name and address, so that the registration of a surname or geographical name does not amount to a complete monopoly. The subsection contemplates that the defendant's name or address consists of or contains another's registered trade mark (*Céline*). So in *Reed Executive plc v Reed Business Information Ltd*, the claimant's mark REED was included in the defendant company's name REED ELSEVIER, and in *IBM Corporation v Web-Sphere Ltd*, WEBSPHERE (without a hyphen) was a registered trade mark of the claimant. A company can rely on the defence when it was using its trading name rather than its registered name: *Hotel Cipriani Srl v Cipriani (Grosvenor Street) Ltd* [2010] RPC 485. The recast Directive will, however, limit this defence to use of personal names and addresses, as was originally intended.

15.4.4.2 Descriptive use

Paragraph (b) permits the use of 'indications concerning the kind, quality, intended purpose . . . or other characteristics of the goods or services', so that one trader can make reasonable descriptive use of another's mark (see *Hölterhoff v Ulrich Freiesleben*). An example would be where a garment manufacturer states on the care label 'Contains LYCRA' (which is a registered trade mark of the Du Pont Corporation). Such use is permissible as long as it does not overstep the limits of the proviso to the subsection. Similarly, a car dealer may advertise that it carries out the servicing of BMW cars (Case C-63/97 *BMW v Deenik* [1999] ECR I-905), or that it is a VOLVO specialist (*AB Volvo v Heritage (Leicester) Ltd* [2000] FSR 253), and a fizzy drinks manufacture can state that its product contains NUTRASWEET.

15.4.4.3 Use for spare parts and components

Finally, para (c) creates a defence where use of the trade mark is necessary to indicate the intended purpose of a product or service (in particular, as accessories or spare parts).

A manufacturer of automotive parts may wish to state that 'these brake pads are suitable for use on the following models of FORD cars'. Whilst para (b) therefore enables the rival manufacturer to indicate the *internal* characteristics of his product ('contains NUTRASWEET'), para (c) is more concerned with its *external* attributes, such as compatibility with the products of others.

The scope of para (c) was considered by the ECJ in Case C-228/03 *The Gillette Company & Gillette Group Finland Oy v LA-Laboratories Oy* [2005] ECR I-2337. It ruled that the phrase 'accessory or spare part' was used in Article 6 by way of example and should not be given a narrow meaning. Use of a competitor's trade mark was 'necessary' in order to provide the public with comprehensible and complete information about the intended purpose of the product. Such use was necessary if that information could not be provided by a third party without employing the trade mark. That use must, in practice, be the only means of providing such information.

15.4.4.4 The proviso

Section 11(2) (like Article 6 of the Directive) is qualified by the proviso that such use must be in accordance with honest practices in industrial or commercial matters. The proviso seeks to balance the interests of the trade mark owner with those of other traders. Its wording can be traced to Article 10*bis* of the **Paris Convention** for the Protection of Industrial Property 1883, where it forms the definition of unfair competition. The proviso to s.11(2) therefore requires the court to consider the defendant's motives in making use of the registered mark and to examine all the surrounding circumstances.

The ECJ has on several occasions offered guidance as to the meaning of the proviso. In Case C-100/02 *Gerolsteiner Brunnen GmbH v Putsch GmbH* [2004] ECR I-691, relying on its earlier remarks in *BMW v Deenik*, it declared that the phrase 'honest practices' expressed the duty of third parties 'to act fairly in relation to the legitimate interests of the trade mark owner'. Later, in *The Gillette Company & Gillette Group Finland Oy v LA-Laboratories Oy*, the ECJ added that:

> use of the trade mark will not be in accordance with honest practices...if it gives the impression that there is a commercial connection between the [defendant] and the trade mark owner; it affects the value of the trade mark by taking unfair advantage of its distinctive character or repute; it entails the discrediting or denigration of the mark; or where the [defendant] presents its product as an imitation or replica of the product bearing the trade mark of which it is not the owner.

It has since clarified what is meant by 'unfair advantage' in Case C 487/07 *L'Oréal v Bellure* at [50] as being where the third party seeks to ride on the coat-tails of the senior trade mark in order to benefit from its power of attraction, reputation and prestige, and to exploit the investment made by the owner of the senior mark without paying compensation.

As a result of the ECJ's rulings in *Putsch* (which was applied in *Reed Executive plc v Reed Business Information Ltd*) and *Gillette*, s.11(2) should *not* be seen as the converse of trade mark use, as previously suggested by the Court of Appeal in *The European Ltd v The Economist Newspaper Ltd* [1998] FSR 283. Instead, in accordance with the policy in *Arsenal v Reed*, it should be asked whether there has been trade mark use by the defendant. If there is not trade mark use, then that is an end of the case. If there has been trade mark use, what then needs to be considered is whether the defendant's conduct has breached the 'duty to act fairly'.

Case C-63/97 *BMW v Deenik* [1999] ECR I-905

Guidance from the ECJ on the application of the proviso can be found in *BMW v Deenik*. The case also involved a discussion of the Article 7 **exhaustion of rights** defence. Mr Deenik ran a garage in the Netherlands, specialising in the sale of second-hand BMW cars, and in the repair and servicing of such cars. He was not part of the dealer network run by BMW. The car manufacturer sued him for trade mark infringement, taking particular objection to the way in which his advertisements described him as a 'BMW specialist'. In reply, Mr Deenik relied on the defences in Article 6(1)(c) (the origin of s.11(1)(c)) and Article 7. The ECJ stated that Article 7 was the relevant defence to the sale of second-hand cars but that Article 6(1)(c) was appropriate to the activities of repair and servicing. It then proceeded to apply the same test to each defence, noting that both defences sought to achieve a balance of interests, Article 7 balancing the rights of the trade mark owner with the interests of the internal market, Article 6 balancing the rights of the trade mark owner with those of other traders. Whilst use of another's trade mark may be legitimate as a means of informing consumers about the nature of the defendant's business, such use would not be permitted if it was contrary to the duty to act fairly in relation to the legitimate interests of the trade mark owner. Therefore if the advertisements for Mr Deenik's business either misled consumers into thinking that there was a commercial connection with BMW (in particular that the defendant was part of the dealer network) or if they sought to take unfair advantage of the distinctive character or repute of the trade mark, they would lose the benefit of both defences.

It can thus be seen, both from the ruling in *Deenik* and that in the later case of *Gillette*, that there is an element of consumer protection in the defence.

AB Volvo v Heritage (Leicester) Ltd [2000] FSR 253

BMW v Deenik was relied on by Rattee J in *AB Volvo v Heritage (Leicester) Ltd*. Here, all the circumstances surrounding the defendant's use of the claimant's trade mark were examined. The defendant, having lost its status as an approved dealer of the claimant car manufacturer, continued to describe itself on headed paper and other advertising materials as an 'independent Volvo specialist', which was true. However, of particular significance was the fact that the words 'independent' and 'specialist', placed adjacent to the registered mark, appeared in much smaller lettering. Rattee J concluded that the effect of the use of the claimant's trade mark would be to mislead the public into thinking that the defendant was still an authorised franchisee. He confirmed that the test under the proviso is objective. No reasonable motor service provider would think that the use complained of was in accordance with honest practices in that line of business.

In *IBM Corporation v Web-Sphere Ltd*, the court had no hesitation in rejecting the defence of use of own name under s.11(2)(a) because the defendant's conduct clearly took it outside the scope of the proviso. The defendant had changed its corporate name to Web-Sphere shortly after the successful launch of IBM's product of that name. Lewison J held that it was difficult to avoid the inference that the new company name had been chosen to take advantage of IBM's goodwill, as no convincing explanation had been advanced for the

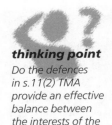

thinking point
Do the defences in s.11(2) TMA provide an effective balance between the interests of the trade mark owner and other traders?

change. In *Redd Solicitors LLP v Red Legal Ltd* [2012] EWPCC 54, HHJ Birss decided that had the defendant firm of licensed conveyancers bothered to check before registering their company name, they would have discovered the existence of the claimant, a leading intellectual property law firm. The recast Directive will in effect codify the ECJ's ruling in *BMW v Deenik* by giving examples of what does not amount to acting in accordance with honest practices.

15.4.5 **Prior rights**

In common with other intellectual property registration systems, s.11(3) contains a saving for earlier rights. It is based on Article 6(2) of the Directive, but unfortunately uses wording which does not match exactly that deployed in the Directive. The main difference is that s.11(3) requires that the earlier right must have been used continuously, a condition not imposed by the Directive. 'Earlier right' here bears a different meaning from that found in s.5 when dealing with relative grounds for refusal. Here it means only an unregistered trade mark or sign which has been used continuously in such a manner that it would be protected under the laws of passing off. The **prior use** must predate whichever is the earlier of two events, the use *or* the registration of the claimant's mark. The fact that the defendant must be able to satisfy the court that it would be able to succeed in a passing off action imposes a considerable evidential burden.

15.4.6 **Statutory acquiescence**

Section 48 (based on Article 9 of the Directive) creates a very limited form of statutory acquiescence. It provides that where the proprietor of an earlier trade mark or other earlier right has acquiesced for a continuous period of five years in the use of a registered mark, they can no longer seek a declaration that the junior mark is invalid, nor can they oppose the use of the later trade mark (ie, sue for infringement), unless the registration of the latter was obtained in bad faith. The circumstances in which s.48 will apply are therefore the same as those arising under s.11(1). *Both* marks must be registered with the later mark being on the Register as a result of failure to oppose or an unsuccessful opposition by the owner of the senior mark. The practical effect of the section is that where there are conflicting registered marks, the proprietor of the first mark has just five years in which to challenge the second mark under s.47. Once the junior mark is protected against challenge by virtue of s.48(1), its proprietor is, by virtue of s.48(2), in exactly the same position as the owner of the senior mark, and so cannot challenge the validity of the senior mark. The section therefore, when it applies, creates a stalemate so that the two marks are forced to co-exist for the future.

The scope of Article 9 was considered by the ECJ in Case C-482/09 *Budejovicky Budvar NP v Anheuser-Busch Inc* [2011] ECR I-8701, yet another episode in the long-running dispute between the two rival producers of BUDWEISER beer. It advised the Court of Appeal that 'acquiescence' in the Directive is a concept of EU law. A proprietor cannot be held to have acquiesced unless it was in a position to prevent the use of the rival mark but chose not to do so intentionally and with full knowledge of the facts. The five-year period only starts to run once the following conditions are satisfied: the later mark has been registered (assuming it was done so in good faith); the later mark has been put to use; and the owner of the earlier mark knows of both the registration and use of the later mark.

The ECJ's criteria should be compared with the general equitable defence of acquiescence which is available against a claim for the infringement of any intellectual property right. The general defence of acquiescence involves a positive misrepresentation by the claimant, and an intimation to the defendant, on which the defendant relies to their detriment, that the right in question will not be enforced (*Film Investors Overseas Services SA v Home Video Channel Ltd* Times, 2 December 1996). Mere delay in commencing infringement proceedings does not amount to acquiescence (*Farmers Build Ltd v Carier Bulk Handling Materials Ltd* [1999] RPC 461).

15.4.7 **Comparative advertising**

15.4.7.1 The old law

The law prior to 1994, based on the decision of the Court of Appeal in *Bismag Ltd v Amblins (Chemists) Ltd* (1940) 57 RPC 209, confirmed in the later case of *Chanel Ltd v Triton Packaging Ltd* [1993] RPC 32, was that comparative advertising was trade mark infringement, because, in the words of the 1938 Act, such use by the defendant amounted to 'importing a reference' to the claimant or the claimant's mark. In some extreme instances, comparing the defendant's and claimant's products, their attributes, and prices in an inaccurate manner, could also amount to **malicious falsehood** (*Compaq v Dell* [1992] FSR 93), a form of common law liability which survives the 1994 changes. The pre-TMA United Kingdom law (that is, treating comparative advertising as trade mark infringement) was not unlike that found in Germany where, until recently, comparative advertising was regarded as a form of unfair competition.

15.4.7.2 TMA s.10(6)

There was a change of policy in the United Kingdom in 1994 when it was decided that in the interests of better consumer information, the law on comparative advertising should be de-regulated. In consequence s.10(6) was introduced providing (in essence) that a trade mark is not infringed where it is used to identify the goods or services as those of the proprietor of the mark. The wording does not actually refer to comparative advertising and potentially covers other situations. Nevertheless, references to *Hansard* indicate that s.10(6) was intended to reverse the previous law on comparative advertising as a form of trade mark infringement, 'in the best interests of competition and therefore in the interests of the consumer' (*Hansard* (HL) 24 February 1994, col 738). Cases decided under s.10(6) have all involved comparative advertising.

It is sometimes said that TMA s.10(6) (which does not have a counterpart in the Directive) creates a fourth category of trade mark infringement. Such statement must be open to doubt in view of Bornkamm's analysis of the 'triad of protection' and in view of the ECJ's frequent pronouncements that Articles 5 to 7 constitute a complete code of the trade mark owner's right. Further, close examination of its legislative history shows that the provision started out in the family of clauses in the Trade Marks Bill dealing with defences to infringement, but was moved to what ultimately became s.10 because 'the provision and its relationship with the Directive would be clearer' (*Hansard* (HL) 24 February 1994, col 736). In addition, the opening words of the subsection, 'nothing in the preceding provisions . . . shall be construed as preventing the use of a registered mark' point to the fact that it operates by way of defence, not a cause of action. Indeed, it has been suggested that s.10(6) is the domestic equivalent of the exhaustion of rights defence (*Scandecor Development AB v Scandecor Marketing AB* [2001] 2 CMLR 645, HL). The conclusion must be, nevertheless, that s.10(6) is misplaced in the provision dealing with infringement and should logically be located with other defences in s.11.

Two further criticisms can be made. First, as was said at the time of its enactment, the Government should have waited to see what was the effect of the Comparative Advertising Directive (Directive 97/55/EC of the European Parliament and of the Council of 6 October 1997 amending Directive 84/450/EEC concerning misleading advertising so as to include comparative advertising [1997] OJ L 290/18, now consolidated as Directive 2006/114/EC of the European Parliament and of the Council of 12 December 2006 [2006] OJ L 376/21) (hereafter 'the CAD'). It would have been better, it was said, to leave the TMA silent on comparative advertising, to rely instead on the descriptive use defence under s.11(2)(b) and, if need be, introduce an appropriate amendment once the EU legislative process was complete. In the event, the United Kingdom chose to implement the CAD in such a way that it had no direct impact on the TMA.

A second criticism (one frequently voiced by the judiciary) was that the section is badly drafted. The opening words are qualified by a two-limbed proviso which states that any such use otherwise than in accordance with honest practices in industrial and commercial matters shall be treated as infringement, if the use without due cause takes unfair advantage of, or is detrimental to, the distinctive character or repute of the mark. In effect what the proviso is saying is that comparative advertising will not be permitted where it amounts to unfair competition (the first half of the sentence repeating Article 10*bis* of the Paris Convention, explained earlier) because the defendant's conduct amounts to unfair competition. The proviso is, to say the least, tautologous.

thinking point
Given the criticisms of s.10(6), was the Government wise to 'jump the gun' before the CAD was passed?

15.4.7.3 Case law on s.10(6)

Several cases have analysed the wording of s.10(6), the last of which was *British Airways plc v Ryanair Ltd* [2001] FSR 541. The decision in *Ryanair* reinforced the trend evident from the outset, namely the reluctance of the judiciary to find in favour of the trade mark owner under s.10(6). The case has the added advantage that it involved two advertisments published just before the operative date of the United Kingdom's implementation of the CAD which enabled Jacob J to explore the relationship between s.10(6) and this Directive. The first advertisement was withdrawn after a number of complaints to the Advertising Standards Authority, the second was the subject of an action for trade mark infringement and malicious falsehood. In regard to the second, Jacob J summarised the law as it then stood on comparative advertising as a defence to trade mark infringement. He stated that the primary objective of s.10(6) was to permit comparative advertising and as long as the use of the competitor's mark was honest, there was nothing wrong in telling the public of the relative merits of competing goods and services. However, an advertisement which was significantly misleading was not honest. The onus was on the registered proprietor to show that the requirements of the proviso existed. The phrase 'honest practices' was to be interpreted objectively, through the eyes of a reasonable audience, ie 'would a reasonable reader be likely to say, upon being given the full facts, that the advertisement is not honest?' Industry-wide codes of practice should be ignored; rather, the advertisement was to be assessed through the eyes of the relevant public. Words were to be given their natural meaning as judged by the general public, who were used to 'hype', and minute textual analysis of the advertisement was to be avoided, as this is something that the reasonable reader would not do. The advertisement was to be considered as a whole. The TMA was not to be used to enforce a more puritanical standard than the general public would expect.

With regard to the impact of the CAD, Jacob J noted that this had amended the earlier Misleading Advertising Directive, but not the Trade Marks Directive so that there was no obligation to interpret the TMA in the light of the CAD. Although the CAD refers to trade marks and although comparative advertisements will usually involve use of other traders' marks, it was as if the Trade Marks Directive and the CAD existed in parallel universes.

15.4.7.4 The Comparative Advertising Directive

> **The Comparative Advertising Directive**
> ....
>
> The CAD starts from a different premise than s.10(6). Whilst the TMA is based on the assumption that comparative advertising is acceptable *unless* it is contrary to honest practices in industrial and commercial matters, the CAD provides that comparative advertising is acceptable *only* if it is *not* misleading. The CAD, in Article 4 of its consolidated version, lays down a number of positive criteria to be met:
>
> - the advertisement must compare goods or services meeting the same needs or intended for the same purpose;
> - it must objectively compare one or more material, relevant, verifiable and representative features of goods and services, which may include price;
> - it must not discredit or denigrate the trade marks, trade names, other distinguishing marks, goods, services, activities or circumstances of a competitor;
> - it does not take unfair advantage of the reputation of a trade mark, trade name or other distinguishing marks of a competitor;
> - it does not present goods or services as imitations or replicas of goods or services bearing a protected trade mark; and
> - it does not create confusion among traders, between the advertiser and a competitor, or between their trade marks.

15.4.7.5 Implementation of the CAD in the United Kingdom

Taking advantage of the discretion conferred on it by the CAD, the United Kingdom chose to implement its provisions by means of administrative regulation. Under the Business Protection from Misleading Marketing Regulations 2008 (SI 2008/1276) (replacing the two previous versions of the Control of Misleading Advertisements Regulations), enforcement is by way of complaint to the Advertising Standards Authority which can direct an advertisement to be withdrawn (just as it had done as regards the first advertisement in the *Ryanair* case, on the grounds that it was contrary to good taste). The Regulations do *not* have any effect on TMA s.10(6). The choices open to the trade mark owner are that if it is felt that a competitor has indulged in unfair comparative advertising, it is better by far (and considerably cheaper) to make a complaint under the Regulations than to bring an action for trade mark infringement.

15.4.7.6 The ECJ's view

case close-up

Case C-533/06 *O2 Holdings Ltd v Hutchinson 3G Ltd* [2008] ECR I-4231

The relationship between comparative advertising and liability for trade mark infringement was considered by the ECJ in Case C-533/06 *O2 Holdings Ltd v Hutchinson 3G Ltd* [2008] ECR I-4231. Here the claimant mobile phone company used bubble images coloured blue to advertise its services and had registered pictures of bubbles (in blue) as trade marks. The defendant's television advertising campaign compared its prices with those of the claimant using black-and-white bubble imagery. It was accepted before the Patents Court that the price comparison was accurate, that the advertisement was not misleading, and that there was no suggestion of any trade connection between the two companies. At first instance it was held that although the use of the bubble imagery fell within s.10(2), compliance with the CAD provided a defence under s.11(2)(b). The Court of Appeal sought the ECJ's guidance.

The ECJ began by saying that the use of a competitor's trade mark in a comparative advertisement was use for the advertiser's own goods and services and therefore *prima facie* infringement. However, the CAD was intended to promote comparative advertising. Further, Recitals 13 to 15 of the consolidated version cross-referred to the Trade Marks Directive and so it was necessary to read the CAD into the limitations on the trade mark owner's rights. The trade mark owner could not object to the use of an identical or similar sign by a third party in a comparative advertisement which complied with the CAD. Compliance with the CAD is therefore a complete defence to trade mark infringement unless the advertisement gives rise to a likelihood of confusion.

thinking point

Can the ECJ's interpretation of the CAD in O2 be reconciled with its statements in Bellure *that there is liability per se for 'taking unfair advantage' of another's mark?*

This means that most direct comparative advertisements ('our washing powder is cheaper than your washing powder'), where the consumer is alerted to the fact that there are two rival producers, will get the protection of the defence. Only an indirect comparison, where the consumer does not appreciate that there are two different sources of supply and consequently confuses the two, will amount to infringement. The ECJ added that the trade mark owner could not object to the use by a third party of a similar sign if this did not give rise to a likelihood of confusion, regardless of whether the advertisement satisfied all the conditions of the CAD.

The recast Directive will make clear that use in a comparative advertisement in a manner contrary to the CAD is trade mark infringement.

The net effect of *O2 Holdings Ltd v Hutchinson 3G Ltd* is that the law of passing off and the law of trade marks now achieve the same outcome. As ever with trade mark infringement issues, everything depends on the consumer's perception. This is entirely in accordance with the Court's earlier statements in *Arsenal*, *Opel* and *Céline*. How the consumer views the advertisement was to the fore in Case C-159/09 *Lidl SNC v Vierzon Distribution SA* [2010] ECR I-11761. The case concerned a dispute between two rival supermarkets as to the price of the average shopping basket. The ECJ ruled that it was important that the products were interchangeable, so that if the advertiser selected products which had different features which affected the average consumer's choice, the advertisement would be misleading.

15.4.7.7 Copyright infringement by comparative advertisement

One final point about s.10(6) needs to be made, if indeed the provision has any sort of role to play after the decision in *O2 Holdings Ltd v Hutchinson 3G Ltd*. The subsection sought to provide a specific defence to trade mark infringement, but where the advertisement takes copyright material belonging to the claimant as well as its trade mark (for example, if the front covers of rival magazines are compared) then s.10(6) has no bearing on the issue of copyright infringement, the defences to which must be found in the CDPA: *Macmillan Magazines Ltd v RCN Publishing* [1998] FSR 9; *IPC Media Ltd v News Group Newspapers Ltd* [2005] FSR 752. It is unlikely that the defence of fair dealing will apply.

cross reference
See section 9.5.

15.5 Loss of registration

15.5.1 Introduction

Intellectual property litigation tends to be aggressive. A claimant contemplating an infringement action should consider whether their right is liable to be challenged. In the case of trade marks, entry of a mark on the Register is only *prima facie* evidence of its **validity** (TMA s.72). The wording of s.72 has two consequences: first, registration can never be totally guaranteed (TMA s.70); and second, the onus is placed on the defendant to challenge the registration. A defendant who is sued for trade mark infringement, besides denying that infringement has been made out or raising one of the statutory defences, will usually try to counterclaim that the mark should be removed from the Register. The grounds of such a counterclaim will be:

- the registered mark should be revoked under TMA s.46 because it has been mismanaged by its owner since the date registration was completed. Mismanagement comprises non-use, generic use or deceptive use; and/or
- the mark should be declared invalid under s.47, on the ground that it failed to comply with TMA s.3 or s.5 at the time it was registered.

15.5.2 The difference between revocation and invalidity

In contrast to patents and registered **designs** where the two terms are interchangeable, trade mark law draws a very precise distinction between revocation and invalidity. They bear completely different meanings. Revocation relates to the conduct of the proprietor *since* registration, conduct which in some way has 'tainted' a previously valid mark. It is essentially concerned with failure to look after the trade mark, to nurture it, since it was registered. The effect of a successful revocation application is that the mark is removed from the Register for the future (from the date of the application to revoke) unless the tribunal directs otherwise. In the context of an infringement action, revocation of the claimant's mark will not exonerate the defendant from past acts of infringement, although it will enable the defendant to continue using their sign in the future. Invalidity, on the other hand, relates to the fact that the trade mark should never have been registered in the first place because at the time it was registered, it did not comply with the TMA. A declaration of invalidity is backdated to the time the mark was filed, so is a much more effective tactic for a defendant to argue than revocation. Invalidity means that the registration never existed (so the defendant cannot have infringed) whilst revocation removes the mark from the Register only for the future, leaving the defendant still liable for acts of past infringement. The actions for revocation and invalidity are independent: *T-Mobile (UK) Ltd v O2 Holdings Ltd*, Appointed Person, 13 December 2007. The difference between revocation and invalidity of trade marks is illustrated in Diagram 15.2.

Diagram 15.2
The difference between the revocation and invalidity of trade marks

Period A | Period B

Date of registration
1 October 2003

Date when infringing
conduct commences
1 October 2007

Date of application to
remove mark
1 October 2008

Notes:

1 If the mark is successfully removed under s.46 TMA (revocation), this will normally operate from 1 October 2008 onwards. Liability for infringement during Period B is *not* affected.

2 If the mark is successfully removed under s.47 TMA (invalidity), this will operate from 1 October 2003. The mark is treated as if it never existed and so *cannot* be infringed.

15.5.3 **Revocation**

An application to revoke a registered trade mark can be brought by any person: there is no requirement of *locus standi*. The application can be made directly to the Trade Marks Registry or it can be raised by way of a counterclaim in opposition or infringement proceedings. There are three grounds of revocation listed in TMA s.46(1).

15.5.3.1 Revocation for non-use

TMA s.46(1) contains two separate objections to a mark on the basis of non-use. They comprise five years' non-use of the trade mark since it was first entered on the Register (s.46(1)(a)) and any continuous five-year period of non-use (s.46(1)(b)). If you don't use it you lose it! The policy behind revocation for non-use (stated in *Imperial Group v Philip Morris* [1982] FSR 72) is that the Register should be an accurate reflection of marks currently in use. To stockpile marks in case of possible future need or to register a mark as a pre-emptive strike against a competitor is contrary to this policy.

Under s.46(1)(a), the five-year period runs from the date the registration process is completed, not the date of application (*BON MATIN Trade Mark* [1989] RPC 537), whilst under s.46(1)(b), any continuous period of non-use counts. An application for revocation can be brought as soon as the five-year period has elapsed. The onus is then on the trade mark owner to show that the mark has been used (TMA s.100). The only qualification is that no revocation application can be brought where use is recommended before the application to revoke is made. However, no account is taken of use which is recommended during the three-month period before the application to revoke if the trade mark proprietor already knew that the application to revoke might be made (s.46(3)). Granting a **licence** to use the mark is not evidence of use, simply evidence of preparations to use the mark: *Philosophy Inc v Ferretti Studios SRL* [2003] RPC 287.

Section 46(1)(a) and (b) both require the proprietor to make 'genuine' use of the mark.

Case C-40/01 *Ansul BV v Ajax Brandbeveiliging BV* [2003] ECR I-2439
. . . .

Use is 'genuine', according to the ECJ in Case C-40/01 *Ansul BV v Ajax Brandbeveiliging BV* [2003] ECR I-2439, where the mark is used in accordance with its essential function. In other words, the mark must guarantee the identity of the origin of the goods or services for which it is registered, in order to create or preserve an outlet for those goods or services. Genuine use does not include token use for the sole purpose of preserving the rights conferred by the mark. When assessing whether use of the trade mark is genuine, regard must be had to all the facts and circumstances, particularly whether other traders would regard the use as justified to maintain or create a share in the market for the goods or services protected by the mark. The court should also consider the nature of those goods or services, the characteristics of the market, and the scale and frequency of use of the mark.

In *Ansul* itself (which concerned the activities of the trade mark owner supplying parts and chemicals to maintain fire-extinguishers which it had previously sold), the ECJ added that the fact that a mark is not used for goods newly available on the market but for goods that were sold in the past does not mean that its use is not genuine. It suffices if the proprietor makes actual use of the same mark for component parts that are integral to the make-up or structure of such goods, or for goods or services directly connected with the goods previously sold and intended to meet the needs of customers of those goods. In other words, the nature of the goods and the market for them has to be considered. Also relevant, as in *POLICE Trade Mark* [2004] RPC 693, is the size of the trade mark owner's business. This does not mean that there is one rule for big businesses and one for small firms: rather it is an element in deciding whether the use of the mark has been genuine. In the same way, the quantum of use should be considered, but this does not mean that a small number of sales cannot be genuine use. It all depends on the facts of the case. So, in Case C-442/07 *Verein Radetzky-Orden v Bundesvereinigung Kameradschaft 'Feldmarschall Radetzky'* [2008] ECR I-9223 putting the mark on headed paper sufficed in the case of a voluntary non-profit organisation.

The *Ansul* ruling has been applied by the Court of Appeal in *Laboratoires Goëmar SA v La Mer Technology Inc* [2006] FSR 49. In overturning the decision of Blackburne J, it held that although the volume of sales had been small (only £800 worth had been despatched to one intermediary who had then gone into liquidation) and had not been to members of the public, the transactions in question had been at arm's length so that title to the goods had been transferred. That transfer of title had been with a view to creating a retail outlet for the goods. This was not token use for the purpose of protecting the mark from revocation, but genuine use as required by the Directive. It was the quality of the use that mattered, not the quantity.

Under similar provisions under the 1938 Act, the nature of the use made by the proprietor was crucial. Promotional use did not count: see *KODIAK Trade Mark* [1990] FSR 49 where it was held that use of KODAK on T-shirts was not enough to maintain the registration for clothing, as the use was advertising KODAK films, not indicating the origin of the T-shirts. Under the current law, the rulings of the ECJ in *Arsenal v Reed*, *Opel* and *Céline* are likely to be relevant. What amounts to 'trade mark use' for the purposes of infringement will be appropriate in deciding what amounts to use for the purpose of maintaining a registration. In Case C-495/07 *Silberquelle GmbH v Maselli-Strickmode GmbH* [2009] ECR I-137 the ECJ ruled that there had not been genuine use of the trade mark (WELLNESS for drinks) where the proprietor had affixed it to bottles of alcohol-free drinks which it then gave away free to customers who bought items of clothing sold under the same mark. The drinks mark (as opposed to the clothing mark) had been correctly revoked for non-use. In this area, just as in other areas of trade mark law, the views of the consumer will be relevant.

case close-up

ORIENT EXPRESS Trade Mark, Appointed Person, 31 October 2008

In *ORIENT EXPRESS Trade Mark*, Appointed Person, 31 October 2008, the Appointed Person upheld the decision of the Hearing Officer that there should be partial revocation for non-use of the trade mark ORIENT EXPRESS. The trade mark owner had appealed against the decision, arguing that two of the products to be deleted from the specification of goods (whisky and olive oil) were covered by the use of the name 'Orient Express Gift Boutique' on board the trade mark owner's trains, arguing that the Hearing Officer had misapplied the ECJ's ruling in *Céline*, where it was suggested that use of a name over a shop could be trade mark infringement. The Appointed Person stated that much depended on the perception of the average consumer, and whether they saw the name of the shop as an identifier of the origin of the goods sold there or merely as an identifier of the retail business carried on there. The key issue was whether use of the mark as the name of the on-board shop was use 'in relation to' the goods concerned. Here there was evidence that the shops had sold other companies' goods: it was therefore arguable that the name did not operate as a badge of origin for the goods concerned so that there had not been genuine use.

Under s.46(1)(a) or (b), the proprietor can prevent revocation by showing that there existed proper reasons for non-use. 'Proper reasons' means obstacles arising independently of the will of the proprietor rather than incompetence or inefficiency on the part of the trade mark owner: *MAGIC BALL Trade Mark* [2000] RPC 439. The ECJ has stated (in Case C-246/05 *Armin Häupl v Lidl Stiftung & Co KG* [2007] ECR I-4673) that obstacles to non-use must have a direct relationship with the trade mark, so that its use is impossible or unreasonable and that these must be independent of the will of the proprietor. This will be a heavy burden to discharge.

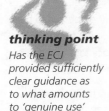

thinking point
Has the ECJ provided sufficiently clear guidance as to what amounts to 'genuine use' in the context of revocation?

Alternatively, the proprietor can show that the mark has been used in a form differing in elements which do not affect the distinctive character of the mark. This alternative argument against revocation is very narrow, so that using NEUTRALIA when what was registered was NUTRALIA did not suffice to avoid revocation for non-use (*Neutrogena v Golden Ltd t/a Laboratoires Garnier*) (the first syllable, though only one letter different, conveyed a totally different meaning to the consumer, suggesting that the product was ph-neutral rather than that it was derived from nuts). Likewise, using similar but different cartoon drawings of penguins from those which were registered did not prevent revocation (*United Biscuits (UK) Ltd v Asda Stores Ltd* [1997] RPC 513), and using VENICE SIMPLON ORIENT EXPRESS differed significantly from the registered mark (ORIENT EXPRESS) so that the owner could not rely on s.46(2) (*ORIENT EXPRESS Trade Mark*).

15.5.3.2 Revocation because the mark has become generic

Under s.46(1)(c) a registered trade mark will be revoked if, in consequence of the acts or inactivity of the proprietor, the mark has become the common name in the trade for the product or service for which it is registered. In other words the mark has become generic, the name of the product itself. Consider the name ASPIRIN. Originally this was a registered trade mark of Bayer AG but is now the name for a painkiller. Other trade marks which have been lost due to becoming generic include LINOLEUM, CELLOPHANE and YO-YO.

Section 46(1)(c) will come into play both where the trade mark owner has misused the mark personally, and where they have done nothing to stop others' misuse. Whether the mark has become the common name in the trade for the product is assessed through the eyes of the average consumer: Case C-371/02 *Björnekulla Fruktindustrier AB v Procordia Food AB* [2004] ECR I-5791. This has the effect of reversing the old United Kingdom law in *DAIQUIRI RUM Trade Mark* [1969] RPC 600 (HL) which asked whether other traders used the mark as the common name for the product. The trade mark owner must therefore ensure that the use of the mark, whether by the owner in its advertising or by others, does not lead the public to use it generically.

thinking point

In the light of the ECJ's ruling in Björnekulla Fruktindustrier AB v Procordia Food AB, *consider whether the trade mark HOOVER for vacuum cleaners is liable to be revoked for having become generic in the eyes of the consumer.*

15.5.3.3 Revocation because of deceptive use

Under s.46(1)(d), the last ground of revocation is that in consequence of the use made of it by the proprietor, the mark is liable to mislead the public. The leading decision under the 1938 Act was *GE Trade Mark* [1973] RPC 297 (HL) which emphasised the 'clean hands' doctrine as the basis for this category of revocation. Under the TMA, the deception must arise because of the use of the mark by its owner, which suggests positive misconduct. One suggested example of deceptive use can be found in the somewhat complex facts of *Scandecor Developments AB v Scandecor Marketing AB* [2001] 2 CMLR 645. Here, the House of Lords was prepared (until the case was settled voluntarily) to refer to the ECJ the question of whether the failure to exercise quality control over an **exclusive licensee** by the trade mark proprietor, so that the public associated the mark with the licensee, amounted to deceptive use under s.46(1)(d).

On the limited ECJ authority so far available, it seems that this ground of revocation is narrower than the 'clean hands' doctrine in *GE Trade Mark*, and forms a mirror image of one of the Absolute Grounds for refusal where a mark will be rejected under TMA s.3(3)(b) if it is deceptive.

case close-up

Case C-259/04 *Elizabeth Emanuel v Continental Shelf* [2006] ECR I-3089

A famous fashion designer had registered her name as a trade mark in 1994. Having subsequently **assigned** her business to a company, becoming its employee before ultimately resigning, she opposed a number of further applications to register her name made by the eventual successors of her business, arguing that the marks were deceptive under TMA s.3(3)(b). She also sought revocation of the earlier registration under s.46(1)(d) on the ground that it had become deceptive as to the origin of the goods. The ECJ ruled that the wording of the Directive required there to be actual deceit or a sufficiently serious risk that the consumer would be deceived. Although a consumer might be influenced by the name 'Elizabeth Emanuel' when buying a garment, the characteristics and qualities of that garment remained guaranteed by the business which owned the mark. Therefore the name itself could not be regarded as being of such a nature as to deceive the public.

The ECJ reached its conclusion in the *Emanuel* case by considering the functions performed by trade marks (set out in its ruling in *Arsenal*), adding that the public interest ground underlying Article 3(1)(g) (the parent of TMA s.3(3)(b)) was consumer protection. Its remarks about the interpretation of 'deceive' echo those of AG Colomer, who stated that Article 3(1)(g) referred to the intrinsic characteristics of the trade mark. The sign must confuse the public by virtue of its inherent qualities, containing incorrect information, which must be deceptive from an objective point of view. The ECJ added that the fact that a mark consisting of the name of an individual had been assigned did not of itself render the mark deceptive (otherwise such marks could never be capable of assignment). There might be circumstances where the **assignee** of the mark misled consumers into thinking that the named individual was still associated with the business. That might amount to fraudulent conduct, but that would not affect the trade mark itself.

15.5.3.4 Partial revocation

Section 46(5) provides for partial revocation. The objection may be in respect of only some of the goods or services of the registration, so that the effect of partial revocation will be to leave the mark on the Register but with a reduced **statement of goods and services**. The threat of revocation, particularly for non-use, coupled with the broader protection accorded to registered marks under s.10, means that there is no need for a trade mark **applicant** to seek protection for a wide range of goods and services (unless, of course, they do actually trade in such a way).

Several cases have considered how the court ought to approach the task of reducing the scope of the registration in cases of partial revocation, bearing in mind that there is a balance to be struck between the proprietor, other traders and the public. The problem is that the **classification** of goods and services set out in Sch. 4 to the Trade Mark (Amendment) Rules 2001 (derived from the Nice Agreement) contains items with a very wide scope. Consider as examples 'computer programs' in Class 9 (*Mercury Communications Ltd v Mercury Interactive (UK) Ltd* [1995] FSR 850) and 'printed matter' in Class 16 (*MINERVA Trade Mark* [2000] FSR 734). 'Beers' was held too wide as a statement of goods when all that the trade mark owner had supplied was 'bitter beer': *David West t/a Eastenders v Fuller Smith & Turner plc* [2003] FSR 816. Even 'household containers' (*Premier Brands UK Ltd v Typhoon Europe Ltd*) is a category covering a wide range of items. The problem therefore, as stated in the last-mentioned case, and over which there has been some debate, is whether it is necessary for the court to 'dig deeper' into how the trade mark owner has actually used the mark. The solution, suggested by the Court of Appeal in *Thomson Holidays Ltd v Norwegian Cruise Lines Ltd* [2003] RPC 586, is to use the viewpoint of the reasonably informed consumer of the product in question. The court should consider the nature of the proprietor's business and then decide how the notional consumer would describe such use. Here the consumer would have described the claimant's business as 'package holidays' and so its registration of FREESTYLE would be cut back accordingly, with other services being deleted from the registration.

15.5.4 Invalidity

An application to have a trade mark declared invalid can be made directly to the Trade Marks Registry or it can be raised by way of a counterclaim in opposition or infringement proceedings. A declaration of invalidity is based on the simple premise that the trade mark was registered in error. The effect of a successful application for a declaration of invalidity is that the mark is removed from the Register retrospectively, that is from the date of the original registration. In contrast to revocation, this will exonerate the defendant from past acts of infringement, and consequently is a much more effective tactic to pursue. Like revocation, invalidity may be total or partial, so that partial invalidity results in the mark staying on the Register but with a reduced statement of goods and services.

The grounds on which a trade mark can be declared invalid are set out in TMA s.47(1). The subsection covers two things, first that the mark was registered in breach of s.3. However, under the proviso to s.47(1) (which equates to the proviso to s.3(1)), where the mark was registered in breach of s.3(1)(b), (c) or (d), the plea of invalidity may be overcome where the mark has acquired factual distinctiveness since the date of registration. The proviso to s.47(1) therefore operates in the same way as the proviso to s.3(1), with one difference. The latter requires that factual distinctiveness be acquired by use *before the date of application* to register the trade mark. The former requires that factual distinctiveness be acquired by use *between the date of registration and the date of the application for the declaration of invalidity*. Apart from this, the effect of the two provisos is the same. The evidence required under s.47(1) will presumably have to comply with the criteria for acquired distinctiveness set out by the ECJ in Cases C-108/97 and 109/97 *Windsurfing Chiemsee Produktions und Vertriebs GmbH v Boots und Segelzubehor Walter Huber* [1999] ECR I-2779.

cross reference
See section
14.4.2.5.

The second ground of invalidity is that the mark was registered in breach of s.5, unless the owner of the prior right consented. However, and in contrast to challenge under s.3, the standing to seek a declaration of invalidity under s.5 is much more constrained. Under The Trade Marks (Relative Grounds) Order 2007 (SI 2007/1976), only the owner of the earlier right can bring an action under s.5; and The Trade Marks (Proof of Use) Regulations 2004 (SI 2004/946) requires such an action to be brought within five years of the registration of the junior mark. Whilst, therefore, it is not fatal if the owner of the earlier right fails to bring opposition proceedings or is unsuccessful in them, they must nevertheless act within the time limits. No one else can challenge the mark for conflict with earlier rights.

Summary

This chapter has explained:

- the issues which have to be decided in a trade mark infringement action, including whether the defendant's conduct falls within the scope of the claimant's registration, whether there are any available defences and whether the mark is vulnerable to a counterclaim;

- the meaning of the key statutory provisions together with the case law which has interpreted the same; and

- the role of the consumer in deciding matters such as trade mark use, the scope of the trade mark owner's protection, and whether comparative advertising infringes.

❓ Reflective question

The decision of the European Court of Justice in *Arsenal v Reed* is a disaster for business. Its ruling on what constitutes trade mark use is so wide there is a real danger that powerful brands will become unfair monopolies.

Discuss.

📖 Annotated further reading

Bornkamm, Judge J. 'Harmonising Trade Mark Law in Europe: the Stephen Stewart Memorial Lecture' [1999] *IPQ* 283

Explains the relationship between ss.10(1), 10(2), and 10(3) TMA and how they create a 'triad of protection' for the trade mark owner.

Dawson, N. 'Non-Trade Mark Use' [2012] *IPQ* 204

Considers the role of trade mark functions in the context of infringement.

Norman, H. 'Davidoff v Gofkid: Dealing with the Logical Lapse or Creating European Disharmony' [2003] *IPQ* 342

Explains how the ECJ set about dealing with the apparently unfair treatment accorded to marks with a reputation when used on similar goods in circumstances where there was no confusion.

Norman, H. 'Time to Blow the Whistle on Trade Mark Use' [2004] *IPQ* 1

The requirement of trade mark use both under the 1938 Trade Marks Act and the 1994 Act. It also analyses the decision in *Arsenal v Reed* and the consequences of the ECJ's wide view of what constitutes 'taking unfair advantage' of a trade mark.

Simon Fhima, I. *Trade Mark Dilution in Europe and the United States* (2011), Oxford University Press

A comprehensive survey and analysis of the protection of trade marks against dilution in two different legal systems.

Simon Fhima, I. 'Dilution by Blurring—A Conceptual Road Map' [2010] *IPQ* 44

Considers the theoretical justifications for dilution.

Simon Fhima, I. 'Exploring the Roots of European Dilution' [2012] *IPQ* 25

Discusses the way in which pre-harmonisation national trade mark laws might have influenced the emerging EU jurisprudence.

Spence, M. 'Section 10 of the Trade Marks Act 1994: Is There Really a Logical Lapse' [2001] *EIPR* 423

Explains the potential gap between s.10(2) (where likelihood of confusion must be proved) and the original wording of s.10(3) which required a mark with a reputation to be used on dissimilar goods.

Exhaustion of rights

Learning objectives

Upon completion of this chapter, you should have acquired:

- an understanding of the meaning of the term 'exhaustion of rights' and how it operates as a defence to an action for the infringement of any intellectual property right;

- an understanding of the origin of the defence in the case law of the ECJ under Articles 34 and 36 of the Treaty on the Functioning of the European Union and the arguments used by the Court in such case law;

- knowledge of the different rights of the intellectual property owner in relation to parallel and infringing imports;

- knowledge of the circumstances in which a trade mark owner can still object to parallel imports from within the EEA; and

- knowledge of the different treatment accorded to goods which have first been marketed outside the EEA.

Introduction

This chapter is devoted to one specific defence which, dependent on the facts, can be raised in any intellectual property infringement action, namely exhaustion of rights. Because of the nature of global trade, it is most often encountered in trade mark infringement actions, hence the location of this chapter as a sequel to trade mark infringement.

16.1 Definitions and key issues

16.1.1 The meaning of 'exhaustion of rights'

The term '**exhaustion of rights**' denotes that the ability of an intellectual property owner to object to the unauthorised conduct of third parties is spent. The right becomes unenforceable. In consequence, further dealings in **patented**, **trade marked** or **copyright** goods cannot be challenged, even though infringing conduct has been committed by a third party. In common with other statutory defences, exhaustion of rights is not absolute. Much depends on the circumstances of the case. Indeed, the complexity of the case law 'would astonish the average consumer' (*per* Jacob LJ in *Boehringer Ingelheim KG v Dowelhurst Ltd* [2004] ETMR 902 at [79]).

16.1.2 Geographical scope

Like intellectual property rights themselves, exhaustion of rights has a territorial effect. It applies within a geographical area. Exhaustion, therefore, *could* be domestic only, that is, it could operate within a single country, such as the territory of the United Kingdom. The consequence of confining exhaustion to the territory of a particular state would be that once the intellectual property owner has placed patented, trade marked or copyright goods in circulation *within* that country, no objection could be made to further dealings in those goods. Importation of goods from elsewhere could be stopped as they would not be 'national' products. An example of exhaustion of trade mark rights being confined nationally (decided by the Court of Appeal under the Trade Marks Act 1938) is *Colgate-Palmolive v Markwell Finance* [1989] RPC 497, where toothpaste imported (somewhat circuitously) into the United Kingdom from Brazil via Nigeria was held to infringe the **claimant's** registrations, even though the claimant had manufactured the product itself. A significant fact of the case, however, was that the imported product contained different ingredients from the domestic version of the product, which could have caused customer disappointment and harm to the claimant's business.

Alternatively, exhaustion of rights could apply internationally. The right to object to further dealings in the goods would be spent no matter where the goods were first put into circulation by the intellectual property owner. An example of international trade mark exhaustion (decided prior to the 1994 reforms) is *Revlon Inc v Cripps & Lee Ltd* [1980] FSR 87, where a differently constituted Court of Appeal held that the claimant corporate group could not rely on its United Kingdom rights, whether under the law of registered trade marks or **passing off**, to object to the importation of shampoo from New York. With regard to passing off, there was no misrepresentation as to the commercial source of the goods, as they had originated with the claimant corporate group. Concerning **infringement** of the REVLON registered trade mark, the whole corporate group was taken to have consented by implication to the use of the mark and to the disposal of the goods. The application of international exhaustion in the *Revlon* case was no doubt helped by the way in which the Revlon corporate group had organised its structure and by the fact that there was no contractual or other stipulation that the goods were not for sale outside the USA. That the grade of shampoo imported from New York had not been previously made available to United Kingdom customers does not seem to have troubled the court.

There is, however, a third possibility. The application of a national approach to exhaustion of rights conflicts with the fundamental principle of the internal market of the EU. The internal market views all 28 Member States as a single territory, within which the four freedoms (free movement of goods, persons, services and capital) operate. National boundaries are to be disregarded. Further, the effect of the **EEA** Agreement is that the three EFTA countries adhering to the EEA (Norway, Iceland and Liechtenstein) are treated as part of the EU for the purposes of the four freedoms. Harmonisation Directives enacted in order to give effect to the four freedoms (such as the various intellectual property Directives) also apply throughout the EEA. Free movement of goods within the EEA therefore requires that exhaustion of rights operates on a regional not national basis.

16.1.3 The role of exhaustion of rights

Exhaustion of rights as a defence to trade mark infringement is found in s.12 of the Trade Marks Act 1994 (hereafter, 'TMA'), based on Article 7 of the First Trade Marks Directive (Council Directive 89/104/EEC of 21 December 1988 on the approximation of the laws of Member States relating to trade marks [1989] OJ L 40/1, now codified as Directive 2008/95/EC of the European Parliament and of the Council of 22 October 2008 [2008] OJ L 299/25) ('the Directive'). However, exhaustion of rights is a defence to an action for infringement of *any* intellectual property right. Similar provisions are in various other harmonisation Directives dealing with copyright, **designs** and biotechnological patents.

16.1.4 Issues to be determined in a case involving exhaustion of rights

As a defence to trade mark infringement, the issues to be determined by a court dealing with the defence will be similar to those raised in any infringement action, namely:

- has there been infringing conduct? Exhaustion is normally pleaded where the defendant has *imported* trade marked goods from another country. Importation is an infringing act under s.10(4)(c) TMA. Similar provisions, listing importation as infringing conduct, can be found in the Patents Act 1977 s.60, the Registered Designs Act 1949 s.7, as amended ('RDA'), and the Copyright, Designs and Patents Act 1988 s.18 ('CDPA'). There are also cases where some other person has previously imported the goods, and the claimant wishes to object to dealings by the defendant which are subsequent to the act of importation, such as resale, advertising or after-sales service;

- does the case fall within the 'triad of protection' afforded to the trade mark owner under ss.10(1), 10(2) or 10(3) TMA? Normally, the applicable provision will be s.10(1) as the goods will have originated from the claimant or someone acting with the claimant's consent, and will have been marked with the claimant's own trade mark;
- is the defence of exhaustion of rights available on the facts of the case, that is, because the goods were first marketed with the trade mark owner's consent within the EEA? If so:
- does the claimant nevertheless have a valid reason to oppose further commercialisation of the goods because the defendant's activities have in some way undermined the trade mark?

16.1.5 **Theoretical issues**

cross reference
See section 1.4 and section 12.4.

Exhaustion of rights applies to all forms of intellectual property. It has been argued (see van der Merwe, 'The Exhaustion of Rights in Patent Law with Specific Emphasis on the Issue of Parallel Importation' [2000] *IPQ* 286) that the defence of exhaustion should apply differently to the various types of intellectual property rights. In Case 40/70 *Sirena v Eda* [1971] ECR 69, the Advocate General suggested that patents merited greater respect and therefore a higher degree of protection than trade marks, so the exhaustion doctrine should be applied less rigorously to patents. The value judgement inherent in this statement raises (again) the justifications for intellectual property rights and the specific economic role which each plays. In relation to trade marks in particular, the debate about the commercial functions which trade marks perform permeates the case law on exhaustion of rights.

thinking point
Can you think of any arguments which could be made against a rule which states that intellectual property rights are exhausted on first sale of the product?

16.2 # The origin of exhaustion of rights

16.2.1 **Provisions in the Treaty on the Functioning of the European Union ('TFEU')**

The origin of the defence of exhaustion of rights is to be found in key provisions in the **TFEU**, the new name for the Treaty of Rome after the coming into force of the Treaty of Lisbon in December 2009. The case law of the ECJ on these provisions has been crucial to the development of the defence. That case law is now encapsulated in Article 7 of the Directive, so that the Directive's provisions should always be referred to first (*per* AG Sharpston in Case C-348/04 *Boehringer Ingelheim v Swingward Ltd and Dowelhurst ('Boehringer II')* [2007] ECR I-3391 at [15]).

The origin of exhaustion of rights

439

16.2.2 **Free movement of goods**

Part III of the TFEU sets out the policies of the EU, namely the four freedoms mentioned earlier. The fundamental rule in Article 34 TFEU (formerly Article 28 EC) is that goods should be able to move freely between Member States. Article 34 is not, however, absolute. Article 36 TFEU (formerly Article 30 EC) contains a list of exceptions to the principle of free movement, but being a derogation to the basic rule, it should be strictly construed (*per* AG Sharpston in *Boehringer II* at [5]).

Article 34 TFEU declares that 'quantitative restrictions on imports and all measures having equivalent effect shall be prohibited between Member States'. When considering the development of exhaustion of rights, the principle of the supremacy of EU law declared in Case 6/64 *Costa v ENEL* [1964] ECR 585 should be remembered. Free movement of goods as an EU principle prevails over any national rule to the contrary, unless the latter can be justified under Article 36.

Further, the deceptively simple wording of Article 34 has been held by the ECJ to have direct horizontal effect, so that it can be relied upon by a defendant to proceedings for the infringement of any intellectual property right.

> **case close-up**
>
> ### Case 58/80 *Dansk Supermarked v Imerco* [1981] ECR 181
> ....
>
> An example is to be found in Case 58/80 *Dansk Supermarked v Imerco* [1981] ECR 181. Here, to celebrate 50 years in business, the claimant had commissioned commemorative china from an English company. The china was decorated with photographs and engravings of Danish castles, copyright in the pictures belonging to the claimant. The intention was that the claimant would market the china in Denmark, as part of a publicity campaign. The contract allowed the manufacturer to sell any 'seconds' in England, on condition that resale to Scandinavia was prohibited. The defendant supermarket chain nevertheless acquired some 'seconds' which it proposed to sell through its shops in Denmark. The ECJ advised the Danish Supreme Court that neither the law of copyright nor trade marks could be used to stop the sale of goods which had been lawfully marketed in another Member State. However, Danish laws on consumer protection could be relied on to enforce the proper labelling of the china as sub-standard when sold in Danish shops.

The last observation is that Article 34 has been given a broad interpretation by the ECJ, in line with its judicial activism in developing the internal market. The Court has ruled that the phrase 'quantitative restrictions' means 'measures which amount to a total or partial restraint of . . . imports, exports or goods in transit' (rather than simply 'quotas') in Case 2/73 *Geddo v Ente Nazionale Risi* [1973] ECR 865; and that 'measures of equivalent effect' means 'all trading rules enacted by Member States, which are capable of hindering, directly or indirectly, actually or potentially, intra-Community trade' in Case 8/74 *Procureur du Roi v Dassonville* [1974] ECR 837. Thus Article 34 covers not just national rules which discriminate against imported goods, but rules which, although applying equally to domestic and imported goods alike, make it more difficult to import products from another Member State: Case 120/78 *Rewe-Zentrale v Bundesmonopolverwaltung für Branntwein* [1979] ECR 649. In other words, it covers both direct and indirect discrimination against imported goods.

16.2.3 Free movement of services

A parallel provision to Article 34 is Article 56 TFEU, which provides that Member States cannot place restrictions on the freedom to provide services. The Treaty adds (in Article 57) that goods and services are mutually exclusive. In terms of items covered by intellectual property rights, patented and trade marked products will always be regarded as 'goods' and so subject to Article 34. Copyright **works** which are tangible (including films and videos) will also be regarded as 'goods'. However, EU law distinguishes the right to sell tangible copies of works from the right to hire them, these rights in turn being quite separate from the right to control the performance of the work in public, 'performance' in relation to films including both cinematic exhibition and broadcast, whether by terrestrial signal, satellite, cable or over the internet. Intangible copyright works which are treated as 'services' (and hence governed by Article 56) are broadcasts and the performance right in films.

16.2.4 The derogation to Article 34: Article 36

Article 36 TFEU contains a list of circumstances which permits Member States to restrict the free movement of goods. The one which concerns us is 'the protection of industrial and commercial property'. For present purposes it can be assumed that the phrase equates to 'intellectual property'. Taken at face value, the first sentence of Article 36 appears to allow intellectual property rights to take precedence always over the free movement of goods. However, what is equally important is the second sentence of the Article, which provides that 'such prohibitions or restrictions shall not, however, constitute a means of arbitrary discrimination or a disguised restriction on trade between Member States'.

The combined wording of Articles 34 and 36 at first glance creates circularity. Free movement of goods may not be restricted, except to protect intellectual property, but not where such protection restricts trade. The answer to this conundrum lies in the difference between **parallel imports** and **infringing imports**. Distinguishing between the two is vital to an understanding of the cases. Mercifully, the distinction is a question of fact, simply requiring the identification of the commercial origin of goods.

16.2.5 The difference between parallel and infringing imports

The difference between parallel and infringing imports is determined by answering the following factual question: 'who first put these goods into circulation?'

16.2.5.1 First marketing with the intellectual property owner's consent

Where the first marketing (ie in the country of export) was by the intellectual property owner or by another person acting with the owner's express consent (such as a subsidiary or associated company, a **licensee** or a distributor) then those goods are treated as parallel imports. In this instance, the second sentence of Article 36 prevails. For the intellectual property owner to object to further dealings in the goods is 'a disguised restriction on trade' and so free movement of goods takes precedence over intellectual property rights. Intellectual property rights in the Member State of import cannot be used to object to further dealings in those goods unless, in the words of Article 7(2) of the Directive, there exist 'legitimate reasons for the proprietor to oppose further commercialisation of the goods'.

16.2.5.2 First marketing by an unconnected third party

Where, however, the goods were first marketed by an unconnected third party (such as a competitor or counterfeiter) then the intellectual property owner can always rely on their rights in the country of import to prevent importation and sale. Such goods are infringing imports, so the first sentence of Article 36 prevails over the desired goal of the internal market. The conduct of a competitor or counterfeiter, if unchecked, would destroy the right in question (whether patent, design, copyright or trade mark) which would be contrary to Article 345 TFEU which declares that 'this Treaty shall in no way prejudice the rules in Member States governing the system of property ownership'. The internal market gives way to the rights of the intellectual property owner, even if this does reinforce national boundaries.

The ECJ was initially somewhat reluctant to accept that the achievement of the internal market had to be tempered in the interests of the intellectual property owner in the case of infringing imports (see Case 119/75 *Terrapin v Terranova* [1976] ECR 1039). It has, however, now recognised that the value of intellectual property rights should be protected in such circumstances.

case close-up

Deutsche Renault AG v Audi AG [1993] ECR I-6227
· ·
Audi sought to stop Renault using its mark QUADRA in Germany, where Audi had already registered its mark QUATTRO for motor vehicles. Despite the argument that to allow Audi to keep Renault cars out of the German market would be contrary to the principle of free movement of goods, the Court accepted that the function of Audi's trade mark (to guarantee the origin of goods) would be seriously undermined if a rival car manufacturer could be allowed to use a confusingly similar name for its products.

thinking point
How easy is it to differentiate between infringing and parallel imports?

The only way that such fragmentation of the internal market could be avoided is by use of the unitary **EU trade mark**. However, the EU institutions long ago recognised that such a system had to be voluntary and that national trade mark laws had to be allowed to run in parallel to it. Traders have to be free to choose whether to obtain trade mark protection regionally or nationally, depending on the scope of their business activities. The necessary consequence is that national intellectual property rights do create barriers to the free movement of goods.

16.2.6 Extension of Article 36 to cover intellectual property services

On the face of the Treaty, Article 36 does not apply to Article 56. There is nothing in the Treaty which gives Member States specific reasons to restrict the freedom to provide services. However, the ECJ has shown its creativity by applying the derogation found in Article 36 TFEU to services. It has declared that Article 56 does not prevent national rules for the protection of intellectual property from being applied, provided that this does not amount to a disguised restriction on trade between Member States. Hence, in Case 62/79 *Coditel v Ciné Vog (No 1)* [1980] ECR 881 it upheld the right of a film copyright owner to control when and where a film was first exhibited to the public in a Member State, regardless of whether the film had been 'released' elsewhere.

16.2.7 **Concepts deployed by the ECJ**

The way in which the ECJ has resolved the circularity of wording in Articles 34 and 36 TFEU reveals the nature of the balancing exercise which the Court has to perform. Not only does it have to reconcile the territorial nature of national intellectual property rights with the stated Treaty objective of achieving the internal market, it has to take into account the interests of the right-holder, other traders and consumers. To this end, the Court has deployed three particular arguments when creating its case law on exhaustion of rights. None of the reasoning used by the ECJ is totally transparent. However, ultimately each concept which the Court has advanced is concerned with whether the intellectual property owner is objecting to parallel or infringing imports.

16.2.7.1 Existence and exercise

The first argument utilised by the Court has been to say that there is a difference between the 'existence' and 'exercise' of intellectual property rights. The criteria for deciding whether and how such rights are to be created is left to the laws of the Member States, but the way in which such rights are exploited by their owners is a concern of EU law. Such exploitation (whether this consists of granting **licences** or suing for infringement) might have the effect of partitioning the internal market along national boundaries. Seeking to rely on national rights to prevent parallel importation from other Member States is a disguised restriction on trade.

The existence-exercise dichotomy has been criticised as being tenuous and difficult to apply. One of the critics is F-K Beier ('Industrial Property and the Free Movement of Goods in the Internal European Market' (1990) 21 *IIC* 131) who argues that the better approach is to consider the demarcation between legitimate and improper use of intellectual property rights. Indeed, if an intellectual property right exists, then the sole purpose of such existence is for the right to be exercised; conversely, if a right is being exercised, that presupposes its existence.

16.2.7.2 Specific subject matter and essential function

The other two concepts used by the Court are based on the notion that each form of intellectual property has a 'specific subject matter' and an 'essential function'. In relation to patents, the 'essential function' is to reward creativity, whilst the 'specific subject matter' is to allow the proprietor the exclusive right to use the **invention** to make industrial products and to put them 'into circulation for the first time, either directly or by the grant of licences to third parties, as well as the right to oppose infringements' (Case 15/74 *Centrafarm v Sterling Drug Inc* [1974] ECR 1147 at [9]). In relation to trade marks, 'the specific subject matter' contains two elements, namely the guarantee that the owner of the mark has the exclusive right to use it to put goods in circulation for the first time, and protection for the owner against those who wish to take unfair advantage of the status and repute of the trade mark by selling products illegally bearing that mark (Case 16/74 *Centrafarm v Winthrop BV* [1974] ECR 1183 at [8]). The 'essential function' of a trade mark is 'to guarantee the identity of the origin of the trade-marked product to the consumer or ultimate user, by enabling him, without any possibility of confusion, to distinguish that product from products which have another origin [and to] be certain that a trade-marked product has not been subject at a previous stage of marketing to interference…such as to affect the original condition of the product' (Case 102/77 *Hoffmann-La Roche v Centrafarm* [1978] ECR 1139 at [10], repeated in Recital 11 to the consolidated version of the Directive).

The ECJ has not yet declared what the primary function of copyright protection is, except in the case of films. Here, influenced by French cultural tradition, it has stressed the role of copyright in ensuring that the film maker can control the exploitation of the film through its public exhibition: *Coditel v Ciné Vog (No 1)*.

thinking point

Are the arguments advanced by the ECJ to justify the distinction between parallel and infringing imports as clear as they might be?

16.2.8 Interchangeability of the case law

Decisions made in patent cases are generally applicable to trade marks and vice versa. However, care needs to be taken in relation to copyright cases for a number of reasons. Copyright is a bundle of rights. EU law distinguishes between the right to control the reproduction of the work, the right to distribute (ie sell) tangible copies of the work, the right to control the hire of copies and the right to control the performance of the work, whether by cinematographic exhibition or by some other intangible means, such as by broadcast or the internet. First sale of copyright works will exhaust the distribution right (Cases 55 & 57/80 *Musik Vertrieb Membran v GEMA* [1981] ECR 147) but not the other rights (Case 158/86 *Warner Bros v Christiansen* [1988] ECR 2605). The right to control rental of the work can never be exhausted: Case C-61/97 *Egmont Films A/S v Laserdisken* [1998] ECR I-5171.

16.2.9 Summary

The first sentence of Article 36 TFEU allows the intellectual property owner the right of first marketing and the right always to object to the conduct of an infringer (because this goes to the specific subject matter of the right). The owner, however, cannot object to the conduct of a parallel importer of products as this amounts to a disguised restriction on trade.

16.3 The case law of the ECJ: parallel imports from within the EEA

16.3.1 Early cases: reliance on competition law

The initial jurisprudence of the ECJ on exhaustion of rights arose in the context of competition law. The simple reason for this was that the provisions in the then Treaty of Rome dealing with free movement of goods had a transitional period of 12 years, so that it was 1970 before such provisions could be relied on by litigants before national courts. As a result, early cases show the Court attempting to fit the facts of the cases into Articles 101 and 102 TFEU (formerly

Articles 81 and 82 EC). These prohibit, respectively, restrictive agreements which distort intra-EU trade and the abuse of a dominant position. Whilst in some cases, the use of competition law as the vehicle to create the exhaustion of rights defence was non-controversial, in other cases the facts did not really fit the criteria of competition policy, so the ECJ's reasoning appears strained.

case close-up

Cases 56 & 58/64 *Consten & Grundig v Commission* [1966] ECR 299

The first time the ECJ considered the way in which intellectual property rights could be used to partition what was then called the common market was in Cases 56 & 58/64 *Consten & Grundig v Commission* [1966] ECR 299. Grundig, a German maker of hi-fi equipment, appointed Consten to be its exclusive distributor for France. The arrangement gave Consten the right to register Grundig's mark GINT in its own name in France (whether this amounted to a trade mark **assignment** or licence is irrelevant for present purposes). Consten brought a trade mark infringement action against another trader who had attempted to import Grundig products into France, thereby undercutting Consten (price competition is one of the hallmarks of parallel imports case law). Rather than fight the trade mark infringement action, the other trader complained to the EU Commission that the exclusive distribution agreement breached competition law because it distorted trade between Member States. The ECJ upheld the Commission's decision that intellectual property rights could not be used to partition the common market along national boundaries.

At the time, the decision caused consternation, as it had been assumed that intellectual property agreements fell outside the scope of competition policy. A further assumption had been that what was then Article 85 of the Treaty of Rome (now Article 101 TFEU) prohibited only horizontal restrictive agreements rather than vertical restraints. In other words, it was thought that EU competition policy had been intended to operate against cartels of undertakings at the same level in the supply chain (for example, collaboration between rival manufacturers or rival retailers) rather than agreements between manufacturers and distributors.

The ECJ had an early opportunity to consider the effect of owning intellectual property rights in the context of Article 86 of the Treaty of Rome (now Article 102 TFEU) in Case 24/67 *Parke Davis v Probel* [1968] ECR 55. A Dutch **patentee** sought to stop the importation of pharmaceuticals from Italy and was met by the argument that it was abusing its dominant position by exercising its patent right in this way. That argument was rejected. Mere ownership of intellectual property rights, said the Court, did not place an undertaking in a dominant position for the purposes of EU competition policy. What has to be understood from the Court's somewhat Delphic pronouncement is that the products in question were not in fact parallel imports. They had originated from a firm which essentially was taking advantage of the then lack of patent protection for pharmaceuticals in Italy to replicate the patentee's product. Had the case occurred today, these would have been treated as infringing imports.

16.3.2 The foundation cases

Once the free movement of goods provisions were fully effective, it did not take long for the ECJ to set out the foundations of the defence of exhaustion of rights.

case close-up

Case 78/70 *Deutsche Grammophon v Metro-SB-Grossmärkte* [1971] ECR 487

Case 78/70 *Deutsche Grammophon v Metro-SB-Grossmärkte* [1971] ECR 487 concerned sound recordings made by Deutsche Grammophon (DG), a German firm specialising in classical music records. In Germany, at the time, DG was able to require its retailers to sell the recordings at a particular price. It had appointed another company, Polydor, to sell the records in France. Metro, a German supermarket chain, acquired copies of the records in France from Polydor and imported them into Germany where it sold them below list price. The ECJ held that by selling the records in France, DG had exhausted any right it might have to object to their importation and resale in Germany.

case close-up

Case 15/74 *Centrafarm v Sterling Drug Inc* [1974] ECR 1147 and Case 16/74 *Centrafarm v Winthrop BV* [1974] ECR 1183

The ECJ took matters further in *Centrafarm v Sterling Drug Inc* and *Centrafarm v Winthrop BV*. The cases form a classic example of a third party entrepreneur (Centrafarm) using parallel importation to exploit price differentials, and illustrate the Court's vision of the importance of establishing the internal market. Sterling-Winthrop was a multi-national pharmaceutical group. All patents were held in the name of the USA parent company (Sterling Inc) whilst the relevant trade marks were registered in the name of local subsidiaries. Centrafarm purchased medicines in the United Kingdom (where the prices were low) and transported them to the Netherlands where the prices were higher. It was sued for patent and trade mark infringement. The ECJ ruled that the attempt by the Sterling-Winthrop group to rely on its rights to keep out parallel imports was incompatible with the free movement of goods. Further, the different companies in the corporate group were to be treated as a single undertaking. The consent of one company to the marketing of the goods within the common market bound all.

16.3.3 The meaning of 'put on the market'

A key phrase in the *Centrafarm v Winthrop* ruling, repeated in Article 7(1) of the Directive, is that the trade mark right doesn't entitle its owner to object to the use of the mark 'in relation to goods which have been put on the market in the Community by the proprietor or with his consent'. What does 'put on the market in the Community' mean? Does it mean that the goods have been driven through a Member State on a lorry or displayed in a shop or kept in a warehouse? Or must there have been a transfer of ownership through an act of sale? The answer was provided by the ECJ in Case C-16/03 *Peak Holding AB v Axolin-Elinor AB* [2004] ECR I-11313. The Court ruled that 'put on the market' requires that goods have been sold, either to members of the public, or to another trader who has the power of disposal over them. Where goods have been kept in a warehouse by the trade mark owner, or displayed in a shop without being sold, then they have not been 'put on the market'. However, once goods have been supplied to another trader, even if there is a clause in the contract prohibiting resale within the EU, the goods are treated as having been 'put on the market', so the defence of exhaustion applies. The trade mark owner cannot use trade mark rights to stop the resale of the goods, even though there might be liability for breach of contract.

The ECJ has since confirmed this in Case C-405/03 *Class International BV v Colgate Palmolive* [2005] ECR I-8735 where a consignment of imported AQUAFRESH toothpaste had been stored in a warehouse before being sent to another non-EEA country. The issue was whether the goods were to be treated as having been 'put on the market' so that the trade mark owner could object to their importation. The Court ruled that mere entry into the EU was not enough. Goods must be introduced into the EU for the purpose of putting them on the market, ie for the purpose of resale, so that where goods were merely in transit, no infringing conduct had been committed. Similarly, in Case C-281/05 *Montex Holdings Ltd v Diesel* [2006] ECR I-10881, goods which were in transit to a Member State where there was no trade mark protection could not be treated as infringing goods in an intermediate country where there was such protection. The corollary of these two rulings was that the trade mark owner was unable to ask customs authorities to impound imported goods as counterfeit unless there was clear evidence that they were about to be supplied to EU consumers: Cases C-446/09 and C-495/09 *Philips/Nokia* [2012] ETMR 248. This gap will be closed by draft Article 10(5) of the proposed 'recast' Trade Marks Directive.

The ECJ has also stated that where goods such as 'perfume testers' are supplied without transfer of ownership and with a prohibition on their re-sale, they have not been 'put on the market' for the purposes of Article 7: Case 127/09 *Coty Prestige Lancaster Group GmbH v Simex Trading AG* [2010] ECR I-4965; Case C-324/09 *L'Oréal SA v eBay International* [2011] ECR I-6011. It remains to be seen whether brand owners utilise these two rulings as a means of limiting the effect of the doctrine of exhaustion.

16.3.4 **The importance of consent to first marketing**

The wording of Article 7(1) reveals the key element in the defence of exhaustion, namely consent. It took the ECJ quite some time before consent to the first marketing of the goods was clearly spelled out in case law: the Court misled itself for a time in cases where, historically, there had been a change of ownership of the mark even though there was no connection between the trade mark owner and the importer at the time of the case.

16.3.4.1 The effect of a change of ownership of the mark

The scenario to be imagined is that Company A owns parallel national trade mark registrations in a number of Member States, for example, France, Germany and the United Kingdom, but then sells its entire French business to Company B, including the French trade mark registrations. The question to be answered is whether, because of this change of ownership, Company A can now keep trade-marked goods originating from Company B out of Germany and the United Kingdom, and conversely whether Company B can keep the branded goods of Company A out of France.

The difficulty with the cases is that initially, the ECJ treated such goods as if they were parallel imports. It did so as a result of adopting something called the 'common origin' doctrine. The doctrine came about at a time when the Court was obliged to use competition law as the basis of its decisions on exhaustion of rights, and when it was keen to develop the common market. In its enthusiasm to treat all Member States as a single entity, it all but destroyed the value of trade marks. Mercifully (albeit some 20 years later) it set the record straight.

The 'wrong turning' taken by the ECJ occurred in *Sirena v Eda*. Here, there had been parallel trade mark registrations for shaving cream in Germany and Italy. In 1937, ownership of the German mark had been transferred to an unrelated company. Many years later, the Italian trade mark owner sued for infringement when shaving cream bearing the trade mark was imported from Germany. The ECJ treated the 1937 assignment as having continuing effect for the purposes of competition law (a proposition which completely misunderstands the nature of change of ownership) and ruled that the assignment partitioned the market. The Italian trade mark owner could not stop the imports from Germany, even though its links to the German trade mark owner were historical only.

case close-up

> ### Case 192/73 *Van Zuylen Frères v Hag AG* [1974] ECR 731 ('*Hag I*')
>
> The ECJ further developed this 'common origin' doctrine in Case 192/73 *Van Zuylen Frères v Hag AG* [1974] ECR 731 ('*Hag I*'). It ruled that even an involuntary change of ownership (by Government expropriation at the end of World War II) did not break the link between the original German owner and the Belgian registration for KAFFEE HAG, so that the current Belgian owner could not object to coffee imported from Germany. The Court's attention was focused on historical origin of the *trade mark* rather than the common origin of the *goods*.

Apart from its failure to appreciate the nature of property transactions, the ECJ's ruling in *Hag I* had the effect of undermining many successful brands, as trade marks often change hands as companies merge, expand and diversify.

The change of thinking began in Case 19/84 *Pharmon v Hoechst* [1985] ECR 2281 where the ECJ ruled that where a parallel patent had been the subject of a **compulsory licence** in the Member State of export, the patentee in the Member State of import could object to the imported patented product as they had not given voluntary consent to the marketing of the goods. In due course the ECJ reconsidered its ruling in *Hag I* in Case C-10/89 *SA CNL-Sucal NV v Hag GF AG* [1990] ECR I-3711 ('*Hag II*'). Here, the German trade mark owner objected to imports of KAFFEE HAG coffee coming from Belgium. The Court, no doubt impressed by arguments that consumers would be confused by the availability of two versions of the KAFFEE HAG product, reversed its previous decision, concentrating not on the history of the mark, but whether the owner of the mark in the importing state had consented to the first marketing of the goods. It changed its mind about the effect of voluntary assignments in Case C-9/93 *IHT Internationale Heiztechnik GmbH v Ideal-Standard GmbH* [1994] ECR I-2789, holding that where a German company had sold off its French business, trade-marked sanitary ware imported from France into Germany by the new owners could be stopped. This reversed the decision in *Sirena*, although the Court added, as an afterthought, that it reserved the right to look behind an assignment to see if it was an attempt to partition the market.

16.3.4.2 The difference between an assignment and a licence

The effect of the cases discussed in the previous sections can be summarised as follows. The treatment of trade marks which have been assigned and those which have been **licensed** is different. A change of ownership of the mark means that **assignor** and **assignee** can keep each other's products out of their respective territories (in line with the decision in *Audi v Renault*, discussed earlier). However, imports from a licensee, because they have been marketed with the consent of the brand owner, are subject to the full force of the exhaustion defence. In other words, whether exhaustion applies depends entirely on the trade mark owner's consent to the goods being put into circulation in the internal market.

Nevertheless, in some cases the trade mark owner may even be able to object to the circulation of licensed products.

case close-up

Case C-59/08 *Copad SA v Christian Dior Couture SA* [2009] ECR I-3421

Dior had concluded a trade mark licence agreement with a company called SIL for the manufacture and distribution of luxury underwear. The contract stipulated that, in order to maintain the repute and prestige of the trade mark, the licensee would not sell to discount stores and the like without the prior written consent of the **licensor**. Facing economic difficulties, SIL asked Dior permission to market the goods outside of its selective distribution network, but Dior refused. Nevertheless, SIL supplied goods to Copad which ran a discount store. Dior sued both companies for trade mark infringement, arguing both breach of the licence and that lack of consent meant that there was no exhaustion of rights. The ECJ ruled first, that Article 8(2) of the Directive (which contains an exhaustive list of when conduct by a licensee amounts to trade mark infringement) entitled Dior to sue its licensee for trade mark infringement: it was conceivable that the sale of luxury goods by a licensee to third parties which were not part of a selective distribution network might affect *the quality of the goods themselves*, a factor listed within the Article. Second, although goods marketed by a licensee were put on the market with the consent of the trade mark owner, where, as here, the licence did not amount to absolute and unconditional consent (because of the wording of Article 8(2)), the contravention of the terms of the licence meant that there was no exhaustion of rights. Finally, where, as here, luxury goods were marketed in contravention of the terms of a licence agreement but this was not sufficient to trigger Article 8(2), the proprietor could rely on Article 7(2) of the Directive and could therefore oppose further commercialisation of the goods, but only where it could be established that the resale of the goods could damage *the reputation of the trade mark*.

cross reference

See section 17.3.4.2.

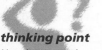

thinking point

How important is the role of consent in the defence of exhaustion of rights?

16.4

Copad is a significant case for a number of different reasons. It strengthens the argument that the trade mark acts as a guarantee of quality rather than origin. Further, it emphasises the importance of quality control provisions in a trade mark licence and makes clear that a licensee who breaches these will be liable for trade mark infringement, not just breach of contract. Also, it establishes that where there is breach of quality control provisions in a licence, the goods will have been put on the market *without* consent so that Article 7(1) does not apply and that even if selling to a prohibited retailer doesn't affect the condition of the goods, it may still give the trade mark owner the right to oppose further commercialisation under Article 7(2) because of damage to the mark.

Exceptions to exhaustion

Over almost four decades, the ECJ has gradually developed exceptions to the defence of exhaustion of rights. In each case, it has said, there are valid reasons why the intellectual property owner can stop the importation of the goods (or, in some cases, object to post-importation conduct). The case law is now expressed in Article 7(2) of the Directive, which provides that the defence of exhaustion shall not apply 'where there exist legitimate reasons...to oppose further commercialisation of the goods, especially where the condition of the goods is changed or impaired after they have been put on the market'. Article 7(2) is an exception to the free movement of goods, and should not be generously construed (*per* AG Sharpston in *Boehringer II* at [13]). In applying Article 7(2), the Court has endeavoured to strike a balance between the interests of a number of key players, namely the intellectual property owner, enterprising importers and consumers. It may be questioned whether as the law currently stands the ECJ has got the balance right, or whether the scales have been tilted too far towards the rights of the intellectual property owner.

16.4.1 Exception 1: alteration of the goods

The first exception to the defence occurs where the parallel importer alters the imported goods. Most (but by no means all) of the cases have concerned pharmaceutical products. As P. Koutrakos explains ('In Search of a Common Vocabulary in Free Movement of Goods: The Example of Repackaging Pharmaceuticals' [2003] *ELR* 53), the pharmaceutical market differs considerably from others. The market is dominated by a handful of large, multi-national companies. Size matters because of the research and development costs; further, the time gap between the identification of a new chemical compound and its marketing as an effective pharmaceutical treatment is considerable, so that it takes many years to recoup investment. There are complex EU and national rules for the approval of medicines, and government intervention means that there are significant price differentials between Member States. Nevertheless, medicines are global products. They are needed by patients wherever they live. The products are easy to transport. However, local prescribing and dispensing practices vary enormously. Last, and perhaps most importantly, information about the product needs to be given in the local language. Patients need to know about when and how much of the medicine to take.

These factors provide some of the reasons why importers wish to alter imported pharmaceuticals. It is no good supplying tablets in blister-packs of 10 if doctors only prescribe in multiples of seven. Patients used to the United Kingdom trade mark for the product will not recognise the mark used in Italy for the same product. Patients in the United Kingdom will want to read the dosage instructions in English not Spanish.

The word 'alteration' includes repackaging, rebranding, relabelling and over-stickering. As these terms are crucial, it will be useful to explain the differences between them. These differences are set out in Table 16.1.

Such alteration of the goods is, according to the ECJ, *prima facie* infringement of the trade mark right, although there is not an irrebuttable presumption to this effect (*per* Jacob LJ in *Boehringer Ingelheim KG v Dowelhurst Ltd* at [80]). Alteration entitles the trade mark owner to oppose importation and converts the parallel importer into an infringer. At first glance this appears to run contrary to both the origin function of trade marks and the principle of the internal market. What the ECJ has done, as part of its balancing exercise, has been to create *cumulative* guidelines with which the importer must comply in order to render the importation of the altered goods unobjectionable. The guidelines apply equally to repackaging,

Table 16.1

Repackaging, rebranding, relabelling and over-stickering: definitions and differences

Term	Meaning
Repackaging	Where the importer leaves the internal packaging intact, but replaces the exterior carton, this being printed in the language of the Member State of import (this should be distinguished from where the internal packaging is altered, for example cutting up blister packs of tablets).
Rebranding	Where the importer removes the trade mark used on the Member State of export and replaces it with that used in the Member State of import (because the trade mark owner uses different marks in different countries).
Relabelling	Where the importer removes existing product labels (including those containing batch codes) and replaces them with its own (possibly inferior) labels.
Over-stickering	Where the importer leaves the original internal and external packaging intact, but then applies an additional label printed in the language of the Member State of import to the outside of the packaging.

thinking point

Is the identical treatment accorded to repackaging, rebranding, relabelling, over-stickering and de-branding justified?

rebranding and relabelling: Case C-143/00 *Boehringer Ingelheim v Swingward Ltd and Dowelhurst* ('*Boehringer I*') [2002] ECR I-3759 (*per* AG Jacobs at [86]). The Court disagreed with the advice of AG Sharpston at [42] in *Boehringer II* that over-stickering should not receive the same treatment and instead held that such conduct equally amounted to trade mark infringement (at [29]–[32]). It has now added that the removal of packaging ('de-branding') has the same effect as re-packaging: Case C-324/09 *L'Oréal SA v eBay International* [2011] ECR I-6011.

16.4.1.1 Repackaging the goods

case close-up

Case 102/77 *Hoffmann-La Roche v Centrafarm* [1978] ECR 1139

The rights of the trade mark owner where the goods have been repackaged were first considered by the ECJ in *Hoffmann-La Roche v Centrafarm*. VALIUM tranquilliser tablets sold in the United Kingdom were repackaged by Centrafarm so as to make them acceptable to the prescribing practices of the German market, the importer re-affixing the trade mark together with its own name and address to the outside of the repackaged product. Such conduct was held to infringe the trade mark because it undermined its function of guaranteeing the quality of the goods. The Court went on to provide the first repackaging guidelines. The initial four *Hoffmann-La Roche* conditions were that:

- the trade mark owner's conduct must have the effect of partitioning the market. Example of such conduct would be where the goods in question are sold in yellow boxes in Italy but blue boxes in the United Kingdom, or where tablets are supplied in blister packs of seven in the United Kingdom, but packs of 10 in Germany;
- the importer must state that the goods have been repackaged;
- notice must be given to the trade mark owner;
- the repackaging must not affect the condition of the goods. This is termed 'physical impairment' and includes the adequacy of any replacement instruction leaflets which the importer adds to the product, *per* AG Jacobs in *Boehringer I*.

The balancing act referred to earlier is evident in the guidelines. The interests of the trade mark owner are met by the requirement that the goods must not be adversely affected by the repackaging, otherwise the essential function of the trade mark is damaged. Equally, the interests of the internal market are met, because the trade mark owner's conduct is examined objectively (ie without reference to the owner's intentions) to see whether it has the *effect* of reinforcing national boundaries. The other two guidelines (marking the goods to show that they have been repackaged, and giving notice), whilst underpinning the guarantee function of the mark, appear procedural in nature. The importer in Case 1/81 *Pfizer Inc v Eurim-Pharm* [1981] ECR 2913 successfully complied with these guidelines, thereby escaping liability for infringement.

16.4.1.2 Rebranding the goods

case close-up

Case 3/78 *Centrafarm v American Home Products* [1978] ECR 1823

The importer not only repackaged the product but changed the trade mark from that used in the United Kingdom (SERENID) to that used in the Netherlands (SERESTA). The importer was held to have infringed the latter registration when it imported the goods into the Netherlands. The ECJ accepted that the trade mark owner had good reason (language differences) to have different marks in different Member States, but added the warning that if different marks were chosen simply to partition the internal market, the parallel importer would be at liberty to change the marks without incurring liability.

The difficulty with the ruling is that whereas that in *Hoffmann-La Roche* had demanded an *objective* assessment of whether the trade mark owner's conduct divided the internal market, here the Court appears to contemplate a *subjective* test where that conduct consists of having different marks for different Member States. The ECJ has now removed this discrepancy.

16.4.1.3 Relabelling the goods

Relabelling occurred in Case C-349/95 *Frits Loendersloot v George Ballantine & Sons Ltd* [1997] ECR I-6227, which for once did not involve pharmaceutical products. Importers of whisky had removed the labels on the bottles, replacing them with their own. The original labels had included batch numbers, required under EU foodstuffs law to enable the recall of faulty products, but the numbers were also used by the trade mark owner to prevent counterfeiting and to follow dealings in the goods with a view to finding out whether particular traders had breached conditions of sale by supplying known parallel importers. The ECJ held that the removal of labels amounted to trade mark infringement. The use of the labels did not lead to artificial partitioning of the market.

16.4.1.4 Over-stickering

In contrast to the facts of *Ballantine*, over-stickering does not involve the removal of any material from the product. Instead, a label is placed onto the exterior packaging, with the objective, at least in the case of pharmaceutical goods, of providing the patient with additional information in their own language. The additions to the *Hoffmann-La Roche* guidelines, discussed next, have added a requirement of proportionality: the importer's over-stickering, where it is the *minimum* that can be done to achieve access to the market, will avoid liability, provided that the labels are of appropriate quality.

16.4.1.5 The additions to the *Hoffmann-La Roche* guidelines

In two subsequent rulings, the ECJ added to the *Hoffmann-La Roche* guidelines. In Cases C-427/93 *Bristol-Myers Squibb v Paranova*, C-71/94 *Eurim-Pharm v Beiersdorf* and C-232/94 *MPA Pharma v Rhône-Poulenc* ('*Paranova I*') [1996] ECR I-3457, the Court said that the power of the trade mark owner to oppose repackaging would be limited where repackaging was necessary to market the product in the importing Member State. It also said that the importer must supply samples of the goods to the trade mark owner if asked to do so, and that the repackaging must not be untidy, of poor quality, or likely to injure the reputation of the mark (referred to as the 'mental impairment' of the mark). In Case C-379/97 *Pharmacia & Upjohn SA v Paranova A/S* ('*Paranova II*') [1999] ECR I-6927 it declared that the repackaging must be objectively necessary to enable the importer to have access to the market. *Paranova I* was the first case to be heard by the ECJ under the provisions of the Directive. Its restatement of the rights of the trade mark owner under Article 7(2) has since been adopted with approval in *Boehringer I* and *Boehringer II*.

> **case close-up**
>
> **Case C-348/04 *Boehringer Ingelheim v Swingward Ltd and Dowelhurst* ('*Boehringer II*')** [2007] ECR I-3391
>
> . . . .
>
> In *Boehringer II*, the ECJ (at [21], [32]) summarised the restatement thus. Under Article 7(2) of the Directive, a trade mark owner may legitimately oppose the further marketing of a pharmaceutical product which has been repackaged, rebranded, relabelled or over-stickered unless:
>
> - repackaging is necessary for market access;
> - the repackaging does not affect the original condition of the product;
> - the new packaging clearly states who repackaged the product and the name of the manufacturer;
> - the presentation of the repackaged product is not such as to be liable to damage the reputation of the trade mark and of its owner; and
> - the importer gives notice to the trade mark owner before the repackaged product is put on sale, and, on demand, supplies a specimen of the repackaged product.

A number of matters in this definitive restatement require further elaboration, namely necessity, 'mental impairment', marking the goods as having been repackaged, the giving of notice, the supply of samples and the burden of proof.

Necessity

The requirement that the importer must show the need to repackage has been part of the case law since *Paranova I*. The number of requests for preliminary rulings under what is now Article 267 TFEU which this has generated shows the inherent difficulty of the concept.

The need to repackage will be a direct result of the conduct of the trade mark owner partitioning the market. Such conduct might consist of choosing different forms of packaging for different Member States, or different trade marks for different Member States (the ECJ in *Paranova I* made clear, in contrast to its earlier ruling in *Centrafarm v American Home Products*, that the choice of different marks for different states was to be determined objectively not subjectively). It was initially thought the need to repackage had to be in response to restrictions imposed by national legislation (for example, prohibiting the use of particular names as trade marks, as in *Paranova II*) or of local prescribing practices, but the ECJ in *Paranova II* made clear that 'necessity' meant simply whether the importer had to change the goods in order to gain market access. Necessity itself was to be determined objectively. In *Boehringer I*, it said that 'market access' included overcoming consumer resistance to over-stickered boxes (thereby justifying the replacement of the outer packaging) but did not extend to the importer's attempt to secure a commercial advantage (ie by free-riding on the success of the claimant's trade mark).

In *Boehringer II*, the ECJ said (at [33–39]) that the requirement of necessity was concerned solely with *whether* the goods had to be reboxed. It did not extend to *how* they were reboxed. To hold otherwise would place an intolerable burden on national courts who would have to take 'numerous decisions on trivial details of pattern and colour', matters not within their judicial remit (*per* AG Sharpston at [54]).

Mental impairment

The requirement that the importer must not cause harm to the reputation of the trade mark was first established by the ECJ in *Paranova I*. This appears to run contrary to the origin function of trade marks and has not been well received by the United Kingdom judiciary: see *Zino Davidoff SA v A&G Imports Ltd* [1999] 2 CMLR 1056; *Glaxo Group Ltd v Dowelhurst Ltd (No 2)* [2000] FSR 529. Nevertheless, it does accord with the wider view of trade marks set out by the ECJ in Case C-206/01 *Arsenal Football Club v Matthew Reed* [2002] ECR I-10273. In line with this, the Court stated in *Boehringer I* that the legitimate interests of the trade mark owner must be respected. Further, in *Boehringer II*, the ECJ confirmed (at [43]) that whilst such damage must be serious, it is not limited to defective, poor quality or untidy packaging. Instead, both the 'inappropriate presentation' of the trade mark and an incorrect suggestion of a commercial link between the trade mark owner and the importer are capable, in principle, of causing damage. Whether 'de-branding', 'co-branding', obscuring the original trade mark, failing to state the ownership of the original mark or printing the name of the importer in capital letters does damage the reputation of the trade mark is a question of fact for the national court to decide in the light of the circumstances of each case (*Boehringer II* at [47]).

Despite this advice, when *Boehringer II* returned to the national court, the Court of Appeal held that the defendant's conduct in repackaging and over-stickering the claimant's pharmaceutical products had not caused mental impairment: *Boehringer Ingelheim v Swingward* [2008] EWCA Civ 83.

Marking the goods as repackaged

This is one of the original *Hoffmann-La Roche* guidelines. Surprisingly, the Court seems less concerned that it should be strictly applied, in contrast to some of the other repackaging conditions. In Cases C-400/09 and C-207/10 *Orifarm v Merck, Sharp & Dohme; Paranova v Merck, Sharp & Dohme* [2011] ECR I-7063 it stated that as long as consumers weren't misled, it didn't matter that the name which appeared was not that of the actual repackager but another company in the same corporate group which held the marketing authorisation. What was required was to indicate that someone other than the trade mark owner had repackaged the goods.

Notice

Likewise, the requirement for the importer to given notice to the trade mark owner that the goods have been repackaged originated in *Hoffmann-La Roche*. It has frequently been questioned. One of the key issues in *Boehringer I* was whether the importer had to give notice in person to the trade mark owner. Laddie J, when making the reference, had thought it sufficient if the owner learned of the repackaging from another reliable source. Further, how much notice has to be given? Laddie J thought that 48 hours' notice was enough but the ECJ declared that the trade mark owner had to be given a reasonable time to react and so stipulated that the notice period had to be 15 working days. Notice had to be given by the importer in person.

The matter was revisited in *Boehringer II*, where the Court of Appeal sought further guidance on the penalty to be imposed should the importer comply with all the other guidelines but fail to give the correct notice. AG Sharpston suggested that as notice was a procedural requirement, it ought to attract a less severe remedy than that awarded for breach of the other guidelines. That was not to belittle the importance of giving notice. It was an important safeguard for the trade mark owner and save in the most exceptional cases, failure to give notice would normally be deliberate. The ECJ disagreed on the remedies point: the trade mark owner's right to prevent parallel importation of products marketed in breach of the requirement to give prior notice is no different from the right to object to counterfeit goods. Awarding the same remedy for failure to give notice as for dealing in counterfeit goods is not contrary to the principle of proportionality, although it is for the national court to determine the amount of the financial remedy: *Boehringer II* at [55–64]).

Samples

case close-up

Case C-276/05 *The Wellcome Foundation Ltd v Paranova Pharmazeutika Handels GmbH* [2008] ECR I-10479

. . . .

The need to submit samples was the subject matter of the reference in Case C-276/05 *The Wellcome Foundation Ltd v Paranova Pharmazeutika Handels GmbH* [2008] ECR I-10479. Wellcome was the **registered proprietor** in Austria of the mark ZOVIRAX. Paranova had sold the tablets (bought elsewhere in the EEA) in new packaging, which bore the phrase 'Repackaged and imported by Paranova' in large print, and gave notice to an associated company, enclosing samples of the packaging. The claimant objected that the defendant had not explained the reasons for the re-packaging, had not stated where it had bought the tablets (in fact they had been purchased in Greece where the original packs contained different quantities of the tablets), and had not justified using such large print and asked for samples of all re-packaging. The defendant refused. The ECJ stated that the requirement to supply samples was to enable the trade mark owner to check that the condition of the product was not affected and that the presentation of the product was not likely to damage the reputation of the mark. It was for the national court to decide here whether the packaging did damage the reputation of the mark. It was up to the importer to show necessity to repackage, and to produce sufficient information to enable the proprietor to decide whether repackaging was necessary.

The burden of proof

In *Boehringer II*, the ECJ saw fit to depart from the Opinion of AG Sharpston. It stated (at [51–53]) that the burden of proof lay on the importer to establish all the conditions set out in para [32] of its ruling. However, with regard to the condition that the repackaging must not affect the original condition of the goods and the condition that the presentation of the product must not affect the trade mark's reputation, it was enough to furnish evidence that led to a reasonable presumption that the condition was fulfilled. As regards mental impairment, the onus then switched to the trade mark proprietor (who was best placed to assess whether the repackaging was liable to damage his reputation and that of the trade mark) to prove that they had been damaged. The Court added that an EU rule regarding the burden of proof was essential to meet the policy set out Recital 10 to the consolidated version of the Directive, namely that trade marks should receive the same level of protection in all Member States.

thinking point

Do the ECJ's guidelines for a parallel importer who wishes to repackage goods give too much power to the trade mark owner?

16.4.2 Exception 2: advertising and after-sales service

Two cases illustrate how the exhaustion defence can apply to conduct occurring after goods have been imported. Equally they show how the trade mark owner can object if such conduct affects the essential function of the mark. Both cases make use of the concept of mental impairment first set out in *Paranova I*. In Case C-337/95 *Parfums Christian Dior SA and Parfums Christian Dior BV v Evora BV* [1997] ECR I-6013, the trade mark owner sued for infringement where luxury perfumes were sold in a cut-price chemist's shop, arguing that the positioning of the goods (next to disposable nappies) and the manner of advertising (on cheap leaflets) undermined the 'aura of luxury' associated with the mark. The ECJ ruled that although Article 7(1) applied to post-importation conduct (such as resale), it was for the national court to decide whether the manner of resale caused harm to the mark. Similarly, in Case C-63/97 *BMW v Deenik* [1999] ECR I-905, the Court said that any sales of second-hand cars by the defendant must not create the mistaken impression on the part of customers that Mr Deenik was part of the authorised BMW dealer network, nor must the manner of sale cause harm to the reputation of the mark.

16.4.3 Exception 3: rental rights

The ECJ has ruled that a copyright owner's exclusive right to control the rental of copies of films (created by Council Directive 92/100/EEC of 19 November 1992 rental right and lending rights and on certain rights related to copyright in the field of intellectual property [1992] OJ L 346/61, now codified as Directive 2006/115/EC of the European Parliament and of the Council of 12 December 2006 [2006] OJ L 376/28) (hereafter 'the Rental Rights Directive') is not exhausted by sales of copies of the film, indeed the rental right is incapable of being exhausted: Case C-61/97 *Egmont Films A/S v Laserdisken* [1998] ECR I-5171.

A more complex issue is the supply of computer software. Pumfrey J in *Microsoft Corporation v Computer Future Distribution Ltd* [1998] ETMR 597 assumed that where software is licensed (even though supplied on a physical medium such as a CD-ROM) then the manufacturer could object to subsequent dealings as there was no transfer of ownership of the intangible right. However, in Case C-128/11 *UsedSoft GmbH v Oracle International Corp*, 3 July 2012, the ECJ ruled that exhaustion applies not only where the software is supplied on a physical medium, but where it is distributed by means of downloads from a website. The Court added that a perpetual licence involved a transfer of the right of ownership of the copy.

16.5 Case law of the ECJ: parallel imports from outside the EEA

We mentioned at the start of this chapter that it is possible for exhaustion of rights to apply internationally. Marketing of the goods anywhere in the world with the consent of the owner of the intellectual property right would mean that no objection could be made to further dealings in those goods. We consider here the case law of the ECJ on international exhaustion. As harmonisation Directives have led to a change in the law, we set out the pre- and post-harmonisation rules.

16.5.1 The position prior to harmonisation

Where the goods were first marketed in a non-EEA Contracting State and then imported into the EU, the ECJ ruled (in Case 51/75 *EMI v CBS* [1976] ECR 811) that this was not a matter of EU law because Article 34 TFEU only applied to the free movement of goods *between* Member States. Accordingly, it was up to the Member State of import to decide whether imports from outside the EU could be stopped. Subsequently, Case C-352/95 *Phytheron International SA v Jean Bourdon SA* [1997] ECR I-1729 added a qualification. The Court said that where the trade mark owner agreed to the initial importation of the goods into the EEA, then the goods became EU goods and therefore subject to the principle of intra-EU exhaustion of rights. Again, it may be observed, consent to the goods being placed on the market is the key.

The difficulty with the *EMI v CBS* ruling (see Norman, 'Parallel Imports from Non-EEA Member States: the Vision Remains Unclear' [2000] *EIPR* 159), was that Member States did not have a uniform attitude towards the principle of international exhaustion, so that non-EEA goods received different treatment in different Member States, depending upon which was the Member State of import and, further, which form of intellectual property right was involved. For example, Germany adopted a theory of international exhaustion of rights with regard to trade marks but not with regard to patents. Even within the United Kingdom, case law on trade marks was inconsistent, as illustrated by the two contrasting Court of Appeal decisions in *Revlon Inc v Cripps & Lee Ltd* and *Colgate-Palmolive v Markwell Finance* discussed at the start of this chapter.

16.5.2 The position post-harmonisation

Once the EU began enacting harmonisation Directives, the question was whether Article 7 of the Directive (and indeed the equivalent provision in other intellectual property Directives) removed the discretion left to Member States by *EMI v CBS* to deal with parallel imports from non-EEA Member States in accordance with their own national laws. If (as was logical) Member States no longer had any discretion, but had to apply a single EU rule, should the latter impose a doctrine of international exhaustion or only EU-wide exhaustion of rights?

case close-up

Case C-355/96 *Silhouette International Schmied GmbH v Hartlauer Handelsgesellschaft mbH* [1998] ECR I-4799

. . . .

The answer came in Case C-355/96 *Silhouette International Schmied GmbH v Hartlauer Handelsgesellschaft mbH* [1998] ECR I-4799. Silhouette, a manufacturer of spectacle frames at the 'upper end' of the market, sold them under the trade mark SILHOUETTE. In Austria, the frames were supplied to specialist opticians, elsewhere they were supplied through local subsidiaries or distributors. The case came about because Silhouette had 21,000 pairs of spectacles which it no longer required as they were, fashion-wise, out of date. It entered into a contract whereby the goods were sold to an intermediary who was under strict instructions to require the purchaser to resell only in Bulgaria or the states of the former Soviet Union and not to export them to other countries. Predictably, Hartlauer (with whom Silhouette had previously refused to do business because it did not conform to the prestigious image to which Silhouette aspired) acquired the goods and offered them for sale in Austria.

The ECJ ruled that there should be no doctrine of international exhaustion, so that the trade mark owner could object to the importation of the spectacle frames into Austria. EU Member States had to apply intra-EU exhaustion of rights only. The reasoning of the Court is brief. It said that because of what is now Recital 10 to the Directive, trade marks must receive the same level of protection in all Member States, so that in the interests of the internal market, there must be a single rule in order to ensure a 'level playing field'. Articles 5 to 7 of the Directive are a complete code of the trade mark owner's rights. To recognise international exhaustion would reduce the trade mark owner's protection. The key phrase in Article 7, namely 'put on the market in the Community...by the proprietor or with his consent' meant that there should only be intra-EU exhaustion of rights.

The decision in *Silhouette* was extensively criticised because it led to the creation of 'fortress Europe' and because it ignored the origin function of trade marks. Nevertheless, Judge David Edwards has argued that the ECJ had little choice but to adopt a policy of intra-EU exhaustion (see 'Trade Marks: Descriptions of Origin and the Internal Market' [2001] *IPQ* 135). Despite the criticism, the Court confirmed its thinking in *Silhouette* in Case C-173/98 *Sebago Inc & S.A. Ancienne Maison Dubois v S.A. G-B Unic* [1999] ECR I-4103. At the same time, it dealt with a recurring argument as to the meaning of the word 'consent' in Article 7. The importer had tried to argue that consent could be implied from a course of dealing, so that once one consignment of goods (here, shoes made in Central America) had been imported into a Member State, all subsequent assignments should be treated as entering the EU with consent. The ECJ dismissed this argument. The wording of its earlier rulings in *Centrafarm v Winthrop*, *Dior* and *Deenik*, together with the text of Article 7, made plain that consent had to be given for each individual batch of goods rather than product lines.

thinking point

Why should a trade mark owner be able to object to goods he has placed in circulation in Singapore or the USA when he cannot object (subject to the repackaging rules) to goods he has placed in circulation somewhere in the EEA?

16.5.3 **The sequel to *Silhouette***

Predictably, United Kingdom judges were not impressed by *Silhouette* and *Sebago*. Indeed, before the rulings were given, Jacob J had hinted (in *Northern & Shell v Condé Nast* [1995] RPC 117) that he favoured a doctrine of international exhaustion. Although Scottish courts had applied *Silhouette* (see *Zino Davidoff SA v M&S Toiletries* [2000] 2 CMLR 735), Laddie J refused to do so in *Zino Davidoff SA v A&G Imports Ltd* [2000] Ch 127. Here, aftershave made in Singapore had, through a chain of dealings, reached the United Kingdom, despite the attempts by the trade mark owner to impose contractual obligations on each purchaser of the goods not to import the goods into the EU. Laddie J, clearly concerned at the enhancement of the trade mark owner's rights, tried to sidestep *Silhouette* by treating consent as a matter of national contract law. Nevertheless, he referred to the ECJ a number of questions on international exhaustion. The ECJ, in a remarkably forthright ruling, insisted that there should be no international exhaustion of rights in EU law.

---

case close-up

Case C-414/99 *Zino Davidoff SA v A&G Imports Ltd* [2001] ECR I-8691
. . . .

The ECJ repeated that Articles 5 to 7 of the Directive were a complete harmonisation of the owner's rights. In the interests of the internal market these provisions had to be consistently applied. First marketing outside the EEA did not exhaust the trade mark owner's rights. Further, 'consent' was a concept of EU intellectual property law. Article 7 was a derogation of the rights found in Article 5 of the Directive, and must therefore be narrowly construed, so that consent was the decisive factor. Consequently, the intention of the trade mark owner to renounce the Article 5 rights must be unequivocally proved. This had to be express, although (exceptionally) consent could be implied. However, said the Court, consent could *not* be implied from failure to communicate an import ban to all subsequent purchasers, from the fact that a warning notice was not placed on the goods, from the absence of any appropriate contractual reservations in any agreement transferring ownership of the goods, nor from the owner's silence. It was also irrelevant that retailers/wholesalers did not pass on the trade mark owner's reservations. Finally, said the Court, the onus of proof was on the importer to show consent, not on the trade mark owner to show lack of consent.

Predictably, the *Silhouette/Davidoff* principle that there should be no international exhaustion of rights continues to attract criticism. One argument is that the *Davidoff* ruling smacks of protectionism. Another which is frequently rehearsed is that consumers are denied the opportunity to buy cheap, non-counterfeit goods made outside the EU. The EU Commission, having initiated research into the effect of the case law, has stated that it does not think consumers are being harmed by the rulings and has indicated that it does not intend to overturn the cases by legislative means. Given the forthright tenor of the *Davidoff* ruling, it looks unlikely that the ECJ can be persuaded to change its mind. The recast Directive will make no change here.

The case law on exhaustion of rights is represented diagrammatically in Diagram 16.1.

Diagram 16.1

*Exhaustion
of rights*

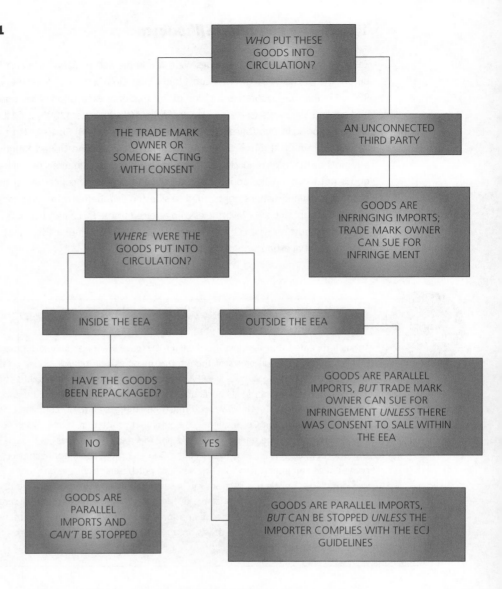

16.5.4 **An example of lack of implied consent**

Despite the statement in *Davidoff* that consent must be express not implied, parallel importers of non-EEA goods continue to argue that the facts of the case demonstrate implied consent. An example is *Roche Products Ltd v Kent Pharmaceuticals* [2007] ETMR 397. The claimants manufactured a product for self-checking of glucose levels. The goods had been supplied to the Dominican Republic for use in clinical trials. Some units were later found in France where the defendant bought them and transported them to England. The packaging bore a 'CE' mark and instructions in three European languages. The defendant argued that the packaging amounted to implied consent to sale within the EEA. It was held that the presence of the CE mark showed that the goods had been formally approved for sale in the EU, but this was an indication of quality control and did not amount to consent to the product being placed on the market within the EEA. It could not be said that the trade mark owner had unequivocally renounced its rights.

16.5.5 **The position in EEA Contracting States**

As stated earlier, those EEA Contracting States who are not EU Member States (Iceland, Liechtenstein and Norway) are obliged to observe the four freedoms in the TFEU and are subject to the various harmonisation Directives. It was initially held by the EFTA Court that these states retained the discretion accorded to them under *EMI v CBS* and so were free to apply the principle of international exhaustion to goods imported into their territory from outside the EEA: Case E-2/92 *Mag Instrument Inc v California Trading Company Norway* [1998] 1 CMLR 331. This raised the intriguing question of whether parallel importation into one of the three EEA Contracting States could be the means to sidestep the *Davidoff* ruling. However, the EFTA Court has since changed its mind (in *L'Oréal Norge AS v PerAarskog AS* [2008] ETMR 943) and ruled that non-EU EEA member states cannot unilaterally maintain a rule of international exhaustion of rights.

16.5.6 **The application of *Silhouette/Davidoff* to other forms of intellectual property right**

To what extent do *Silhouette* and *Davidoff* apply to other forms of intellectual property? Logic dictates that if trade marks are considered the least deserving of protection (see the remarks in *Sirena v Eda*), then the principle of no international exhaustion of rights ought to be more easy to justify in relation to copyright, designs and patents.

The application of *Silhouette* and *Davidoff* will depend on there being in place a harmonisation Directive containing wording similar to that of Article 7 of the Trade Marks Directive. In the absence of any harmonisation measure, then the ruling in *EMI v CBS* would still operate, thus leaving Member States free to decide for themselves whether or not to recognise international exhaustion of rights.

16.5.6.1 Designs, copyright and analogous rights

There has been extensive harmonisation in relation to designs, copyright and other analogous rights (such as computer software and databases). All the relevant Directives contain the defence of exhaustion of rights, with the presence of the key phrase 'put on the market within the Community'. The Directives therefore contemplate EU-wide exhaustion of rights (a point supported by the Commission's *travaux préparatoires*) so the *Silhouette* and *Davidoff* rulings are applicable.

However, United Kingdom law is not entirely in accord with this policy. The tortuous wording of s.18 CDPA does (rather imperfectly) reflect that of the Rental Rights Directive and so applies intra-EU exhaustion to the restricted act of issuing copies. However, the problem lies in the wording of s.27(3) CDPA, which provides one of the definitions of 'infringing copy' for the purposes of secondary infringement. It declares that an article is also an infringing copy if it has been or is proposed to be imported into the United Kingdom and its making in the United Kingdom would have constituted an infringement of copyright or breach of an **exclusive licence**. The presence of the phrase 'would have constituted' indicates that a court hearing an infringement action is required to make an assumption about where the article was made, ie, that it was made in the United Kingdom rather than in the actual place of manufacture. But by whom is this hypothetical making done, the actual maker of the copy or the importer?

cross reference
See section 9.3.2.

Dealing with the equivalent provision in the Copyright Act 1956, Browne-Wilkinson J in *CBS v Charmdale* [1980] 2 All ER 807 thought that the court was only required to make one assumption, so that the hypothetical making was by the actual maker. In the particular case, this meant that sound recordings made in the USA and then imported into the United Kingdom in breach of contract were treated as having been made in the United Kingdom by the actual maker, the copyright owner itself. This had the effect of creating international exhaustion of rights.

An alternative approach can be found in the New Zealand case of *Barson v Gilbert* [1985] FSR 489 (the relevant legislation being virtually identical to that in the United Kingdom). The court thought that two assumptions should be made, namely that the copy was made in the country of import not the country of origin, and that the making was done by the importer itself. This was vital, it said, to protect the interests of the exclusive licensee. The consequence was that there could be no international exhaustion.

It may be noted that s.27(3) doesn't just repeat the wording of the 1956 Act, it adds a new variation, namely that importation is breach of an exclusive licence. Consequently, non-EEA copyright articles will be subjected to a régime of international exhaustion if there is no exclusive licensee appointed, but no international exhaustion if there is. This is hardly consistent with the EU policy of having a level playing field. Further, given that there is no system of copyright registration, how is the importer supposed to find out whether there is an exclusive licensee? In addition to this practical point, the fact that one alternative under s.27(3) gives rise to international exhaustion is a breach of EU law. It has been confirmed by the ECJ in Case C-479/04 *Laserdisken ApS v Kulturministeriet* [2006] ECR I-8089 that Member States no longer have a discretion to maintain any doctrine of international exhaustion of rights in relation to copyright.

16.5.6.2 Patents

cross reference
See section 4.3.1.3.

In respect of patents, however, the only harmonisation measure in place so far is that dealing with biotechnological inventions (Council Directive 98/44/EC of 6 July 1998 on the legal protection of biotechnological inventions [1998] OJ L 213/13), Article 10 of which contains the standard exhaustion of rights provision. This means that as regards patents within the scope of the Directive, the *Silhouette/Davidoff* rulings will apply, but all other patents will be left to domestic law under *EMI v CBS* (until, that is, the Unified Patent comes into effect).

United Kingdom law as regards exhaustion of patent rights again favours the importer. The effect of *Betts v Willmott* (1871) LR 6 Ch App 239, as applied by Jacob J in *Roussel Uclaf v Hockley International Ltd* [1996] RPC 441, is that although a **patentee** can potentially stop the importation into the United Kingdom of patented goods first marketed outside the EEA, to succeed they must show that the restriction has been brought to the attention of each and every undertaking in the chain of supply. This imposes a heavy evidential burden and has the effect of introducing international exhaustion 'through the back door'. A similar attempt to use contract law to sidestep intra-EU exhaustion failed in *Davidoff*.

Summary

This chapter has explained:

• the role of exhaustion of rights as a defence to an action for the infringement of any intellectual property right;

• the development of a doctrine of intra-EU exhaustion of rights by the ECJ;

• the principal exceptions to the defence; and

• how the intellectual property owner can object to the parallel importation of non-EEA goods.

Reflective question

In developing its case law on exhaustion of rights under Article 7 of the Trade Marks Directive, the Court of Justice has all but forgotten the origin function of trade marks.
Discuss.

Annotated further reading

Beier, F.-K. 'Industrial Property and the Free Movement of Goods in the Internal European Market' (1990) 21 *IIC* 131
Argues that the concepts deployed by the ECJ in explaining exhaustion of rights are not as clear as they could be.

Edwards, Judge D. 'Trade Marks: Descriptions of Origin and the Internal Market' [2001] *IPQ* 135
Argues that the ECJ had no choice but to reach the conclusion it did in *Silhouette*.

Koutrakos, P. 'In Search of a Common Vocabulary in Free Movement of Goods: The Example of Repackaging Pharmaceuticals' [2003] *ELR* 53
Explores the problems found in the repackaging cases.

Annotated further reading

Norman, H. 'Parallel Imports from Non-EEA Member States: the Vision Remains Unclear' [2000] *EIPR* 159

An examination of the *Silhouette* decision.

Tritton, G. 'Parallel Imports in the European Community' [1997] *IPQ* 196

Discusses the repackaging cases in detail.

Van der Merwe, A. 'The Exhaustion of Rights in Patent Law with Specific Emphasis on the Issue of Parallel Importation' [2000] *IPQ* 286

Argues that different intellectual property rights should receive different treatment in the exhaustion of rights defence.

Part 7

Property rights and exploitation

Dealings in intellectual property rights

Learning objectives

Upon completion of this chapter you should have acquired:

- an appreciation of the economic importance of dealings in intellectual property rights;

- an understanding of the two basic ways of dealing with intellectual property rights;

- knowledge of the United Kingdom statutory provisions which govern such transactions;

- an understanding of the arguments which may be raised in an attempt to challenge certain copyright transactions; and

- background knowledge of how European Union law on free movement of goods affects dealings in intellectual property rights and how competition law, whether national or EU, may impinge on such dealings.

Introduction

One of the key features of intellectual property rights is, naturally, that they have some (but not all) of the characteristics of property. Although generally of finite duration, and (in the case of registrable rights) always at risk of cancellation for invalidity, they can nevertheless be bought and sold, bequeathed and mortgaged. Under International Financial Reporting Standards, intangible assets have to be shown on corporate balance sheets. Frequent surveys are conducted to establish which is the most successful trade mark (in 2009, Google was declared the first $100 billion brand; Apple is currently the top global brand) or which pharmaceutical company has the most valuable patent portfolio (Pfizer Inc is presently the largest such company).

We examine in this chapter the United Kingdom statutory requirements governing transactions in intellectual property rights. This is a prelude to chapter 18 where we consider how United Kingdom law does (or perhaps does not) protect those who wish to exploit such rights. We also consider how such transactions may be challenged, how EU law imposes certain consequences on assignments and licences of intellectual property rights, and how competition law may curtail freedom of contract in dealings with such rights.

17.1 The difference between being the creator and the owner of the right

When considering the statutory requirements for intellectual property transactions, it is important always to remember the key distinction between being the creator and being the owner of the right. Being the creator does not necessarily mean that you have the ability to enter into transactions with others.

17.1.1 Patents

In the case of **patents**, there is the popular image of the sole inventor coming up with revolutionary ideas in his workshop. The reality is that most inventors are employed by large companies. Although the inventor has the right to be named in a patent (Patents Act 1977 s.13), and may in certain instances be entitled to compensation where the **invention** is of outstanding benefit (s.40), the patent will belong to the employer where the criteria set out in s.39(1) apply. The employer will thus have the rights of exploitation set out in the Patents Act s.60 as well as the rights of property found in s.30, but equally will have borne the research and development costs and the financial risk of developing the patented product or process.

17.1.2 Copyright

Similarly with **copyright**. Section 11(1) Copyright Designs and Patents Act 1988 ('CDPA') provides for the **author** of a work (as defined in s.9) to be the first owner. However, where a literary, dramatic, musical or artistic work, or a film, is made in the course of employment (but not any other category of work), the employer is first owner 'subject to any agreement to the contrary'. Being an author does not guarantee that you will own the work, essential if an **infringement** action is to be brought (*Beloff v Pressdram Ltd* [1973] RPC 765, *Gabrin v Universal Music Operations Ltd* [2004] ECDR 18) or if the work is to be **assigned** or **licensed** (*R Griggs Group Ltd and others v Evans and others* [2005] FSR 706). Further reference to s.9, as supplemented by s.178 CDPA, (the definition section for Part I of the Act) reveals that in respect of entrepreneurial copyrights like films, sound recordings, broadcasts and computer-generated works, the statutory definition of 'author' does not always reflect creative input. For example, in the case of sound recordings, the producer is first owner, this being defined as the person who made the arrangement for the recording; in the case of a typographical arrangement, it is the publisher.

The common law tradition is to treat copyright as a commodity. In certain industries, such as entertainment and media, there is extensive use of contractual arrangements so that ownership of copyright is far removed from those whose creative efforts are being exploited. In the case of a film, for example, copyright works created by the authors of the story, the screenplay, the dialogue, the costume designers and the composer of the music (to name but five) will have been assigned in advance to a third party, usually the production company.

17.1.3 Commissioned works

By contrast, s.11(1) CDPA has an unexpected outcome where a work is **commissioned**. Contrary to a popular misconception, under the CDPA commissioning a work does not confer any right of ownership. In consequence, someone who pays to have a work created for them has to ensure that appropriate contractual provisions are in place with the author which either operate to assign the copyright to the commissioner (under ss.90 or 91 CDPA) or at the very least give the commissioner a **licence** to use the work. Should the contract fail to do so, then the court may if it thinks fit imply such a provision in the interests of business efficacy, but the court will only imply the absolute minimum to make the contract work.

case close-up

Ray v Classic FM plc [1998] FSR 622

The paradigm case dealing with commissioned works is *Ray v Classic FM plc* [1998] FSR 622. Here, the defendant radio station had asked the **claimant** to create a database of classical music, the contract stating that the claimant was to be treated as a consultant not an employee. It was held that the defendant did not have any right of ownership. Lightman J restated the principle that in the case of a commissioned work the author was entitled to retain the copyright in the absence of an express or implied term to the contrary effect. The mere fact that an author had been commissioned to produce a work was of itself insufficient to entitle the commissioner to the copyright. In order to imply some rights to fill a hole in the contract, the court should award only the minimum necessary to give the commissioner what the parties to the contract must have intended to confer and in the present case that was the grant of a licence to the defendant to exploit the work. The amount of the purchase price which the commissioner had promised to pay could be relevant. It was only in the rarest cases that an **assignment** rather than the grant of an **exclusive licence** would suffice.

Several cases provide a contrast to *Ray v Classic FM*, showing that the courts are not averse to allocating the ownership of copyright despite the apparent wording of the contract.

case close-up

R Griggs Group Ltd and others v Evans and others [2005] FSR 706

A freelance designer had been commissioned by an advertising agency on behalf of its client (the claimant) to combine two existing **trade marks** for DOC MARTENS footwear so as to produce a new logo. When the claimant subsequently sued a third party for infringement, the latter claimed it was the owner of copyright in the logo as the result of an assignment taken from the freelance designer. The Court of Appeal, confirming the decision of Peter Prescott QC sitting as a Deputy High Court Judge, held that the claimant had equitable ownership of the copyright, because in the circumstances this was the minimum necessary to satisfy the 'officious bystander' test for an implied term in the law of contract. The designer had no conceivable further interest in the work being created and was not able to confer property rights on anybody else.

In *Ibcos Computers Ltd v Barclays Mercantile Highland Finance Ltd* [1994] FSR 275 the dispute was about ownership of copyright in an agricultural machinery traders' accounting program written at a time when the claimant and defendant were partners. Jacob J decided that both legal and equitable ownership was vested in the partnership because this was necessary to give the partnership 'business efficacy'. Further, copyright in an earlier, general purpose program which had been incorporated into the disputed software also vested in the claimant (as successor in title to the partnership) because of a clause in the defendant's post-employment contract which stated that 'P recognises that all PK software are the sole property of PK', hardly the wording one would expect to see for the assignment of copyright. Last, in *Hutchison Personal Communications Ltd v Hook Advertising Ltd* [1996] FSR 549 the defendant advertising agency had, through one of its employees, designed a logo for a new mobile phone company. Although clause 8 of the contract stated that copyright in all the artwork should belong to the agency, the court decided that statements made when the agency was bidding for the work resulted in an implied promise that if it was appointed, it would hand over all copyright to the claimant. The difference between these three cases and the decision in *Ray v Classic FM* perhaps lies in the fact that the contract in the last-mentioned case had been very carefully drafted and left no room for doubt as to the ownership of the copyright.

thinking point

Does the absence of any statutory rule on commissioned works, when taken in conjunction with the decisions in Ray v Classic FM *and* Griggs v Evans, *provide for sufficient certainty?*

Some fundamental issues

17.2.1 **Lack of coherence**

As Vaver has pointed out (in 'Reforming Intellectual Property Law: An Obvious and Not-So-Obvious Agenda: The Stephen Stewart Memorial Lecture for 2008' [2009] *IPQ* 143) the rules on ownership, transfer and licensing of intellectual property rights require rationalisation. They need to be clear and identical wherever possible, and there should be consistency of terminology.

With regard to the last point, Vaver says, there is a labelling problem. For example, legislation may refer to either the 'owner', 'proprietor' or 'holder' of the right and it is unclear whether being an owner differs from being a proprietor or a holder. Only an appellate court could provide that answer.

cross reference
See chapter 11.

Likewise, the statutory provisions on employees are inconsistent, differing from one right to another. In the case of the Community design right, the employer owns the right if the employee did the work 'in the execution of his duties or following the instructions given by his employer'. For copyright, the rule is (as mentioned earlier) framed in much more general language, namely that certain works (but not all works) created 'in the course of employment' belong to the employer 'subject to an agreement to the contrary'. With **unregistered design right**, s.215 CDPA uses the same words as s.11(2) but does not mention the ability to 'contract out' of the basic rule. As the appearance of an **article** might be protected simultaneously under both copyright and unregistered design right, this lack of consistency is not only illogical but likely to cause practical problems. By contrast, the provisions in the Patents Act dealing with employee-inventors are stated to be 'notwithstanding anything in any rule of law' which appears to oust any common law rules on ownership. The criteria for when an invention is owned by the employer are set out with far greater precision than in copyright and could well produce a different outcome where creative activity at work leads to both types of right being created.

There are similar discrepancies with regard to co-ownership and even more inconsistencies with regard to how the various intellectual property rights are to be licensed. Last, Vaver points out, the consequences for failing to comply with the statutory provisions are not what they appear at first glance. The Patents Act s.30(6) declares that failure to comply with its requirements renders the transaction 'void' and the CDPA s.90(3) states that non-compliance renders it 'ineffective', it being unclear whether these two words have identical meaning. However, it is still possible that the defective disposal can take effect in equity. We consider how equitable title to intellectual property rights might arise later. For the present, we can conclude that the need for an overarching intellectual property code is apparent.

17.2.2 **Distinction between an assignment and a licence**

The two most common forms of transactions concerned with the ownership of intellectual property rights are an assignment and a licence. It is important to keep the two separate, although in the case of some copyright contracts the courts have had difficulty in determining, from the wording used by the parties, exactly which has been created.

In brief, an assignment involves the outright transfer of ownership from the current owner (the **assignor**) to the new owner (the **assignee**). It may be voluntary (ie by way of gift), but in most cases will be for consideration, usually the payment of a lump sum but sometimes for periodic royalties. Just as with the conveyance of land or the giving of a present at Christmas, the original owner 'drops out of the picture' and is replaced by the new owner. Nevertheless, in the case of copyright, certain rights, for example an author's **moral rights** and a **performer's right** to object to illicit recordings of a performance, cannot be assigned. Despite the transfer of the legal ownership of copyright, they survive for the benefit of the original creator, subject to the conditions of the CDPA being satisfied. Lest it be thought that the meaning of 'assignment' is too simple to require explanation, even the ECJ has failed to understand the nature of such a transaction and for a time treated it as having continuing effect for the purposes of **exhaustion of rights** (see Case 40/70 *Sirena v Eda* [1971] ECR 69 and Case 192/73 *Van Zuylen Frères v Hag AG* [1974] ECR 731 ('*Hag I*')).

cross reference
See chapter 10.

By contrast, a licence is basically permission to use the right. The orthodox view in United Kingdom law is that this is a personal right and does not give the **licensee** any proprietary interest: *CBS v Charmdale Records* [1980] 2 All ER 807; *Northern & Shell plc v Condé Nast & National Magazine Distributors Ltd* [1995] RPC 117. Its effect is to provide immunity from liability for infringement. However, in many instances statute confers certain procedural advantages on licensees so that they can bring infringement proceedings in their own name. These, however, are procedural rights and do not have any proprietary implications.

A licence can take several forms, namely exclusive, non-exclusive and sole. An exclusive licence means that the licensee is the only person who can exploit the right in the territory in question, this being to the exclusion even of the owner of the right. A **non-exclusive** licence means, therefore, that other licensees may be appointed to operate in parallel to the first licensee. A **sole licence**, by contrast, means that no other licensee can be appointed, but the owner of the right can exploit it at the same time as the licensee. In practice, one often encounters documents entitled 'sole and exclusive licence' which is, in fact, a contradiction in terms.

17.2.3 **Intangible personal property rights**

In England and Wales, property rights are divided into realty and personalty. The latter is subdivided into choses in possession (ie assets which can be handed over physically) and choses in action (intangible assets enforced by litigation rather than by taking possession of them). According to Firth and Fitzgerald (in 'Equitable Assignments in Relation to Intellectual Property' [1999] *IPQ* 228) it is arguable that with two exceptions, intellectual property rights are choses in action even though they may appear to share some of the characteristics of real property. The two exceptions are patents which are declared by Patents Act s.30(1) *not* to be things in action; and **confidential information** which has been stated by the House of Lords and, more recently by the Court of Appeal, not to be capable of ownership but to rest on the conscience of the confidant (*Boardman v Phipps* [1967] 2 AC 46 at pp. 127–8 *per* Lord Upjohn and *Douglas v Hello! Ltd (No 2)* [2005] 4 All ER 128 at [119]).

The general rule for the assignment of choses in action can be found in the Law of Property Act 1925 ('LPA') s.136, which requires a written document, signed by the assignor and with notice being given to the other party to the chose. All intellectual property statutes follow this basic template, with each requiring the right in question to be assigned in writing, the assignment to be signed by the person disposing of the right, and (in the case of registrable rights) the change of ownership being entered on the relevant register. Notification to the **United Kingdom Intellectual Property Office ('UKIPO')** can therefore be equated to the need in s.136 LPA to give notice to the other party to the chose. The consequences of failing to register the change of ownership used to vary from right to right, but as a result of the Enforcement Directive (Directive 2004/48/EC of the European Parliament and of the Council of 29 April 2004 on the enforcement of intellectual property rights [2004] OJ L 157/45) there has been standardisation. The single rule is that the new owner is not awarded costs in any subsequent infringement action should there be delay in recording the transaction.

Failure to comply with the requirement of writing does not necessarily mean that the transaction has no effect. As Firth and Fitzgerald explain, it is possible (depending on the circumstances) for equitable title to pass, so that the assignee, as equitable owner, can demand completion of the appropriate formalities because of the equitable maxim that 'equity looks on that as done which ought to be done'. The assignor in effect becomes trustee for the assignee. The right to specific performance will only arise where value was given for the assignment. However, being an equitable owner (ie a beneficiary under a bare trust) is not something which can be entered on the relevant register, as the Registered Designs Act 1949 ('RDA'), Patents Act 1977 and Trade Marks Act 1994 ('TMA') all declare that no notice of any trust, whether express, implied or constructive, is to be entered on the register. The equitable owner must therefore go to court for the discretionary remedy of specific performance to compel completion of the legal formalities to make them the owner of the right in law.

Whilst s.136 LPA provides a template for changing the ownership of intellectual property rights, there is no similar provision with regard to giving permission to use such a right. How intellectual property licences are to be effected and recorded at UKIPO therefore depends on the wording of each intellectual property statute. There is no standard pattern, proof again that an overarching code is overdue.

> ### *thinking point*
>
> *Given the global nature of intellectual property law, does it make sense for someone to be able to claim equitable ownership of a right in England and Wales when statute declares that failure to comply with the appropriate formalities renders an assignment of 'no effect'?*

17.3 United Kingdom statutory requirements

17.3.1 Patents

17.3.1.1 Ownership of patents

Section 30(1) Patents Act 1977 declares that any patent is personal property but without being a thing in action. The reason for not treating patents as choses in action is unclear, although

Firth and Fitzgerald, quoting Cornish, suggest that this may be something to do with the historical fact that patents were granted by virtue of the Crown Prerogative. No other category of intellectual property right is so treated. The section goes on to state that a patent (and indeed, a patent application) can be assigned or mortgaged and can pass by operation of law or on death. Any assignment or mortgage, and any assent (such as by the personal representative of the previous owner) must be in writing and signed, otherwise it will be void. The section also provides for patents to be licensed but is silent as to any formal requirements for such licence. There is a separate provision (s.31) dealing with property rights under Scottish law. Section 36 goes on to deal with where a patent is granted to two or more persons, providing that such co-ownership is to be by way of equal undivided shares, in other words creating a tenancy in common. Where there is co-ownership, one co-owner cannot enter into any property transaction (such as an assignment or licence) without the consent of the other.

Section 32 by implication requires all transactions affecting patents to be recorded at UKIPO, by stating that rules may make provision for the registration of transactions, instruments or events affecting rights in patents, though the section itself does not list which 'transactions, instruments or events' are to be so recorded. The duty to record is emphasised by the *bona fide* purchaser rule set out in s.33: any person who claims to have acquired property rights in a patent is to be entitled as against someone claiming under an earlier transaction if that earlier transaction had not been registered and there was no knowledge on the part of the person claiming under the later transaction. The need to register is further reinforced by s.68 (amended as a result of the Enforcement Directive). The original version of the section provided that failure to record a transaction meant that a claimant was not to be awarded a pecuniary remedy for any acts of infringement committed between the date of the transaction and the date of its recordal. The amended version merely provides for the penalty to be the non-award of costs.

case close-up

Thorn Security Ltd v Siemens Schweiz AG [2008] EWCA Civ 1161

The provisions discussed in the previous section were considered by the Court of Appeal in *Thorn Security Ltd v Siemens Schweiz AG* [2008] EWCA Civ 1161, a case which shows that s.68 (whether in its original or amended version) is not as well drafted as it might be. The question here was whether a company merger under Swiss law (which differed significantly from United Kingdom law as to the mechanism for achieving a merger) amounted to an assignment which had not been promptly recorded in the register of patents. It had been held at first instance that an assignment had to involve a consensual document so that a Government order transferring assets on merger did not suffice. The Court of Appeal disagreed. A narrow literal approach to s.68 was to be avoided, and instead a purposive interpretation was adopted. It was wide enough to cover both consensual and administrative transfers of ownership.

17.3.1.2 Licensing of patents

The Patents Act provides for a number of different ways in which a patent can be licensed to others.

Voluntary licences can be exclusive or non-exclusive. An exclusive licensee has procedural rights to bring an infringement action in their own name under s.67, but if the licence has not been recorded on the register, then under s.68 the licensee is denied costs in any infringement action. No procedural rights are given to a non-exclusive licensee, so that they are dependent on the co-operation of the **patentee** to sue infringers. A well-drawn licence will usually contain a provision requiring the patentee to sue infringers if requested by the licensee to do so.

By contrast to a voluntary licence, a patent may be the subject of a **compulsory licence** any time after the third anniversary of its grant. The reason why the patentee can be forced to license the invention is basically failure to exploit it. The rules on compulsory licences (set out in Patents Act 1977 s.48, as amended by SI 1999/1899) draw a distinction between where the patentee is a **WTO** proprietor and where they are not, with regard to the criteria to be satisfied before the licence can be granted and the steps which the intending licensee must observe. The terms of the licence are determined by UKIPO. Alternatively, the patentee can ask that the entry on the Register be endorsed to the effect that **licences of right** are available (s.46 Patents Act, as amended), thus inviting others to request a licence, the terms of which may be decided by the UKIPO. Such an application may be made at any time after **grant** and has the advantage of halving subsequent **renewal fees**.

Last, under s.55, the Crown has extensive powers to exploit patents.

17.3.2 **Copyright**

One of the major characteristics of copyright is its fragmentary nature. Each right listed in s.16 CDPA, as was said in *CBS v Charmdale Records* at p. 811, can be divided vertically or horizontally. So, for example, the right to reproduce the work, whether in all forms or a particular form, the right to distribute such copies, the right to perform the work, the right to communicate the work and, for certain works, the right of adaptation, can each be dealt with separately, not just in the United Kingdom, but in any state which is a contracting party of the **Berne Convention**, the **Universal Copyright Convention** or the WTO. Different people can own or be licensed to exploit different aspects of the same copyright in different countries. This presents the immediate problem that the lack of any system of registration makes keeping track of who is entitled to the ownership or exploitation of each right very difficult.

cross reference
See section 7.3.5.

17.3.2.1 Assignment

Assignment of copyright is dealt with by s.90 CDPA. The usual declaration is to be found in s.90(1), namely that copyright is transmissible in the same way as other forms of personal property, ie by assignment, by testamentary disposition or by operation of law. As with any form of intellectual property, no particular form of wording is required. In the case of testamentary dispositions, there is the practice of appointing literary executors who will deal only with the deceased author's rights, thus separating copyright from the rest of the estate. Further, s.93 provides that in the case of an *unpublished* work (whether this consists of the original document or some other form of recording of a literary, dramatic, musical or artistic work, or a 'material thing' embodying a sound recording or film) a bequest of the author's personal estate (whether general or specific) will carry with it the relevant copyright.

As might be expected from the fragmentary nature of copyright, s.90(2) provides for total or partial assignment, 'partial' being as to which rights are assigned or for a particular period of time. The subsection therefore contemplates copyright reverting to the author (or their estate) after a fixed period. However, in the case of a poorly worded document, the court may find it difficult to decide whether what has been created is an assignment or a licence, in the same way as provisions in contracts of commission may lead to uncertainty as to whether the commissioner is entitled to a licence of the work or to demand that ownership be transferred.

Section 90(3) requires any assignment to be in writing and signed by the assignor (who of course may not be the original owner) if it is to be 'effective'. The ability of a court to treat an imperfect transaction as an assignment in equity was discussed earlier.

Last, s.91(1) provides for the automatic assignment of a work to be created at some date in the future where the prospective owner purports to assign such copyright in writing. The provision should be seen as a balancing mechanism to the absence of any right of ownership of the commissioner of any work covered by Part I of the Act.

Copyright legislation is always playing 'catch up' with technology. The consequence is to create problems of interpretation of copyright contracts where, subsequent to the drafting of the agreement, there has been either a change in law or a change in technology or both.

case close-up

Governors of the Hospital for Sick Children v Walt Disney [1966] 2 All ER 321

An example is to be found in *Governors of the Hospital for Sick Children v Walt Disney* [1966] 2 All ER 321. Here, J.M. Barrie, the author of *Peter Pan* (a play written in 1904 and adapted into a book in 1911, and consequently governed by the Copyright Act 1842), had, in 1919, granted an exclusive licence to an American film company to produce all his works in cinematograph form. At the time, all films were silent films, and further, under the 1911 Copyright Act there was no protection for films as such. Subsequently, the licence was transferred (with permission) to Walt Disney. In 1939 a further agreement allowed Disney to make a cartoon version of the *Peter Pan* story, but in the meantime Barrie had assigned his copyright and any residual performing rights to what is now Great Ormond Street Hospital (the hospital has perpetual rights to control the public performance, commercial distribution, communication to the public and adaptation of the work by virtue of s.301 CDPA). By the 1960s, the hospital proposed to license another company to make a sound film based on Barrie's book. The majority of the Court of Appeal agreed with the contention that the 1919 agreement was not intended to cover 'talking' films as these were not in the parties' contemplation at the time.

17.3.2.2 Reversionary interests

In a number of cases, copyright ownership might revert (ie return) to the author or his estate. There are three instances when this can occur. First, where a partial assignment under s.90 CDPA is limited in time, the copyright will revert automatically to the previous owner (who of course might not be the author) when the relevant period has expired. Second, where legislation extends the duration of copyright, Government policy has sometimes provided that any additional period of protection should belong to the author. Finally, in one instance, Parliament thought it appropriate (in a paternalistic way) to provide for the return of rights to the author or his estate on the assumption that the impoverished author might have sold his or her rights for a pittance and so deserved some sort of belated recompense when the work subsequently proved to be popular. This last category is in one sense legislative history (being found only in the 1911 Act), although because of the longevity of copyright it is still producing contemporary case law. All three categories cause problems because of the absence of any registration system. Someone claiming to be entitled to a reversionary interest will have to produce all relevant documents creating a chain of title.

Reversionary interests when copyright term is extended

When the 1911 Copyright Act extended the period of protection (in accordance with the Berne Convention) to the author's life plus 50 years, it provided in s.24 that existing works were entitled to this extended term. The section went on to state, however, that where before the operative date of the Act (1 July 1912) the author of an existing work had assigned the copyright, at the date when, but for the 1911 Act copyright would have expired, it was to revert to the author or his estate unless there was an agreement to the contrary. This was interpreted in *Coleridge-Taylor v Novello & Co* [1938] Ch 850 to apply only to pre-1912 assignments. Any assignment subsequent to the date of the Act would be covered by another provision, s.5(2), explained later.

cross reference
See section 8.5.2.

A different approach was adopted when a similar situation arose in 1995 when s.12 CDPA had to be amended as a result of the Copyright Term Directive (Council Directive 93/98/EC of 29 October 1993 harmonising the term of copyright protection [1993] OJ L 290/9, now codified as Directive 2006/116/EC of the European Parliament and of the Council of 12 December 2006 [2006] OJ L 372/12). In broad terms, Regulations 16 and 17 of The Duration of Copyright and Rights in Performances Regulations (SI 1995/3297) provide that any extended or revived copyright belongs to the person who was the owner immediately before the commencement of the Regulations (for extended copyright) or who was the owner immediately before it expired (for revived copyright). In other words, there is no reversion of copyright to the author, so that the 'windfall' of the extended term (as it was described in the *Coleridge-Taylor* case) goes to the current owner.

Reversionary interests to protect the author

The 1911 Act provided, paternalistically, a means to protect an author against the consequences of having assigned their rights to a work which subsequently proved to be successful. The proviso to s.5(2) declared that where an author, as first owner, had assigned copyright in a work *after* the date of the Act, the copyright was to revert to his estate 25 years after the death of the author. The section did not apply to collective works, nor where copyright was bequeathed by will.

Section 5(2) is internally inconsistent, because although being intended to protect the author, it in fact benefits the author's heirs. It also does not fit in with the entrepreneurial view of copyright, nor with the Berne Convention, and was abandoned by the 1956 Act although the latter's transitional provisions preserve its effect for pre-1957 assignments.

thinking point
Do reversionary interests in copyright have a proper place in the twenty-first century?

The loophole in s.5(2) is that it does not control the right to dispose of the reversionary interest. As a property right, this can, of course, be dealt with by assignment. The loophole was exploited to the full in *Chappell & Co v Redwood Music Ltd* [1981] RPC 337, where the defendant publishers worked out the implications of s.5(2) and approached the personal representatives of various deceased composers and obtained from them assignments of their reversionary interests. Although this was a test case involving only 27 songs, at dispute were an estimated 177 estates of deceased composers and up to 40,000 pieces of music. The House of Lords held that reversion under s.5(2) was automatic and operated to divest the claimant, the original assignee of the songs, of the copyright. The composers' personal representatives were free to deal with the reversionary copyright as they thought fit and so the defendant had the better title. The Court of Appeal has since held in *Novello & Co Ltd v Keith Prowse Music Publishing Co Ltd* [2005] RPC 578 that there is nothing to stop a composer himself from disposing of his reversionary interest prior to his death.

17.3.2.3 Copyright licences

Just like the Patents Act, the CDPA provides for licences of copyright to be granted and for such licences to be binding on the owner's successor in title unless that person is a *bona fide* purchaser for value (s.90(4)) although this section is silent as to formalities. Section 92(2) adds that in the case of an exclusive licence (which must be in writing) the licensee is to have the same rights against a successor in title as they have against the person granting the licence. Section 101 confers procedural advantages on an exclusive licensee by stating that they are to have the same rights and remedies (except against the owner) 'as if the licence had been an assignment'. Despite this wording, the nature of an exclusive licence of copyright is to confer a personal right on the licensee so that they are not to be treated as the owner of the right (*CBS Ltd v Charmdale*). Changes made to the CDPA as a result of the Information Society Directive (Directive 2001/29/EC of the European Parliament and of the Council of 22 May 2001 on the harmonisation of certain aspects of copyright and related rights in the information society [2001] OJ L 167/10) now give similar rights to a non-exclusive licensee provided the licence is in writing (s.101A).

17.3.3 **Designs**

17.3.3.1 Registered designs

The RDA (as amended by the Intellectual Property (Enforcement etc) Regulations 2006 (SI 2006/1028) now contains three new provisions, ss 15A, 15B and 15C, which set out the basic rules on property rights. Prior to the 2006 changes, there were no stipulations in the Act as to dealings in **registered designs**, an omission which the courts refused to rectify: *Oren v Red Box Toy Factory Ltd* [1999] FSR 785 at [42].

Section 15A proffers the standard declaration that registered designs and applications for the same are personal property (in Scotland, incorporeal moveable property), whilst s.15B declares that registered designs may be dealt with in the usual way, that is, by way of assignment, testamentary disposition, by operation of law or by charge. Assignments must be in writing and signed by the assignor. Any dealing in a registered design is subject to any rights previously entered on the register. Any assignment or transmission of a registered design must be entered on the designs register (RDA s.19), normally by the person acquiring the right, although s.19(2) does provide for the original owner to apply for the transaction to be recorded. Further, where an unregistered design right also subsists in a registered design, the change of ownership in the registered design is not to be recorded unless the registrar is satisfied that the new owner is also entitled to a corresponding interest in the unregistered design right (RDA s.19(3A)).

Section 15B(7) declares that licences may be granted without specifying what formalities may be required, but in the case of exclusive licences, under s.15C these must be in writing and signed by the proprietor before the exclusive licensee is given the usual procedural right of being able to bring infringement proceedings in their own name. The rights of the exclusive licensee are spelled out in more detail in s.24F. The licence is to be entered on the register under s.19(1) RDA.

As with patents, there are provisions in the RDA as to Crown use of registered designs, the details of which are to be found in the First Schedule to the Act.

17.3.3.2 Unregistered design right

Section 222 CDPA declares that the United Kingdom unregistered design right is to be treated as personal property (in Scotland, moveable property) and can be transferred by assignment, testamentary disposition or by operation of law. Unlike registered designs, there is no provision for an unregistered design to be charged by way of security, yet another instance of the lack of consistency in the rules on the ownership of intellectual property rights. For an assignment to be effective, it must be in writing and signed by the assignor. Section 222(2) (which appears to have been copied in its entirety from section 90(2)) provides for an assignment to be partial, either with regard to the right transferred or for a fixed period of time. Given that s.226 CDPA only gives the design right owner two exclusive rights (in contrast to the multiple rights conferred on a copyright owner), namely making articles to that design or making a design document which enables such articles to be made, the logic of allowing partial assignments is questionable. Further, given the very short duration of unregistered design right (again, in contrast to copyright) the notion of a temporary transfer of ownership followed by a reversionary interest seems odd.

Part III CDPA is the one area of the Act where at present commissioning the work gives rise to a right of ownership. The Intellectual Property Act 2014 will remove the references to commissioned designs. The net result is that s.223 at last makes sense. The provision is a mirror image of s.91 whereby an automatic assignment of a design to be created in the future results from a written agreement signed by the prospective owner (to be determined under the rules found in s.215) so that the assignee becomes the legal owner as soon as the design comes into existence. The denial of ownership to a commissioner is therefore balanced by the ability to provide contractually for the handing over of title once the design is created.

Section 224 CDPA provides that where a registered design is assigned, such assignment also carries with it any unregistered rights unless there is an intention to the contrary. The parallel provision in RDA s.19(3B) states that the assignment of the unregistered design right shall be taken to be also an assignment of the right in the registered design unless a contrary intention appears.

Finally Part III CDPA provides for the granting of a licence to exploit an unregistered design right (s.222(4)). No formality is prescribed, although for the procedural advantages conferred by s.225 on an exclusive licensee to apply such an arrangement must be in writing and signed by the design right owner. Licences, whether granted by the design right owner under s.222, or by a prospective design right owner under s.223, are stated to be binding on the whole world except a subsequent *bona fide* purchaser for value and without notice (actual or constructive) of the licence.

Crown use of unregistered designs is provided for by ss.240 and 241 CDPA.

thinking point

Are the differences in detail between the statutory provisions on assignments and licences of patents, copyright and designs justifiable, or is this just a case of sloppy drafting?

17.3.4 **Trade marks**

The TMA, being the youngest of the quartet of United Kingdom legislation dealing with intellectual property rights, proves to be the most detailed, but also contains illogicalities as a result of provisions being 'cut and pasted' from the other Acts without consideration as to whether these are appropriate.

TMA 1994 s.22 declares that a trade mark is personal property. This is added to by s.27 which states that even a pending application for a trade mark is property. Although there is good practical reason for such a provision (similar ones appear in the RDA and in the Patents Act) in that a business may want to transfer all of its rights, regardless of whether these have matured to registration, there is an apparent conflict with s.2 TMA which declares that 'a registered trade mark is a property right obtained by the registration of the trade mark under the Act'.

The TMA provides for there to be co-ownership of a trade mark, but subtly changes the rules as to how this takes effect. The Trade Marks Act 1938 had provided for co-ownership of marks to be by means of joint tenancy, but s.23 of the 1994 Act declares that co-ownership of a trade mark creates a tenancy in common subject to any agreement to the contrary. This appears to have been copied from s.36 of the Patents Act 1977 with no thought being given as to whether it is appropriate to have a trade mark held in undivided shares. As with other legislation, s.26 states that no details of any trust is to be entered on the Register.

17.3.4.1 Assignment

In order to understand the wording of the TMA, it is necessary to consider how trade marks have been treated as items of property in the past. Our starting point is s.24(1) TMA which states that trade marks are transmissible in the same way as other forms of personal property, and can be assigned with or without the **goodwill** of the business. The House of Lords in *CIR v Muller & Co's Margarine Ltd* [1901] AC 217 explained the meaning of 'goodwill' as 'the attractive force which brings in custom' and 'that which distinguishes an old business from a new'. Goodwill is itself a species of personal property. The reference to 'goodwill' in s.24 has to be understood in the light of a fundamental principle of trade marks at common law. Prior to the Trade Marks Act 1938 the rule was that an assignment of a trade mark had to be in conjunction with the transfer of the goodwill of the business in which it had been used: *Bowden Wire Ltd v Bowden Brake Co Ltd* (1914) 31 RPC 385. In other words, a trade mark could never be separated from goodwill, and any attempt to do so would render the trade mark invalid. In the language of the old law, assignment in gross of a trade mark was not possible.

However, prior to the Trade Marks Act 1938 it was possible to assign a mark with partial goodwill but only where the business could be subdivided into separate activities, such as happened in *Sunbeam Motor Car Co's Application* (1916) 33 RPC 389 where the assignor had made both cars and bicycles. However, it was not possible to assign a trade mark 'together with such of the goodwill as relates to the mark' where the assignor remained in the same line of business as that relating to the mark as that would destroy the link between the mark and its supporting goodwill: *Sinclair's Trade Mark* (1932) 49 RPC 123.

To return to current law, s.24(2) TMA provides that a partial assignment of a trade mark is possible, either as to some of the goods or services, as to locality or as to manner of use. This appears to have been copied from the later provision on partial licences. Whilst the ability to 'split' a mark in relation to particular goods and services is at first glance unobjectionable, it could cause customer confusion. It should also be asked whether it is in fact possible to divide a mark geographically without infringing EU law and how it is even possible to divide a mark so that A can use it in one manner and B in another.

Further, and in contrast to the 1938 Act, there is no longer any mechanism for objecting to deceptive assignments, either by individuals or at the instance of the Registry. The Government's view was that any deception caused by an assignment could be remedied by a third party seeking **revocation** of the registration under s.46(1)(d).

Case C-259/04 *Emanuel v Continental Shelf 128 Ltd* [2006] ECR I-3089

. . . .

The ECJ's ruling in Case C-259/04 *Emanuel v Continental Shelf 128 Ltd* [2006] ECR I-3089 indicates that Government assumptions about deceptive assignments were wrong. The Court said that under both Articles 3 and 12 of the First Trade Marks Directive (Council Directive 89/104/EEC of 21 December 1988 on the approximation of the laws of Member States relating to trade marks [1989] OJ L 40/1, now codified as Directive 2008/95/EC of the European Parliament and of the Council of 22 October 2008 [2008] OJ L 299/25) ('the Trade Marks Directive') 'deceptive' means that the mark must objectively deceive as a result of its *inherent* qualities. Consequently, where the trade mark was a person's name and had been assigned as part of the business, it did not deceive the public even if it created the mistaken impression that that person took part in the creation of the goods for which the mark was used. There could be no revocation of the mark for its having become deceptive under s.46(1)(d) (the enactment of Article 12) nor could a later application for the same mark by the assignee be challenged by the former owner under s.3(3)(b) (corresponding to Article 3(1)(g)).

The formalities for the assignment of a trade mark are to be found in s.24(3). This requires a written document signed by the assignor. More importantly, s.25 requires the transaction to be recorded on the Register. As with other types of intellectual property, failure to record an assignment exposes the assignee to the risk of a *bona fide* purchaser for value and the inability to claim costs in any post-assignment infringement action. Despite this, the TMA should be viewed as an exercise in deregulation when compared with the convoluted procedure which had to be followed under the 1938 Act in the case of an assignment without goodwill.

Unregistered trade marks, in accordance with the *Bowden Wire* principle, must still be assigned with the goodwill of the business. This has been confirmed in *Iliffe News & Media Ltd v Commissioners for HM Revenue & Customs* [2012] UKFTT 696 (TC). Regrettably, the procedure available under the 1938 Act where a 'family' of marks, some registered, some not, could be assigned together without goodwill has been removed. The Government must have assumed that the liberalising effect of the TMA would lead to a reduction in the number of unregistered rights.

17.3.4.2 Licences

The current provisions on licensing of trade marks have their bases in Articles 8 and 10 of the Trade Marks Directive. The former declares that a trade mark can be licensed for some or all of the goods for which it is registered and for the whole or part of the Member State concerned, adding that licences can be exclusive or non-exclusive. The latter deals with the requirement to use a mark (reflected in TMA ss.46(1)(a) and (b) with regard to revocation for non-use) adding in Article 10(3) that use of the trade mark with the consent of the proprietor is deemed to constitute use by the proprietor.

Article 8(1) of the Directive has its counterpart in s.28(1) TMA which states that a trade mark licence can be general or limited, either as to some of the goods or services, as to a locality or as to manner of use (we may note that this latter phrase does not appear in the Directive). When reading s.28 and its related provisions, it is important (just as with trade mark assignments) to understand how trade mark law has evolved over the last century. Prior to the 1938 Act, the common law rule was that to grant a licence of a trade mark was to invalidate the mark because the licence broke the connection between the mark and the goodwill of the proprietor's business: *Bowden Wire Ltd v Bowden Brake Co Ltd*. It was, however, recognised in due course that this harsh rule did not apply in relation to use of the mark within a corporate group: *RADIATION Trade Mark* (1930) 47 RPC 37.

The 1938 Act (also in s.28) introduced the possibility of licensing marks. Perhaps because of the *Bowden Wire* case it did not use the word 'licence' as such, but instead talked about the licensee being the 'registered user' of the mark. The procedure in that Act for recording licences on the Register was bureaucratic and cumbersome. Both **licensor** and licensee had to join in the application to record, and had to provide clear evidence to the Registrar that *at the time of the application* the **registered proprietor** had the right to exercise quality control (this normally consisted of either parent/subsidiary relationship, the existence of a patent licence, or else evidence of the contractual terms found in the trade mark licence itself, such as those which would enable the proprietor to inspect the licensee's premises or to demand samples). Further, the Act gave the Registrar discretion to refuse to record a licence (evidence again of the paternalistic policy of the 1938 Act). However, the Act did contain one weakness. As was pointed out in *BOSTITCH Trade Mark* [1963] RPC 183 the wording of the legislation was entirely permissive ('application may be made') so that failure to apply to record a registered user agreement was not fatal to the mark's **validity**.

To return to the TMA, the formalities for trade mark licences are to be found in s.28(2). In contrast to patents and copyright, the TMA requires *all* licences to be in writing. Section 28(3) provides for the licence to bind any successor to the licensor, unless there is an agreement to the contrary. Sublicences may also be granted 'where the licence so provides' (s.28(4)).

It is in relation to the recording of licences on the Register that there is the biggest contrast with the 1938 Act. Section 25(2) requires 'all **registrable transactions**' (which phrase includes licences) to be entered on the register. The sanctions for failing to record are threefold. First, the transaction will be ineffective against a subsequent *bona fide* purchaser, second the procedural rights given to the licensee by ss.30 and 31 will not be available, and (in accordance with the Enforcement Directive) no costs may be awarded in subsequent litigation for acts of infringement committed between the date of the transaction and the date of registration (ss.25(3) and (4) as amended). However, there is a degree of relaxation in comparison with the old law in that s.25(1) contemplates that it will be the licensee who applies to record the licence (which reflects the sanctions for failing to record) although application may also be made 'by any other person claiming to be affected by such transaction'.

The TMA draws a distinction between exclusive and non-exclusive licensees, 'exclusive licensee' being defined by s.29 in orthodox language. Section 31 confers procedural rights on the exclusive licensee (in effect to bring infringement proceedings in their own name) whilst other licensees are given lesser rights by s.30, ie to bring proceedings in their own name only after the proprietor has refused a request to sue on behalf of the licensee. Despite both provisions treating the licensee as if they were the owner of the mark, orthodox theory is that trade mark licences do not give any proprietary rights to the licensee but simply confer personal rights which prevent the licensee from being sued for infringement: *Northern & Shell plc v Condé Nast & National Magazine Distributors Ltd*.

The need for quality control

There is one issue which is a particular feature of trade mark licences, and that is the need for quality control. The reason is in part attributable to trade mark function.

case close-up

Re American Greetings Corporation's Application [1984] 1 All ER 426

....

The significance of quality control under the 1938 Act was made apparent in *Re American Greetings Corporation's Application* [1984] 1 All ER 426. Here, multiple trade mark applications had been filed in connection with the application to record a number of licences for the merchandising of a character called 'Hollie Hobby' (a little girl in a gingham dress accompanied by a cat). The House of Lords confirmed that the Registrar had been correct to reject the applications and the licences because what had been done amounted to 'trafficking in a trade mark' (prohibited by s.28(6) of the 1938 Act). The mark was being treated as a commodity in its own right. Even though there were quality control provisions in each of the licences, the scale of the merchandising activity was such that there was no link between the proprietor and the goods so that the mark no longer indicated origin.

483

Further, in *JOB Trade Mark* [1993] FSR 118, it was held that a 'bare' licence under which the licensor had no control over the quality of goods sold by the licensee potentially made the registration revocable for non-use.

cross reference
See section 14.2.

It is a matter of speculation whether these two cases survive under the TMA. First, it is now possible to make multiple class applications rather than having to file individual applications for each class of goods and services. Second, Article 10(3) of the Trade Marks Directive states use with the consent of the proprietor suffices to prevent revocation for non-use. However, might uncontrolled licensing make the mark liable to revocation under s.46(1)(d) because it is liable to deceive? The matter was considered at some length by the House of Lords in *Scandecor Development AB v Scandecor Marketing AB* [2001] 2 CMLR 645 (a complex contractual dispute which should never have come to court). Their Lordships were prepared to refer questions to the ECJ about this link between uncontrolled licensing and revocation, but at the last moment the case was settled and so the questions were never put. However, in view of the ECJ's reasoning in *Emanuel v Continental Shelf* 'deception' as an element of s.46(1)(d) requires the mark itself to be inherently deceptive, so it seems unlikely that sloppy licensing could lead to revocation. Last, however, there is a lingering doubt as to whether filing multi-class trade mark applications accompanied by multiple licences (an aspect of character merchandising) may amount to making an application in 'bad faith' for the purposes of s.3(6) (see *Knoll AG's Trade Mark* [2003] RPC 175).

Licensing of unregistered trade marks

One unresolved question is whether unregistered trade marks can be licensed. It might be assumed that the *Bowden Wire* principle still applies because of the need to maintain the link between the trade mark and the goodwill of the proprietor's business. However, there are *obiter* remarks both at first instance and in the Court of Appeal in *GE Trade Mark* [1969] RPC 418 at p. 454 (Graham J) and [1970] RPC 339 at p. 391 (Cross LJ) the consensus being that providing quality control is *in fact* exercised, a licence does not render an unregistered trade mark invalid.

17.3.5 **Know-how**

Know-how, which is commercially valuable but non-patentable information protected by means of confidentiality agreements, is not a property right and so is incapable of assignment. It can, however, be licensed. As know-how is a non-statutory right there are no provisions as to the requirements of such a licence. The inference is that a know-how licence *could* be made orally. However, common sense dictates that as the key feature of such an agreement is to preserve the secrecy of the information, then a clearly worded written contract is essential.

thinking point
Would it be a good idea for all intellectual property legislation to provide (like the TMA) that all licences should be made in writing?

17.4 Challenging the validity of copyright transactions

Many industries make extensive use of contractual arrangements in order to place the ownership of copyright in the hands of those wanting to exploit works commercially. Creators often have to accept the terms which are offered to them, but in so doing may have no access to independent legal advice. Thus an aspiring author may have to accept the standard terms offered by a publisher; a musician in the early stages of their career may not appreciate how unfavourable are the terms offered by a record label or a management team.

Brownsword (in 'Copyright Assignment: Fair Dealing and Unconscionable Contracts' [1998] *IPQ* 311) explains that English law has no general doctrine of good faith in contracts but instead has developed piecemeal solutions to deal with unfairness (*Interfoto Picture Library Ltd v Stiletto Visual Programmes Ltd* [1989] QB 433 *per* Bingham LJ at p. 439). Brownsword further suggests that in relation to unfair intellectual property bargains it might be possible to invoke the Unfair Contract Terms Act 1977. Significantly, however, Sch. 1 to that Act specifically excludes intellectual property agreements from its application. We must therefore look to the common law to find a way to protect our aspiring author or budding rock star. Two arguments have been used over the years, namely restraint of trade and inequality of bargaining power.

17.4.1 Restraint of trade

case close-up

Schroeder Music v Macaulay [1974] 1 WLR 1308

The argument that a publishing agreement was in restraint of trade was successfully deployed in *Schroeder Music v Macaulay* [1974] 1 WLR 1308, although the terms of the disputed contract were one-sided in the extreme. Here M, a young composer, entered into a standard form agreement with the defendant music publishers in which he handed over the copyright in any songs he might write during the term of the contract. The deal was initially for five years but was extended automatically if royalties exceeded £5,000, an amount described by Lord Reid (at p. 1312) as representing a 'very modest success'. There was no obligation on the defendant to publish the songs, but it could assign the contract at any time whilst the composer could not. Equally, the publisher could end the agreement by giving one month's notice but the composer could not.

The House of Lords had no hesitation in granting the declaration sought by the composer that the agreement was void as being in restraint of trade. In passing, Lord Diplock (at p. 1315) remarked that the public policy which the court was implementing was not some nineteenth-century theory about freedom to trade, but 'the protection of those whose bargaining power is weak against being forced by those whose bargaining power is stronger to enter into bargains that are unconscionable'. The fact that this was a standard form contract, the terms of which were being offered by a party whose bargaining power enabled it to say 'take it or leave it', did not raise a presumption that the bargain was unconscionable, but did require the court to be vigilant to ensure that it was not.

17.4.2 Inequality of bargaining power

Lord Diplock's words in the *Macaulay* case were seized upon by Lord Denning in *Lloyds Bank Ltd v Bundy* [1975] QB 326 at p. 339 where he argued that there was a general jurisdiction to set aside contracts where there was inequality of bargaining power:

> By virtue of it, the English law gives relief to one who, without independent advice, enters into a contract upon terms which are very unfair or transfers property for a consideration which is grossly inadequate, when his bargaining power is grievously impaired by reason of his own needs or desires, or by his own ignorance or infirmity, coupled with undue influences or pressures brought to bear on him by or for the benefit of the other.

case close-up

Clifford Davis v WEA Records [1975] 1 WLR 61

Lord Denning himself then made use of this principle in *Clifford Davis v WEA Records* [1975] 1 WLR 61. Here, two members of the 'Fleetwood Mac' pop group had signed a management agreement with the claimant under which they assigned the worldwide copyright in any songs they might write over the next 10 years, promising to produce one song a month, whilst there was no undertaking from the claimant to publish their work. Having fallen out with the claimant, they composed some new songs which the defendant had recorded and proposed to release. The Court of Appeal held that the terms of the bargain were 'manifestly unfair'. The assignment of copyright had been for consideration which was grossly inadequate, and undue influence had been brought to bear on them. They had not had access to independent legal advice. The assignment of copyright was invalid and would be set aside.

The two lines of thinking, namely restraint of trade and undue influence, were blended together in *O'Sullivan v Management Agency & Music Ltd* [1985] QB 428. The claimant, who became a successful composer and singer, had at the age of 23 entered into a series of agreements with the defendant management company. At the time, he trusted implicitly the defendant's chairman who managed a number of other high-profile pop stars. This enabled the court to conclude that the defendant and its related companies stood in a fiduciary relationship with the claimant, such that undue influence could be presumed, particularly as the claimant had not been offered independent legal advice. Such undue influence rendered the contracts voidable rather than void, but the court nevertheless ordered the contracts to be set aside and required the defendant to **account** for all the profits made from the arrangement. However, credit was to be given for the skill and labour in promoting the claimant and making a significant contribution to his success, so that the defendant was entitled to a reasonable remuneration including a small profit element albeit one considerably less than would have been received had independent advice been offered.

The willingness of Lord Denning to find that a contract had been vitiated by inequality of bargaining power should be contrasted with the views of the House of Lords in *National Westminster Bank v Morgan* [1985] AC 686. Their Lordships expressly disapproved *Lloyds Bank v Bundy*, stating that a court should not presume undue influence simply from the parties' relationship without more. It had to be shown that the transaction had been wrongful in that it had constituted a manifest and unfair disadvantage to the person seeking to avoid it; in other words, there had to be victimisation. They added that it was questionable whether there was any need in the modern law to erect a general principle of relief against inequality of bargaining power, but, conversely, there was no precisely defined law setting limits to the equitable jurisdiction of a court to relieve against undue influence.

Despite the perceived conservatism in *National Westminster Bank v Morgan*, Nicholls J (as he then was) was able to use the case to set aside some of the disputed agreements in *Elton John v James* [1991] FSR 397, a case decided shortly after *Morgan*, but only reported some six years later. The facts of the case follow the familiar pattern, that of a singer-songwriter (and also his lyricist) signing a series of publishing, recording and management agreements at a time when he was very young (in fact a minor), without receiving independent legal advice, which had it been obtained would have shown the one-sided nature of the deal. Nicholls J stated that the present position (following *Morgan*) is that two ingredients are required before the court will set aside a transaction on the ground of undue influence, namely a relationship in which one person has a dominating influence over another and, second, a manifestly disadvantageous transaction resulting from that influence. Here, to have tied two young men at the beginning of their career to a publishing agreement for six years represented an unacceptably hard bargain. The defendant had assumed a dominating rôle over the claimants so that the original publishing agreement was unfair.

17.4.3 **Conclusion**

The cases discussed in the previous section, viewed historically, show a trend of moving away from the now-discredited principle of inequality of bargaining power. What is required is clear evidence from which the court may conclude that there has been undue influence. This will no longer be presumed, but must be shown to have existed as a result of the parties' relationship.

thinking point
Would the CDPA benefit from having a provision which enabled a copyright assignment to be challenged on the ground that it was unreasonable, or do the general contractual principles set out earlier provide adequate protection for the naive but talented creator?

In turn, that relationship must have led to the imposition of contractual terms which are manifestly unfair to the creator.

17.5 Intellectual property transactions and the internal market

One of the challenges facing the ECJ over the last four decades has been to reconcile the territorial nature of intellectual property rights with the concept of the EU internal market in which all 28 Member States are treated as a single entity. What emerged as the key to understanding the relationship between Article 34 of the **Treaty on the Functioning of the European Union ('TFEU')** (formerly Article 28 EC) which contains the principle of the free movement of goods and Article 36 TFEU (formerly Article 30 EC) which provides for a derogation from this in order to protect intellectual property is the factual distinction between infringing and **parallel imports**. The importation of infringing products can always be stopped by the intellectual property owner because such goods undermine the specific subject matter of the right (Case C-317/91 *Deutsche Renault AG v Audi AG* [1993] ECR I-6227). Parallel importation of goods first marketed by the intellectual property owner elsewhere within the EU cannot be prevented (subject to certain specific exceptions), as this amounts to a disguised restriction on trade: Case 15/74 *Centrafarm BV v Sterling Drug* and Case 16/74 *Centrafarm v Winthrop* [1974] ECR 1183.

cross reference
See further chapter 16.

487

17.5.1 Assignment and licensing of intellectual property rights and the free movement of goods

As a result of the ECJ's case law, imports originating from an assignee or licensee of the intellectual property right in the exporting Member State now receive different treatment.

17.5.1.1 Article 30 TFEU and intellectual property assignments

It took almost 25 years before the ECJ reached a proper understanding of the effect of an assignment of intellectual property rights. The starting point of its case law is *Sirena v Eda*, decided before the transitional period for the implementation of the Articles dealing with free movement of goods was complete and hence coloured by the fact that the Court was trying to utilise principles of competition law to decide the issues. Although the trade mark registration in Germany had been assigned by its Italian owner in 1937, it was held that the assignment had continuing effect so that imports of shaving cream from Germany to Italy in the 1960s could not be stopped, even though there was no economic link between the owner of the Italian trade mark and the goods. To treat the assignee's products as parallel imports was considered by the Court as vital as part of its mission in establishing what was then called the common market. Such reasoning, however, is fundamentally flawed as it fails to appreciate the property law aspects of assigning a trade mark. This lack of understanding of property law was perpetuated by the ECJ's decision in *Van Zuylen Frères v Hag AG*, where it treated coffee imported into Belgium from Germany as parallel imports even though the Belgian registration for KAFFEE HAG had been seized by the Government as part of war reparations before being sold to the claimant. The defect in the Court's reasoning was to focus on the common origin of the trade mark (ie the history of its ownership) rather than on whether the goods had originated from the trade mark owner in the Member State of import.

The correction of these errors began in Case 19/84 *Pharmon v Hoechst* [1985] ECR 2281 (a case concerned with the compulsory licensing of patents) where for the first time the Court focused on the question of whether the intellectual property owner had consented to the marketing of goods. As the goods had been put into circulation in the Member State of export without the agreement of the patentee, the patentee was able to object to their importation into another Member State. The process of correction was completed in two later cases, namely Case C-10/89 *SA CNL-Sucal NV v Hag GF AG* [1990] ECR I-3711 ('*Hag II*') where the Court accepted that an involuntary assignment broke the connection between the original owner and the intellectual property right in question; and Case C-9/93 *IHT Internationale Heiztechnik GmbH v Ideal-Standard GmbH* [1994] ECR I-2789 where *Sirena* was reversed, so that a voluntary assignment of an intellectual property right has the same effect. The net effect of *Ideal Standard* is therefore that where one of several parallel trade mark registrations is assigned in Member State A to an unrelated company, that will break the connection with the original trade mark owner based in Member State B. Both assignor and assignee can therefore keep the other's branded products out of their respective territories. Because they are independent legal entities with no economic connection to the other, neither has consented to the goods being put into circulation in the Member State of export. However, the Court added (at [59]) that where two businesses entered into a series of trade mark assignments with a view to partitioning the internal market, such an arrangement would breach EU competition law, so that it was necessary to analyse the context, the commitments underlying the assignment, the intention of the parties and the consideration for the assignment in deciding whether it was a collusive bargain.

17.5.1.2 Article 30 TFEU and intellectual property licences

Licences of intellectual property rights are permission to use the right in question. Consequently, the intellectual property owner has given consent to the use of the right so that the right becomes exhausted on first sale of the goods anywhere in the **EEA**. To seek to use a trade mark to prevent the importation of goods marketed under licence elsewhere within the EEA partitions the internal market along national boundaries and so is an abusive exercise of the right: Cases 56 & 58/64 *Consten & Grundig v Commission* [1966] ECR 299. Further, it doesn't matter whether first marketing was carried out by a licensee or an associated company of the intellectual property owner: although the doctrine of corporate personality might suggest that holding and subsidiary companies are to be treated as separate undertakings, for the purposes of the free movement of goods they are to be regarded as a single entity (*Centrafarm v Winthrop*).

The defence of exhaustion of rights applies equally to the sale of patented products (Case 15/74 *Centrafarm BV v Sterling Drug* [1974] ECR 1147) and the sale (but not rental or exhibition) of copyright works (Case 78/70 *Deutsche Grammophon v Metro-SB-Grossmärkte* [1971] ECR 487).

17.5.1.3 Trade mark licences and quality control

We considered earlier the importance of quality control in trade mark licences and how it was argued in *Scandecor* that failure to supervise the licensee might affect the ability of the trade mark to remain on the register. However, a recent ECJ case has shown that the presence of quality control provisions in a trade mark licence may give the trade mark owner enhanced powers in the context of the free movement of goods.

case close-up

Case C-59/08 *Copad SA v Christian Dior Couture SA* [2009] ECR I-3421
. . . .

Case C-59/08 *Copad SA v Christian Dior Couture SA* [2009] ECR I-3421 shows that breach of the terms of a licence (at least one involving luxury goods) may entitle the proprietor to sue the licensee under Article 8(2) of the Trade Marks Directive because the quality of the goods might be affected (one of the conditions set out in Article 8(2)). Further, because of the quality control clause, the licence does not amount to absolute and unconditional consent so that there can be no exhaustion of rights. A further argument is that even if such contractual breach does not trigger the right to sue under Article 8(2), the proprietor can rely on Article 7(2) of the Directive and can oppose further commercialisation of the goods, but only where it could be established that the resale of the goods could damage the reputation of the trade mark.

thinking point

Does the Copad *decision undermine the fundamental principle found in* Centrafarm v Winthrop *that marketing by a licensee anywhere in the EEA exhausts the intellectual property right?*

17.6 Intellectual property transactions and competition law

17.6.1 General remarks

It is beyond the scope of this book to deal in depth with the application of competition law to intellectual property. What follows, therefore, is no more than a very general overview. A more detailed account can be found in ch 12 of Jones and Sufrin, *EU Competition Law*.

As Anderman explains (in ch 1 of *The Interface between Intellectual Property Rights and Competition Policy*), competition policy and intellectual property rights have evolved historically as two separate systems of law, each with its own goals and the means of achieving those goals. Each has the common goal of promoting innovation and economic growth, but intellectual property law seeks to do this by granting exclusive rights whilst competition law seeks to do this by regulating commercial agreements and monopolies in order to maintain effective competition. He further points out (in ch 2 of the same) that historically there was a period when a misunderstanding of intellectual property rights led the EU competition authorities to place unduly strict limits on the exercise of such rights. A particular example of this was in the area of patent licensing. More recently, he says, a more realistic approach has been adopted and there is express recognition of the positive contribution which intellectual property rights make to competition.

17.6.2 EU and national law

EU competition law is a product of the decisions of the EU Commission under its original task of applying Articles 101 and 102 TFEU (formerly Articles 81 and 82 EC). In turn, judicial review of these decisions, initially by the ECJ, and then by the General Court generated a considerable body of jurisprudence. Such case law has been supplemented by secondary legislation (in the shape of Regulations), in particular those dealing with frequently encountered types of restrictive agreements.

Centralised enforcement of EU competition law proved to be costly and time-consuming, especially once the 2004 enlargement of the EU was contemplated. The Council of Ministers therefore adopted Regulation 1/2003 on the implementation of the rules on competition laid down in Articles 81 and 82 of the Treaty ([2003] OJ L1/1) in order to decentralise the enforcement of competition law. It gives a greater role to national competition authorities and the courts of Member States. As Jones and Sufrin observe, the Regulation entails the voluntary surrender of some of the Commission's powers. The other major impact of the Regulation was to replace the centralised notification and authorisation system and to make the whole of Articles 101 and 102 directly applicable.

United Kingdom competition law is to be found in the Competition Act 1998 which came into force on 1 March 2000. The Act introduced EU competition law principles into domestic law. It contains provisions parallel to Articles 101 and 102 TFEU, namely Chapter I prohibitions (dealing with restrictive agreements) and Chapter II prohibitions (dealing with the abuse of dominant position).

17.6.3 Restrictive agreements

Article 101 TFEU prohibits as incompatible with the internal market all agreements, decisions and concerted practices between undertakings which may affect trade between Member States and which have as their object or effect the prevention, restriction or distortion of competition. The Commission (and EU courts) have generally adopted a broad interpretation of the key words in the Article.

17.6.3.1 Vertical and horizontal restraints

One fundamental issue is the difference between vertical and horizontal restraints. This involves an analysis of the position of the parties in the relevant product market. Are they on the same level in the chain of manufacture and supply of goods or services or not? If they are on the same level and so are in effect competitors (for example both are manufacturers) then any agreement between them is a horizontal agreement. The most obvious example of a horizontal agreement would be a cartel under which the parties agree to price fixing or market sharing. If, however, the parties are not on the same level (for example one is a manufacturer and the other is a retailer) then the agreement is a vertical one. The premise of competition law is that agreements between competitors are likely to be more dangerous than agreements between non-competitors. It was assumed in the early days of competition law that intellectual property licences, normally being vertical agreements, would be unobjectionable. It therefore came as a shock when the ECJ held in *Consten & Grundig v Commission* that vertical agreements could be void under Article 101 TFEU. The Court held that intellectual property licences which use the territorial nature of the right in question (here a trade mark) to partition the internal market by reinforcing national boundaries in order to shield the licensee from price competition from parallel importers was a prohibited restrictive agreement.

17.6.3.2 Patent licences

In the case of patent licences, the policy of the EU Commission has changed significantly over the years. It will be useful first to consider the sorts of clauses which a patentee would wish to insert in a patent licence.

First, and fundamentally, there will be a transfer of technology. The patent may be combined with know-how (ie how to exploit the technology more efficiently) or with related software, trade marks, copyrights and/or designs. Whatever the exact subject matter of the licence, it will grant permission to use the intellectual property rights concerned, although this may be limited to a particular 'field of use' (for example, the use of a patented process to make one particular type of product). In return for this permission, the licensee will undertake to pay royalties, which may be periodic or by way of lump sum. The calculation of such royalties is a matter for negotiation, but, for example, there may be a clause stating that a minimum royalty is payable in any event.

The licensor may want to insert other provisions which are essential to protect their interest in the patent, such as an obligation on the licensee to use their best endeavours to promote the patented product, a duty not to sublicense, and to assist with the pursuit of infringers. In return, the licensee may demand that they be made an exclusive licensee, particularly if the start-up costs of the manufacturing process are considerable. Alongside exclusivity will be the geographic territory of the licence: it may be worldwide, but given the territorial nature of intellectual property rights, is more likely to be confined to a particular country. One particular aspect of territorial protection is that it may be reinforced by a contractual term banning the licensee from exporting from the territory (an active ban) or from responding to potential customers from outside the territory (a passive ban).

Other provisions might oblige the licensee to grant back to the licensor any improvements which are made to the invention: such 'grant-back' obligations could be by way of an assignment, or an exclusive or non-exclusive licence. The licensor may also seek to impose a 'tie-in', that is to require the licensee to purchase particular ingredients from them. Such products may be either essential or non-essential to the exploitation of the patent. There may be a clause prohibiting the licensee from challenging the validity of the patent (an obvious temptation because if the patent is invalid the information it contains is public knowledge and so theoretically free for anyone to use). There may be a desire to prolong the duration of the licence beyond the lifetime of the youngest patent, although this type of clause should be distinguished from a provision which obliges the licensee to keep know-how secret after the licence has ended. Last, the licensor may attempt to impose restrictions on the licensee's freedom to trade by, for example, fixing prices or dictating their choice of retail outlets.

The initial reaction of the EU Commission was benign. In its 1962 'Christmas Message' it indicated that even exclusive patent licences did not fall within Article 101 provided the restrictions did not go beyond the 'scope of the patent'. That, however, changed in the 1970s. In a series of decisions, the Commission held that a number of favourite provisions *were* restrictions on competition, namely: the grant-back of improvements unless by means of non-exclusive licence; 'tie-ins' for non-essential goods; 'no challenge' clauses; prolongation of the licence beyond life of the youngest patent; and restrictions on freedom to trade. It was, however, accepted by the ECJ that exclusivity could be justified under certain circumstances. In Case 258/78 *Nungesser v Commission* [1982] ECR 2015 the Court adopted a far less strict approach than the Commission, taking into account economic considerations and the need to encourage new technology (in this case the development of new varieties of maize).

Since 1984, there have been a number of EU Regulations granting block exemption from Article 101(3) for patent licences which comply with the certain requirements. A Block Exemption does not provide the parties with a standardised agreement; rather it lists those clauses which are acceptable under competition law and those which are not. The latest Block Exemption is Commission Regulation (EC) 772/2004 of 27 April 2004 on the application of Article 81(3) of the Treaty to categories of technology transfer agreements (the Transfer of Technology Block Exemption, 'TTBER'), [2004] OJ L 123/11. It is considerably wider than it predecessors, as it includes software and designs as well as patents and know-how. The TTBER is accompanied by a detailed Commission Notice containing Guidelines for the application of the TTBER: [2004] OJ C 101/2. The two documents have to be considered as a whole.

The basic premise of the TTBER (which applies only to bilateral agreements) is to draw a distinction between agreements between competitors and agreements between non-competitors. It will only apply to exempt licences from breach of competition law where certain market thresholds are not exceeded (Article 3). These thresholds vary depending on whether the agreement is between competitors or non-competitors. Besides setting out when exclusivity is permitted (Article 2), it lists impermissible hardcore restrictions (Article 4). The presence of any of these in an agreement will remove the entire agreement from the protection of the Block Exemption. Article 5 lists excluded restrictions: these restrictions are not exempted but their presence does not remove the protection of the Block Exemption. Again, the hardcore restrictions and the excluded restrictions differ depending on whether the agreement is between competitors and non-competitors. The TTBER applies only to agreements which concern the *production* of contract products, ie it does not cover patent pooling agreements, the licensing of R&D or agreements whose primary object is the sale and purchase of products rather than their production.

The TTBER is due to expire on 27 April 2014: at the time of writing details of its replacement are not available.

17.6.3.3. Trade mark licences

Unlike patent licenses, trade mark licences have not attracted as much attention from the EU Commission, but when considering the competition law aspects, the difference between horizontal and vertical agreements must be kept in mind.

One particular category of horizontal trade mark agreement is a trade mark delimitation agreement. This is an agreement entered into in order to settle litigation, particularly where one party opposes or objects to the use of an allegedly confusingly similar trade mark. A number of Commission decisions on such contracts culminated in the ECJ's ruling in Case 35/83 *BAT Cigaretten-Fabriken GmbH v Commission* [1985] ECR 363. Here the Court stated that an agreement will be outside Article 101 if there is a genuine risk of confusion and the agreement does not attempt to divide markets within the EU. The subsequent enactment of the Trade Marks Directive means that there is now a harmonised approach to when there is a likelihood of confusion, but nevertheless, the encouragement to settle litigation found in the United Kingdom's Civil Procedure Rules has to be balanced against the impact of competition law.

One particular type of trade mark vertical agreement which did attract the Commission's attention is a franchising agreement. Franchise agreements relate to the licence of particular business methods, enabling the franchisor to set up a uniform network for the distribution of goods or services (for example photocopy shops, hairdressers or pizza shops). The franchisee is enabled to set up business with an established entrepreneur using a tried and tested format. Franchise agreements were considered by the ECJ in Case 161/84 *Pronuptia de Paris GmbH v Schillgallis* [1986] ECR 353 where it was held that two clauses essential to franchise agreements did not amount to a restriction on competition. These were a ban on the franchisee opening a shop of a similar nature for a reasonable period after the end of the contract; and selling the shop without the franchisor's consent. Similarly, other clauses such as laying out the premises in a particular manner, only selling approved products, and getting all advertising approved did not fall within Article 101.

Although there was subsequently a Block Exemption dealing with franchise agreements, these now fall within the Vertical Restraints Block Exemption, the latest version of which is Commission Regulation 330/2010 of 20 April 2010, [2010] OJ L 102/1, effective 1 June 2010. The Regulation also applies to selective distribution agreements. Like the TTBER, the Vertical Restraints Block Exemption uses a market share test (Articles 3 and 9), below which threshold vertical restraints are presumed to be beneficial to competition (Recital 6), as long as they do not contain certain prohibited clauses (listed in Articles 4 and 5). Agreements not satisfying the Regulation will fall outside its protection. Certain types of provision are considered to render the agreement non-exemptable, including retail price maintenance, cross-supply restrictions and customer allocation to a given distributor.

Because of the combined effect of the TTBER and the Vertical Restraints Block Exemption, the only trade mark licences not covered by Block Exemptions are those involving merchandising agreements. These presumably would still fall within the scope of Article 101 TFEU if restrictive of competition.

17.6.3.4 Copyright licences

There have been few decisions on copyright licences, although it is clear that any agreement which partitions the market along territorial boundaries may fall within Article 101 TFEU: Case

19/77 *Miller International Schallplatten GmbH v Commission* [1978] ECR 131; Case 262/81 *Coditel v Cine Vog (No 2)* [1982] ECR 3381.

thinking point

Does the treatment of intellectual property licences under Article 101 TFEU and the various Block Exemptions recognise, in Anderman's words, the positive contribution which intellectual property rights make to competition?

17.6.4 **Abuse of dominant position**

Article 102 TFEU declares that any abuse by one or more undertakings of a dominant position within the internal market or in a substantial part of it shall be prohibited as incompatible with the internal market in so far as it may affect trade between Member States. It goes on to list particular forms of abuse, such as directly or indirectly imposing unfair purchase or selling prices or other unfair trading conditions; limiting production, markets or technical development to the prejudice of consumers; applying dissimilar conditions to equivalent transactions with other trading parties, thereby placing them at a competitive disadvantage; and making the conclusion of contracts subject to acceptance by the other parties of supplementary obligations which, by their nature or according to commercial usage, have no connection with the subject of such contracts.

The application of Article 102 to intellectual property rights requires consideration of three separate issues.

17.6.4.1 Ownership of intellectual property rights

It was held by the ECJ at a fairly early stage of the development of competition law that mere ownership of an intellectual property right did not breach Article 102 because of the negative nature of the right: Case 24/67 *Parke Davis v Probel* [1968] ECR 55. Therefore although ownership of a patent, copyright, design or trade mark confers a statutory monopoly, this is not the same as an economic monopoly and does not mean that its owner is in a dominant position. However, how the owner chooses to exploit that right may well have implications under competition law.

17.6.4.2 Refusal to license

More relevant to Article 102 is if the proprietor declines to deal with potential licensees (the terms of any licence actually granted will fall under Article 101). The ECJ held in Case 238/87 *Volvo v Veng* [1988] ECR 6211 that a refusal to license copyright in relation to car replacement parts was not automatically a breach of Article 102 but might be in certain circumstances, depending on the nature of the proprietor's conduct and whether that was abusive; for example, whether it was arbitrary, whether unfair prices were charged and whether there was a continuation of supply of parts for out-of-date models.

Case C-241–242/91P *RTE v Commission (Magill Intervening)* [1995] ECR I-743

. . . .

Refusal to license was given a much more detailed examination by the ECJ in Case C-241–242/91P *RTE v Commission (Magill Intervening)* [1995] ECR I-743. The refusal of three broadcasting organisations in the 1980s (the BBC, ITV and RTE) to license Magill so that he could publish a multi-channel TV guide (common in mainland Europe but at the time unusual in the United Kingdom and Eire) was held to be a breach of EU competition law. The Court did not deny that the organisations had copyright in their respective lists of programmes but did hold, in effect, that such copyright was secondary to the broadcasters' main product, television programmes, and that they were using their market power to stifle the publication of a new product for which there was public demand. One might speculate that the hidden message of the case was that the Court considered the threshold for copyright protection in the United Kingdom and Eire was too low, but did not have the jurisdiction to comment on the point.

The Court revisited the issue of when a refusal to license copyright can amount to an abuse of dominant position in Case C-418/01 *IMS Health GmbH v NDC Health GmbH* [2004] ECR I-5039. The case concerned IMS' alleged copyright in a database of regional sales information about pharmaceutical products and its refusal to license others. The ECJ declared that three conditions had to be satisfied before a refusal to license copyright was a breach of Article 102 TFEU. First, the undertaking requesting the licence must intend to offer new products not offered by the copyright owner and for which there was a potential consumer demand; second, the refusal could not be justified by objective considerations; last, the refusal had to have the effect of eliminating all the copyright owner's competitors in that market.

495

17.6.4.3 Collecting societies

Certain copyrights (particularly music) are usually managed on behalf of authors by collecting societies. For a composer to have to obtain royalties from someone who controls premises each time a piece of music is performed on those premises would be manifestly inconvenient.

Copyright collecting societies tend to be territorial, and so deal with particular categories of copyright work within a particular country, although there exists a network of reciprocal arrangements between various societies whereby royalties are collected on behalf of each other's members. Of concern under Article 102 are the terms on which membership is provided and on which copyright is licensed to potential users. As Rosenblatt explains (in 'Copyright Assignments: Rights and Wrongs—the Collecting Societies' Perspective' [2000] *IPQ* 187) collective administration, in contrast to individual copyright agreements, may not offer the most favourable terms to every right holder in every circumstance, nor to every user. The majority of European collective societies operate on an exclusive basis, usually acquiring the rights they administer by way of assignment.

In *Re GEMA* [1971] CMLR D35, the Commission decided that the German copyright collecting society had infringed competition law because its membership rules tied authors to it for too long a period and in respect of too many rights. Cases decided by the ECJ include Case 127/73 *Belgische Radio en Televisie v SABAM* [1974] ECR 51 where the Court recognised the benefits of collective administration but emphasised the need for collecting societies, when drafting their membership rules, to take account of all interests and to try to balance the needs of authors and composers with effective management of their rights.

The relationship between copyright collecting societies and those wishing to exploit the works has been considered by the ECJ in a number of referrals to it by national courts under Article 267 TFEU. In Case 22/79 *Greenwich Films v SACEM* [1979] ECR 3275 the Court suggested that the activities of SACEM (the principal French copyright collecting society) should be considered in their totality as their licensing system as a whole might be considered to partition the internal market, even with regard to the granting of extra-territorial licences. SACEM's policy with regard to the licensing of music for use in discothèques has been the subject of extensive litigation in France, culminating with the referral to the ECJ in Cases 395/87 and 241–242/88 *Ministère Public v Tournier; Lucazeau v SACEM* [1989] ECR 2521, 2811. The Court stated that the imposition of significantly higher royalties on specific forms of exploitation might be evidence of the abuse of a dominant position unless the royalty rate could be objectively justified. Most recently, in Case C-52/07 *Kanal 5 Ltd, TV 4 AB v Föreningen Svenska Tonsättares Internationella Musikbyrå (STIM) upa* [2008] ECR I-9275, it was held that there was no breach of competition law where the remuneration model for commercial TV channels was based partly on the channels' revenue (ie it was a flat rate reflecting the commercial success of that channel) unless there was another means of identifying more precisely which musical works had been broadcast, as long as this did not involve disproportionate costs. However, the society might breach Article 102 if it treated commercial and public sector broadcasters differently where they were in fact offering equivalent services, unless this different treatment could be objectively justified. In all of these cases, it should be remembered that the ECJ was giving advice to the application of EU competition law by national competition authorities, so of necessity the conclusions as to the status of collecting societies under Article 102 tend to be expressed in general terms.

At the time of writing, the EU is in the process of enacting a Directive on collective management organisations: its objectives are to improve the corporate governance of such bodies, to set common standards for multi-territorial licensing and to help expand the availability of online music.

17.6.5 **Summary**

EU competition law, by means of Articles 101 and 102 TFEU, controls the ways in which intellectual property rights may be licensed and managed. Of necessity, this law is complex and highly specialised and is driven by the need to achieve the 'level playing field' of the internal market.

Summary

This chapter has explained:

- the ways in which intellectual property rights can be dealt with contractually;
- the United Kingdom statutory formalities which govern such transactions; and
- the constraints imposed on such dealings, whether at common law, under the EU's free movement of goods rules, or under competition law.

Reflective question

Intellectual property law would benefit by having in place a simple rule that any contract dealing with such rights must be fair and just.

Discuss.

 # Annotated further reading

Anderman, S.D. *The Interface between Intellectual Property Rights and Competition Policy* (2007), Cambridge University Press

The book surveys the relationship between competition policy and intellectual property rights in the major trading blocks of the world (the EU, USA and Japan), in some selected smaller economies and also considers some specific issues, including parallel imports, technology transfers and economic theory.

Brownsword, R. 'Copyright Assignment: Fair Dealing and Unconscionable Contracts' [1998] *IPQ* 311

Discusses the cases where copyright assignments have been set aside.

Firth, A. and Fitzgerald, J. 'Equitable Assignments in Relation to Intellectual Property' [1999] *IPQ* 228

Puts dealings in intellectual property rights into the broader context of legal and equitable assignment of choses in action.

Jones, A. and Sufrin, B. *EU Competition Law: Text, Cases and Materials* (5th edn, 2014), Oxford University Press

A detailed account of all aspects of competition law, with ch 12 dealing with competition law and intellectual property rights.

Rosenblatt, H. 'Copyright Assignments: Rights and Wrongs—the Collecting Societies' Perspective' [2000] *IPQ* 187

Discusses the role of collecting societies in the administration of copyright with reference to the competition law aspects of the contracts with their members.

Vaver, D. 'Reforming Intellectual Property Law: An Obvious and Not-So-Obvious Agenda: The Stephen Stewart Memorial Lecture for 2008' [2009] *IPQ* 143

Considers ways in which United Kingdom intellectual property law could be reformed, with particular reference to formalities for assignment and licensing.

Protection for image, character and personality merchandising

Learning objectives

Upon completion of this chapter, you should have acquired:

- an understanding of what is meant by 'character merchandising' and the theoretical difficulties which its legal recognition presents;

- knowledge of the various means which are available under United Kingdom law to protect image, character and personality merchandising;

- an understanding of the limitations and deficiencies of each type of protection; and

- an appreciation of how other jurisdictions provide protection for merchandising activities.

Introduction

In this chapter, we consider the protection (or rather, lack of protection) afforded under United Kingdom law to merchandising activities. Merchandising, economically speaking, is an important industry. Consider, as examples, the value of goods sold to fans by football clubs and other sporting organisations and worn as 'badges of allegiance', the sale of memorabilia associated with celebrities, the endorsement of goods and services by famous people, and the way in which a whole range of items can be used to promote films such as *Harry Potter* or *Jurassic Park*, or concert tours by rock stars such as the Rolling Stones.

These commercial activities have, as their foundation, contractual arrangements between the person or company claiming to 'own' a name or image, and those undertakings who wish to make and sell legitimate (or 'authorised') goods on their behalf. Such contracts will have, as their subject matter, intellectual property rights. Legal protection for merchandising has a twofold effect, operating in a positive way for the 'owner' of the name or image to exploit their intellectual property rights by licensing others; and, in a negative sense, as a means of suing those who wish to 'free-ride' on the success of a particular name or image. Protection of merchandising brings together a number of different areas of intellectual property law, namely copyright, registered and unregistered design right, registered trade marks, passing off and breach of confidence. We shall therefore select the relevant aspects of each and apply them to the practice of merchandising to judge their effectiveness. Each area of law has its own deficiencies, some more than others. Brief reference will be made to the law in other jurisdictions in order to demonstrate that in the United Kingdom, the law does not always accord with perceived commercial needs.

One question to be asked is whether such denial of protection is defensible. Isn't it the task of the law to uphold expectations? Conversely, the tacit assumption that misappropriation of fame is wrong should be challenged. Why should the value of success be a protectable commodity in the same way as the copyright in a novel or the invention of a life-saving drug?

18.1 Challenges, justifications and definitions

18.1.1 The reasons for inadequate protection for merchandising under United Kingdom law

One question which is frequently asked is why United Kingdom law accords such poor protection to merchandising activities. Carty suggests (in 'Advertising, Publicity Rights and English

Law' [2004] *IPQ* 209) there is a judicial antipathy to fame. British courts, she states, have always been sceptical about creating monopoly rights in nebulous concepts such as names, likenesses or popularity (there is a long-established principle that there is no property right in a name, *Day v Brownrigg* (1878) 19 Ch D 294). In the absence of a right of personality in United Kingdom law, celebrities who wish to prevent the exploitation of their name or image are forced (unsuccessfully) to find a category of intellectual property right to fit the facts of the case. This distorts existing causes of action (see Klink 'Fifty Years of Publicity Rights in the United States and the Never Ending Hassle with Intellectual Property and Personality Rights in Europe' [2003] *IPQ* 363). Other torts have occasionally proved useful, such as the action for defamation in *Tolley v Fry* [1931] AC 33, where an amateur golfer successfully claimed that the use of his picture in an advertisement for chocolate implied that he had been paid a fee for endorsing the product. Equally, a claim for **malicious falsehood** (an analogous form of protection) was upheld in *Kaye v Robertson* [1991] FSR 62. Intellectual property protection has generally been less effective.

Apart from the fact that intellectual property rights do not 'map' well onto the protection of fame, there are other reasons why the cult of celebrity receives scant judicial recognition. First, brands and images are part of twenty-first-century popular culture. Any particular brand or image could therefore be regarded as in the public domain and part of the 'cultural commons', available for all to use. Alternatively, there is the argument that someone who has already courted publicity should not be able to complain if further use is made of their name or image (see Lord Woolf in *A v B (a Company)* [2002] 3 WLR 542, at [11(xii)]). Last, over-protection for celebrities could stifle freedom of speech (as an example, see the arguments put forward by the German Government in *Von Hannover v Germany (No 1)* (2004) 40 EHHR 1).

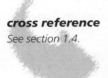

cross reference
See further chapter 3.

18.1.2 **Justifications for protecting merchandising activities**

Carty identifies three common reasons often advanced to justify the protection of merchandising. These are misappropriation (derived from Locke's labour theory of property), the protection of personal autonomy and dignity as an aspect of personality (favoured by Hegel), and economic justifications. Economic justifications for the protection of merchandise include the need to provide incentives for creativity, allocative efficiency, and preventing consumer misinformation, the last-mentioned, which is the narrowest of the economic arguments, being the one favoured by Carty. None of the reasons for having intellectual property rights in general is totally convincing, and is rarely adverted to in case law. As Carty demonstrates, there are equally valid objections to the justifications for protecting for merchandising. Ultimately, it seems, clients and lawyers simply assume that merchandising is a 'good thing', with little analysis.

cross reference
See section 1.4.

18.1.3 **Definitions of character merchandising**

A number of definitions of character merchandising have been suggested. 'That activity is one in which a notable public figure lends his name to a particular product or range of products so as, apparently, to endorse that product. The consequence relied on is that the consumer comes to regard goods bearing that name as having the approbation of or **licence** from his or her "idol" ' (*per* Morritt LJ in *ELVIS PRESLEY Trade Marks* [1999] RPC 567 at p. 594). 'The reason large sums are paid for endorsement is because . . . those in business have reason to believe that the lustre of a famous person, if attached to their goods or services, will enhance the attractiveness of those goods or services to their target market' (*per* Laddie J in *Irvine v Talksport Ltd* [2002] 2 All ER 414 at [39]). The drawback of both of these pronouncements is that they are limited to product endorsement by a celebrity, whereas the scope of merchandising activities is considerably broader.

case close-up

Lorimar Productions v Sterling Clothing [1982] RPC 395

The most comprehensive definition of character merchandising is that given in the South African decision of *Lorimar Productions v Sterling Clothing* [1982] RPC 395 at p. 398 by Van Dijkhorst J. He stated that it involves:

> the use of characters, locations, names, titles and logos from TV series, feature films or other entertainment programmes for promotions and the sales of products and services. It is alleged that modern buying habits are highly responsive to image-related advertising. If carefully chosen merchandise is marketed in overt association with a popular film, TV series, celebrity, fictitious character or the like, that merchandise will enjoy a greater consumer demand than could have been expected for the unadorned product.

His comments should be seen in the light of the facts of the case. It involved an unsuccessful attempt by the television company responsible for the series *Dallas* to bring actions in **passing off** to prevent the use of the names DALLAS and SOUTH FORK for, respectively, clothing and restaurant services. The case was therefore concerned with merchandising based on the *names* of fictitious characters or places. The basis of the decision was that the public, on seeing the defendants' use of the **claimant's** names, would not assume that there was any link between the parties. They were in separate fields of commerce, so that the defendants had not made an actionable misrepresentation to the effect that the claimant had approved or endorsed the use of the names. A further, perhaps doubtful, assumption was that the public were not used to the concept of character merchandising.

cross reference
See chapter 13.

The reasoning in *Lorimar* shows how a strict application of the criteria for passing off can lead to the denial of a remedy for conduct which could be considered to be misappropriation or 'free-riding'. In turn, it invokes two further debates. First, should passing off (indeed, intellectual property in general) be responsive to the needs of business, as suggested by Lord Diplock in *Erven Warnink BV v Townend & Sons* [1979] AC 731, or should it remain confined to its well-established criteria, so that where these are not satisfied, the claimant is left without a remedy, however wrong the defendant's conduct may seem (see Lord Scarman in *Cadbury-Schweppes v Pub Squash Co* [1981] RPC 429)? Second, if Lord Scarman's thinking is adopted, and the passing off criteria are strictly applied, is this a reason to introduce separate, possibly statutory protection against **unfair competition**, or at the very least, protection against misappropriation, as advocated by some writers? Misappropriation as the basis of intellectual property protection has, however, been rejected judicially (see *Victoria Park Racing v Taylor* (1937) 58 CLR 479 at p. 509 (*per* Dixon J) (Australian HC) and *Moorgate Tobacco v Philip Morris* [1985] RPC 291 at pp. 236–40 (*per* Deane J) (Australian HC)).

cross reference
See section 1.2.

Merchandising activities, however, go far beyond the use of fictitious names from television programmes or films, as happened in *Lorimar*. They can involve the use of the *appearance* of characters from films (such as Darth Vader from *Star Wars*), television (*Teletubbies*) or comics (*Judge Dredd*). In connection with the last-mentioned example, an increasing number of characters from comics are being turned into films, such as Batman, Superman and Spiderman, a point not without significance in the discussion which follows of the use of **copyright** to protect merchandising activities. Consider also the commercial needs of a sporting organisation (such as Manchester United in football, Ferrari in motor racing) to protect its name and emblem, celebrity endorsements (where a person's name or image is used to suggest approval of another's goods or services), as well as where a celebrity's name or image is used to sell memorabilia (whether the celebrity is alive or dead). Such a variety of circumstances suggests that a wide range of legal devices needs to be deployed.

thinking point
How many examples of merchandising activities can you think of?

There are several means whereby legal protection can be afforded to the merchandiser, namely copyright and design law, the law of registered trade marks, passing off and **breach of confidence**. None provides a complete solution.

18.2 # Possible means of protection: copyright

18.2.1 Copyright drawings

The simplest way in which character merchandising can be protected under the law of copyright is where a fictitious character started out as a cartoon drawing. As long as the drawing is **original**, copyright will subsist in it under s.4(1)(a) CDPA 1988, irrespective of artistic quality. The same applies where the character started out as a doll or puppet (as in *Allen v Redshaw* [2013] EWPCC B1), which could be regarded as a 'sculpture' for the purposes of s.4. 'Sculpture' would also be the relevant category of copyright work where the character began life as a figure made out of plasticine-like material, such as those in the *Wallace and Gromit* films.

The significance of claiming copyright for such creations is that the rights will be **infringed** by copying the work and issuing copies to the public (s.17 and s.18 CDPA). In particular, s.17(2) CDPA provides that a **work** is infringed if it is reproduced in any material form, and s.17(3) adds to this by stating that a two-dimensional artistic work is infringed by a three-dimensional reproduction and vice versa. Hence, in *King Features v Kleeman* [1941] AC 417, POPEYE dolls and brooches were held to be infringing reproductions of the claimant's comic strips. Clearly, therefore, whether the character was created for inclusion in a film or whether it started life in a comic, with the stories later being adapted for film, copyright protection is a powerful weapon.

Where the copyright owner itself uses the cartoon character in the manufacture of articles, this will amount to exploitation by an industrial process. The former restriction on the term of protection to 25 years for such an artistic work found in s.52 CDPA has been repealed by the Enterprise and Regulatory Reform Act 2013.

The copyright owner may, however, have difficulty in suing for infringement where the defendant merely takes the idea of the character, because copyright protects expression not ideas. Nevertheless, in *Mirage Studios v Counter-Feat Clothing* [1991] FSR 145 (the *NINJA TURTLES* case), where the defendant took the claimant's concept of humanoid turtles when producing its own designs for T-shirts, Browne-Wilkinson VC held that there was an arguable case of copyright infringement. At first glance, such reasoning appears to protect ideas not their expression. Discounting the fact that this was an application for interim relief, the case is unique in United Kingdom law, not only for its particular findings of fact as regards the practice of merchandising but also for the way in which it combined the principles of passing off and copyright to secure a remedy for the claimant. The passing off aspect of the case is discussed further later.

cross reference
See section 7.4.

A further difficulty which may occur should the owner of a copyright drawing sue a third party for copying the artistic work is that the defendant may seek to rely on the defence found in s.51 CDPA. Section 51 has the effect of preventing the claimant suing for copyright infringement because the original drawings for the character are 'design documents' for an **'article'** which is not an artistic work in its own right. Consequently, the principal argument available to the copyright owner will be that the cartoon drawing was not *for* an article, which would place the matter outside s.51, or that the drawing was for an artistic work such as a sculpture, which equally ensures that the defence does not apply. Should either of these arguments not succeed, the only course of action open will be for the claimant to rely on any **unregistered design right** in the drawings for the character.

cross reference
See section 11.3.2.

Successful reliance on s.51 occurred in *BBC Worldwide Ltd v Pally Screen Printing Ltd* [1998] FSR 665 where the defendant had applied pictures of the *Teletubbies* characters to T-shirts. Laddie J held that the claimant could not sue for copyright infringement. The decision should be treated with caution, as arguably the design was applied *to* an article (the front of the T-shirt) rather than being used to produce the 'shape or configuration' *of* a three-dimensional article (to quote the language of s.213 CDPA). However, the claimant's case was hampered by other difficulties which clearly had a bearing on the court's discretion to deny interim relief.

case close-up

Lucasfilm Ltd v Ainsworth [2009] FSR 103 (Mann J); [2011] 3 WLR 487 (Supreme Court)
. . . .

A much more clear-cut case which explores in some detail the relationship between something which is a three-dimensional artistic work and something which is simply an article protected by unregistered design right is *Lucasfilm Ltd v Ainsworth* [2009] FSR 103 (Mann J); [2011] 3 WLR 487 (UKSC). At issue was whether the Stormtrooper helmets for the film *Star Wars* could be regarded as either sculptures or works of artistic craftsmanship and so protectable under the law of copyright. At first instance Mann J had concluded that they were neither. A sculpture, he said, should have, as part of its purpose, a visual appeal in the sense that it might be enjoyed for that purpose alone, whether or not it might have another purpose as well. The purpose was that of the creator. An artist (in the realm of the visual arts) created something because it had visual appeal which was to be enjoyed as such. It had to have the intrinsic quality of being intended to be enjoyed as a visual thing. Mann J also held that the Stormtrooper helmets for the film *Star Wars* were not works of artistic craftsmanship, concluding (at [131]) that 'for a work to be to be regarded as one of artistic craftsmanship it must be possible fairly to say that the author was both a craftsman and an artist. A craftsman is a person who makes something in a skilful way and takes justified pride in their workmanship. An artist is a person with creative ability who produces something which has aesthetic appeal.' In light of these observations, the end result was that the helmets fell squarely within the s.51 defence so that the action for copyright infringement was barred. The Supreme Court agreed with his conclusions.

18.2.2 **Names and titles**

Copyright also subsists in original literary works (ss.1(1)(a) and 3 CDPA), but there can be no copyright in a single word or name. In *Francis Day and Hunter Ltd v Twentieth Century Fox Corporation* [1940] AC 112, it was held that there was no copyright in the song title *The Man Who Broke the Bank at Monte Carlo*. Similarly, in *Exxon Corporation v Exxon Insurance Consultants International Ltd* [1981] 3 All ER 241, it was held that there was no copyright in the invented word trade mark EXXON despite the vast amount of research and effort which went into its creation. Copyright is therefore of no assistance to the production company who wants to promote the name of a film or television series through merchandising activities, nor the names of a fictitious place occurring in the plot of a film, nor the name of a character such as Sherlock Holmes.

18.2.3 **Photographs**

Other forms of copyright which might assist the merchandiser are films and photographs. Taking a photograph from a film, for example, to make a transfer to be printed on T-shirts or to make posters or postcards will be infringement of copyright in the film (*Spelling-Goldberg Productions Inc v BPC Publishing Ltd* [1981] RPC 283; s.17(4) CDPA). In the case of photographs, copyright protection will be available if the personality (or their management company) is the owner of the copyright in the photograph and that photograph is applied to a range of goods or services without consent. But this does not stop the unauthorised exploiter from taking an independent photograph of the personality and applying it to the goods or services concerned (see *Lyngstad v Anabas Products Ltd* [1977] FSR 62 (*ABBA*), *Irvine v Talksport Ltd*), because, of course, independent creation is always a defence to copyright infringement. Where a third party takes their own photograph, then the celebrity will be forced to rely on passing off as the means of protection, unless the circumstances in which the photograph was taken give rise to a claim for breach of confidence. Similarly, should a drawing of a celebrity be created by a third party, in the absence of any written agreement transferring copyright to the celebrity, the ownership of copyright in the drawing will vest in the **author** (or their employer) and the famous person will have no right to object to the commercial reproductions of the picture.

The availability of passing off is heavily dependent on the facts of the case, but for now we can consider two contrasting decisions where the claimants had to rely on passing off because they did not own copyright in the relevant photographs. In *ABBA*, Oliver J concluded that no relief in passing off was available to the group to prevent unauthorised merchandise, as they were not in the business of selling goods and so were not in competition with the defendant. By contrast, in *Irvine*, the claimant had already entered into a number of commercial arrangements where his image was used to endorse various products and so had the requisite business **goodwill** which could be protected against the defendant's unauthorised use of his likeness. The fact that the defendant had not committed copyright infringement was therefore irrelevant.

cross reference
See section 8.1.2.2.

Even if the celebrity does own the copyright in any photographic image, copyright protection is limited. In *Merchandising Corporation of America Inc v Harpbond Ltd* [1983] FSR 32, a portrait of the singer Adam Ant wearing his new 'Prince Charming' make-up was held not to be infringement of the copyright in the photograph on which it was based because there had not been substantial taking from the photograph, a conclusion similar to that reached in *Bauman v Fussell* (1953) [1978] RPC 485. Also, it was held that there was no copyright in the singer's make-up because it was too transitory in nature: 'a painting is not an idea; it is an object; and paint without surface is not a painting'.

thinking point
How effective is the law of copyright in protecting merchandising activities?

Finally, the photograph of the celebrity may have been taken in circumstances where the celebrity regards it as media intrusion. Here the law of copyright is not relevant. Instead, recourse is necessary to the law on breach of confidence.

18.3 Possible means of protection: designs

18.3.1 Registered designs

The current law of **registered designs**, reflecting the wording of the EU Designs Directive (Directive 98/71/EC of the European Parliament and of the Council of 13 October 1998 on the legal protection of designs [1998] OJ L 289/28), protects 'the appearance of the whole or a part of a **product** resulting from the features of, in particular, the lines, contours, colours, shape, texture or materials of the product or its ornamentation' (Registered Designs Act 1949 ('RDA'), s.1(2) as amended). The positive criteria for registrability are that the design must be 'new' and have **individual character**, the latter requirement being assessed through the eyes of the **informed user**. In the case of merchandise (such as dolls, ceramic figures or toys) such person is likely to be the average buyer of these products for a retail chain. None of the exclusions from registrability appear to be relevant. The scope of protection, under s.7 RDA, would enable the designer to stop any third party from using the design. 'Use' comprises making, offering, putting on the market, importing, exporting or using a product in which the design is incorporated or to which it is applied, or stocking such a product for those purposes. The presence of the indefinite article ('a') in the infringement provision means that there will be liability if the design applied by the third party to an article other than that for which the design was registered.

case close-up

> *Spice Girls Ltd's Application* (16 August 1999)
>
> One argument raised in the past was whether a registered design could still be 'new' if it consisted of the likeness of a famous person. Under the previous version of the RDA, the answer was that it could. In *Spice Girls Ltd's Application* (16 August 1999) the pop group sought **cancellation**

of a series of designs registered in the name of Girl Power Toys Ltd, on the ground, *inter alia*, that the designs were not new. The Registrar held that the prior publication, in order to destroy **novelty**, had to be prior publication *of a design*, that is, 'features applied to an article'. Just because images of the group were in the public domain did not mean that the *design* was not new. One of the authorities cited was *Dean's Rag Book Co Ltd v Pomerantz & Sons* (1930) 47 RPC 485, where a registration for a design for a 'Mickey Mouse' doll was allowed even though the shape of Mickey Mouse was well known from earlier cartoons: 'Images or photographs of individual persons are not a design until they are applied to some article of manufacture'. However, the registration in the *Spice Girls* case was cancelled because of lack of consent by the individual members of the group, and because dolls bearing the likenesses of the group had previously been sold.

It is arguable that the same result would be reached under the wording of the amended RDA. The definition of novelty (based on the wording of the Designs Directive) is that no identical or similar *design* has previously been made available to the public, and 'design' means 'the appearance of a product'. Novelty is therefore only lost if articles have previously been made available, rather than the image which is applied to those articles. It would, however, be a matter of interpretation by the ECJ under Article 267 of the **Treaty on the Functioning of the European Union ('TFEU')** (formerly Article 234 EC).

18.3.2 **Unregistered design right**

Should the creator of the character choose to rely on unregistered design right rather than registered design or copyright, then it will be necessary for the design to meet the criteria for protection set out in s.213 CDPA. Taking as examples a doll in the likeness of a celebrity, or a toy model of a racing car, protection would be available for the shape or configuration of that article. Again, the exclusions in s.213(3) appear not to be relevant and the requirement of originality, in the copyright sense, would be easy enough to satisfy. Interesting arguments might be raised, however, concerning the requirement that the shape must not be **commonplace** in the design field in question. If the design field is toy cars, how commonplace is the design?

thinking point
To what extent does the law of registered and unregistered designs provide a mechanism for protecting merchandising activities?

Design right does, however, provide narrower protection than copyright, with only one restricted act, namely copying the design by the commercial manufacture of articles to that design (CDPA s.226) and is *de facto* limited to a period of five years from first marketing because of the availability of **licences of right** during the last five years of the term of protection (CDPA s.237). Should, however, there be both copyright and design right in the same drawing, then copyright will prevail (CDPA s.236).

18.4 **Possible means of protection: registered trade marks**

It might be thought that the TMA improved the protection available to merchandisers. The list of what can be a trade mark under s.1 is much broader than before and the scope of protection

cross reference
See section 12.4.

in an infringement action is far greater than under the Trade Marks Act 1938. Despite that, the law of registered trade marks continues to present a significant number of challenges to those seeking legal protection for legitimate merchandising activities. When examining the difficulties which await the owner of the image, current United Kingdom law should be evaluated critically in the light of the ECJ's pronouncements about trade mark function in Case C-206/01 *Arsenal Football Club v Matthew Reed* [2002] ECR I-10273. For convenience, merchandising issues arising under the law of registered trade marks are subdivided into registrability, loss of registration (whether by way of **revocation** or **invalidity**), infringement and licensing.

18.4.1 Registrability

In relation to the registrability of names and images, current practice is set out in detail in the Trade Marks Registry Works Manual (available online from the **United Kingdom Intellectual Property Office ('UKIPO')** website). Where appropriate, we refer to the Manual.

18.4.1.1 Registrability of names

Despite the 'fresh start' which might have been expected under the TMA, two key cases decided under the previous law form the basis of the current policy on the registration of names of celebrities, namely *TARZAN Trade Mark* [1970] RPC 450 and *ELVIS PRESLEY Trade Marks*. In *TARZAN*, the Court of Appeal held that although the name had been an invented word at the time Edgar Rice Burroughs had written the first of his stories about the character, at the date of the application to register the name for films and toys, it was no longer invented, but instead had a 'direct reference to the character or quality of the goods' (to quote the language of s.9(1)(d) of the Trade Marks Act 1938, the counterpart of which is s.3(1)(c) TMA). The same objection was raised in the *ELVIS PRESLEY Trade Marks* case. The name did not indicate to the consumer that there was a connection in the course of trade between toiletries and Elvis Presley Enterprises (the singer's successors), simply that the mark commemorated the singer. It told consumers about the nature of the goods, not their origin.

The principal grounds of challenge to registering the name of a celebrity under the TMA will be the **Absolute Grounds** of refusal found in ss.3(1)(b) and (c). In other words, the name will either be devoid of distinctive character (it doesn't say to the consumer 'I am a trade mark') or it will describe the characteristics of the goods. In particular, in relation to deceased celebrities, the public may not perceive the name as indicating commercial origin, rather the name will simply commemorate the person in question. The thinking in *ELVIS PRESLEY Trade Marks* was transposed into the 1994 Act in *DIANA, PRINCESS OF WALES Trade Mark* [2001] ETMR 254 and *JANE AUSTEN Trade Mark* [2000] RPC 879. Both decisions should be considered critically in light of the decision of the ECJ in *Arsenal Football Club v Matthew Reed*. The ECJ thought the perceptions of the consumer (who need not be the original purchaser) went beyond simply recognising the commercial origin of the goods. If the trade marks in *Arsenal* could be infringed even though the purchasers of football shirts and scarves saw the marks as 'badges of loyalty', then arguably the names of deceased personalities could be registrable even though they may be regarded as a form of commemoration.

ECJ case law on the Absolute Grounds of refusal require ss.3(1)(b) and (c) to be applied in a concrete manner, that is, in relation to the goods and services of the application and through the eyes of the average consumer who is deemed to be reasonably well informed, reasonably

observant and circumspect. In relation to the registration of famous names, the Trade Marks Registry Works Manual draws a distinction between different types of goods. Where the name is to be used on printed publications, sound recordings or films, for example, such use implies some form of control or guarantee, so that the name is *prima facie* registrable. Where, however, the goods are what the Registry calls 'mere image carriers' (posters, photographs, transfers and figurines) the name will be seen by consumers as simply descriptive of the subject matter of the product.

case close-up

LINKIN PARK Trade Mark Application (7 February 2005)

An application of the Registry's practice occurred in the decision of the Appointed Person in *LINKIN PARK Trade Mark Application* (7 February 2005). Just as in the *TARZAN* case, it was accepted that the trade mark (the name of a rock group) was an invented word when the group was formed, but by the date of the application to register the mark for posters was no longer so. The Appointed Person concluded that the mark was therefore descriptive of the characteristics of the goods because a fan of the group, had they gone into a shop selling posters, would have asked for 'a LINKIN PARK poster'. What the decision overlooks, however, is that the applicant company had been specifically formed as a merchandising vehicle for the group. Further, the posters in question were not necessarily posters *of* the group. Just like books, 'posters' as the goods of the registration are content neutral and can depict anything.

thinking point

Is the policy set out in the Trade Marks Registry Works Manual and in the LINKIN PARK Trade Mark Application *decision in accord with the ruling of the ECJ in* Arsenal v Reed?

18.4.1.2 Registrability of three-dimensional shapes

Any attempt to register the likeness of the character or celebrity as a three-dimensional trade mark (for example in respect of dolls or figurines) might be met by the objection under s.3(2)(c) TMA, namely that the shape gives substantial value to the goods. In other words, consumers buy the goods primarily for their shape and not for any other purpose. If a film company decides to make toys in the shape of one of its popular characters (for example, 'Darth Vader' from *Star Wars*), or if a car manufacturer launches a range of toy cars as scale models, s.3(2)(c) would logically prevent the registration of the various shapes as a trade marks, because the items are 'collectibles'. The shape gives substantial value to the goods.

18.4.2 **Loss of registration**

18.4.2.1 Protection against revocation for non-use

A further problem is that use of the name or likeness of a character or celebrity on promotional goods may not suffice to protect the trade mark against **revocation** for non-use under s.46(1)

(a) or (b) TMA especially if the consumer sees the mark as commemorating the celebrity rather than indicating origin. Under the 1938 Act, promotional use of the KODAK mark on T-shirts was not enough to protect the trade mark owner against revocation in *KODIAK Trade Mark* [1990] FSR 49: the mark had been used to sell photographic equipment not clothing. By contrast, it has been suggested (albeit by way of *obiter*) that promotional use does suffice under the TMA: *Premier Brands UK Ltd v Typhoon Europe Ltd* [2000] FSR 767.

However, more specific guidance has been given by the ECJ in two cases referred to it under Article 267 TFEU. First, the Court offered general guidance as to the meaning of 'use' in Case C-40/01 *Ansul BV v Ajax Brandbeveiliging BV* [2003] ECR I-2439, a case which relies heavily on the ruling in *Arsenal* as to what constitutes 'trade mark use'. Use is 'genuine' where the mark is used in accordance with its essential function. In other words, the mark must guarantee the identity of the origin of the goods or services for which it is registered, in order to create or preserve an outlet for those goods or services. When assessing whether use of the trade mark is genuine, regard must be had to all the facts and circumstances, particularly whether other traders would regard the use as justified to maintain or create a share in the market for the goods or services protected by the mark. The court should also consider the nature of those goods or services, the characteristics of the market, and the scale and frequency of use of the mark. Second, and particularly relevant to merchandising activities, in Case C-495/07 *Silberquelle GmbH v Maselli-Strickmode GmbH* [2009] ECR I-137 the ECJ ruled that there had not been genuine use of the trade mark (WELLNESS for drinks) where the proprietor had affixed it to bottles of alcohol-free drinks which it then gave away free to customers who bought items of clothing sold under the same mark. The drinks mark (as opposed to the clothing mark) had been correctly revoked for non-use.

cross reference
See section 15.3.2.

In this area, just as in other areas of trade mark law, the views of the consumer will be relevant, especially in view of the ECJ's pronouncements in relation to infringement in Case C-48/05 *Adam Opel AG v Autec* [2007] ECR I-1017 and Case C-17/06 *Céline SARL v Céline SA* [2007] ECR I-7041.

18.4.2.2 Protection against invalidity

Even if the Registry permits registration of a mark to be used in merchandising, this will not stop a third party seeking a declaration that the mark is **invalid** under one or more of the Absolute Grounds. A counter-argument that the trade mark owner may seek to raise is that the mark, although initially contrary to s.3(1), has been saved by factual distinctiveness acquired since registration (s.47(1) TMA). This raises the same question as in relation to revocation, namely whether promotional use suffices for acquired distinctiveness. In *Arsenal v Reed*, at first instance, Laddie J held that the football club had made sufficient use of its marks to defeat the counterclaim for a declaration of invalidity.

case close-up

The Rugby Football Union v Cotton Traders Ltd [2002] EWHC 467

A different outcome occurred, however, in *The Rugby Football Union v Cotton Traders Ltd* [2002] EWHC 467. In what was basically a contractual dispute, the RFU had sued its former **licensee**, claiming *inter alia* infringement of its **EU trade mark** registration for a modified version of the English Rugby Rose symbol. Lloyd J upheld the defendant's counterclaim for a declaration of invalidity, on the ground that the registered mark was not perceived by the public as a badge of origin but as a national emblem. In contrast to the facts of *Arsenal v Reed*, the English Rugby Rose had never been used for swing tickets or neck labels, a different rose symbol being used for that purpose, but instead was emblazoned on the front of rugby jerseys, so that neither at the date of application for registration nor at the date of the counterclaim for invalidity was the mark distinctive of the goods or associated with the RFU. At the time of the decision, Lloyd J did not have the benefit of the ECJ's ruling in *Arsenal v Reed* as to what constitutes 'trade mark use', albeit such a wide approach must now be tempered by the Court's subsequent pronouncements in *Adam Opel AG v Autec* and *Céline SARL v Céline SA*. However, is it really the case that an individual team (in whatever sporting discipline) can benefit from trade mark protection in its merchandising activities but a national side cannot?

thinking point

Can the decision in The Rugby Football Union v Cotton Traders Ltd *be reconciled with the ruling of the ECJ in* Arsenal v Reed?

18.4.3 **Infringement**

18.4.3.1 Infringement: 'trade mark use'

When it comes to the unauthorised use of the name or likeness of a character or celebrity on merchandise, the most obvious argument which the alleged infringer may raise is that what they have done does not amount to 'trade mark use' for the purposes of s.10 TMA. Under the pre-1994 law, the application of a slogan as decoration to T-shirts was held not to amount to trade mark use in *Unidoor v Marks & Spencer plc* [1988] RPC 275 because it was merely decorative, and did not indicate origin. By contrast, the ECJ has indicated that in the case of a trade mark with a reputation, decorative use may amount to infringement for the purposes of s.10(3): Case C-408/01 *Adidas-Saloman AG and Adidas Benelux BV v Fitnessworld Trading Ltd* [2003] ECR I-12537 at [38–41] as long as the consumer makes a mental link between the decorative matter and the registered mark. Further, the meaning of 'trade mark use' was extended radically by the ECJ in *Arsenal Football Club v Matthew Reed*. The Court ruled that even if goods are bought by football fans as a 'badge of loyalty', this still amounts to trade mark use, because the fan will assume that the football club is responsible for the quality of the goods. By analogy, if an Elvis Presley fan buys a cup bearing Elvis' name or picture, would this amount to trade mark use for the purposes of infringement, assuming, that is, that the name or image had been successfully registered as a trade mark? Would the Elvis fan think they were buying something for which Elvis' successors had been responsible, or would they think that this merely commemorated his life?

The statement in *Arsenal* that the views of the end user are what matters can therefore be a double-edged sword. The answers offered by the ECJ in *Adam Opel AG v Autec* to the question of whether a reproduction of the claimant's trade mark on a model car infringed depends entirely on what the end user thinks. If the customer thinks the model car was made by the trade mark owner, there is infringement; if the customer thinks the model is simply a faithful replica of the full-sized car there is no liability. One can easily transplant this case into the Elvis example, or into the scenario where the defendant is offering unauthorised reproductions of Formula 1 racing cars.

18.4.3.2 Infringement: descriptive use

cross reference
See section 15.4.4.4.

One of the defences to infringement found in s.11(2) TMA is that the use of the mark has been to describe the characteristics of the goods. This is, however, qualified by the proviso that such use must not be contrary to honest practices in industrial and commercial matters. This phrase is the definition of unfair competition in Article 10*bis* **Paris Convention**. In the context of defences to trade mark infringement, the ECJ has explained that the proviso to s.11(2) involves 'the duty to act fairly in relation to the legitimate interests of the trade mark proprietor' (Case C-100/02 *Gerolsteiner Brunnen GmbH v Putsch GmbH* [2004] ECR I-691).

case close-up

> **Bravado Merchandising v Mainstream Publishing** [1996] FSR 205
>
> An example of the descriptive use defence being used in the context of merchandising activities is *Bravado Merchandising v Mainstream Publishing* [1996] FSR 205. The defendant had published an unauthorised biography of the pop group 'Wet Wet Wet' entitled *A Sweet Little Mystery—Wet, Wet, Wet—The Inside Story*. It was held that although all the elements of trade mark infringement had been established, the defence of descriptive use in s.11(2)(b) came to the rescue. The case should be treated with a degree of caution, partly because of the concessions made by counsel as to the requirement of trade mark use, and because it pre-dates many key ECJ decisions, in particular *Arsenal v Reed*, *Adidas v Fitnessworld* and *Putsch*. However, the case is entirely consistent with the policy of UKIPO in relation to celebrity names on 'image carriers' set out in *LINKIN PARK Trade Mark Application* and discussed earlier.

thinking point

Does the ECJ's requirement that the perception of the consumer is all important in deciding whether a registered trade mark has been infringed have any implications for merchandising?

18.4.4 Merchandising and quality control in trade mark licences

Celebrities who wish to make money out of their image, or the creators of films and television programmes who wish to take advantage of the success of their work will often register trade marks as the first step in the merchandising process. Assuming that the difficulties listed earlier can be overcome, and registration is obtained, the next step is to enter into a series of trade mark licences with those who wish to exploit the name or image in question.

The TMA made the business of trade mark licensing more straightforward than its predecessor. It declares that a trade mark is personal property (s.22) so that it can be **assigned** like any other form of intangible personal property, whether with or without the goodwill of the business (s.24). 'Goodwill' means 'the attractive force which brings in custom' and 'that which distinguishes an old business from a new' (*per* Lord McNaghten in *CIR v Muller & Co's Margarine Ltd* [1901] AC 217). Further, under s.28(1) TMA, a trade mark can be licensed, either in a general or in a limited manner, partial licences being either as to some of the goods or services, as to a locality, or as to manner of use. A trade mark licence (whether **exclusive** or **non-exclusive**, general or partial) must be in writing and signed by the trade mark proprietor (s.28(2)). A trade mark licence will bind the proprietor's successor in title unless it says otherwise. The licensee can grant sublicences unless there is a provision to the contrary. However, like any other transaction affecting the property right in the mark, the licence must be recorded at the Trade Marks Registry (s.25, as amended). Failure to do so means that the licensee is at risk from the later arrival of a *bona fide* purchaser of the mark, and the licensee will not obtain the procedural rights conferred on them by the TMA. Failure to record the licence within six months of its being granted (or as soon as practicable thereafter) means that the claimant will not be awarded costs in any subsequent infringement action.

An exclusive licensee (as defined in s.29) is given certain procedural rights by s.31. However, even though the licensee can bring infringement proceedings in their own name, this does not give them any proprietary rights over the trade mark. A trade mark licence simply confers personal rights: *Northern & Shell v Condé Nast* [1995] RPC 117.

The critical clause which must be present in a trade mark licence is one imposing an obligation on the licensee to comply with the proprietor's instructions as to the quality of the goods. The proprietor must be able to dictate quality and to ensure that the obligation is being observed. The sorts of clauses which are normally inserted in a trade mark licence are those requiring the licensee to submit samples periodically, or those which permit the proprietor to enter the licensee's premises with a view to checking the quality of the goods being made there.

cross reference
See section 12.4.

The reason why quality control is so important is because it impinges on the functions which trade marks fulfil. Under the 1938 Act, where the only recognised function was that of indicating origin, to license a trade mark without an effective system of quality control undermined the origin function and rendered the trade mark deceptive. Further, if the trade mark proprietor was willing to grant an unlimited number of licences to other firms, then that would amount to 'trafficking in a trade mark', a practice which meant that the Registrar could refuse to register any licence relating to that mark: *Re American Greetings Corporation's Application* [1984] 1 All ER 426 (HL).

The prohibition on 'trafficking in a trade mark' (that is, treating the mark as a commodity in its own right) is no longer in the United Kingdom legislation. However, the presence of quality control is relevant as regards the revocation of trade marks. It had been held under the 1938 Act that where the trade mark owner failed to exercise contractual rights of control (in effect leading to a 'bare' licence of the mark) the mark would be at risk for revocation for non-use, because the use of the mark accrued to the licensee not the **licensor**: *JOB Trade Mark* [1993] FSR 118. This is not the case under the TMA, because any use with consent is enough to prevent revocation under s.46(1)(a) or (b). However, might uncontrolled licensing make the mark liable to revocation under s.46(1)(d) because it has become deceptive? The matter was considered at some length by the House of Lords in *Scandecor Development AB v Scandecor Marketing AB* [2001] 2 CMLR 645 (a complex contractual dispute which should never have come to court). Their Lordships were prepared to refer questions to the ECJ about this link between uncontrolled licensing and revocation, but at the last moment the case was settled and so the questions were never put. However, in view of the ECJ's reasoning in Case C-259/04 *Emanuel v Continental Shelf 128 Ltd* [2006] ECR I-3089 'deception' as an element of s.46(1)(d) requires the mark itself to be *inherently* deceptive, so it seems unlikely that sloppy licensing could lead to revocation. The Court said that under both Articles 3 and 12 of the First Trade Marks Directive (Council Directive 89/104/EEC of 21 December 1988 on the approximation of the laws of Member States relating to trade marks [1989] OJ L 40/1, now codified as Directive 2008/95/EC of the European Parliament and of the Council of 22 October 2008 [2008] OJ L 299/25) ('the Directive') 'deceptive' means that the mark must objectively deceive as a result of its inherent qualities. Applying that in the merchandising context, failure to exercise quality control no longer has any implications for revocation.

Nevertheless, there is another ECJ ruling which does suggest that there is a positive reason to insist on quality control provisions in a trade mark licence, and to ensure that they are enforced, because in the context of **parallel imports** this gives the trade mark owner enhanced powers.

case close-up

Case C-59/08 *Copad SA v Christian Dior Couture SA* [2009] ECR I-3421

Case C-59/08 *Copad SA v Christian Dior Couture SA* [2009] ECR I-3421 shows that breach of the terms of a licence (at least one involving luxury goods) may entitle the proprietor to sue the licensee for infringement under Article 8(2) of the Directive because the quality of the goods might be affected (one of the conditions set out in Article 8(2)). Further, because of the quality control clause, the licence does not amount to absolute and unconditional consent so that there can be no **exhaustion of rights** within the **EEA**. A further argument is that even if such contractual breach does not trigger the right to sue under Article 8(2), the proprietor can rely on Article 7(2) of the Directive and can oppose further commercialisation of the goods, but only where it could be established that the resale of the goods could damage the reputation of the trade mark.

thinking point
How important do you think provisions as to quality control in trade mark licences are in the context of merchandising?

This aspect of the law of registered trade marks should be compared with the passing off cases on character merchandising, particularly the decisions in *Children's Television Workshop Inc v Woolworths (NSW) Ltd* [1981] RPC 187 (the *MUPPETS* case) and *NINJA TURTLES*. It was highly significant in both cases that the owners of the images had inserted effective quality control provisions in their licences. Further, in each case, the court commented adversely on the poor quality of the defendant's goods.

(18.5) # Possible means of protection: passing off

Copyright law is incapable of protecting the name of a character or the title of a film or television series. In the absence of trade mark registration, passing off would appear to be the most logical means of providing protection for a name. It might be thought that the claimant simply has to satisfy the 'classic trinity' established by Lord Oliver in *Reckitt & Colman Products Ltd v Borden Inc* [1990] 1 WLR 491, namely reputation, misrepresentation and damage. Further, there is no rule that the claimant and defendant must be trading in the same or related fields in order to succeed in passing off (*Lego Systems A/S v Lego M Lemelstrich Ltd* [1983] FSR 155, *Harrods v Harrodian School* [1996] RPC 697). Despite this last point, the lack of a common field of activity is often fatal to a claim for passing off in character merchandising cases. This is not because a common field of activity is an express requirement for liability, but rather lack of direct competition between claimant and defendant means that the consumer is not misled by the defendant's implied misrepresentation of approval or sponsorship. If the misrepresentation does not create a material reliance, so that the consumer alters their economic behaviour, then there is no harm to the claimant's goodwill. Instead, all the defendant has done, in Carty's words, is to cash in 'on the feel-good factor or magnetism of the celebrity'.

cross reference
See section 13.2.

18.5.1 **Protecting the names of real or fictitious characters**

In United Kingdom passing off actions where the claimant has sought to protect the *names* of characters or celebrities (whether real or fictitious), the defendant (ie the copyist) has generally succeeded. The reason for this outcome is, quite simply, that no harm has been done to the claimant's business. If the claimant makes films or television programmes, then the goodwill in that business is not diminished if a third party makes and sells merchandise. If the claimant is an individual celebrity actor or singer trying to protect their image against lookalike or soundalike imitations, then again they have no business goodwill to protect. Arguments that the public are used to merchandising activities and expect the claimant to have approved or endorsed the products are normally dismissed out of hand by the judges.

One case where the claimant was successful was *Shaw Bros v Golden Harvest* [1972] RPC 559, where the Hong Kong court granted protection for the name of a martial arts film character, 'the one-armed swordsman'. However, both claimant and defendant were in the same line of business, that is, they were both film producers, so harm to goodwill by competition was established.

United Kingdom cases have not been so kind. In *Wombles v Wombles Skips* [1977] RPC 99 (*WOMBLES*), the creator of the WOMBLES (characters in a children's television programme who liked to clear up rubbish) was unable to prevent the defendant trading under the name 'Wombles Skips' (a business specialising in waste removal). The lack of a common field of activity meant that there was no harm to goodwill. The identical outcome in the South African DALLAS decision (*Lorimar v Sterling*) has already been noted. Even the names of real people (as opposed to fictitious characters) have received similar treatment, so that the group ABBA were unable to prevent third parties producing merchandise bearing the name of the group: *Lyngstad v Anabas*. In *ELVIS PRESLEY Trade Marks*, the Court of Appeal remarked (at pp. 593 and 597) that the fame of Elvis Presley was as a singer, not as a producer of toiletries. There was no reason why he or any organisation of his should be concerned with toiletries so as to give rise to some perceived connection between his name and the product. There should be no assumption that only a celebrity or his successors could ever market or license the marketing of his own character. 'Monopolies should not be so readily created.'

To make matters worse, there are instances where the interloper has successfully sued the official licensee of the right for passing off, for the simple reason that having come to the market first, the free-rider has established their own goodwill in the name. The classic example of this is *Taverner Rutledge v Trexapalm* [1977] RPC 275 (*KOJAK*), where the official licensee from the makers of the KOJAK television series was sued for passing off by a sweet manufacturer who had been selling KOJAK lollipops for some time. It was the sweet manufacturer who had established goodwill in the name, and the 'rightful' licensee was harming the copyist's goodwill. The licensee's rights in the name (which had not been registered as a trade mark and the goodwill of which related only to television programmes) were 'as writ in water' (*per* Walton J). Similarly, the official licensee of NASA, the United States space agency, had no rights against a clothing manufacturer who had been selling leisure wear under the same name: *Nice and Safe Attitude Ltd v Flook* [1997] FSR 22.

18.5.2 **The public perception of merchandising**

Despite the remarks in the previously discussed cases of *Lyngstad v Anabas* and *Lorimar v Sterling* to the effect that the public do not expect the owner of the image to have endorsed the defendant's product, some United Kingdom cases have shown a slightly more realistic awareness of the public perception of merchandising.

case close-up

> **IPC Magazines Ltd v Black and White Music Corp** [1983] FSR 348
>
> The claimant sought an interim **injunction** to restrain the defendants from releasing a record named after, and containing a song about, the claimant's science-fiction cartoon character JUDGE DREDD. JUDGE DREDD enjoyed a cult following and, by the time of the case, both the drawings and the name had been the subject of merchandising agreements (it may be observed that the case was some years before the making of the *Judge Dredd* film). The claimant argued that it had suffered damage under two headings, namely damage to the reputation of its character, and damage to its existing licensing operations. It was alleged that others would be encouraged to use the character without seeking licences. Goulding J was prepared to accept that misrepresentation had been established because members of the public might think that the record was approved by the claimant. But the claimant had failed to show damage to reputation (the record was 'no worse' than others in the charts) and there was no evidence that others would use the character without a licence.

thinking point

Do judicial pronouncements on the public perception of the licensing of names and images accord with reality?

18.5.3 **Protecting the appearance of a character**

The most significant decision under United Kingdom law is that in the *NINJA TURTLES* case. However, as Browne-Wilkinson VC relied heavily on *Children's Television Workshop Inc v Woolworths (NSW) Ltd* [1981] RPC 187 (the *MUPPETS* case) it will be useful to consider this first.

18.5.3.1 An Antipodean approach

case close-up

Children's Television Workshop Inc v Woolworths (NSW) Ltd [1981] RPC 187 (the *MUPPETS* case)

In the *MUPPETS* case, the claimant was the producer of the television series SESAME STREET and the creator of the MUPPETS. The MUPPET characters had been licensed in Australia for a wide variety of products including soft toys. All licensed products were manufactured under strict quality control. The defendant **commissioned** the making of cheap imitation MUPPET soft toys and sold them through its WOOLWORTHS stores. Copyright protection was not available to the claimant because the design of the MUPPETS should have been registered under the then Australian registered design law but had not been. Nevertheless, the court granted interim relief. The court applied the 'classic trinity' of passing off to the facts of the case. The claimant had established a reputation: the evidence showed that the public would recognise the toys as the MUPPET characters from SESAME STREET. Further, the public was aware of the practice of character merchandising and would associate the toys with the claimant, hence there was misrepresentation. The parties were operating in a common field of activity. Both were concerned with getting MUPPET toys on the market, albeit through licensing arrangements rather than manufacture in the case of the claimant. The defendant was passing off its goods as those of the claimant made under licence. Lastly, the defendant's toys were 'lousy imitations', thus causing damage to the claimant's goodwill.

18.5.3.2 The *NINJA TURTLES* case

case close-up

Mirage Studios v Counter-Feat Clothing [1991] FSR 145 (the *NINJA TURTLES* case)

The claimant owned copyright in the drawings for the characters TEENAGE MUTANT NINJA TURTLES. It did not manufacture or market the goods itself, being concerned mainly with the creation of cartoons, films and videos depicting the characters. However, a major part of its revenue was derived from royalties received under various licensing agreements made with those who wished to use the characters to sell goods (over 150 licences had been granted in the United Kingdom). Each licence contained quality control provisions. The defendant also made drawings of humanoid turtles (in sporting guise), relying on the turtle concept rather than the claimant's actual drawings. The defendant licensed its drawings to certain manufacturers to reproduce the images on clothing. Browne-Wilkinson VC granted the claimant an injunction for the reason that there was an arguable case of copyright infringement. Also, the essential requirements for passing off propounded by Lord Diplock in *Warnink v Townend* had been made out. The public had mistaken the defendant's turtle characters for the claimant's turtles and they 'expect and know that where a famous cartoon or television character is reproduced on goods, that reproduction is the result of a licence granted by the owner of the copyright or owner of other rights in that character'. An important part of the claimant's business consisted of licensing the copyright in the NINJA TURTLES drawings and there would be loss of royalties if the unauthorised exploitation of the drawings was allowed. The licensing right would be significantly reduced by placing turtle pictures on inferior goods.

Two key points to note about the decision in *NINJA TURTLES* are that:

- there was a common field of activity. The claimant was able to show extensive merchandising activities. Both parties were in the business of licensing pictures of turtle characters, although neither was actually concerned in the manufacture or selling of the goods;
- the claimant was licensing copyright material. Passing off exists to protect the goodwill in a business, and here, the claimant's business included licensing activities rather than just making films. Harm to the claimant's goodwill was therefore caused by the defendant's conduct.

The existence of copyright material also enabled Browne-Wilkinson VC to distinguish earlier United Kingdom authorities (*WOMBLES, KOJAK* and *ABBA*) because these were concerned with the licensing of names (in which there was no copyright, and therefore no separate business in licensing their use) and to express his preference for the Australian authorities, chiefly the *MUPPETS* case. Whether or not this intertwining of passing off and copyright was doctrinally sound, the case has the merit of providing an effective remedy for unauthorised merchandising.

18.5.4 Celebrity endorsements

Another type of merchandising activity which has received judicial scrutiny in the context of passing off is where the name of an organisation or a famous person is used to endorse a product. If the organisation or person has not agreed to the use of their name, this may amount to passing off. Until recently, the cases revealed the possibility of two different outcomes, depending on whether the name in question was that of a professional body or a commercial organisation on the one hand, or an individual on the other. For example, in *BMA v Marsh* (1931) 48 RPC 565, the British Medical Association was able to prevent a pharmacist placing the letters BMA above his shop; and in *Walter v Ashton* [1902] 2 Ch 282, the *Times* newspaper could prevent its name being used to sell bicycles. By contrast, in *Sim v Heinz* [1959] RPC 75, it was held that there was no misrepresentation of endorsement where the defendant's television advertisement for its soup imitated the voice of a famous actor. In *McCulloch v May* (1947) 65 RPC 58, the presenter of children's radio programmes could not restrain the sale of breakfast cereal using his name ('Uncle Mac') as there was no common field of activity. Lastly, in *Stringfellow v McCain Foods (GB) Ltd* [1984] RPC 501, a nightclub owner unsuccessfully argued that the defendant had committed passing off when it had called its oven chips 'Stringfellows'. The public would not be misled into thinking that the claimant had approved the product.

18.5.4.1 Australian cases

Again, Australian cases have shown a more generous attitude to celebrity endorsements. In *Henderson v Radio Corporation Pty Ltd* [1969] RPC 218, it was accepted that a common field of activity is not an essential requirement for passing off. Passing off, it was said, is established on proof of misrepresentation and it is not necessary to prove actual damage. It is enough that the claimant has been deprived of the right to approve the product for a fee. Thus, in *Henderson* itself, well-known professional ballroom dancers were held entitled to prevent the sale of a dance music record which carried their photograph.

thinking point
Consider whether the blending of copyright and passing off in NINJA TURTLES was theoretically unsound or justified in terms of the outcome of the case.

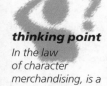

thinking point
In the law of character merchandising, is a cartoon character better protected than a pop star?

517

In two later cases, involving the actor Paul Hogan and his fictitious film character 'Mick "Crocodile" Dundee', the Australian courts went considerably further, bearing in mind that in both cases the misrepresentations involved a mixture of celebrity endorsement of the type found in *Henderson* and taking the appearance of the character of the type found in the *MUPPETS* case. In *Hogan v Koala Dundee Pty Ltd* (1988) 83 ALR 187 the defendant used both the name DUNDEE and the image of a koala bear wearing clothing reminiscent of that worn in the *Crocodile Dundee* films by Paul Hogan. An injunction was granted, the court accepting that the public are familiar with the practice of character merchandising and will believe that an image-bearing product is produced under licence from or with the approval of the image owner. In *Pacific Dunlop Ltd v Hogan* (1989) 87 ALR 14 the defendant had advertised its shoes by means of a parody of the 'knife' scene from the first *Crocodile Dundee* film. What was taken here could hardly be said to be copyright material (one line of dialogue) yet the court was prepared to grant a remedy on the basis that passing off *ought* to cover the intentional misappropriation of personality, or 'image filching'. The crucial factor in each case appears to be the misappropriation by the defendant rather than any harm to goodwill caused by customer confusion.

18.5.4.2 A change of heart in the United Kingdom

case close-up

Irvine v Talksport Ltd [2002] 2 All ER 414

A significant change of attitude to celebrity endorsement as a category of passing off can be found in *Irvine v Talksport*. The important points to note about the case are:

- the claimant was already in the business of entering agreements for the use of his name and/ or image to sell goods and services and therefore had a business goodwill to protect. This finding of fact enabled Laddie J to distinguish the practice of endorsement from what might be termed 'mere' merchandising, such as occurred in the *DIANA, PRINCESS OF WALES Trade Mark* case;

- Laddie J rejected the requirement of common field of activity in *McCulloch v May* (although it had already been discredited by the Court of Appeal in *Harrods v Harrodian School*), preferring instead the thinking of the Australian court in *Henderson v Radio Corporation Pty Ltd*; and

- Laddie J was prepared to recognise the fact that the public is aware of the practice of celebrity endorsement.

As Carty observes, although *Irvine v Talksport* at face value appears to comply with the strict requirements of passing off, it has the potential to be expanded by subsequent cases into a tort of misappropriation. Carty further argues that the 'classic trinity' should continue to be strictly applied, so that passing off should not merely prevent 'cashing in on fame'. Liability should only occur where there is a real message of endorsement, leading to a material reliance on the misrepresentation. Conjuring up a vague impression of association with the celebrity should not suffice. This would then lead to consistency with the decision of the Court of Appeal in *Harrods v Harrodian School*, to the effect that simply to hint at 'official' approval or sponsorship may not be enough for liability if there is not origin confusion. The public must have a mistaken belief that the claimant actually endorsed the defendant's product.

Another example of passing off being used successfully to protect the name and image of an individual is *Clark v Associated Newspapers* [1998] 1 All ER 959. Here, a well-known politician and author was able to get an injunction to restrain a newspaper from publishing a column entitled 'Alan Clark's Secret Election Diary'. The defendant had failed to do enough to prevent the public from being misled into thinking that the claimant had actually written the column when he had not. A significant factor was that the claimant had already published some of his memoirs ('The Alan Clark Diaries') which had proved highly successful. He therefore had a reputation as an author which was capable of protection.

Last, *Irvine v Talksport* has been used to justify the outcome in *Fenty v Arcadia Group Brands Ltd* [2013] EWHC 2310 (Ch). The singer Rihanna successfully sued the defendant for passing off in respect of T-shirts bearing her image. Birss J noted that the claimant, through her companies, ran a very large merchandising and endorsement operation. He considered that the thinking in *Irvine*, although declared by Laddie to be concerned only with endorsement, was equally applicable to merchandising activities, though he stressed that the case was not about image rights. There had been misrepresentation here because a substantial number of customers would be deceived into thinking that this was an authorised image.

thinking point
Should there be more effective protection against the unauthorised misappropriation of celebrity?

18.6 Possible means of protection: breach of confidence

One aspect of breach of confidence which is relevant to merchandising is the extent to which celebrities can control the use of their image in the media. However careful a celebrity may be in their choice of photographer and the use of contractual arrangement to control the use of so-called 'exclusive' photographs, ownership of photographic copyright does not prevent someone else taking their own photograph, a problem exacerbated not just by the activities of the paparazzi but also by the advent of digital cameras and camera phones.

At one time, it was said, there was no general law of privacy (*Kaye v Robertson*) and, indeed, no law of personality in the United Kingdom. A celebrity who was photographed in a public place had little redress, unless that photograph was taken surreptitiously (*Naomi Campbell v MGN* [2004] 2 AC 457; *Murray v Express Newspapers* [2009] Ch 481). The result, however, was different if the photograph was taken on private premises: *Theakston v Mirror Group Newspapers*, Ouseley J, 14 February 2002; *Shelley Films v Rex Features* [1994] EMLR 134.

The decision of the European Court of Human Rights in *Von Hannover v Germany (No 1)* has had a significant impact in relation to celebrities wishing to control the activities of paparazzi. The case imposes a positive obligation on Member States of the European Convention on Human Rights ('ECHR') to protect an individual against the unjustified invasion of their private life by another individual, and a further obligation on the courts of a Member State to interpret domestic legislation in a way which will achieve that result (*Douglas v Hello! Ltd (No 2)* [2005] 4 All ER 128 (CA) at [49]). The means to achieve such protection against the invasion of privacy is to adopt the cause of action formerly described as breach of confidence, taking into account the rights found in Article 8 and 10 ECHR (*Douglas v Hello! Ltd (No 2)* at [53]). The action is properly called the misuse of personal information (*Naomi Campbell v MGN* at [14] *per* Lord Nicholls) and the correct test is to ask whether the claimant had a reasonable expectation of privacy (*Naomi Campbell v MGN* at [21], again *per* Lord Nicholls), viewed through the eyes of a reasonable person with the claimant's sensibilities (*per* Lord Hope at [99]; *Murray v Express Newspapers*).

Use of the action for breach of confidence to prevent unwelcome photographic intrusion appears to go far beyond the events of *Douglas v Hello! Ltd (No 2)* (CA). Here, a significant fact was the reliance on confidentiality undertakings to ensure that the claimants' wedding remained as private an event as possible, so as to prevent the taking of unauthorised photographs, such that the House of Lords thought that the case could just as well have been treated as an action for 'classical' breach of confidence rather than misuse of personal information: *Douglas and Zeta-Jones v Hello! Ltd* [2008] 1 AC 1 *per* Lord Hoffmann at [124]. Another instance of the effective use of a duty of confidence (this time implied rather than express) to restrain publication of photographs is *Creation Records v News Group Newspapers* [1997] EMLR 444, where Michael Mann QC held that the photographer sent by *The Sun* to cover the photo-shoot for the new Oasis CD should have known that the event was secret.

By contrast, the basis of the complaint in *Von Hannover v Germany (No 1)* was the repeated publication in magazines and newspapers of photographs of Princess Caroline of Monaco and her family going about their daily business rather than attending official functions. The photographs had been taken in public, and there were no confidentiality agreements attempting to control their dissemination. The Court observed that the sole purpose of the various publications was to satisfy readers' curiosity, rather than contribute to any debate of general public interest. The Court also remarked on the intrusive nature of repeated photography amounting to harassment, and the effect of technology in helping disseminate such photographs to a broad section of the public. The judgment therefore shifts the balance between Article 8 and Article 10 ECHR in favour of the individual's right to respect for private and family life.

There are signs that the decision in *Von Hannover v Germany (No 1)* has the potential to go beyond photographic intrusion and protect the celebrity from so-called 'kiss-and-tell' biographies. In *McKennitt v Ash* [2007] 3 WLR 194, the claimant was a very successful composer and performer of folk music. The defendant was a former friend who had worked closely with the claimant in connection with merchandising activities and who had accompanied her on tour. The defendant wrote a book called *Travels with Loreena McKennitt: My Life as a Friend*. The claimant sought to restrain publication on the basis of breach of privacy and/or breach of confidence. Eady J, subsequently confirmed by the Court of Appeal, held a significant shift had taken place between freedom of expression and the legitimate interest of the citizen to have their private lives protected. Even public interest had to yield to effective protection of private life. A number of passages in the book would fall within a reasonable expectation of privacy. The defendant would have been aware, at the time of and prior to publication, that much of the book would cause distress because of its intrusive nature. The passages complained of breached the claimant's reasonable expectation of privacy and should not have been published. The claimant was entitled to an injunction and to £5,000 **damages** for hurt feelings and distress. The same judge also decided the later case of *Mosley v News Group Newspapers* [2008] EWHC 1777, where he held that the claimant's right to privacy under Article 8 ECHR was not trumped by the newspaper's freedom of expression under Article 10 to disclose sado-masochistic behaviour 'in the public interest'. Nevertheless, in *Von Hannover*

thinking point

To what extent can the action for breach of confidence enable celebrities to control the dissemination of unwelcome photographs or biographies?

v Germany (No 2) [2012] ECHR 228 the ECtHR emphasised that the balance between Article 8 and 10 depends very much on the facts of the case. Whilst the earlier ruling treated the photographic intrusions into the Princess's daily life as simply satisfying readers' curiosity, in the later case the circumstances had changed. The Princess's father was gravely ill so it was a matter of public concern that she and her family continued regardless with their skiing holiday.

One other significant catalyst for change should be noted. In Case C-161/10 *Olivier Martinez v MGN* [2011] ECR I-10269, the ECJ ruled that under the Brussels Regulation (Council Regulation EC 44/2001 of 22 December 2000 on Jurisdiction and the Recognition and Enforcement of Judgments in Civil and Commercial Matters, [2001] OJ L 12/1), where a claimant's personality rights had been infringed by publication of private information on a website, proceedings could be brought in a number of Member States. These were either the Member State where the damage to the personality right was caused (here, France); or the Member State where the publisher was established (here the United Kingdom); or any other Member State where the online content was accessible. This meant that the claimant could object to the story published by the *Sunday Mirror* in France or in the United Kingdom or in any other Member State where the internet publication caused damage to his rights.

cross reference

See section 3.5.5.

Returning to the issue of photographic intrusion, if the *obiter* comments in *Douglas v Hello! Ltd (No 2)* (CA) and *Douglas and Zeta-Jones v Hello! Ltd* (HL) are followed, it also seems probable that an interim injunction is more likely to be granted to restrain the publication of unauthorised images, because of the unique ability of photographs to invade a person's privacy, not just once, but repeatedly, each time the photograph is published. What is unclear, however, is whether, should publication actually occur, more than nominal damages are to be awarded, particularly if the images are not very flattering. The Court of Appeal in *Douglas v Hello! Ltd (No 2)* did not disturb the award of damages to the claimants, a conclusion which is at odds with its remark to the effect that interim relief should have been granted. It may be that the underlying basis of the complaint was not so much invasion of privacy, but a loss of control over the right of publicity. Privacy and publicity are, of course, but two sides of the same coin, but need to be kept distinct. One is personal, the other is commercial.

Summary

This chapter has explained:

- the meaning of 'character merchandising' as a commercial activity;

- the choice of intellectual property rights which can be utilised in such an activity, together with the limitations on such rights; and

- the potential of United Kingdom law to provide better protection for merchandising activities in the future.

Reflective question

Would United Kingdom law benefit from the introduction of a right of personality?

Annotated further reading

Carty, H. 'Advertising, Publicity Rights and English Law' [2004] *IPQ* 209

Examines the decision in *Irvine v Talksport* and argues that the case should not be developed into a broader action for misappropriation of image.

Jaffey, P. 'Merchandising and the Law of Trade Marks' [1998] *IPQ* 240

Explores the role of passing off and registered trade marks in merchandising, arguing that the activity should be better protected.

Klink, J. 'Fifty Years of Publicity Rights in the United States and the Never Ending Hassle with Intellectual Property and Personality Rights in Europe' [2003] *IPQ* 363

Compares the position of celebrities under USA law with the difficulties encountered in various European legal systems in connection with merchandising rights.

Walsh, C. 'Are Personality Rights Finally on the UK Agenda?' [2013] *EIPR* 253

Argues that the ECJ's ruling in *Martinez v MGN* might help to fill the gaps in passing off, trade mark law and breach of confidence.

Glossary

Absolute Grounds Objections which may be raised against an application for a registered **trade mark** which concern the inherent nature of the trade mark itself. *Trade Marks Act 1994 section 3*.

Abstract One of the documents which must be provided when applying for a **patent**. It should contain a concise summary of the **invention** (normally in no more than 150 words), setting out the technical field to which the invention belongs, the problem addressed by the invention, its solution, and the invention's principal use(s). The purpose of the abstract is to facilitate searching. *Patents Act 1977 section 14*.

Account of Profits An equitable monetary remedy which seeks to transfer to the **claimant** the net profits made by the defendant. In some circumstances it can be a more effective means of redress than an award of **damages**.

Additional Damages In cases only of **copyright** and **unregistered design right infringement**, the award of additional compensation by a court where the defendant's conduct has been particularly flagrant. *CDPA 1988 sections 97 and 229*.

Advertisement Part of the procedure for the registration of a **trade mark**. Once it has been accepted for registration by the Trade Marks Registry after **examination**, the mark is advertised in the *Trade Marks Journal*. Owners of earlier rights wishing to lodge an **opposition** to the application have a maximum period of three months within which to do so. *Trade Marks Act 1994 section 38*.

Amendment In the case of **patents**, the **description** or **claims** may be amended, usually to avoid **prior art** or some other objection to **validity**. Amendment may be during application or after **grant**. An amendment of the description may not introduce matter extending beyond that disclosed in the application, and an amendment of the claims may not extend the scope of protection. An unallowable amendment to the description or claims is a ground of **revocation**. *Patents Act 1977 sections 19, 27, 72 and 76*. In the case of **trade marks**, an amendment to an application to register may *only* restrict **the statement of goods or services** or correct the **applicant's** details. *Trade Marks Act 1994 sections 39, 44*.

Anticipation In order to be patentable, an **invention** must be new, that is, is not form part of the state of the art. The state of the art comprises everything which has been made available to the public in the United Kingdom or elsewhere before the **priority date** of the invention. **Prior art** will anticipate an invention where it contains an **enabling disclosure**, that is, it enables the **skilled addressee**, without undue burden, to put the invention into effect.

Applicant A person or organisation seeking to obtain a **patent**, **registered design** or **trade mark**.

Article The subject matter of **unregistered design right** protection.

Assignee The person receiving the ownership of the intellectual property right as a result of the transfer.

Assignment The transfer of the ownership of an intellectual property right from one person or organisation to another. To be effective, the assignment must be in writing. In the case of registrable intellectual property rights, the change of ownership must be recorded on the relevant register of **patents**, **registered designs** or **trade marks**. Hence:

Assignor The transferor of the ownership of the intellectual property right.

Author In the case of **copyright**, the creator of a **work**. In order for a work to attract United Kingdom copyright, the author must be a **qualifying person**. In the case of works covered by the **Berne Convention**, it is the author's life which will determine the duration of protection, and it is the author who is given a number of **moral rights**.

Berne Convention The Berne Convention for the Protection of Literary and Artistic Works. The principal multilateral **copyright** convention, first signed at Berne in 1886 and last revised in Paris in 1971. It is administered by **WIPO** and obliges Contracting States to observe the principle of **national treatment**. It covers literary, dramatic, musical and artistic works and films, and stipulates that copyright protection is to arise automatically without the need for any formality such as registration or the use of a copyright notice.

Breach of Confidence The unauthorised use or disclosure of **confidential information** which has been communicated in circumstances (express or implied) when a duty of confidence arises.

Cancellation In the case of **registered designs**, the removal of a design from the register on the grounds that it is invalid. The equivalent of **revocation** in the law of patents. *Registered Designs Act 1949 section 11*.

Certification Mark A particular type of **trade mark** protectable through registration at the Trade Marks Registry. Its function is to signify that goods or services comply with certain objective standards in respect of origin, material, mode of manufacture, quality, accuracy or other characteristics. Regulations governing the use of a certification mark must be submitted to and approved by the Registrar of Trade Marks. *Trade Marks Act 1994 section 50*.

Claim Located at the end of a patent **specification** after the **description** of the **invention**. It is a statement of the extent of the monopoly **granted** by the patent. It is to be interpreted purposively through the eyes of the **skilled addressee** (in the light of the description and any drawings) so as to combine a fair degree of protection for the patentee with a reasonable degree of certainty for third parties. A claim may relate to a **product** or a **process**, and a patent usually contains a number of claims, some of which may be independent of each other. *Patents Act sections 14, 125*.

Claimant Under the Civil Procedure Rules, the person (formerly called 'plaintiff') who institutes proceedings against another by issuing a claim form.

Classification In the case of **trade marks**, the system of classifying goods and services for the purposes of trade mark registration. Under the **Nice Agreement** for the International Classification of Goods and Services 1957, there are 34 classes of goods and 11 classes of services in respect of which a mark may be registered. There is also an International Patent Classification System and an International Classification System for Designs. All of these Treaties are administered by **WIPO**.

Co-authorship In **copyright**, where the author of a musical **work** and the author of a literary work collaborate in order that the two works be used together. *CDPA 1988 section 10A*.

Collective Mark A particular type of **trade mark** protectable through registration at the Trade Marks Registry. Its function is to indicate who is entitled to use the mark, normally members of an association which owns the mark. It may imply a guarantee of objective standards, but does not have to do so. Regulations identifying who is authorised to use the mark, the conditions of membership and the conditions of use must be submitted to and approved by the Registrar of Trade Marks. *Trade Marks Act 1994 section 49*.

Commission An agreement whereby one person (the commissioner) requests another to create a copyright work or a **registered** or **unregistered design** and undertakes unconditionally to pay for it in any event. The effect of the agreement, however, is that ownership of the design remains with the creator unless there is an express agreement to the contrary, or the court implies a term vesting ownership in the commissioner.

Common General Knowledge Background information deemed to be possessed by the notional **skilled addressee** of a patent **specification**.

Commonplace An **unregistered design** cannot be protected if it is commonplace in the design field in question, even if it is **original**. 'Commonplace' has been judicially defined as 'trite, trivial, common-or-garden, hackneyed, or of the type which would excite no peculiar attention in those in the relevant art.' *CDPA section 213*.

Comptroller The official title of the Head of the United Kingdom Intellectual Property Office (**UKIPO**) (the Comptroller General of Patents, Designs and Trade Marks) (now also called the Chief Executive).

Compulsory licence A **licence** which the owner of a United Kingdom **patent** may be ordered to grant against its will. The intending **licensee** must previously have made efforts to obtain a voluntary licence on reasonable commercial terms and have been refused. The reason why such a licence may be ordered is failure on the part of the **patentee** to exploit the patent. The order granting such a licence is made by the United Kingdom Intellectual Property Office (**UKIPO**), who will also settle the terms of the licence. *Patents Act 1977 section 48*.

Confidential Information Secret information (ie information not in the public domain) which, provided that it has been disclosed in circumstances imposing a duty of confidentiality, is protectable by means of an action for **Breach of Confidence**. The information must not be useless, trivial, vague or immoral and must be capable of being identified and certain.

Contributory Infringement In the case of a **patent** (where it is properly called 'indirect infringement'), supplying the essential means for putting the invention into effect, knowing that those means are suitable for putting the invention into effect. Liability does not arise in the case of the supply of a staple commercial product. *Patents Act 1977 section 60*. In the case of a registered **trade mark**, applying a registered trade mark to material intended to be used for labelling or packaging goods, as a business paper, or for advertising goods or services, knowing or having reason to believe that the application of the mark is not authorised. *Trade Marks Act 1994 section 10*. In the case of **copyright**, making, importing, possessing in the course of a business, or selling or hiring, an article specifically designed or adapted for making infringing copies; permitting the use of premises for an infringing performance; and in the context of infringement of a work by public performance, supplying apparatus for the playing of sound recordings, the showing of films or receiving images or sounds by electronic means. In each case the defendant must know or have reason to believe that the equipment or premises would be used to infringe copyright. *CDPA 1988 sections 24–26*.

Convention Country In the case of **patents, registered designs** and **trade marks**, a country which is a Contracting State of the **Paris Convention** or of the **WTO**; in the case of **copyright**, a country which is a Contracting State either of the **Berne Convention, the Universal Copyright Convention or the Rome Convention** or of the **WTO**. In the case of **Performers' Rights**, a Contracting State either of the **Rome Convention** or the **WTO**.

Copyright The category of intellectual property right which protects **works**, provided they are **original**, recorded in a material form, and the **author** is a **qualifying person**. The exclusive rights conferred by copyright are to reproduce the work, issue copies of it to the public, perform the work in public, communicate the work to the public and adapt the work. *CDPA 1988 sections 1, 16*.

Damages The common law monetary remedy for the **infringement** of an intellectual property right. Such an award is tortious in nature, that is, it seeks to restore the claimant to the position they would have been in had the infringing conduct not been committed. The measure of damages may be either lost profits (for **trade mark** infringement and for **patent** infringement where the **patentee** intends to manufacture the patented product themselves) or (in most other cases) a reasonable **licence** fee.

Database Right The category of intellectual property right which protects a collection of independent **works**, data or other materials, arranged in a systematic or methodical way and individually accessible by electronic or other means. The database must be the result of a substantial investment, either qualitatively or quantitatively in the obtaining, verification, or presentation of its contents. Such database confers on its owner the right to prevent extraction and/or re-utilisation of the whole or a substantial part, evaluated qualitatively and/or quantitatively, of the contents of the database. *Copyright and Rights in Databases Regulations 1997 Articles 12–16.*

Description The first part of the patent **specification** in which the **patentee** is required to set out a description of the **invention** clearly and concisely so that it can be performed by **the skilled addressee**. Failure to do so renders the description **insufficient**. *Patents Act 1977 section 14.*

Dilution Harm caused to the advertising power of a **trade mark** with a reputation. Under EU law, such harm can take one of three forms: detriment to the distinctive character of the mark ('whittling away' or 'blurring'); detriment to the repute of the mark ('tarnishment' or 'degradation'); or taking unfair advantage ('parasitism' or 'free-riding'). *Trade Marks Act 1994 sections 5(3), 10(3).*

Disclosure In the context of litigation, a court order requiring a party to the litigation to disclose certain documents. *Civil Procedure Rules Part 31.* In **patent** law: (a) the requirement that the **description** of the **invention** discloses it sufficiently for it to be performed by the notional **skilled addressee**; and (b) in relation to **novelty**, the question of whether an item of information is part of the **prior art** as a result of having been made available to the public. *Patents Act 1977 sections 14(3) and 2.*

Discovery In the context of litigation, a court order requiring the defendant to reveal the name or names of parties who have committed an infringing act. In the context of patent law, one of the list of matters excluded from patentability and often described as the opposite of an **invention**. *Patents Act 1977 section 1(2).*

EEA The European Economic Area, that is the current 28 Member States of the European Union together with those members of the European Free Trade Area (EFTA) which have agreed to join the EEA, namely Norway, Iceland and Liechtenstein. The four freedoms found in the **Treaty on the Functioning of the European Union (TFEU)** (formerly the Treaty of Rome) (free movement of goods, persons, services and capital)

together with EU competition policy apply in the EEA. Consequently, internal market harmonisation Directives implementing the four freedoms (in particular, those dealing with intellectual property) extend to the EEA Contracting States.

Enabling Disclosure In **patent** law: (a) the requirement that the **description** of the **invention** in the patent **specification** be clear and complete enough to enable the notional **skilled addressee** to perform the invention; (b) in relation to **novelty**, the requirement that the **prior art** must enable the skilled addressee to carry out what is claimed in the later patent in order for the prior art to be an **anticipation** of that patent.

EPC The European Patent Convention 1973, promulgated by the Council of Europe, which creates a regional system for the centralised grant of patents. Membership of the Convention is open to any country which is a Contracting State of the Council of Europe. The 2000 revisions to the Convention came into force on 13 December 2007.

EPO The European Patent Office, the body established under the **EPC** with responsibility for granting **European patents**.

EU Design A unitary design effective throughout all the Member States of the EU. It may be registered or unregistered. Registered EU designs may only be obtained from **OHIM**. *Council Regulation (EC) No 6/2002 on Community designs.*

EU Patent The intended patent effective throughout all the Member States of the EU, granted by the **EPO** designating the EU as its territory of protection. Not implemented as the *Draft Regulation on the EU Patent 2009* together with the accompanying subsidiary legislation was declared incompatible with the **TFEU**. Replaced by the **Unitary Patent**.

EU Trade Mark A unitary **trade mark** effective throughout all the Member States of the EU. It cannot be acquired by use, but only by registration at **OHIM**. *Council Regulation (EC) No 40/94 on the Community trade mark, repealed and codified by Council Regulation (EC) No 207/2009 on the Community trade mark.*

European Patent A patent granted by the **EPO** in Munich for all or some of the Contracting States of the **EPC**. Once granted, such patents become national patents in the relevant designated states.

Examination In the context of registrable intellectual property rights (patents, registered designs and trade marks) the scrutiny of the application by the United Kingdom Intellectual Property Office (UKIPO). In the case of **patents**, such examination will, at the request of the applicant, entail a **preliminary examination** to ensure compliance with the legislation, and a **substantive examination** to determine patentability. In the case of **registered designs**, the examination will be to ensure that the application complies with rules made under the legislation, is by the rightful owner and meets the definition of design and the criteria for protection. In the case of **trade marks**, examination is to ensure compliance with the legislation and that there is no objection to the mark under **the absolute grounds of refusal.** *Patents Act 1977 sections 17–18; Registered Designs Act 1949 section 3A, Trade Marks Act 1994 section 37.*

Exceptions to Patentability Certain items which although possessing technical character are denied patent protection on grounds of public policy, namely **inventions** contrary to morality, plant and animal varieties, and methods of treating animals and humans. *Patents Act 1977 section 1(3), Schedule A2 and section 4(A)(1).*

Excluded Subject Matter In relation to **patents**, certain items which are deemed not capable of patent protection as such, usually because they are of a non-technical or abstract nature. *Patents Act 1977 section 1(2).*

Exclusive Licence A **licence** in which the **licensor** undertakes neither to exploit the intellectual property right themselves nor to grant a licence to anyone else.

Exhaustion of Rights A defence to an action for the **infringement** of a **trade mark**, **patent**, **design** or **copyright** in which the defendant argues that the owner of the right in question cannot object to further dealings in the goods because those goods (which are **parallel imports**) have been put into circulation with the consent of the proprietor. Such defence arises where the goods were first put into circulation in the **EEA**, but not where they were first sold anywhere else in the world. *Trade Marks Act 1994 section 12; CDPA 1988 section 18.*

Filing Date The actual date on which the relevant formalities for an application for a **patent**, **registered design** or **trade mark** are completed. The period of protection is always calculated from this date. The **validity** of the patent, registered design or trade mark will be assessed as of this date, unless the application claims **priority** from an earlier filing in another **Convention country**, in which case validity is assessed by reference to the earlier date.

Freezing Injunction Formerly known as a *Mareva* injunction, an interim order of the court restraining a party from removing from the jurisdiction assets located there; or restraining a party from dealing with any assets whether located within the jurisdiction or not. The objective is to ensure that there are enough of the defendant's assets within the jurisdiction to compensate the **claimant** should the claim succeed. *Civil Procedure Rules Part 25.*

Geographical Indications A name or other indication which identifies that a product comes from a particular region or locality, such that a particular quality or characteristic is attributable to its geographic origin. Protected in the EU under *Council Regulation (EC) No 510/2006 on the protection of geographical indications and designations of origin for agricultural products and foodstuffs.*

Goodwill Intangible personal property belonging to a business protectable at common law through the action of **passing off**. Goodwill is local and depends on the existence of customers within the United Kingdom. It is 'the attractive force which brings in custom' or 'that which distinguishes a new business from an old'.

Grant The technical term for the registration of a United Kingdom **patent**, reflecting its historical origin as an exercise of the Crown prerogative.

Individual Character One of the two principal criteria for the protection of a **registered design**, under both United Kingdom and EU law. *Registered Designs Act 1949 section 1B(3).*

Industrial Application One of the key requirements of **patentability**. It means that the **invention** must be useful and not speculative. *Patents Act 1977 section 4.*

Industrial Property The term previously used to describe those intellectual property rights falling within the scope of the **Paris Convention**, namely **patents**, **registered designs** and **trade marks**, in contrast to 'intellectual property', a term used until the mid-1960s to refer just to copyright and related rights. 'Intellectual property' is generally used today to refer to all categories of rights.

Informed User The hypothetical person through whose eyes the **individual character** of a **registered design** is assessed. *Registered Designs Act 1949 section 1B(3).*

Infringement Conduct by a third party who does not have the consent of the intellectual property owner which amounts to a 'trespass' on the exclusive right granted by statute to the owner of the right in question. *Patents Act 1977 section 60, Registered Designs Act 1949 section 7, Trade Marks Act 1994 section 9, CDPA sections 16–27 and 226.*

Infringing Imports Goods imported into the United Kingdom when they have been made elsewhere without the consent of the intellectual property owner, either by a competitor or counterfeiter.

Injunction A court order directing that certain acts do or do not take place or continue. An injunction may be ordered in all cases in which it appears to the court to be just and convenient to do so. *Senior Courts Act 1981 section 37 and Civil Procedure Rules Part 25.*

Insufficiency An objection which may be made to a **patent** application, as well as being a ground of **revocation** of a granted patent, to the effect that the **description** of the invention does not disclose the invention clearly and completely enough for it to be performed by **the skilled addressee.** *Patents Act 1977 section 14(3), section 72(1)(c).*

Integer An element or part of a patent **claim**.

Invalidity The argument that a registered intellectual property right should never have been entered on the register because it fails to comply with one or more statutory requirements, so that it should be removed from the appropriate register. Such removal is retrospective to the **filing date**.

Invention The subject matter of patent protection, something which according to the EPO must have technical character, that is, there must be a physical entity or concrete product, man-made for a utilitarian purpose.

Inventive Concept The 'epitome' or 'essence' or 'kernel' of an invention. It is derived from an analysis of the claims in the light of the problem which the **patentee** was trying to solve. Not to be confused with **inventive step**.

Inventive Step One of the key requirements of **patentability**. An **invention** has inventive step if it is not obvious to **the skilled addressee**. *Patents Act 1977 section 3*.

Joint Authors In **copyright**, where two or more people have contributed to the creation of a literary, dramatic, musical or artistic **work**. It must not possible to identify their respective contributions. *CDPA 1988 section 10*.

Know-how Technical information, not necessarily patentable, but of economic value, which is secret, substantial and identifiable. It is capable of being licensed, although any such **licence** must comply with the requirements of EU and United Kingdom competition law.

Licence Permission (normally contractual) to exploit an intellectual property right. Such permission means that the **licensee** cannot be an infringer. A licence (nb the English as opposed to US spelling of the noun) confers personal rights only and is not proprietary in nature. Hence:

Licence of right In the case of **patents**, the **patentee** may at any time after grant apply to the United Kingdom Intellectual Property Office (**UKIPO**) to have the patent endorsed 'licence of right'. The endorsement acts as an invitation to third parties to apply for a licence. In the case of a dispute as to the terms of an intended licence, the terms may be settled by the United Kingdom Intellectual Property Office (UKIPO). The advantage of the endorsement is that renewal fees are halved. *Patents Act 1977 section 46*. In the case of **unregistered design right**, during the last five years of the term of protection, a potential infringer can demand a licence of right to exploit the design. In the case of a dispute as to the terms of an intended licence, the terms may be settled by the United Kingdom Intellectual Property Office (UKIPO). *CDPA 1988 section 237*.

Licensee The person to whom a **licence** is granted.

Licensor A person granting a **licence** of an intellectual property right.

Madrid System The system for the international registration of **trade marks** administered by **WIPO**.

Malicious Falsehood A common law tort analogous to defamation. It involves an untrue statement which disparages the **claimant's** goods or business, made with malice, which causes pecuniary loss in respect of the claimant's office, trade, profession, calling or business.

Moral Rights Those rights accorded to the **author** of a literary, dramatic, musical or artistic work or film under the provisions of the **Berne Convention** 1886 which are separate from the **copyright** in the **work** and which remain personal to the author, and, after the author's death, their successors. Moral rights comprise the right to be identified as author and the right to object to derogatory treatment of the work. *CDPA 1988*

sections 77, 80. Similar moral rights are now accorded to performers: *The Performances (Moral Rights etc) Regulations 2006*.

National Treatment One of the fundamental principles of the **Berne Convention**, the **Paris Convention** and **TRIPs**. Any Contracting State to these conventions is required to provide the same protection under domestic law to foreign nationals as it does to its own nationals.

Neighbouring Rights Rights which are regarded in some countries as analogous to **copyright**. Such rights are covered by the **Rome Convention**, namely phonograms (sound recordings), performances and broadcasts. Under United Kingdom copyright law, sound recordings, and broadcasts are treated as copyright **works**, whilst performer's rights are dealt with by Part II of the CDPA.

Nice Agreement The Nice Agreement for the International Classification of Goods and Services 1957, under which there are 34 classes of goods and 11 classes of services in respect of which a **trade mark** may be registered. The Agreement is administered and periodically revised by **WIPO**. *Trade Mark (Amendment) Rules 2001 Schedule 4*.

Non-exclusive Licence A **licence** which does not prevent the **licensor** from appointing other **licensees** nor from exploiting the intellectual property right itself.

Novelty In relation to **patents**, one of the key requirements of **patentability**. The information contained in the **patent** must not have been made available to the public anywhere in the world before the **priority date** of the patent. However, in order to destroy novelty, the prior art must contain an **enabling disclosure**. *Patents Act 1977 section 2*. In relation to **registered designs**, one of the key requirements of registrability, the meaning being the same as in the law of patents. *Registered Designs Act 1949 section 1B*.

Observations The ability of a third party to make informal written representation to the United Kingdom Intellectual Property Office (**UKIPO**) concerning a published **patent** application as to its **patentability** or an advertised **trade mark** application as to whether it should be registered. A person who makes observations does not become party to the proceedings. *Patents Act 1977 section 21; Trade Marks Act 1994 section 38*.

Obviousness The converse of **inventive step** in the law of **patents**. Whether an invention is obvious is judged through the eyes of the notional **skilled addressee** in the light of their **common general knowledge**. *Patents Act 1977 section 3*.

OHIM The Office for Harmonisation in the Internal Market (Trade Marks and Designs). The EU institution responsible for the registration of **EU Trade Marks** and **EU Designs**.

Opposition In the case of **trade marks**, the procedure whereby formal objections can be raised by the owner of an earlier right to a later application. In the case of **patents**, there is no system of opposition under United Kingdom law (although there was under the Patents Act 1949), but a **European Patent** can be opposed at the **EPO** during the nine-month period after it has been granted. *Trade Marks Act 1994 section 38*.

Original The principal criterion which must be satisfied for either **copyright** or **unregistered design right** to arise. In United Kingdom law it means 'not copied', ie that the **work** or design originated with the **author** or designer, but EU Directives emphasise the author's intellectual creativity.

Orphan Work A work protected by copyright for which no right holder has been identified. Directive 2012/28/EU of the European Parliament and of the Council of 25 October 2012 on certain permitted uses of orphan works [2012] OJ L 299/5 provides the framework to enable the digitisation and dissemination of such works and must be implemented by October 2014.

Parallel Imports Goods to be imported into the United Kingdom which have been placed in circulation in another country, either by the United Kingdom intellectual property owner, or by their subsidiary or **licensee** or someone else acting with their consent.

Paris Convention The Paris Convention for the Protection of Industrial Property. The principal multilateral convention dealing with **industrial property**, ie **patents**, **registered designs** and **trade marks**. It was first signed at Paris in 1883 and last revised in Stockholm in 1967. Besides laying down minimum standards for the registration of such rights, it also deals with **unfair competition**. It is administered by **WIPO** and obliges Contracting States to observe the principle of **national treatment**.

Passing Off The protection available at common law to protect unregistered **trade marks**. To succeed in an action for passing off, the **claimant** must prove that the name, mark or other symbol which has been used in the course of trade has acquired reputation or **goodwill**; that the defendant has made a misrepresentation to customers in the course of trade to lead such customers to believe that the claimant is responsible for the goods or services supplied by the defendant; and that such misrepresentation has or will cause damage to the claimant's goodwill.

Patent The category of intellectual property right which protects an **invention** (that is, something having technical character) provided it possesses **novelty** and **inventive step**, and is susceptible of **industrial application** and not **excluded** from patent protection. The exclusive right conferred by the **grant** of a patent is to make, dispose of, offer to dispose of, use, import or keep a patented product, to use or offer for use a patented process, or dispose of, offer to dispose of, use, import or keep a product derived directly from a patented process. *Patents Act 1977, sections 1, 60*.

Patentability The criteria which must be met by an **invention** in order for a patent to be granted. These are **novelty**, **inventive step**, susceptibility of **industrial application** and not falling within the list of **exceptions** and **exclusions**. *Patents Act 1977 section 1*.

Patentee The person to whom a **patent** is granted.

PCT The Patent Co-operation Treaty 1970, administered by **WIPO**. It facilitates the simultaneous multiple filing of national patent applications.

Performers' Rights Protection accorded to those who undertake live dramatic performances, musical performances, readings of literary works or performances of variety acts. Such protection is separate from any copyright which may or may not subsist in the work being performed. In order to be protected under United Kingdom law, the performer must be a **qualifying individual** or the performance must take place in a **qualifying country**. *CDPA 1988 sections 180, 181*.

Plant Variety Right The category of intellectual property rights (sometimes called plant breeders' rights) which protects botanical material. A plant variety means a plant grouping within a single botanical classification of the lowest known rank which is distinct, uniform, stable and new. Protection may be granted either by the United Kingdom Plant Variety Rights Office under the *Plant Varieties Act 1997* or by the EU Plant Varieties Office under *Council Regulation (EC) No 2100/94 on Community plant variety rights*. The relevant international convention is the International Convention for the Protection of New Varieties of Plants 1961 (UPOV).

Preliminary Examination A step in the procedure for the **grant** of a United Kingdom **patent**, in which the Patent Examiner will scrutinise the application to determine whether it complies with the formal requirements of the Act. Such step must be initiated by the patent **applicant**. *Patents Act 1977 section 17*.

Prior Art Information of any kind which has been made available to the public at the **priority date** of a **patent**. It is against this state of the art that the patent application is compared in order to decide whether it meets the requirements of **novelty** and **inventive step**. *Patents Act 1977 sections 2, 3*. Similarly, in the case of registered **designs**, the application is compared with the prior art to see if it is new and has individual character. *Registered Designs Act 1949 section 1*.

Prior Use In the case of patents, registered designs and registered trade marks, a defence to an infringement action, whereby the defendant alleges that its use commenced before the **priority date** of the claimant's patent, design or trade mark. *Patents Act 1977 section 64; Registered Designs Act 1949 s7B; Trade Marks Act 1994 section 11(3)*.

Priority The ability of an **applicant** for a United Kingdom **patent**, **registered design** or **trade mark** to backdate the United Kingdom filing to an earlier national filing in another **Convention country**. Convention priority must be claimed within 12 months in the case of a patent application, and within six months in the case of registered designs and trade marks. In each case the applicant for and subject matter of the United Kingdom filing must be the same as the earlier Convention application. *Patents Act 1977 section 5, Registered Designs Act 1949 section 14, Trade Marks Act 1994 section 35*.

Priority Date The date at which the **validity** of an application for a **patent**, **registered design** or **trade mark** is decided. Such date will be the actual filing date of the application in the United Kingdom, unless the **applicant** claims **priority** from an earlier filing in another **Convention country**, in which case validity is determined as of the earlier date. *Patents Act 1977 section 5, Registered Designs Act 1949 section 14, Trade Marks Act 1994 section 35.*

Process Claim A statement in a **patent** which claims a monopoly in how to make something or how to use something or how to do something.

Product The subject matter of **registered design** protection.

Product claim A statement in a **patent** which claims a monopoly in a tangible thing.

Publication In the case of **patents**, an application will be automatically published in the *Patents Journal* 18 months after it is filed, unless the **applicant** withdraws it beforehand or unless the information it contains is thought to be prejudicial to the defence of the realm or the safety of the public, in which latter case the United Kingdom Intellectual Property Office (**UKIPO**) may prohibit its publication. The fact that a patent has been granted will also be published in the *Patents Journal*. *Patents Act 1977 sections 16, 22 and 24.*

Public Interest 'In the public interest' is a defence to the action for **breach of confidence**, and is also a defence to **copyright** infringement. To justify their wrongdoing, the defendant must show that it is in the interests of society that confidential information is disclosed or an act of copyright infringement is committed.

Qualifying Country In respect of **Performers' Rights**, a state which is a party either to the **Rome Convention** or to the **TRIPs** Agreement. *CDPA 1988 section 208.*

Qualifying Individual In respect of **Performers' Rights**, a performer who is entitled to protection under United Kingdom law by virtue of being a subject of or resident in a **qualifying country**. In respect of the artist's resale right (a category of **moral right**), the artist must be a national of an **EEA** Contracting State or of a state listed in the relevant Regulations. *CDPA 1988 sections 180, 181, 206; The Artist's Resale Rights Regulations 2006.*

Qualifying Performance In respect of **Performers' Rights**, a performance which is protected under United Kingdom law either because it has been given by a **qualifying individual** or because it has taken place in a **qualifying country**. *CDPA 1988 sections 180, 181.*

Qualifying Person One of the factors used to determine whether a **work** is entitled to protection under United Kingdom **copyright** law, or whether an **unregistered design right** is entitled to United Kingdom protection. *CDPA 1988 sections 153–159, 213(5), 217–220.*

Registered Design Under both United Kingdom and EU law, the category of intellectual property right which protects the appearance of the whole or part of a **product** which results from the lines, contours, colours, shape, texture or materials of the product or its ornamentation. To be registered, the design must have **novelty** and **individual character**. Registration of a

design confers on its proprietor the exclusive right to use the design and any design which does not produce a different overall impression on the informed user, 'use' comprising making, offering, putting on the market, importing, exporting, using or stocking a product in which the design is incorporated or to which the design is applied. *Registered Designs Act 1949 sections 1, 7.*

Registered Proprietor The person whose name appears on the register of patents, the register of designs or the register of trade marks as the owner of the right in question.

Registrable Transaction A property dealing in respect of a registered **trade mark**, the details of which must be entered on the trade marks register. Failure so to record may affect the award of costs in an **infringement** action. Such dealings include **assignments**, **licences**, mortgages, probate assent and court orders. *Trade Marks Act 1994 section 25.*

Relative Grounds An objection which may be raised against an application for a registered **trade mark** which involves a comparison of the mark with earlier rights. Such rights are usually previously registered trade marks, whether on the United Kingdom, EU or International registers, or **well-known marks**, but can also be earlier copyright or designs, and earlier unregistered marks which are entitled to protection under the law of **passing off**. Such objection can only be brought by the owner of the earlier right. *Trade Marks Act 1994 section 5.*

Renewal Fees In the case of United Kingdom **patents**, **registered designs** and **trade marks**, the fees which must be paid in order to keep the right alive. For patents, renewal fees are payable annually, from the fifth year onwards; for registered designs, renewal fees are payable every five years on four occasions only, giving a maximum term of 25 years; in the case of trade marks, renewal fees are payable every 10 years on an unlimited number of occasions. In each case, the **filing date** is the date from which the calculation of the renewal date is made. *Patents Act 1977 section 25; Registered Designs Act 1949 section 8; Trade Marks Act 1994 sections 42–43.*

Restoration The return to the register of a **patent**, **design** or **trade mark** which had previously lapsed due to non-payment of a renewal fee. *Patents Act 1977 section 28; Trade Marks Act 1994 section 43; Registered Designs Act 1949 section 8.*

Revocation In the case of **patents**, the total or partial removal of a patent from the register of patents, as from the **filing date**, on the grounds that it is not a patentable **invention**, has been granted to the wrong person, has an insufficient **description** or has been the subject of impermissible **amendment** either to the description or the **claims**. *Patents Act 1977 sections 72–74.* In the case of registered **trade marks**, the total or partial removal of a trade mark prospectively from the register on the ground that it has been the subject of mismanagement *since* the date of registration. Mismanagement comprises non-use, generic use or deceptive use. Revocation of a registered mark does not normally remove liability for acts of infringement committed between the date of registration and the date of removal from the register. *Trade Marks Act 1994 section 46.*

Rome Convention The International Convention for the Protection of Performers, Producers of Phonograms and Broadcasting Organisations. The principal multilateral convention dealing with so-called **neighbouring rights**, namely performances, sound recordings and broadcasts. It was signed at Rome in 1961. It is administered by **WIPO** and obliges Contracting States to observe the principle of **national treatment**.

Search Order Formerly known as the *Anton Piller* order, an interim order made by a court before the hearing of the action. It requires the defendant to admit the **claimant's** solicitor to premises for the purposes of preserving evidence of infringing conduct. *Civil Procedure Act 1997 section 7 and Civil Procedure Rules Part 25.*

Search Report In the case of **patents**, the report produced by the Patent Examiner which identifies documents against which the patent application is to be compared for the purposes of **novelty** and **inventive step**.

Sign The subject matter of **trade mark** protection.

Skilled Addressee The hypothetical person to whom a **patent specification** is deemed to be addressed. The qualifications of such person will depend on the field of technology with which the patent is concerned and the level of sophistication of the **invention**. The skilled addressee is also deemed to have the **common general knowledge** of those working in that area. Such person does not possess a spark of inventiveness, but would conduct experiments deemed to be technically worthwhile.

Sole Licence A **licence** of an intellectual property right whereby the owner of the right undertakes not to appoint any other **licensees**, but remains free to exploit the right itself.

Specification One of the documents which must be provided when applying for a **patent**. It will consist of a **description** of the invention and the **claims**, and must be accompanied by any drawings referred to in the description. *Patents Act 1977 section 14.*

Statement of Goods and Services A **trade mark** registration must be in respect of particular goods or services, as listed in the **Nice Agreement**. A statement of the goods and/or services in respect of which the mark is to be registered must be included on the trade mark application form.

Substantive Examination A step in the procedure for the **grant** of a United Kingdom **patent**, in which the Patent Examiner will scrutinise the application in the light of the **Search Report** to determine whether the application complies with the **patentability** requirements of the Act. Such step must be initiated by the patent **applicant**. *Patents Act 1977 section 18.*

Sufficiency The requirement in **patent** law that the **description** of the **invention** must be clear and complete enough to enable the **skilled addressee**, armed with **common general knowledge**, to perform

the invention. Insufficiency is a ground of **revocation**. *Patents Act 1977 sections 14, 72.*

Threats Action A civil action brought against any person who unjustifiably threatens another with proceedings for the **infringement** of a patent, **registered design**, **unregistered design right** or registered **trade mark**. The **claimant** is any person aggrieved by those threats and need not be the direct recipient of the communication that infringement proceedings will be taken. Remedies include a declaration of unjustified threats, an **injunction** against the continuation of the threats, and **damages**. *Patents Act 1977 section 70, Registered Designs Act 1949 section 26, CDPA 1988 section 253, Trade Marks Act 1994 section 21.*

Trade Mark The category of intellectual property right which protects a brand name or any other **sign** used in the course of trade to indicate the commercial origin of goods. Protection may be obtained through registration, or by use. In the case of a used but unregistered mark, protection is by means of the action for **passing off**. To be registered, a trade mark must consist of a sign, which is capable of graphic representation and capable of distinguishing. The sign must not prevented from registration by any of the **absolute** or **relative grounds of refusal**. Registration confers on the proprietor the exclusive right to prevent anyone not having their consent from using in the course of trade an identical or similar sign in relation to the identical, similar or dissimilar goods or services, 'use' comprising affixing the sign to goods, offering or exposing the goods for sale, putting them on the market, stocking the goods or supplying or offering to supply services, importing or exporting goods under the sign, and using the sign on business papers or in advertising. *Trade Marks Act 1994 sections 1, 3, 5, 9, 10.*

Trade Secret Another name for **Confidential Information** in a commercial context.

Treaty on the Functioning of the European Union (TFEU). The name of what used to be called the Treaty of Rome, the renaming being the result of the Treaty of Lisbon.

TRIPs The Trade Related Aspects of Intellectual Property Agreement 1994. One of the agreements overseen by the **WTO**. TRIPs provides for a minimum 'floor of rights' for all major categories of intellectual property. It builds on what has gone before by incorporating the fundamental principles of the **Paris**, **Berne** and **Rome Conventions**, and requires its Contracting States to accede to the latest versions of these (and other) treaties.

Unfair Competition Any act of competition which is contrary to honest practice in industrial and commercial matters. Although the **Paris Convention** 1883 obliges its Contracting States to provide redress against unfair competition, there is no specific action for unfair competition under United Kingdom law.

Unitary Patent The replacement for the **EU Patent**, agreed under the enhanced co-operation procedure of the **TFEU**, consisting of Regulation No 1257/2012 ([2012] OJ L 361/1) implementing enhanced co-operation in the area of the creation of unitary patent protection together with a further Regulation on translation arrangements and the Agreement on the Unified Patent Court, which will take effect only in those Member States which have agreed to it.

United Kingdom Intellectual Property Office (UKIPO) The name since 2007 of the United Kingdom Patent Office.

Universal Copyright Convention (UCC) First signed in Geneva in 1952, with the revised version being signed in Paris in 1971, it is administered by the United Nations Educational, Scientific and Cultural Organisation not **WIPO**. It provides for **copyright** protection for 'literary, scientific and artistic works' but such protection is less than that found in the **Berne Convention**. The UCC requires use of the © symbol accompanied by the name of the copyright owner and the date of first publication as the maximum formality a contracting state can require in order to protect a work originating from another contracting state.

Unregistered Design Right Under United Kingdom law, the category of intellectual property rights which protects the shape or configuration (whether internal or external) of the whole or part of an **article**. The design must be **original**, not **commonplace**, and recorded. Design right confers on its owner the exclusive right to reproduce the design for commercial purposes by making articles to that design. The criteria for the protection of an EU unregistered design right are different, corresponding to those for a **registered design**. *CDPA 1988 sections 213, 226.*

Utility Model A type of intellectual property right obtainable in certain countries (not the United Kingdom) similar to a patent and granted for technical **inventions** which are new but involve a small **inventive step**. It is cheaper and quicker to obtain than a patent (there is no **prior art** search to assess **validity**) and has a shorter term of protection. The EU Commission proposed the introduction of utility model protection for the EU in 1997 but no progress has been made.

Validity Whether a **patent, registered design** or **trade mark** meets the substantive requirements of the relevant legislation so as to qualify for protection.

Variant A difference between the wording of a **claim** in a **patent** and the defendant's alleged infringing product or process. Whether this difference falls within the language of the claim (and so infringes the patent) is determined through the eyes of the **skilled addressee**, the claim being given a purposive construction.

Well-known mark A **trade mark** which is accorded special protection under the **Paris Convention** and the **TRIPs** Agreement. Whether a mark is well known depends on a number of factors, including the degree of recognition of the mark in the relevant sector of the public, the duration, extent and geographical area of its use, the duration and geographical area of its promotion, the extent of any registrations for the mark, and the record of its successful enforcement. *Trade Marks Act 1994 section 56.*

WIPO World Intellectual Property Organisation. A specialist agency of the United Nations established in 1967 which is responsible for the promotion of the protection of intellectual property throughout the world by means of co-operation between States. It oversees and administers a number of multilateral treaties dealing with intellectual property. These treaties are categorised by WIPO itself as protection treaties (establishing minimum standards for the various categories of IP rights), global protection systems (which facilitate multiple national filings), and classification treaties.

Work The subject matter of **copyright** protection. In United Kingdom law, copyright protects literary, dramatic, musical and artistic works, films, sound recordings, broadcasts and printed editions. *CDPA 1988 section 1.*

WTO World Trade Organization. The international organisation which came into being as a result of the Uruguay Round of the General Agreement on Tariffs and Trade 1986–1994. Its principal objective is to promote free trade between states by overseeing and enforcing the rules of international trade. It oversees a number of international agreements, including the **TRIPs** Agreement. A key element of WTO is its dispute resolution mechanism.

Index

Introductory Note

References such as "178–9" indicate (not necessarily continuous) discussion of a topic across a range of pages. Wherever possible in the case of topics with many references, these have either been divided into sub-topics or only the most significant discussions of the topic are listed. Because the entire work is about 'intellectual property', the use of this term (and certain others which occur constantly throughout the book) as an entry point has been minimized. Information will be found under the corresponding detailed topics.

DIRECTIONS: *straightforward law*

Studying the law can be a difficult task and as a student you want to know that you are on the right track and getting to grips with the key issues.

Books in the *DIRECTIONS* series effectively set you on your way. Without assuming prior legal knowledge, each book shows students where to start and offers a sufficiently detailed guide through the subject.

Each *DIRECTIONS* book is written by an experienced teacher or teachers who are passionate about making their subject understood. Topics are carefully and logically structured and clearly explained, making use of real life examples. Engaging learning features accompany the lively writing style, helping students effectively grasp each subject.

   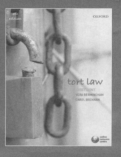 

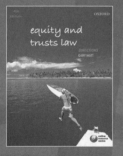  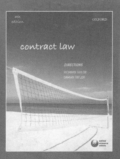 

Titles in the series include:

contract law

criminal law

equity and trusts law

intellectual property law

human rights law

land law

public law

tort law

EU law

For further details about titles in the series visit

www.oxfordtextbooks.co.uk/law/directions/

Revision & study guides from the **No.1** legal education publisher

When you're aiming high, reach for credible, high quality revision and study guides that will help you consolidate knowledge, focus your revision, and maximise your potential.

 ## Oxford's Concentrate series

When you're serious about success

Oxford's **Q&A** series

Don't just answer the question: nail it